D0041736

# PAULINE KAEL

BRIAN KELLOW

# PAULINE KAEL

## A LIFE IN THE DARK

VIKING

VIKING
Published by the Penguin Group
Penguin Group (USA) Inc., 375 Hudson Street,
New York, New York 10014, U.S.A.
Penguin Group (Canada), 90 Eglinton Avenue East, Suite 700, Toronto,
Ontario, Canada M4P 2Y3 (a division of Pearson Penguin Canada Inc.)
Penguin Books Ltd, 80 Strand, London WC2R 0RL, England
Penguin Ireland, 25 St. Stephen's Green, Dublin 2, Ireland
(a division of Penguin Books Ltd)
Penguin Books Australia Ltd, 250 Camberwell Road, Camberwell,
Victoria 3124, Australia (a division of Pearson Australia Group Pty Ltd)
Penguin Books India Pvt Ltd, 11 Community Centre,
Panchsheel Park, New Delhi – 110 017, India
Penguin Group (NZ), 67 Apollo Drive, Rosedale, Auckland 0632,
New Zealand (a division of Pearson New Zealand Ltd)
Penguin Books (South Africa) (Pty) Ltd, 24 Sturdee Avenue,
Rosebank, Johannesburg 2196, South Africa

Penguin Books Ltd, Registered Offices: 80 Strand, London WC2R 0RL, England

First published in 2011 by Viking Penguin, a member of Penguin Group (USA) Inc.

3 5 7 9 10 8 6 4 2

LIBRARY OF CONGRESS CATALOGING-IN-PUBLICATION DATA
Kellow, Brian.
Pauline Kael : a life in the dark / Brian Kellow.
p. cm.
Includes bibliographical references and index.
ISBN 978-0-670-02312-7 (alk. paper)
1. Kael, Pauline. 2. Film critics—United States—Biography. I. Title.
PN1998.3.K34K46 2011
791.43092—dc23
[B]    2011021798

Printed in the United States of America
Set in Adobe Caslon Pro
Designed by Francesca Belanger

To my father, Jack Kellow,
who loves shoot-'em-ups

To my mother, Marjorie Kellow,
who loved *The Godfather* and *Prizzi's Honor*,
and thought '40s women's pictures were "crap"

And most of all
to my brother, Barry Kellow,
whose movie love turned out to be contagious

# INTRODUCTION

In the beginning, even the French had their doubts about Louis Malle's *Murmur of the Heart*. The director's 1972 film was a memory piece that drew on elements of his own childhood. In it, a timid fifteen-year-old boy grows increasingly distant from his bourgeois French father and increasingly attached to his freewheeling Italian mother. After a bout with scarlet fever reveals that the boy has a heart murmur, his mother takes him to a health spa, where, free from the constraints of their ordinary lives, mother and son are drawn closer than ever—so close, in fact, that one night, on the heels of a boozy Bastille Day celebration, they wind up in bed together, quite gently and quite naturally making love to each other.

When Malle turned in his script for *Murmur of the Heart*, the Centre National du Cinéma refused to come across with any support at all. The script, they complained, depicted "too many erotic sequences . . . in which all manner of perversions are evoked with a disturbing complacency." Malle was stunned by the reaction. "I certainly did not set out to do a film about incest," he later recalled. "But I began exploring a very intense relationship between a mother and her son, and I ended up pushing it all the way."

*Murmur of the Heart* went on to enjoy an immense worldwide critical and financial success, and one of its most celebrated admirers was Pauline Kael, who for years had been upending conventional, academically correct notions of film criticism, first as a freelance contributor to a string of film journals and, since 1968, from a truly enviable and distinguished platform as one of two regular authors of the column "The Current Cinema" in *The New Yorker* magazine. To Kael *Murmur of the Heart* was one of the most refreshingly complex and honest views of family life she had ever experienced. Malle was to be commended for seeing "not only the prudent, punctilious surface" of the bourgeois experience "but the volatile and slovenly life underneath." She noted that advance word on the picture centered on its shock value, because of the element of incest. But for Kael, "the only shock is the joke that, for all the repressions the bourgeois practice and the conventions they pretend to believe in, they are such amoral, instinct-satisfying creatures that incest doesn't mean any more to them than to healthy animals. The shock is that in this context incest *isn't* serious—and that, I guess, may really upset some people, so they won't be able to laugh."

In 1976 she found herself addressing an overflow audience at Mitchell Playhouse in Corvallis, Oregon, home of Oregon State University. For years Kael had been keeping up a hectic schedule of appearances around the country, drawing huge crowds as her fame grew and more and more readers were hanging on her opinions of the latest movies. Although she had little patience for many of the questions that she was asked at these lecture tours, she relished the opportunity to come together with movie-lovers—young ones, especially—during this fertile period of filmmaking that had sprung up in the late 1960s and was still flourishing.

At Mitchell Playhouse she was introduced by Jim Lynch, an associate professor of English at Oregon State, who delighted her by introducing her as "the Muhammad Ali of film critics." She proceeded to give a stimulating talk on the current state of movies, then took questions from the audience.

"How many times do you see a movie before you write about it?"

"Only once," replied Kael.

"What about *Persona*?" asked one senior member of Oregon State University's English faculty. "I had to see it three times before I felt I had any real grasp of it at all."

"Well," said Kael, "that's the difference between us, isn't it?" The line played less insultingly than it might read, and she laughed as she said it. Then she went on to explain that she felt the need to write in the flush of her initial, immediate response to a movie. If she waited too long, and pondered the film over repeated viewings, she felt that she might be in danger of coming up with something that wouldn't be her truest response.

Someone else in the audience persisted with a question along similar lines: "But if you were going to see one movie again, which one would it be?"

"I'd always rather see something new."

After a few minutes of back and forth, a man in the audience raised his hand and asked about *Murmur of the Heart*, which Kael had reviewed for the October 23, 1971, *The New Yorker*. He told her that, having seen the film again recently, he had found it sentimental and unconvincing, and wondered if she still recalled it with enthusiasm.

"Yes," said Kael, "I do."

*"Really?"* pressed the questioner.

After a stiff silence punctuated only by the clearing of throats and the rustling of programs, Kael fixed her gaze on the man for a moment and gave him a catnip smile.

"Listen," she finally asked. "Do you remember your first fuck?"

"Sure," he answered, flushing, struggling to hang on to his composure. "Of course I do."

"Well, honey," said Kael, after another perfectly weighed silence, "just wait thirty years."

This was the Kael that her army of readers at *The New Yorker* had come to worship—bold, clear-eyed, pithy, a brilliant critical thinker unafraid of a flash of showmanship. *Do you remember your first fuck?* was, as well as a laugh line, a perfect description of the effect that Pauline always wanted the movies to have on her. She had made similar pronouncements on many occasions. She had discovered her passion for the screen early on, as a child growing up in the farming community of Petaluma, California. It was a passion that grew during her adolescence; through her time as a student at Berkeley; her hard-scrabble years when she struggled at a demoralizing series of dead-end jobs to support herself and her only child, Gina; her protracted apprenticeship as a critic for obscure film magazines; up to her emergence, when she was nearing fifty, as the most famous, distinctive, and influential movie critic *The New Yorker* ever had. And her love of the movies reached its apex from the late 1960s through the mid-1970s, a period she regarded as equivalent to some of the great literary epochs in history. Her involvement with her subject matter was anything but casual; it was as tumultuous and irrational and possessive as the most volatile love affair. "Definitely her engagement was libidinal," observed her friend the film critic Hal Hinson. "She took notes constantly at screenings, that nubby little pencil going constantly throughout the movie. That engagement was as erotic as any erotic engagement could be. . . . Pauline's presence was essential, and you felt what she felt: that she was at the center of the culture, and that movies were at the center of the culture."

"I am the most grateful human being in the whole world for what Hollywood has given me," Joan Crawford once said with straight-faced sincerity, in a late-career interview. "It's given me my education—it's given me everything that I've ever earned." Pauline Kael, who dismissed Crawford as an actress, might easily have said something along those lines. Her love of the movies was nothing short of life-giving: It sustained her in ways that nothing and no one else in her life ever could, or ever did.

# CHAPTER ONE

From the beginning of her career Pauline Kael seemed intensely proud of the fact that she came from the American west. There were elements of both careerism and reverse snobbery in this: She took great pains to paint herself as a western rebel, an independent, plain-speaking thinker who owed nothing to what she considered to be the hidebound thinking of the East Coast literary and critical establishment. While she often gave the impression of being a second- or third-generation Californian, her parents were actually only in the process of settling into their life on the West Coast at the time she was born.

For most of her life, Kael's mother, Judith Yetta Friedman, projected the identity of the classic displaced person. She was born on December 21, 1884, in Pruszków, Poland, a town whose population hovered around 16,000 in the early years of the twentieth century. Kael later claimed that her mother's father was a tax collector for Tsar Alexander II.

Judith prized a solid, first-rate education above most other things in life, but during her formative years, such a thing was mostly out of reach for even the brightest of young women. A proper education was a privilege reserved for men, and Judith never stopped resenting the way women were denied opportunities in the Old World. "Judith Kael resented her lot in life, which was to be a breeder," said her grandson, Bret Wallach. Pauline Kael may well have had her mother in mind when she reviewed the 1983 film *Yentl*, directed by and starring one of her favorite performers, Barbra Streisand. Based on a short story by Isaac Bashevis Singer, *Yentl* tells the story of a young woman who, yearning to become a religious scholar, disguises herself as a boy and enrolls in a yeshiva. Though never an ardent feminist in the traditional sense, Kael, more than most critics at the time, liked *Yentl* and particularly responded to Streisand's portrayal of the title character, "who runs her fingers over books as if they were magic objects."

Judith eventually married Isaac Kael, born in Pruszków on August 18, 1883. Isaac's family background was not nearly as elevated as Judith's, which appears to have been a source of conflict between them for much of their married life, as Judith grew increasingly resentful of being consigned to the role of housewife and mother.

During the late nineteenth and early twentieth centuries, more than two million Jews, a great number of them from Russia and Poland, arrived on American shores. Isaac emigrated to the United States in 1903, with Judith following two years later; Isaac's younger brother Philip (who married one of Judith's sisters) would join them in 1907. They settled into the epicenter of New York's Jewish ghetto—the grim, poverty- and disease-ridden slums of Hester Street, where Jewish peddlers shoved their pushcarts up and down the dirty streets, hawking fish, meat, household items, novelties. Isaac made a living by selling caps. Within a short time the couple started a family: Louis, born February 27, 1906, and Philip, born May 12, 1909. The chilly disposition that Judith showed later in life may have had its roots in the miserable experience of these difficult early years in New York. Soon the family sought out a healthier place to live, with greater opportunities. The Kaels did eventually manage to live for a brief time in the Catskills town of Mountain Dale, New York, where their third child, Annie, was born on September 23, 1912.

For some time Isaac and Judith had been aware of a thriving community of Jewish chicken ranchers in Petaluma, a picturesque town in Sonoma County, California. In 1904 a Lithuanian named Sam Melnick had settled there and gained a foothold as its first Jewish poultry farmer. Once word of Melnick's success got around—thanks in large part to articles and advertisements in *The Jewish Daily Forward*, the most widely read Yiddish daily newspaper in America—many Jewish immigrants made the trek westward.

The decision of the Kaels to become part of this Jewish community had no particular religious motivation; both Isaac and Judith had been and would remain highly secular Jews. But in Petaluma they would have the chance to live among their own people in what sounded like a beautiful setting, with plenty of fresh air and room for the children to play. They also knew that in a farming community, poor people almost always have an easier time coming by food than they do in the city. So in 1912, along with Judith's parents and Isaac's brother Philip, the Kaels packed up their belongings and headed to California.

In 1912 Petaluma, which lies thirty-five miles north of San Francisco, was a tiny town—its population was around 7,500—surrounded by rolling hills and sprawling dairy farms with signs hawking farm-fresh eggs and milkshakes. With its dirt roads and hitching posts and frame houses, it seemed to belong to the Old West more than to the twentieth century.

In 1878, a Canadian named Lyman C. Byce had arrived in Petaluma, and soon began raising poultry there. In 1879, he and Isaac Dias invented the first egg incubator, which revolutionized the poultry industry. Farmers could produce a far greater number of chicks, and business began to boom. Ranches sprang up that eventually developed the capacity to produce anywhere from 100,000 to 1.8 million eggs annually. The Petaluma Valley became dotted with stock and poultry feed mills, egg-packing plants, and box factories. At the railroad station was a sign depicting an enormous hen sitting on a stack of eggs that trumpeted Petaluma's sobriquet "The Egg Basket of the World."

On their arrival the Kaels moved into a two-story house at 219 Fifth Street, until Isaac found a nine-acre farm five miles west of town, near Middle Two Rock Road. On the property was a large frame house, with a couple's house and bunkhouse out back. The Kaels got their poultry business off the ground with a flock of white Leghorns. As was the case with most Jewish immigrants in the area, their lack of experience wasn't much of an obstacle. Maintaining a chicken ranch wasn't overly complicated and didn't require a huge initial outlay of cash, but it was hard work; the eggs had to be gathered and sorted and cleaned by hand, then packed up to go to market. Year by year their business grew, and Isaac ultimately built up the ranch to the point where it could accommodate five thousand chickens. He and Judith also added to their family. On November 30, 1913, another daughter, Rose, arrived. And on June 19, 1919, their fifth and last child, Pauline, was born at Petaluma General Hospital. In a few short years the family's life had improved to an almost unimaginable degree, and the future seemed to hold great promise.

At home, however, the atmosphere was far from harmonious. From the beginning, Judith—or Yetta, as she was often called—loathed life on the farm. A woman who, during her privileged youth in Poland, had scarcely had reason even to boil an egg was now harvesting and cleaning them for long hours each day. Then there was the kale that had to be grown, picked, and mixed into the chicken feed, on top of cooking for the ranch hands. Judith was angry and frustrated much of the time, and the harder she worked, the more distant she grew toward her children. Anne Kael Wallach's son, Bret Wallach, who remembered visiting Judith in the late 1940s, described her as someone whose "affection radiated at about two degrees above absolute zero." However frustrated she may have been, Judith did show a certain motherly concern for her three daughters, and as time went on, she grew determined that Anne, Rose, and Pauline would have the educational opportunities that had eluded her.

Judith's unhappiness made a sharp contrast with Isaac Kael's own good-natured gregariousness. He was a man who naturally expected good things to unfold before him and made no attempt to hide his delight when they did. He had great drive and energy and confidence, and his children adored him.

The Jews who settled in Petaluma generally fell into one of two groups— those who allied themselves with the Labor Zionist movement in Israel, and those who sought to improve social conditions for American Jews; outsiders were quick to tag the latter group as "radical," even "Red." To Kenneth Kann, author of *Comrades and Chicken Ranchers*, an oral history of farm life in Petaluma, the town was "a community of idealists, people who were not so concerned with making a lot of money, people who preferred the agricultural life over the sweatshops and the pushcarts of the city." The so-called radicals were, in Kann's view, individuals who "retained a Jewish identity, but they were people with a national and a world perspective."

To Isaac and Judith Kael, it was plain that such an intellectually inquisitive community needed a proper social gathering place, and Isaac became one of the founders of the Jewish Community Center of Petaluma. Plans for the center got under way in 1924, but when it became apparent that the community hadn't raised enough money to pay for its construction, Isaac traveled to San Francisco and appealed to the wealthy Haas family of the Levi Strauss Company, well known for their support of Jewish cultural enterprises. The Haases came up with a sizable gift, and with Judith serving tirelessly on the building committee, the Jewish Community Center of Petaluma opened on August 2, 1925. Its activities were focused on Jewish cultural and religious issues; the individual organizations that made the center their home included both the men and women's branches of B'nai Brith, Hadassah, and Poale Zion. Jewish performers and lecturers on Jewish topics visited the center, spurring the locals to engage in colorful and often heated debates on topics of international significance. Sometimes the locals themselves banded together to perform readings from Yiddish literary classics.

To Kenneth Kann, the community of Petaluma Jews "bore an unmistakable resemblance to the *shtetl*, the Jewish village of Tsarist Russia." Certainly the Jewish farmers' customs seemed quite alien to many of their gentile neighbors, and their relations were not always harmonious. In school the Jewish children were frequently subjected to racist slurs by their gentile classmates. Annie Kael, for instance, was a good student and generally well accepted, but even though her gentile friends were allowed to come to the Kael house to visit, the reverse did not hold true. The success of the Jewish Community Center, however, made Isaac something of a local golden boy, and many of the prominent gentiles in Petaluma held him in high esteem. Still, the esteem was qualified. One local dignitary referred to him as "the one white Jew in Petaluma." Many local Jews were given bank loans on the condition that Isaac cosign for them, which he was more than happy to do.

This early part of Pauline's childhood unfolded in an ambience of comfort and security. She enjoyed life on the farm and, though she was too young to have much to do with the egg business, she liked spending time outdoors in the temperate climate. At many of the meals, nearly everything on the table came from the land—chicken, eggs, and vegetables and fruits directly from the garden. The film critic Stephanie Zacharek, who met Pauline in the early 1990s, observed that "she loved to eat and cook, and she was very conscious of what she ate and the quality of the food. She said, 'It's because I grew up in the country, and we always had fresh vegetables and eggs. That was part of where I came from.'"

Despite being an agricultural community, Petaluma was fertile ground for any child interested in reading and writing and ideas. The community overflowed with the traditional Jewish love of culture and learning. Many of its ranchers subscribed to the Yiddish-language newspapers from New York and engaged in spirited debate about world issues. "Such wonderful evenings we had talking about books in Petaluma," recalled Basha Singerman, a Russian immigrant whose family moved to the area early in the twentieth century. "Yiddish books—the classical writers, history, politics. Books were our life in Petaluma." And there were silent movies in town, which the entire family attended. Pauline remembered sitting on her father's lap and being enthralled by the "flickers" if impatient with their intertitles: "We were so eager for the movie to go on that we gulped the words down and then were always left with them for what, to our impatience, seemed an eternity, and the better the movie, the more quickly we tried to absorb and leap at the printed words, and the more frustrating the delays became."

From the beginning it was clear to the family that Pauline was exceptionally clever. She learned to read at an early age, and both Isaac and Judith encouraged her interest in books. As a small child, she devoured L. Frank Baum's Oz books, collections of fairy tales, and Edith Maude Hull's torrid *The Sheik*, filched from her older brothers. She was extremely precocious, and her older siblings delighted in the astonishing observations that routinely popped out of her mouth. Like her sisters, Pauline was diminutive. (Family members jokingly referred to them as the "Three Amazons.") Rose was industrious and earnest, eager to fit in with her peers; Anne was a quiet, disciplined, and bright student; and Pauline was the talkative one who couldn't help but call attention to herself, the one whose intellect was the most obvious and least conformist.

Isaac's success and popularity in Petaluma no doubt encouraged him to indulge in his principal vice: pursuing other women. By the mid-1920s he had developed a reputation as one of Petaluma's smoothest ladies' men. There was one particular widow whom he joined for frequent dalliances. As a way of covering up his motives, he often brought along Pauline, who would play outside while her father paid court.

Throughout her writing career, and even to an overwhelming degree throughout her personal life, Pauline was extraordinarily reluctant to discuss her childhood and adolescence. Stephanie Zacharek remembered that she would talk about her past "only in a vague sort of way." Even people who felt that they knew her quite well realized at some point or other that she had revealed next to nothing about the dynamics of her family life, especially her relationship with her mother. When Kenneth Kann called Pauline to interview her for *Comrades and Chicken Ranchers*, she provided him with a one-sentence reply:

"Chicken ranching? I can't remember a thing about it. But just ask me about the Mystic Movie Theater in Petaluma."

In the early 1960s, before New Journalism had really taken hold and it had become acceptable for reporters to impose their own personalities on their work, no one really expected a movie critic to share personal information in a review. So it came as something of a surprise when Pauline did just that in her *Film Quarterly* review of Martin Ritt's 1963 Western drama *Hud*. She felt that the material had been misinterpreted by both those who made it and the critics who reviewed it. To them, the character of Hud, played by Paul Newman at his most virile and attractive, was meant to symbolize the moral decay that had infected the country. Audiences, meanwhile, seemed to react to him— understandably, given the glamour casting of Newman—as "a celebration and glorification of materialism—of the man who looks out for himself." Pauline agreed with popular sentiment, adding that she appreciated *Hud*'s accurate depiction of the West—"not the legendary west of myth-making movies like the sluggish *Shane* but the modern West I grew up in, the ludicrous real West . . . The incongruities of Cadillacs and cattle, crickets and transistor radios, juke-boxes, Dr Pepper signs, paperback books—all emphasizing the standardization of culture in the loneliness of vast spaces." In her analysis of the honest, unro-mantic way Ritt had depicted life on a western ranch, she offered a very personal memory:

The summer nights are very long on a western ranch. As a child, I could stretch out on a hammock on the porch and read an Oz book from cover to cover while my grandparents and uncles and aunts and parents didn't stir from their card game. The young men get tired of playing cards. They either think about sex or try to do something about it. There isn't much else to do—the life doesn't exactly stimulate the imagination, though it does stimulate the senses. . . . I remember my father taking me along when he visited our local widow: I played in the new barn which was being constructed by workmen who seemed to take their orders from my father. At six or seven, I was very proud of my father for being the protector of widows.

And later:

My father, who was adulterous, and a Republican who, like Hud, was opposed to any government interference, was in no sense and in no one's eyes a social predator. He was generous and kind, and democratic in the western way that Easterners still don't understand: it was not out of guilty condescension that mealtimes were communal affairs with the Mexican and Indian ranchhands joining the family, it was the way Westerners lived.

It was an unusual point of view for an educated woman to hold in the 1960s: Rather than resenting her father for his infidelity to her mother, Pauline seemed almost to take pride in it. In her adult years, Pauline would be drawn steadily to similarly unapologetic, confident, and self-reliant males—as friends, sometimes as lovers, and often as objects of professional admiration.

By mid-1928 Isaac Kael had reached his peak of prosperity, having built the ranch up to the point where it could accommodate a capacity of twenty-five thousand chickens and having amassed a stock portfolio totaling more than $100,000. But because he had bought the bulk of his securities on margin, they didn't really belong to him, and he then made a terrible misjudgment in selling short. As the market continued to rise, however, he was forced to lay his hands on more cash in order to maintain control of his stock. "He put up everything he had as security, and still he was short," remembered Louis Kael. With such a huge amount of stock debt, Isaac was in no way prepared for such turbulence in the marketplace, and eventually he was washed up.

He quickly found that he had become a pariah, as far as the other chicken ranchers were concerned, and the people who had always seemed to look up to him were now plainly uneasy, avoiding him when he ran into them on the street. There was nothing for Isaac to do but pull up stakes and move to San Francisco, where he hoped he might be able to piece together a new life for his family.

# CHAPTER TWO

Isaac Kael was only forty-five when he lost the Petaluma ranch, and initially, at least, he was confident that he was capable of two more decades of solid work. Taking into account the expertise he had developed during his years as a chicken rancher, he decided it would make sense to go into the retail poultry and produce business. When the Kaels arrived in San Francisco, he immediately sprang into action and, using most of the little money that was left, leased three separate stores. As he had no equipment, no license, and no product, he sent Louis, now in his early twenties, to the Jewish Welfare Foundation to take out a series of modest loans to help launch his new business.

Isaac enjoyed a few reasonably profitable months as a poultry retailer and greengrocer until October of 1929 and the Wall Street crash, after which it became a constant struggle to keep the business going. He tried to put on a brave front by taking the produce salesmen out for nice lunches; in private, however, his confidence began to desert him. He pined for the days when he had been a man of influence in Petaluma, and succumbed to bouts of nerves and melancholy.

Judith was forced to work in the grocery store, and she despised catering to the public even more than she had disdained life on the farm. Her disposition worsened, and with Louis and Philip out on their own, the three daughters still at home all gradually withdrew, in different ways, from her. Pauline's niece Dana Salisbury believed that "Pauline had no patience or even any kind of feeling for her mother." Nevertheless, Judith remained a powerful spur to her daughters' education, constantly putting money aside in the hope that one day they would all be able to attend a four-year college. She was delighted when Annie—who now called herself Anne—was accepted as a freshman at Berkeley. According to Salisbury, Anne felt that "these ideas had saved her life. Reading and listening to music had given her a whole world, and she was thrilled to be able to pursue the life of the mind at Berkeley."

Judith's advocacy was not something that Pauline spoke about easily in later years. But she carried a sense of it inside her. In her review of James Toback's 1978 movie *Fingers*, she observed, "All of us have probably had the feeling of being divided between what we got from our mother and what we got from our father, and no doubt some of us feel that we've gone through life trying to please each of them and never fully succeeding, because we have always been torn between them."

By the time Pauline reached high school, it was clear to her family that she was a girl with an intense intellectual drive and wide-ranging talents. "The youngest in a large family has a lot of advantages," she once said. "You pick up a fair amount of knowledge from your older siblings, and your parents don't worry too much about you." Not only was she unusually well-read for some-one her age, she had learned to play the violin, and her teacher was certain that if she kept working at it, she could become a superb musician. Most of the time she played classical music, and she went regularly to hear Alfred Hertz guest-conduct the San Francisco Symphony, but Gershwin and Elling-ton ultimately proved to be as much her taste as Dvořák and Mozart. At San Francisco's Girls' High School, which she attended from age fourteen, Pauline was the only violinist in the school orchestra. She also was a member of the debating club, and with her quick wit and already solid reasoning skills was an expert debater, at one point going up against Lowell High School's Carol Channing. A photograph taken in June 1933 reveals Pauline to be the small-est girl in the group, with big glasses, a mass of brown hair, and a shrewd-looking expression that suggests a much older and more mature woman.

In her warm and friendly yet strong and commanding voice—her diction was immaculate—she could hold forth on an amazing range of topics for one so young. Already she was seized by the power of reading and acquiring more knowledge; like W. B. Yeats's Wandering Aengus, she had a fire in her head. She spoke in beautifully complete sentences, but she also loved slang and four-letter words, "shit" being a favorite. She was very funny, and her family delighted in her extroverted side. "I was quick to understand things," she once told the film historian Sam Staggs. "I can remember members of the family asking me to repeat gags I'd pulled on them when we had company."

While it was an impressive achievement for her older sisters to have grad-uated from Berkeley, Pauline was not very enthusiastic about their career choices as teachers. She herself had no interest in teaching, which she con-sidered a very ordinary profession. She recognized that Anne was a talented educator, and was always fond of her, even though they had completely dif-ferent temperaments. As a child, Anne had exhibited a temper, but as she grew older, she became more even-keeled—although her calm demeanor masked a strong will.

Rose, on the other hand, was Pauline's bête noire from an early age, as

Rose resented what she viewed as her younger sister's egocentricity. Pauline, for her part, soon grew enormously critical of Rose's middlebrow taste in reading material. Rose favored *Liberty* and *Collier's* magazines and Zane Grey Westerns, while Pauline valued the works that Anne passed her way, including Sherwood Anderson's *Winesburg, Ohio* and Willa Cather's *My Ántonia*.

Recalling the sisters' relationship as adults, Dana Salisbury said, "Pauline looked down with such contempt on my aunt Rose. Pauline loved to be in charge. She had ideas. She was the intellectual. Pauline considered herself smarter than everyone else, and Rose was more conventional in her behavior and refused to kowtow." As a result Rose and Pauline often squared off against each other, leaving Anne to play the role of the calming oldest sister.

Life in San Francisco was much to Pauline's liking. The Kaels were now living in an infinitely more diverse and cosmopolitan place, which was fine with Pauline, who always maintained a neutral, detached attitude toward her own Jewish past. Like Rose and Anne, she in no way identified herself, even humorously, as a "nice Jewish girl," with all that term's connotations, and friends from the later part of her life do not remember her ever using Yiddish expressions in conversation, even in the offhand way that many urban gentiles do. Only in her thirst for knowledge and culture did Pauline embrace traditional Jewish values, but throughout her life she refrained from thinking of them as "Jewish." To her, that sort of self-identification was the essence of straitjacketed thinking, and she would have none of it.

San Francisco also placed her in much closer proximity to the arts. Like all other cities, it had been hard hit by the effects of the Depression, yet its performing arts thrived. While audience numbers may have declined during the peak Depression years, touring companies continued to view San Francisco as the most important stop on their West Coast schedule. Martha Graham and Trudi Schoop gave dance recitals; Charlotte Greenwood, Leo Carillo, Ethel Waters, and many other great stars of the New York stage appeared at the President, Tivoli, Curran, and Orpheum theaters. Top-balcony seats at the Curran were only fifty cents, and as they were growing up, Pauline and her sisters attended concerts and plays as often as they could. One of the plays that thrilled Pauline most was a 1932 touring production of *Cyrano de Bergerac*, starring Richard Bennett.

And there were the movies. The city was full of grand-scale picture palaces, and Pauline went as often as she could to the Fox, the Roxie, the Castro, and to the Paramount over in Oakland. As a young girl discovering the talkies, she found herself especially drawn to the tough gangster movies that Warner Bros. turned out with the beginning of sound. Of all the studios at the time,

Warners seemed most committed to portraying the ways that American life had been altered by the Depression in what were, by Hollywood standards, realistic terms. Its stories were built around hardened gangsters, wised-up chorus girls and dance-hall hostesses, ruthless and enterprising crime bootleggers and syndicate bosses. These down-and-dirty archetypes had great appeal for American audiences, who saw something of their predicament in the lives of the characters onscreen, who, after all, were just caught up in the business of trying to get ahead. With their no-frills settings and uncomplicated lighting, these films were easy and inexpensive to produce, and were turned out by the week during the early '30s. With her own natural tough-mindedness, Pauline responded to them immediately; years later, when she came to write about them, she was amazed by how much they had stayed with her. The crime drama from this period that meant the most to her was *I Am a Fugitive from a Chain Gang* (1932), which she would eventually dub "one of the best of the social-protest films—naïve, heavy, artless, but a straightforward, unadorned story with moments that haunted a generation." As a girl, she was shattered by the moment at the end of the movie when the starving hero, James Allen (Paul Muni), is asked, "How do you live?" His face a study in pure anguish, he replies, "I steal."

Pauline was most taken with the independent spirit of the smart, fast-talking heroines of screwball comedies and progressive women's dramas. She later observed that in the 1930s, "The girls we in the audience loved were delivering wisecracks. They were funny and lovely because they were funny. A whole group of them with wonderful frogs in their throats. They could be serious, too. There was a period in the early '30s when Claudette Colbert, Ann Harding, Irene Dunne and other actresses were running prisons, campaigning for governor or being doctors and lawyers." Many of these were made prior to the 1934 establishment of the Production Code, devised by the Motion Picture Producers and Distributors of America to ensure that the screen presented a safe and sanitized view of American life.

Pauline's lifelong love of movie comedy also began in the '30s. She never liked Chaplin—whom she regarded as a tear-pulling fraud—but soaked up the screwball farces of the first decade of the talkies and fell in love with their quick-witted stars—Claudette Colbert, Carole Lombard, Lee Tracy, and Cary Grant. The change in her own family's fortunes had helped give her a deep understanding of the ways in which the Depression era had given birth to screwball. She felt that the best comedies of the time "suggested an element of lunacy and confusion in the world; the heroes and heroines rolled with the punches and laughed at disasters. Love became slightly surreal; it became stylized—lovers talked back to each other, and fast. Comedy became the new romance, and trading wisecracks was the new courtship rite. The cheerful, washed-out heroes and heroines had abandoned sanity; they were a little crazy, and that's what they liked in each other. They were like the wisecracking soldiers in service comedies: if you were swapping quips, you were alive—you hadn't gone under." She also developed a great love for the manic, eye-spinning antics of the Ritz Brothers, and she wanted to yelp in pain when her friends failed to perceive their worth. "She was crazy, ga-ga, over my dad," recalled Harry Ritz's daughter, Janna Ritz. Pauline loved to ask people she met which performers they liked best, the Ritz Brothers or the Marx Brothers—if the answer was the Ritz Brothers, Pauline thought a person might turn out to be worth her time.

One of Pauline's favorite actresses of the '30s was Barbara Stanwyck. Decades later, she was one of the first critics to grasp fully the power and seamlessness of Stanwyck's craft, which was simple and spare and true, devoid of the sentimental, laid-on effects in which so many other female stars of the time indulged. Of Stanwyck's performance in the 1930 drama *Ladies of Leisure*, directed by Frank Capra, she wrote, "Though she came from the theatre, Barbara Stanwyck seemed to have an intuitive understanding of the fluid physical movements that work best on camera; perhaps she had been an unusually 'natural' actress even onstage." To Pauline, Stanwyck represented a "remarkable modernism" and was "an amazing vernacular actress." This observation about Stanwyck was crucial to understanding the aesthetic that would later make Pauline famous, controversial, and deeply misunderstood. She loved movies—and literature—that made honest, direct, and imaginative use of plain American speech.

Pauline was less pleased with many of Hollywood's more high-minded efforts. The antithesis of Warner Bros., Metro-Goldwyn-Mayer was a kind of celluloid confectionary, turning out big-budget movies marked by exquisite set designs, costumes, and lighting. No one could argue with the high level of the studio's craftsmanship, but it seldom had more than a passing resemblance to real life. The studio's head, Louis B. Mayer, was a martinet committed to presenting squeaky-clean, sentimental, wholesome entertainment, with a view of American life that bordered on propaganda; when she eventually wrote about MGM pictures, Pauline delighted in puncturing their grandiosity and high-mindedness. She would come down particularly hard on the studio's number-one female star, Norma Shearer—in Pauline's view, a thoroughly phony actress who in MGM's 1931 *Private Lives* rose to the level of acting "halfway human," but who most of the time never made it even that far.

Even as a girl, Pauline was flat-out bored by the figure of the ladylike, long-suffering heroine—a staple of the movies, in various incarnations, for decades to come. (She was stubbornly resistant to the charm of Irene Dunne, despite Dunne's talent and versatility.) She was instinctively drawn to actresses who could unapologetically portray toughness and sexuality and independence, actresses who went against the grain, such as Miriam Hopkins in *The Story of Temple Drake* (1932). While she never made any outrageous claims for Greta Garbo's acting ability, she was, like so many others, spellbound by the actress's "extraordinary sensual presence." She did consider Garbo capable of great artistry, but in her adolescence was already beginning to form the notion that it was not necessary for movie stars to be brilliant actors, so long as the audience was somehow seduced by their presence. Garbo was the most seductive of all 1930s stars, and Pauline understood early on that she had the power to make the audience surrender to her. She didn't apologize for responding to performers' physical beauty, whether they were women or men. She could enjoy a second-rate actress such as Paulette Goddard because she was "shiny and attractive."

There were two female stars of the time who Pauline placed above all the rest—Katharine Hepburn and Bette Davis. It isn't surprising that a high-spirited, rebellious, and fiercely intellectual girl like Pauline would make such an instant connection with both actresses: Each was a blazingly original talent who fought hard to make sure that her own view of herself came through on the screen. Hepburn, with her casual superiority and tough-mindedness where men were concerned, and Davis, with her sizzling, neurotic intensity, refused to be shoved into the glamorous, conventional leading-lady mold; on film, they radiated independence, and their impact was overwhelming, in ways that their audiences weren't always quite able to figure out. Both were also well known for refusing to melt into the Hollywood system, for defying the studio bosses—a fact that was not lost on Pauline, for whom the Hepburn of the '30s was a kind of beacon for all the strong-minded American women who were under the ever-present pressure to compromise their standards. Writing of Hepburn's drama *Christopher Strong* (1932), Pauline recalled a scene that had haunted her as a young woman. In the film Hepburn played a daring aviatrix who falls in love with a distinguished married man. After their first night together, the man asks that she withdraw from flying in the match she has entered. Pauline observed:

> I don't know of any other scene that was so immediately recognizable to women as a certain kind of *their* truth. It was clear that the man wasn't a bastard, and that he was doing this out of anxiety and tenderness—out

of love, in his terms. Nevertheless, the heroine's acquiescence destroyed her. There are probably few women who have ever accomplished anything beyond the care of a family who haven't in one way or another played that scene. Even those who were young girls at the time recognized it, I think, if only in a premonitory sense. It is the intelligent woman's primal post-coital scene.

Bette Davis's explosive energy, Pauline felt, made the actress "the embodiment of the sensational side of '30s movies . . . vibrantly, coarsely *there*." In the '30s Davis's material didn't resonate with Pauline the way Hepburn's did, but she relished Davis's ability to transcend it with her own audacious style. A ramshackle movie such as *Dangerous* (1935) was still worthwhile because of the way Davis "hypes it with an intensity that makes you sit up and stare." A weeper like *Dark Victory* (1939) might have struck Pauline as "a gooey collection of clichés," but Davis made it worthwhile by the way she "slams her way through them in her nerviest style." She felt that Davis, more than any other screen actress, was able to reflect the neuroses that gnawed at Depression-era American women.

There was one movie genre whose appeal eluded Pauline from the beginning. Although she admired John Ford's influential *Stagecoach* (1939)—she later wrote that it presented a view of the American past "that made the picture seem almost folk art; we wanted to believe in it even if we didn't"—most Westerns left her cold. She didn't buy the male fantasy of the mythical past that the Western sold to the public, and she hated the treatment of the Indians as monsters more appropriate to a horror movie. Isaac was a great lover of movie Westerns, and Pauline later recalled that he always said it didn't matter if it was any good or not, or if he'd already seen it. "I think I understand what my father meant," Pauline observed in the mid-1960s. "If you're going for *a* Western (the same way you'd sit down to watch *a* television show), it doesn't much matter which one you see."

It might have been expected that Pauline would become an English literature major once she reached college, but she avoided that route, possibly because she worried that she might be pigeonholed into a teaching career. Instead, after graduating from Girls' High School in the spring of 1936, she enrolled that fall at the University of California at Berkeley as a philosophy major. In view of her excellent high school record, Berkeley awarded her an alumni-sponsored scholarship for her first year.

Founded in 1868, Berkeley had come to be regarded by many as the apotheosis of modern academic freedom. Unlike the Ivy League colleges in the east, Berkeley at the time was anything but exclusive: Proof of a legitimate high school diploma, along with proof of a solid background in the arts, sciences, and humanities and a solid B average, was usually a guarantee of admission. The emphasis was on electives, with a minimal number of required courses.

Along with the relatively enlightened academic atmosphere came the beautiful campus setting. The Greek Theater, the Sather Gate, the Doe Library were all impressive works of architecture free of institutional chill. There were eucalyptus groves, bountiful gardens and creeks, and plenty of open spaces. There was a lively off-campus scene, too. The Sather Gate Bookstore was widely known as one of the finest retail book outlets in the state. There were good restaurants, such as the Varsity, that fell within student budgets. The Campus Theater, on Bancroft, was a haven for those who loved foreign-language films. And at the Berkeley Music House, classical music lovers could go into a soundproof booth and get to know the latest recordings without ever having to plunk down cash for them.

During her freshman year Pauline immersed herself in English and philosophy courses. For both semesters she scored a solid B in philosophy, earning an A in English. She also excelled in public speaking, but did less well in French, earning a B during the first semester and a C in the second. She took no further language courses for the rest of her time at Berkeley, and the pattern of her freshman year was to be repeated over her sophomore and junior years: excellent grades in her philosophy and literature courses, lower ones in the classes she took simply to fill a requirement, such as economics.

In high school Pauline had been frustrated by her teachers' persistent attempts to force-feed their students material that was good for them: history that reeked of academic correctness, literature with carefully worked out, socially and morally responsible themes. It was learning deemed socially constructive rather than learning that opened up the mind, training it to think in daring, critical ways. At Berkeley she encountered a whole new set of frustrations. For one thing, she wasn't allowed to write her papers in colloquial English. Pauline responded to literature, music, and art with a kind of no-holds-barred intensity, but she found that her professors criticized her for injecting her personal voice into her essays. Humor was seldom welcome at all. The conversational style that she naturally favored was frowned upon; she was asked to remove "I" from her essays and use "one" instead. It was a kind of chilly formality, "term-paper pomposity," as she would come to label it, that went against her natural writing instincts.

But she was a serious student, with a fierce competitive streak, and mindful of the importance of succeeding at Berkeley. So she set to work, trying her best to turn out essays in her own individual voice, in ways that wouldn't alienate the professor and result in a poor grade. She was a great lover of the works of contemporary English novelists such as Henry Green, Ivy Compton-Burnett, Elizabeth Bowen, and Rosamond Lehmann, and in one essay, written midway through her time at Berkeley, she compared the leading British authors with their American counterparts:

> The English are the inheritors of civilization and style, and the current writers know how to use them. They write with grace and assurance; the words mean what they intend them to mean; the rhythms fall where they should. They use the English language with authority. The American writer, caught in his clumsy despair, can scarcely withstand envy and resentment.
>
> But the English, for their part, have more to resent in us than our dollars! The freshness . . . of American writing, the qualities that have made American novels an influence abroad, are as little accessible to them as their authority is to us.

This argument took hold of her early on, and once she became a film critic, it would figure very strongly into the way she wrote about American and European movies.

Pauline's years at Berkeley were a time of great discovery, as she lost herself in the novels of Dostoyevsky, Melville, Hawthorne, James, and Woolf. She loved to make her way through an author's entire oeuvre, becoming, as she put it, "immersed in a sensibility." Henry James's novels would prove an exception to Pauline's habit of binge reading, as it took ten years for her to familiarize herself with the author's work, with breaks in between. Early on she was most deeply drawn to *The Bostonians*, James's 1886 account of the conflict between the hard-bitten suffragette Olive Chancellor and Basil Ransom, a staunch conservative from the old South, as they both fight to control the future of Verena Tarrant, a charismatic rising star on the public lecture circuit. James hints strongly that Olive is a repressed lesbian whose designs on Verena are motivated by sex, as well as by her commitment to the movement, but Pauline was less intrigued by this than she was by Olive's audacious, monomaniacal character—by her pure determination to get what she wants. Already, Pauline was getting a sense of how hard most women had to fight to hold on to their ambitions and ideals, to hold fast against the threat of compromise.

To Pauline, *The Bostonians* made a fascinating contrast with the immaculately wrought, complex subtleties of James's later works, such as *The Golden Bowl* and *The Ambassadors*. She regarded it as "the liveliest of his novels, maybe because it has sex right there at the center, and so it's crazier—riskier, less controlled, less gentlemanly—than his other books." *The Bostonians* possessed "a more earthly kind of greatness." It became one of the seminal books of her early life, and her reaction to it provides a key to her developing literary sensibilities. Years later, reviewing the 1984 James Ivory film of *The Bostonians*, she would put forth the theory that James's original was "the best novel in English about what at that time was called 'the woman question,' and it must certainly be the best novel in the language about the cold anger that the issue of equal rights for women can stir in a man."

For extra money Pauline worked as a teaching assistant, reading papers for a number of courses. Later she had a job as assistant to a chemist who created makeup for performers. One of his clients was the skating star Sonja Henie, then at the height of her movie fame. Taking note of Pauline's fair complexion, the chemist asked her to be the "test girl" for Henie's makeup. "She would come in and inspect the cream on my arms," Pauline later told Sam Staggs. "I don't believe she ever spoke a word to me; she would talk to the chemist while fingering the patches on my arms."

Pauline managed to keep up her generally good grades while pursuing an intense social life. The Bay Area in the 1930s was a good place to be for anyone who loved jazz as much as she did, and she later claimed that she went out dancing every single night in the many top jazz clubs that had sprung up around the city. One of her favorite performers was Turk Murphy, a trombonist who earned a big Bay Area following playing in the dance bands of Will Osborne and Mal Hallet. She delighted in Murphy's Dixieland jazz; she also loved dancing to the big-band sounds of Glenn Miller, Guy Lombardo, and others who frequently played at San Francisco's best hotels. For Pauline, music, like movies, didn't have to be immaculately polished to give intense pleasure. Sometimes it was much better if it wasn't polished at all. She developed a passion for the singing of the trombonist Jack Teagarden; she recalled thinking, *Oh, that's how to do it. You don't need a voice; you just sing.*

And always, there were movies. During her student years at Berkeley, Pauline first came under the spell of the films of Jean Renoir. She was entranced by *La grande illusion*, the director's brilliant 1937 World War I drama—an attempt to make a pacifist statement as Hitler was on the brink of annexing Austria and Czechoslovakia. She was full of admiration for Renoir's evenhanded treatment of the story's aristocrats and plebeians, and wrote in 1961, "Renoir isn't a sociologist or a historian who might show that there were heroes and swine in both groups." She also responded to the fact that Renoir was an instinctive filmmaker who never stuck too slavishly to the script. She found *La grande illusion* "a triumph of clarity and lucidity; every detail fits simply, easily, and intelligibly. There is no unnecessary camera virtuosity: the compositions seem to emerge from the material. It's as if beauty just happens (is it necessary to state that this unobtrusive artistry is perhaps the most difficult to achieve?)." She was also mesmerized by Renoir's 1939 *La règle du jeu*, which she would one day call "perhaps the most influential of all French films, and one of the most richly entertaining." This comedy about a country-house party run amok appealed to her on its own terms, but she also was drawn to its underdog status. It had been mutilated prior to its 1939 release, slashed again after its opening, then stifled completely by the Vichy government, as well as by the Nazis, before being restored in 1959. Pauline grew to love Renoir's best films beyond measure; he was, perhaps, the most kindred spirit of any director she would encounter until she came upon the 1970s masterworks of Robert Altman.

Despite her natural competitive bent and a strong need to dominate, she had no trouble finding friends among the Berkeley student body. She had become part of a circle that included Ida Bear, a writer, and Virginia Holton Admiral, an Oregon-born painter and poet (and later the mother of the actor Robert De Niro). There was also Violet Rosenberg, her closest woman friend. Like Pauline, Violet was passionately interested in art and politics and did not suffer fools, and the two become inseparable companions. Violet was deeply proud of Pauline's intellect and her fearlessness in expressing her opinions, and in the years to come she would prove a loyal friend. "There was always a circle of people around Pauline," Violet later recalled. "People came to her. They were magnetized."

Pauline also became attached to two men who were to count among the most important relationships of her life. Robert Duncan, a young poet who shared many of Pauline's left-leaning political interests, would become one of her most cherished friends. Duncan was a renegade almost from the beginning of his life—one of the most unorthodox lives that could possibly have been found in 1930s and '40s America. He was born in Oakland just six months before Pauline. His mother died in childbirth, and his father, Edward Howard Duncan, put him up for adoption soon thereafter. His foster parents were an architect named Edwin Joseph Symmes and his wife, Minnehaha

Harris, who were devoted to spiritualism and the occult. At their home in Bakersfield, the Symmes family hosted séances the way some couples hosted canasta games, and they informed their son that he was descended from a line of people who had perished in the lost city of Atlantis. The Symmeses were hostile toward modern science, which they believed would cause the New World to be engulfed in flames during their son's lifetime, just as Atlantis had been decimated by flood and earthquake. Small wonder that young Robert made his way through his early school years as a misfit—a cross-eyed, conspicuously effeminate though fiercely quick-witted boy who acquired the unfortunate nickname "Sissie Symmes." Like Pauline's, Duncan's family suffered serious reversals in the wake of the Wall Street crash, and like Pauline, he came through it with a strong sense of himself intact. In 1936 Duncan entered Berkeley as a scholarship student, and soon he was immersed in writing poetry and exploring radical politics, significantly as editor of the American Student Union's *Campus Review*, which the university effectively disowned. Duncan, during his years at Berkeley still known as Robert Symmes, was an English major who was also taking introductory philosophy courses, and it was there that he met Pauline.

She responded immediately to his strong and commanding personality. "He was attracted to strong-mother-archetype women he could talk to on an equal basis," recalled Duncan's friend Jack Foley. "He wanted real, substantive discussions." Duncan had a great sense of his own sexual power, and he could be enormously flirtatious and seductive. He was an equally charismatic presence on the public podium, and when he read from his own poetry, the effect could be spellbinding. He was a rather handsome man, but his crossed eyes made people slightly uneasy; they never quite knew whether he was looking at them.

Midway through his time at Berkeley, Duncan left the American Student Union behind for the Young People's Socialist League; Pauline and Virginia Admiral often joined him at the organization's meetings. Duncan would leave Berkeley in 1938 for an abortive fling as a student at North Carolina's progressive Black Mountain College, then move on to Philadelphia, where he began his first serious relationship with a man, an older instructor he had known at Berkeley. But he and Pauline were to maintain a frequent correspondence for the next decade, sometimes writing to each other several times a week.

For years the rumor persisted that the two had been secretly married for a time. They weren't, but Pauline felt a powerful attraction to Duncan, as a surviving fragment of a letter she wrote to him indicates. He had indicated to her that he felt a certain pressure from their circle of friends for them to become romantically involved—hardly an unusual situation for a gay man to come up against in those conformist times. "Don't be foolish—you don't love me—you will never love me," Pauline responded to him with remarkable clearheadedness. Duncan had been flirting with the idea of psychoanalysis, and Pauline was encouraging: "For Christ's sake be analyzed!" she wrote. "Be analyzed if only because you need the self-knowledge for your work, your art."

In her review of the 1973 Barbra Streisand–Robert Redford romantic drama *The Way We Were*, Pauline seems to have tipped her hand a bit with respect to her Berkeley years. Watching the scenes set at Columbia University during the 1930s, with the driven, obsessive Katie trying to rally student support for Stalin, trying—and failing—to perfect a short story for her fiction-writing class, Pauline may have felt a bit as if she were seeing the ghost of her seventeen- and eighteen-year-old self. Like Katie, Pauline did dabble in left-wing radical politics during her college years—she was more intrigued by Trotskyism than anything—but with the passage of time, as her review of *The Way We Were* revealed, she took a much cooler attitude toward leftist politics: "[T]here appears to be nothing between Communist involvement and smug indifference. . . . Implicitly, the movie accepts the line the Communist Party took— that it was the only group doing anything, so if you cared about peace or social injustice you had to join up." She was fairly quick to step away from her own flirtation with the Communist Party, largely because of her natural suspicion of anything that smacked of dogma.

The person at Berkeley with whom Pauline was destined to be most intimately involved was, like Robert Duncan, a poet: Robert Horan, with whom she also shared classes. Horan was attractive, with a keen, alert mind, and discussion—often angry—immediately formed the foundation of their friendship. Kael found Horan stimulating company because, like her, he was obsessed with just about anything concerning the arts. It became routine for the two of them to stay up all night arguing about poetry, fiction, movies, music, painting.

In a number of ways Horan exerted greater influence over her than Duncan did. For one, their shared enthusiasm for the arts got her to rethink the academic path she had been on since her freshman year. Pauline's principal instructors felt that a good grounding in philosophy, public speaking, and English literature would prepare her beautifully for law school. But her involvement with Horan made her see herself increasingly as a writer. She wasn't quite sure which form appealed to her most, but she instinctively began moving toward playwriting, and Horan encouraged her every step of the way.

He also became her lover. Sex may never have been the engine in their mercurial friendship, but at the time it was not surprising that a young man and woman who shared such intensity, along with so many common interests and ideas, should match up. She loved Horan, but she also understood and, on some level, accepted his attraction to men. Certainly there is no evidence, in her many letters from this period, that she considered those men any real threat to her relationship with him. Her own attitude toward gay men was quite open and sympathetic, and later, when Horan showed an interest in settling into a permanent relationship with a woman, she did her best not to be judgmental. She was happy to be involved with a man as attractive and stimulating as Horan, but she had no great designs on marrying him, and she sat back to see which direction it all would take.

# CHAPTER THREE

)

**B**y her senior year Pauline had compiled a solid, if far from outstanding, academic record. She might well have gone on to do graduate work in English, or, given her oratory skills, to success as a law student. But during her final year at Berkeley, her grades fell apart. Her first semester in 1939 was a disaster: She completed only a single course in political science and failed to pass Philosophy 12, Philosophy 199, and Economics 199a. The university gave her a chance to make up the courses before placing her on any official form of academic probation. She petitioned to have the failing grade removed, but her request was denied. Later, in 1940, she made up Philosophy 199 with a B, but she never completed the other two classes, and she finished her time at Berkeley a few credits short of a degree. Decades later, when interviewers occasionally asked her why she hadn't managed to graduate, Pauline was quick to say that she had had around six credits left when she ran out of money.

In the future she would offer other accounts of her final academic year. To some she said that she had been a teaching assistant for several courses. When she had caught the flu during her senior year, she had realized that she could either grade the final papers in all the courses or study for her own finals, but she didn't have the strength to do both—therefore, she had opted to help the other students graduate. To her friend Daryl Chin, she once said that she had taken the money put aside for her final semester and gone to New York, where she treated herself to a theatergoing binge that included Lillian Hellman's *The Little Foxes*, starring Tallulah Bankhead.

In fact, the events of her senior year suggest that she was tired of student life, and that the thought of returning for one more semester was anathema to her. She longed to be rid of the restrictive, unreal atmosphere of campus life and to go out in the world, finding her way as a writer. By summer she was desperate for money, and decided to join her sister Anne in a sublet apartment, where she began determining in what direction she would set out as a writer.

At Berkeley she and Bob Horan had discovered the literary criticism of R. P. Blackmur, whose ability to illuminate the social context of great literature resonated deeply with both of them. Pauline loved the passionate tone of Blackmur's writing, and later she would always be flattered when her criticism was compared with his. Reading his comments on Henry James's *The Wings of the Dove*, one can easily see how his intensely personal voice had a profound influence on her:

> When I was first told, in 1921, to read something of Henry James—just as when I had been told to read something of Thomas Hardy and something of Joseph Conrad—I went to the Cambridge Public Library looking, I think, for *The Portrait of a Lady*. It was out. The day was hot and muggy, so that from the card catalogue I selected as the most cooling title *The Wings of the Dove*, and on the following morning, a Sunday, even hotter and muggier, I began, and by the stifling midnight had finished my first reading of that novel. Long before the end I knew a master had laid hands on me. The beauty of the book bore me up; I was both cool and waking; excited and effortless; nothing was any longer worth while and everything had become necessary. A little later, there came outside the patter and the cooling of a shower of rain and I was able to go to sleep, both confident and desperate in the force of art.

The immediate question, though, was exactly how she was going to survive. Fortunately, during her student years, she had figured out how to live reasonably well on very little, and despite her horror at the thought of becoming a housewife, she mastered a number of solid, practical skills. She was adept at sewing and was a good cook, able to fix herself inexpensive meals by shopping at San Francisco's markets, where the freshest produce was available for very little.

Still, she needed *something* to live on, and she was lucky to be able to count on friends and relatives. Anne, by now teaching at Polytechnic High School near Commerce Street, was always a soft touch, and there was Robert Duncan, who had split from his lover in Philadelphia and by 1940 was living in Woodstock, New York, as part of a commune organized by James Cooney, editor of *The Phoenix*, a countercultural publication with a pacifist point of view. Duncan was working on the magazine and contributing pieces to it, and during this period he became friendly with Henry Miller and Anaïs Nin, both of whom had recently returned to America after years of living in Europe. Both were impressed with Duncan's talent and encouraged him to continue writing poetry. Duncan had a bit of money to send to Pauline, and did so on a few occasions, always with her assurance that she would pay him back when she could.

In addition to working at her writing, Pauline took in everything on the local arts scene that piqued her interest. She had become addicted to reading

*The Partisan Review*, a literary quarterly with a heavy accent on politics that had been published since the mid-'30s. On the musical front she had discovered Aaron Copland's *Piano Variations*, in which the composer explored more abstract musical ideas than usual. She constantly attended art openings throughout the Bay Area and kept up with all the new movies, writing to Violet Rosenberg, who now lived in Santa Paula, her impressions of them. She enthused over John Ford's *The Long Voyage Home*, which she considered "a wonderful movie . . . really the most exciting photography—at least the most sustained in quality, I've seen in the movies yet." It's an interesting reaction, given her later antipathy toward Ford's large-scale, elegiac Westerns and her dislike of the director's *The Grapes of Wrath* (also released in 1940). Also, the use of the superlative in singling out an aspect of a film—"the most sustained in quality"—was to become one of the defining characteristics of Pauline's style as a movie critic; in time, it would draw her both an army of admirers and a loud chorus of detractors.

By March 1941 Robert Horan was working on the staff of *The San Francisco News*. Happy enough with his job, he was also consumed by writing poetry, and Pauline had plenty of opportunity to monitor his progress and offer her criticism, since they were by now living together in an apartment at 930 Post Street. Horan worked at the paper from 4:30 a.m. to 12:30 p.m., which suited Pauline, an inveterate night person, perfectly. She would sit up reading voraciously until it was time for Horan to leave for work, then she would join him for a predawn breakfast at one of the neighborhood diners. Their romance, which had always been of an on-again, off-again nature, was going through a cooling period—enough so that in mid-March 1941, Pauline wrote to Vi of a new affair that had presented itself:

> I'm fairly sure that in the long run it would turn out disastrously. But he remains the only exciting new mind I've met in the last year or so— remarkably brilliant—but it's all just too much trouble for now and I prefer to let things drift. Besides, it would be so damned much trouble to "hook" him properly. (About thirty-five, wife dead, has small daughter, is a musician of quality, studied music and philosophy, and has fun around town with a lady prof from Mills . . . get the idea?

She continued with her round of moviegoing, regaling Vi with her sharp and often somewhat eccentric reviews of what she'd seen. Indeed, the comments about movies in her letters of this period form a kind of intriguing preview of what would become her critical voice. Predictably, she found the Margaret Sullavan–Charles Boyer weeper *Back Street* "fairly dull" and Preston Sturges's brilliant *The Lady Eve* (Barbara Stanwyck, again) "awfully vulgar-funny—really quite something." She considered *Meet John Doe* "not too poor" for a film directed by Frank Capra, whose relentless glorification of American individualism was already grating on her. More unexpectedly she recommended that Violet Rosenberg take in *So Ends Our Night*, John Cromwell's 1941 drama about Nazi Germany—not for its social and political content, but for "the most beautiful shot of Frances Dee, standing in a European marketplace."

In her social life she was feeling misunderstood, a fairly common condition for her. She beseeched Vi to come back to San Francisco to live, because there were so few people who really seemed to grasp her ideas about the arts and the world scene, and she desperately missed the conversations they used to have. "Communication (orally) with people around seems even more difficult than it used to be," she wrote. "I'm getting more tired than ever of having to get basic ideas accepted before you can go on to talk about the things you're interested in talking about."

By May, she was feeling better about herself, buoyed up by the intense work that she and Bob Horan were doing together. They had teamed up for what she described as "a rather complex essay" on three formidable literary critics, R. D. Blackmur, Kenneth Burke, and Lionel Trilling. They hoped to sell the piece to one of the top national magazines as the first step toward launching their reputation as serious critics. "We've been working together just about every waking moment we could find," she wrote to Vi, "and he's just been swell and wonderful to work with . . . By now we know the workings of each other's mind too well for disparities from sentence to sentence."

While Horan and Pauline often disagreed violently about the art exhibits they took in together, they were more in accord when it came to modern poetry. In particular they shared a great love of Dylan Thomas's early works, relishing the raw power of poems such as "And Death Shall Have No Dominion." "It was tremendous fun," Pauline remembered. "We were both young and a little bit crazy, in the sense that practical things didn't matter the way matters of the mind did—matters of mind and emotion."

Ultimately Pauline and Horan were beginning to feel stifled by living in San Francisco, and they began spending hours plotting a move to New York. Horan was desperate to be in the vortex of cultural activity in America, but given Pauline's strong connection to the West Coast, she had mixed feelings about the enterprise. Much as she loved the Bay Area, however, she had to admit that San Francisco was really the biggest small town in America, and later observed that it was like Ireland: If you really wanted to do something important, you needed to get out.

In November 1941 Pauline and Horan finally made the break and left for the East Coast. They hitchhiked across the country, dropping into a number of burlesque houses along the way. They arrived in Manhattan to find they were flat broke, and camped out for several nights at Grand Central Station, homeless in the city they had dreamed of for so long. Several nights later Horan was wandering the streets, trying to lay his hands on some money so they could eat. He was standing in front of Saks Fifth Avenue when he attracted the attention of two men who were returning home from a performance at the Metropolitan Opera. Horan was weaving back and forth, pale and exhausted, and fearing that he might be seriously ill, the two men stopped and began to talk to him.

It turned out to be a lucky break for Horan, since the pair were both well-known composers—Samuel Barber and his lover, Gian Carlo Menotti. They had met a decade earlier when they were students at Philadelphia's Curtis Institute of Music; by now, both had several major successes behind them. Barber, at age thirty-two, had enjoyed his greatest triumphs in the concert hall, with his lushly romantic Violin Concerto and his elegiac *Adagio for Strings*. Menotti, one year younger than Barber, had shown that his gifts lay on the opera stage: two short works, *Amelia Goes to the Ball* and *The Old Maid and the Thief*, had done well, and his third stage work, *The Island God*, had recently had an unsuccessful world premiere at the Metropolitan Opera.

The composers were immediately taken with Horan and invited him to come to their apartment on East Ninety-fifth Street, where they gave him food and liquor, and invited him to spend the night. Horan protested that he couldn't take them up on their offer because Pauline was waiting for him at Grand Central. But they persisted, and Horan quickly arranged for Pauline to stay with a friend on Fifth Avenue, while he moved in with Barber and Menotti—not just for a night but for the long term. The two composers gave him the affectionate nickname "Kinch."

Pauline, left to make her own way in New York, would continue to have conflicted feelings about the degree to which Barber and Menotti had suddenly dominated Horan's life. Finding herself feeling antagonistic toward them, she recorded some of her feelings in a series of notes that appear to have been preparation for a play script she wanted to write. The "trouble with Bob is he feels guilty. First, *feels* as tho [sic] he's whoring," she wrote. "All right— maybe these homos have fine rich mature relationships—what good is that going to do me? I can't be a homo no matter how hard I try, or how commercial I get." (The latter remark underscored her feelings that it was easier to break into New York's artistic circles if you happened to be a gay man.) She accepted Horan's attraction to men; what was more difficult for her to accept was the deepening influence that his new mentors had over him.

Horan's defection left her feeling excluded, which marked the real beginning of her career-long antipathy toward New York and the East Coast artistic establishment. Her upbringing in rural California contrasted wildly with the backgrounds of so many writers and artists she was to meet during her early years in New York, many of whom had come up through the more traditional routes—a cosmopolitan childhood, tony prep schools, Ivy League universities—where they began to make the connections that would serve them later in their careers. By nature Pauline loved painting herself as a rebel, and she found that her Petaluma background was a great help in doing so.

What Pauline needed immediately, in order to survive in New York, was a job. She quickly found one—little to her liking—as governess for a wealthy East Side family. While it gave her access to literary teas and performances at the Metropolitan Opera, she loathed the work itself and resented the fact that she had to dress in proper sports clothes. "I haven't invested a sou in pleasure clothes," she wrote to Vi. "So anything you could send would be most gratefully snatched at—but for heaven's sake, don't send the taffeta if you can still look terrific in it."

She was appalled by the cost of housing in New York City but managed to earn enough at her job to afford an apartment in the upper reaches of Park Avenue, just north of the street's most elegant apartment houses, where the neighborhood began to melt into East Harlem. By late May she no longer had the governess's post and was frantically looking for work. She spent a good deal of her spare time taking in art shows—and disliking much of what she saw, including an exhibition of Max Ernst's paintings and the opening of a Henri Rousseau exhibit at the Museum of Modern Art. Most of the paintings she encountered only intensified her love of Picasso and Miró and Klee. The Nindorf Gallery boasted a generous selection of Klees, and Pauline found that every few weeks she returned there to "look at them all over and feel delighted."

Sentimental 1940s movies mostly left her cold, although she enjoyed Bette Davis's 1942 hit, *Now, Voyager*, which she later dubbed "a schlock classic," and *Casablanca*, which had a "special, appealingly schlocky romanticism." But she was repulsed by *Mrs. Miniver*, which she and Samuel Barber saw at Radio City Music Hall; Pauline found it a mawkish tribute to the British gentry, and she was horrified when it won the Academy Award for Best Picture of

1942. She detested the general run of war movies—remembering their characters as being "patriotic and shiny-faced. Wiped clean of any personality"—and was appalled by the racist manner in which all German and Japanese were portrayed. Propaganda, whether it glorified Americans or demonized the enemy, was inescapable in Hollywood's war pictures, and Pauline longed for the screen to depict American life with some degree of authenticity.

Her letters from this period consistently indicate her low opinion of most of the people she encountered in New York artistic circles. She had come east hoping to be challenged and invigorated, but after only a few months, she was disappointed. (There is also a suggestion of frustration that people she regarded as mediocrities were ahead of her on the career path—more adept than she at playing the New York game.) She thought that New York's arts world was blighted by "a heavy confusion of young men and not so young men living together and shopping around, or being married to fierce young ladies who have other fierce young ladies. And all of them making infantile efforts for a chic wit, for a maximum of attention. . . . The place is cluttered up with 'promising' young poets who are now thirty-five or forty writing just as they did fifteen years ago or much worse."

For some time Isaac Kael had been in failing health. He had suffered from hypertension in his later years; eventually he had a stroke, after which he was confined to a wheelchair. On November 11, 1942, Isaac died in Alameda, California. His death was reported by Rose, the child who had looked after him most. Pauline's grief was of an unusually private nature. She never said much to friends about her reaction to his death, and her surviving letters make no mention of it; she had never been an introspective person, and her father's passing did nothing to change that fact. If anything, it only intensified her feelings of restlessness: Isaac had died without seeing her achieve anything of significance, and she became ever more mindful of how quickly time passes when one is trying to establish a career.

She had landed a job at a publishing house—her letters to Vi do not indicate which one—but the salary was abysmal, and the constant struggle for cash was leaving her feeling depleted. During the first part of 1943, she switched apartments, finding a fairly spacious flat at 135 East Twenty-eighth Street, complete with fireplace, skylight, and built-in bookshelves—but no furniture, which meant that she spent her weekends scrounging in junk and antiques shops for used tables and chairs.

She remained hard at work on her short stories and playwriting, constantly reworking them to try to get them in salable shape. She also kept Vi informed

of the gossip about their old school friends. The big news was that, in a startling about-face, Robert Duncan was planning an April wedding to an
acquaintance of Pauline's named Marjorie McKee. "Pleasing news for a
change," noted Pauline, "altho [*sic*] I can't dare to imagine how it may
work out."

Pauline continued, however, to be a fairly stubborn transplant to New York,
and her letters reveal very little sense of optimism about the future. She was
flailing about, constantly battling anxieties about money and increasingly filled
with doubt and ambivalence about her current situation. It was also harder than
she had guessed to establish a relationship with a man—the kind of relationship
she thought she wanted. There were plenty of opportunities for casual sex;
servicemen regularly propositioned her on the street and in bars, and when she
turned them down, as she often did, they would try to make her feel guilty by
telling her that the girls at home were the ones for whom they were fighting.

She kept in close touch with Bob Horan, who by now was spending much
of his time at Capricorn, Barber and Menotti's country retreat in Mount Kisco,
New York, north of the city. Horan had always had a serious interest in music,
and he was in his element, discussing music theory with two celebrated composers. He was also turning out to be a potent influence on both men, encouraging them to explore abstract painting and modern dance. Eventually
Barber wrote the *Capricorn* Concerto, a modern take on the Baroque concerto
grosso, featuring solo instrumental writing for flute, oboe, and trumpet—
which Barber claimed represented himself, Menotti, and Horan, respectively.

Pauline enjoyed the stimulating environment at Capricorn, and Horan
saw to it that she was a frequent weekend guest. Designed by the architect
William Lescaze, Capricorn was later described by Horan as "a modern but
not *moderne* chalet set into the side of the mountain and overlooking Croton
Lake and the hills." The house was spacious and spare, with a terrace in back
that was ideal for summertime lunches. "One would have to be an imbecile,
not to succumb to the beauty and the quiet. I feel miserable when I have to
catch a train back to the city," Pauline wrote to Vi.

Horan frequently stayed with Pauline when he was in New York, and she
seemed relieved that their relationship had become less complicated. "Bob is
terribly sweet to me these days when he comes to stay," she told Vi, "but there's
a kind of bony structure missing there that I think I should always be too well
aware of—despite his obvious talents and mind, and the very good understanding we have. . . . I've never felt so good about living alone."

Her low opinion of much of the mainstream fare being offered in New
York continued unabated. She was shocked by the quality of most of the plays

of the 1943 fall season and was especially dismayed by *Dream Girl*, Elmer Rice's female version of the Walter Mitty fantasy, and baffled by the acclaim for the performance of Mrs. Rice, Betty Field. But by early 1944, there were more personal concerns nagging at her—one of which was the prospect of her sister Rose's visit in late February. By now Rose had married Myron Makower and embarked on a teaching career, but her proper, settled status seemed only to inflame the animosity between the two sisters.

Pauline was also becoming extremely possessive about her spare time, trying to protect as much of it as she could in order to work at her writing. But with too many friends and acquaintances dropping by the Twenty-eighth Street apartment in the evenings or on weekends, she was beginning to feel as if she had never left Berkeley. In the meantime, Horan's own writing flourished: Some of his poems had been accepted by *The Kenyon Review*, and he was providing the text for *The Unicorn*, a dance work that Menotti was composing for Martha Graham. Pauline, stalled in her tracks, was not entirely enthusiastic about her friend's full-speed-ahead career progress. She told Vi that she found Horan's recent work "hurried and a little too chic. Success doesn't come that easily if you're really serious—and I just don't think he is at the moment." Deep down, she feared that Horan might never turn out anything of real substance.

She was far more impressed with the progress of Robert Duncan. In 1944, the distinguished editor Dwight Macdonald had launched an exciting new magazine of contemporary thought called *Politics*. Pauline considered it the finest publication of political commentary she had come across; it reflected Macdonald's strong, anarchist point of view, and it never cheated the issues. For some time she had admired Macdonald's work as editor of *The Partisan Review*, and she was excited when she learned he was starting up a rival magazine. In late 1943 she had written him a kind of fan letter: "I am looking forward to a magazine which will stand for the principles and position you represented on *Partisan Review*; if there are to be policy-forming discussions, I should be very interested in attending them."

In August 1944 *Politics* published a groundbreaking essay by Duncan called "The Homosexual in Society," a gutsy and powerful piece of work in which Duncan spoke up for a group "who have suffered in modern society persecution, excommunication, and whose intellectuals, whose most articulate members, have been willing to desert that primary struggle, to beg, to gain at the price if need be of any sort of prostitution, privilege for themselves, however ephemeral." The essay provoked widespread comment and gave a substantial boost to Duncan's literary reputation.

Pauline soldiered on in New York, thanks to periodic loans from Vi, but in the fall of 1944 her money worries worsened when she impulsively quit her job at the publishing house. Not only was she bored with the stodgy, good-old-boy atmosphere of the place, but she had become incensed when an anticipated raise to $175 monthly showed up as only $106.

At home she was absorbed in recordings of Beethoven, Purcell, Mozart, and Stravinsky. In the fall of 1944, she accompanied Samuel Barber to a New York Philharmonic concert that featured Stravinsky conducting a program that included some of his own works. After the concert, Barber launched a lengthy denunciation of Stravinsky, both as composer and conductor. Pauline defended him point by point until Barber sighed that Stravinsky was just a fad with her. Pauline replied, "At least I don't have a fad for *your* music." Barber responded with a frozen silence that lasted for weeks. "He has pride and vanity at a maximum," Pauline wrote to Vi. "*Nobody* is ever rude to him— and I'm afraid the poor dear will take some time recovering."

She limped through the following year with a string of odd jobs. Her greatest literary discoveries of 1945 were the works of Marcel Proust, which she made her way through in four weeks of concentrated reading. "I almost feel as if it had become a layer of my sensibility by now," she told Vi. "When you get to know a book that well it seems to get *into* you."

She was fascinated by the news that her old Berkeley classmate Virginia Admiral had left Robert De Niro, Sr., and gone off to live with Manny Farber, the film critic of *The New Republic*. This was bound to pique her interest, since for some time she had followed Farber's reviews with great enthusiasm. Born in Arizona, Farber had certain things in common with Pauline—a Berkeley education, an interest in other forms of art (he went on to distinction as an abstract painter), and an intense dislike of overly formal, schematic "masterpiece art, reminiscent of the enameled tobacco humidors and wooden lawn ponies bought at white elephant auctions decades ago," which, he felt, "has come to dominate the over-populated arts of TV and movies. The three sins of white elephant are (1) to frame the action with an all-over pattern, (2) install every event, character, situation in a frieze of continuities, and (3) treat every inch of the screen and film as a potential area for prizeworthy creativity." He much preferred what he called "termite art," which he characterized as something that "feels its way through walls of particularization, with no sign that the artist has any object in mind other than eating away the immediate boundaries of his art." He believed that the movie critic's objective was to dig into the truth of a film and get it across to his readers. He once said, "I can't see any difference between writing about a porno movie and an Academy

Award movie—both are difficult objects." His writing was at once jazzy and direct and intellectually rigorous. Pauline admired many things about him, including his iconoclastic wit and his fondness for lively B movies, and his theory about white elephant art vs. termite art would be an important influence on her own development as a critic.

There were other movie critics that Pauline had admired over the years, and each of them cast some degree of influence over her as she began thinking more seriously about the art of the film. One was Graham Greene, who began reviewing films for *The Oxford Outlook* while still a student, and from 1935 to 1940 he reviewed by the week, mostly for the *London Spectator*. Greene was never afraid to rail about the blindness of the British Board of Censors, or to berate his British readers for not taking cinema seriously enough. Pauline agreed with his observation that "an excited audience is never depressed; if you excite your audience first, you can put over what you will of horror, suffering truth." It was a point of view that led him in some surprising directions, such as his feeling that Alfred Hitchcock "amuses but he doesn't excite. . . . He hasn't enough imagination to excite; he doesn't convince." He felt that Hitchcock concentrated on his big moments at the expense of everything else that was going on in the movie: opinions that served as a blueprint for the critical position that Pauline would later hold on Hitchcock.

Another critic Pauline admired enormously was Otis Ferguson, who wrote for *The New Republic* beginning in 1930. Ferguson possessed a keen appreciation of the director's contribution, but he also understood that movies were mostly the product of a factory system. "Movies are such common and lowly stuff," he once wrote, "that in intellectual circles we often find ourselves leaping, like trout for flies, after something in a new offering that promises to set it off from the average run, something of special interest or fame, in short any branch of art certified to have nothing to do with that of making pictures." Ferguson was anything but predictable. He could easily overlook the studied and self-conscious artiness of John Ford's *The Grapes of Wrath*, which he considered a masterpiece, yet he raised loud objections to the knowing machinations of *The Wizard of Oz*, in which he found Frank Morgan, as the Wizard, "the only unaffected trouper in the bunch; the rest either try too hard or are Judy Garland. It isn't that this little slip of a miss spoils the fantasy so much as that her thumping, overgrown gambols are characteristic of its treatment here: when she is merry the house shakes, and everybody gets wet when she is lorn."

But the reviewer whose work Pauline admired most was James Agee, who was on the staff of *Time* from 1941 to 1948; during most of this period he also reviewed for *The Nation*. Agee was a superb prose stylist, and although he could be sharp, he was never strident and seemed to speak with the voice of reason. He was capable of dismissing a big sentimental hit in a few sentences, as in his evaluation of Leo McCarey's Academy Award–winning story of two priests, *Going My Way*: "It would have a little more stature as a 'religious' film if it dared suggest that evil is anything worse than a bad cold and that lack of self-knowledge can be not merely cute and inconvenient but also dangerous to oneself and to others." He could accomplish more in a limited space than any other movie critic, and his adeptness at seeing right through an actor's performance was unparalleled. He was stunningly prescient about the turn that Bette Davis's career was in the process of taking by the mid-1940s. In his essay on her 1945 release, *The Corn Is Green*, in which she played a dedicated schoolteacher in a Welsh coal-mining town, Agee saw all too clearly that the spontaneity and raw grasp of realism that had made many of Davis's earlier performances so magical had begun to elude her as her importance within the movie industry grew:

> It seems to me that she is quite limited, which may be no sin but is a pity; and that she is limiting herself beyond her rights by becoming more and more set, official, and first-ladyish in mannerism and spirit, which is perhaps a sin as well as a pity. In any case, very little about her performance seemed to me to come to life, in spite of a lot of experienced striving which often kept in touch with life as if through a thick sheet of glass. To be sure, the role is not a deeply perceived or well-written one, and the whole play seems stolid and weak. I have a feeling that Miss Davis must have a great deal of trouble finding films which seem appropriate, feasible, and worth doing, and I wish that I, or anyone else, could be of use to her in that. For very few people in her position in films mean, or could do, so well. But I doubt that anything could help much unless she were willing to discard much that goes with the position—unless, indeed, she realized the absolute necessity of doing so.

This appreciation of the decline of early gifts—gifts that come so much more easily before actors and directors become officially sanctioned stars—was a theme that Pauline would return to often once she began her own reviewing career.

But perhaps Agee's greatest gift as a critic was an ability to wrestle with his feelings about a movie in a way that involved the reader. Covering Preston Sturges's 1944 farce *The Miracle of Morgan's Creek*, he admitted that he found the movie "funnier, more adventurous, more intelligent, and more encouraging than anything that has been made in Hollywood in years." But he went on to say:

> Yet the more I think about the film, the less I liked it. There are too many things that Sturges, once he had won all the victories and set all the things moving which he managed to here, should have achieved unhindered, purely as a good artist; and he has not even attempted them. He is a great broken-field runner; once the field is clear he sits down and laughs. The whole tone of the dialogue, funny and bright as it often is, rests too safely within the pseudo-cute, pseudo-authentic, patronizing diction perfected by Booth Tarkington. And in the stylization of action as well as language it seems to me clear that Sturges holds his characters, and the people they comically represent, and their predicament, and his audience, and the best potentialities of his own work, essentially in contempt. His emotions, his intelligence, his aesthetic ability never fully commit themselves; all the playfulness becomes rather an avoidance of commitment than an extension of means for it.

It was this ability to dig deep beneath the surface of the movie, to take into account the audience's role in the picture, and to examine what the director's particular style might mean in the context of what was happening in contemporary life, that Pauline most loved about Agee's criticism. There were points, however, at which she parted company with him. She took issue with his fondness for plain, bare-bones, unadorned drama without a trace of vulgarity or over-the-top flair. He wanted movies to be "cleansed" of excess, but Pauline couldn't help but feel that this "virtue may have been his worst critical vice."

The critic who most consistently irritated Pauline was the country's most powerful one: *The New York Times*'s Bosley Crowther. He had come to the *Times* in 1940, taking over as screen editor and chief movie critic from Frank Nugent, who had gone to Hollywood to become a screenwriter. Crowther's writing style was ponderous and schoolmasterish, lacking in any real wit. He was constantly on the march against vulgarity and sensationalism, two qualities that Pauline believed could make for hugely entertaining movies. Crowther sought to maintain a certain numbingly correct objectivity. "Any critic writing for a large publication cannot be extremely personalized," he once stated. "He must realize that other persons have their own opinions." Pauline dismissed this as "saphead objectivity" and found some of Crowther's opinions—such as his belief that the best actors are the ones who maintain the most consistent popularity—downright loopy. In his high-minded insistence that "pictures are a great intellectual exercise and have great power to influence people in their thinking," Pauline felt that Crowther completely missed the fun and vitality that movies were capable of bringing to audiences. She also resented his power and influence; because he was generally hailed as America's most powerful critic, his *Times* reviews could affect whether people elsewhere in the country saw a film. In her denunciation of Crowther, she was once again squaring off against the East Coast establishment.

Pauline found her situation in New York increasingly untenable: She couldn't live on her unemployment insurance, and she found herself waiting until a check—from Vi or Bob Horan or Robert Duncan, or from one of her odd freelance jobs—came through so that she could pick up her clothes at the dry cleaners, or purchase some new stockings. She was filled with invective for the "eastern college people" who swoop down on the best publishing jobs, because "they'll work for almost anything (since they don't need the money). . . . I've seen so many really incompetent people get jobs in preference to good people." On a visit to Capricorn, she and Barber got into a violent argument about some artistic point, and Barber, who by now perceived her as a threatening influence on Horan, lit into her without mercy. No invitation for a weekend at Capricorn had been issued since, and if Horan had traveled into the city, he hadn't bothered to contact her.

By the fall Pauline had to acknowledge that New York was not working out for her. Deeply disappointed, she packed her things and moved back to San Francisco. Her years in New York seemed to her to represent one stinging defeat after another, and she felt no closer to success than she had been when she left Berkeley.

# CHAPTER FOUR

On her return to the West Coast Pauline moved in temporarily with her mother, who was living on her own and in declining health. Their time together was apparently pleasant, for when Pauline found an apartment of her own at 355 Fulton Street, she felt guilty about leaving Judith. She cast around for a newspaper job, trying (unsuccessfully) to master typing. She worked for a time as a clerk at Brentano's, where her total income for 1946 was $156.65, and then found a position at Houghton Mifflin. She was grateful for the money, but she complained to Vi, "I don't think properly on the typewriter and I have been composing hundreds of business letters so that my poor mind is a cesspool of business English."

Her timing in coming back to San Francisco, however, was excellent, as she was about to witness one of the most explosive flowerings of the arts in the city's history. One of the crucial figures of the period—in many ways, the woman who triggered the beginning of it—was the poet and translator Madeline Gleason, who launched the first Festival of Modern Poetry at San Francisco's Lucien Labaudt Gallery in April of 1947. This landmark event unfolded over the course of two evenings. Among the poets featured were the activist Muriel Rukeyser; the anarchist Kenneth Rexroth, who had for some years been cultivating a growing presence in San Francisco; and Robert Duncan, who had returned to the Bay Area following the collapse of his marriage to Marjorie McKee and had enrolled at Berkeley as a student in medieval and Renaissance literature. The event was the catalyst for what came to be known as the Berkeley Renaissance of the 1940s, which in turn would feed into the later San Francisco Renaissance. The local audience for poetry readings began to grow. Both Duncan and Jack Spicer had a following from their classes at Berkeley; they began to have discussion groups in their homes in which young poets would read from their works, and soon more and more people were crowding into their salon evenings. While the city had long been home to major individual writers such as Frank Norris, Bret Harte, and Jack London, the poetic activity of the 1940s and '50s would make it a genuine bohemian literary center.

Pauline was, by nature, distrustful of such movements. She admired the highly personal tone that many of the Berkeley poets employed, but she was not one who easily succumbed to the romance of underground causes; she suspected that those involved in them were guilty of self-consciousness at best, self-promotion at worst. Much as she revered artistic achievement, she also had a pragmatist's love of mainstream success and failed to see why a group of obscure poets should congratulate themselves for being known only to a tiny sector of the reading public. Her own connection to the postwar flowering of avant-garde activity was a more personal one: She had become a friend and lover of the poet James Broughton.

Born in Modesto, California, in 1913, Broughton claimed that the defining experience of his life had taken place at age three, when he received a visitation from an angel named Hermy, who proclaimed that, however he might resist the calling, he would one day be a poet. "He offered me three gifts that he said would come in handy: intuition, articulation, and merriment," recalled Broughton. "Poets, he explained, believe in the unbelievable, worship wonder, celebrate life. Despite what I might hear to the contrary the world was not a miserable prison, it was a playground for a nonstop tournament between stupidity and imagination. If I followed the game sharply enough I could be a useful spokesman for Big Joy." At this point, Broughton recalled, Hermy pulled a sparkler from between his legs and showered him with stars, disappearing into the night, just as Broughton's mother entered the room to check on him.

A visionary like Broughton might have seemed an unlikely match for a wisecracking, skeptical, resolutely earthbound woman like Pauline, but they had a number of things in common: a California upbringing, a deep feeling for the natural beauty of the west, a difficult mother (like Judith, Broughton's mother, Olga, was born into comfortable circumstances and was disappointed by the life her husband had carved out for them), and a great love of the arts. Broughton was an immensely likable man—attractive, dynamic, witty, openhearted, and bisexual. Again, Pauline was making a mistake that heterosexual women in the arts often made: They were surrounded by attractive, bright men unafraid to engage in emotional discourse, and they mistakenly thought that a passionate friendship could turn into an enduring romance. And the men, lacking strong gay role models, did their best to conform to what the women wanted them to be.

"He looked like he was the concept that Marlowe was working on in *Doctor Faustus*," Broughton's friend Ariel Parkinson said of him. "He was the concept of Mephistopheles!" He also had a remarkably strong sense of self that had made it possible for him to withstand years of adversity that might have sunk a lesser man. James Broughton was the child of a socially ambitious mother who, in her son's words, "adored babies but disliked children." The daughter of the president of the San Francisco Bank, she married a man she held in contempt for not being a more aggressive wage-earner. Broughton's father had died in his mid-thirties, and his mother set about finding herself a new husband; her principal requirement was that he had to be financially secure. But many of her suitors recoiled in the presence of her effeminate son. After Olga came home one night to discover her son decked out in her beaded chiffon evening gown and lamé cloche, she decided that he needed to be taken in hand and given a crash course in masculinity. She passed the responsibility for this on to her current beau, who saw to it that young James wound up in a military academy in San Rafael.

Educated at Stanford (where his lovers included the future writer and gay activist Harry Hay), Broughton had enjoyed a limited success with his play *Summer Fury* and was buoyed up by the enthusiastic climate for avant-garde work in San Francisco, venturing into experimental filmmaking. The Bay Area was home to a number of nonnarrative filmmakers who would receive considerable acclaim, including Stan Brakhage and Kenneth Anger. Pauline circulated among them, and once she and Broughton met, she helped sew costumes and do miscellaneous production work on his dreamlike early film *Mother's Day* (1948), which Broughton intended as a comment on the tyranny of motherhood, and how it affects children. But Pauline's involvement in the California underground cinema movement remained limited. "She deplored little magazines, little theater, little films," Broughton wrote. "She valued the big time, the big number, the big screen."

"She was not sympathetic to avant-garde enterprise and did not make any particular attempt to deal with it in her writing," observed Ernest Callenbach, longtime editor of *Film Quarterly*. "Documentary was also something that bored her. Broughton said to me once, 'You have to remember that Pauline is an Ibsenist.' It's perfectly true! What she was interested in was plot and character. The visual side of film, although she had an immense visual memory and could remember things well, didn't interest her as critical material. She was so focused on people and the way the story was told as a drama that she would neglect the things that would make movies interesting." The filmmaker Bruce Baillie agreed that Pauline could be waspish about avant-garde movies. "She liked the word 'precious,'" Baillie recalled. "She liked to say, behind the scenes, 'Those precious filmmakers hold on to every single bit of film and have no discretion'—that kind of thing. But between these tirades, she was also very loving and encouraging to us." Pauline did attempt to persuade

Broughton to head for Hollywood and gain a foothold there, arguing that he would never truly be able to test his own talents unless he tried to make it in Los Angeles.

Broughton had been staying in a small house at 60 Lower Crescent Avenue in Sausalito, and soon Pauline talked her way into moving in with him. His sister, Marjorie Broughton, recalled that Pauline lived by her own rules and sometimes shook up the neighbors: She had a habit of parading in front of the living room windows in her bra, and on one occasion, she removed her bra and waved it out the window at passersby. Still, her presence was a boon in many ways. She flew into a frenzy of cleaning and cooking and interior decorating, leaving Broughton somewhat puzzled by this burst of domestic attentiveness, but she was such vibrant company that it was easy enough to go along with her.

Then, in early 1948, she informed Broughton that she was pregnant. He was stunned, then angry: He believed that she had for some time wanted to have a child and had blatantly manipulated him into being the father. Pauline assured him that she would make no demands on him, of a financial or any other kind. But Broughton wanted nothing to do with the child. Although he claims in his memoir that he was not aware of its existence until many years later, he told a different story to Joel Singer, who remembered, "He 'threw her out.' I heard that phrase countless times over the years, and it was certainly related to her being pregnant. He felt deceived. He had no intention of being a father at that time."

She broke the news of her pregnancy to her mother and to her siblings. Rose was shocked and disappointed, feeling that her sister was making a grave mistake, and several of Pauline's friends felt that she never fully forgave Rose for not supporting her in a time of stress. Not surprisingly, it was Anne who responded with the greatest equanimity; "Pauline is Pauline" had long been her summing-up of the tumultuous events in her youngest sister's life. She also had the support of many close friends. In the spring of 1948, she received a letter from Robert Horan, still residing at Capricorn, who expressed regret that "what sounded like such a solid thing for a while" with Broughton "had to explode into these fragments." He also said that "excepting the fact that for a few infantile hours I even pretended the child was mine!, I couldn't be happier about it."

Pauline was happy, too. Decades later, while she was having dinner with the food critic Meredith Brody, the subject of abortion arose. Pauline was in favor of reproductive rights for women, but when Brody praised a mutual friend for her work on pro-choice issues, Pauline stiffened. "When it happens to you," she said, "you will think of the child growing inside of you and the person that you were making love to—and I guarantee you, you won't be able to do it."

It was decided that Pauline would leave town to have her baby. She moved down to Santa Barbara, renting a place at 1108 Bath Street. At Santa Barbara's Cottage Hospital on September 21, 1948, she gave birth to a five-pound, fifteen-ounce daughter whom she named Gina James. The birth certificate stated that the mother's name was "Mrs. Pauline James" and the father's, "Lionel James," a writer. She adored having a child and received help both from friends and her sister Anne. "The pictures of Gina are a delight," Robert Horan wrote to her in the summer of 1949. "I have one set up on my desk, and it stares at me with those deep and curious eyes, as if to say 'What in heaven are *you* doing?'" By June 1950, Gina had begun her toilet training. She was also quite talkative, and she often spoke in the first person: "I'm Gina!" "I'm a baby!"

The first year of Gina's life was difficult for Pauline. While some writers have strained to portray her as an early feminist, nothing could be further from the truth. To Pauline, leading a life on her own was not really a virtuous act. While she was sorry that Broughton had exited her life, she regretted not having a husband only in the sense that having one would have made it easier to get along financially.

Pauline eventually wrote of her relationship with Broughton in a one-act play called *Orpheus in Sausalito*. Subtitled "a farce for people who read and write," it dealt with the breakup of the freethinking Beth Thomas and Richard Trowbridge, a poet with a mother complex and conflicted feelings about success. "The world doesn't find you," Richard says. "You have to go knock on doors, hat in hand, if you want your art to be accepted." *Orpheus in Sausalito* wasn't much of a play and is really interesting only as a biographical reference point. Its dialogue is self-consciously smart and the characterizations don't naturally spring to life.

Eventually, the personal chaos that *Orpheus* attempted to portray would make its way into her writing life in a more significant way. Both as an early audience member and, later, as a critic, Pauline always objected to patness, an avoidance of examining emotional complexity onscreen. In her film reviews she would repeatedly champion pictures that did not back away from portraying outwardly puzzling, seemingly contradictory situations that nevertheless had a potent truth all their own. When she described a film that portrayed a "messy" situation, she usually meant it as a compliment.

Because of the demands of motherhood, Pauline's employment

opportunities were limited; it made the most sense for her to pursue freelance writing assignments that she could do at home. While still living in Santa Barbara, she was able to pick up occasional book-reviewing assignments with *The Santa Barbara Star*, covering recent releases such as Budd Schulberg's *The Disenchanted* and Rose Macaulay's *The World My Wilderness*. In her review of May Sarton's May-December love story *Shadow of a Man*, in November 1950, she hit on what would become one of her most frequently revisited topics—technical control and manipulation at the expense of emotional involvement:

> There is not an unintelligent line in *The* [*sic*] *Shadow of a Man*. From her first sentence, May Sarton shows distinction of mind: her intentions are of the highest, her integrity cannot be challenged, her craftsmanship is remarkably sustained. . . . Craftsmanship, this surface poise and control, this careful maturity, isn't enough. The writers one cares about are controlled on a different level: the controlling mind and vision allow for a surface variety and spontaneity—even allow for mistakes.

After her stint in Santa Barbara, she moved back to San Francisco and into a small apartment at 2490 Geary Street. She also wrote an original story for the screen and submitted it, with high hopes, to the Columbia Pictures story department. Called "The Brash Young Man," it was rooted in Pauline's frustrating experience in New York and her fear of losing her renegade outsider status. It centered on a character named Benjamin Burl, "brash, confident, pugnacious," who for years has been struggling to achieve literary success. Although he has talent, not one of his several novels has sold well, and his publisher has all but given up on him. Benjamin is very much a back number when he makes one more attempt at a novel. To his astonishment it catches on with the public and becomes a big seller. Benjamin becomes a belated literary "discovery," but success ruins his life:

> He became modest and shy. All the fun had gone out of things: there was no one to quarrel with and shout at; he didn't have to convince people of his genius—they all agreed with him.

Benjamin becomes morbidly depressed. He longs for the days when someone would say something derogatory about his books. He gets what he's looking for in Amanda Magill, a glamorous, sharp-tongued reviewer who sums up his life by writing: "Mr. Benjamin Burl's infatuation with himself has become a national romance." Amanda has a genius for pointing out to

Benjamin that he is a fraud whose talent consists of indulging in literary tricks. The story synopsis ends with Amanda standing over Benjamin as he begins a new novel, smiling, shaking her head and pronouncing, "no"—much to Benjamin's delight.

All in all, "The Brash Young Man" consisted of a seventeen-page synopsis, but it took one of Columbia's readers only a little more than three pages to dismiss it: "about the substance and quality of a slick-paper magazine story." The reader offered a plot rewrite that would conform more closely to the commercial formula for a big-screen romantic comedy but ended with the observation that "its first best chance would be with the magazines." "The Brash Young Man" went nowhere, but it is quite revealing about Pauline's own defensiveness where her career was concerned, her frustration at having her talents consistently overlooked, and her fears of what commercial success might bring.

The next several years were to be among the leanest and most stressful of Pauline's life. They were marked by a maze of unfortunate jobs, taken only out of the desperate need to provide for her daughter. In 1951 a doctor examining Gina detected a heart murmur, and it was eventually discovered that she had been born with a congenital defect: a sizable hole that would require delicate and complicated surgery. Pauline, devastated, had already faced times when she couldn't scrape together enough money to stay ahead of the rent and keep herself and her daughter properly fed; now she was facing a potentially crippling mountain of medical bills. The consensus was that it might be better to wait to perform the necessary surgery until Gina was a little older and stronger. Anxiety over Gina's health became a constant in Pauline's life.

It also signaled the real beginning of what was to be a deep, lifelong, mutually dependent bond between mother and daughter. Many of Pauline's friends, sometimes teasingly, sometimes seriously, often told her that she was a classic Jewish mother. What they appeared to mean was that she was a nervous mother, worrying over her daughter's condition. But as Gina grew older, friends and family members sensed another characteristic of classic Jewish motherhood: the conviction that her child was destined to be some kind of creative genius.

While she was determined to see to it that the health issues that threatened Gina were vanquished, having a fragile daughter fulfilled her needs in some way that she could never quite bring herself to admit to anyone. All her life she had wanted to be at the center of someone's universe—but on her own strict terms. The spell that Gian Carlo Menotti noted that she cast over Bob

Horan had faded; by now Horan's relationship with Menotti and Barber had run aground, and he was no longer a member of the household at Capricorn, all of which had triggered a nervous collapse. Robert Duncan, too, had pulled away from her and gone his own way. In the early 1950s Pauline might have been unsure of most aspects of her future, but she was certain of one thing: Gina needed her more than anyone else ever had.

On November 21, 1952, Judith Kael died at the age of sixty-seven, after a long battle with cancer. Both Philip and Louis were living in Los Angeles by this time, so responsibility for looking after their mother had fallen to Rose, Anne, and Pauline. Most of the caring for Judith seems to have been absorbed by Rose, which served only to heighten the animosity between her and Pauline.

Pauline stumbled along in her writing life. She was accumulating a pile of play scripts, comedies mostly, but she seemed to realize that they weren't as good as they needed to be. She kept scribbling away in what spare time she could find in the middle of the constant chaos of trying to make ends meet. She coached students in a wide range of subjects. She ran a laundry and tailoring business, Kent Cleaners, just off Market Street in San Francisco, which entailed an inconvenient streetcar ride from her apartment. She took on ghostwriting assignments from time to time.

Still, she prided herself on being able to make do with little. Her struggles didn't make her hell-bent on success; in some ways, they seemed to deepen her natural distrust of people with money. Decades later, Pauline was chatting with her son-in-law, Warner Friedman, about the whole nature of struggle and hard times.

"I was never hungry in my life," said Warner.

Pauline went silent and stared at him for a long moment.

"You never were?" she finally asked, stunned and a little angry.

Even when things were at their worst, Pauline had one constant source of pleasure—going to the movies. The end of World War II had signaled the beginning of a new era in American moviegoing. During the war, most of the major Hollywood studios had lost tremendous ground abroad because the European markets were all but closed during hostilities, leaving Hollywood's export efforts concentrated on the United Kingdom and Latin America. European filmmaking was by necessity cut back dramatically while the war was on, but there were some remarkable examples of filmmaking under duress—notably Marcel Carné's *Les enfants du paradis*, made during the occupation of Paris, and Roberto Rossellini's stunning *Rome, Open City*, filmed while the Allied and Axis forces were shooting it out in the streets of Rome. With the end of the war there was suddenly a generous supply of foreign films pouring into the United States. American audiences were now finding their way to movies like Vittorio de Sica's *The Bicycle Thief*, whose unvarnished honesty was a welcome change to the surfeit of overglamorized, manipulative Hollywood products, full of crashing Max Steiner scores, gauzy photography, and implausible happy endings. Pauline had fallen under the spell of de Sica and the other Italian neorealists while she was still involved with James Broughton. De Sica's *Shoeshine* had actually been one of her indelible movie-going experiences:

When *Shoeshine* opened in 1947, I went to see it alone after one of those terrible lovers' quarrels that leave one in a state of incomprehensible despair. I came out of the theater, tears streaming, and overheard the petulant voice of a college girl complaining to her boyfriend, "Well, I don't see what was so special about that movie." I walked up the street, crying blindly, no longer certain whether my tears were for the tragedy on the screen, the hopelessness I felt for myself, or the alienation I felt from those who could not experience the radiance of *Shoeshine*. For if people cannot feel *Shoeshine*, what *can* they feel? . . . Later I learned that the man with whom I had quarreled had gone the same night and had also emerged in tears. Yet our tears for each other, and for *Shoeshine*, did not bring us together. Life, as *Shoeshine* demonstrates, is too complex for facile endings.

But it was a movie Pauline disliked that was to provide the unexpected turning point in this difficult phase of her life. In the fall of 1952, as she and a friend were sitting in a Berkeley coffeehouse arguing about a film they had both seen recently, sitting nearby was Peter D. Martin, who recently had launched a magazine, *City Lights*, devoted to film commentary. Martin was intrigued by the stream of articulate, independent opinion he heard Pauline expressing, and he asked her if she would like to review the new Chaplin picture, *Limelight*, for *City Lights*.

*Limelight* was a heavy-handed, strangely charmless tale of a down-at-the-heels English comic, Calvero (played by Chaplin), written off by his peers and public, who gets one last chance to show what he can do. The press treated it respectfully, but Pauline found it embarrassingly sentimental and, with its irritating references to Chaplin's own neglect in Hollywood, nothing more than a testament to himself.

Her review reveals that her critical voice was still in the process of assembling itself, but all the intimations of what she would become are there. She wrote that Chaplin, at this point in his career, was playing to a "somewhat segmented art-film audience," and no longer the mass audience that had thrilled to his performances as the Little Tramp. "When the mass audience becomes convinced that the clown who had made them laugh was really an artist, they felt betrayed," she observed. She thought that Chaplin had become too serious, so that his view of his character, Calvero, was fatally high-minded: "The Chaplin of *Limelight* is no irreverent little clown; his reverence for his own ideas would be astonishing even if the ideas were worth consideration. They are not—and the context of the film exposes them at every turn."

She thought the stage benefit that provides the climax of the film, in which Calvero proves that his comedic gifts have not deserted him after all and dies in the wings, was "surely the richest hunk of self-gratification since Huck and Tom attended their own funeral." Chaplin, she felt, was trying to even the score with those who had attacked him for his morals or his politics, or those who had simply forgotten him. To her, the central conceit, the lie of the movie, was driven home in the scene in which Calvero praises the young ballerina (Claire Bloom) he has rescued: "My dear, you are a true artist, a true artist." "The camera emphasis on Chaplin's eyes," wrote Pauline, "the emotion in his voice, are intended to give depth to his words. This ghastly mistake in judgment and taste—this false humility which proclaims his own artistry in the act of asserting another's—is not a simple mistake. It is integral to the creative mind which produces a *Limelight*."

Pauline had managed her first piece of writing about the medium that meant more to her than any other. While she continued to work on her stories and play scripts, deep down she had the feeling that, at the age of thirty-three, she might have found herself as a writer at last.

P auline's official debut as a movie critic was well timed, for she was beginning what would become her life's work in an atmosphere of amazing creative ferment. By the mid-1950s Berkeley was known as the Athens of the West. The poets who had read at Madeline Gleason's festival at the Lucien Labaudt Gallery in 1947 had grown in numbers and influence. In addition to Robert Duncan and Kenneth Rexroth, there were Allen Ginsberg, Robert Creeley, Philip Whalen, and Gary Snyder, who together formed one of the most vital and progressive communities of poets in U.S. history. The most important event of this period took place on Friday, October 7, 1955, when Rexroth organized a reading at San Francisco's Six Gallery that would soon become legendary. The poets that night included Snyder, Whalen, and Ginsburg, who gave an unforgettable reading of his explosive poem "Howl," a cri de coeur against the complacency of the Eisenhower years (and, by extension, against the effect that it had on artists). Nothing like it had ever been experienced, and it was clear that American poetry had discovered a thrilling new voice.

This eruption of new poetry was only one part of the San Francisco renaissance. Jazz clubs, avant-garde performance spaces, and small, experimental presses were plentiful. In 1953, Peter D. Martin and Lawrence Ferlinghetti founded the City Lights bookstore, devoted exclusively to selling paperbound books. (Previously, paperbacks had been available mostly on racks in drugstores and groceries; City Lights gave them a new respectability and became a magnet for local artists in the process.) Ferlinghetti went on to launch City Lights Publishers, which brought out "Howl" in 1956.

Across the bay, Berkeley was enjoying a renaissance of its own. The leading bookstores included U.C. Corners, where all the international newspapers and film magazines could be found; Cody's; the Circle, where the literary quarterly *Circle* magazine was published in the back; and Moe's, a magnet for secondhand-book hounds. Telegraph Avenue and Channing Way were dotted with first-rate classical record stores staffed by well-informed clerks. What had been a relatively bucolic town with all the conventional trappings of university life was in the process of transforming itself into a lively arts and intellectual center.

Pauline was about to become a significant player in this world. Her review of *Limelight* in *City Lights* had attracted some positive attention from literary figures of note, among them Mary McCarthy. With her first real encouragement, she worked on several pieces on spec through 1954, one of which, "Morality Plays Right and Left," was a lengthy discursive essay. (She had already come to recognize that her love of jazz was revealing itself in her own writing: She was fond of riffs, as she came to think of them—the extended, brilliant, sidetracking discussions that veered off from the main crux of her argument but always reconnected to it in the end.) Ostensibly her topic was Twentieth Century–Fox's 1954 Cold War thriller *Night People*, starring Gregory Peck, about the effort to rescue a U.S. soldier who has been kidnapped in Berlin. Pauline found the film to be a reflection of the U.S. government's love affair with its own image and disapproved of its oversimplification of complex issues. Her wide-ranging discussion probed the dangers of pandering to the public, something studios were aggressively doing with the popular widescreen technology, designed to help people forget about television and get back into the theaters:

> The new wide screen surrounds us and sounds converge upon us. Just one thing is lost: the essence of film "magic" which lay in our imaginative absorption, our entering into the film (as we might enter into the world of a Dostoyevsky novel or *Middlemarch*). Now the film can come to us—one more consummation of the efforts to diminish the labor (and the joy) of imaginative participation.

Members of the U.S. government were also guilty of pandering, notably Senator Joseph McCarthy, whose anti-Communist attacks were about on the level with the sentiments expressed in *Night People*:

> When Senator McCarthy identifies himself with *right* and identifies anyone who opposes him with the Communist conspiracy, he carries the political morality play to its paranoid conclusion—a reductio ad absurdum in which right and wrong, and political good and evil, dissolve into: are you for me or against me? But the question may be asked, are not this morality and this politics fundamentally just as absurd and just as dangerous when practiced on a national scale in our commercial culture? The world is *not* divided into good and evil, enemies are *not* all

alike. Communists are *not* just Nazis with a different accent; and it is precisely the task of political analysis (and the incidental function of literature and drama) to help us understand the nature of our enemies and the nature of our opposition to them. A country which accepts wars as contests between good and evil is suffering from the delusion that the morality play symbolizes real political conflicts.

"Morality Plays Right and Left" was initially accepted by one of the publications Pauline most revered, *The Partisan Review*, but was eventually taken by the British film journal *Sight and Sound* in 1954. *Sight and Sound*'s editor, Penelope Houston, wrote that the section on *Night People* was "the type of thing I have been trying to get hold of for a long time; it is so much better for these things to be written by an American than by a journalist on our side." The cofounding editor of *The Partisan Review*, Philip Rahv, responded enthusiastically to Pauline's lively critical voice, but he was consistently troubled by the length of her pieces and always urged that they be cut.

1955 was a pivotal year for Pauline. She had become friends by then with Weldon Kees, one denizen of the Bay Area who genuinely deserved to be called a Renaissance man. Kees was a native of Nebraska who had enjoyed early success publishing short fiction in a string of distinguished literary quarterlies. During World War II, he moved to New York City, where he did a fairly good job of taking the town by storm. He published his first book of poems, *The Last Man*, in 1943 and went on to write for a wide range of newspapers and magazines, including *The New York Times*. He also became a highly skilled abstract painter and a gifted jazz pianist. In 1950 he left New York for San Francisco, where he became part of the circle that included Pauline and James Broughton; he provided the musical score for Broughton's film *The Adventures of Jimmy*. Kees and Pauline had many passions in common, including the movies and New Orleans jazz, which Kees performed locally every chance he got.

Kees was also a fixture on Berkeley's KPFA-FM, the first listener-supported radio station in the United States, which aimed to provide its audience with a respite from America's commercially dominated pop culture and to spread liberal ideas beyond the confines of academia—to reach out to the common citizen and bring him into a discussion of art, politics, and ideas. The ultimate, idealistic goal was to create a more enlightened society—a particularly urgent objective in the age of McCarthyism.

One of KPFA's popular programs was a weekly show featuring Kees called *Behind the Movie Camera*. Seeing in Pauline a kindred movie-lover, he invited her to be a guest on his program several times, as he enjoyed her scorching directness and her provocative views about what was going on in the movie industry.

Unfortunately, Kees was a deeply troubled man, given to fierce mood swings and prolonged feelings of desolation. One day he asked Pauline sadly, "What keeps *you* going?" For years, she blamed herself for failing to perceive the depth of his emotional state. On July 19, 1955, his Plymouth Savoy was found just north of the Golden Gate Bridge. No suicide note was found, and his body was never recovered.

In the aftershock of Kees's disappearance, KPFA asked Pauline to step in as a semiregular film critic. The station manager made it clear that they would not be able to pay her for her broadcasts, but she judged that the exposure and the chance to hold forth for a regular audience would be hugely beneficial. She was broadcasting to a subscription audience of more than four thousand, whose educational background and income level were well above the norm. She was also surrounded by other broadcasters who shared many of her ideas about the regrettable division between classical and contemporary music. Among them was Alan Rich, KPFA's music director, who joyously combined Mozart and Bach with Schoenberg and David Diamond. She was also delighted to find KPFA such a strong proponent of jazz, notably by way of Phil Elwood's highly informative regular program.

Pauline was a natural on the radio, firing off her opinions of the latest movies in crisp diction, even occasionally saying "rah-ther" and almost consistently pronouncing "movies" as "myoovies." She could sound almost cultivated, an occasional affectation that her friend Donald Gutierrez teasingly called her "Mrs. Lamont of the Air" voice. But her radio pieces, almost always carefully written out beforehand, were notable for their wit, drive, and guts, and slowly, she began building a loyal, growing band of listeners.

One of them was Edward Landberg, who operated a revival theater located at 2436 Telegraph Avenue. A physician's son who had been born in Vienna in 1920, Landberg had come to New York City at the age of nine. He had ambitions to become an author, and after graduating from the University of Iowa's prestigious writers' program, he slaved away at scattered teaching jobs at Berkeley, at Ithaca College, and in France. Eventually he wound up in Mexico City, teaching Shakespeare and writing movie reviews for an English-language newspaper, *The Mexico City News*, a job that ended when his opinions inflamed some of the advertisers. Thinking that he might be better off showing movies than writing about them, Landberg leased a screening room in Mexico City and was soon making a decent amount of money exhibiting films on a weekly basis. He had pleasant memories of his time in Berkeley, so moved back there, found a defunct market on Telegraph Avenue, and rented and renovated it. There were columns dividing about two-thirds of it, so he had the idea of turning the space into two separate theaters. The result was the Berkeley Cinema Guild, which Landberg opened in 1951 and always claimed was the first twin art house in the United States. (At times, he claimed it was the first in the world.)

Most of the time movies were shown simultaneously in the two theaters. The larger one, the Cinema Guild, had two hundred seats and was reasonably long and narrow, with the screen positioned somewhat high, meaning that the best place to sit was in the back. The smaller theater, holding around one hundred seats, was the Studio. It was wider and shorter than the Guild and offered better general seating. Landberg began programming according to his own taste, which mostly ran toward European film.

One evening Ed Landberg heard Pauline broadcasting on KPFA, and after telephoning to compliment her on the program, they arranged to meet. "She was the closest thing to somebody who had my kind of vision about movies," Landberg recalled. "Not that she did have. But she was more intelligent than most people who had anything to do with movies. One day, when I was over at her place, I happened to graze her breast with my hand, and she kind of looked up at me and said, 'What have you got to lose?'"

Landberg and Pauline had not been romantically involved for very long when Pauline made it known that she would like to write program notes for the Cinema Guild. "I hadn't written notes," said Landberg, "because I wasn't into audience manipulation. But she wrote some notes, and one thing led to another." The Cinema Guild was doing well enough, but almost immediately Pauline saw that it could be made into a bigger attraction than it was, and she decided that she was the person to make that happen. Her notes, written on fold-out programs, were available at the theater, mailed out to local moviegoers, and distributed to some of the neighborhood businesses, and they caught on almost immediately. Although the programs were very carefully printed, with thoughtfully selected photographs and Pauline's incisive descriptions of the movies, plus the monthly calendar running down the center, they were anything but public relations fluff. Pauline didn't hesitate to poke fun at some of the films being shown at the Guild, but even when she was taking swipes at them, her energetic critical tone seemed only to make people all the more determined to turn up to see them.

Soon enough she was taking an aggressive hand in programming as well, pressing Landberg to show more vintage American movies from the 1930s

and '40s—screwball comedies, gangster dramas, film noir, musicals. "There
was a little resistance to the notion that there was something good to be said
about American musicals," recalled Stephen Kresge, who worked on the Cinema Guild's staff for several years. "When we first showed *Gold Diggers of
1933*, there wasn't anyone walking out, but I think there was a lot of puzzle-
ment as to why this was thought to be fun. She started that whole revival of
American musicals having a place in the canon. They were willing to accept
things like *Casablanca* and so on, but . . . There was nothing quite so hidebound and stuffy as a Berkeley intellectual at that time. They were inhibited
by European values and philosophy that she no longer had any use for. She
wanted to open the windows and let in some air."

Many of the double bills were delightfully unexpected: Ingmar Bergman's
medieval allegory *The Seventh Seal* was paired with the Beatrice Lillie comedy
*On Approval*, Clouzot's thriller *Diabolique* with Frank Capra's comedy *Arsenic
and Old Lace*, Laurence Olivier's 1953 *The Beggar's Opera* with René Clair's
*Sous les toits de Paris*, which Pauline described in her notes as "one of the first
imaginative approaches to the musical as a film form." Sometimes there was
a thematic connection, as with the English comedies *The Man in the White
Suit* and *Lucky Jim*, or Pauline's "corruption-in-Mexico" double bill of John
Huston's *Treasure of the Sierra Madre* and Luis Buñuel's *Los Olvidados*. Frequently Pauline's notes were hilariously personal and direct: when the Guild
showed Howard Hawks's *Red River*, she wrote that the film was "not really
so 'great' as its devotees claim (what Western is?) but it's certainly more fun
and superior in every way to that message movie *The Gunfighter*, which Dwight
Macdonald, in the November *Esquire*, puts forward as 'the best Western'
because it showed 'movie types behaving realistically instead of in the usual
terms of romantic cliché.'"

Pauline was not deeply enamored of much of the pre- and postwar British
cinema, but she had a great fondness for some of the great Ealing comedies,
such as *The Happiest Days of Your Life*, as well as Laurence Olivier's stirring
1955 version of *Richard III*, and she saw to it that they all got generous exhibition. With her exceptional taste, as well as the rapidly growing popularity
of her program notes, hers began to become the voice of the Berkeley Cinema
Guild. Audiences picked up, and the Friday and Saturday night showings
often had lines down Telegraph. Audience members were almost giddy with
a sense of discovery of so many hard-to-locate movies. Carol van Strum, who
became a friend of Pauline's in these years, remembered the thrill of receiving
her movie education at the Cinema Guild. "My parents hardly ever went to
the movies," said van Strum. "Part of it was me: they took me to see *Drums*

*Along the Mohawk*, and I got so scared I never wanted to go back. I missed *The Third Man*, Buster Keaton, W. C. Fields—and it was magic finding them at the Guild." The exhibitors who supplied the prints began to notice the Guild's success and began to talk about changing the way they were going to charge. "They were doing it on a nightly rental basis," said Stephen Kresge. "Then they found out that many weekends, the Cinema Guild was grossing the highest of any of the theaters in Berkeley."

It was becoming well known around the Bay Area that Pauline was the prime mover responsible for putting the Cinema Guild on the map. Friendly, gregarious, and bawdy, she was becoming something of a local character. She dressed down—with her finances in the shape they were in, it was impossible to do anything else—and locals grew accustomed to seeing her up on a ladder changing the Guild's marquee, a hip flask filled with Wild Turkey dangling from a belt loop. Landberg, on the other hand, struck people as cold and diffident. "Landberg was very remote," recalled Ariel Parkinson, widow of the poet and Berkeley English professor Thomas Parkinson. "He almost *cultivated* the image of the faceless man. The theater was a fully cooperative enterprise, or at least it seemed to me. I think it's a shame that people don't remember Ed Landberg, but then he was very self-effacing. Pauline was the one."

Pauline's relationship with Landberg was more in the nature of a meeting of minds, and even that was a bit shaky, as Landberg was a peculiar, somewhat morose man who seemed unable to express joy and enthusiasm in the same way Pauline did. She tried her best to see him as a man of quality and refinement and was encouraged by certain gestures on his part; he had given her a gift of a recording of Gluck's opera *Orphée et Eurydice*, and she clung to this as evidence that he would make a good match for her. Landberg also provided a degree of financial security, and she thought that at last she might be able to establish a bit of stability for herself and for Gina. If she was searching for a father figure for her daughter, however, she was doomed to be disappointed: Landberg made no secret of his dislike for children in general and showed no interest in Gina whatsoever.

Despite all the reasons she shouldn't have, Pauline married Edward Landberg. She later told friends that she had cried all through the ceremony, knowing that the marriage was a mistake. She also liked to tell the story that on their wedding night, Landberg fell asleep.

Gina's observation that her mother never told the same story twice is borne out in Pauline's puzzling and perverse account of her marriages. Although she delighted in confusing reporters by suggesting to them that she had married two or three times, she was married only once, to Landberg. "We were married for something like a year," Landberg said decades later. "It was very brief. I didn't find her sexually attractive, among other things. She was also very bossy, and it wasn't a happy marriage. It was out of mutual interest." (Attempts to track down a marriage certificate yielded nothing; Landberg claims not to remember where the marriage took place.) Friends and colleagues agreed that they were a bizarre match. "Pauline and Ed Landberg came for dinner one night," remembered Ariel Parkinson. "They struck me as having a very tenuous relationship to one another. They weren't on the same set of vibrations, really."

Pauline did gain one important thing in her brief union with Landberg—a big step up in living quarters: a handsome, redwood-shingled two-story Craftsman home at 2419 Oregon Street in Berkeley. In the small front yard was a magnificent deodar cedar tree, and in the back was a small garden. The house had a decent-sized front room, a spacious living room with a separate dining area, a kitchen with redwood cabinets, and three upstairs bedrooms. Pauline loved it, and when she and Landberg purchased it, she lost no time in putting her own personal stamp on it, beginning with her vast assortment of books. The downstairs of the house was quite dark, but she had a remedy for that. Pauline was drawn to color, and for years she had been collecting a number of brilliant Tiffany lamps. At the time, they were regarded by many as gaudy junk, but Pauline made a point of picking them up for very little at garage sales and antique shops. She loved the bright, warm pools of light that they cast around the room. The kitchen floor was done in a pattern of bright, Harlequin-colored square tiles by Harry Jacobus: sea green, black, salmon, yellow, mauve. It became her house, not Landberg's—and soon that was true in the literal sense. Out the back door, on the other side of the small garden, the newlyweds had a little couple's house built. In a matter of months the marriage had become so rocky that it became Landberg's new home; he came into the big house mostly for meals and to discuss Cinema Guild business with Pauline, but it was clear that their marriage was doomed. As Landberg bluntly put it, "I soon found out that I couldn't stand this woman."

At the Cinema Guild, Pauline supervised all the details of presentation, taking great care to choose the music that was piped in before and in between screenings. Always she selected pieces that connected in some way to what was being shown. One thing she didn't involve herself in were the theater's financial affairs. That was Landberg's territory, and he watched over it obsessively. At each showing of a movie he would stand in the back counting the heads in the audience. Then he would check the ticket count, and if the two numbers didn't match, the theater staff was expected to make up the difference.

. . .

In 1956 Pauline turned out her finest essay to date. Originally published in *The Berkeley Book of Modern Writing, No. 3* by William Phillips and Philip Rahv, "Movies, the Desperate Art" was a critical view of what Pauline felt was the deplorable level of expensive, wide-screen filmmaking in the mid-1950s. It was a chaotic period in Hollywood: The postwar demand for greater realism, and the rise of the Actors Studio in New York, with its emphasis on sense-memory as a way of creating an authentic, emotional moment pulled out of the actor's personal past, had paved the way for more adult performers and subject matter. This was all good news to Pauline, who was pleased to see the emergence of pictures such as Elia Kazan's *A Streetcar Named Desire* (1951), Fred Zinnemann's *From Here to Eternity* (1953), Richard Brooks's *The Blackboard Jungle* (1955), and Charles Laughton's *Night of the Hunter* (1955, scripted by James Agee). However, there was a danger, Pauline felt, in the new quest for more serious and complicated emotional subject matter, which was exemplified by George Stevens's *A Place in the Sun* (1951) and *Shane* (1953). Stevens, who had delighted her with warm, human dramas such as *Alice Adams* (1935) and thrilling, tongue-in-cheek adventures like *Gunga Din* (1939), had become a self-appointed Minister of Relevance; his movies now wore their serious intentions on their sleeve.

But a parallel universe was rising in 1950s Hollywood, and it was a place where none of the new dramatic content had much currency. The wide-screen spectacle had grown out of the movie studios' desperation to compete with the onslaught of television. To Pauline, big-screen romances such as *Three Coins in the Fountain* (1954) and biblical spectacles like *The Robe* (1953) and *The Egyptian* (1954) had set moviemaking back decades. "Like a public building designed to satisfy the widest public's concept of grandeur," Pauline wrote in "Movies, the Desperate Art," "the big production loses the flair, the spontaneity, the rhythm of an artist working to satisfy his own conception. The more expensive the picture, the bigger the audience it must draw, and the fewer risks it can take." She was not impressed with the so-called visual splendor made possible by the wide-screen process; she deemed it "about as magical as a Fitzpatrick travelogue."

The new breed of stars—Tony Curtis, Janet Leigh, Esther Williams—likewise disheartened her, because they were not "protagonists in any meaningful sense; they represent the voice of adjustment, the caution against individuality, independence, emotionality, art, ambition, personal vision. They represent the antidrama of American life." And with this assembly line of movies designed not to threaten anyone, to please as wide an audience as possible, she could see that newspaper critics were bound to praise the popular and pan the problematic until they lost their way entirely.

This was Pauline in one of her most accomplished roles: the Cassandra of film criticism, predicting nothing less than a cultural holocaust if the movies continued to go down the same, self-defeating path. And the blight, she warned, had already infected critics everywhere, who had "been quick to object to a film with a difficult theme, a small camera range, or a markedly verbal content (they object even when the words are worth listening to). Because action can be extended over a wide area on the screen, they think it must be—or what they're seeing isn't really a movie at all."

Overall, the essay was a thrilling demonstration of Pauline's credo that a critic's voice should never be objective. It was only through subjective means that a critic could convey what was in her heart and mind to the reader. "Movies, the Desperate Art" was a milestone in Pauline's early career. Only three years after she had published her first review, she had found her voice and what would become her greatest subject and the continuing passion of her life: the confluence of what happened onscreen and what happened in life.

With the house on Oregon Street, Pauline at last had a real workspace where she could spread out and be genuinely productive. Where the two front rooms divided, she set up a movie screen and constantly ran 16 mm films on a giant projector. She wrote at a drafting table, often standing up, a cigarette in one hand and a glass of Wild Turkey in the other, with her favorite Bessie Smith records playing. She stayed up late at night, reading obsessively and scribbling articles to submit to *The Partisan Review*.

The house became a gathering place for local movie-lovers, writers, poets, musicians. She fussed over what they were reading. She became upset with her friend Linda Allen, who loved Isak Dinesen, which Pauline considered far too head-in-the-clouds; instead, she pressed Allen to read Colette. Anne Kael Wallach was a frequent visitor. She was now a highly respected English teacher at Berkeley's Lowell High School; she would be fondly remembered by generations of Lowell students as a quietly exacting but kindly Mrs. Chips. Pauline remained extremely fond of her oldest sister, and when Anne's husband, Max Wallach, had difficulty making a success of his business, Pauline lent him money. She was known for being generous to her young artist friends—even something of a soft touch. She also managed the difficult feat of being brutally honest about their creative work while at the same time showering them with generosity. "She was one of the most ethical people I ever knew," said David Young Allen, a young Texan whom Pauline met after he had enrolled as a student at Berkeley and come to work as a projectionist at the Cinema Guild. "I would sometimes clean house for her when I was a student. She was always cooking soup, or sometimes doing her hand laundry. Sometimes she was a little insulting. She said to me, 'You are a kind of a semi-fuck-up, honey.' I would get pissed at her, but she was so funny—and she wasn't wrong."

For Gina, the constant crowd of artist friends created an atmosphere in which she had to compete for her mother's attention. She craved a more conventional home life, one in which the dinner hour wouldn't be interrupted by phone calls that had to be answered "Cinema Studio and Guild!" What bothered her most, however, were the stricken reactions that many of Pauline's friends had to her opinion of their work. Some of them were quite devastated by her pronouncements, and while Pauline seemed oblivious to it all, Gina internalized the friends' hurt feelings.

Employees of the Cinema Guild and invited members of the audience also regularly gathered for parties at Oregon Street, where Pauline laid out a generous supply of California wine and homemade lasagne and shepherd's pie and roast chicken. The hostess always had the best time of all, pouring bourbon, mingling with everyone, cigarette in hand, enthusiastically holding forth on the latest developments in the film industry. Sometimes, when she would get particularly excited about a point she was making, she would give a little backward kick with her heel. "Her mind was always moving five times faster than most other people's minds," said Donald Gutierrez, who worked at the Cinema Guild for a brief time. "But she had an engaging habit of indicating that she didn't understand some point of view or poem. She would say, 'Beats me—what do you think about that?' Kind of a compliment of sorts."

She had two beloved basenji dogs, Polly and Bushbaby, who frolicked with the guests, and several of her friends noted the irony that a compulsive talker like Pauline chose to have dogs who couldn't bark. There was an upright piano in the living room with characters from *The Wizard of Oz* painted on it, and Pauline loved to sing Gilbert and Sullivan songs, *The Mikado*'s "The Moon and I" being a particular favorite. She liked to joke that through the doors of 2419 Oregon Street passed the best-educated and worst-looking people in the world. "She had a motherly side," recalled Ernest Callenbach, "especially to young people who needed help. I think that's why she was sympathetic to certain directors. She thought she could be their den mother. She could be very bitchy to people, but she had a very soft, sweet side, which many people refused to admit was there."

Robert Duncan often turned up at Oregon Street. Gregarious and uninhibited, he added a lot to the parties, despite his disconcerting habit of scratching his rear end in front of other people. Perhaps because he had developed an enviable reputation as a poet, she seemed to have mixed feelings about her old friend. For years she had harbored a strong prejudice against almost anyone who came from the world of academia; she professed to believe that most literature professors were second-rate, affected hacks who made their living off the work of real writers. One night Duncan arrived at Oregon Street, having just come from the home of Thomas Parkinson, the noted Berkeley English professor with a keen interest in the avant-garde. When Duncan announced where he had been earlier in the evening, Pauline lit into him with a vengeance, asking him how he could possibly associate with people like Parkinson, whom she considered a mediocre academic. And many other times, she would snipe about Duncan as soon as he wasn't around. "She started damning his poems," said Gutierrez. "Here's someone she seemed to approve of, and then as soon as he was out the door, she was slamming him. I thought, *Well, if she said that about him, what would she do to me?* It developed a distrust on my part." It seemed much easier for her to extend generosity to her younger friends, the ones who were struggling to find their way.

Around this time, Pauline enjoyed some of the benefits of a widening reputation. In 1958 Ernest Callenbach was approached to become editor of a new, California-based magazine, *Film Quarterly*. He declined and suggested Pauline to the magazine's founder, August Fruge. But when Pauline and Fruge spoke, it was clear that they didn't agree on matters of editorial content. Pauline told Fruge that she would accept the post only if she could be guaranteed no editorial interference of any kind, an assurance Fruge refused to give. In the end, Callenbach did accept the job, which he held from 1958 to 1991.

Gina benefited from Pauline's marriage to Edward Landberg in that there were now funds available for the heart surgery that had been put off for so many years. (Pauline's niece Dana Salisbury, believed that getting the money for the operation was Pauline's principal motive in marrying Landberg.) It was delicate surgery, but it was successful, and Gina proceeded through a long and difficult recovery period with Pauline looking after her every minute.

Even though she was still a young girl, Gina was usually not excluded from the parties. She was bright and precocious, although still remarkably small for her age. Guests got used to her coming downstairs in her pink bathrobe, watching the movies that Pauline was screening and taking in the heady conversation that was swirling around her. Gina was a student at Bentley, a reputable private school in Oakland. Pauline monitored her education carefully and, critical of teachers as always, decided that her daughter wasn't being taught properly. After a tremendous row with one of Gina's instructors, Pauline removed her from Bentley and home-schooled her until she was eighteen. She claimed that it was designed to give Gina a more substantial education, but Anne Wallach always believed that the break had come because Pauline loved to stay up late and didn't want to be bothered getting Gina off to classes.

It was a dramatic move that shocked many of Pauline's friends and relatives, and they worried that Gina was being deprived of a normal childhood. Gina herself had extremely conflicted feelings about being removed from school. While she was accustomed to having a close relationship with her mother, she missed the camaraderie of her classmates. Pauline's involvement with her daughter could also be unpredictable. "Her attention to Gina would go on and off like a searchlight," said Stephen Kresge. "There would be a boom, giving Gina an overwhelming amount of attention, and the next minute, Pauline was off on the next thing. This happened not just with Gina but with others, and they weren't too thrilled. They loved it when the spotlight was on them and were miffed when it wasn't. But that was Pauline. Whatever she was doing, she was doing with all of herself, and she wasn't about to waste time."

Landberg and Pauline had become increasingly incompatible, and neither one had much difficulty reaching the decision to separate. Since their working relationship had been mutually beneficial, they saw no reason not to continue it, and Pauline assumed management of the theater while Landberg, though still nominally in charge, went to Los Angeles to take filmmaking courses at UCLA.

One evening in the spring of 1961, the Cinema Guild had the most celebrated visitor in its history. Jean Renoir had been invited by Berkeley's Council of Regents to occupy a chair, an appointment that had turned out to be a mostly pleasant experience for the veteran director. Renoir was cheerful and outgoing; he had a good rapport with the Berkeley students and was heartened by their enthusiasm for film. Almost immediately it was clear to him that the Cinema Guild was part of the reason for the high level of expertise among the young local movie buffs, and when Pauline programmed his 1951 film *The River*, he attended the screening and the after-party at Oregon Street. The evening had its bumpy moments: Renoir nearly became apoplectic when one of the guests asked him if he edited his own films; he angrily responded, "Does a poet edit his own poetry?"

Throughout the night, however, Pauline was in a state of bliss. "She was overwhelmed in his presence," remembered Donald Gutierrez, "so that she didn't bother to introduce me." David Young Allen recalled that Pauline was in a state of high anxiety preparing for Renoir's visit. "She got Gina and me out of the house," Allen said. "She didn't want interference. She came down with lipstick on and sort of a nice chartreuse sweater. She took the trouble to look nice." Renoir was quite heavy at the time, and when he sat down on one of the good-quality chairs that Pauline had picked up in an antiques shop, he went right through it. But she was too ecstatic in the great man's presence to care in the least.

In the end Pauline's success with the Cinema Guild turned out to be too much for Landberg. After his sojourn in Los Angeles, which he followed up with a trip to Mexico, he returned to Berkeley in late 1961. When he discovered how Pauline had essentially taken over the Cinema Guild by signing the program notes, he was furious, accusing her of stealing all of the theater's publicity. The two of them quarreled bitterly over the issue of the copyright on the notes, and Landberg announced that she was to cease and desist in all matters of programming; he was going to regain control of his own theater. He accused several of the Guild staff members of treason, causing them to resign on the spot. In 1962 Pauline ended her association with the Cinema Guild. Eventually Landberg had a dispute with the landlord, who now wanted him to pay rent plus a percentage. He refused and wound up letting the Cinema Guild fold. He had acquired another theater, the Cinema, on Shattuck Avenue, and eventually he astounded local audiences by playing the Japanese epic *Chushingura* there for forty-three consecutive weeks. But his Cinema Guild audiences felt abandoned: A great institution had come to an end.

# CHAPTER SIX

O nce again Pauline was left without a steady source of income. As her fame had grown locally, she had appeared more and more frequently on KPFA. She continued to lobby hard for payment—cofounder Lewis Hill and the station manager, Trevor Thomas, calmly listened to her demands and refused. She was writing critical pieces for *The Partisan Review* and *Film Quarterly*, but her work yielded minimal income. She petitioned *The San Francisco Chronicle* for a reviewing job, but nothing came of it. She fretted over money, wondering how she was going to provide for Gina and if she would ever be able to build a proper, functioning life for herself.

It wasn't only KPFA's refusal to put her on salary that made Pauline feel antagonistic toward its management. It was what she considered their middle-of-the-road editorial voice. She felt that the station had something in common with *Sight and Sound* and other film journals: While they prided themselves on their liberal point of view, and their editorial content, which was superior to the commercial norm, they were in fact stodgy, predictable, and drearily well-intentioned. She constantly criticized the station—sometimes on the air—for its self-congratulatory attitude and lack of programming flair. (KPFA, trying to maintain a proper atmosphere of free speech on the airwaves, did little to protest.) Pauline found the station's lack of response to suggestions and any criticism of their programming policies an adequate explanation of the fact that after thirteen years, it had a total of only eight thousand subscribers.

She also encouraged her colleagues to rebel whenever possible. "She was kind of a champion of mine in times when I was in a little bit of trouble at KPFA," remembered the station's music director, Alan Rich. On his weekly music review program, Rich's critical arrows were often aimed at the San Francisco Symphony. Unfortunately, several of the Symphony's major donors were also viewed by KPFA's management as potential patrons of the station, and from time to time, Lewis Hill made his objections known to Rich. "I remember running into Pauline on Telegraph Avenue," said Rich, "and she, at the top of her lungs, started yelling about how good I was, and how dare they give me a hard time."

Pauline's weekly broadcasts, meanwhile, were covering many of the new European movies that were catching on with American art-house audiences. One of the most exhilarating movements in world cinema then was the Nouvelle Vague (New Wave). The many champions of the New Wave during the late 1950s and early '60s prized its style of looking at movie storytelling—a more complex, relaxed, intuitive means of portraying characters and situations onscreen. Those at the forefront of the New Wave carried on loudly about the stagnation and lack of imagination that had blighted French cinema since the end of the war, arguing that it had never moved ahead in any innovative way, having been crippled by the hard financial times that cast a pall over the postwar years.

New Wave filmmakers were not too concerned with plot symmetry and conventional narrative technique; they wanted to get at the absolute truth of a situation, often in jagged and allusive ways. If the final result challenged or even puzzled the audience, so much the better. Among the notable characteristics of the New Wave was a preference for location shooting over studio-made sets, a sense of the absurd, an overall feeling of cinema verité—an attempt to portray life as it really was, not as moviegoers had grown accustomed to seeing it manipulated. There was some irony in this, since many of the New Wave directors—François Truffaut, Jean-Luc Godard, and Claude Chabrol, among others—had begun their careers by writing for the French film magazine *Cahiers du Cinéma*, a scholarly journal that consistently paid homage not only to the Italian neorealist movement, but to commercial Hollywood studio product. The *Cahiers* critics were at the forefront of the new movement of auteurists, intent on reevaluating the achievements of many screen directors they considered underrated, and linking their films to one another in terms of style and theme. They elevated the works of studio directors such as Nicholas Ray and Douglas Sirk to a level of appreciation that Americans had not shown them. The *Cahiers du Cinéma* group revered directors who left a conspicuous visual "signature" on their movies, and, like police detectives trying to connect a disparate set of clues, they loved searching for visual links among the directors' films. John Ford, with his painterly instinct in depicting the Old West, and Alfred Hitchcock, the most unapologetically commercial director of all, were held up by the New Wavers as cinema geniuses par excellence.

In 1959, the crucial year for the New Wave, three films premiered at the Cannes Festival and went on to tremendous international success. The first, Marcel Camus's *Black Orpheus*, with its relentless impressionistic score by Luiz Bonfa, was by no means a characteristic New Wave effort, but the other two,

Alain Resnais's *Hiroshima, Mon Amour* and François Truffaut's *The 400 Blows*, were landmark events in world cinema. These films had unexpected rhythms, perversities of editing, scenes of great complexity, ambiguity, and beauty. *The 400 Blows*, in particular, was full of unforgettable sequences, with Henri Decae's camera impassively observing the characters in long, fluid takes. The lack of a conspicuously controlled and controlling directorial tone struck audiences as wildly exciting—even liberating.

Pauline was intrigued by many of the New Wave efforts; their discarding of traditional storytelling structure greatly appealed to her. But on general principle she was not about to give her wholehearted embrace to any trendy new movement, and was meticulous about examining each of the New Wave films individually, believing that they differed wildly in their merits. To her, *Hiroshima, Mon Amour* fell far short of being a significant piece of work. She argued against the film in a provocative article called "Fantasies of the Art-House Audience," which she published in the Winter 1961–62 issue of *Sight and Sound*. "I would like to suggest that the educated audience often uses 'art' films in much the same self-indulgent way as the mass audience uses the Hollywood 'product,' finding wish fulfillment in the form of cheap and easy congratulation on their sensitivities and their liberalism," she wrote. (She added that she used "large generalizations in order to be suggestive rather than definitive.") She was instinctively suspicious of the acclaim heaped on *Hiroshima, Mon Amour* by the American press—notably *Esquire*'s critic Dwight Macdonald, who compared Resnais with Joyce, Picasso, Berg, Bartók, and Stravinsky. To her, the praise that greeted *Hiroshima, Mon Amour* amounted to "incense burning." She was determined to let her readers know that she was one critic not taken in by the repetitive, stilted dialogue, written by the experimental novelist Marguerite Duras, and the movie's controlled, self-consciously hypnotic tone, which she found not at all profound, merely irritating. Most of all, she was troubled by the educated audience's reverence for the film: "audiences of social workers, scientists, doctors, architects, professors—living and loving and suffering just like the stenographer watching Susan Hayward. . . . It is a depressing fact that Americans tend to confuse morality and art (to the detriment of both), and that, among the educated, morality tends to mean social consciousness."

The acclaim for *Hiroshima, Mon Amour* disturbed her as much as the mixed reception for the film that she considered to be the best of the New Wave group: Jean-Luc Godard's *Breathless* (1960), the story of a young, amoral Parisian hood (Jean-Paul Belmondo) who goes on a crime spree while trying to get himself and his girlfriend (Jean-Seberg) to Italy. Pauline was fascinated by the way Godard had managed to make two characters who cared nothing about anything or anyone both attractive and appealing: They were so detached from the world that impulsiveness was a way of life for them. She found *Breathless* funny and sexy and playful and consistently surprising. It worked on the audience in a way that was unusual for movies at the time; those who saw the film found that it was almost impossible to regulate their responses to what was unfolding on the screen. This style and technique resonated with Pauline—it was another example of her attraction to "messiness" on screen—and in her KPFA review of the film, it is easy to sense her exhilaration:

> The codes of civilized living presuppose that people have an inner life and outer aims, but this new race lives for the moment, because that is all that they care about. And the standards of judgment we might bring to bear on them don't touch them and don't interest them. They have the narcissism of youth, and we are out of it, we are bores. These are the youthful representatives of mass society. They seem giddy and gauche and amusingly individualistic, until you consider that this individualism is not only a reaction to mass conformity, but, more terrifyingly, is the new form that mass society takes: indifference to human values.
>
> Godard has used this, as it were, documentary background for a gangster story. . . . But *Breathless* has removed the movie gangster from his melodramatic trappings of gangs and power: this gangster is Bogart apotheosized and he is romantic in a modern sense just because he doesn't care about anything but the pleasures of love and fast cars.

The New Wave movies were considered by KPFA to be ideal editorial content for its listening audience, and Pauline continued to cover them in her broadcasts. One of her favorites was Antonioni's *L'Avventura*, which she felt was easily the best film of 1961. Yet her review of it revealed a certain weakness in some of her writing about European movies. She seemed to have a bit more trouble hitting the bull's-eye with some of the new French and Italian films than she did when dealing with American product. Her assessment for KPFA of *L'Avventura* is a case in point; it's a bit fuzzy, lacking a strong central point. In fact, when she called it "a study of the human condition at the higher social and economic levels, a study of adjusted, compromising man—afflicted by short memory, thin remorse, easy betrayal," she sounded perilously close to the mealy pomposity of Bosley Crowther and other critics she had been railing against for years.

When it came to reviewing Hollywood product, however, she was in full command. One of her most provocative broadcasts was the one in which she took on *West Side Story*, which was released in December of 1961 and went on to sweep that year's Academy Awards, including Best Picture and Best Director (Robert Wise). Pauline considered the movie perfect fodder for her KPFA show: Here was a blatantly commercial movie trying equally blatantly to achieve some level of "artistry" through its dramatic cinematography, gimmicky editing, crashing stereophonic sound, and its relentless attempt to make some relevant statement about street gangs and the folly of modern youth. The combination worked magic with nearly all the major critics. In *The New York Times*, Bosley Crowther hailed the movie as a "cinematic masterpiece"; in *The New Republic*, Stanley Kauffmann called it "the best musical film ever made." *West Side Story* might have been made just so Pauline could knock it off its pedestal. She loved classic, comedy-driven movie musicals such as *Singin' in the Rain* and *The Band Wagon*, but she thought *West Side Story* was, in both conception and execution, a big, loud, pretentious bore:

> The irony of this hyped-up, slam-bang production is that those involved apparently don't really believe that beauty and romance *can* be expressed in modern rhythms—for whenever their Romeo and Juliet enter the scene, the dialogue becomes painfully old-fashioned and mawkish, the dancing turns to simpering, sickly romantic ballet, and sugary old stars hover in the sky. . . . If there is anything great in the American musical tradition—and I think there is—it's in the light satire, the high spirits, the giddy romance, the low comedy, and the unpretentiously stylized dancing of men like Fred Astaire and the younger Gene Kelly. There's more beauty there—and a lot more humanity—than in all this jet-propelled ballet.

A specific leitmotif had begun to emerge in Pauline's reviews of this period: scorn for critics who heaped praise on movies that she felt in no way deserved it. Pauline took to regularly clipping reviews from *The New York Times*, *Time*, *The New Republic*, and other publications and quoting them derisively in her own pieces. In her KPFA review of Billy Wilder's 1961 comedy *One, Two, Three*, which she found "overwrought, tasteless, and offensive—a comedy that pulls out laughs the way a catheter draws urine," she took *Show*'s Arthur Schlesinger to task for calling the film an "irresistible evocation of the mood of Mark Twain"; in the same review, she also took swipes at Stanley Kauffmann, Dwight Macdonald, and *The New Yorker*'s Brendan Gill. In her review of *The Innocents*, Jack Clayton's adaptation of Henry James's *Turn of the Screw*, she dug into Crowther and the *London Observer*'s Penelope Gilliatt for mis-interpreting the aims of the movie.

Crowther was a prime target when she wrote about the creative explosion in British cinema, which had sprung up at roughly the same time as the French New Wave. The British movie industry had been moribund for years: The great days of the Ealing comedies were past, and what Britain mostly produced now were tame costume dramas and cozy mysteries. But the industry came roaring back to life in the late 1950s when a group of directors—Tony Richardson, Karel Reisz, and Lindsay Anderson, among others—turned out a remarkable string of pictures about contemporary British life. One that Pauline particularly took to heart was Richardson's version of John Osborne's play *Look Back in Anger*, starring Richard Burton as the hopelessly lost modern man Jimmy Porter, raging against the stranglehold of the British class system. "The injustice of it is almost perfect," says Jimmy. "The wrong people going hungry. The wrong people being left. The wrong people dying."

Pauline was incensed by Crowther's fatuous dismissal of Jimmy as "a conventional weakling, a routine cry-baby, who cannot quite cope with the problems of a tough environment, and so, vents his spleen in nasty words." For *Look Back in Anger* was "about the failures of men and women to give each other what they need, with the result that love becomes infected. And it is about class resentments, the moral vacuity of those in power, the absence of courage. It's about humanity as a lost cause—it's about human defeat." She found it exhilarating that filmmakers such as Richardson had the courage to confront the bleakness of modern British life onscreen. She had admired Jack Clayton's *Room at the Top* for its uncompromising portrayal of Joe Lampton (Laurence Harvey), an aggressive young Yorkshire man trying to get ahead. The picture had an intimacy and candor that the British cinema hadn't gone near—it was as new as the black-and-white photography of Freddie Francis, depicting the stifling British cityscapes with their bleak row houses and factories spewing soot from their chimneys.

Those who didn't like Pauline's work objected to her caustic tone and what they perceived as her superior, even slightly condescending, attitude, and they often used her bashing of fellow critics as evidence against her, claiming that her lack of collegiality bordered on the unprofessional. But to Pauline, it was essential to draw attention to the ways in which she felt critics had strayed from the path. She believed that they wielded enormous power with the public, and it pained her to see them guiding their readers to what she considered the wrong kind of movies and not giving a fair shake to the ones she felt deserved to be widely seen. Even though she was unpaid, she increasingly approached her reviewing job with a missionary zeal.

She also shook up KPFA by making comments that, decades later, would be viewed as downright callous. From 1960 on, the once-inviolable Production Code had been diluted, and it was now easier for frank subject matter to make it to the screen in some form or another. One of the more controversial movies of 1961 was William Wyler's version of Lillian Hellman's play *The Children's Hour*, a groundbreaking success when it premiered on Broadway in 1934. It deals with a pupil in a girl's school who circulates the malicious lie that her two women teachers are having an affair, causing one of the women to confront her long-repressed lesbianism. The play had been filmed by Wyler in 1936 as *These Three*, but the strictness of the Code meant that it dealt with a conventional heterosexual triangle. By 1961 the play's original content could be played out onscreen, even if the producers covered themselves by casting two enormous box-office stars, Audrey Hepburn and Shirley MacLaine, in the leads. Pauline, however, found the movie stodgy and labored. "Aren't we supposed to feel sorry for these girls because they're so hard-working and because, after all, they don't *do* anything—the lesbianism is all in the mind. (I always thought this was why lesbians needed sympathy—that there isn't much they *can* do.)" It was a careless remark, an example of Pauline the Entertainer, going for an easy laugh. Decades later, in more socially conscious times, it would be taken as evidence in the case that some of her detractors sought to build against her.

In addition to her film criticism on KPFA, Pauline also attacked some of the institutions responsible for bringing films to the Bay Area. One of her favorite targets was the San Francisco Film Festival, launched in 1956 by Irving M. Levin, who came from a family of San Francisco theater owners. Pauline considered Levin and his wife, Irma, to be the most ill-equipped people imaginable to run a festival, an opinion shared by many in San Francisco's arts community, who viewed them as using the Film Festival to secure a niche for themselves among San Francisco's cultural elite. Pauline believed that the festival was crippled by its self-congratulatory atmosphere, and its tendency to confer genius upon anyone with any connection to the world of film. The truth, she said in her broadcast of November 22, 1961, was that those who had paid $2.50, expecting to see a movie of quality, emerged from the festival "sleepy and bored, asking, how could they have picked that movie?"

She admired the technical skill behind the year's biggest film, David Lean's *Lawrence of Arabia*, and also admired Peter O'Toole's performance in it, though she felt that the complex political situation the movie attempted to set forth—British relations with the Arabs and Turks during World War I—was never adequately sorted out so the audience really could understand what was going on; she also was temperamentally indisposed to like such a big, square spectacle, with every detail carefully calculated and put in its proper place. She felt that one of 1962's most revered pictures, *To Kill a Mockingbird*, was too dutiful and not imaginative enough in its dramatization of Harper Lee's prizewinning novel about racial tensions in the south, with Gregory Peck's heralded performance as the scrupulously fair-minded lawyer Atticus Finch on the whole typical of what she had found him to be back in the 1940s—a plodding, hardworking, uninspired actor.

One picture of 1962 that she immediately loved but didn't write about was the Western *Ride the High Country*, which not many people saw on its initial, poorly managed release. It was important to Pauline, however, because it was directed by the gifted, rebellious Sam Peckinpah, who came to films after several years of working in television. *Ride the High Country* was an intriguingly self-referential reunion of two veteran stars—in this case, Joel McCrea and Randolph Scott—playing two aging ex-lawmen hired to transport a gold shipment through dangerous mountain territory. But it was the director's contribution that made Pauline sit up and take notice. Always on the march against pretense, Pauline believed that the Western, especially under the influence of John Ford and George Stevens, had become increasingly pompous and self-important throughout the 1950s. *Ride the High Country* impressed her with its honesty and as an example of beautiful and imaginative filmmaking. She would later call it "the most simple and traditional and graceful of all modern Westerns." MGM's neglect of the film only made Pauline get behind the picture all the more. She was beginning what would be a career-long advocacy for directors she considered misunderstood and mistreated, and Peckinpah was one whom she would champion with especially intense devotion.

The early 1960s continued to be arduous years for Pauline. She was now a woman in her forties with a child to support, and she seemed no closer to figuring out how to earn a living than she had been when she was in her early twenties, just out of Berkeley. There was an increasing number of assignments from *Film Quarterly*, *Sight and Sound*, and *The Partisan Review*, but while they kept her name alive in film-criticism circles, none of them paid more than a pittance.

At KPFA, tensions between Pauline and management continued to build, and on December 8, 1962, she vented her feelings about the station's programming. She craved provocative, intense political discussions rather than what she termed KPFA's preference for "interviews with Quakers and Unitarians":

> Do you really want to be endlessly confirmed in the opinions you already hold? Don't you even want to hear a good case made for other points of view, so that you can test and sharpen your own theories? . . . I sometimes get the impression that KPFA likes the loose, vague, tiresome political interviews and discussions because they make the station seem like an open platform for anyone who wants to talk. I think this impression is deceptive because so much of the talk seems to be of the same general nature. The consequences of this kind of programming are that the air is full of droning sounds, that no other speakers are obtainable. More likely, no one from KPFA has ever approached them.

She had also grown weary of the station management's continued prodding of their unpaid commentators to make on-air pitches for donations and to recruit new subscribers:

> And you I suppose will go on guiltily turning your dollars over to this station, feeling that with each contribution you are a better person for it. You're paying off the liberal debt. You feel as if you're really doing something even if no one will tell you exactly what. It's all a big union of self-sacrificing dedicated staff and self-sacrificial listeners. A kind of osmosis. They give you guilt. You give them money.

KPFA's management was stunned by this public airing of grievances, although it was really no different from what she had long been saying to them directly. Relations between Pauline and Trevor Thomas deteriorated until finally she decided she had had enough, and on her March 27, 1963, broadcast, she resigned over the air. She calculated that she had delivered around one million words over the station's airwaves, and she had come to the conclusion that "a million words delivered without remuneration is a rather major folly." After considering the matter, she had decided that "if KPFA is not a station where we can have open discussions of station policy and get answers to questions, then I see no reason to donate my time. . . . If they want me back on the air, they can pay me. . . . After a million words for love, I think I should turn professional."

The response from listeners was overwhelming; Thomson received so many canceled subscriptions and angry letters accusing him of suppression that he had to send out a form letter, assuring subscribers that Pauline had not been fired, "although some of her charges made that an attractive possibility." Thomas went on to assure listeners that Pauline was welcome to return to the station anytime she liked.

In 1963 Pauline applied for a grant from the Guggenheim Foundation to support her during the writing of a book she had been contemplating for some time. She planned it as a serious look at the state of contemporary movies, with special emphasis on the audience's response to them—a particular interest of hers—and what that response said about the way the culture was changing. In spite of the fact that she had regularly badgered him in her essays, she lost no time in contacting *Esquire*'s Dwight Macdonald for a letter of reference. Although Pauline considered herself the better writer of the two, she was fond of Macdonald; their frequently opposing views of many of the new movies had not derailed their mutual respect for each other. (Macdonald's son Nick had also developed a crush on Gina.) In the fall of 1963 Macdonald wrote to Pauline, "Despite your implacable harassment of me in print, I have, as a good Christian atheist, turned the other cheek and written a fulsome recommendation of your project to the Guggenheim people." He told her that he hoped she got the fellowship because her project was "one of the best I've read in many years of (mostly unsuccessful) recommending people for Guggenheims. Maybe THE best." In his letter to the Guggenheim Foundation, Macdonald wrote that Pauline was right when she said in her application that "the most urgent task for American film criticism" was to provide "a rationale for . . . Critical practice." He felt that Pauline's proposed book was desperately needed in order to show that "cinema has become, in the last five or six years, the liveliest and most interesting of the arts." He urged that the Guggenheim award her as large a grant as possible, because his impression was that "Miss Kael has little income independent from what she earns by her pen."

In March of 1964 Pauline wrote to Macdonald thanking him for his assistance: The Guggenheim grant had come through. Immediately she began making plans to travel, for although she had been writing for several years about foreign-language films, she had never visited Europe. That summer she returned to New York for the first time in years. staying with an old friend, the film writer and psychoanalyst Dan Rosenblatt. Rosenblatt had a floor-through apartment on Patchen Place in Greenwich Village, which delighted Pauline with its bohemian character. He was also well connected with the management of the New York Film Festival, which was set to open in the fall of 1963, and suggested that it should include some substantive panel discussion along with all the screenings. The result was an evening at the Donnell Library on East Fifty-third Street, moderated by Rosenblatt and featuring three provocative critics—Pauline, Dwight Macdonald, and John Simon. Pauline respected Simon's formidable intellect but was wary of him, feeling that many of his opinions were needlessly sadistic and abusive.

For his part Simon was far from an unqualified admirer of Pauline. He recognized her writing ability and respected her sharp wit and her gutsiness as a critic. "She had a style that appealed to a lot of people: those who loved to read, ignorant movie buffs, other critics," he said. "Even critics who didn't agree with her had to admit that she had a real style. And not many people have such a style." But Simon was disturbed by her acceptance of so much that he considered vulgar and lowbrow; he felt that as someone who aspired to be a critic of the first rank, she should hold to a higher aesthetic standard.

Simon also found her problematic on a personal level. "Her main trouble was, of course, that she did want to be a force in the field, an influence, someone you had to reckon with, no matter what," he observed. "In other words, a kind of arrogance." Simon was always suspicious of Pauline's lust to become a powerful player in criticism; to him, this degree of ambition was something that threatened to compromise or even undermine a writer's critical judgment. For most of their careers Pauline and Simon would keep a careful distance from each other, and she didn't go out of her way to denounce him in print. "She felt that it would make me more important than I am," said Simon.

The panel discussion by Pauline, Macdonald, and Simon at the Donnell Library made for a lively and provocative evening, with much of the debate centering on two 1963 releases, *Hud* and *8½*. The discussion of *Hud*, in particular, pointed up some of the ideas about audience reaction that would intrigue Pauline throughout her career. She felt that the movie had "marvelous ambiguity and split in the content." The audience, she felt, was completely on the side of the heel-hero, "enjoying Hud's anarchism, his nihilism, his rejection of the role of the government." The movie caught her completely by surprise with its ending, in which Hud isn't redeemed for his coarse, self-centered behavior: Instead of cleaning up his act, as he would have done had the movie been made a few years earlier, he rapes the family housekeeper, Alma (played by Patricia Neal).

Macdonald dismissed her concerns about the division between audience and critical reaction by arguing, "That's sociology. That's not criticism." Simon, for his part, said, "I am worried about Pauline Kael's position. What she says identifies her in my mind hopelessly not only with the audience, which is bad enough, but with a kind of audience that loves movies so indiscriminately that it is not merely content to accept almost anything that comes its way gratefully for what it is, but will even work overtime inventing a rationale which will somehow justify the inadvertencies and the shortcomings and in some cases even the stupidities of what they see." He also accused her of being one of the critics who imposed an idea on the film that was unjustified simply "to assuage their own boredom." Pauline laughed. "I've never been bored, John, except sometimes, you know, caught by lecturers."

Her views on *8½* were even more controversial. Critics had lined up to applaud Federico Fellini's view of the fantasy life of a bored, creatively stymied director. Unlike nearly all of her major critic colleagues, Pauline hadn't warmed to Fellini's *La Dolce Vita*, which had been released to immense worldwide success in 1960 but which had struck her as a work that "wants to be a great film—it cries out its intentions." While admiring its cleverness, she felt that Fellini had misstepped in using Rome's beautiful people as stand-ins for the aimlessness of modern life, and she was temperamentally unresponsive to any attempt to dramatize the anxieties and fears of a creative artist who had the good fortune to be rich and famous. She found *8½* alienating as well, because it was "surprisingly like the confectionary dreams of Hollywood heroines, transported by a hack's notions of Freudian anxiety and wish fulfillment. *8½* is an incredibly externalized version of an artist's 'inner life'—a gorgeous multi-ringed circus that has very little connection with what, even for a movie director, is most likely to be solitary, concentrated hard work."

She was likewise troubled by the art-house audience's enthusiasm for two other movies released in 1961: Antonioni's *La Notte* and Alan Resnais's *Last Year at Marienbad*, both of which explored the angst of modern times, the futility and ultimate failure of human intimacy. While many critics found them daringly experimental and intellectually thrilling, Pauline thought them stultifying and empty—all surface posing and no real substance. "And isn't it rather adolescent to treat the failure of love with such solemnity?" she asked, with the rhetorical question that had become one of her stylistic trademarks. "For whom does love last? Why try to make so much spiritual desolation out of the transient nature of what we all know to be transient, as if this transiency somehow defined our time and place?" *Marienbad*, in particular, was offensive to her: "Enthusiasts for the film," she wrote, "start arguing about whether something happened last year at Marienbad, and this becomes rather more important than what happens on the screen in front of them—which isn't much. The people we see have no warmth, no humor or pain, no backgrounds or past, no point of contact with living creatures, so who cares about their past or future, or their present?" She criticized all three films in a persuasive essay titled "The Come-Dressed-as-the-Sick-Soul-of-Europe Parties," which *The Massachusetts Review* published in the winter of 1963.

In this viewpoint, she often found herself pitted against her colleagues. Colin Young, an editor at *Film Quarterly* and later head of UCLA's film school, used to tangle with her often, particularly on the subject of Antonioni. "Pauline had her blind spots," said Young. "I remember once being at an Academy screening of foreign-language nominees, and in the toilet after the screening of *La Notte*, I overheard two guys who were peeing. They were saying, 'What's the matter with this guy? He's good-lookin', he's got a good job, he's got a beautiful wife, a mistress—why the fuck is he so miserable all the time?' Pauline would have said 'Here here' to these guys. She couldn't stand all this agonizing. She was a frontier plainswoman."

# CHAPTER SEVEN

During the early 1960s Pauline's reviews had drawn a devoted and gradually growing following among readers of film criticism. The numbers were modest: Her work had appeared only in small-circulation publications and listener-supported radio broadcasts. She was a little like the flickering beacon from a lighthouse far off on the West Coast, only dimly perceived in the east. She needed either a major platform or a major critical piece to raise her visibility. Very soon, she got both.

The critical piece was "Circles and Squares," a lengthy polemic that she finished early in 1963 against the auteur theory. The premise of auteurism was that the strong, individual personality of a talented director was always visible in his films, and that it was necessary to examine how that personality provided crucial links in his entire oeuvre. Even if the film in question happened to be a routine product of the Hollywood studio system, the auteurists held that a good director's signature could be found if one knew how and where to look for it. The greater the talent, the clearer the indication of a powerful sensibility and characteristic visual style. Directors such as Jean Renoir, Max Ophuls, Robert Bresson, Alfred Hitchcock, Howard Hawks, and John Ford were all heroes to the auteurists, because their films displayed distinctive themes and stylistic traits. The rise of auteurism was a significant development in the gradual rise of the director in the general public consciousness, and many previously overlooked artists—including such figures as Phil Karlson and Joseph H. Lewis—who had languished in the shadows of the all-powerful stars were delighted to have attention refocused on their own efforts.

A prime example of an auteur hero is Douglas Sirk, the gifted German director who turned out a series of highly polished tearjerkers in the 1950s. The scripts assigned Sirk to direct were often clichéd romantic dramas, but he brought a striking edge to them. He considered the American family corrupt and unhealthy, and his films displayed a tension and pessimism that made many other directors' portrayal of family life seem utterly fraudulent.

In 1962 auteurism attracted major notice in the United States when Andrew Sarris, then film critic for *The Village Voice*, wrote an essay about it for the Winter 1962–63 edition of *Film Culture*. "Notes on the Auteur Theory" laid out Sarris's criteria for directors to achieve auteur status: the display of technical competence of a high order, a recognizable personal style or voice that could be traced from one film to another, and a powerful ability to convey interior meaning. As Sarris later said, "The strong director imposes his own personality on a film; the weak director allows the personalities of others to ran rampant." He believed that the auteur theory was a crucial tool for understanding film history in that it allowed for the revelation of a kind of directorial autobiography, and the essay brimmed with affection for many little-known, overlooked, and misunderstood films. In his book *The American Cinema: Directors and Directions 1929–1968*, Sarris wrote, "Ultimately, the auteur theory is not so much a theory as an attitude, a table of values that converts film history into directorial autobiography. The auteur critic is obsessed with the wholeness of art and artist. He looks at a film as a whole, a director as a whole. The parts, however entertaining individually, must cohere meaningfully. This meaningful coherence is more likely when the director dominates the proceedings with skill and purpose."

"Notes on the Auteur Theory" was widely discussed in film-critic circles, and though it met with some skepticism, to be sure, its central premise was enthusiastically received, and would eventually result in Sarris's developing an elaborately worked-out ranking of directors, which ranged from the "pantheon" (which included John Ford, D. W. Griffith, Charles Chaplin, Jean Renoir, Max Ophuls, Orson Welles, Josef von Sternberg, F. W. Murnau, Ernst Lubitsch, Fritz Lang, Alfred Hitchcock, Buster Keaton, Howard Hawks, and Robert Flaherty) to the bottom rank of "miscellaneous" directors in whose work Sarris could discern no striking personality (a group that numbered such figures as Gordon Douglas, Victor Fleming, Joshua Logan, Richard Quine, and W. S. Van Dyke).

Sarris was a critic whose opinions would vex Pauline for decades to come. She considered him an intelligent man capable of remarkable insight, and anything but negligible. But many of his ideas about movies struck her as absurd.

She found the auteur theory fundamentally unconvincing: It made no sense to give the director total credit for a work that inevitably reflected the personalities of the screenwriter, the cinematographer, and the actors, as well. She liked to use *Casablanca* as an example of the wrongheadedness of the theory, pointing out that if the character of the cynical hero Rick Blaine had been played by Robert Cummings rather than by Humphrey Bogart, it was a fair guess that the result would have been a poor picture. She decided to seize the moment and asked Ernest Callenbach if she could publish a broadside against Sarris and the other auteur critics in *Film Quarterly*. Callenbach, who had admired Sarris's essay, was somewhat taken aback, but agreed to accept Pauline's piece, "Circles and Squares," for the magazine's Spring 1963 issue.

Her first objection to the auteur theory was that she felt it attempted to elevate relatively minor studio product. In "Notes on the Auteur Theory," Sarris, as an example of tracking a director's signature, pointed out a similar storytelling technique in a scene from Raoul Walsh's 1935 Alice Faye musical *Every Night at Eight* and in one from his 1941 Humphrey Bogart crime drama, *High Sierra*. His conclusion: "If I had not been aware of Walsh in *Every Night at Eight*, the crucial link to *High Sierra* would have passed unnoticed. Such are the joys of the auteur theory."

Pauline thought it ridiculous to bother discussing a comparison between a movie she considered poor (*Every Night at Eight*) with one she considered below-par (*High Sierra*), and she went on to ask why Walsh was to be praised for merely repeating a given technique several years later. Was this really a sign of artistic growth? And why did the auteur theory even have to come into play in such an analysis? "Would Sarris not notice the repetition in the Walsh films without the auteur theory?" she asked. A first-class critic, she argued, didn't need to lean on a theory of any kind: "The greatness of critics like Bazin in France and Agee in America may have something to do with their using their full range of intelligence and intuition, rather than relying on formulas."

She admitted that Sarris's emphasis on "technical competence" sounded reasonable enough on the surface, yet she found it misleading, pointing out that "the greatness of a director like Cocteau has nothing to do with mere technical competence: His greatness is in being able to achieve his own personal expression and style. And just as there were writers like Melville or Dreiser who triumphed over various kinds of technical incompetence, and who were, as artists, incomparably greater than the facile technicians of the day, a new great film director may appear whose very greatness is in his struggling toward grandeur or in massive accumulation of detail. An artist who is not a good technician can indeed create new standards, because standards of technical competence are based on comparisons with work already done."

Moving on to the next argument—that of "the distinguishable personality of the director as a criterion of value"—Pauline shifted into higher gear. "The smell of a skunk is more distinguishable than the perfume of a rose; does that make it better?" She was particularly disturbed by the auteur critics' elevation of Hitchcock, a director whose work had exasperated her over the years. She felt that Sarris was correct about Hitchcock's personality being readily identifiable, but felt it was not a quality that should necessarily elicit critical praise. Comparing Hitchcock with a director whose work she deeply admired, Carol Reed, Pauline wrote that Hitchcock's signature was easier to spot than Reed's "because Hitchcock repeats while Reed tackles new subject matter." She believed that Hitchcock's signature was "not so much a personal style as a personal theory of audience psychology, that his methods and approach are not those of an artist but a prestidigitator. The auteur critics respond just as Hitchcock expects the gullible to respond. This is not so surprising—often the works auteur critics call masterpieces are ones that seem to reveal the contempt of the director for the audience."

Pauline then penetrated Sarris's "inner circle," with its concentration on "interior meaning," which by Sarris's definition was "extrapolated from the tension between a director's personality and his material." Here Pauline's anger was almost palpable, as she denounced this aspect of the theory as "the opposite of what we have always taken for granted in the arts, that the artist expresses himself in the unity of form and content. What Sarris believes to be 'the ultimate glory of the cinema as an art' is what has generally been considered the frustrations of a man working against the given material." Again, she felt that the theory was conferring virtues on undistinguished studio product that simply weren't there. "Their ideal auteur is the man who signs a long-term contract, directs any script that's handed to him, and expresses himself by shoving bits of style up the crevasses of the plots. If his 'style' is in conflict with the story line or subject matter, so much the better— more chance for tension."

The end result of all this, she believed, was that some of the least-deserving movies, and directors, were often candidates for the greatest critical praise. She had seldom liked the work of Otto Preminger; with the exception of his stylish early melodramas like *Laura*, she found his films crude and heavy-handed. But Preminger was a hero to the auteur critics, who praised his characteristic use of the tracking camera. Pauline was having none of it: "I suspect that the 'stylistic consistency' of say, Preminger, could be a matter of his *limitations* and that the only way you could tell he made some of his movies was that he used the same players so often (Linda Darnell, Jeanne Crain, Gene Tierney, Dana Andrews, et al., gave his movies the Preminger look.)"

In 1964 Pauline and Andrew Sarris first came face to face while she was on her Guggenheim-sponsored stay in New York, when she phoned Sarris and asked if he could meet her for a drink. He was stunned at the invitation from a woman he assumed hated him, and hesitated. But Pauline wouldn't be put off. "What's the matter?" she demanded. "Won't your lover let you go?" At the time, the word "lover" had specific connotations. At the time, Sarris was living with his mother in Kew Gardens, Queens. Half-fearing that she really would think he was gay if he didn't turn up, he took the subway into Manhattan and met Pauline, Gina, and Dan Rosenblatt at a midtown restaurant.

"She was always on the boil," Sarris observed. "It was a sort of temperamental difference between us. She was a very lively writer, and she was very readable. I give her a lot of credit for what she did. I think that a lot of people who professed to like her were a bit condescending to her. Even her supporters. There was something unthreatening about her as opposed to people like Mary McCarthy, who really knew how to get at you. And Pauline had a way of getting at people, but she didn't really threaten them."

That night Pauline was bold, confident and inquisitive, Sarris retiring and uneasy, wanting to be anywhere else but sitting across the table from his critical adversary. "I wasn't as worldly and aggressive as she was about sex," Sarris recalled. "About who was gay and who wasn't. I wasn't an expert on such things." There were other matters to discuss, however, than the sexual politics of their film-critic colleagues. "Pauline acted as if I were a great menace of American criticism," Sarris said. "I wasn't getting any money for these pieces. I had no sense that I was being read, even. She talked about going to different places and people would say, 'What about what Andrew Sarris said?' She provided me with the first indication I had that I was being read."

However passionately felt and persuasively argued, to what extent was "Circles and Squares" a careerist move? By taking such a hard public line against another respected critic—at the time Sarris was, by his own admission, hardly the widely read critic he later became, but he was one of the darlings of intellectual and academic film circles—Pauline was clearly clamoring for attention. In "Circles and Squares" she believed she was taking the position of good common sense, challenging the auteurists' dubious claims. In her aggressive, can-you-believe-this? tone, she was practically daring the movie-loving public not to take her side of the argument. At this, she was enormously successful. Sarris himself admitted that Pauline's "attack on the theory received more publicity than the theory itself." In the end Pauline's hostility toward the auteurists was, more than anything, a matter of taste: She could not believe that any thinking person would prefer the work of an erratic filmmaker like Nicholas Ray over that of a proficient, gifted craftsman like John Huston.

One of the misconceptions about "Circles and Squares" was that it engendered a lifelong feud between the two critics. Although Sarris did bring up the disagreement in occasional articles over the next several decades, Pauline put the matter squarely behind her. There was a certain clean detachment in many of her broadsides against other critics, and she was often astonished to learn that the objects of her critical wrath were under the impression that she hated them personally. Again, her behavior betrayed a certain naïveté: She could not always understand why a fellow critic whom she had roundly criticized might feel threatened by her.

Certainly the reading public's response to her essay—which wouldn't become fully clear for years to come—would make it clear to both Pauline and Sarris that they had arrived at a greater level of recognition than they had ever had before. Their meeting was historic, in a sense. They had no way of knowing that in the years ahead, their highly individual points of view would line up critics on either side of a dividing line, pro-Kael and pro-Sarris. And that division would become part of one of the most fascinating chapters in the history of movie criticism.

# CHAPTER EIGHT

The mid-1960s was a good time for Pauline to be coming into her own as a writer: The postwar flourishing of the art-house circuit and the explosion of interest in new foreign films meant that there were now more opportunities for film critics than ever before. Movies were no longer just a great common pastime, like Saturday afternoon baseball games. Now they were playing a more significant role in the culture as people became interested in exploring the connections between cinema and contemporary life. Hit films stayed in theaters longer and were dissected in national magazine cover stories, on television and radio talk shows, and in film studies courses, and movies were well on their way to demonstrating to the world that they really were the liveliest art.

The change had been coming since the 1950s when, in the flush of postwar prosperity, Americans became more inquisitive about the arts. "Growing numbers of middle-class consumers felt it their responsibility to be au courant," wrote the social historian Todd Gitlin in his book *The Sixties: Years of Hope, Days of Rage*. "They were accumulating coffee-table books, subscribing to *Saturday Review* and the Book-of-the-Month Club, buying records, briefing themselves about art." By the following decade the national fascination with arts and culture had taken on a decidedly different shade of meaning with the assassination of John F. Kennedy and the tremendous upheaval wrought by the civil rights movement and the Vietnam War. Young audiences, in particular, wanted more from the movies than mere entertainment. There was still an enormous audience for Walt Disney family pictures and fluffy comedies, but people had also developed an appetite for films that conveyed the anxieties of the times. Movies such as *The Manchurian Candidate*, *Seven Days in May*, and *Dr. Strangelove, Or: How I Learned to Stop Worrying and Love the Bomb* became extremely popular among college students and in intellectual communities. (In the previous decade, many of the most downbeat movies, such as *Sweet Smell of Success*, *Twelve Angry Men*, and *A Face in the Crowd*, had been box-office failures, perhaps because they seemed too dark and pessimistic.) "The rock 'n' roll generation," wrote Gitlin, "having grown up on popular culture, took images very seriously indeed; beholding itself magnified in the funhouse mirror, it grew addicted to media which had agendas of their own—celebrity-making, violence-mongering, sensationalism."

This new climate had its effects even in movie-critic circles. For years many reviewers at major newspapers and magazines had acceded to studio publicists in exchange for access to the biggest movie stories and star interviews. But during the 1960s a number of critics began to speak out and show a much more independent spirit than had previously been the case. In 1963 Judith Crist, then movie critic of *The New York Herald-Tribune*, found herself at the center of a major standoff with a leading studio. When she slammed that year's Easter attraction at Radio City Music Hall—*Spencer's Mountain*, a sentimental family drama starring Henry Fonda and Maureen O'Hara—in both the daily and Sunday editions of the *Herald-Tribune*, Warner Bros. retaliated the following Monday by withdrawing an invitation to an upcoming screening and, more crucially, by pulling all of its advertising from the paper. Radio City Music Hall followed suit, and because the theater's advertising provided income for the newspaper seven days a week, fifty-two weeks a year, the loss was felt immediately. The *Herald-Tribune*'s publisher, Jock Whitney, and editor, Jim Bellows, held firm, running an editorial affirming their support for Crist and her right to say what she thought. "The Associated Press picked up the editorial and transmitted it coast to coast," Crist remembered, "and it made a nice little fuss."

The message was clear: With the steady collapse of the once-powerful studio system and the immense publicity machine that operated within it, the public was forming a new, closer connection with movie critics. As personalities they were becoming better known via radio and television; starting in 1964, Crist would become a familiar face via her appearances on NBC's *Today Show*. Talk show hosts frequently invited Pauline and Andrew Sarris, who were far more in tune with the latest trends in filmmaking, and the new audience it had created, than *The New York Times*'s Bosley Crowther, who increasingly resembled a relic from another era. As the subject matter of movies became more and more provocative, Crowther began to seem more and more out of touch—particularly in his distaste for onscreen violence.

The public's appetite for writing about film was also growing. Only a few years earlier "film studies" was an all but nonexistent category in book publishing. Now there was a demand for film history, theory, and biography, and for published screenplays. Pauline spent all of her spare time hard at work on her own book project, and although a few friends tried to talk her out of her plan to call it *I Lost It at the Movies*, she held fast. The title precisely conveyed its tone—wicked, funny, provocative—and, in terms of her own development as a moviegoer, was absolutely to the point.

She had acquired a New York agent, the estimable Robert P. Mills, and in the summer of 1963 he phoned her with the news that *I Lost It at the Movies* had been accepted for publication by the Atlantic Monthly Press. She received an advance of $1,500 (a year later, the publisher would increase that sum by an additional $1,000), and that, combined with her Guggenheim money and her genius for managing to survive on very little, permitted her to settle down and finish the book.

Despite her hard work on the manuscript, she was tempted by the occasional plum freelance assignment. One came her way in late August 1963, when Robert B. Silvers, the recently appointed editor of *The New York Review of Books*, asked if she would be willing to write a 1,500-word review of *The Group*, Mary McCarthy's new novel about eight bright and promising Vassar graduates. The book had caused a sensation with a surprisingly frank sex scene and an equally detailed sequence in which one of the women gets fitted for a diaphragm. Only a few weeks after publication, it was well on its way to becoming one of the year's most popular and critically praised novels. Pauline, who had liked much of McCarthy's work in the past, snapped up the assignment, which Silvers asked her to turn around in two weeks.

Pauline's review offered a fresh point of view about McCarthy's achievement:

> "*The Group* is the book that Mary McCarthy's admirers have been waiting for." The dust jacket is wrong: this is the book that people who have never liked Mary McCarthy before will admire. Her Vassar girls, misled by "progressive" ideas, are the women as victims so dearly beloved of middle-class fiction. . . . It's like a Hollywood movie: the girl who wants "too much" gets nothing, is destroyed; the girl waiting for the right man gets the best of Everything. . . . As a group, the girls are as cold and calculating, and as irrational and defenseless and inept, as if drawn by an anti-feminist male writer. Those who want to believe that the use of the mind is really bad for a woman, unfits her for "life," miscellanies her, or makes her turn sour or nasty or bitter (as in the past, Mary McCarthy was so often said to be) can now find confirmation of their view in Mary McCarthy's own writing.

This opening salvo was the strongest part of her assessment; elsewhere, her review did not represent her best work. In dissecting the problems with

McCarthy's overall conception of the book, she seemed to circle without ever quite landing. A few days after she had submitted the review, she received a letter from Elizabeth Hardwick, editorial adviser at *The New York Review of Books* (and a close friend of McCarthy). Hardwick apologized for the magazine's tight deadline and then politely, if somewhat condescendingly, rejected the piece, without offering Pauline an opportunity to make revisions. Hardwick told Pauline that it was "rather fruitless to care so much about how fairly or unfairly womankind is treated in this or any other book," that such questions, unless treated in an entirely new way, "seem a bit tired and irrelevant." She added that the piece Pauline had submitted did not seem up to her best work.

Pauline delivered the manuscript for *I Lost It at the Movies* early in the summer of 1964. The Atlantic Monthly Press's director, Peter Davison, wrote to her in mid-July that he was returning the manuscript with "the general recommendations which are truly not too radical." In general Davison was delighted with the condition of the book, but he stressed that "some of the very best pieces were marred by being too long. In fact, I was deterred from full appreciation by boredom!"

By the fall, word had gotten around the publishing industry that *I Lost It at the Movies* was, potentially, at least, a hot project—so much so that Marcia Nasatir, special projects editor at Bantam Books (and future vice president of production at United Artists), wrote to Pauline in October asking to see the manuscript, with an eye toward bringing out a paperback edition.

The intense social upheaval of the 1960s had a curious effect on the arts—and, more particularly, on the audiences for the arts, in whom a certain restless spirit was now in evidence. People who read or attended the theater, concerts, and movies were unsure of what they wanted, and even more unsure of exactly how to react once they had gotten settled into their seats. On the music scene, serial composition had won overwhelming favor with the academic community and music critics; the result was that geniuses such as Aaron Copland more or less lost their footing musically, or in the case of Samuel Barber, languished completely.

In her essay "Is Phoenix Jackson's Grandson Really Dead?" Eudora Welty commented on reader reaction to her famous short story "A Worn Path," in which an old Mississippi country woman, Phoenix Jackson, makes the trek into Natchez to get medicine for her grandson. Many of Welty's readers wrote to her, intrigued by the idea that Phoenix's grandson had already died, that the old woman was making the trip out of habit—the implication being that this somehow improved the story. It was an interpretation that disturbed Welty. "It's *all right*, I want to say to the students who write to me, for things to be what they appear to be, and for words to mean what they say." More and more people seemed to be having some sort of breakdown of identity in relation to what they consumed; they were learning not to trust their own reactions to what they experienced in the arts. This might have been regarded as a healthy sign, as a breaking out of complacent patterns and a reaching toward something new and different—but there were many who did not view it that way, and Pauline was one of them. She expressed her concerns on this subject in an essay called "Are Movies Going to Pieces?" which was published in December 1964—her first appearance in a large-circulation periodical, *The Atlantic Monthly*.

"Are Movies Going to Pieces?" was a lively examination of what she believed to be the increasing incomprehensibility of many of the new pictures being produced. The New Wave classics might have been free-form, but they had a strong, unified vision behind the experimental style; some of the more recent movies seemed to throw logic and cohesion and structure out the window in search of something more sensational or self-consciously "artistic," and it disturbed her that viewers didn't seem to be wise to the trend. Television, with its constant interruptions, might be partly responsible for audiences' acceptance of gaping lapses of logic in movies, of the breakdown of a reliable storytelling method. But she sensed that there was much more to it than that, and she felt that the true cause was to be found in the chaotic pace of modern life: Audiences were so revved up emotionally that they had lost the ability to discern when a movie's form and structure had let them down.

It was a film that not many saw which crystallized Pauline's concerns: Robert Wise's *The Haunting* (1963), a haunted-house thriller in which the horror is unseen. In her essay she reported what had become one of her favorite reviewing habits: scrutinizing the audience as a way of sorting out what was happening to the movie industry. She reported that at the showing of *The Haunting* that she had seen, the few people in attendance "were restless and talkative, the couple sitting near me arguing—the man threatening to leave, the woman assuring him that something would happen. In their terms, they were cheated: nothing happened. And, of course, they missed what was happening all along." From this point, she drew a connecting line to another of her favorite targets, the art-house audience, which she felt "accepts lack of clarity as complexity, accepts clumsiness and confusion as 'ambiguity' and as style."

She was careful to warn her readers that, while she didn't want to be branded as a "boob who attacks ambiguity and complexity," she did believe that even complex subject matter should be expressed as lucidly as possible. The fracturing of narrative, the habit of taking simple ideas and stories and rendering them "complex" through superficially tricky and dazzling technical means, meant that "more and more people come out of a movie and can't tell you what they've seen, or even whether they liked it."

Having placed "Are Movies Going to Pieces?" with the widely read *Atlantic Monthly*, Mills was now able to sell Pauline's essay "Old Movies Never Die" to *Mademoiselle*, which, despite being a women's fashion magazine, had for years published a good deal of quality nonfiction and fiction. "Old Movies Never Die" was a fairly routine roundup of '30s movies, and she herself thought little of it when it was eventually published in the July 1965 issue. But she was delighted with the money and exposure that publication in another wide-circulation magazine brought her.

On March 11, 1965, *I Lost It at the Movies* was published. It had an advance sale of 5,227 copies—an excellent showing for a book about film by an author whose name was still relatively unknown to the general reading public. The Atlantic Monthly Press gave it a significant push with full-page ads in trade publications such as *Library Journal* and the American Library Association's *Booklist*, and smaller ads in such prestigious venues such as *The New York Review of Books*, *The New Republic*, *The Kenyon Review*, and *The New York Times Book Review*. The prepublication reviews from the trade press were encouraging. *Library Journal* stated, "There are very few American film critics whose collected writings would maintain the high level of this book," while *Publishers Weekly* found "the artistry, literacy, fine style and clearheaded reasoning of this criticism is outstanding" and predicted that it should be an "explosively controversial book." The exacting *Kirkus Reviews* wrote, "Never dull, blazingly personal, provokingly penetrating . . . Miss Kael is a 'find.'"

But one review counted the most—that of *The New York Times Book Review*, which appeared on March 14, 1965. The reviewer was Richard Schickel, a former editor at *Look* magazine and the author of the acclaimed study *The Movies*. His review began:

> I am not certain just what Miss Kael thinks she lost at the movies, but it was assuredly neither her wit nor her wits. Her collected essays confirm what those of us who have encountered them separately over the last few years, mostly in rather small journals, have suspected—that she is the sanest, saltiest, most resourceful and least attitudinizing movie critic currently in practice in the United States.

After calling Pauline's "the surest instinct for movies and movie-making since James Agee," Schickel concluded:

> That she is able to analyze her instinct so well and so wittily and to convey its findings without the slightest sense of strain makes her criticism seem like art itself, something of a mystery and something of a miracle. In the end, one is a little awed by the mystery, more than a little grateful for the miracle. Miss Kael may have lost something at the movies, but in her book we have found something—the critic the movies have deserved and needed for so long.

Among the congratulatory letters she received was one from James Broughton, who wrote that it was "always gratifying when a friend who has worked hard for a long time finally makes a substantial breakthrough." He signed it, "My good wishes to you and Gina."

Pauline was pleased by the attention she received from the personnel at the Atlantic Monthly Press, particularly the senior editor William Abrahams, who would work closely with her for years to come. (She would always address him as "Billy dear" in her letters.) Although she was quick to point out when something was not to her liking, the publisher's staff generally found her to be a very cooperative author, eager to comply with most of the interviews that she was asked to do.

In late March she spent the better part of a month in New York, doing publicity for the book. During that trip, she began giving more serious thought to an idea she had recently been tossing around—returning to New York full-time. Maintaining payments on the Oregon Street house had become a burden, and while she had an attractive offer of $10,300 from UCLA to lecture during the 1965–66 academic year, she admitted to Bob Mills, "I don't really want to do it—I'd rather be in the east for awhile. So I'm stalling on acceptance."

Although the thought of paying Manhattan rents was unappealing, she could no longer come up with any excuses for not living in the nation's publishing capital. Besides, now that she had a solid success under her belt with *I Lost It at the Movies*, she would in a sense be going back a star. Still, after all her years of struggle, and having on some level adjusted herself to being in a state of perpetual difficulty, the prospect of major success was somewhat daunting, somewhat complicated. Like Benjamin Burl in her long-ago story "The Brash Young Man," she found that the idea of finally being on the inside, when for so many years she had been pressing her face against the window, took some degree of mental adjustment. "I think there was a moment when she realized that she was going to be really successful," said David Young Allen. "I remember her lying on the couch with her hand on her head and she said something—she had to go through a whole process. She went through a struggle to make the transition in her mind." Her friend Dan Talbot, who owned the prestigious art house the New Yorker Cinema on Manhattan's West Side, telephoned her and said, "I know you love California, but come east—this is where you belong."

The Atlantic Monthly Press signed an agreement with Bantam Books for the latter to bring out the paperback version, Marcia Nasatir having persisted in her enthusiasm for the book and having made the attractive offer of $15,000 for the rights. By fall the paperback edition was in production, but Pauline was not happy with Bantam's ideas for the cover. Robert Mills wrote to Nasatir that he shared Pauline's disappointment, because "the cover seems to illustrate the title rather than the contents, and also looks a little bit like a Grove Press comic book." She asked some of her artist friends to whip up some rough sketches for a cover, and these were used as the basis for the jacket design in its final form. Pauline was an astute judge of a cover's commercial possibilities, and for the rest of her career, she would not hesitate to express her opinions on an art department's efforts on her behalf. Her efforts to make *I Lost It at the Movies* a commercial prospect paid off: It would sell in the neighborhood of 150,000 copies—astonishing for a book on the movies.

By summer the decision that had been gnawing at her for months was made: She would move to New York. The Oregon Street house was sold, and Pauline and Gina went through the arduous process of packing up their belongings, among which books far outnumbered everything else. She had asked several of her friends in New York to be on the watch for available apartments, and Dan and Toby Talbot helped her locate one on the West Side of Manhattan, at 670 West End Avenue—with enough room for the basenjis.

While they were getting ready to take possession of the apartment, Pauline and Gina stayed with Robert and Tresa Hughes at their West Side flat. Robert had been a protégé of Colin Young at the UCLA film school, and Tresa was a respected stage actress. "In the evenings, especially, Bob and Pauline drank and talked," said Tresa Hughes. "There were all these F.O.O. F.s around—Friends of Old Film." Pauline transferred the party atmosphere of the Oregon Street house to her Manhattan dwelling—even the temporary one. Frequently when Tresa came home from the theater, the apartment was still full of Pauline's movie cronies, talking, drinking, and often violently disagreeing.

These relationships were now the closest thing to an emotional life that Pauline had. Her New York friends all had the impression that she was essentially through with men. Perhaps her feeling on the matter was best observed in *Wearing the Quick Away*, a one-act monologue she had written in the 1940s. "People shouldn't marry you if they can't accept you as you are," her character says. "These men get to acting as though this *change* was what they married you for and you cheated them by not turning into something else."

*I Lost It at the Movies* turned out to be a potent calling card: Pauline was constantly being asked to make lecture appearances, and *Holiday* magazine offered her $750 for a 2,000-word piece, "The Incredible Shrinking Hollywood," which eventually ran in its March 1966 issue. What she craved most, though, was a steady movie-reviewing berth. Over the summer Robert Mills worked hard trying to find one for her, and by summer's end, it appeared that *McCall's* (which called itself the "first magazine for women") was seriously interested. With its emphasis on features dealing with home and beauty, it was hardly the sort of place Pauline might have imagined would offer her a staff position, but Robert Stein, the magazine's editor, was trying to reshape the readership by seeking out cultural coverage with a bit more gravitas. By the mid-1960s Stein recognized that there was a wide, new audience of young women with college degrees who might be looking for something a little more serious in tone in a standard-issue women's magazine. By early October Mills had concluded negotiations with Stein: *McCall's* would sign Pauline for a six-month trial period, to commence in February 1966. During that time she would turn in one monthly column of no more than 2,500 words, for which she would be paid $1,500—a good salary for the time. At last she would be able to make a real living solely as a film critic.

While she was waiting for the *McCall's* assignments to begin, she accepted a number of lecture engagements. One of them was an invitation to speak at a conference of educators held at Dartmouth College in October 1965. The speech that resulted may not have been what the conference's officials had in mind, but it was a perfect distillation of Pauline's feelings about the worst traps of academia. "It's Only a Movie" was a persuasive argument against film studies courses in American universities. In it, Pauline referred to her early, rebellious student attitudes. Sitting down to try to prepare a film course, she said, served only to remind her "how my thumbnails got worn down from scraping the paint off my pencils as the teacher droned on about great literature. I remembered music appreciation with the record being played over and over, the needle arm going back and forth, and I remembered the slide machine in art history and the deadly rhythm of the instructor's paper. Teaching a course in film studies," she said, "goes against the grain of everything I feel about movies, and against the grain of just about everything I believe about how we learn in the arts."

What academic instructors seemed incapable of recognizing about genuine movie-lovers, she argued, was that film represented "a world more exciting than the deadening world of trying-to-be-helpful teachers and chewed-over texts." Film, like jazz and popular music, had an advantage over other traditional art forms because it had not received a cultural stamp of approval in advance; it was "something we wanted, not something fed to us." She went on:

> Surely only social deviates would say to a child, "What's the matter with you, why don't you want to go to the movies?" Kids don't have to get all dressed up or go with an adult the way they do to a Leonard Bernstein concert, shiny and flushed with the privilege of being there. No cultural glow suffuses the Saturday afternoon movie audience; they are still free to react as *they* feel like reacting, with derision or excitement or disappointment or whatever. . . . Going to a movie doesn't wind up with the horrors of reprimands for your restlessness, with nervous reactions, tears, and family disappointments that you weren't up to it. It's only a movie. What beautiful words. At the movies, you're left gloriously alone. You can say it stinks and nobody's shocked.

She also penned an intriguing essay for *The Atlantic Monthly*: "Marlon Brando: An American Hero." The title may have suggested a straightforward, starry-eyed appreciation, but what evolved was something rather different: an attempt to explain why Brando, only sixteen years after the beginning of his screen career, seemed to be parodying himself. Pauline placed the blame on the unspoken conspiracy of both journalists and the movie industry to ridicule him. She also lit into the corrupt studios, which, in her view, usually reacted to a star's rising power and fame by launching "large-scale campaigns designed to cut him down to an easier-to-deal-with size or to supplant him with younger, cheaper talent." Still, Brando's talent could not be disguised. "His greatness is in a range that is too disturbing to be encompassed by regular movies," she wrote. She found him "still the most exciting American actor on the screen. The roles may not be classic, but the actor's dilemma is."

By far Pauline's biggest undertaking in the fall of 1965 was an assignment from *Life*: a report on the filming of Mary McCarthy's *The Group*. The producer, Charles K. Feldman, had bought the movie rights, and now United

Artists, the studio making the picture, had assigned it to the quickly rising director Sidney Lumet. Although he had turned out several pictures that had met with great critical praise, including *Twelve Angry Men*, *Long Day's Journey into Night*, and *The Pawnbroker*, none had been a commercial success. Given the book's popularity, it was expected that *The Group* would be one of the big screen events of the year, and *Life* felt it warranted major coverage in the magazine. The success of *I Lost It at the Movies* led *Life* to Pauline, even though she had never done a piece of straight reportage. (It is doubtful that anyone at the magazine knew or cared about her history with McCarthy's novel and *The New York Review of Books*.)

Initially Sidney Lumet was delighted to have Pauline covering the picture, as he had been following her work for some time and found her one of the most perceptive and articulate critics to come along in years. "The only thing she was really lacking," said Lumet, "which I feel is true of many critics, is any *technical* knowledge of how a movie is made." He gave her complete access to the filming, which was being done entirely in New York. On the set Pauline kept herself in the background, never interrupted a shot, never asked questions at tense or inappropriate times. To the actresses she was rather intimidating, despite her low profile—"rather brusque and strict" was how Shirley Knight, playing Polly, the group member who wants only a simple and fruitful marriage, remembered her.

It was a challenging shoot. There were many locations, and often, a key scene would involve as many as eight people—a daunting task from the cameraman's point of view. Pauline watched as Lumet worked with great speed and authority, a highly professional director who was cordial to most of the cast and crew. Still, she couldn't help but feel that he was applying too many of the abrupt, unsubtle, time-saving techniques he had picked up during his years directing for television. He was extremely generous with actors, but Pauline wasn't sure that he always sensed the most imaginative way of pulling a performance out of them; she believed that he had a tendency to settle for a take that was only passable. (Jessica Walter, who played Libby, the bookish girl with ambitions to succeed in the publishing industry, disagreed: "I remember doing so many takes. Sidney always wants it to be a hundred and fifty percent plus. Never did I see him accept the passable." Shirley Knight concurred that Lumet insisted on many takes, but she questioned the outcome. "He'll do a bunch of takes, and there'll be a take that is really *the* one, and everything goes together," observed Knight. "And he wants you to duplicate it.")

Lumet and Pauline had a very friendly relationship during the weeks that she observed on the set. Not long after *The Group* had wrapped, Lumet invited her to his apartment for dinner. Also present was Lumet's close friend the show-business caricaturist Al Hirschfeld, with his wife, Dolly. "We had a good dinner and a lot to drink," recalled Lumet. "Oh, boy—did Pauline like to drink. Al had the greatest equanimity of any person I've ever seen. But I could see he was rankled by Pauline, and they got into an idiotic discussion about the function of a critic." The argument went back and forth, until Hirschfeld finally raised his voice slightly and demanded of Pauline, "What do *you* think the function of a critic should be?"

"My job," snapped Pauline, "is to show *him*"—pointing at Lumet—"which way to go."

Lumet never saw her again. "I thought, this is a very dangerous person. When she had arrived in New York, she had just come from San Francisco, and I thought, poor kid—she's probably lonely as hell. Little did I know what I was dealing with."

"The Making of *The Group*" was the most ambitious project Pauline had undertaken, and the result was anything but a piece of conventional reportage. But by 1965 the movement that would come to be known as the "New Journalism" was under way with a new breed of journalists—Tom Wolfe, Gay Talese, Joan Didion, Michael Herr—employing some of the storytelling techniques of fiction, turning reporting from something dutifully responsible into a highly personal and creative art, which, as the historian Marc Weingarten observed, "changed the way their readers viewed the world."

The New Journalism movement had been evolving for years, but one article that put it center stage appeared in *New York*, the Sunday supplement of *The New York Herald-Tribune*, in April 1965. It was written by the young Tom Wolfe, and the name of it was "Tiny Mummies! The True Story of the Ruler of 43rd Street's Land of the Walking Dead!"—an attack on the famously polished and discreet editorial practices of *The New Yorker*'s editor in chief, William Shawn. To a young renegade such as Wolfe, Shawn's prudish tastes and obsessively controlled line editing had rendered a once-vital magazine rather dull. As journalism, "Tiny Mummies!" was pure provocation.

Pauline, who had always abhorred the idea of an objective tone in her critical writing, was intrigued by the New Journalists, and "The Making of *The Group*" was very much in step with their methods. In *Picture*, her celebrated 1951 account of the filming of MGM's *The Red Badge of Courage*, Lillian Ross was meticulously detached, never intruding on the story she was telling. By contrast, Pauline was quick to register shock, dismay, amusement, embarrassment.

When "The Making of *The Group*" was completed, it had grown to about 25,000 words—far too long for *Life* to consider publishing. Pauline was enraged that the magazine would turn down an effort on which she had worked so hard in good faith, and she complained loudly to Robert Mills about it, but there was nothing her agent could do: The piece was about ten times longer than anything that *Life* normally published. What the magazine did put into print were Pauline's observations of the eight lead actresses, in an article titled "A Goddess Upstages the Girls." Pauline was particularly tough on Candice Bergen, whom she portrayed as a vapid dilettante with no interest whatsoever in the craft of acting. "What really offended me was the way she wrote about Candy Bergen," Sidney Lumet recalled. "One of the things Pauline attacked her for was sleeping during rehearsals, for daring not to listen to my brilliant, forty-minute speeches. I adored Candy for just that. For anyone at eighteen—that beautiful, that intelligent, with so much of life ahead, to be a devoted actress by that point, would have struck me as a hopeless neurotic—someone who I could find anywhere between Forty-second and Fifty-second Street. Pauline was asking for someone to be as obsessive as she was."

*The Atlantic Monthly* eventually bought the entire piece for $1,900, but Pauline refused the cuts that the editors suggested, and by the fall of 1966, the *Atlantic* had dropped it. Perhaps it was not only the article's length but its tone that made editors so nervous. It was Lumet who came off worst in Pauline's essay, as he was portrayed essentially as an aggressive, ambitious whiz kid from television who was hungry for a commercial movie hit, the kind of director who was apt to get hired in these artistically bankrupt times because "he would not try to reshape the scenario or risk holding up production to do something unscheduled; he wouldn't plead for a few extra days to get something right."

"The Making of *The Group*" would not see the light of day until 1968, when it was published in Pauline's second book, *Kiss Kiss Bang Bang*. "I had heard it was going to be butchery, and I never read it," Lumet claimed. "If there's an unpleasantness to avoid, I avoid it."

# CHAPTER NINE

auline's first column for *McCall's* appeared on schedule in the magazine's February 1966 issue. "The Function of a Critic" was a reprise of some of the ideas set forth in "It's Only a Movie":

> Appreciation courses have paralyzed reactions to modern music, painting, poetry and even novels, but movies, ignored by teachers as a Saturday afternoon vice, are one of the few arts (along with jazz and popular music) Americans can respond to without cultural anxieties.
>
> This, unfortunately, is beginning to change. At art houses and film festivals, audiences are beginning to show the same kind of paralysis. They seem to think that a highly praised movie or a movie selected for a festival must be art, and if they don't respond to it, they are uncomfortable about saying so. They no longer trust themselves. Ultimately, if this fear of authority develops even in movie audiences, our responses will contract, movies will join the paralyzed high arts. There are already signs of this. At a recent opening, I said to the manager, "It was wonderful, but I was puzzled. I couldn't tell whether the audience liked it or not." He answered, "They're waiting for the reviews."

Initially the editors of *McCall's* seemed pleased with her tough, smart writing, and in the March issue she covered a number of new releases, including the movie that would turn out to be John Ford's last, *Seven Women*, starring Anne Bancroft as the head of a group of women missionaries in 1930s China. Pauline observed that sitting through *Seven Women* was "rather like watching an old movie on TV and thinking, 'No, no, they're not *really* going to do that next'—but they do, they do, and superior as you feel to it, you're so fascinated by the astounding, confident senselessness of it all that you can't take your eyes off it." In the same column, she lamented that Laurence Olivier's magnificent *Othello* had been preserved only in a cheap filmed version of the play, not in a proper screen transcription with the full arsenal of technical possibilities at his disposal.

In the April issue, however, she ventured into more controversial territory with her review of David Lean's *Doctor Zhivago*. This mammoth, meticulously detailed screen version of Boris Pasternak's 1958 bestseller about the Russian Revolution had long been anticipated as one of the big movie events of the year, and it was already on its way to becoming one of the top-grossing films of all time. Pauline loathed the hype for the picture as much as she loathed Lean's meticulously detailed and worked-out style of moviemaking, with every response carefully calculated, every shade of meaning put properly in place. She dismissed it as "stately, respectable and dead" and likened it to "watching a gigantic task of stone masonry executed by unmoved movers. It's not art, it's heavy labor—which, of course, many people respect more than art." She went on to predict that it would further accelerate the race for superspectacles "that will probably have to bankrupt several studios before a halt is called."

Pauline always claimed that none of the *McCall's* editors attempted to dictate to her how to review a particular movie. It was one thing for her to dismiss a run-of-the-mill film that either made or lost a little money, and quite another for her to attack such a prestigious picture that had found its cultural niche so quickly. Still, the editors at the magazine gave her the benefit of the doubt for the moment.

Dwarfing even *Zhivago*, however, was *The Sound of Music*, which had been released in March of that year and would soon surpass *Gone With the Wind* as the top-grossing film of all time. A big, handsome film, shot in spectacular Technicolor in Austria, brimming with wholesomeness, *The Sound of Music* confirmed what *Mary Poppins* and *My Fair Lady* had shown the year before: that the movie musical wasn't dead at all; provided it was big and splashy and colorful enough, it could be box-office gold. *The Sound of Music* also single-handedly rescued its studio, Twentieth Century–Fox, where production had slowed to a trickle after the devastating failure of the astronomically expensive *Cleopatra*. *The Sound of Music*'s soundtrack album was an enormous success; an entire generation of parents and children memorized the songs at home, and then treated themselves to repeat viewings of the movie. And in the spring of 1966, *The Sound of Music* beat *Doctor Zhivago* for the Academy Award as Best Picture of 1965.

Because it had been released months before she began work at *McCall's*, Pauline had not reviewed *The Sound of Music* for the magazine. But in April 1966, when MGM released its own big entry in the family-musical sweepstakes—*The Singing Nun*, starring Debbie Reynolds—Pauline took it as an opportunity to annihilate retrospectively *The Sound of Music*, which she predicted would prove to be "the single most repressive influence on artistic freedom in movies for the next few years."

While she herself was not immune to the movie's basic appeal, as she acknowledged,

> You begin to feel as if you've never got out of school. . . . This is the world teachers used to pretend (and maybe still pretend?) was the real world. It's the world in which the governess conquers all. It's the big lie, the sugarcoated lie that people seem to want to eat. They even seem to think that they should feed it to their kids, that it's healthy, wonderful "family entertainment" . . . Why am I so angry about these movies? Because the shoddy falseness of *The Singing Nun* and the luxuriant false-ness of *The Sound of Music* are part of the sentimental American tone that makes honest work almost impossible.

Taking such a morally indignant tone was a risky move, for while her righteous anger might have had its place in one of the small film or literary quarterlies, to attack a movie that the world had taken to its heart in a big-circulation women's magazine such as *McCall's* struck many readers as unsuit-able and oddly misplaced.

By mid-May, it was announced that Pauline and *McCall's* would part company, a story that was big enough news to merit coverage in *Newsweek*. "The reviews became less and less appropriate for a mass-audience magazine," Stein told *Newsweek*. "I still think she's one of the best movie critics around. My hiring her was, I thought, a noble experiment. The experiment did not work out."

Pauline did not look back on her brief stint at *McCall's* with rancor and celebrated her departure from the magazine by taking Gina on a trip to Europe in late May 1966. While they were stopping off in London at the Mount Royal Hotel, Robert Mills wrote to her that she had earned $1,000 in royal-ties for *I Lost It at the Movies* and $1,500 from the latest *McCall's* payment. "What would you like us to do with all this money?" he asked.

Mills cast around for another regular reviewing job, and while Pauline and Gina were still abroad, he received an offer: *The New Republic* wanted her to be its regular movie columnist, to replace one of the critics she admired least, Stanley Kauffmann, who was leaving for what would be an extremely short-lived stay as drama critic for *The New York Times*. Founded in 1914 by Herbert

Croly and Walter Lippmann, the magazine had long been known for its in-depth essays on politics and culture that generally embraced a liberal point of view. By the 1960s its political stance was harder to pin down. While it had come out against the Vietnam War, it was also sharply critical of the wave of protest and activism that had swept across America in mid-decade. Its circulation was anything but mass—it hovered on either side of 50,000—and its editor, Robert Evett, offered Pauline terms that were not nearly as lucrative as the *McCall's* deal had been—twenty-four columns a year at $300 each. Still, she believed that as an outlet for her talents, *The New Republic* made more sense than *McCall's* had.

Her debut column appeared on October 8, 1966—"The Creative Business," another analysis of the artistic bankruptcy rampant in Hollywood—after which she settled down to the business of reviewing movies. Her October 22 column featured reviews of two sprawling epics, *Hawaii* and *The Bible*, and surprisingly, for someone who had always harbored an antipathy to the grandiosity of David Lean's films, she liked both. *The Bible* was directed by John Huston, and she preferred his approach to the "ploddingly intelligent and controlled" work of Lean; she thought *Hawaii* was superbly edited, and that its director, George Roy Hill, "compensates for his inexperience in the medium by developing strong characterizations that succeed in binding the material."

It was a disagreement over *Hawaii* that led Pauline to one of the most enduring of her friendships with a colleague. Joseph Morgenstern was a young critic at *Newsweek* who had been invited to appear on the entertainment reporter Pat Collins's radio show to discuss current films. When he arrived at the studio, he found that Pauline was also a guest. "I could hardly get a word in edgewise," Morgenstern remembered. "The talk turned to *Hawaii*. At the time, I thought it was just a big, clumsy movie. Pauline said vociferously on the radio that it has a social conscience, talks about smallpox, this and that. But she overpraised it, as was her wont. I couldn't believe what I was hearing on the air, and I said it. That goaded her. And as soon as we got off the air, she said, 'That was fun, honey. Let's have a cup of coffee!'" It was the beginning of a thirty-six-year friendship.

It had begun to bother Pauline that the youth audience, in particular, didn't seem more discriminating about the movies it considered "great." All that seemed to matter was that they felt hip. She regarded this as the worst sort of narcissism, while at the same time dreading that her lack of enthusiasm for many of the new pictures might brand her as some kind of hidebound reactionary. She was particularly troubled by some of the films coming out of

Britain, with their bouncing pop-music scores, fast editing, and accelerated camerawork taking in the gritty streets of mod London.

In her November 5, 1966, column for *The New Republic*, "So Off-beat We Lose the Beat," she complained that *Morgan!* was nothing more than "a modernized version of an earlier, romantic primitivist notion that people are conformists, animals are instinctively 'true' and, of course, 'free.'" She suspected that *Morgan!* was "so appealing to college students because it shares their self-view: they accept this mess of cute infantilisms and obsessions and aberrations without expecting the writer and director to straighten it out or resolve it and without themselves feeling a necessity to sort it out." Yet she was intrigued by the wild enthusiasm the youth audience showed for it and for *Georgy Girl*. In an obvious jab at Dwight Macdonald, she added, "And if it be said that this is sociology, not aesthetics, the answer is that an aesthetician who gave his time to criticism of current movies would have to be an awful fool. Movie criticism to be of any use whatever must go beyond formal analysis."

By December Robert Mills felt confident in requesting a raise per *New Republic* column, as Pauline "could find good use for another one or two hundred dollars a check." In a short time, however, friction developed, as she often had a difficult time confining herself to the assigned word count. The lack of communication also disturbed her: Sometimes her column was dropped from an issue without explanation. When it did appear in print, it was often in a significantly altered form—either cut or, worse yet, rewritten, with observations and word choices that were not her own. She complained to Mills, but the editors continued to make wholesale changes without consulting her.

Pauline was beginning to turn up as a frequent guest on radio programs and film-critic panel discussions. But their organizers began to anticipate her appearances with equal parts excitement and dread, since she behaved with a candor that sometimes crossed over into rudeness. One such episode took place in the spring of 1966, when Judith Crist invited her to appear on a radio program she was hosting. The other guest was Ginger Rogers, who was about to open on Broadway as Carol Channing's replacement in the hit musical *Hello, Dolly!*

Pauline had praised Crist's critical integrity, and when she showed up to tape the radio show, all seemed promising. "Judy Crist!" she shouted as she got off the elevator. "The *one tough critic* in New York!" The program got under way, and Crist began questioning Ginger Rogers about *Kitty Foyle*, the 1940 soap opera that had earned her a Best Actress Academy Award. Rogers began to speak about how her agent had tried to discourage her from doing *Kitty Foyle*, and how she had persisted and wound up winning the Oscar. "Your agent was right," snapped Pauline. Rogers, looking as if she was about to burst into tears, was shocked into silence, leaving Crist to vamp about *Kitty Foyle* and other matters.

On another occasion, Pauline and Crist had both served on a critic's panel at Lincoln Center for the Performing Arts. During the discussion, Pauline lit into her favorite bogeyman, Bosley Crowther, and Crist angrily shouted her down, telling her that she should lay off Crowther—that he had his parish and Pauline had hers. Later, Pauline asked Crist to join her for a cup of coffee. "She wanted to explain to me," recalled Crist, "that when she was running her theater in Berkeley, running the Cinema Guild, she had to put up posters that featured banner reviews by Bosley in big print. She resented that he was the most important critical voice in the country; she'd harbored it for years." That year Universal Pictures dropped Pauline from its list of complimentary invitational press screenings. The alleged reason was her behavior at a screening of the studio's new Ross Hunter–produced soap opera, *Madame X*. The studio felt that Pauline's derisive hoots and audible comments in the screening room had adversely influenced the other critics. For a time she would have to pay to see Universal's pictures in a theater—her preferred setting, anyway, as she could then monitor the reactions of the audience.

The movie of 1966 that perplexed Pauline most was Antonioni's *Blow-Up*, a study of the fast-paced, empty life of a high-fashion photographer (David Hemmings) in swinging London. It was a strikingly filmed and brilliantly edited murder mystery, and this part of the film she found quite successful. But few things vexed her as much as unearned seriousness, and it was here that she felt *Blow-Up* went off the rails. The basic idea that *Blow-Up* seemed to be setting forth—that the photographer's life represented illusion and the murder reality—struck Pauline as impossibly facile, and she also felt that its implicit message that the mod scene represented the spiritual aridity of the times was nothing but a pompous, moralizing pose. While Antonioni had tapped into the alienation and unresponsiveness of modern youth, he had missed "the fervor and astonishing speed in their rejections of older values; he sees only the emptiness of pop culture."

In her reviewing career to date, Pauline had shown a powerful gift for defending the great talents she believed had been prevented from doing their best work by Hollywood; Orson Welles's *Falstaff* provided her with another such opportunity. After *Citizen Kane* and *The Magnificent Ambersons*, Welles's career had consisted mainly of giving hammy performances in a string of mediocre pictures and trying to amass enough cash to finance a project that might restore his reputation as a director. He had come tantalizingly close with *Othello*, finally released in 1955 after years of stop-and-start filming, and *Touch of Evil*, a wholly original thriller set in a Mexican border town, but both films received minimal distribution and flopped.

In the 1960s he had one more chance, with *Falstaff* (later known as *Chimes at Midnight*), which he had been shooting in Europe for years. It was an amalgamation of several Shakespeare plays, with the most poignant part of *Henry IV, Part I* at its center: Prince Hal's recognition of his destiny and gradual pulling away from Falstaff. Pauline admitted that technically, the movie was a mess, showing many signs of its chaotic filming, but she found "the casting superb and the performance beautiful." The Battle of Shrewsbury, she felt, ranked with "the best of Griffith, John Ford, Eisenstein, Kurosawa—that is, with the best ever done." And yet its technical defects were preventing it from getting proper distribution. "And Welles—the one great creative force in American films in our time, the man who might have redeemed our movies from the general contempt in which they are (and for the most part, rightly) held—is, ironically, an expatriate director whose work thus reaches only the art-house audience."

*The New Republic* continued to tamper with her copy, and by the summer of 1967 she realized she could not continue for much longer. She resigned her post, using her latest royalty check for *I Lost It at the Movies* to take Gina to Europe for a few weeks. She was not at all sure that another steady reviewing job would present itself.

Pauline was distressed that the creative ferment that had burst out of France and Britain at the end of the '50s seemed to have dried up. It was particularly sad to see what had happened to François Truffaut, who had taken on the ill-advised *Fahrenheit 451* and was now preparing what would turn out to be a hollow parody of his idol, Alfred Hitchcock, *The Bride Wore Black*. One of the few French directors to keep his hold was Jean-Luc Godard, whose *Band of Outsiders* Pauline had admired. She felt that *Breathless* and *Band of Outsiders* derived their spark from the fact that they were "movies made by a generation bred on movies . . . Godard is the Scott Fitzgerald of the movie world, and movies are for the sixties a synthesis of what the arts were for the post–World War I generation—rebellion, romance, a new style of life." Unfortunately, *Band of Outsiders* failed to intrigue American audiences and played in New York for only a single week in March 1966.

American movies, Pauline believed, were in a shambles. She was certain that she had been right about the dangerous example set by *The Sound of Music*. Big, expensive, self-important pictures seemed to be all that interested the studios. Very seldom did she see anything that reflected the current climate in America in a serious or challenging way, and she had come to fear that perhaps there wasn't even a public for such movies. Impressed as she had been by Truffaut's and Godard's early films, she had stopped short of genuine capitulation to them: that degree of abandon she still reserved for an American movie.

And then, on August 4, 1967, *Bonnie and Clyde* opened at the Montreal Film Festival.

The picture had first gone into development in 1963, when David Newman and Robert Benton, both staff art directors at *Esquire*, had gotten together to write a treatment based on the legendary Depression-era crime sprees of Clyde Barrow and Bonnie Parker. Like Pauline, Newman and Benton were impatient for the American film to move forward, and their telling of the story of Bonnie and Clyde showed the influence of the French New Wave filmmakers. When it was released, it was clear that the restless, often violent spirit of the '60s pervaded practically every frame of the movie.

Versions of the story of Bonnie and Clyde had reached the screen many times before—in Fritz Lang's *You Only Live Twice* (1937) and Joseph H. Lewis's *Gun Crazy* (1950), among others—but never with such complexity, such wit, such unexpected shifts of tone, the wild, jaunty scenes of the early part of the picture leading seamlessly into the more violent and disturbing second half. Warren Beatty's Clyde and Faye Dunaway's Bonnie were so vital and attractive that it was easy for those watching the movie to accept them as folk heroes; the film seemed to embrace them as stand-ins for all those disenfranchised by the worst economic disaster in U.S. history, and the audience wanted them to get away with everything. There was a remarkable scene midway through the picture in which Bonnie and Clyde shoot up a house that has been repossessed by the bank—and, with the fervor of a student protester, the owner joins them in shooting out the windows and the bank's sign. In the horrifying finale the couple dies in a shower of bullets—agonizingly and yet, somehow, beautifully—in a staggering orgy of violence. This was tough stuff for audiences at the time, but the director, Arthur Penn, and Beatty gambled that contemporary moviegoers would connect with what was happening on the screen.

At first it appeared that their gamble might fizzle. Warners opened *Bonnie and Clyde* in a string of mostly undistinguished theaters in mid-August

1967. Some of the reviews—from Judith Crist and a few others—were positive, but many of the most important ones were not, and the most important one of all was, of course, written by Pauline's bête noire, Bosley Crowther, in *The New York Times*. Long known for his abhorrence of violence, Crowther found the portrayal of Bonnie and Clyde nothing less than an act of moral repugnance. He denounced the film as "a cheap piece of bald-faced slapstick comedy that treats the hideous depredation of that sleazy, moronic pair as though they were as full of fun and frolic as the jazz-age cut-ups in *Thoroughly Modern Millie*."

From the moment she saw *Bonnie and Clyde*, Pauline was one of the film's most enthusiastic champions. It excited her as no movie had in years. If a picture as thrillingly bold and original as *Bonnie and Clyde* could come out of a climate that was desperate to create another *Sound of Music* or *Doctor Zhivago*, there might yet be amazing possibilities in store for American movies. The trouble was, she had not had an opportunity to write about it. She had submitted a lengthy essay to *The New Republic* during the month that she departed from the magazine, but the editors considered it overlong and refused to run it.

There was one place where length would not be an issue: *The New Yorker*. The magazine had already featured Penelope Gilliatt's very favorable notice, but Pauline knew that the magazine's editor, William Shawn, had been following her work for some years. Shawn was a serious moviegoer and he had been particularly intrigued by Pauline's writings on Godard in *The New Republic*. She had already made her *New Yorker* debut in the June 3, 1967, issue with an article titled "Movies on Television," in which she discussed the mixed blessing of reencountering old films on the small screen. Robert Mills now called William Shawn with an offer: Would he be interested in publishing a 7,000-word essay on why *Bonnie and Clyde* represented a moment of enormous importance in America's pop culture?

In terms of the impact it would have on her career, it was the most important essay Pauline would ever write. It ran in *The New Yorker*'s issue of October 21, 1967, and it opened on a strong note of defiance, in one of her favorite devices, the rhetorical question:

How do you make a good movie in this country without being jumped on? *Bonnie and Clyde* is the most excitingly American movie since *The Manchurian Candidate*. The audience is alive to it. Our experience as we watch it has some connection with the way we reacted to movies in childhood: with how we came to love them and to feel they were ours— not an art that we learned over the years to appreciate but simply and immediately ours. When an American movie is contemporary in feeling, like this one, it makes a different kind of contact with an American audience from the kind that is made by European films, however contemporary. Yet any movie that is contemporary in feeling is likely to go further than other movies—go too far for some tastes—and *Bonnie and Clyde* divides audiences, as *The Manchurian Candidate* did, and it is being jumped on almost as hard.

She felt that the screenwriters had tapped into something very important in that "they were able to use the knowledge that, like many of our other famous outlaws and gangsters, the real Bonnie and Clyde seemed to others to be acting out forbidden roles and to relish their roles. In contrast with secret criminals—the furtive embezzlers and other crooks who lead seemingly honest lives—the known outlaws capture the public imagination, because they take chances, and because, often, they enjoy dramatizing their lives."

She could tell from the vibe in the theater that "*Bonnie and Clyde* keeps the audience in a kind of eager, nervous imbalance—holds our attention by throwing our disbelief back in our faces. To be put on is to be put on the spot, made the stooge in a comedy act. People in the audience at *Bonnie and Clyde* are laughing, demonstrating that they're not stooges—that they appreciate the joke—when they catch the first bullet right in the face." In a sense *Bonnie and Clyde* played the audience in a way that wasn't unlike the way Hitchcock had been playing them for years. But it did so with a cleanness and open-heartedness that Hitchcock could never come near. Part of the genius of Penn's direction had such sleight of hand; he was driving the vehicle, but both hands weren't clenched fiercely on the steering wheel. "Audiences at *Bonnie and Clyde* are not given a simple, secure basis for identification," Pauline wrote; "they are made to feel but are not told *how* to feel."

One of the many ways that *Bonnie and Clyde* ushered in a new era in American moviemaking was with its stunningly direct portrayal of violence and its effect on our lives. Accusing the film of romanticizing crime and promoting violence was an easy, facile way of attacking it, and many critics and columnists had taken it. Arthur Penn objected to this in a *New York Times* interview that appeared a few weeks after the movie's release. "The trouble with the violence in most films," he said, "is that it is not violent enough. A war film that doesn't show the real horrors of war—bodies being torn apart and arms being shot off—really glorifies war." Pauline agreed, writing that "the whole point of *Bonnie and Clyde* is to rub our noses in it, to make us pay our dues for laughing. The dirty reality of death—not suggestions but blood and holes—is necessary. . . . *Bonnie and Clyde* needs violence; violence is its meaning." And she cautioned against people who saw "*Bonnie and Clyde* as a danger to public morality; they think an audience goes to a play or a movie and takes the actions in it as examples for imitation. They look at the world and blame the movies." *Bonnie and Clyde* had done contemporary audiences a favor, she felt, because "it has put the sting back into death." At last, it seemed that the American film might be on its way to growing up, as she had longed for it to do for decades. The ultimate cinematic seduction she had dreamed of for so long might now actually be on the verge of happening.

Pauline's review did not, as was often claimed, turn around *Bonnie and Clyde*'s fortunes single-handedly. The movie had been doing well in its single-theater bookings in a number of major U.S. cities, but Warner Bros. had never put much promotional muscle behind it, and by mid-October, it was being yanked from theaters to make way for the studio's new release, *Reflections in a Golden Eye*, starring Marlon Brando and Elizabeth Taylor.

But the fascination with *Bonnie and Clyde* continued, and in December *Time* ran a lengthy cover story about the movie's impact on the culture. Early in 1968 Warren Beatty strong-armed Warners into giving the picture a well-orchestrated rerelease, and this time, there were long lines at the box office everywhere. It was nominated for ten Academy Awards, including Best Picture, in competition with another of the year's trendsetting films, Mike Nichols's *The Graduate*. (Both lost to the much tamer *In the Heat of the Night*—but even that, via its exploration of racial tensions in a Mississippi murder case, was indicative of a changing Hollywood.)

The management of *The New York Times*, meanwhile, had taken note of the movie's resonance and decided that the time had come for their chief film critic to step down, and December of 1967 marked the end of Bosley Crowther's twenty-two-year reign. He continued on staff for a time as a special reporter, but he was devastated that the success of *Bonnie and Clyde* had unseated him from the powerful position he had held for so long.

In an act of counterpoint so perfect it might have come out of an old movie, Pauline's fortunes rose at the precise moment that those of her old nemesis collapsed. She had been out of work since *The New Yorker*'s piece on *Bonnie and Clyde* had run, and with the holidays approaching, she was in bed with the flu. Uncharacteristically for her, she had sunk into a state of dejection and self-pity. The irony of her situation seemed particularly nasty: Just as the movies were showing signs of having the dust blown out of them, she seemed further than ever from her dream of making a living as a film critic.

For weeks William Shawn had been pondering some of the points Pauline had raised in her essay on *Bonnie and Clyde*. *The New Yorker* had a long history of movie critics who traded in light, above-it-all dismissals of the pictures they reviewed, a school of criticism that owed much more to the brittle wit of a Dorothy Parker than to the searching curiosity of a James Agee; John McCarten, particularly, had represented this school of criticism, peering at the movies he covered as imperiously as Eustace Tilley, the magazine's icon, peered through his monocle. Shawn decided that a different approach was needed. He wanted someone in tune with the way movies were now, who could speak to the rabid movie-loving audience that had come along in the last decade. Pauline's piece on *Bonnie and Clyde* had been a test, and she had passed. Shawn phoned her and told her that he wanted her to succeed Brendan Gill as movie critic for six months a year, alternating with Penelope Gilliatt. She was to begin in January.

It is tempting—however wrongly—for those of us examining the lives of writers, actors, and other artists of the mid–twentieth century to see those lives unfold with the rhythm and pace of an old-fashioned three-act Broadway play. Act I entails the long, slow study and preparation for a brilliant career, Act II the vintage years of that career, Act III the inevitable decline to the end.

Pauline's Act I had lasted an unusually long time. At age forty-eight, her prolonged apprenticeship was finally completed. What she felt now was the opposite of stage fright: it was an inability to remain standing in the wings any longer, a driving urgency to make her entrance and get on with the best part of the play.

# CHAPTER TEN

By the mid-1960s *The New Yorker* had long since attained iconic status among its readers. The longtime subscribers who stacked copies of the magazine on their coffee tables felt that it brought something into their homes that no other magazine could come close to offering. In those days the magazine focused principally on cultural and literary matters; while it did frequently run profiles of political figures, it was not primarily concerned with up-to-the-minute journalism that probed troubling social issues and the machinations of contemporary politics. The image of New York that the magazine presented to its readers everywhere was that of a sophisticated, unconventional city where it was possible to seek out the very best in culture twenty-four hours a day, a place where the traditional values and habits of thought that might hamstring the rest of the country did not come into play. A reader in the Midwest or on the Pacific Coast might never come close to touching down at LaGuardia Airport—yet he could feel, through the pages of *The New Yorker*, that he possessed an intimate knowledge of the city and of the city's sensibility. In 1940 a piece of promotional literature outlined the magazine's ethic succinctly: "You cannot keep *The New Yorker* out of the hands of New York–minded people, wherever they are. For, unlike the myriad points in which New York–minded people live, New York is not a tack on a map, not a city, not an island nor an evening at '21.' *The New Yorker* is a mood, a point of view. It is found wherever people are electrically sensitive to new ideas, eager for new things to do, new things to buy, new urbanities for living."

Many longtime readers of the magazine, however, had begun to feel that the image of sophistication it peddled was as outmoded as the old black-and-white movies featuring chic café singers on nightclub sets the size of the roof of the Empire State Building. These critics believed that *The New Yorker* had fallen out of touch with the world to the point of ossification. And their target for blame was William Shawn.

*The New Yorker* was perhaps the supreme illustration of the principle that any good magazine is a reflection of its presiding editor's tastes and ideas. Shawn had started his career at the magazine as a reporter for the front-of-book section "Talk of the Town" in 1933. In only a few years he had become

managing editor for fact, and in 1952, he was promoted to the top job, succeeding the magazine's founding editor, Harold Ross. *The New Yorker* was
Shawn's passion; he devoted himself to it, with an attention to minutiae that
might have astounded even the most workaholic editors in chief of the day.
Shawn followed many of the precepts established by Ross: He did not believe
that a magazine succeeded by sending out reader surveys and frantically chas-
ing what it believed its readers' strongest interests to be. He believed that a
good editor compelled readers to become interested in what *he* was interested
in by presenting the material in the clearest, best balanced, and most lucid
way.

But as the 1960s became the most chaotic decade in American memory,
Shawn's chorus of critics grew steadily louder. They complained that the pulse
of modern life simply was not present in the magazine; they believed there
was a way for *The New Yorker* to retain its impeccable journalistic standards
and still come closer to depicting life as it was really being lived.

There was no real indication that Shawn was displeased with the job that
his writers had been doing with "The Current Cinema" over the years. "William Shawn respected, admired, and enjoyed the movie reviews of John
McCarten and Brendan Gill, both of whom he regarded as talented writers
who were funny, witty, sharp, and independent," observed Lillian Ross, a *New
Yorker* staff writer since the 1940s, and Shawn's longtime companion. "He
liked the way both writers took a light-hearted view of much Hollywood
product, while—never grim or cranky—they prized the movies of unique
artists like Bergman, Renoir, Kurosawa, Fellini, et cetera. Above all else,
Shawn loved writers' humor in their pieces."

Shawn brought a number of new critical voices to the magazine during
the mid-1960s. In 1966 he hired Michael Arlen to write "The Air," a regular
column on television. George Steiner began contributing his erudite, deeply
informed book reviews. Harold Rosenberg, the esteemed proponent of modern American art, joined the staff as art critic. Shawn was an avid moviegoer
who sensed that something new and exciting was happening in the world of
film and decided that Pauline would be an excellent choice to cover it. Brendan Gill, whom Pauline regarded as something of a dinosaur, had desired a
change of pace and was reassigned to review theater; it was decided that
Pauline would cover film reviewing for the months of September through
March. Penelope Gilliatt, a former critic for the London *Observer* who had
successfully completed a kind of test run at the magazine during the summer
of 1968, would take over from April to August.

In a business in which the relationship between writer and editor is often a prickly, contentious one, Shawn had the loyalty of the great majority of those who contributed to *The New Yorker*. It was unusual for any editor in chief to be as closely involved in line editing as Shawn was; every major article that appeared in the magazine bore his stamp. Shawn was, along with many of his subeditors, dedicated to the highly manicured style for which the magazine had long been famous. Those lapidary sentences and smoothly flowing paragraphs that appeared in the magazine each week had been worked over by many people before they made it into print, which led to criticism that there was a kind of sausage-grinder mentality at work in *The New Yorker*'s editorial process. Pauline, for one, thought that all the obsessively careful editing sometimes yielded a rather uniform, almost generic *New Yorker* tone.

There were certain oddities about the daily workings at *The New Yorker*. The magazine's fact-checking department was considered the finest in the industry. Accuracy had been a priority since 1927, when the magazine had published a profile of Edna St. Vincent Millay so filled with inaccuracies that a lawsuit had been threatened. Sometimes, however, the clinging to factual accuracy crossed over from obsessive to irrational. John Simon recalled that he once submitted a piece of light verse to *The New Yorker* called "A Short Social History of the Condor." "It was totally fictitious," he remembered, "a fantasy about the history of the condor through the ages, including Europe, where there never *was* any condor." He sent it in to the magazine and soon received an enthusiastic letter from Katharine White, the poetry editor, praising it and telling him how wonderful it was to discover a new light-verse writer, something the magazine had been searching for for some time. "The only thing she wanted me to do," remembered Simon, "was to give her the factual basis for the poem. I said, 'That's like asking the Brothers Grimm to give the factual basis for fairy tales.' I was told by one of the editors that there was a big editorial meeting at which they took up this matter. And the decision finally was that they couldn't do it."

As she began her first stint of movie reviewing for the magazine, Pauline was shocked when she saw what had been done to her copy. It seemed that there was scarcely a sentence that hadn't been rearranged and turned upside down, emerging with an entirely different accent and rhythm from what she had initially written. She had worked hard to develop a spontaneous, intimate, conversational tone in her writing, but after it had been through *The New Yorker*'s cleansing process, it didn't sound so very different from many other articles. "I think a certain Anglophilia crept into it very early on—when it was founded, really," Pauline once told an interviewer. "It started out with a sort of English tone and a kind of elite sophisticated Manhattan tone which was fake English." Each week, when the first galley proof arrived, she went through it and carefully restored her original meaning and rhythm, writing very precisely in the margins in order to minimize editorial confusion in the second stage of galleys. Then she went to Shawn's office to discuss the matter.

When she was hired, Shawn had given Pauline a handshake agreement that her copy would not be changed without her permission. As a courtesy to his writers, he made clear to them that if they felt that the magazine's editing had violated their intentions, they were free to withdraw their articles and still receive payment. Shawn didn't go back on his word with Pauline, but he didn't give up without a fight, either. While many of his writers gratefully accepted his editorial handiwork, Pauline's highly theatrical negotiating sessions with Shawn soon became the stuff of *New Yorker* legend. She often compared him with a pit bull, but she proved to be more than his equal in their arguments. She appreciated his urging her toward greater clarification of her thoughts on the page, but she reminded him over and over that she had to sound the way she sounded—otherwise there was no point.

Certainly, Pauline and Shawn were never likely to be truly compatible. He was an old-style gentleman through and through, who behaved with an imperturbable politeness. No matter how abusively someone might treat him, he seemed almost incapable of responding with anything but patient kindness. Jane Beirn, who served as his secretary for three years in the early 1970s, remembered, "Mr. Shawn was always polite and courteous to *everyone* he dealt with. Even if he wound up rejecting the work of people who came to see him, he would sit and talk with them, and they would walk out on air. I think he was so lovely and charming and complimentary that some of them may have gotten down to the lobby before they realized that the answer was 'no.'"

Pauline was amused by Shawn's courtly manners, but it appears that she never believed them to be entirely sincere, either; she felt his behavior had the ring of passive aggression. Nearly all staff writers referred to him as "Mr. Shawn"; Pauline made a point of calling him "Bill" early on in their working relationship and made no attempt to purge the "goddammit"s and "shit"s from her conversations with him.

Shawn's many quirks and phobias have been well documented by various chroniclers of the magazine's history. He detested the cold and dressed warmly almost year-round. Even on hot days at the office, when the air-conditioning might be on the blink, he would put on a blazer to receive visitors. At lunches with authors, at the Algonquin Hotel, just a block from the magazine's offices at 25 West Forty-third Street, Shawn's guests might gorge themselves on steak and martinis, while he ate a bowl of cereal or a slice of toasted pound cake. He prided himself on being the soul of propriety—yet he maintained his relationship with Ross throughout all the years of his marriage to his wife, Cecille. He abhorred the increasing violence and tension of daily life in New York—yet he had given Pauline the space for her lengthy essay on the shockingly violent *Bonnie and Clyde*.

A number of *New Yorker* staff members agreed with Ross's view that Pauline "seemed to seek combat" with Shawn. Pauline was wise enough to realize that at last she had an editor willing to give her the number of words she needed. Indeed, Shawn was famous for his generosity to writers and often hesitated to suggest a word length, preferring to think that the size and scope of the piece would be dictated by the subject matter. With Pauline, he insisted on one rule only: that her written attacks on other critics come to a halt. Such things, he told her, had no place in *The New Yorker*.

There was nothing remotely posh about *The New Yorker*'s working environment. The corridors were dingy and disorderly, and the walls seemed always to be in need of a fresh coat of paint. It was a far cry from the plush image of New York publishing promoted in movies like *The Best of Everything*. "*The New Yorker* has a long-standing tradition of squalor with which I am loath to interfere," Shawn once said. When she first joined the magazine staff, Pauline did most of her writing at home but was given a small, nondescript office that she generally used on the days when her pieces were going through various stages of proofs, to make long-distance telephone calls, and to answer mail—and also as a rest stop before and after her wrangles with Shawn.

What is most striking about her reviews in her first years at *The New Yorker* is their relative brevity; she would sometimes cover two or three films in a single column of "The Current Cinema," and if the movie didn't warrant extensive comment, she typically kept her review fairly succinct. She didn't belabor the plots of bad movies; she often used her reviews of them to make a particular point about a trend she saw in films in general, or about an actor she felt might be seriously going off the track. She often raised her continued concern about the corrupting influences of television. The fast-paced economics of television production had been turning up for years on the big screen. In early 1968 Pauline observed:

The emotional shorthand of television—climaxes with a minimum of preparation—has been developed so that the audience won't get away. Like the flip-page sex that authors of pulps now put in, so that the man in the drugstore can open the book anywhere and reach within a few pages a passage that makes him want to buy, the television director learns to keep socking the viewers so they won't get bored, so he won't lose them. They may have just tuned in, and he's got to hold them for the commercial. . . . The men who have learned these lessons graduate to movies, where they try to keep up the same mechanical pace irrespective of subject or meaning, and where, increasingly, they're working with the flip-page sex authors, who have mastered the knack of turning out a book in ten days and can produce a TV script or a movie script with the practiced indifference to quality of a short-order cook. And as this kind of material floods the market and gives audiences immediate sensations (audiences that may very possibly be interested only in excitation and be indifferent to theme anyway), the very notion of movie art, or even craftsmanship, begins to seem old-fashioned, "classical"—too slow in development perhaps, or too painstaking, or too "personal."

In Hollywood, the old studio heads such as Darryl F. Zanuck and Jack L. Warner—men who, whatever their shortcomings, had cared and known a great deal about the craft of moviemaking—were now retired, and they had been replaced by bright young business-school graduates with a lust for making money, some crude understanding of basic marketing techniques, and no real interest in film at all. At the same time, however, there were signs of progress in terms of taking on adult subject matter. Several films released in 1968 took on the still-controversial subject of homosexuality, but Pauline wasn't at all sure how much it mattered if the results were mostly negative; the films were a spotty bunch, ranging from the serious (*The Fox*) to the sensationalistic (*The Detective*). During her first year at *The New Yorker* Pauline reviewed several of them, and Rod Steiger starred in two. This was safety-net casting at its best: Few actors were less likely to be suspected of actually being gay than Steiger, particularly since his Academy Award–winning turn in 1967 as the bigoted small-town Mississippi sheriff in Norman Jewison's *In the Heat of the Night*. The first of his 1968 films, *No Way to Treat a Lady*, was released in March and directed by one of Pauline's least favorite directors, Jack Smight (who came from television). It was a black comedy, with Steiger as a cross-dressing, mother-dominated psychopath who spends his spare time strangling women. Pauline wrote that Steiger's "presence is so strong that he often seems to take over a picture even when he isn't the lead. This is true of George C. Scott, too, and actors this powerful just don't fit into ordinary roles. The answer, of course, is that they need extraordinary ones—great roles." But in Steiger's case, the best that Hollywood could come up with was "this fag phantom of the opera."

It was a line that would haunt her years later, when a faction of gay readers accused her of having used her pages in *The New Yorker* to indulge in bald-faced homophobia. Certainly her choice of the word "fag" was questionable, yet she was using it for a specific purpose—to convey the crude, low-grade quality of both Rod Steiger's role and the film's coarse, low-comedy attitude toward gay men. In this particular context, "homosexual" would have lacked the zing she was after.

A more complicated matter was *The Sergeant*, released, strangely enough, during the Christmas season of 1968. In it Steiger played a career military man who develops an obsessive passion for a young private in his outfit. The movie was clearly an attempt to make a serious statement about the damage wrought by repression, but it also showed that the price paid for throwing off repression was often tragic. (The sergeant finally kisses the private, then, out of disgust, kills himself.) The outcome was a dreary film that was really all about the "daring" casting of Steiger, an excuse to let him exercise his acting skills; the audience could practically feel the actor asking for their approval, but Pauline wasn't sure that he'd gotten it. "Does playing a homosexual paralyze him as an actor?" she wondered. "He gives such a tense, constricted performance it's almost as if he didn't want to convince anybody." But the nerviest part of her review, again, would come back to plague her years later:

> There is something ludicrous and at the same time poignant about many stories involving homosexuals. Inside the leather trappings and chains and emblems and Fascist insignia of homosexual "toughs" there is so often hidden our old acquaintance the high-school sissy, searching the streets for the man he doesn't believe he is. The incessant, compulsive cruising is the true, mad romantic's endless quest for love. Crazier than Don Juan, homosexuals pursue an ideal man, but once they have made a sexual conquest the partner is a homosexual like them, and they go on their self-defeating way, endlessly walking and looking, dreaming the impossible dream.

Since her writing about the films of Jean-Luc Godard had propelled William Shawn's interest in having her at *The New Yorker*, it seemed fitting that two Godard pictures opened during her first year on the magazine's staff. There were few major directors of the time with whom Pauline felt more inwardly connected; Godard's jangly, modern tempo was *her* tempo. She had not liked *Vivre sa vie*, his 1962 drama with Anna Karina, because she suspected there was nothing much happening behind the heroine's opaque presence. But his more recent efforts, including *Band of Outsiders* and *Masculin féminin*, had pleased her; she considered them "a volatile mixture of fictional narrative, reporting, essay, and absurdist interludes" whose frenzied, pop-art spirit was an ideal reflection of the chaotic times.

The first of his 1968 films, released in March, was *La Chinoise*, a biting satire of a bunch of young revolutionaries who attempt to use terrorist techniques to pull off a Maoist takeover. *La Chinoise* was aptly described by the Godard scholar Richard Brody as "less a document of Maoist thought, action, or organization than a collage of Maoist graffiti and paraphernalia." The movie had been loosely organized, to say the least; Godard admitted to his close associates that he had given little thought to a cohesive story line, instead peppering the film with fast and furious references to figures such as Sartre and Malraux and Rosa Luxemburg, which vexed many members of the art-house audience. But Pauline respected Godard for not making the effort to explain the allusions that flew by so quickly:

> We all know that an artist can't discover anything for himself—can't function as an *artist*—if he must make everything explicit in terms accessible to the widest possible audience. This is one of the big hurdles that defeat artists in Hollywood; they aren't allowed to assume that anybody knows anything, and they become discouraged and corrupt when they discover that studio thinking is not necessarily wrong in its estimate of the mass audience. Godard, like many American novelists, works in terms of an audience that is assumed to have the same background he has.

Unlike so many American filmmakers, who repackaged old genres to make them palatable for a late-'60s audience, Godard was a fresh, original thinker; Pauline found his films "funny, and they're funny in a new way."

But it was Godard's *Weekend*, released in October, that excited her more than any European film had in years. Pauline believed that by this time, Godard's craft was so brilliantly confident that he had become the equal of James Joyce among filmmakers. She predicted that Godard would "probably never have a popular, international success; he packs film-festival halls, but there is hardly enough audience left over to fill small theaters for a few weeks."

*Weekend* is a study of a greedy, bourgeois French couple (Jean Yanne and Mireille Darc) who leave on a trip to make sure the wife's dying mother has provided for them in her will. Along the way they are plunged into a nightmarish traffic jam that leads to complete chaos—including the rape of the wife, portrayed in a disturbing, seriocomic tone. Pauline considered the director's vision of the true hell of the modern materialistic world to be "a great original work." There were sequences that excited her so much she could hardly wait to get her reactions down on the page—particularly the wife's confession to her husband of a heated erotic episode with her lover, and the virtuoso filming of the traffic jam, in which the camera tracks its way through the cars that have come to a standstill, until it comes to the reason for the delay: a horrific, bloody accident that has attracted a crowd of gawkers. The movie's ending stunned audiences: The couple become prey to a gang of cannibalistic hippies who slaughter and cook the husband; the wife winds up feasting on his flesh.

It was the most potent comment on the decay of modern French society that any filmmaker had dared to make, and Godard's touch throughout was sure, brazen, and perpetually unexpected. Pauline felt that he had become one of the few directors who had really done what a great artist was supposed to do: He had enlarged the way in which his public saw the world around it.

In the spring of 1968 Penelope Gilliatt took over for Pauline, as planned. Pauline took advantage of her first layoff to get ready for the big event of the year—the publication of her second book by the Atlantic Monthly Press. Its working title had initially been *Movie Watching*, then *All About Movies*, both of which Pauline had rejected as being too tame. She finally settled on *Kiss Kiss Bang Bang*, words she had once seen on an Italian movie poster. She considered the phrase "perhaps the briefest statement imaginable of the basic appeal of the movies. This appeal is what attracts us, and ultimately what makes us despair when we begin to understand how seldom movies are more than this."

Robert Mills had sold *Kiss Kiss Bang Bang* to the Atlantic Monthly Press for an advance against royalties of $8,500. In the end it included reviews from *The New Republic* and *McCall's*, as well as "The Making of *The Group*," which at last would appear in its entirety. The most attention-getting feature of the book was "Notes on 280 Movies: From *Adam's Rib* to *Zazie*." Taking up the book's final 143 pages, "Notes" was quite a surprising feature in those days before such general movie guides as *Leonard Maltin's TV Movies* and *Video Hound*; several of the pieces were slightly reworked versions of the notes she had written for the Berkeley Cinema Guild. Despite the occasional peculiar observation ("Katharine Hepburn is probably the greatest actress of the sound era"), the "Notes" were pithy and highly original. There was also a last-minute inclusion, Pauline's *New Yorker* essay on *Bonnie and Clyde*, and because the book was already in page proofs, she was charged $306 for inserting the piece in the late stage of production. Pauline also did her own index, compiling some two thousand index cards.

The Atlantic Monthly Press brought out *Kiss Kiss Bang Bang* as one of its big releases in the spring of 1968, and again the reviews were excellent. In *Newsweek* her friend Joseph Morgenstern proclaimed her a "she-Shaw of the movies" and pronounced *Kiss Kiss Bang Bang* "blessedly brilliant." Walter Kerr, the esteemed drama critic of *The New York Times*, reviewed the book for his newspaper's Sunday *Book Review*:

> If Miss Kael has a particular bent as a film critic, it is in the direction of social psychology. Almost always she wants to know what a film *means* to the people who make and see it, how it squares with—or falsifies—their lives, how it functions as truth or untruth in the immediate environment. . . .
>
> When you disagree with Miss Kael, you do not become irritable or want to tell her to shut up. You see—in the candor with which she records her own case history, in the intense curiosity she brings to the implications of what she is seeing and responding to—that she has earned her right to her hardheadedness, her decisiveness. She went to the movie with us, and as we walk home gesticulating, she can say anything she pleases. That's why we're walking home—to discuss the damn thing.

In June, William Abrahams wrote to Robert Mills that *Kiss Kiss Bang Bang* was "going great guns at the moment," and that Atlantic was so encouraged that it was expanding the book's advertising campaign. By late August it had earned back its advance, and Pauline was collecting royalties. Peter Davison was pleased to be able to send Robert Mills a check for $2,684.90 for royalties on both of Pauline's books. And a substantial paperback sale had been made to Bantam Books, with a release set for the spring of 1969.

One of the book's most ardent admirers was Louise Brooks, the silent-era actress who had established new levels of sexual candor with her revealing performances in G. W. Pabst's *Pandora's Box* and *Diary of a Lost Girl* and had in recent years turned out a number of startlingly perceptive articles on film. She had corresponded with Pauline for a number of years, ever since Pauline had tried to get Brooks to fly from her home in Rochester, New York, to speak before a showing of *Pandora's Box* at the Berkeley Cinema Guild. Brooks thought her "the best film critic since Agee." Pauline had sent her a copy of *Kiss Kiss Bang Bang*, to which Brooks responded, "You could have knocked me over with Audrey Hepburn." She mentioned several parts of the book that she had pored over with fascination: "Going through the index I have sampled some of your views on my loves and hates. And I don't care what you write about anyone as long as I have found you love Garbo." She closed with the kind of shrewd observation she was known for: "Your picture on the dust cover made me think of Dorothy Parker when she was young in a moment of happiness."

One thing that Pauline most lamented about the movies of the 1960s was the absence of genuine stars. For her this had always been one of the elemental pleasures of going to the movies: being bowled over by an astonishing talent who genuinely belonged on the screen. Realism was always welcome, but Pauline craved the charge of something more. "In life," she wrote, "fantastically gifted people, people who are driven, can be too much to handle; they can be a pain. In plays, in opera, they're divine, and on the screen, where they can be seen in their perfection, and where we're even safer from them, they're *more* divine."

In the fall of 1968 she found the star she'd been waiting for in Barbra Streisand. When Pauline resumed her duties at *The New Yorker* that September, her first review was of Streisand's debut film, *Funny Girl*. It was titled simply, "Bravo!" and the word was aimed at Streisand alone—certainly not at her costar, the almost preternaturally passive Omar Sharif, and not at the director, William Wyler. Pauline's review nearly vibrated with the thrill of discovery.

"It has been commonly said," Pauline wrote, "that the musical *Funny Girl* was a comfort to people because it carried the message that you do not need to be pretty to succeed. That is nonsense; the 'message' of Barbra Streisand in *Funny Girl* is that talent is beauty." She went on:

Most Broadway musicals are dead before they reach the movies—the routines are so worked out they're stiff, and the jokes are embalmed in old applause. But Streisand has the gift of making old written dialogue sound like inspired improvisation; almost every line she says seems to have just sprung to mind and out. Her inflections are witty and surprising, and more surprisingly, delicate; she can probably do more for a line than any screen comedienne since Jean Arthur, in the thirties.

Streisand posed a formidable challenge to audiences, even those who had rushed out to buy her records but weren't yet at ease with her as a screen presence. She conveyed the idea that she was exactly what she appeared to be—a kooky, unvarnished, undiluted Jewish girl from Brooklyn. Her looks were perhaps more charismatically mercurial than those of any movie actress since Bette Davis: She could be crude and horsey-looking one minute, ravishingly beautiful and glowingly expressive the next—just as her singing voice could go from powerful to exquisitely tender and vulnerable in a split second. Many of the men in the audience didn't know quite what to make of her, and neither did some of the male critics. In a stunningly misguided review in *The New York Morning Telegraph*, Leo Mishkin wrote of Streisand's spectacular star turn, "She is not quite up to the task as yet of carrying a whole motion picture by herself," adding, "The one thing you cannot fault her with is that she is unique. But it takes time to get used to her."

Pauline found that Streisand was more than just a naturally adept funny girl—she was a beguiling actress as well. In the picture's second half, when Fanny Brice's story got bogged down in heartbreak, Streisand showed her deep well of self-respect as an actress: "She simply drips as unself-consciously and impersonally as a true tragic muse. . . . She doesn't 'touch' us for sympathy in the Chaplinesque way by trying to conceal her hurt. She conceals nothing; she's fiercely, almost frighteningly direct."

Pauline did not yet know Streisand personally, but she must have seen in Streisand a great deal of herself. Like Streisand, Pauline was a smart Jewish girl who had refused to alter, even modify her singular talent and her independent approach to life. Each was uncompromising about how she wanted her talent to be presented to the public, and in the years ahead, Pauline would follow Streisand's career with a close fascination she reserved for very few actors.

It was when writing about performers that Pauline's gift for imaginative analysis was expressed at its finest. She could not only give an acute assessment of a performance but could offer fascinating insights about what it revealed about the actor's relationship with his public, or why a particular piece of casting had turned out to be wrongheaded, and even damaging to a career. Shortly after *Funny Girl* opened, Julie Andrews's latest vehicle, *Star!*, a biography of the stage actress Gertrude Lawrence, was released by Twentieth Century–Fox. A musical about Gertrude Lawrence, an actress whose fame was by that time quite remote, was an odd, risky choice for a big-budget film, but it had its intriguing side: The director, Robert Wise, and the screenwriter, William Fairchild, didn't want to do a standard rags-to-riches show-business biopic; instead they wanted to explore Lawrence's selfish, manipulative side, and in the process, reveal an untapped side of Andrews's talents.

Pauline, however, found the results misguided: "Glamour is what Julie Andrews doesn't have," she wrote. "She does her duties efficiently but mechanically, like an airline stewardess; she's pert and cheerful in some professional way that is finally cheerless." There was a certain tough determination underneath Andrews's dependable smile that Pauline found the most interesting thing about her, but in the end the actress "merely coarsen[ed] her shining nice-girl image, becoming a nasty Girl Guide." *Star!* opened in classy road-show engagements, but it was pulled from circulation by July 1969, and reedited and rereleased a few months later as *Those Were the Happy Times*. It flopped all over again, and Pauline was delighted when Streisand unseated Andrews as the movies' number-one female musical star.

October 1968 also saw the release of James Goldman's *The Lion in Winter*, an uneasy blend of bitchy high comedy and historical drama, starring Peter O'Toole as Henry II and Katharine Hepburn as Eleanor of Aquitaine. Hepburn had recently moved to the front of the herd of the movie industry's sacred cows: Her longtime companion Spencer Tracy had died the year before, and she subsequently won the Academy Award for their last film together, *Guess Who's Coming to Dinner?* It was considered a form of cinematic sacrilege not to respond to her gracefully aging beauty and no-nonsense Yankee spirit. If Streisand had become Pauline's new movie love, Hepburn plummeted from her pantheon at almost precisely the same moment. Hepburn had always struck Pauline as the toughest and least maudlin of golden-age movie stars—even Bette Davis had done her share of lugubrious soapers, but Hepburn had, for the most part, retained a crisp dignity in the roles she played. But now, Pauline complained, her idol had let her down by succumbing to the public's affection for her, and by playing up to them and begging them for that affection:

> When an actress has been a star for a long time, we know too much about her; for years we have been hearing about her romances or heartbreaks, or whatever the case may be, and all this carries over into her presence on the screen. And if she *uses* this in a role, she's sunk. When actresses begin to use our knowledge about them and of how young and beautiful they used to be—when they offer themselves up as ruins of their former selves—they may get praise and awards (and they generally do), but it's not really for their acting, it's for capitulating, and giving the public what it wants: a chance to see how the mighty have fallen. . . . When Hepburn, the most regal of them all, contemplates her blotches

and wrinkles with tears in her anxious eyes, it's self-exploitation, and it's horrible.

Pauline was all too accurate about the rewards for this kind of performance: The following year, Hepburn won her third Oscar and, for the first time in her career, found herself on an exhibitors' list of the top ten box-office stars.

By the late summer of 1968, Pauline had decided to give up the flat at 670 West End Avenue. She and Gina found a large, high-ceilinged apartment at the Turin, at 333 Central Park West. The apartment was on the twelfth floor, and it had a spacious living room with a commanding view of Central Park. The Turin, which had been completed in 1910, was designed by Albert Joseph Bodker in the New Renaissance style. It was a famous building on the West Side because of the intensity of its social life, and many leftist writers and academic types lived there. The doyenne of the building's left-leaning thinkers was a West Side socialite named Roz Roose, who threw regular parties and weekend brunches that became famous gatherings. Roose worked assiduously in trying to get Pauline to attend, but she succeeded only once, and then Pauline remained for only a few minutes, as she was bored by the other guests. "She hated that kind of thing," said Jane Kramer, the distinguished writer who penned many of *The New Yorker*'s "Letter from Europe" columns. "Pauline was the least pretentious person."

As she always had, Pauline turned the living room into the place where she wrote. She still worked at the drafting table she had brought with her from California. On the table was an inkstand filled with paper clips, a jar of pencils, an electric pencil sharpener, and, inevitably, the many little scraps of memo pads on which she took notes during movie screenings. She sat in a straight-backed chair with a pillow folded over on the seat. During her six months at *The New Yorker*, it was from this spot that she maintained a fiercely demanding schedule. Her rough copy was due each week on Tuesday, but she saw several films for each one she wrote about, and she might not see until Monday night the main movie she would choose to cover. Often she would hand-write several drafts, and that meant staying up all night on Monday, fortified with bourbon and cigarettes, to get her copy to *The New Yorker* on time. Jane Beirn recalled that "there was always a fair amount of drama in getting the copy out of Penelope Gilliatt," but that Pauline was extremely strict and disciplined about observing her deadlines. One of the advantages to working all night, she said, was that she got to see some spectacular Tuesday morning sunrises over Central Park.

But Pauline's routine was also punishing for Gina, whose job was to type her mother's drafts before they were submitted to *The New Yorker*. As she went to bed, Pauline would leave her final handwritten copy in the living room, and by the time she arose, Gina would have neatly typed it. Sometimes Gina had to type more than one version and have it ready, usually with Pauline's penciled-in last-minute emendations, by the time *The New Yorker*'s messenger arrived to pick it up. Gina turned twenty in 1968 and was still very much functioning as her mother's right hand. Gina complained about her situation to a number of people, but she usually did it in a quasi-humorous way, so it was easy enough to dismiss. "Gina was a lovely girl," remembered Tresa Hughes. "I always felt she was a slave—or rather, on a leash."

Certainly those close to the family felt that Pauline made little attempt to encourage Gina to widen her horizons. It was obvious to everyone that Pauline loved her, but she had also grown accustomed to the steady, dependable role that Gina played—as secretary, driver, reader, sounding board—and she was loath to give her up. Gina was a constant in her life, and now that Pauline lived in New York, where she was not nearly as much at ease as she had been in Berkeley, having her daughter close by was more important than ever. "I think she had more of a sense of fellowship and community on the West Coast," observed Hughes. "Here, it was sort of dispersed. She didn't really have her coterie."

Although Pauline definitely had her favorites among directors, her *New Yorker* reviews were, from the beginning, full of surprising reactions. She went out of her way to praise a movie that few saw, *Greetings*, directed by a twenty-eight-year-old filmmaker named Brian De Palma. *Greetings* wasn't in the macabre vein of the later films that made De Palma famous but was an off-kilter comedy about three young New Yorkers trying to keep from being drafted, and it had been shot in two weeks for very little money. Rutanya Alda, who played a supporting role in the film, recalled how the tiny budget made it essential to work fast and accurately: "Brian would say, 'I've got only three minutes of film—we've got to get the scene in three minutes.'" Locations were snapped up wherever they could arrange them cheaply: one sequence in a bookstore was shot at three in the morning without the owner knowing about it. Pauline acknowledged that some of *Greetings* was a mess, but she also recognized a vibrant, original talent; *Greetings* went on to win the Silver Bear Award at the Berlin International Film Festival, and Pauline noted De Palma as a talent to watch.

During her first year at *The New Yorker* she also experienced some unexpected reversals of opinion. Her longtime readers were particularly caught off guard by her review of Ingmar Bergman's *Shame*. For years she had struggled with Bergman's body of work and had come to the conclusion that she had no temperamental affinity for much of it. She loved the humanity the director showed toward the foolish lovers of *Smiles of a Summer Night*, and the contemporary wit and sensibility he brought to his medieval allegory *The Seventh Seal*. But *Wild Strawberries*, a major breakthrough for Bergman on the international art-house circuit, had left her both dissatisfied and unconvinced, and once he had gone into his long series of films that probed man's attempt to unravel the mystery of God's silence, Pauline had gradually lost interest. It was not simply, as some have suggested, that Bergman's tempo was too slow for her, or that she disliked contemplative films; it was that she questioned the profundity of the dilemmas he was setting forth on the screen. She was deeply suspicious of the way Bergman had been turned into a cultural hero by college students who, she felt, didn't grasp how simpleminded many of his ideas were. ("I did my own share of soul-wrestling," she once said, referring to her youth, "and it's not too tough to do.") She was uncomfortable with the sort of unwritten contract Bergman had with his audience, in effect asking to take them by the hand and explore the spiritual crises that were plaguing his own life, over and over, in film after film.

Pauline believed *Shame*, however—a study of the ravaging effects of war on a married couple (Max von Sydow and Liv Ullmann) living on an island—to be a significant artistic step forward for Bergman. *Shame* succeeded, in her view, because he had reversed direction and made "a direct and lucid movie . . . Bergman has pulled himself together and objectified his material. There are no demons, no delusions. Everybody is exactly who he appears to be, so we can observe the depth and complexity of what he is. There is no character who may or may not represent Bergman; he is not lost in the work but is in control of it, and is thus more fully present than before." She thought that *Shame* had an "almost magical lack of surprise; it has the inevitability of a common dream." There is a strong indication that she was comparing Bergman with Godard when she offered this observation:

> In film, concentrating on a few elements gives those elements such importance that the material can easily become inflated, and the method is generally attempted by people who overvalue their few ideas and have little sense of the abundance of ideas that must go into a good movie. Bergman was not in such straitened intellectual circumstances, but he

was given to inflation of "dark" and messy ideas. The order he imposed
on his chamber dramas was a false order. The films looked formal and
disciplined, but (as often happens in movies) that "abstract" look con-
cealed conceptual chaos. If a movie director cannot control both his
thematic material and the flux of visual material, it is far better to have
inner order and outer chaos, because then there is at least a lot to look
at—different people and things and places to distract one—even if it is
disorganized, while if the movie looks formally strict but the ideas and
emotions are disturbed, the viewer may feel that the fault is in himself
for not understanding the work, or, worse, feel that this kind of artistic-
looking, disturbing ambiguity is what art *is*.

Inner order and outer chaos: it was a theme she would return to again and
again in future reviews, and one that her critics, many of them guilty of mis-
reading her, would take up as ammunition against her.

At *The New Yorker*, Pauline had many of the luxuries that most writers can
only dream of—a generous-minded editor who, despite his attempts at interference, permitted her to write in her own true voice; no crippling space
restrictions; an enthusiastic and informed readership.

Her main problem was money. Initially the magazine paid her $600 per
column. Over a six-month period that meant an annual income in the neighborhood of $14,000—which, after taxes and set off against New York's high
cost of living, she found very difficult to live on. She told friends that she
wanted Shawn to fire Penelope Gilliatt and give her the reviewing job year-
round, so at least she could make a more respectable living. "She was sore
because she was only paid half a salary, and salaries in those days were so
awful," recalled Jane Kramer. "But it was a very benevolent place, on the other
hand. A paternalistic benevolence." Pauline had a limited appetite for pater-
nalism: It galled her that she was rushing to meet weekly deadlines when
many of the magazine's old-guard writers, cronies of Shawn's from the war
years and after, were getting money on their monthly "drawing accounts"
when they hadn't turned in a word of copy for years.

Her limited income made it all the more crucial for her to book as many
speaking engagements as she could during her six months off from the magazine. (Since the success of her two books, Robert Mills's office was flooded
with offers.) She also had an arrangement with *The New Yorker* to take on
outside writing assignments during her time off. In mid-1968 she accepted a

major assignment from Willie Morris, the enterprising young editor of *Harper's*, who had successfully lured an impressive array of new writers to his magazine, and the long essay she published in the magazine's February 1969 issue, "Trash, Art and the Movies," was perhaps her boldest statement yet of her own moviegoing personality.

"There is so much talk now about the art of the film," Pauline wrote, "that we may be in danger of forgetting that most of the movies we enjoy are not works of art." Again, she encouraged audiences to respond to what they genuinely enjoyed—not to second-guess themselves as they might have been taught to do in school. And if what they enjoyed was a cheap youth exploitation picture like *Wild in the Streets*, that was fine, "because it's smart in a lot of ways that better-made pictures aren't." Movies like *Planet of the Apes* and *The Thomas Crown Affair* couldn't possibly be defended as works of art, she wrote.

> But they are almost the maximum of what we're now getting from American movies, and not only these but much worse movies are talked about as "art"—and are beginning to be taken seriously in our schools.
>
> It's preposterously egocentric to call anything we enjoy art—as if we could not be entertained by it if it were not; it's just as preposterous to let prestigious, expensive advertising snow us into thinking we're getting art for our money when we haven't even had a good time.

The genuine movie-lover knew in his gut that what movies had to offer was not an academic study in perfect artistic unity. "At the movies we want a different kind of truth," Pauline wrote, "something that surprises us and registers with us as funny or accurate or maybe amazing, maybe even amazingly beautiful," whether that was a line, a scene, a performance that somehow had resonance. Audiences needed to understand that a low-grade picture like *Wild in the Streets* "connects with their lives in an immediate, even if a grossly frivolous way, and if we don't go to movies for excitement, if, even as children, we accept the cultural standards of refined adults, if we have so little drive that we accept 'good taste,' then we will probably never really begin to care about movies at all."

Pauline's championing of the lowbrow—the good, vital lowbrow—was really a plea for some degree of emotional honesty on the part of the audience.

"I don't trust anyone who doesn't admit having at some time in his life enjoyed trashy American movies," she confessed. "I don't trust *any* of the tastes of people who were born with such good taste that they didn't need to find their way through trash."

This was not a unique point of view among movie critics. Joseph Morgenstern shared it, as did Judith Crist, who often used the phrase "trash—but delicious," to get through to her students at Columbia University. But Pauline took it in a new direction by pointing to the folly of the reverse perspective: the attempt to identify "art" in movies that were merely a smokescreen of directorial manipulation. She focused on some notable recent examples: *Petulia*, *The Graduate*, and *2001: A Space Odyssey*—all critically acclaimed box-office hits. She regarded *Petulia* as a pitiful attempt to take advantage of the pessimism and alienation that Americans had come to feel in the turmoil of the 1960s, and dismissed it as "obscenely self-important." Kubrick's *2001*, with its view of the blissful potential of space, where anything was possible, rendering the petty existence of life on Earth irrelevant, was "a celebration of cop-out" and fundamentally an expression of the oversize ego of its creator. She felt that, like many directors, Kubrick had fallen into the trap of the Big Idea, and along the way, he had abandoned his early promise (*The Killing*, *Paths of Glory*) and had come "to think of himself as a myth-maker." The ultimate, redeeming value of trash, she argued in her summing up, was that it leaves us wanting, hoping for more—"Trash has given us an appetite for art."

In October 1968 she had had an opportunity to test these theories when Twentieth Century–Fox sneaked into release a little movie called *Pretty Poison*, a psychological thriller about a bizarre loner (Anthony Perkins) who impresses a young girl (Tuesday Weld) by telling her that he's a CIA agent; the twist is that the girl is much more disturbed than he is. *Pretty Poison* showed some of the influence of *Bonnie and Clyde*. (The tag line for the movie was "She's such a sweet girl. He's such a nice boy. They'll scare the hell out of you.") Fox hated the film and wanted to cut it drastically. But Richard Zanuck, who had taken over from his father as head of the studio, pointed out that if *Pretty Poison* was cut much further, it wouldn't be possible to sell it to television, because it wouldn't fit a standard time slot. So Fox opened it in New York at the out-of-the-way Riverside Theatre at Ninety-sixth Street and Broadway.

On a gray, chilly day, Pauline telephoned Joseph Morgenstern at *Newsweek* and asked if he had heard anything about the film. Morgenstern hadn't, so the two of them headed for the Riverside, where there were only three other people in the audience. They both loved the movie and rushed back to their respective desks to write about it. In particular, it gave Pauline an opportunity to indulge in one of her favorite pastimes—bashing the studios:

> When I discovered that *Pretty Poison* had opened without advance publicity or screenings, I rushed to see it, because a movie that makes the movie companies so nervous they're afraid to show it to the critics stands an awfully good chance of being an interesting movie. Mediocrity and stupidity certainly don't scare them; talent does. This is a remarkable first feature film by a gifted young American, Noel Black—a movie that should have opened in an art house—and it was playing in a vast and empty theatre, from which, no doubt, it will depart upon the week. And the losses will be so heavy that the movie companies will use this picture as another argument against backing young American directors.

*Pretty Poison* was Pauline's kind of movie—a story of mayhem told with an appealingly subversive point of view and unexpected twists and turns—but it had the chintzy look of a cheap TV show and a tinny TV-style musical score by Johnny Mandel. Even the film's screenwriter, Lorenzo Semple, Jr., felt that she had overpraised it. "When she was on somebody's side, they could do no wrong for a while, which actually clouded her critical judgment, in my opinion," Semple said. "Loyalty is nice, but in many ways she was better as a cultural critic than a movie critic. Her weakness was her extreme, idiosyncratic views, sui generis, of things. I generally agreed with her, and she liked good movies rather than bad movies. But I do think she often made up her mind whether she liked the movie and *looked* for reasons *why* she liked it."

When the New York Film Critics Circle met to vote on its awards for 1968, a deadlock occurred between two movies in the Best Screenplay category. Pauline insisted on a compromise choice for *Pretty Poison*, and managed to win the majority of voters over to her side.

After the awards ceremony, she had dinner with Semple. "I'm going to bring a friend along," she told him, and showed up with six people. Semple recalled it a "a habit of hers when she went out to dinner. You'd get stuck with a very substantial check. I always considered it sort of amusing, but I know a couple of people who gritted their teeth—'Don't ask Pauline to go out to dinner with you. You'll pay for it.'"

In the summer of 1969 Pauline made another trip to Europe—this time as part of a honeymoon party. She had become good friends with the young writer Gary Carey, who edited a magazine called *The Seventh Art*. Carey had planned to go to France with Pauline and Gina, when he decided to get married. Pauline liked his intended, Carol Koshinskie, and no one saw any reason to make a change in plans. Gary and Carol were married on July 5, 1969, and a little more than a week later joined Pauline, Gina, and another friend, the pianist Marvin Tartack, in the south of France. For three weeks they all traveled together, jammed into a tiny Volkswagen, eating at one three-star restaurant after another in Toulouse, Marseilles, and other towns.

The success of *Bonnie and Clyde* had signaled a hunger for something new in film, but the process of reshaping the audience was a chaotic one: The two years following *Bonnie and Clyde* witnessed an industry flailing about, not really sure of what moviegoers wanted or exactly how they were going to give it to them.

This was the theme Pauline took up when she returned to *The New Yorker* in September. Her first column marked the beginning of what would become a tradition: her revisiting of several of the movies that had opened during her six-month layoff, movies that she thought had been misinterpreted by Penelope Gilliatt or that she simply felt compelled to weigh in on herself. In 1969 she was most interested in commenting on the pictures that had become big box-office hits over the summer: *Midnight Cowboy* and *Easy Rider*. *Midnight Cowboy* was the story of Joe Buck (Jon Voight), an aspiring stud from Texas who moves to New York City to strike it rich as a gigolo, only to wind up hustling closeted gay men in hotel rooms and public restrooms. Pauline thought that John Schlesinger's attempt to portray the soulless squalor of modern urban life had a pessimistic tone that was like "the spray of venom," and that what audiences really responded to was not the picture's "grotesque shock effects and the brutality of the hysterical, superficial satire of America" but "the simple, *Of Mice and Men* kind of relationship at the heart of it"—Joe Buck's alliance with the grimy, tubercular con man Ratso Rizzo (Dustin Hoffman).

*Easy Rider*, released in July, had made history by becoming the first movie made by and for the counterculture to become a massive commercial hit. Wrapped for somewhere around $500,000, it was reported to have made its entire cost back in one week of release; it went on to gross more than $19 million. This study of two druggie bikers (Peter Fonda and Dennis Hopper) drifting around the country barely had any plot at all, but it was a raw expression of youthful paranoia about the dangers represented by Middle America. While Pauline knew that it wasn't particularly a good movie in any artistic sense, she was fascinated by what it offered its public. "What is new about *Easy Rider*," she wrote, "is not necessarily that one finds its attitudes appealing but that the movie conveys the mood of the drug culture with such skill and in such full belief that these simplicities are the truth that one can understand why these attitudes are appealing to others. *Easy Rider* is an expression and a confirmation of how this audience feels; the movie attracts a new kind of 'inside' audience, whose members enjoy tuning in together to a whole complex of shared signals and attitudes." The significance of both films was that they continued the dialogue with the audience that had been established in *Bonnie and Clyde*— a dialogue that Pauline had hoped to see continue for years.

If it was individual artists such as Dennis Hopper who were going to enrich that dialogue, it was the studios, Pauline feared, who might well succeed in silencing it altogether. Too much was at stake now; it was more important than ever for her to exhort her readers to support the true artists, the good films that enlarged the moviegoing experience, and cut down the tired, the dead, the formulaic, the meretricious. From this point on, she would dig even deeper in her writing than she had before, pointing out the connections between the movies and the times from which they sprang. In the years to come her reviews took on even greater immediacy, her own excitement over what she'd just experienced in the screening room practically exploding on the page. She began to write as if her own moviegoing life depended on it— and to her, it did.

Given her sense of what she believed was about to burst through in the movies, it was axiomatic that she would reserve her fiercest attacks for the filmmakers she considered the ones who best knew how to play the studio's political games and milk the audience. Since they were, in her view, standing in the way of the genuine artists, she began to pounce on them with a reformer's zeal. When she returned to *The New Yorker* in the fall of 1969, she took aim at the director George Roy Hill, whose Western *Butch Cassidy and the Sundance Kid* had just opened.

*Butch Cassidy* took some of the thematic material of Sam Peckinpah's *The Wild Bunch*—the dying frontier at the fadeout of the nineteenth century—and plastered a free-spirited, youth-movement sensibility on it. It was this low cunning that bothered Pauline most. Hill came from television, and although she thought there was "a basic decency and intelligence in his work," she felt he didn't "really seem to have the style for anything," certainly not for this "facetious Western," with its relentlessly jokey, chummy tone.

*Butch Cassidy* was, as Pauline predicted, a huge hit, but it drew mixed reviews. In *Life*, Richard Schickel wrote that while he enjoyed the picture, its anachronistic, late-'60s dialogue consistently "destroys one's sense of mood and time and place." Pauline agreed. "The dialogue is all banter, all throwaways, and that's how it's delivered; each line comes out of nowhere, coyly, in a murmur, in the dead sound of the studio. (There is scarcely even an effort to supply plausible outdoor resonances or to use sound to evoke a sense of place.)"

This observation triggered a response from Hill, one that made Pauline cackle with glee when she read it to her friends:

> Listen, you miserable bitch, you've got every right in the world to air your likes and dislikes, but you got no goddam right at all to fake, at my expense, a phony technical knowledge you simply don't have.
>
> I fought the studio to the bloody mat in order to get authentic sound. . . . The picture was shot 90% on location and when it was over and I didn't have all the sound I wanted I took some horses and a couple of guys and on my own expense went out into the hills for two days and recorded the kind of sound I wanted myself. And I resent the hell out of a smart ass critic trying to show off their technical acumen and building up their image for their readers by pretending they can tell the "dead sound of a studio," and that their ear is so marvelously acute that they know that "scarcely any attempt was made to supply outdoor resonances." . . . You didn't like the sound, say so, but cut out that bullshit about how you know where it was done and made.

If Pauline considered George Roy Hill a prime example of the kind of middling talent that could flourish in Hollywood, she found Paul Mazursky the kind of original artist she believed the industry should be nurturing.

A former actor who had performed with the West Coast edition of the Second City comedy troupe, Mazursky directed his first picture, *Bob & Carol & Ted & Alice*—a comedy about two married couples, one relatively open-minded (Robert Culp and Natalie Wood), the other strictly conventional (Elliott Gould and Dyan Cannon), who decide to face the sexual revolution head on by experimenting with other partners—in 1969. The script was funny without being epigrammatic; the comedy arose from character, as the four people began to pursue their own arousal—physicality with no strings attached. Unlike so many other directors of the time, Mazursky wasn't concerned with making a long-winded commentary about the corruption of America's moral values. He didn't score points off his characters but seemed to love all of them; he treated them satirically, but the satire was warmhearted and generous-spirited.

*Bob & Carol & Ted & Alice* had the distinction of being the first American picture to open the New York Film Festival. There was tremendous buzz about it, and its ad campaign, featuring the four lead actors in bed together, would become one of the iconic movie images of the time. Those behind the picture were nervous about its reception, to the point of apologizing for it in advance. "Americans talk a lot about marital infidelity," Mazursky said in the movie's publicity notes. "But they are secretly shocked by it. I know if I told my wife I had been unfaithful to her . . . that would be the end." Its producer, Mike Frankovich, told the New York *Daily News*, "I felt obliged to note that I did not believe the film would have an adverse effect on American morals." Even Elliott Gould, who had the image of being one of the hippest of young actors, had reservations about accepting the role of Ted. "When it was offered to me, I turned it down," he admitted. "I was afraid of it. I thought it seemed to be, to some degree, exploitative."

The film festival audience loved *Bob & Carol & Ted & Alice*, but many of the initial reviews were negative—none more so than Vincent Canby's in *The New York Times*. Canby found the film "unpleasant" and populated by characters who were "cheerful but humorless boobs, no more equipped to deal with their sexual liberation than Lucy and Desi and Ozzie and Harriet."

At 8:30 on the morning Canby's notice appeared, Mazursky was sitting at home, dejected, when his phone rang. "I read Canby's review," Pauline told him. "He's a schmuck. I loved the movie, and I'm going to give it a great review." This was the sort of line-crossing that many critics frowned on, but Pauline thought nothing of it. She was certain that there was no way she could be bought, no way she could wind up in the pocket of anyone in the film industry, no matter how powerful. Therefore, she saw no reason why she couldn't flex her muscles a little and fraternize with directors.

"*Bob & Carol & Ted & Alice* is a slick, whorey movie," she wrote in *The New Yorker*, "and the liveliest American comedy so far this year." She loved Mazursky's freedom with his actors, his way of "letting the rhythm of their interplay develop." She felt that he had "taken the series of revue sketches on the subject of modern marital stress and built them into a movie by using the format of situation comedy, with its recurrent synthetic crises." She particularly loved Dyan Cannon's performance, writing that she "looks a bit like Lauren Bacall and a bit like Jeanne Moreau, but the wrong bits."

The two women met at a screening in Manhattan not long after the release of *Bob & Carol & Ted & Alice*. "Someone tapped me on the shoulder from behind," recalled Cannon, "and it was Pauline. She said, 'I'm a fan'—and she said that didn't come easily with her. I said, 'So am I a fan.' And I was. Her voice was so strong, and she didn't care what we thought of it, and she seemed to be true to it, always."

Another artist who benefited from Pauline's critical support in the fall of 1969 was the documentary filmmaker Frederick Wiseman, whose new movie *High School*—a pitilessly straightforward look at the futility and frustration of life at Philadelphia's Northeast High School—also played at the New York Film Festival. *High School* resonated deeply with Pauline, and she called Wiseman "probably the most sophisticated intelligence to enter the documentary field in years." What emerged most powerfully in her review of *High School* was her rage at what she believed to be the inadequacy of her own education. She found the teachers shown in the film to be "the most insidious kind of enemy, the enemy with corrupt values who mean well." She loved the film's unflinching treatment of teachers, the same kind of teachers she had grown to despise as a girl and had been railing against ever since:

> *High School* is so familiar and so extraordinarily evocative that a feeling of empathy with the students floods over us. How did we live through it? How did we keep any spirit? . . . Here it is all over again—the insistence that you be respectful; and the teachers' incredible instinct for "disrespect," their antennae always extended for that little bit of reservation or irony in your tone, the tiny spark that you desperately need to preserve your *self*-respect.

Pauline immediately grasped what Wiseman was trying to get at in *High School*. "Many of us grow to hate documentaries in school," she wrote in her by now familiar student-rebel tone, "because the use of movies to teach us something seems a cheat—a pill disguised as candy—and documentaries always seem to be about something we're not interested in." Wiseman, on the other hand, never stooped to didacticism. He took a dispassionate view of the audience's common experience.

Wiseman, who became a friend of Pauline's and often dined with her and Joe Morgenstern, recalled, "Joe is a very soft-spoken, kind guy. I think that she was attracted to people who were not tough, or not tough in any obvious way." After her review of *High School* appeared, the film turned up on about two hundred screens each month—amazing statistics for a documentary. Wiseman found himself the center of generous critical attention and didn't mind that she reviewed his work only sporadically thereafter. "The impression I had was that she felt I didn't need her," he said, "and that she was saving her space for people who did."

For many longtime readers of "The Current Cinema," Pauline's increasingly expansive style took getting used to; after she returned to her reviewing post in 1969, a number of complaining letters landed on William Shawn's desk. "Dear Sir: I think I've figured it out. Pauline Kael is the Long Winded Old Lady," wrote one subscriber. "Six full columns to review *The Arrangement* in the Nov. 22 issue must stand as the ultimate in long-windedness. Oh for the days of John McCarten and Brendan Gill!" "There was a time," wrote one reader from Virginia, "when a man could open up the magazine and learn from John McCarten in one very pungent paragraph why the movie stank. Today we have to learn how the condition of the director's psyche, and that of all of us, has an effect on the movie condition as it is today, in 75,000 words." Many of the readers who wrote complaining letters about Pauline were initially thrown by her intimate, conversational tone and her fondness for slang. It was not unusual for her to receive a few letters every month wanting to know why she hadn't been properly educated, and when she was going to learn how to write in a way becoming to a *New Yorker* contributor; at least one reader even went so far as to ask her when she was going to take off her cowboy boots and become a proper lady writer.

But to younger readers—always a key demographic for any magazine or newspaper—Pauline was becoming a heroine. In the dialogue between screen and audience, many young film fans considered this fifty-one-year-old woman from Berkeley the ideal moderator. She shared their enthusiasms, she had a clear sense of who her audience was, and she delighted in guiding them and tracking their progress. "They're looking for 'truth'—for some signs of emotion, some evidence of what keeps people together," she wrote. "The difference between the old audiences and the new ones is that the old audiences wanted immediate gratification and used to get restless and bored when a picture didn't click along; these new pictures don't click along, yet the young audiences stay attentive. They're eager to respond, to love it—eager to *feel*."

Some of her fans had now taken to phoning her at home to ask her opinion of various films, and she was generally good about fielding these calls. Her number was also close to that of the Thalia Theater, one of the leading revival houses in Manhattan, and while she initially considered the "wrong number" calls for the theater a nuisance, she began to keep a schedule for the Thalia handy and cheerfully told callers what was playing that day, just as she had at the Cinema Guild.

If she was on deadline, however, she sometimes pretended to be her own secretary. Ruth Perlmutter, who was running a repertory film program at Philadelphia's Walnut Theater in the late '60s, once phoned her to ask which Robert Bresson film she should program. Pauline, posing as her own secretary, informed Perlmutter that Ms. Kael was on deadline. Perlmutter played along and asked the "secretary" what she thought of *Au Hasard, Balthasar*.

"Grim," said Pauline, and excused herself and hung up.

Late in 1969 Pauline used her column for some intriguing speculation about the future of two actresses she admired—Jane Fonda and Barbra Streisand. Fonda had spent most of the '60s trying to make her mark as a sexy comedienne, but her films—*Sunday in New York*, *Any Wednesday*, *Barefoot in the Park*—were commercial in the flimsiest sense, and by the end of the decade, most critics regarded her as a case of potential wasted. Then, late in 1968, she was offered the screen version of *They Shoot Horses, Don't They?*, Horace McCoy's 1935 novel about a group of desperate people competing in a brutal dance marathon in Hollywood. Fonda played Gloria, a would-be actress who can't get into Central Casting; her ferocious anger is all she has left to hang on to. "How're you going to feed it?" she snaps to a pregnant competitor (Bonnie Bedelia). When her own partner (Red Buttons) is dying of a heart attack on the floor, Gloria screams at him, "I'm tired of losing!" In the end, Gloria breaks down completely when her new partner (Michael Sarrazin) accidentally rips one of the silk stockings she'd stopped riding streetcars for a month in order to afford. She asks him to shoot her, to put her out of her misery—and he calmly grants her wish.

Fonda's tough, economical performance dazzled Pauline. "She doesn't try to save some ladylike part of herself," she wrote, "the way even a good actress like Audrey Hepburn does, peeping at us from behind 'vulgar' roles to assure us she's not really like that." Pauline went on to predict that Fonda stood "a good chance of personifying American tensions and dominating our movies in the seventies as Bette Davis did in the thirties."

Streisand, meanwhile, opened at the end of the year in Twentieth Century–Fox's gargantuan screen version of the Broadway smash *Hello, Dolly!*, a project Pauline regarded as a horrible waste of the actress's talents. "Somewhere along the line," she wrote, "Hollywood got the idea that musicals were 'family entertainment'—and had to be wholesome and overproduced and full of mugging actors and cloying ingénues and a processed plot and all the rest of the paraphernalia that has made so many people say 'I can't stand musicals.'" Streisand, she argued, was in a perfect position to take musicals in a new direction—contemporary and smaller-scale, scored with the pop music that the public "is alive to." She was encouraged that even the $20-million-plus excesses of *Hello, Dolly!* couldn't camouflage Streisand's gifts as a sexy comedienne and singer. But Pauline insisted that the actress needed "to be liberated from period clothes and big-studio musical arrangements . . . Streisand could inaugurate a new kind of musical, because she uses song as Astaire used dance, expressively, to complete a role and make it a myth."

The new year began with Luchino Visconti's *The Damned*, which had opened to widespread critical acclaim. It distressed Pauline to see her colleagues throwing bouquets at this slow-moving, overlong drama about the changing fortunes of a wealthy German family during the rise of the Third Reich. One of the most widely discussed aspects of *The Damned* was the long sequence depicting a beer party thrown by the Brownshirts that turns into a men's orgy. It didn't possess the slightest hint of eroticism, but many reviewers hailed it as an example of the daring possibilities created by the screen's new permissiveness. Pauline believed that Visconti was "not using decadence as a metaphor for Naziism but the reverse: he's using Naziism as a metaphor for decadence and homosexuality." The trouble, she thought, was that "Visconti, though drawn to excess, lacks the gifts of an F. W. Murnau or a Fritz Lang; he's *carefully* flamboyant." *The Damned* provided a good example of one of the dangers of the screen's new openness: too many critics who should have known better rushed to praise it simply because of its flashy sensationalism, combined with the gravity of its Nazi Germany setting. Pauline was one of the few critics to review the result, not the concept, confessing, "I have rarely seen a picture I enjoyed less."

Then, in mid-January 1970, she was seduced once again. The movie was Robert Altman's *M\*A\*S\*H*, brought out by Twentieth Century–Fox. Even the backstory of the film was bound to appeal to Pauline's rebellious streak: It was made by a group of artistically brilliant, rule-breaking, authority-defying bad boys under what basically amounted to the cover of darkness. The director was Robert Altman, a forty-four-year-old director who had grown up in Kansas City and had a low-level, stop-and-start career, mostly in television. The publicity handout for *M\*A\*S\*H* described him as "a B-25 pilot in World War II, freelance magazine writer and producer of many prize-winning documentary films." (Next to this last credit, Pauline scribbled "such as?") He had worked extensively in television, directing episodes of *Bonanza*, *Bus Stop*, *Combat!*, and *Alfred Hitchcock Presents*. His most recent feature had been *That Cold Day in the Park*, starring Sandy Dennis, and Pauline had loathed it.

*M\*A\*S\*H* had started life as a novel by the pseudonymous Richard Hooker. Ring Lardner, Jr., had reviewed the book—a comedy about doctors serving in the Korean War—for *The New York Times* and thought it would make a terrific picture. Lardner's agent, George Litto, approached the producer Ingo Preminger at Twentieth Century–Fox about the idea of turning it into a movie. Lardner wrote the script, which Fox liked, and when Preminger asked Litto whom he thought might direct it, he suggested one of his other clients— Robert Altman. No one at Fox knew who Altman was, so they sent out the script to more than a dozen of the most successful comedy directors—from George Roy Hill to Blake Edwards—all of whom passed on it, seeing it as nothing more than a string of vignettes. Litto pressed Altman once more. Having met with nothing but rejection from their other directorial candidates, Fox reluctantly signed him up.

"Bob had gotten fired from Warners on a movie called *Countdown*," George Litto recalled, "because he had all the actors talking at the same time." In *M\*A\*S\*H* he adopted the same technique, in an attempt to dispense with traditional story setups and exposition and to come right in on the action as if he were jumping into the middle of a cocktail-party conversation. Rene Auberjonois, who played the chaplain who goes by the name of Dago Red, recalled an episode that underlined the essence of what Altman was after on film. One night Altman and Auberjonois were walking down Eighth Avenue in Manhattan after a play. There was a lot of street traffic, and suddenly Altman stopped and asked Auberjonois, "Did you hear that?" "He was referring to a conversation that we had both sort of heard," recalled Auberjonois, "between two people coming toward us, but you could only hear a small section of it. But that small section told you everything. You could extrapolate on that and have a complete scene and a whole story out of it, but you had only to hear a few broken sentences. And I think that was the key—that you don't hear most of what is going on around you. But what you do hear is enough to tell you the whole story."

*M\*A\*S\*H* was a wartime comedy in which not one shot was fired. It was not a piece of military slapstick, like *Operation Madball*. It was a counterculture comedy: The setting may have been a MASH unit during the Korean War, but the audience's association was naturally with the war in Vietnam; in fact, specific references to Korea had been deleted. The trio of flip, rebellious doctors, played by Elliott Gould, Donald Sutherland, and Tom Skerritt, chased women, drank to excess, pulled cheap practical jokes on fellow officers, and thumbed their noses at anything resembling authority; it was their only way of coping with the insanity into which they'd been unwillingly thrust.

Nobody paid much attention to *M\*A\*S\*H* while it was in production, as studio executives were preoccupied with two enormously expensive World War II pictures that were undergoing various budget and production difficulties, *Tora! Tora! Tora!* and *Patton*. That suited Altman: There were certain passages that he didn't want the powers-that-be seeing in rushes, for fear they might get nervous and start looking over his shoulder, interfering with what he wanted to put on the screen. He used fog filters to give the scenes a fuzzy, unfocused, dirty look—clarity was the last thing he was after. *M\*A\*S\*H*'s surgery scenes, in which the doctors wisecracked their way through the most gruesome procedures, were graphic—realistic without being sensationalistic. These moments were seamlessly juxtaposed with other hilarious scenes—the doctors pulling down the side of the tent while the officious Hot Lips Houlihan (Sally Kellerman) is taking a shower; Hawkeye (Donald Sutherland) asking the pompous surgeon Frank Burns (Robert Duvall) about the sounds Hot Lips makes in bed; and the "Last Supper" sequence, in which the well-endowed, libidinous dentist Painless Pole (John Schuck) decides that he wants to commit suicide.

Even some of the people working on *M\*A\*S\*H* weren't at all sure what Altman was up to. "I remember the sound engineer—an old-school, Twentieth Century–Fox elderly guy," recalled Auberjonois. "I remember him sitting there after a take, and he threw up his hands and said, 'I don't know how they're going to make *anything* out of this.'" The film was full of overlapping dialogue and barely heard asides, but once he began cutting the picture with the film editor Danford B. Greene, Altman showed an uncanny ability to pull it all together. The scenes in *M\*A\*S\*H* had a comic rhythm unlike anything that had ever been put on film. Even some of the actors hadn't been sure of Altman's approach at first. "Donald Sutherland and I became very close during the process," said Elliott Gould, "and we didn't get Bob. And Bob thought we wanted to have him fired. We didn't. We just didn't get him. Thank goodness he let us reshoot something, and subsequently, we became great, great friends."

No one involved with the picture had any sense that it might turn out to be an immense hit. "We were completely under the radar," said Auberjonois. "I seem to remember going into the commissary at Fox and sitting down and opening the menu to get lunch, and there would be the Doctor Dolittle Salad and the *Hello, Dolly!* Chowder, but there was nothing about *M*A*S*H*." There was plenty of indication that Fox executives had backed the picture only because they knew Mike Nichols was shooting the screen version of Joseph Heller's mammoth bestseller *Catch-22* over at Paramount, and they felt Fox needed to be ready with its own antiwar comedy.

Once they finally saw the finished product, however, they didn't understand what they had. Its freewheeling, plotless structure bore no relation to anything they'd ever experienced. The head of the editing department at Fox predicted that *M*A*S*H* would go straight to drive-in release. Altman later claimed, "This picture wasn't released—it escaped." And then the reviews began to appear.

Although *The New York Times*'s Roger Greenspun liked the performances and admitted that the film was funny, he didn't really respond to Altman's techniques; most of the other important reviews, however, were quite positive—and leading the way was Pauline's in *The New Yorker*. She titled her column "Blessed Profanity" and pronounced *M*A*S*H* "a marvelously unstable comedy, a tough, funny, and sophisticated burlesque of military attitudes that is at the same time a tale of chivalry. It's a sick joke, but it's also generous and romantic—an erratic, episodic film, full of the pleasures of the unexpected." It was perhaps the movie's unexpected spirit that appealed to her most; she appreciated that "competence is one of the values the movie respects—even when it is demonstrated by a nurse (Sally Kellerman) who is a pompous fool." Pauline also loved the film's subversive sensibility and language ("I've rarely heard four-letter words used so exquisitely well in a movie, used with such efficacy and glee. I salute *M*A*S*H* for its contribution to the art of talking dirty") and Altman's use of sound: "When the dialogue overlaps, you hear just what you should, but it doesn't seem all worked out and set; the sound seems to bounce off things so that the words just catch your ear."

Like a great opera singer, she saved the best she had to give for the aria's climax:

> Many of the best recent American movies leave you feeling that there's nothing to do but get stoned and die, that that's your proper fate as an American. This movie heals a breach in American movies; it's hip but not hopeless. A surgical hospital where the doctors' hands are lost in

chests and guts is certainly an unlikely subject for a comedy, but I think
*M\*A\*S\*H* is the best American war comedy since sound came in, and
the sanest American movie of recent years.

The movie that "escaped" wound up becoming one of the year's biggest
successes, and Altman would always claim that *M\*A\*S\*H* saved Fox (whose
executives finally perceived that movies for the new audiences, rather than
overdressed musicals, were the way to go). What was most interesting about
Pauline's reaction to *M\*A\*S\*H*, given that Altman would soon become the
director most closely associated with her tastes and sensibility, is that her
review is remarkably succinct and in scale. She didn't overreact to anything,
didn't proclaim the arrival of a new moviemaking messiah—as she well might
have done had *M\*A\*S\*H* appeared later in her career. But clearly she had
perceived Altman's greatest talent. In Elliott Gould's words, "His pictures
showed life taking its course."

*M\*A\*S\*H* became one of the most potent symbols of the New Hollywood;
contrary to expectations, it buried Mike Nichols's highly anticipated adaptation of Joseph Heller's *Catch-22*, which would have a disappointing release in
June 1970.

Pauline's attitudes toward pomposity and self-righteousness versus authenticity in screen drama were briskly consistent without being stiffly predictable.
In February of 1970 Irvin Kershner's *Loving* took her by surprise. It gave the
talented George Segal, an actor Pauline had admired for years, a great role as
a failed artist, plodding along while trying to provide for his wife and family,
but never losing sight of the fact that he wasn't what he once dreamed of
becoming. "After so many movies that come on strong with big, flamboyant
truths," Pauline observed, "a movie that doesn't pretend to know more than
it does but comes up with some small truths about the way the middle class
sweats gives us something we can respond to; it gives us something we desperately need from the movies now—an extension of understanding." Like
Altman, Kershner earned her praise by shunning the easily theatrical and
manipulative and simply showing life as it was lived.

Late in February Pauline's third book of criticism was published by Little,
Brown. Again, her book had a sexy title, and also one that reflected her secure
status at *The New Yorker*—*Going Steady*. It included all of her *New Yorker*
reviews, plus "Trash, Art and the Movies." By now a new book by Pauline
was treated as something of a publishing event. "Pauline Kael is my favorite

movie critic," John Leonard stated in the opening of his *New York Times* review. It was a rave, with suggestions throughout that she had moved beyond the position of a mere film critic and into the pantheon of significant writers. Leonard admitted, "While I miss the polemics and the reviews of other reviewers that made her first two collections such evil fun"—the very thing that William Shawn had insisted on purging from her work—"I care about Miss Kael's criticism as literature. Her reviews can be read before, immediately after, and long after we have seen the movie that inspires or exasperates her."

Appearing before that positive notice, however, was a more probing one in the Sunday *New York Times Book Review*, written by Charles T. Samuels, a member of the English faculty at Williams College and already a prominent film commentator. Seizing on some of Pauline's comments in "Trash, Art and the Movies," Samuels suggested that Pauline might be more of a reviewer than a genuine critic, less an aesthetician than a social historian. In "Trash, Art and the Movies," Pauline had written, "One doesn't want to talk about how Tolstoi got his effects but about the work itself. One doesn't want to talk about how Jean Renoir does it; one wants to talk about what he has done." To Samuels, this was a warning sign. "By neglecting to analyze technique," he wrote, "Miss Kael can do no more than assert that a given film is new, or beautiful, hoping that her language will provide the reader with something parallel to the qualities implicit in the work of art." And underneath her consistent refusal to delve into formal analysis, Samuels went on—in the pointed yet cautious tone so often adopted by academics—was the implication that she ultimately came down on the side of trash rather than the side of art:

> About film art, she reminds her readers not to be solemn, and so does not bore them with the exegesis that is needed to justify her opinions. Instead, she arms them against the cultural stigma of Philistinism and creates some of her best epithets in behalf of avowed trash. No wonder, then, that Pauline Kael is so popular. She combines high spirits with low seriousness—a winning combination in movies and now, it seems, in their criticism.

If it had been fair for her to rail unrelentingly against academia so many years, it was fair for academia to strike back, and that, clearly, was part of Samuels's agenda. He revealed as much when he wrote with self-contained derision, "In her youth, as the author avows, she was a farm girl harried by schoolmarms spoon feeding her classics. The movies were her escape from 'respectable,' therefore emasculated, culture and she assumes that they function as a similar antidote for us all." With these words Samuels laid the foundation of an argument against Pauline's work that would grow louder and more insistent in the years ahead.

Unlike many critics who insisted on maintaining a stance of complete neutrality and distance toward their subjects, Pauline enjoyed making a blatant show of her support. When she was in the company of artists of whose work she approved, she could be enormously warm and encouraging. Many of her colleagues, among them Joseph Morgenstern, were uncomfortable with this aspect of her personality, but Pauline saw no reason to remain aloof in such circumstances.

She was also quite willing to confront the artists she considered failures and could be dismissive and fault-finding with them. Because she believed she was simply expressing her honest opinion rather than seeking to do harm, she was often naïvely baffled when the objects of her scorn reacted negatively to her criticism. A mutual friend had put her together with Mart Crowley, whose *The Boys in the Band*—the story of a group of gay men who play out their longings and regrets in high, bitchy style during a birthday celebration—had been a tremendous hit Off-Broadway and then had transferred to Broadway for another highly successful run. Pauline attended a performance of the piece in the company of the playwright and afterward, at the home of the mutual friend, she excoriated Crowley, telling him she found the play empty, cheaply theatrical, and superficial. As they talked and drank, Pauline became ever more abusive, until Crowley, stunned and wounded, got up and retired to another room. After a couple of hours, during which she got increasingly drunk, Pauline sought out Crowley to tell him that the next time she saw him he would no doubt be very rich and famous. (William Friedkin's screen version of *The Boys in the Band* was even more offensive to her; she thought Friedkin had compounded the play's problems with too many lingering close-ups aimed at currying sympathy for his poor, suffering-through-their-wisecracks characters.)

In March 1970 Pauline—more unwillingly than ever—again made way for Penelope Gilliatt to take over "The Current Cinema." She continued to complain to her friends that, while *The New Yorker* might offer a lively, informed readership—she delighted in the letters she constantly received from her readers—it did not, on a six-month schedule, pay enough to allow her to live comfortably in New York.

The city itself continued to challenge her. After five years she still hadn't grown accustomed to its noise and chaos and aggression; she once told a reporter that while her tone on the printed page might be quite assertive, she was not, in life, a particularly assertive person. (This was only partly true; in an argument, she could be quite formidable.) She despised the greased machinations of the city's social network, the way so many gifted and deserving individuals were looked down upon because they didn't have money or an Ivy League education—while socially connected people of lesser talent generally had an easier time of it.

She was often most comfortable in the company of people like herself, who came from the West Coast or the Midwest—anywhere but the carved-in-marble runway to success that New York represented. She answered as much of her fan mail as she could, often in great detail. If a young film fan approached her, either at a screening or by mail, telling her that he wanted to be a critic, she was usually happy to provide good counsel. Several close friends attributed this to her egalitarian, West Coast roots, the simple background that she might not care to discuss in any depth, but that clearly she had not forgotten.

In time she found an escape—a spacious, turreted Victorian house in Great Barrington, Massachusetts, a small, attractive town right on Route 7, in the heart of the Berkshires. It was a lovely, graceful, unspoiled area, near the Housatonic and Green rivers. Two Berkshire Heights Road stood on a four-and-a-half-acre lot and was in a state of decay, but the asking price—$37,000—was attractive, and she and Gina decided to go to work on it. The down payment and costly repairs virtually depleted Pauline's savings, but she considered it a sound investment. She looked forward to the day when she and Gina would be able to move there full-time. As she told a reporter years later, "I never adapted to New York. I feel better in the country."

On May 26, 1970, Pauline received an Award in Literature from the American Academy of Arts and Letters and the National Institute of Arts and Letters. It was presented to her "for her film criticism, written fast, out of a desire to respond to new movies before they have settled into history. Her exacting standards and her enthusiastic recognitions of excellence have been a stimulus to the quality of film-making and film-viewing." The $3,000 she was given was as welcome as the honor itself.

She occupied herself in the summer of 1970 with reading, and clipping articles from *The New York Times*, *The Atlantic Monthly*, and other publications that might be useful reference points when she resumed her *New Yorker* duties in September. She also paid close attention to Penelope Gilliatt's columns in "The Current Cinema," and remained frequently baffled by Gilliatt's cloudy style. A brilliant, well-read woman, Gilliatt possessed a formidable intellect that Pauline respected. Her reviews were much shorter than Pauline's, but they were often vaporous, their central points difficult to identify. It is possible that Shawn prized this very quality in Gilliatt's writing, simply because it provided such a startling contrast with Pauline's own style, but for those who loved the latter, the six months that Gilliatt was on reviewing duty were an opportunity to pass over the pages of "The Current Cinema" as quickly as possible. In the spring of 1971, one disgruntled reader vented his frustration to Shawn in the form of a poem:

> Gimme a P,
> Gimme a G,
> But don't send Gilliatt back by sea.
> Give 'er the fare, give 'er the fare
> To get to England
> Quick!
> By air.

Gilliatt was a sweet-natured woman who was generally well liked by her colleagues at *The New Yorker*. She did, however, have a serious drinking problem. Patrick Crow, an editor at the magazine, remembered sitting in O'Lunney's Bar near *The New Yorker* offices and seeing Gilliatt saunter in in mid-afternoon and toss down four Scotch and sodas. When the bartender asked her if she wanted a fifth, she replied that she had to go to the office and read proof. She was constantly plagued by money worries, and while she needed her post at *The New Yorker* to maintain any reasonable kind of lifestyle, she seemed unable to perform her critic's duties without the aid of a drink. Her friend Jane Kramer recalled that Gilliatt "could focus under the most intense sedation—alcohol, God knows what pills she was taking. Most people would be conked out. But with Penelope . . . it focused her mind. She wrote some of her best fiction that way."

Pauline was convinced that Shawn was effectively holding her back by not giving her the chance to write "The Current Cinema" year-round. She had clearly demonstrated her connection to the younger readers that the magazine's advertising department coveted, and while Gilliatt may have possessed a keener sensitivity to certain European films, she was not tuned in to the tenor of the times in the way that Pauline was. Pauline's resentment of Gilliatt's presence at the magazine grew by the day. She was not uncivil to her, but she spent plenty of time complaining about Gilliatt to friends and colleagues.

"My sense was that they stayed out of each other's way almost intentionally," said Jane Kramer. "Penelope, during a lot of that time, would have been happy to see Pauline. I'm not sure Pauline would have been happy to see Penelope. She talked to me about it in these terms: 'I can't believe that I am not in every week—this other mind has nothing to do with what I can say.' I know that there's something to be said for having comparative critical voices, but I'm not sure that when you've got something like Pauline, you don't stick to it as the one critical voice, because it creates a vocabulary that people attach themselves to."

For years Gilliatt had written striking pieces of fiction, and recently, she also had her eye on a screenwriting career. The instinctively competitive Pauline, who believed that she had put any ambition to do creative writing strictly behind her, could not help but feel that Gilliatt was in danger of outdistancing her by pursuing areas of writing apart from reviewing films.

One of Pauline's responsibilities, apart from her departmental reviewing, was to provide capsule reviews of the many films that were being shown in repertory and art cinemas around New York. Sally Ann Mock, who worked on the front-of-book "Goings On About Town" section, often found herself in the position of negotiating an uneasy truce between Pauline and Gilliatt. "My personal feeling—more than personally—is that Pauline did not have any respect, particularly, for Penelope," said Mock. "I ran into several problems with both of them, actually. One would write a blurb, maybe on an older film. In the fall and winter Pauline would write a blurb, and in the spring Penelope would come in and want to rewrite it. And in the fall Pauline would want to rewrite Penelope. I finally said, 'I can't do this.'" Gardner Botsford, the editor of "Goings On About Town," eventually put a stop to this practice. Pauline's complaints about Gilliatt continued unceasingly—but it would be years before "The Current Cinema" became hers alone.

CHAPTER TWELVE

By the early 1970s the view of New York City as the center of dazzling glamour and chic romanticism—the view that Hollywood had peddled in pictures ranging from *The Awful Truth* to *Breakfast at Tiffany's*—was dead and buried. The New York that now emerged onscreen was a city that was closer to the everyday experience of the people who lived there. The crime rate was high and growing higher, the decades-long decline of Harlem had reached its nadir, and Times Square had become a playground for junkies and hookers. *Midnight Cowboy* had shown the seedy realities of Manhattan street life and won an Academy Award for Best Picture in the process.

Still, it would be a mistake to dismiss the New York of the late '60s and early '70s as a completely bleak, fear-ridden place where pleasure was hard to come by. The city was, among other things, a haven for committed movie-lovers, who had an astonishing number of repertory cinemas and art houses from which to choose. In those pre-home-video days, there was plenty of moviegoing activity to be found in all parts of Manhattan. On seedy Avenue B, there was the Charles, where the rats and mice often scurried over the customers' feet. There was the Bleecker Street Cinema and also Theatre 80 Saint Marks, where the projector was situated behind the screen and customers could sink down in the lumpy seats and lose themselves in scratchy prints of thematically paired double features—two Bette Davis vehicles, *Jezebel* and *In This Our Life*, or everyone's favorite French Revolution bill, *A Tale of Two Cities* and *Marie Antoinette*.

Uptown, there was the Regency on Sixty-seventh Street, which once ran Luis Buñuel's masterpiece *Belle de Jour* for close to one full year. On Broadway between Eighty-eighth and Eighty-ninth Streets was the New Yorker Theater, launched by Pauline's friends Dan and Toby Talbot. The Talbots had opened the theater on March 17, 1960, with a screening of Olivier's *Henry V* and Albert Lamorisse's short film *The Red Balloon*. That initial run grossed $10,000, and soon the New Yorker became the most popular place on the West Side to take in first-class foreign-language films and hard-to-find Hollywood classics. The New Yorker later gained a bit of on-camera immortality when Woody Allen shot a scene there for his 1977 comedy *Annie Hall*—the one in which Alvy Singer (Allen) clashes with a pontificating academic type who is mangling the theories of the media expert Marshall McLuhan.

A few blocks uptown, on Ninety-fifth Street just west of Broadway, was the reassuringly run-down Thalia, where the seats were on a slight incline, and friends of old film could encounter some of the most difficult-to-find old Hollywood classics. (The Thalia was also featured in *Annie Hall*.) And on 107th Street, the Olympia showed a constantly rotating program of old Spanish-language films. Over the years, even more repertory cinemas would crop up all over town, in some unlikely neighborhoods, proving Toby Talbot's assertion that "there was an obvious hunger for film. Our patrons were as interested in *who* made the film as in what it was *about* and *who* was in it. They cared about visual style and wanted to follow a director's body of work."

Pauline delighted in the public's growing excitement about what was happening in film. She felt she was at the vertex of the most thrilling burst of activity taking place in the arts, and although she often attended the theater, she commented to friends that generally she didn't find it nearly as exciting as film. The commercial theater, in her view, was still trading on tired conventions and predictably "serious" forms of audience manipulation, and had not succeeded in really connecting with the times, as the movies now showed every promise of doing.

With all of the enthusiasm New Yorkers showed for the movies, it wasn't surprising that the activities of the New York Film Critics Circle were more frequently reported than they had been in years. Pauline was, by 1970, an integral member, having been admitted in 1968, following her appointment at *The New Yorker*. When it was founded in 1935, the NYFCC had been composed of newspaper critics only, but over time, the membership restrictions had been relaxed to include prominent magazine reviewers as well. From its inception the NYFCC had earned a reputation for going its own way, its members being less susceptible to a movie's box-office standing than were the voting members of the Motion Picture Academy. As far back as the 1940s, the NYFCC sometimes awarded top prizes to performers not even nominated in that year's Oscar race—Ida Lupino in *The Hard Way*, Tallulah Bankhead in *Lifeboat*. Pauline believed it was important to uphold the integrity of the group, as she believed that a good critic's review was the only genuine truth on which moviegoers could depend: Everything else, she was fond of saying, was nothing but advertising in one form or another.

The NYFCC operated under a fairly simple system: Nominations were made by writing down one name or title per category on a folded slip of paper. Any selection lacking at least two votes was eliminated. On successive ballots members ranked first-, second-, and third-place choices on a point system—and the balloting continued until one choice had a clear two-thirds majority. All of the balloting was secret; no critic was permitted to take the floor and argue the case for his favorites unless a stalemate occurred.

Because the NYFCC held to such strict rules, there was practically no opportunity for personality clashes to arise among its various members. Only occasionally was there a disruption of the circle's orderliness—as in 1969, when Renata Adler, who had briefly succeeded Bosley Crowther as chief movie critic of *The New York Times*, announced that she could take no more of the meeting and stormed out, insisting that she had to see her analyst immediately—and whatever alliances and rivalries revealed themselves, did so subtly. Judith Crist remembered that "at one end of the table were the intellectuals [Adler, Stanley Kauffmann, Andrew Sarris] and the rest of us were the ink-stained newspaper people." Pauline would attend the meetings in her regulation outfit—plain slacks, simple blouse, and sneakers—and sit passively, a Sibyl-like smile on her face, as she cast her votes. "I always felt that there was an assumption that there was tension between Pauline and Judith," remembered Kathleen Carroll, who covered movies for the *Daily News*. "Competitive, no question. Both very bright and ambitious. I think most of us in the group really felt it."

At the time Pauline was far less widely known than Crist, who was unquestionably the most recognizable name and face in the NYFCC. In 1968 Clay Felker had hired her to become the first film reviewer of the trend-setting *New York* magazine, and she was also the movie critic for the mass-circulation *TV Guide* and film commentator for the popular morning newsmagazine series *The Today Show* on NBC-TV. It was estimated that between *TV Guide* and *The Today Show*, Crist's sharp and succinct opinions reached more than 23 million people, and that her income hovered between $45,000 and $50,000 annually. (Pauline's *New Yorker* salary was a pittance by comparison.) An indication of Crist's celebrity came in September 1968, when *TV Guide* ran a full-page ad in *The New York Times*, featuring Crist and Bob Hope with the tag line, "Headliners and by-liners help us do the job." Crist's taste in films was generally very good, and like Pauline, she was unafraid to acknowledge her fondness for trash.

If Crist was at this time America's most visible movie critic, there was serious competition coming up fast, courtesy of Rex Reed. As a boy in Texas, Reed had developed a love for the films of golden-age Hollywood. In the late 1960s and early '70s he was in the enviable position of writing about films during an all-new golden age, but he was far less interested in discussing the work of the new directors than he was in glorifying the stars of his youth, a predilection that hardly damaged his standing with the public. In his *Daily News* column he regularly took out after the new breed—he didn't understand Robert Altman at all—and delighted in provocative anti-intellectual comments, such as dismissing Ibsen's *A Doll's House* with, "I have slept through more productions of this dated play than almost anything else I can think of." He possessed a knack for the colorful, often vituperative, personality profile, which helped give him a reputation for "telling is like it is." Middle-aged talk show hosts such as Mike Douglas and Merv Griffin were all too happy to have him spout off about the New Hollywood's lack of decent, human stories, and Reed, with his blend of withering, Waldo Lydecker–style sarcasm and high-mindedness, seemed to satisfy Middle America's view of what a movie critic was supposed to be.

In 1970, Reed appeared as Myron, the sex-change candidate, in Michael Sarne's much-reviled film version of Gore Vidal's bestselling novel *Myra Breckinridge*. (Fellow reviewers reveled in pointing out Reed's complete lack of acting ability.) When they were both at the height of their fame, Reed and Crist had a standoff. Reed had made an unflattering remark on a television talk show about Crist's celebrity endorsements—she had recently done an ad for a popular feminine-hygiene spray—and later, when she was interviewed on television and asked about the Reed incident, she responded, "Well, when he shows up at screenings, the big question is 'Does he or doesn't she?'" "That was the lowest point of my public life," recalled Crist. "The minute it came out of my mouth, I could have killed myself." Later, Reed and Crist patched up their differences, but the episode was evidence of how prominent movie critics were becoming in the pop-culture consciousness.

While Pauline had no interest in engaging in open confrontations with her colleagues, there were very few whom she genuinely respected. After only two years at *The New Yorker*, she believed herself to be superior to all of them. She had little use for the work of Vincent Canby, Renata Adler's replacement as chief film critic of *The New York Times*, whom she regarded as a man of pedestrian taste and middlebrow thinking who just happened to be a better writer than Bosley Crowther. She delighted in calling Joseph Morgenstern and other friends when she read Canby's reviews in the *Times*, crowing over how he had missed a particular point. *Life*'s Richard Schickel was a good critic, but Pauline found him to be pompous and unpleasant. She respected *The Saturday Review*'s Hollis Alpert, even though their opinions on films often diverged, and she acknowledged the formidable intellect, literary background, and linguistic prowess of John Simon, although she found his criticism needlessly cruel and demeaning, and personally, she didn't take to him at all. (Once, at a screening of a particularly trashy film, Simon greeted her by saying, "Pauline! Of course, *you* come to all the finest pictures." She responded by giving him the finger.) Pauline also suspected Simon of not being able to surrender himself to the art form, as she could; she found his knowledge more impressive than his actual responses to film. She was anything but an intellectual snob, however, and was genuinely fond of the man who was arguably the worst writer in the circle, the *New York Post*'s Archer Winsten. (Pauline told friends that she had to admire a man whose great passion in life was for skiing.)

On the whole, however, it was difficult for Pauline to approve of most of her colleagues for one simple reason: Practically all of them had preceded her in the profession. Pauline had a bit of a Magellan complex: It was easiest for her to give her approval when she was discovering a film or director before other critics had. Some of her friends felt that this explained her antipathy toward certain directors—Alfred Hitchcock and John Ford, for example. Andrew Sarris had written expansively about both men early in his career, and Pauline wasn't particularly interested in following his lead. "There were a lot of directors who were off the table for her because they were on Andy's plate," observed Paul Schrader, who began his career as a movie critic before becoming a director in the 1970s. "I always assumed Ford was one of those. Andy beat her to John Ford, and she beat Andy to Jean Renoir." The same principle held true for critics themselves: She wouldn't approve of many of them until the next generation came along—and she was in a position to help shape their career paths and push them toward positions of importance.

In the fall of 1970 Pauline returned to *The New Yorker* with a traditional season-opening think piece designed to exhort her readers to pay attention to what was happening in the movie industry. "Numbing the Audience" was an open attack on the coarsely manipulative tactics of the studios' attempts to latch on to new viewers. After pointing out that most of the films released over the summer had been both artistic and box-office calamities, Pauline declared that those who had engineered the corporate takeovers of the old studio system were going down a road that was certain to run out on them. "It used to be understood that no matter how low your estimate of the public intelligence was, how greedily you courted success, or how much you debased your material in order to popularize it, you nevertheless tried to give the audience something."

Too many of the new pictures, she argued, weren't giving the audience *anything*. For key evidence she pointed to the mass of youth pictures, such as

*Getting Straight*, one of the year's big hits with college audiences. It starred Elliott Gould as Harry Bailey, a candidate for a master's degree in English who had a past as a civil rights activist. There were a few sequences calculated to bring forth cheers from the audience—the police moving in on the campus demonstration; Harry having an emotional meltdown while being grilled in his oral exams by a pompous English professor. Gould was at his most appealing—the archetypal, sexy, brainy, questioning college man of the early 1970s. But Pauline felt that *Getting Straight* was a shameful waste, since "no contemporary American subject provided a better test of the new movie freedom than student unrest. It should have been a great subject: the students becoming idealists and trying to put their feelings about justice into practice. . . . Instead, we've been getting glib 'statements' and cheap sex jokes, the zoomy shooting and shock cutting of TV commercials; plus a lot of screaming and ketchup on the lenses." She was horrified by these movies, which she believed took "the recently developed political consciousness of American students, which was still tentative and searching and (necessarily) confused, and reduced it to simplicities, overstatements, and lies."

Two of the biggest hits of the summer of 1970 were John G. Avildsen's *Joe* and Bob Rafelson's *Five Easy Pieces*. The critical and commercial success of *Joe* came as a surprise: it was a crudely written and acted, modestly budgeted look at the pent-up rage and resentment of the hardworking, play-by-the-rules parents of the hippie generation—Richard Nixon's silent majority. *Joe* was really an old-fashioned melodrama that got a tight grip on its audience by depicting the violence and destructiveness that the older generation was capable of inflicting on the young, and Pauline saw it for what it was—a film "slanted to feed the paranoia of youth." At the picture's violent climax, "members of the audience responded on cue with cries of 'Next time we'll have guns!' and 'We'll get you first, Joe!' " Pauline thought that *Joe*'s "manipulation of the audience is so shrewdly, single-mindedly commercial that it's rather terrifying to sit there and observe how susceptible the young audience is."

She continued to worry that young audiences didn't think deeply enough, didn't read enough. They didn't even, she claimed—though she didn't quote any relevant statistics—go to the movies that often; they simply went to a handful of films over and over again. It also bothered her that audiences cheered the end of *Five Easy Pieces*, in which the social dropout Robert Eroica Dupea (Jack Nicholson) abandons his girlfriend (Karen Black) at a gas station, bums a ride off a trucker, and goes cruising down the freeway, in search of nothing and heading nowhere in particular.

After the Kent State shootings in May 1970, some 4 million American students participated in campus strikes. Pauline thought that American youth was actually in a superb position to work for positive social change, but she was surprisingly conservative on the subject of outright rebellion. In the '60s she had chastised her nephew Bret Wallach for demonstrating against the Berkeley chancellor Edward W. Strong, assuring Bret that Strong was really a good man. She sensed that in the wake of the assassinations of Martin Luther King, Jr., and Robert Kennedy in 1968, the ongoing mess of Vietnam, and the Manson Family murders, young people weren't as interested in working for the good of something as they were in withdrawing from everything. Anger was transmuting itself not into action but into apathy. Too many young people, Pauline worried, were "not caring, and not believing anything. They go numb, like the young girl in *Joe*, looking vaguely for some communal Eden where those without hope can cling to each other, and they accept and *prefer* the loser self-image, not wanting to believe that anything good can happen to them."

It was an observation that revealed Pauline's allegiance—whether or not she cared to admit it—to the period in which she had grown up. For all her unconventional thinking and her strong identification with many in the younger generation of directors and actors, she held to the solidly old-fashioned view that real happiness came through hard work and testing yourself, through identifying a goal and going after it with everything you had. The numbing of the audience that she wrote about in October 1970 was alien to her temperament: She believed that youth should be encouraged to move forward. Instead, the movies were encouraging them to drop out.

There was one person, however, whom she did not encourage to move forward. For a number of years Gina had shown a marked interest in modern dance. Pauline was happy to help fund her studies but stopped short of urging her to explore a career as a dancer. It remained important to her to keep Gina close by, as her typist, first reader, editor. The pattern had long ago been established: The household dynamic centered on Pauline's career. The fact that her fame continued to grow did not mean that she was any more secure in terms of considering living a life on her own. To many of her friends her relationship with Gina, while clearly affectionate, rippled with an evident tension. Gina continued to make world-weary, halfhearted complaints about being enslaved by her mother, but she seemed less able than ever to strike out on her own. To Charles Simmons, an editor at *The New York Times Book Review* who became a good friend of Pauline's in the early 1970s, people missed the point when they criticized Pauline for being overprotective. "She *owned* Gina," stated Simmons.

Pauline could never quite find it within herself to encourage Gina to enter into the mainstream of life. Dana Salisbury felt that Pauline's obliviousness to what might be best for Gina was part of a much larger family emotional blueprint. Salisbury claimed that all three of the Kael sisters were "tone deaf about the effects of things on people. In the case of my mom, I know that it was not deliberate. In the case of Rose, she was unwilling even to consider it. In the case of Pauline, she was above considering it."

The pictures that opened in the fall of 1970 were mostly poor, and Pauline had little good to say about any of them. In November, however, she was delighted to discover Barbra Streisand's latest vehicle, *The Owl and the Pussy-cat*, based on Bill Manhoff's hit Broadway comedy of 1967. Streisand played her first completely contemporary screen role—a New York prostitute who starts a bumpy romance with a neurotic, failed writer, played by one of Pauline's favorites, George Segal. "I think George lifted Barbra, in a way," recalled Buck Henry, who wrote the screenplay. "I was trying to capture Barbra's New York accent and use it in the tawdriest way possible. I begged her to say 'Fuck off'—I wanted her to say it so badly, and she did it wonderfully." The teaming worked beautifully as far as Pauline was concerned. "Were Hepburn and Tracy this good together, even at their best, as in *Pat and Mike*?" she wondered. "Maybe, but they weren't better." Most of all, she thought it was bracing "to see Streisand get out from under the archaic production values of large-scale movies" such as *Hello, Dolly!* She found her "like thousands of girls one sees in the subway, but more so—she is both the archetype and an original, and that's what makes a star."

In addition to the New York Film Critics Circle, Pauline belonged to another prominent critics' group, the National Society of Film Critics. The society tended to be looked on as the bastard cousin of the NYFCC, although it had been founded for valid reasons. Since the city's major newspaper strike in 1962, the NYFCC had accepted magazine critics as members, but it was still perceived as an organization dominated by daily newspaper reviewers. With the demise of *The New York Herald-Tribune* in 1967, only four daily newspapers were still operating, and it was decided that the handful of members of the NYFCC did not really constitute a proper sampling of critical thought in New York. Among the founders of the National Society of Film Critics were Hollis Alpert, Andrew Sarris, Joe Morgenstern, and Pauline. Partly because it was seriously underfunded, the NSFC never developed the cachet of the NYFCC; during some years, the society couldn't afford even a no-frills awards dinner, so honorees were simply notified by mail. The organization, however, had other objectives, one of which was to establish a series of dialogues between critics and some of the most acclaimed film directors of the day. Richard Schickel, who served as chairman of the NSFC in 1970, termed the project "a good idea in theory, a bad one in practice," a point of view that was borne out when David Lean was invited to appear before the group following a special screening of his new film, MGM's *Ryan's Daughter*, at the Ziegfeld Theater on West Fifty-fourth Street in Manhattan.

In the 1960s few directors were as esteemed as David Lean. Both *Lawrence of Arabia* and *Doctor Zhivago* had been enormous worldwide successes and had generally received good press, although some critics understandably preferred his earlier, small-scale work in pictures such as *Brief Encounter* and *Oliver Twist*. *Ryan's Daughter* was a love story, set following the Easter Rising in Ireland, about a country lass (Sarah Miles) who escapes the disappointment of her marriage to a much older schoolteacher (Robert Mitchum) by having an affair with a British soldier (Christopher Jones). Lean gave this essentially simple story his customary grand-scale production, filming in the West of Ireland for more than a year. It was an arduous shoot; rather than use an actual village, Lean sought to construct one of his own, on County Kerry's Dingle peninsula. Initially budgeted at $9 million, *Ryan's Daughter* far exceeded that, while MGM's new president and CEO, James Aubrey, fumed back in Hollywood. This was the era of small films, such as *Joe* and *Five Easy Pieces*, both of which had brought in enormous returns on minimal investments. To Aubrey and the other bosses at MGM, Lean was out of touch with the times. Lean, who had always been a revered prestige director, suddenly found his new picture annihilated by the critics, chief among them Pauline. She had never liked his fussy, meticulous brand of epic filmmaking, which she regarded as all polish and no surprises. His films, she wrote, had "no driving emotional energy, no passionate vision to conceal the heavy labor." *Ryan's Daughter* was nothing more than "gush made respectable by millions of dollars 'tastefully' wasted."

Exactly who led the charge at the NSFC's evening with Lean is open to question; what is certain is that Pauline was one of several critics who subjected the director to some tough questioning. She asked Lean if he really felt he could get away with portraying Robert Mitchum, of all actors, as "a lousy lay." Several members of the group had had a few cocktails and joined in the fray, calling *Ryan's Daughter* unworthy of inclusion in the Lean canon. All of this was devastating to the famously retiring director, who had a long history of shrinking from even the mildest form of criticism. Finally, toward the end of the evening, Lean managed to stammer that Pauline probably wouldn't be satisfied until he turned out a 16 mm picture in black and white. Pauline laughed. "We'll give you color."

The evening, and the torrent of bad reviews that greeted *Ryan's Daughter*'s release, led to a creative paralysis in Lean that lasted until 1984, when he made what turned out to be his final picture, *A Passage to India*.

During the same time, Pauline covered one of the year's biggest hits, *Love Story*, directed by Arthur Hiller. It was based on the runaway success by Erich Segal, which made publishing history in a lowbrow way by becoming the first novelization of a screenplay to climb to the top of *The New York Times* Best Seller List. The paperback, whose cover became one of the iconic images of the early '70s, sold over 4 million copies. Pauline wrote, "The book has been promoted from the start as an antidote to dirty books and movies, as if America were being poisoned by them." The film, she noted, played to both the new and old audience by portraying generation-gap tensions between the hero (Ryan O'Neal) and his stuffy Boston Brahmin father (Ray Milland). In the New York *Daily News*, Kathleen Carroll though that *Love Story* "should bring joy to millions of moviegoers sickened by the overdose of sex and drugs in the movies." Pauline agreed, writing, "It deals in private passion at a time when we are exhausted from public defeats, and it deals with the mutual sacrifice of a hard-working, clean-cut pair of lovers, and with love beyond death."

Although Gina often observed to Pauline's friends that the best way to get along with her was to agree with her, the truth was more complicated than that. Pauline had both a distaste for sycophancy and a need for a certain degree of obeisance, and many of her protégés were often unsure about how much or how little of either to offer. The rules for being in Pauline's good graces were fluid, and if she felt that someone she had supported or believed in had disappointed her, or was on the wrong track critically, she could suddenly become cold and distant. Certainly it was true that if you were a fellow critic, her approval came fastest if you shared her views on movies. She loved to debate, and she was not easily won over by even a persuasive argument; she seldom conceded that the person arguing against her had illuminated a point she hadn't previously considered. She was already fond of saying that she never changed her mind about a movie, a position many other critics found all but impossible to accept. Seeing a movie for a second time years later, at a different point in their lives and with more filmgoing experience behind them, they might have a completely different response. Pauline considered such shifts of opinion a sign of basic critical weakness, an indication that the person hadn't known what he was talking about in the first place.

When it was a matter of mentoring and taking her career advice, many—though not all—of her younger admirers felt that agreeing with her was crucial. One who discovered the price of disagreement was the screenwriter and director Paul Schrader, who had first met Pauline in 1967. Schrader came from a strict Protestant background—his parents were staunch members of the Christian Reformed Church in Grand Rapids, Michigan—and he had entered Calvin College, intending to pursue a career as a minister. But a fading movie theater in Grand Rapids had started showing art films, and Schrader had become enamored of Ingmar Bergman's pictures. Growing up, he had been forbidden to go to the movies at all, and now, as a student, he immersed himself in the art form, running a student-organized film club off campus and reviewing movies for the student newspaper.

During the first night they met, at her West End Avenue apartment, Schrader and Pauline gently argued about movies—she was amused by his worship of Bergman—and drank a good deal, so much so that he wound up spending the night on her living room sofa. The following morning, after she had served him a breakfast of scrambled eggs and toast, Pauline informed him, "You don't want to be a minister. You want to be a film critic. We are going to keep in touch." Given his background, he was highly susceptible to the evangelical streak in Pauline's personality, and once he was back at college, began sending her reviews he'd written, and she would call him and comment on them. Later she pulled strings with Colin Young to get Schrader into the UCLA film school and used her influence to help him land a reviewing job with the *LA Free Press*.

During Christmas 1971 Schrader flew from Los Angeles to New York and met with Pauline. By this time she was regularly approached by the arts editors of newspapers around the country who had openings for film critics; a good word from Pauline usually meant that her candidate got the job. She told Schrader about a position in Seattle, but by now he had begun thinking seriously of trying his hand at writing screenplays and told her that he was afraid leaving Los Angeles for Seattle would put an end to that possibility. Pauline coolly replied that she needed an immediate answer, and Schrader gave her one: no. What followed was a lengthy silence and "some cold chit-chat." Schrader flew back to Los Angeles and went to work on his script. It would be years before he and Pauline reconnected.

One of the frustrations Pauline felt at this time was that the screen's new freedom in tackling both contemporary subjects and contemporary attitudes had given birth to a certain soft-headedness, both in the new audience and among some of the (mostly younger) critics who were writing about the movies. So often, when people rhapsodized about a new film, it was the film's pose, its attitude, that enchanted them, rather than the actual content and substance. In an essay published in *The New Yorker* in January 1971 called "Notes on Heart and Mind," Pauline made it clear that she didn't want her concerns in this area to be misinterpreted as being reactionary. "I don't trust critics who say they care only for the highest and the best," she wrote. "It's an inhuman position, and I don't believe them. I think it's simply their method of exalting themselves." But she saw the dangers in new films that were so freewheeling and "free-spirited" that they lacked any real center or settled for being modish studies in alienation. She was afraid the new pop sensibility wasn't balanced with enough of an artistic, musical, or literary background of genuine substance; she was wary of the new breed of arts-loving intellectuals who had sprung up on college campuses across the country, who rejected much of traditional literature and filled their shelves with "head" reading that combined a pose of depth and meaning with a jazzy, pop sensibility, books such as Herman Hesse's *Siddhartha*, Tolkien's *Ring* books, and Richard Brautigan's *Trout Fishing in America*. She felt that the children of the 1960s "have been so sold on Pop and so saturated with it that they appear to have lost their bearings in the arts."

This led to a number of traps, both for the critic and those reading him. First, it led reviewers to praise rotten movies simply because they were considered in tune with the times. This worked to the critic's advantage, of course: It made him seem an ally of the moviegoing public and also earned him greater name recognition, since his reviews were constantly being quoted in the movie's ads. Much of this, Pauline was sure, smacked of collusion: "In most cases, the conglomerates that make the movies partly own the magazines and radio stations and TV channels, or if they don't own them, advertise in them or have some interlocking connection with them. That accounts for a lot of the praise that is showered on movies." Cover stories on big films always helped magazines boost their newsstand sales, and Pauline knew of many cases in which critics at major newsmagazines were pressured by their editors to write favorable notices of a new release so they could justify placing it on the cover. She found many of the television critics particularly insidious because "they understand that their job is dependent on keeping everybody happy."

Yet, in the end, the tension between the true creative talents in the film industry and the sellouts was an enormous part of what revved Pauline up, made her eager to sit down at her drafting table each week and begin scribbling on her yellow legal pads. She might strongly disagree with John Simon that part of the function of a film critic was to raise the standard of what got made—she wasn't comfortable with the notion of identifying what that standard might be—but believed, as Judith Crist did, that it was imperative to call attention to the best work being done. "I don't have any doubts about movies' being a great art form," she wrote, "and what makes film criticism so peculiarly absorbing is observing—and becoming involved in—the ongoing battle of art and commerce. But movies alone are not enough: a steady diet of mass culture is a form of deprivation. Most movies are shaped by calculation about what will sell: the question they're asking about new projects in Hollywood is 'In what way is it like *Love Story*?'"

The winter season ground on with a run of mostly indifferent films. Pauline admired Eric Rohmer's *Claire's Knee*, but despite her liking of its gently witty script and the "summery richness" of Nestor Almendros's cinematography, it was ultimately too civilized—too tame—for her to embrace fully. She regretted that this story of sexual obsession had "no emotional head of steam when it gets to the subject of sensuality and compulsive attraction." It wasn't until the very end of her six-month reviewing stint that she found a movie she responded to with great enthusiasm: Bernardo Bertolucci's *The Conformist*, which had been shown at the New York Film Festival in September 1970 and was now going into general release. Set in Mussolini's Italy, it cast Jean-Louis Trintignant as Marcello Clerici, a former liberal who has become a quintessentially faceless member of the Fascist machine. Bertolucci loved the look of '30s films, and with his cinematographer, the peerless Vittorio Storaro, he came up with a remarkable look for the movie. Like some of the other reviewers, Pauline was not entirely comfortable with the psychosexual explanation for Marcello's conformity (an attempted seduction, when he was thirteen, by a chauffeur), nor was she at ease with the way Bertolucci equated lavish opulence with decadence, an old movie trope of which she was fast tiring. "Our desire for grace and seductive opulence is innocent, I think, except to prigs, so when it's satisfied by movies about Fascism or decadence we get uncomfortable, because our own enjoyment is turned against us. One wants modern directors to be able to use the extravagant emotional possibilities of the screen without falling into the DeMille-Fellini moralistic bag."

On March 27, in a ceremony held at the Roosevelt Hotel in midtown Manhattan, Pauline received the George Polk Memorial Award for Criticism, conferred by the Department of Journalism of Long Island University. She was in good company: Other honorees were Otto Friedrich (for his book *Decline and Fall*) and Walter Cronkite.

With her review of *The Conformist*, Pauline wrapped up her fourth season at *The New Yorker*. That winter also saw the appearance of "Raising Kane," a major essay she had worked on for several years—a revisionist look at the creation of one of the landmark films of the old studio system, *Citizen Kane*. Part critical analysis, part polemic, part outward-spiraling cultural history, Pauline's article would cement her reputation among her admirers and convince many of her detractors that she was what they had always accused her of being—an irresponsible bully.

# CHAPTER THIRTEEN

W hat was the impetus for Pauline to write "Raising Kane"? Bantam
Books had wanted to bring out a paperback edition of the script,
with an introductory essay by her. She passed on the offer
initially—then, when another writer assigned to the project didn't work out,
she agreed to do it. In September 1968, Pauline received $375, half of the
total advance from Bantam, and set to work. Her contract included the right
to publish the essay separately in a magazine.

More than anything, "Raising Kane" was her call to arms to defend
Hollywood's perennial underdog—the screenwriter. As her own fame as a
critic had grown and she had gotten to know more and more writers, she had
become increasingly aware of how dismissively the writer was treated by the
film business. For decades directors, producers, and stars had wrested writers'
scripts away from them and changed them wholesale. "You have no say at all,"
Arthur Laurents complained to his interviewer Patrick McGilligan in the
late '80s. "Don't you understand? *No writer has any say at all about a movie!*
You can argue, but you can't say. They have the say. That's why they don't like
writers. Because they wish they [themselves] could write. That really is why.
They think, now they'll really fix you . . . now we'll fix you . . . we'll make it
*ours.*"

Pauline knew better than most that there were few more ego-driven animals on the face of the earth than film directors—and Orson Welles, the
young, blazing genius who had come to Hollywood in the early 1940s, commandeered a major studio, and called most of the shots on what became one
of the industry's groundbreaking films, was the embodiment of directorial
ego. By the early 1970s Welles had directed only one commercially successful
picture—1946's *The Stranger*—but with the rapidly growing number of film
studies programs and campus film societies, more and more young people
were discovering his work, particularly his two early masterpieces, *Citizen
Kane* and *The Magnificent Ambersons*. Much had been written about the fate
of both pictures—how, caught in a net of studio and national political
chicanery, they had been deprived of the audience they deserved. Welles
loved to tell these stories in interviews, especially in later years, when his

image as the great misunderstood genius cut down in his prime loomed larger than ever. While Pauline had enormous respect for Welles's talent, she couldn't accept his often-repeated story that he was the one guiding creative force behind *Citizen Kane*. Over the years conversations and casual research had led her to believe that *Kane*'s screenwriter, Herman Mankiewicz, had been the picture's driving creative force. She would use Mankiewicz's years of neglect as a way into the piece, and give auteurism one more drubbing in the process.

In New York Pauline met with John Houseman, Welles's former partner in the Mercury Theatre, who supported her in her belief that Mankiewicz was *Kane*'s true hero. She conducted extensive research on various film-history topics that she thought connected with *Kane*. Unfortunately, she didn't do a great deal of research on the movie itself—partly because she learned that it had already been done.

At some point in mid-1969, Pauline discovered that Howard Suber, a tenure-track assistant professor in the motion picture department at UCLA, had spent years conducting intensive research of his own on *Kane*. Suber, in fact, started a graduate seminar devoted exclusively to the picture's history and influence. The direction and screenplay were closely analyzed, and although Suber failed to entice Orson Welles to visit his classroom, he did succeed in arranging "guest lectures" with *Kane*'s film editor, Robert Wise; key grip, Ralph Hogg; Welles's assistant at the Mercury Theatre, Richard Wilson; and the actress Dorothy Comingore, who played Kane's second wife, the opera singer Susan Alexander. Suber had also gained access to seven drafts of the *Kane* screenplays, which had previously been under lock and key in the RKO studio files. Missing from the archive was "American," the title of Mankiewicz's original, unwieldy first draft, but eventually, Suber tracked that down as well. A pair of noted film scholars, John Kuiper and Richard Dyer MacCann, who were under contract to a small publisher to produce a book on *Kane* that would feature the shooting script, heard about the excellent work Suber was doing. They contacted him with a proposal to write an essay analyzing the development of the screenplay, which they would publish in their book; a three-way contract was signed, and Suber came up with a polished thirty-one-page essay.

For several years Pauline had been making regular appearances as a guest lecturer at UCLA, at the invitation of her old friend Colin Young, now the film school's chairman. On one of these visits she met Suber, greeting him with the comment, "I hear you're pretty good in seminars but boring as a lecturer." Some months after he had signed his agreement with Kuiper and MacCann, Suber received a telephone call from Pauline. She told him about her contract for a book on *Kane*, pointing out that Little, Brown had also secured the publishing rights to the script. What was the point in having two books? she asked Suber. She suggested that the two of them each write an essay for Bantam's book and split the money. She telephoned Kuiper and MacCann, who let Suber out of his contract. When Suber asked Pauline how his agreement with her publishers would work, she replied that she didn't want to bother them at the moment, but she would contact them when the time was right. He agreed and, enthralled to be working on a project with America's most celebrated movie critic, was afraid to ask for a contract between them.

Pauline sent Suber a check for a little over $375, telling him it was half of the advance she had been paid, and he turned over his research materials to her. Over the next several months he frequently queried her about formalizing their agreement with the publisher, and she invariably told him not to worry, and to trust her. Suber's wife warned him that she thought he was being taken advantage of, but he responded, "Why would the biggest film critic in America *need* to screw some little assistant professor at UCLA?"

Herman Mankiewicz had died in 1953, long before Suber began his research, but Suber had spoken with the screenwriter's widow, Sara Mankiewicz, who was all too happy to acknowledge her late husband as *Kane*'s real auteur. She confirmed to Suber that she and Herman had been frequent guests at the spectacular palace hideaway that newspaper publishing tycoon William Randolph Hearst had constructed at San Simeon, the model for *Kane*'s Xanadu. Hearst and Herman were never close; among other things, they were poles apart politically, with Hearst opposing the union movement and Herman coming out in favor of reform-minded Upton Sinclair when he was running for governor of California in 1934. Decades later, Herman and Sara's nephew, the movie producer and director Tom Mankiewicz, recalled that Herman was at San Simeon "all the time, but not as a distinguished visitor—although he certainly was a good screenwriter—but really as a kind of class clown. Herman had this extravagantly famous wit and was always saying outrageous things, and they loved him for that. . . . He was invited as a paid talent, as a paid wit. That was it. And they expected a certain number of bon mots."

Mankiewicz and Marion Davies were drinking buddies, and there were certain details from her life at San Simeon that he appropriated for the character of Susan Alexander—particularly Davies's passion for jigsaw puzzles, which were spread out everywhere at the estate. It is astonishing that Mankiewicz thought he could get away with such a crude invasion of Davies's privacy.

His portrayal of Susan, in fact, showed a baffling combination of hubris, naïveté, and out-and-out stupidity—along with what seems to have been a desire to get caught red-handed. (Perhaps, in this respect, he was like Dorothy Parker, who "atoned" for her lavish weekends with wealthy society folk by lampooning them in her stories.) Mankiewicz seemed to think that if he made Susan Alexander an opera singer without intelligence, class, or talent, no one would link her to Marion Davies, who was an actress with a flair for comedy and, by most accounts, an affable, charming hostess. He was wrong: Davies was shocked by Mankiewicz's betrayal. While Hearst himself was angered that Mankiewicz used him for his portrayal of Kane, it was ultimately just one more blow to his reputation, which had already suffered mightily; Mankiewicz's cruel transformation of Marion into Susan was what determined him to bring down the film.

One revelation involved "Rosebud," the name of young Charles's sled—the symbol of lost childhood happiness that figures in the opening and closing of the picture. "Rosebud," Sara Mankiewicz claimed, was based on one of the many "bitter experiences" that plagued her husband's childhood in Wilkes-Barre, Pennsylvania. Herman's own "Rosebud" had actually been a bicycle he had as a boy. One day, while he was visiting the local library, the bicycle was stolen. "A brand-new bicycle," recalled Sara. "And, as he said, he never, never longed for anything as to get that bicycle back. There was . . . a great deal of *weltschmerz* connected with Herman that few people recognized or realized."

Sara also told Suber that the character of Jed Leland, the drama critic and close friend of Charles Foster Kane (played in the film by Joseph Cotten), included many background details from Herman's own life. In particular, the key scene in which Leland is sent to cover the New York debut of Susan Alexander was taken directly from Herman's days as a drama critic for *The New York Times*, when he had been assigned to review *The School for Scandal*, featuring Gladys Wallis, wife of the railroad and electricity tycoon Samuel Insull. Her performance was inadequate, and Herman got drunk, returned to the *Times* offices, and fell asleep over his typewriter. The scene was re-enacted in *Kane*, with Jed Leland slumped over his typewriter, unable to finish his review of Susan Alexander's catastrophic New York singing debut.

Sara laid out the chronology for Suber as best she could remember it: John Houseman, Welles's collaborator at the Mercury Theatre, had introduced Welles and Mankiewicz to each other around 1937 in New York. Welles had actively solicited story ideas from him, and Mankiewicz had come up with the idea for *Kane*. Sara maintained that Kane himself was intended as an amalgam of Hearst, Insull, and John P. Morgan. In the early spring of 1940, Mankiewicz had gone off to a desert retreat near Victorville, California, and finished the script in several weeks. With him were his secretary, Rita Alexander, and Houseman, who essentially functioned as a story editor. (He was also there to make sure that Mankiewicz, a prodigious drinker, stayed sober enough to complete the job.) Not long before *Kane* was shot, Welles and Houseman had an enormous argument at Chasen's restaurant in Hollywood, which caused a permanent rift between them.

When Pauline read Suber's interview with Sara Mankiewicz, it confirmed her belief that *Kane* had really been Herman's personal and unique vision—not Welles's. Armed with Suber's research, plus what she had undertaken on her own—including an interview with Rita Alexander—Pauline set to work on her essay. Along the way she had discovered a deposition given by Welles in April 1949, when Ferdinand Lundberg, Hearst's biographer, had filed suit against the director, Mankiewicz, and RKO, claiming that his book *Imperial Hearst* was the real basis of Kane. Welles maintained in the deposition that his intention was "to write and produce a work of fiction. As in the case of a great deal of fiction we drew to some extent on our observations of certain aspects of American life and our knowledge of certain types among influential Americans."

It quickly became apparent that three thousand words would not be sufficient to accomplish what was now Pauline's primary goal—to prove that Herman Mankiewicz was indeed the dominant creative force behind *Kane*. A scribbled note on her research papers indicates the direction in which she was heading: "When an actor becomes the role offstage, something fake trails around him, like a magician's cape."

Dorothy Comingore's interview, in particular, yielded some gems, including her recollection that Welles hadn't directed her in the drunken café scene: Comingore insisted that it was a test scene, which was simply put into the film and never retaken by Welles. This information fascinated Pauline, and she delved deeper into her theory that Welles had been misleading people for decades about his omnipotent role in *Kane*.

At some point in 1970 Pauline flew to Los Angeles for her annual lecture at UCLA. Suber met her at the airport and drove her directly to the party in her honor. On the way there he brought up a point he was fond of using to test his students: He asked Pauline how the characters in *Kane* knew that "Rosebud" was Kane's dying word. She answered, as his students normally did, that "Rosebud" is overheard, but Suber pointed out that no one actually hears him say it—he is alone in the room when he utters the word. Thus, the entire puzzle that *Kane* is built around doesn't, strictly speaking, make dramatic sense. As he pulled up to a stoplight on Sunset Boulevard, Suber looked over to check Pauline's response.

"Well," Suber recalled her saying, "it's a trivial point."

Suber finished his essay and mailed it off to Pauline in New York. After that, her phone calls became more sporadic. Then they stopped altogether.

One week in February 1971, Suber's copy of *The New Yorker* arrived in his mailbox as usual. In the section "Onward and Upward with the Arts," he discovered part one of a two-part essay on *Citizen Kane* by Pauline Kael. Some months earlier Pauline had shown her work-in-progress to William Shawn, who agreed on the spot to publish it in the magazine. She made use of the Sara Mankiewicz, Dorothy Comingore, and Richard Wilson interviews. Even worse, she claimed to have discovered, when the picture was released in 1941, that no one actually heard Kane whisper "Rosebud." Nowhere in the piece was Suber's name mentioned. He had not received—nor would he receive— any additional money from Pauline, *The New Yorker*, or Bantam.

When Dorothy Comingore read the article, she was livid. She telephoned Suber, demanding to know how her quotes had ended up in Pauline's piece. Comingore stressed that she had given those recollections to Suber for his use only and threatened to sue Kael. Suber was devastated but also ashamed, feeling that he had somehow been responsible for what had happened. To raise the issue with his department head, Colin Young, would have been to walk into a political quagmire: Not only was he Pauline's close friend, but he could be quite acerbic to the younger members of the faculty. Suber told a few close friends—then tried to put the matter behind him.

"Raising Kane" dominated the pages of the February 20 and 27, 1971, issues of *The New Yorker* and quickly became one of the magazine's publishing events of the year. From its strong opening sentence, *"Citizen Kane* is perhaps the one American talking picture that seems as fresh now as the day it opened"—the essay was a thrilling, audacious piece of writing—if one that indulged in frequent flights of sheer speculation. Early on Pauline launched into an observation sure to rankle many of those who had planted *Kane* at the top of their all-time-best lists. *"Citizen Kane,"* she asserted, "isn't a work of special depth or a work of subtle beauty. It is a shallow work, a *shallow* masterpiece." It was "conceived and acted as entertainment in a popular style (unlike, say, *Rules of the Game* or *Rashomon* or *Man of Aran*, which one does not think of in crowd-pleasing terms.)" To use the "conventional schoolbook explanations for greatness," she explained, was "to miss what makes it such an American triumph—that it manages to create something aesthetically exciting and durable out of the playfulness of American muckraking satire. *Kane* is closer to comedy than to tragedy, though so overwrought in style as to be almost a Gothic comedy."

She linked this idea to what she believed to be *Kane*'s real onscreen antecedents—the fast-talking screwball comedies of the 1930s, an era that had "never been rivaled in wit and exuberance. . . . The '30s were the hardest-headed period of American movies, and their plainness of style, with its absence of false 'cultural' overtones, has never got its due aesthetically." Many of the comedies she cited were set in the newspaper world, depicting tough, aggressive reporters and their hard-driving, duplicitous editors; many of these were written by a small group of smart writers, in exile from the New York newspaper and magazine world, such as Ben Hecht, Charles MacArthur—and Herman Mankiewicz. Pauline felt that it was these writers, rather than the directors whom the auteurists loved to credit, who "may for a brief period, a little more than a decade, have given American talkies their character." She thought it was Mankiewicz's background in this sort of unsentimental comedy that gave *Kane* much of its flavor. Shortly after "Raising Kane" was published, she explained in an interview, "When I got into it and started to research it, it opened up so many interesting areas—particularly when I discovered something about Herman Mankiewicz—his background and what his connections were with Hecht and MacArthur and the whole literary tradition the scripts came out of."

In "Raising Kane," Pauline traced Welles's triumphant arrival in Hollywood, taking care to capture the movie colony's suspicious attitude toward a self-promoting "boy genius" who had managed to be awarded an RKO contract that gave him unprecedented authority. Her description of the industry's discovery that the picture was modeled on Hearst and Davies was vivid and suspenseful: According to her, Mankiewicz had foolishly shown the script to his friend the screenwriter Charles Lederer, who happened to be Marion Davies's devoted nephew—and Lederer had in turn shown it to the Hearsts. She did not hesitate to blame Mankiewicz for his "idiotic indiscretion," which she believed "resulted in the cancellation of the premiere at the Radio City Music Hall, the commercial failure of *Citizen Kane*, and the subsequent failure of Orson Welles."

The ultimate fate of both film and director was, she wrote, sealed by the results of the 1941 Academy Awards, which snubbed *Kane* for both the Best

Picture and Best Director prizes, despite the fact that the film had received the year's most ecstatic reviews. The picture's sole Oscar went to its screenplay—and Welles had to share that with Mankiewicz. She believed that this wounded Welles so deeply that he had to spend the rest of his life claiming credit for more than his share of the film. "Men cheated of their due," she wrote, in a strongly judgmental tone, "are notoriously given to claiming more than their due."

In "Raising Kane" Pauline took repeated, barely disguised swipes at the auteurists. She believed that the worship of directors such as Welles and Fellini approached the ridiculous and that "such worship generally doesn't help in sorting out what went into the making of good pictures and bad pictures." What she didn't do—and what enraged Welles's many champions, devotees, and apologists—was discuss at any substantial length what Welles *did* achieve in directing the film. She did praise his acting performance as Kane, going so far as to say that *The Magnificent Ambersons*, beautiful as it was, suffered because "Welles isn't in it, and it's too bland. It feels empty, uninhabited." She also speculated that Gregg Toland, *Kane*'s cinematographer, had played a previously unsuspected role in the picture's overall look. She pointed to an obscure thriller from 1935 called *Mad Love*, in which Peter Lorre appears onscreen in bald pate, much like the aged Charles Foster Kane. She suggested that Toland might have borrowed the "Gothic atmosphere, and the huge, dark rooms with lighted figures" of *Mad Love* and put them into *Kane*. She had no real evidence for any of these theories, and she had purposely avoided interviewing Welles for "Raising Kane," she explained, because she did not think she could trust anything he might say. "I already know what happened," she had said to Suber when he asked if she would be trying to get an interview with Welles. "I don't have to talk to him."

In fact, the part about *Mad Love* was basically the same sort of movie detective work she had accused the auteurists of peddling. Interestingly, she did not draw a connecting line to a more recent film that may possibly have influenced Welles—Alfred Hitchcock's *Rebecca*. It was released the year before *Kane*, and the opening—the passing through the front gates of the stately Manderley, the scenes with Laurence Olivier and Joan Fontaine standing in enormous rooms with great fireplaces, and the fiery finale, in which the camera slowly moves in to reveal a pillow with the monogram "R" being consumed in flames, just as "Rosebud" is, may well have influenced the look of *Kane*.

At the end of "Raising Kane," Pauline suddenly shifted to a slightly milder, almost apologetic tone. Welles, she wrote, "had been advertised as a one-man show; it was not altogether his own fault when he became one. He was alone, trying to be 'Orson Welles,' though 'Orson Welles' had stood for the activities of a group. But he needed the family to hold him together on a project and to take over for him when his energies became scattered. With them, he was a prodigy of accomplishments; without them, he flew apart, became disorderly." She closed by lamenting that Welles "has lived all his life in a cloud of failure because he hasn't lived up to what was unrealistically expected of him." This was one point on which Welles could not contradict her: Interviewed in the early 1970s, he characterized his career as "98% hustling and 2% moviemaking—that's no way to spend a life."

*The New Yorker* launched "Raising Kane" in a celebratory manner, with a full-page advertisement in *The New York Times,* and letters poured in to *The New Yorker* from enthusiastic readers. The acclaimed screenwriter Nunnally Johnson had had an epistolary acquaintance with Pauline for some time, and Pauline had spoken with him while preparing "Raising Kane." Now Johnson wrote to her that the essay was "a first-rate account and I am a better man for having read it." He added that Sara Mankiewicz wasn't sure whether she liked it or not; she appreciated Pauline's advocacy for Herman but "the references to Mank's drinking must bring up many painful memories." Mostly, though, members of Mankiewicz's family were grateful to Pauline for illuminating the man they believed to be Kane's auteur. "There have always been the Welles idolators," said Tom Mankiewicz. "We just said, 'Herman did everything, and thank you so much, Pauline Kael.'"

With all the acclaim greeting "Raising Kane," Bantam decided the essay was now too important to publish as a paperback original. A deal was made with Little, Brown to bring out a hardcover edition, which would include the shooting script, and in October 1971 *The Citizen Kane Book* appeared. Pauline's essay opened the book, followed by the complete shooting script, illustrated by eighty-one frames from the film, and the cutting continuity of the finished picture.

In *The New York Times,* Mordecai Richler called it "a highly intelligent and entertaining study of a bona fide film classic" and praised Pauline for her "wonderfully sensible reconstruction of the making of *Kane.*" But no matter how persuasively she made the case for Herman Mankiewicz, Richler felt her argument was undercut by the publication of the script, which, despite its merits, he found "superficial and without one quotable line. To Welles, then, however vain and objectionable his manner, rococo his style, must go the ultimate credit for the miracle of *Citizen Kane,*" since in Richler's view "he was the one who did in fact put it all together."

It appears that Welles never contacted Pauline about the article, but Peter Bogdanovich and others claimed he was deeply wounded by Pauline's reduction of his role in *Kane*, feeling that his work on the picture had been undercut once again. The opposition, however, had readied itself on the director's behalf. When the book appeared, *The Village Voice*'s Andrew Sarris angrily rejected Pauline's thesis, but the toughest response came from Bogdanovich in *Esquire*. "The Kane Mutiny" was a lengthy article that was both a level-headed refutation of Pauline's ideas and an expression of righteous anger, and the single worst piece of press she had received to date. Bogdanovich condemned "Raising Kane" as being "loaded with error and faulty supposition presented as fact." Because he had heard Howard Suber's story through his UCLA connections, he explained that Suber and Pauline "were to collaborate in writing the prefatory material to the published screenplay," adding that Pauline took "full credit for whatever use she made of it, and gives none at all to Dr. Suber."

Bogdanovich then proceeded to expose, point by point, the weaknesses in Pauline's research. Not only had she chosen not to consult Welles but she had failed to contact several of the other key players in her story. One was Marion Davies's nephew Charles Lederer, who claimed that he had never—as Pauline had stated—shown the script to Davies. "That is 100 percent, whole-cloth lying," Lederer told Bogdanovich, adding that he had returned the script to Mankiewicz, telling him that he didn't think that Davies would be bothered by the characterization of Susan Alexander. He also told Bogdanovich that the early draft, called *American*, was lugubrious, and that Welles had "vivified the material, changed it a lot, and I believe transcended it with his direction. There were things in it that were based on Hearst and Marion—the jigsaw puzzles, Marion's drinking—though this was played up more in the movie than in the script I read, probably because it was a convenient peg for the girl's characterization." (Lederer's version of this episode is regarded by the Mankiewicz family as highly suspect, since the script reportedly was returned with annotations by the Hearst legal team.)

Bogdanovich quoted George Coulouris, who portrayed Thatcher, the man who becomes young Charles Kane's guardian, dismissing Pauline's essay as "twaddle." The testimony of an actor in thrall to Welles might be questionable. But Bernard Herrmann, the composer of the film's musical score, and famously not a man to play politics in any way, denounced Pauline's research of the film's classic opera sequences, in which Susan Alexander miserably fails her New York debut. Pauline claimed that Welles had pressed Herrmann to create the film's fictional French opera-within-the-film, *Salammbô*, because the first choice, *Thaïs*, involved the expensive proposition of obtaining musical rights. Here she jumped to a conclusion, pointing out that Hearst had once been engaged briefly to Sibyl Sanderson, the American soprano for whom Jules Massenet had written *Thaïs*. Also she reported that Samuel Insull, one of the models for Kane, had built the Chicago Opera House in 1922, and that it had been managed for one disastrous season by the retired diva Mary Garden, in her day a famous Thaïs. But according to Welles, he had simply needed an opera that opened with a big dramatic aria for Susan Alexander, to drive home the point that her career is all but finished the minute the curtain rises. There were no operas in the standard repertory that fulfilled this requirement, since they all had lengthy introductory passages, mostly involving the chorus—so Herrmann simply had to write one.

Bogdanovich suspected that for all of Pauline's knowledge of film history, she did not know much technically about how movies were really made. She had taken Sara Mankiewicz's word for it that the script of *Kane* had changed very little from the first draft, but she had failed to grasp the degree to which scripts change in their long, tortuous evolution. *Kane*'s associate producer, Richard Barr, claimed that "The revisions made by Welles were not limited to mere general suggestions, but included the actual rewriting of words, dialogue, changing of sequences, ideas, and characterizations, and also the elimination and addition of certain scenes."

Bogdanovich's essay for *Esquire* was extremely courageous: For a rising young director, so dependent on popular and critical support, to take on the most celebrated movie critic in the United States showed great conviction and a brave lack of concern about the possible consequences of writing such an article. "The Kane Mutiny," however, did surprisingly little damage to Pauline's reputation. It did, however, represent a serious breakdown of *The New Yorker*'s fact-checking process. Significantly, no transcripts of Pauline's purported conversations with John Houseman, George Schaefer, or Rita Alexander have survived—perhaps because she took no notes. The only research materials in her personal archive, housed at Indiana University's Lilly Library, are copies of Howard Suber's interviews. And Bogdanovich's revelation of her inadequate research efforts did nothing to dissuade her from continuing to chip away at Welles's achievements: In the future she would tell numerous colleagues that she did not believe that the missing reels of *The Magnificent Ambersons* had ever existed—that she felt Welles had simply abandoned the picture.

Decades after the publication of "The Kane Mutiny," Bogdanovich happened to be having dinner with Woody Allen in New York. Allen, who was once quite friendly with Pauline, recalled that he had been with her when she had finished reading "The Kane Mutiny." She was shocked by the evidence that Bogdanovich had stacked up against her.

"How am I going to answer this?" she asked Allen.

"Don't answer," Allen told her.

And she never did.

# CHAPTER FOURTEEN

By the time Robert Altman's *McCabe & Mrs. Miller* opened in June 1971, regular readers of "The Current Cinema" were well accustomed to Pauline's antipathy for the movie Western. In her capsule reviews in the front of *The New Yorker*, she dismissed one revered Western classic after another—*She Wore a Yellow Ribbon, The Gunfighter, The Searchers, Two Rode Together, The Man Who Shot Liberty Valance*. (*Stagecoach* was an exception.) Given her distaste for the genre's conventions and sentiments, perhaps it was inevitable that Pauline would fall as hard as she did for *McCabe & Mrs. Miller*. In *M\*A\*S\*H*, Robert Altman had subjected the military comedy to a kind of deconstruction; with *McCabe & Mrs. Miller*, he did the same thing for the Western.

The basic story, based on a novel by Edmund Naughton, didn't hold a lot of attraction for Altman; it was the atmosphere of a particular time and place that he was after. Set in the rain-soaked and snow-blanketed Pacific Northwest at the turn of the century, *McCabe* was about a small-time hustler who sets out to make his fortune by opening a whorehouse in a remote zinc-mining town. Altman later said that he took great comfort in the story's familiar types—the drifter/loser hero and the good-hearted whore and the mercenary villains—believing they would give the audience an "anchor," so he could concentrate on getting the feeling he wanted into the film.

Altman wanted the film to look like the old daguerreotypes of the turn of the century, and he and the production designer, Leon Ericksen, had worked out a muted color scheme in order to achieve it. Altman and the cinematographer, Vilmos Zsigmond, also hit on the idea of flashing the film (briefly exposing it to light during processing) in order to capture the desired washed-out effect. And in order to achieve a greater sense of realism, Altman encouraged his actors to overlap their dialogue, much of it once again improvised. Any other director might have turned the story into a conventional romance, but Altman later stated, "I don't really care much about the story in a film. . . . I think more about the painting." *McCabe & Mrs. Miller* was shaping up to be the most elliptical Western ever made—it was nearly an impressionistic study of a Western. Yet there was nothing fey or pretentious about it; for all its visual poetry, it also had tremendous bite and grit.

*McCabe* opened in June, and a number of the television critics, who commanded the widest audience, were hostile to it. Rona Barrett said in a broadcast that *McCabe* "saddened and disgusted" her, and that it was "rated R, presumably for rotten." She also noted that at the screening at the Motion Picture Academy, some forty people "got up and walked out, unable to understand the onscreen mumbling."

Under normal circumstances Penelope Gilliatt would have reviewed *McCabe* as part of her regular schedule, but Pauline persuaded both Shawn and Gilliatt to let her step in and write the review in the middle of her layoff. It was the most rapturous notice she had written to date—the first of the "bliss-out" reviews for which she would soon become famous. She opened with this sentence: "*McCabe & Mrs. Miller* is a beautiful pipe dream of a movie—a fleeting, almost diaphanous vision of what frontier life might have been." She found the film "so indirect in method that it throws one off base. It's not much like other Westerns; it's not really much like other movies." She loved the picture's beguiling, allusive style, its almost dreamlike view of another time, and she praised Altman for having given up "the theatrical convention that movies have generally clung to of introducing the characters and putting tags on them. Though Altman's method is a step toward a new kind of movie naturalism, the technique may seem mannered to those who are put off by the violation of custom—as if he simply didn't want to be straightforward about his storytelling." Curiously, she mentioned neither Vilmos Zsigmond's photography, with its innovative use of filters, or the inferior quality of the sound mixing.

*McCabe & Mrs. Miller* seduced Pauline so completely that she became its cheerleader. In the closing paragraph of her review, she confessed her fear that the movie might not find the audience it deserved. "Will a large enough American public accept American movies that are delicate and understated and searching—movies that don't resolve all the feelings they touch, that don't aim at leaving us *satisfied*, the way a three-ring circus satisfies?" Clearly, she was afraid the answer was no. The week that the review was published, she made an appearance on *The Dick Cavett Show*, exhorting moviegoers to get out and support this major work by a brilliant American artist. *McCabe & Mrs. Miller* had had a soft opening, but suddenly, after Pauline's drum-beating on television, box office returns picked up. There is no way of knowing how much Pauline's advocacy had to do with the increase in *McCabe & Mrs. Miller*'s attendance, but Altman swore that it had been a key factor. In the end, although the film never achieved hit status, Pauline helped to make it one of the year's most talked-about movies.

Those who believed that criticism should maintain a coolly objective tone were bothered by the emotional tenor of Pauline's support for the film, and her review confirmed many suspicions that she was incapable of staying within "correct" critical boundaries. It gave her, however, the growing confidence that her impact on readers and audiences was even greater than she had imagined.

When Pauline returned to her *New Yorker* duties in the fall of 1971, she led off with one of the most misleading statements of her career. Her season-opening review was of John Schlesinger's *Sunday Bloody Sunday*, a movie that posed a particular challenge for her: The screenplay was written by Penelope Gilliatt.

"Seeing *Sunday Bloody Sunday* was for me like reading a novel that was very far from my life and my temperament, and that yet when finished it had me thinking," she wrote in the opening of her review. *Sunday Bloody Sunday* concerned a ménage a trois involving a middle-aged Jewish doctor, an uptight female employment officer, and the casually amoral younger man whom they both love. The film's central theme was how people learn to give up their dreams and settle for less than they had once imagined having. The seminal scene took place between Alex (Glenda Jackson) and her mother (Peggy Ashcroft). At the end of a cheerless dinner, Mrs. Grenville tries to tell Alex why she has stayed with her work-obsessed, neglectful husband:

> MRS. GRENVILLE: Darling, you keep throwing in your hand because you haven't got the whole thing. There *is* no whole thing. One has to make it work.
>
> What you don't know is that there was a time when I left him. We had different opinions about everything. Everything seemed impossible.
>
> ALEX: When?
>
> MRS. GRENVILLE: You were three. He left me alone. It was good of him (pause). But I was mad not to know how much I was going to miss him.
>
> You think it's nothing, but it's not nothing.

Pauline's comment about the film's being alien to her own temperament was correct in one sense: She was and always had been intractable with respect to any form of compromise. But its central situation—the sharing of a man with another man—was reminiscent of her own past, with Robert Horan or James Broughton in the role of *Sunday Bloody Sunday*'s central character. She found that "Peter Finch's Dr. Daniel Hirsh is possibly a movie first—a homosexual character who isn't fey or pathetic or grotesque." She loved the fact that *Sunday Bloody Sunday* didn't portray its protagonists as wallowing around in despair—as an American film might have done. Instead "the characters here all are coping; they're not falling apart," and she felt that the movie's sophisticated approach to a delicate emotional situation made it "instantly recognizable as a classic." She pointed out that the director, John Schlesinger, had "lost his stridency"—the quality that had made her dislike *Midnight Cowboy*. But she saved her highest praise for Penelope Gilliatt, who, she felt, had done "what few people who write for the screen think to do: she has kept her self-respect as a writer, and written not down but up. She has trusted the audience. Miss Gilliatt and I are ships that pass each other in the night every six months. It is a pleasure to salute her on this crossing."

Like many other critics, Pauline had ascribed much of the film's artistic success to Gilliatt, a fact that infuriated John Schlesinger. It may well have been an example of her tendency, as William Friedkin described it, to "mistake the film for the filmmaker. If she hated the filmmaker, there was nothing he or she could do." Despite Pauline's generosity in print, Gilliatt's success with *Sunday Bloody Sunday*—she would receive an Academy Award nomination and win the New York Film Critics Circle award for her script—was bound to aggravate Pauline's competitive streak. There were already numerous offers coming in for her to work on a film script, or to serve as a script doctor, but for the moment, she turned them all down. At this point she felt that she could be more of a positive force by staying at *The New Yorker*. Besides, the run of films was beginning to prove enormously exciting—so much so that she could scarcely wait to sit down at her drafting table and get to work.

In October, Columbia released a film made under the aegis of BBS Productions, one of the most enterprising constellations of New Hollywood talent and the company responsible for *Easy Rider* and *Five Easy Pieces*. *The Last Picture Show* was not part of the '70s New Wave, however. Directed by Peter Bogdanovich, it was a piece of traditional narrative about a group of frustrated, confused people—both young and middle-aged—in a dying West Texas town in the early 1950s. It was based on a book by Larry McMurtry, whose fictional Anarene had been inspired by his hometown of Archer City, where the picture was shot. Bogdanovich had definite ideas about the Texas he wanted to depict onscreen. McMurtry was also the author of *Hud*, and Bogdanovich was concerned that there not be a strong visual link between the two films. He objected to *Hud*'s "bland, barren, gray look which is the cliché version of Texas: a big, empty country. That's not what it is at all—Texas is tortured, savage, cruel and broken."

Bogdanovich made the decision to shoot *The Last Picture Show* in black and white—the first major production since 1967's *In Cold Blood* not to be filmed in color. "It's a dismal town," said Bogdanovich, "but I know damn well that in color it would look pretty, no matter how dismal." The film avoided the distracting attitude and pose of hyperrealism—yet it offered an achingly recognizable and resonant slice of life, thanks in large part to Bogdanovich's superb instinct for casting.

Although he had initially toyed with using old-time stars such as James Stewart and Dorothy Malone, he opted for less familiar faces as a means of achieving authenticity: Timothy Bottoms and Jeff Bridges as the high school seniors Sonny and Duane, best friends who end a losing football season with the painful awareness that there will never be another one; Cybill Shepherd in her screen debut as Jacy, the teenaged tease who works her wiles on both boys; Ellen Burstyn as Lois, Jacy's restless, still-beautiful mother; Ben Johnson as Sam the Lion, the town's respected elder statesman; and Cloris Leachman as Ruth, the football coach's depressed and lonely wife. Only Eileen Brennan, as Genevieve, the good-hearted waitress at Sam's café, seemed a bit actressy, as if she'd seen too many Claire Trevor movies.

*The Last Picture Show* received some of the year's most extraordinary press. Andrew Sarris, still smarting over the damage that "Raising Kane" had done to Welles, wrote: "I have visions of Pauline Kael in the year 2001 setting out to prove that Bogdanovich was not the actual auteur of *The Last Picture Show*, but was in fact deeply indebted to Larry McMurtry's novel and to an entire school of Texas novelists."

Pauline's own review of *The Last Picture Show* was positive, yet oddly measured, with more than a suggestion of the backhanded compliment. She was skittish about the possibility that the film—which she correctly predicted would be both a popular and critical success—would play into the hands of conservative filmgoers: that its traditional storytelling style would "turn into a bludgeon to beat other filmmakers with." She praised the film for not taking the direction of "worked-up, raunchy melodrama about tangled lives but, rather, of something closer to common experience." The movie never was "exploitative of human passions and miseries"; instead, it was "a lovingly exact history of American small-town life." She said that the story, with what she took to be its resonances of the *Peyton Place* TV series, was "perhaps what TV soap opera would be if it were more honest—if it looked at ordinary experience in a non-exploitative way, if it had observation and humor. It is perhaps an *ideal* TV show."

She had reservations about the way movies were used in the picture-show sequences. Bogdanovich had used *Father of the Bride*, starring the ravishing young Elizabeth Taylor, for an early sequence that showed Sonny's dissatisfaction with his ill-tempered girlfriend (marvelously played by Sharon Taggart). For the end, when the picture show closes, Bogdanovich chose a clip from a film by one of his idols, Howard Hawks—*Red River*. It was the final "yee-haw" cattle-drive sequence, and he selected it to contrast the mythic lives of the cowboys with the small, aimless lives of those few in the audience on the picture show's closing night.

Pauline found the contrast too obvious and broad. She could remember the endless run-of-the-mill product ground out by the studios in the late '40s and early '50s—films barely more satisfying than a cheap TV episode—and pointed out that even these dismal movies provided bored people with a form of escapism. "For several decades," she wrote, "the generally tawdry films we saw week after week contributed to our national identity—such as it was." Seeing bad movies week in and week out and "still feeling that they represented something preferable to your own existence" was "part of the truth of American experience." She had a point: It wasn't first-class films such as *Father of the Bride* and *Red River* that were representative of the weekly moviegoing experience as much as it was forgettable B pictures.

Bogdanovich, however, felt that Pauline's idea couldn't possibly work in cinematic terms. "Pauline misses the point," he said nearly forty years after her review of *The Last Picture Show* appeared. "We used *Red River* because of the cattle drive—it shows you that the days of that kind of adventure and exuberance and excitement are gone—compared to what we've been seeing from the movie." (It's worth noting that in McMurtry's novel, the movie was *The Kid from Texas*, a B picture with Audie Murphy and Gale Storm. Sonny and Duane, remembering all their date nights at the picture show, are bored with it and walk out on it. McMurtry wrote, "It would have taken *Winchester '73* or *Red River* or some big movie to have crowded out the memories the boys kept having.")

In the same column in which she reviewed *The Last Picture Show*, Pauline covered Dennis Hopper's new work with a perilously similar title: *The Last Movie*, which investigated the impact of a film crew on a band of natives in the Peruvian Andes. She admitted it was a sloppy mess, but she couldn't help observing, "If Bogdanovich replaces Hopper as the hero of the industry—if, to the industry, he becomes the new hot director that everyone should imitate—the most talented moviemakers may be in trouble. Even Nixon could like *The Last Picture Show*." (Sometime later, when Bogdanovich met Richard Nixon, "I told him that Pauline had said it was a picture that even Richard Nixon would like. He slapped his thigh and said, 'I don't know if that's a compliment or not.' Then he said, '*The Last Picture Show*? Black-and-white? Texas? I *did* like that!'")

Although Pauline was careful not to reveal too much of herself directly in her reviews, it had become possible for those who read her closely to get a sense of her position on various political issues—as was the case with her quip about Nixon's liking *The Last Picture Show*. At around this time she also commented that she couldn't understand how Nixon had gotten elected, because she didn't know a single person who voted for him. The remark circulated widely in conservative circles, something that delighted Pauline no end.

It was also possible from reading some of her reviews to discern where she stood in relation to the women's movement—namely, that she kept a healthy distance from it. The bold choices she had made in her personal life—having Gina out of wedlock, doggedly pursuing her chosen profession even in the years when it brought her little income, refusing to stand in Edward Landberg's shadow or to bend to William Shawn—suggested that she had been living her own version of a feminist ideal. She, of course, would never have characterized it that way: feminism reeked too much of dogma for her to be able to take it seriously and join the movement in any specific, organized way. The feminist sensibility, she feared, was a trap that shackled thinking and rendered one unable to come up with fresh and invigorating opinions. Also, she found many of the feminists she knew to have a certain humorlessness—always a cardinal sin. Pauline's idea of being a feminist was to live her life rather like a Jean Arthur career woman: proving herself by doing her work better than any man, but always maintaining a sense of humor about herself.

"I thought Pauline was deaf to feminism," observed Karen Durbin, who worked with her at *The New Yorker* in the early '70s before becoming a film critic. "Not hostile. It just wasn't something she could hear. If she had been younger, my generation, I'm convinced she would have been a feminist firebrand. But as it was, she fought the fight by herself. It seemed to me one of the key insights of women's liberation was the moment when I thought, 'We don't have permission.' That's what we're fighting for. The pure nerve of the way Pauline would say what she thought and not mince anything—it must have been God's own battle for her to create that permission for herself. And she lived by it. But that doesn't mean that there wasn't underneath that permission a tremulous place—'Am I getting away with this?'"

Pauline's review of one of the year's great critical and commercial successes, *The French Connection*, gave clear indications about how she felt living in New York City at the time. More and more films were being shot there, a development that had been actively sought by Mayor John V. Lindsay. But particularly since the success of *Midnight Cowboy*, filmmakers delighted in presenting the starkest, seamiest views of the city ever to wind up on film. The isolation of Tina Balser (Carrie Snodgress) in *Diary of a Mad Housewife*, lost in a maze of her husband's ambition; Jane Fonda as Bree Daniels, the high-priced call girl in *Klute*, racing to get into her apartment because she knows someone is watching her; the junkie (Al Pacino) who says that death is "the best high of all" in *The Panic in Needle Park*; the squalid apartments of Barbra Streisand and George Segal in *The Owl and the Pussycat*—all of it showed New York as a place of bare trees and gray winter skies, where the inhabitants were simply caught up in the frenzy of trying to survive. Pauline continued to struggle with her own feelings of hostility toward the city, where she thought "everyone seems to be dressed for a mad ball." She volunteered to her readers, "It is literally true that when you live in New York, you no longer believe that the garbage will ever be gone from the streets or that life will ever be sane and orderly."

The New York audience fascinated her, because she felt that a large sector of it was so attuned to the explosive rhythm of the city that they demanded to see it reflected on the screen. *The French Connection* was a fact-based account of one of the great narcotics busts in the history of the New York Police Department. The movies were now giving this audience what it wanted: violent, high-tension thrillers and action films geared to this crazed element in the audience, movies that were "often irrational and horrifying brutal."

While other critics reviewed *The French Connection* simply as a virtuoso piece of filmmaking, the embodiment of what would soon become the cliché "high-octane thriller," Pauline insisted on examining it in the context of the realities of contemporary New York, and of the audience that the city's seemingly endless decline had helped to create. She acknowledged that the film was "extraordinarily well made," yet she seemed no more able to share any genuine enthusiasm for *The French Connection* than she had for *The Last Picture Show*, because of what she thought the movie represented: "what we once feared mass entertainment might become: jolts for jocks. There's nothing in the movie that you enjoy thinking over afterward. . . ."

She also stepped apart from the crowd with her review of the film version of the spectacular Broadway hit musical *Fiddler on the Roof.* Despite the handsomeness and vigor of its big-screen translation, *Fiddler* received very mixed notices. Because of Pauline's deep love of musicals, she often felt betrayed by what happened to them once they were transferred to the screen, but *Fiddler on the Roof* surprised her. After acknowledging that the musical comedy was "primarily an American Jewish contribution" to the theater, she called it "probably the only successful attempt to use this theatrical form on the subject of its own sources—that is on the heritage that the Jewish immigrants brought to this country." She thought part of the reason the film worked well was because it was directed by someone she was careful to point out was a gentile, Norman Jewison. She implied that he avoided the pitfalls a Jewish director might have fallen into by laying on the ethnic sentiment too thick. Jewison presented "the Jews as an oppressed people—no better, no worse than others," side-stepping the "self-hatred and self-infatuation that corrupts so much Jewish comedy." Her review demonstrated, once again, her remarkably unsentimental attitude toward her own Jewish heritage:

> Younger members of the audience—particularly if they are Jewish—may be put off by the movie if their parents and grandparents have gone on believing in a special status with God long after the oppression was over, and have tried to prop up their authority over their children with boring stories about early toil and hardship. . . . Too many people have *used* their early suffering as a platitudinous weapon and so have made it all seem fake. And I suppose that *Fiddler on the Roof* has been such a phenomenal stage success partly because it can be used in this same self-congratulatory way—as a public certificate of past suffering.

Her review moved Norman Jewison to write to her: "Thank you for your in *depth* critique. . . . As Sholem Aleichem would simply say—(in his square way)—go in peace—and God be with you!"

One of Pauline's pet theories was that a director's finest work was nearly always done early on; she believed that as most directors aged and became wealthier and more famous, they became concerned with making grander and grander artistic statements, at which point they usually fell flat. And no director of the time was more concerned with the Big Idea than Stanley Kubrick, whose new film, *A Clockwork Orange*, opened at the end of 1971.

Based on the 1962 novel by Anthony Burgess, *A Clockwork Orange* was set in the not-too-distant future, where Britain has degenerated into a completely mechanized, brutal, soulless society. The perfect representative of this moral vacuum is the character Alex (Malcolm McDowell), a callous teenaged punk and head of his "droogs," a gang that steals, tortures, and rapes just for the sheer pleasure of it. Eventually he is arrested and undergoes a brainwashing that neutralizes him, robbing him of his individuality. It was the type of grandiose topic with all the attendant portentousness that typically made Pauline wince. Prior to the film's release, Kubrick held forth on the film's significance in numerous interviews. He told *The New York Times* that Alex symbolized "man in his natural state, the way he would be if society did not impose its 'civilizing' process upon him. What we respond to subconsciously is Alex's guiltless sense of freedom to kill and rape, and to be our savage natural selves, and it is in this glimpse of the true nature of man that the power of the story derives."

Many in the press felt that Kubrick had turned out a genuinely great film, but there were a few dissenters: Richard Schickel disliked the fact that Alex had been "directed toward cuteness at every opportunity," and that his victims were all malignant and grotesque, resulting in "a viciously rigged game." Andrew Sarris predicted that his colleagues in the New York Film Critics Circle and National Society of Film Critics would select *A Clockwork Orange* as the year's best picture, adding "If such a catastrophe has indeed occurred, I disclaim all responsibility."

Pauline believed she had a clear-eyed view of Kubrick's intentions. At the end of the picture, when Alex's former victims turn on him and he reverts to his old, corrupt self, she grasped that Kubrick intended it as "a victory in which we share . . . the movie becomes a vindication of Alex, saying that the punk was a free human being and only the good Alex was a robot." She was deeply disturbed by Kubrick's grotesque portrayal of the victims, which she found "symptomatic of a new attitude in movies. This attitude says there's no moral difference. Stanley Kubrick has assumed the deformed, self-righteous perspective of a vicious young punk who says, 'Everything's rotten. Why shouldn't I do what I want? They're worse than I am.' In the new mood . . . people want to believe the hyperbolic worst, want to believe in the degradation of the victims—that they are dupes and phonies and weaklings. I can't accept that Kubrick is merely reflecting this post-assassination, post-Manson mood. I think he's catering to it. I think he wants to dig it."

While she made it clear that she in no way advocated censorship, she felt that she and her colleagues had to speak out against the "corrupt" morality that so many directors were attempting to force-feed the gullible public:

At the movies, we are gradually being conditioned to accept violence as a sensual pleasure. The directors used to say they were showing us its real face and how ugly it was in order to sensitize us to its horrors. You don't have to be very keen to see that they are now in fact desensitizing us. They are saying that everyone is brutal, and the heroes must be as brutal as the villains or they turn into fools. . . . There seems to be an assumption that if you're offended by movie brutality, you are somehow playing into the hands of the people who want censorship. . . . Actually, those who believe in censorship are primarily concerned with sex, and they generally worry about violence only when it's eroticized. This means that practically no one raises the issue of the possible cumulative effects of movie brutality. Yet surely, when night after night atrocities are served up to us as entertainment, it's worth some anxiety. We become clock-work oranges if we accept all this pop culture without asking what's in it. How can people go on talking about the dazzling brilliance of movies and not notice that the directors are sucking up to the thugs in the audience?

Her impassioned argument, however, fell mostly on deaf ears: *A Clockwork Orange* became an immense success, one of the year's most widely discussed films.

Pauline's concern about audiences' being turned on by violence were nothing if not timely: In the weeks that followed the release of *A Clockwork Orange*, a number of extremely brutal films opened in theaters, including *Dirty Harry*, which marked Clint Eastwood's first appearance as the San Francisco police inspector Harry Callahan. (Pauline would have a lifelong antipathy toward Eastwood, whom she considered minimally talented and absurdly macho.) *Dirty Harry* took as its theme the corruption and unfairness of a legal system that rewards criminals by getting them off on technicalities: Pauline found it a "right-wing fantasy" about the police being "helplessly emasculated by unrealistic liberals."

But the film of the season that caused her the greatest apprehension was made by a director whose work she admired—Sam Peckinpah. She regretted that she had not been able to write about *The Wild Bunch*, Peckinpah's 1969 drama about a gang of over-the-hill outlaws reuniting for a final spree, but the film had made an indelible impression on her by undermining any number of clichés of the Western genre. In Peckinpah's west, innocent women and children were inevitably slaughtered, as those in the audience begged silently for it not to happen. *The Wild Bunch* had a wealth of unforgettable images—the outlaws passing a whiskey bottle back and forth as if it's a holy chalice; brilliant close-ups, such as the army officer averting his eyes as two parts of a train collide; and Pauline's favorite, the blowing up of a bridge, with army horses and riders "falling to the water in an instant extended to eternity." She understood that Peckinpah's unflinching presentation of violence had a positive purpose: to show how truly horrible war and destruction could be, and the toll that they took on the people caught up in them. At the time of the picture's release, she spoke of his aim to "take the façade of movie violence and open it up, get people involved . . . and then twist it so that it's not fun anymore, just a wave of sickness in the gut." Her difficulty with *The Wild Bunch* was that she felt Peckinpah had "got so wound up in the aesthetics of violence that what had begun as a realistic treatment became instead an almost abstract fantasy on violence; the bloody deaths repeated so often and so exquisitely, became numbingly remote."

Peckinpah was provocative and belligerent and a prodigious drinker, and Pauline enjoyed spending time with him, hashing out the imbecilities of the movie industry over bottles of whiskey. She delighted in their friendship and frequently sent him stories or novels she thought he might want to adapt for the screen. One was Christina Stead's *The Man Who Loved Children*; Peckinpah got drunk and read it one night and pronounced it so "profoundly depressing, it makes *The Wild Bunch* look like early Saroyan." She also championed him as director of the screen version of James Dickey's *Deliverance*, which eventually went to John Boorman. Peckinpah became one of Pauline's pet "lost boys"—the ones she believed to be mistreated by the studio executives— and he in turn courted her assiduously, sending her roses whenever she paid a visit to Los Angeles.

Peckinpah's latest was *Straw Dogs*, and Pauline struggled with it more than she had with any other film of the season. With a script by Peckinpah and David Z. Goodman, based on Gordon Williams's novel *Siege at Trencher's Farm*, *Straw Dogs* was a study of what happens when a man who has purposely distanced himself from conflict is forced to confront his enemies and to defend his home and family—to the death. In the film's long, terrifying finale, the pacifist hero (Dustin Hoffman) is forced to use his gifts for precise, strategic thinking to kill the men laying siege to his household, one by one. The final siege sequence lasted for nearly thirty minutes, and while many in the audience found the tension and the violence all but unbearable, they were placed in the inevitable position of cheering the death of each of the thugs.

The film's point of view was troubling both to viewers and, particularly, to the critics who were ever on the lookout for a higher sense of purpose in filmmaking. Peckinpah regarded all such attitudinizing with unconcealed contempt. "You can't make violence real to audiences today without rubbing their noses in it," he told William Murray for *Playboy*. "We watch our wars and see our men die, really die, every day on television, but it doesn't seem real. We don't believe those are real people dying on the screen. We've been anesthetized by the media. What I do is show people what it's really like—not by showing it so much as by heightening it, stylizing it."

There is a heavy, somber, even somewhat cautious tone in Pauline's review of *Straw Dogs* that is quite uncharacteristic of her work: Reading it, one gets the sense that writing it did not come easily. In the end she was forced to conclude that one of her favorite filmmakers had created a compelling but deeply offensive machismo fantasy, in which the hero had to become a killer in order to feel like a real man. "The vision of *Straw Dogs* is narrow and puny," Pauline wrote, "as obsessions with masculinity so often are." She believed that *Straw Dogs* revealed that Peckinpah's "intuitions as a director are infinitely superior to his thinking." Perhaps most of all, she was insulted by the "stale anti-intellectualism" of the hero's being portrayed as weak and cowardly, unable to stay in the United States and deal with the violent changes that were splitting the country asunder.

She was impressed by the staging of the scene in which the hero's wife (Susan George) is raped, and pronounced it "one of the few truly erotic sequences on film." To praise such material in aesthetic terms—she wrote that "the punches that subdue the wife have the exquisite languor of slightly slowed-down motion"—was an exceptionally bold move for a female critic to make in 1972, near the height of the women's movement. But she qualified her praise: "The rape has heat to it—there can be little doubt of that—but what goes into that heat is the old male barroom attitude: we can see that she's asking for it, she's begging for it, that her every no means yes." In an essay on *A Clockwork Orange* in *The New York Times*, Fred M. Hechinger had worried that "The thesis that man is irretrievably bad and corrupt is the essence of fascism." Now Pauline picked up the idea and took it in a different direction: "What I am saying, I fear, is that Sam Peckinpah, who is an artist, has, with *Straw Dogs*, made the first American film that is a fascist work of art."

It was a stunning assertion, and it certainly stunned Peckinpah that Pauline had taken the film's portrayal of Amy to be a kind of statement about the nature of women, as he assumed such regimented thinking to be beneath her. "Fascist, God how I hate that word," he wrote to Pauline a year after her review appeared, "but I suppose every director in his way is a fascist. *Straw Dogs* was about a bad marriage and the subtle incitement of violence by [the protagonist]. It's a funny thing, but I know that couple, which means knowledge has nothing to do with art. As I evidently failed. In a way I made it for you . . . with all the integrity I could, and missed the boat." In his *Playboy* interview, he used stronger words. "Doesn't Kael know *anything* about sex? Dominating and being dominated: the fantasy, too, of being taken by force is certainly one way people make love. . . . I like Kael; she's a feisty little gal and I enjoy drinking with her—which I've done on occasion—but here she's cracking walnuts with her ass."

The movie season, already the most stimulating she had experienced since coming to *The New Yorker*, was about to come to a triumphant close. Despite her scorn for elephantine productions such as *Camelot* and *Paint Your Wagon*, Pauline hoped the screen musical could be revived in some new and invigorating way. Keeping true to the general tenor of her tastes, she believed the musical to be at its greatest when it was tough and sassy, not when it drowned in sentiment. She could barely contain her excitement once she had seen *Cabaret*, Bob Fosse's tough, fearless screen version of the John Kander–Fred Ebb stage hit. Given its source material—Christopher Isherwood's *Goodbye to Berlin* stories, which traced the fate of a disparate group of characters during the rise of Nazism—*Cabaret* was a welcome departure from the world of singing nuns and dancing street gangs that Pauline had come to loathe:

> *Cabaret* is a great movie musical, made, miraculously, without compromise. It's miraculous because the material is hard and unsentimental, and until now there has never been a diamond-hard big American movie musical. The people must have said something like 'Let's do it right— let's use the right people, let's not wreck it the way *Pal Joey* was wrecked, and *The Boys from Syracuse* and *Guys and Dolls* and *Gypsy* and *Sweet Charity* and all the rest. Maybe it won't work at the box office, maybe the movie moguls have basically been shrewd when they insisted on all the softening and spoiling and the big names in the leads, but let's do it right for once anyway.

Pauline loved the score, with its "distinctive, acrid flavor—a taste of death on the tongue." And she loved the fact that the songs didn't spring "organically" from the story: Nearly all of the musical numbers in *Cabaret* took place where they made most sense to take place—on the stage of the cabaret itself.

Fosse had given the audience a bracing view of a society desperately trying to maintain a party atmosphere while ignoring what was happening around them. Not only did he never relax his vision; more surprisingly, he never let it get away from him—never allowed it to become labored and heavy-handed or moralistic. "The grotesque amorality in *Cabaret* is frightening," Pauline wrote, "not because it's weak but because it's intensely, obscenely alive." Most of all, she saw *Cabaret* as glorious evidence of the courage of its filmmaker's convictions, proving that "you can create a new organic whole by style and imagination—if you have enough faith in the audience to do it right."

Only a few weeks after *Cabaret*'s release, *The Godfather* opened and over-shadowed all of the year's other outstanding films. It changed the fortunes of everyone connected with it: most of all, those of its director and co-screenwriter, Francis Ford Coppola; its star, Marlon Brando; and its dynamic young cast members James Caan, Al Pacino, and Robert Duvall. Based on the bestselling novel by Mario Puzo, its depiction of the dark side of New York Italian–American life took the world by storm. More important, as far as Hollywood was concerned, it launched the careers of a prodigiously gifted group of Italian–American directors and actors.

In recent years most of the pictures that had taken on organized crime as a subject hadn't done well, and *The Godfather*'s producer, Robert Evans, felt it was because too many of the characters had come off as walking Italian movie clichés: The audience simply couldn't believe in them. He wanted the brand of realism that he felt only an Italian American could bring to the project, and he engaged Francis Ford Coppola, a gifted young filmmaker who had yet to come up with a hit, to direct. It was Coppola who believed that *The Godfather* should be less of a standard organized crime thriller than an incisive look at the inner workings and dynamics of the Corleone family.

No critic delighted more in its success than Pauline. The list of all-time box-office grosses had never been a badge of honor where she was concerned, but in her review, she celebrated her theory that "the best popular movies come out of a merger of commerce and art." She admired the fact that Coppola had "stayed very close to the book's greased-lightning sensationalism and yet has made a movie with the spaciousness and strength that popular novels such as Dickens's used to have." Pauline found Coppola's work "tenaciously intelligent . . . It's amazing how encompassing the view seems to be—what a sense you get of a broad historical perspective, considering that the span is only from 1945 to the mid-fifties." As for Brando, she considered that his acting had "mellowed in recent years; it is less immediately exciting than it used to be, because there's not the sudden, violent discharge of emotion." To convey fully the impact of his performance, she displayed her own imaginative powers, writing like a fiction writer: Brando reminded her of one of "those old men who carry never-ending grudges and ancient hatreds inside a frail frame, those monsters who remember minute details of old business deals when they can no longer tie their shoelaces."

Best of all, Coppola had been true to his fictional story while adeptly catching the current mood of the country: He had done what so many other heavy-handed directors had been attempting to do and failing. "Organized crime is not a rejection of Americanism," Pauline wrote, "it's what we fear Americanism to be. It's our nightmare of the American system. When 'Americanism' was a form of cheerful, bland official optimism, the gangster used to be destroyed at the end of the movie and our feelings resolved. Now the mood of the whole country has darkened, guilty; nothing is resolved at the end of *The Godfather*, because the family business goes on. . . . *The Godfather* is popular melodrama, but it expresses a new tragic realism."

Pauline's mid-March review of Marcel Ophuls's *The Sorrow and the Pity*, a documentary about the collaboration of France's Vichy government with the Nazis—"one of the most intricately balanced moral dilemmas imaginable"—was her final review of the season, and never before had she found it so difficult to step away from her job for six months. Films had become so amazingly present and alive with the work of so many superb craftsmen (Francis Ford Coppola, Bernardo Bertolucci, Sam Peckinpah) and so many artists capable of revitalizing genres that had long ossified (Robert Altman, Bob Fosse). The confluence of talent and activity exhilarated her so much that she couldn't stop talking about it; often, she told people that she had the best job she could possibly have found.

One of the things that thrilled her most was that this explosion of creativity was being born out of a specific, unique time in history. The subjects and attitudes of current films were providing a kind of living journal of the times; a legitimate movement was afoot, with filmmakers responding to the world around them and putting their visions up there on the screen in new and exciting ways. Best of all, the audiences were with them. The dialogue between screen and audience that Pauline had always envisioned was rising to glorious heights. Later she would compare this period of filmmaking with the great flowering of American writing in the nineteenth century, with the best of the current crop of directors and screenwriters reinvigorating their art form just as Melville, Hawthorne, Emerson, and Whitman had theirs.

"Inexplicably," she wrote in that season-ending column in March 1972, "despite everything—the suicidal practices of the film industry, the defeat of many people of talent, the financial squeeze here and abroad—this has been a legendary period in movies. . . . A reviewer could hardly ask for more from any art, high or popular."

The luckiest people who work in the arts are those who find themselves in just the right place during the perfect confluence of creative activity and an eager, inquisitive public. Pauline was in the vortex. She had reached the apex of her moviegoing life, and she wanted it to go on forever.

# CHAPTER FIFTEEN

After winding up her reviewing at *The New Yorker* in March 1972, Pauline once again plunged into a hectic schedule on the lecture circuit. She always had mixed feelings about this part of the year. Lecture appearances provided her with much-needed income, and she relished the chance to speak with young people about what they responded to in the movies; many of the conversations she had with college students on the road provided her with important material for her *New Yorker* pieces. But she disliked having to associate with faculty members and attending the English Department party that inevitably followed her lecture appearances. She considered most of the English and film studies professors she encountered to be dull, pompous, jealous of her position in the world, or all three. Still, if academia remained generally unattractive to her, she was quite attractive to academia and regularly received offers to become a visiting or regents professor—one example of many being the unsuccessful attempts of the Berkeley professor David Littlejohn to persuade her to join the School of Journalism faculty. She did, however, agree to serve as a member of the Educational Advisory Board of the John Simon Guggenheim Memorial Foundation, a post that allowed her to use her influence to help artists she considered deserving and underfunded.

When she wasn't on the road, she was occupied with the ongoing process of fixing up the house in Great Barrington. She told friends that she dreamed of one day living there full-time, though she could not yet see how such a thing would be feasible in practical terms, given the intensity of her schedule at *The New Yorker* and the necessity of spending so much time in Manhattan. She delighted in telling people what a wonderful job Gina was doing in getting the house into shape—from overseeing repair work to choosing a beautiful selection of soft colors for the walls. One of the things Pauline loved most about the house was its spacious kitchen—a luxury after the cramped quarters in New York. It was a classic country kitchen, with old 1950s appliances and a big, generous sink, and Pauline loved spending time in it, cooking for her friends.

There was an unceasing flow of fan mail, which she was diligent about answering. A brief, casual note of appreciation about something she had written in *The New Yorker* usually got a polite reply written on a postcard, but the more in-depth and thoughtful letters she took more time with; sometimes she even surprised her devoted readers by telephoning to thank them for their words, even if they were uncomplimentary. Sometimes lasting friendships were born out of her correspondence with readers.

One person who wrote to her in the early 1970s was a professor of English literature at the Oregon College of Education, Erhard Dortmund, with whom Pauline would maintain a steady and lively correspondence for thirty years. As with many who came into her orbit, she took an interest in Dortmund's career and encouraged him to submit articles to *The Atlantic Monthly*. Dortmund recalled their friendship as an "improbable one. She was so smart and intuitive and loved all of life's juices . . . she worshipped people with vitality and people with guts and zaniness. She loved zany things. I'm just the opposite. I'm inhibited and not bold, but luckily full of curiosity. At some level, we found common ground. We had similar vibes about many things."

As Gina often pointed out, Pauline liked to be surrounded by people whose feelings about the arts and politics were close to her own. She often told friends that she found it difficult to form a close bond with someone who disagreed with her about more than three movies. More to the point, she relished the company of people who had zest and intensity and appetite for movies, art, music, literature, current events. She had no need to dominate the conversation in a group of people—she found such behavior boorish. Her social self was very much like her moviegoing self: She loved being a spectator. The writer James Wolcott, who became friends with her in the mid-1970s, observed, "She would throw a little dart in, but it was only when someone was going way overboard about something. She never dressed anybody down. She liked being around people who were entertaining."

Pauline was already developing a circle of movie-loving friends, many of them younger critics in whose careers she took an interest. They would meet at screenings and then go out for drinks or dinner afterward, constituting their own floating version of the Algonquin Round Table. But there was a crucial difference: The Algonquin Round Table had been made up of a group of peers; Pauline's group resembled a Renaissance court, where people tended to seek her approval by agreeing with her about the film they'd just seen, or trying to move to the head-of-class position by outdoing each other with sharp, barbed comments.

It was not strictly true that the way to Pauline's heart was through slavish agreement. She could be patient with her acolytes' worship of her, but if it crossed the line into sycophancy, she could distance herself very quickly. Sometimes those who had considered themselves to be rising through the ranks of her inner circle were stunned to find themselves suddenly frozen out. Joe Morgenstern, for one, found the competitiveness and backbiting of Pauline's acolytes repellent: "Sometimes I would just sit there silent as a stone, listening to everybody dish everybody. It was not part of my knowledge, my world, or my inclination. And I thought it was really unseemly. I had a sense that she needed the idolatry, and that kind of nastiness on the part of the courtiers was just an inevitable part of it."

On her return to *The New Yorker* she continued to chafe under the six-month reviewing schedule. Given the success of her books and her ever-growing popularity on the lecture circuit, she rightly believed that she had eclipsed Penelope Gilliatt in importance, *Sunday Bloody Sunday* notwithstanding. She railed to friends about Gilliatt's having missed the point of so many of the movies she reviewed in her spring-summer schedule, and she detested the character of the little old lady that Gilliatt invented in her columns—a kind of surrogate through whom she filtered her own view of the movie. Still, William Shawn remained fiercely loyal to Gilliatt and showed no interest in bringing Pauline on year-round.

Pauline, who prided herself on her ability to size people up, continued to be baffled by Shawn. He loved television comedians—George Jessel was a particular favorite—and he was an avid amateur jazz pianist, frequently performing at the parties he and his wife gave at their apartment. He also was fascinated by everything that was going on in the movies. But Pauline found it all but impossible to reconcile this fun-loving side of Shawn with the repressed, schoolmasterish behavior she saw him exhibit around the office. Her battles with Shawn and the other editors over language choices continued on a regular basis—and sometimes her arguments unleashed themselves in streams of profanity. "She thought that the editorial department should be doing more to establish some kind of line of succession for Shawn," recalled Hoyt Spelman, who worked in the magazine's editorial and marketing departments for years. "She would pick up the phone and talk to me about it." But some of Pauline's friends thought she was churlish to complain about her boss so much. After all, she had the best film-reviewing gig in the world, and a luxury virtually no other critic had: unlimited space.

Pauline generally maintained a cordial presence around *The New Yorker* offices, though she was dismissive of many in the old guard, such as Lillian Ross, whom Joe Morgenstern remembered Pauline characterizing as a "fossil." But she could be exceptionally kind to those she liked—and, as always, she was never a snob about rank. "Pauline was one of the women at *The New Yorker* who paid attention to the female underlings and was friendly to us," remembered Karen Durbin. "We were *very* aware of the women who ignored us or were slightly hostile."

Surprisingly, Pauline took a keen interest in the magazine's business affairs, despite its policy of complete separation of editorial and advertising matters. (The departments were on separate floors, and fraternization between the two was discouraged.) She was amused by the policy of turning down advertising for things such as ladies' lingerie and cigarettes. Spelman often made trips to advertisers to try to clarify *The New Yorker*'s editorial stance, and from the early '70s Pauline was frequently tapped to be the main speaker at advertising and promotion conferences on the West Coast. She was always happy to do it, because she felt the magazine had become far too insular and she wanted to help bring it to a wider audience.

For years Pauline had deplored the lack of first-class movies about the black experience. In "Trash, Art and the Movies," she had claimed that the main distinction of the film version of Lorraine Hansberry's almost universally admired play *A Raisin in the Sun* was that it taught us "that a Negro family can be as dreary as a white family." So she was thrilled to kick off her *New Yorker* stint in the fall of 1972 with a review of *Sounder*, Martin Ritt's drama about the near-collapse of a family of black sharecroppers during the Depression after the father is jailed for stealing food. She had expected a wearisome tribute to poor people that wore its good intentions on its sleeve; instead, she wrote, Ritt "never pushes a moment too hard or too far—the movie earns every emotion we feel. And I think it will move audiences—move them truly, that is—as few films ever have." Pauline thought that Cicely Tyson, as the farm wife and mother, Rebecca, who must struggle along when her husband is sent to prison, had "the singular good fortune to play the first great black heroine on the screen."

One might have expected many critics to embrace *Sounder*, but Pauline's was one of the most laudatory reviews the movie received. In *The New York Times*, Roger Greenspun found that Ritt seemed "to strive for classical plainness, but to succeed only in being ordinary." Lindsay Patterson, also in the *Times*, boasted that he grew up in a small Louisiana town among black and white sharecroppers, and wrote that *Sounder* bore "no resemblance whatsoever to reality as I observed it, and sometimes lived it, among black sharecroppers." Even Richard Schickel, who admired the film, worried about the reaction of the black audience: "Are they available only for fantasies about machismo-bound private eyes? Can they respond to the story of a black man of another generation for whom rage and militancy were simply not available as responses to injustice?" Despite a soft opening, *Sounder* was a hit, building slowly and steadily and proving especially popular in the new marketing technique of group sales; by January 1973, it would gross $3,251,000 on 115 engagements.

Another smart and important film for the black audience appeared that fall—Sidney J. Furie's *Lady Sings the Blues*, a biography of the great Billie Holiday, starring Diana Ross. Pauline, the inveterate jazz-lover, was riveted, even if she found that the film fell far short of its subject in musical terms: Much as she liked Ross's acting, she thought her shallow pop singing was a pale echo of Holiday's emotionally naked performances. Yet *Lady Sings the Blues* pleased her because it wasn't "heavy and glazed," as so many other singer biographies in the past had been. "Factually it's a fraud, but emotionally it delivers. It has what makes movies work for a mass audience: easy pleasure, tawdry electricity, personality—great quantities of personality." It held her, despite its inability to show what drove Holiday musically—what made singing the most important thing in her life. Pauline felt that the entire project was inflected with a pop sensibility, rather than a jazz one. "Pop music provides immediate emotional gratifications that the subtler and deeper and more lasting pleasures of jazz can't prevail against," she wrote. "Pop drives jazz back underground. And that's what this pop movie does to the career of a great jazz singer." She admitted that she had loved *Lady Sings the Blues*, yet she stressed that she didn't "want Billie Holiday's hard, melancholic sound buried under this avalanche of pop. When you get home, you have to retrieve her at the phonograph; you have to do restoration work on your own past."

As much as Pauline had praised several films of the past two years, as much as she obviously felt they were pointing in a new and intoxicating direction for the cinema, close readers of her column may well have had the sense that these pictures were simply preparation for some ultimate, as yet unknown event in her moviegoing life. Her reviews had began to pulsate with an almost palpable sense of anticipation and vulnerability, as if she were preparing herself for an experience so overpowering that she had never fully been able to imagine it. Having proclaimed that the last year had represented a legendary time for the movies, she now seemed poised for the supreme seduction. And it took place on October 14, 1972, the closing night of the New York Film Festival at Lincoln Center, when she experienced Bernardo Bertolucci's *Last Tango in Paris*.

Bertolucci's film had arrived at the festival accompanied by tremendous word-of-mouth excitement. There had not been the usual special screening for the critics, and the top reviewers in New York were vying for a seat at the final night of the festival. They already knew that *Last Tango in Paris* took on extremely adult and difficult subject matter—the MPAA had given it an X rating—and there was considerable talk that the movie was bound to run into difficulty with the notoriously difficult Italian censors. There was a chance that it might be banned altogether. In *The New Leader*, John Simon stated that the film's distributor, United Artists, had had representatives present at the Lincoln Center showing, driving home the point that if the New York reviews weren't strong enough, the censors might succeed in burying the picture.

With a script by Bertolucci and Franco Arcali, *Last Tango in Paris* told the story of Paul (Marlon Brando), a forty-five-year-old American living in Paris who has reached a critical juncture in his life. He and his wife have run a flea-trap hotel, where the wife often conducted affairs right under Paul's nose, including one with a long-term resident of the hotel. As the film opens, Paul's wife has died—a suicide, though the details are intentionally murky. While perusing a vacant apartment he is thinking of renting, he encounters Jeanne (Maria Schneider), a twenty-year-old Parisian girl who is also looking at the apartment. Their attraction to each other is instantaneous, and they surrender to it with total abandon, having sex in the empty apartment. Paul persuades her that they must not know anything about each other—they must not even reveal their names. Paul rents the place, and for several days they meet to have sex. But it wasn't like the sex that had ever been portrayed on the screen before: Because of the emotional intensity behind it, nothing like it had been seen even in a hardcore porn film. *Last Tango*'s most famous moment—when Paul uses a stick of butter to lubricate his sodomy of Jeanne—was hardly the most shocking thing in the film. "Everything outside this place is bullshit," says Paul, as he presses Jeanne to confront her inner core for the first time. He induces her to stick two fingers up his ass. He tells her that he's going to get a pig to fuck her; that he'll vomit in her face and make her swallow the vomit. "Are you going to do all that for me?" she asks. This dialogue stunned the audience, unaccustomed to seeing and hearing real intimacy between a man and a woman on the screen. (It's possible that the most intimate scenes prior to the ones between Paul and Jeanne had been those featuring Oskar Werner and Simone Signoret in the decidedly G-rated *Ship of Fools*.)

Midway through the picture there is a shattering scene in which Paul rails at the corpse of his wife, laid out in the funeral parlor. He tells her that he could never, ever have discovered the truth about her. She was dishonest with him from the beginning—dirtier than the dirtiest street pig, he tells her. He hopes she rots in hell, because "our marriage was nothing more than a foxhole for you, and all it took for you to get out was a thirty-five-cent razor and a tub full of water." Paul is losing himself in Jeanne, attempting to find the truth through erotic means. "Listen, you dumb dodo," he tells her, when she keeps protesting that she's really in love with her young television filmmaker boy-friend (Jean-Pierre Léaud), "all the mysteries that you're ever going to get to know in life are right here."

The scene at the casket was a history-making moment in world cinema. It was doubtful that any screen actor had ever exposed himself so completely and pitilessly as Brando did in that scene; it made his very fine work in *The Godfather* look like child's play—a harmless exercise.

When the lights came on after *Last Tango in Paris* at the New York Film Festival screening, Pauline was almost speechless. Her friend George Malko, who accompanied her to it, recalled her as being "drenched"—unable even to go out for a drink with him to discuss it afterward. Pauline recalled that there was very little chatter among the critics at the party following the screening; most people seemed to be in a state of shock.

Most of the critics planned to wait to review *Last Tango* until it had opened in Italy and then officially in New York in January. But Pauline could not wait; she retired to her desk at the Turin and wrote her lengthy review as if in one great gasp. Her review *had* to be a masterpiece—it was, as far as she was concerned, the most important review she had ever written. Such a risky piece of filmmaking demanded the riskiest piece of criticism she could muster.

The intensity of her response worked both for and against her, winning her a deeper level of loyalty from her *New Yorker* readers who were swept along by her passion for the film, yet ultimately alienating those who felt she had simply overpraised it. Perhaps not even William Shawn was prepared for her opening:

> Bernardo Bertolucci's *Last Tango in Paris* was presented for the first time on the closing night of the New York Film Festival, October 14, 1972; that date should become a landmark in movie history comparable to May 29, 1913—the night *Le Sacre du Printemps* was first performed—in music history. There was no riot, and no one threw anything at the screen, but I think it's fair to say that the audience was in a state of shock,

because *Last Tango in Paris* has the same kind of hypnotic excitement as the *Sacre*, the same primitive force, and the same thrusting, jabbing eroticism. The movie breakthrough has finally come.

The strange, mysterious relationship of sex to intimacy—and the ways in which the two simultaneously feed and contradict each other—was one of the most powerful themes in *Last Tango*, and it was one that Pauline responded to with her whole being. She had a deep respect for the nature of genuine sexual bliss, the eagerness to engage, however fleetingly, in complete surrender to another. As she sat in the darkness at Lincoln Center, dazzled by what was unfolding on the screen, she knew she was witnessing a revolutionary step in the portrayal of human emotions, and that it would be pointless to write about the film with anything less than total abandon.

Brando's performance stunned her. In her review she called up her memory of seeing him on Broadway in *Truckline Café* back in 1946—a performance so visceral that she had thought he was "having a seizure onstage." His work in *Last Tango* was the most revealing work she had ever seen an actor do onscreen. His performance as Paul was "a study of the aggression in masculine sexuality, and how the physical strength of men lends credence to the insanity that grows out of it gives the film a larger, tragic dignity. If Brando knows this hell, why should we pretend we don't?"

She worried that *Last Tango* would be misunderstood, feared, dismissed. She worried that "Americans seem to have lost the capacity for being scandalized"— in other words, that audiences had become numb to raw emotion. They needed to grant themselves the freedom to respond wholeheartedly to the movie, that it "might have been easier on some if they could have thrown things," as the audience had on opening night of *Le Sacre du Printemps*, because she felt that "this is a movie people will be arguing about, I think, for as long as there are movies." And in the final paragraph of her review, she bared herself to her readers, much as Paul encouraged Jeanne to bare herself to him: "I've tried to describe the impact of a film that has made the strongest impression on me in almost twenty years of reviewing."

Her concern that *Last Tango* would be misunderstood turned out to be justified. The only other major reviewer who covered its opening at the festival was Vincent Canby, who expressed very mixed feelings about it. Once the film had its official New York opening at the Trans Lux Theater on the East Side of Manhattan, many of the reviews referred, somewhat derisively, to Pauline's rhapsodic enthusiasm. The final tally, according to *The New York*

*Times*, was twelve favorable, five mixed (including Stanley Kauffmann and Rex Reed), and two negative (John Simon and WPIX's Jeffrey Lyons).

Pauline's review of *Last Tango* did more than anything else to date to boost her reputation as the era's wisest and most searching film critic. United Artists took out a hugely expensive two-page advertisement in *The New York Times* in which her review was reprinted in its entirety. But her impassioned advocacy for the film ultimately worked against her in some ways. She had gone farther out on a limb with her review of *Last Tango* than she had ever gone for any film in her life. "Bertolucci and Brando have altered the face of an art form. Who was prepared for that?" she had written, and, like many audacious statements about art, it was to be held up to ridicule for years to come. Her review of *Last Tango* signaled the beginning of a certain degree of skepticism and mistrust on the part of many readers who had previously been devoted to her opinions; in later years, many would point to it as the first of her seriously misguided reviews.

One person unnerved by Pauline's passion for *Last Tango* was William Shawn. While he generously allowed her ample space for her review and did not try to moderate her position, he did not understand her fascination with the sexual behavior that the picture portrayed. He had barely recovered from an incident earlier in 1972, when Pauline and her good friend the writer and *New York Times Book Review* editor Charles Simmons had gone together to see *Deep Throat*, the era's most talked-about and financially successful porn film. Pauline was intrigued by the movie's publicity and the fact that it made its star, Linda Lovelace, a household name. "I remember we came out of the movie," recalled Simmons, "and I said, 'You know, I never saw a pornographic movie before—that was pretty good.' Pauline said, 'You lost your cherry on a good one.'" She attempted to bully Shawn into letting her review *Deep Throat*, but he drew the line at writing about pornography in *The New Yorker*: His answer was a heated, unequivocal no.

Pauline felt so strongly about the impact of *Last Tango* that she had difficulty discussing it, even with close friends. "I saw *Last Tango*, not with her, but I saw it," recalled Simmons. "I said, 'That was just a dirty movie.' If you did that kind of thing, she would absorb it and not defend it at all." But the failure of so many of her colleagues to share her opinion of the film's value upset her. Her nemesis Andrew Sarris had not been won over by the movie, which he called "stylistically wasteful and excessive." He felt that "its best scenes are isolated from each other, and the dull moments in between stretch into dull minutes." But he saved his sharpest words for a slap at Pauline:

"Under ordinary circumstances, it would be grossly unfair to single out any one film critic for an ego-puffing practice that is beginning to corrode all film criticism. Still, when the one critic in question has been unduly abusive in print toward the excerpted enthusiasms of others, the temptation to turn the tables over a flagrant lapse in critical decorum becomes well nigh irresistible." He also snidely commented that given the five-dollar ticket prices, it would behoove the management of the Trans Lux to pipe in excerpts of *Le Sacre du Printemps*.

At one of Hoyt Spelman's advertising lunches, Pauline was railing to an enthralled table of listeners about Sarris's lack of support for *Last Tango*. Spelman, a great lover of puns, was sitting next to an agency mogul. "That," he whispered to his luncheon partner, "was her last tango with Sarris."

Pauline was never above taking on "serious" writers, particularly those who were the darlings of the literary establishment. And in 1972, few authors occupied such an enviable critical position as Joan Didion, one of the most acclaimed essayists of the New Journalism movement. Didion was unquestionably a superb stylist. She had an eye that moved like a roving camera, picking up revelatory plangent details and never focusing on them too hard or for too long. In the 1960s Didion and her husband, the essayist and novelist John Gregory Dunne, had relocated to Los Angeles, where, in addition to their other projects, they pursued screenwriting careers. In 1970 Didion published a second novel, *Play It as It Lays*, which made use of her Hollywood experience in its account of Maria Wyeth, a sometime actress and model numbly trying to cope with her overwhelming feelings of isolation in Los Angeles. At the time there were a number of women writers who were connecting with a wide readership by making modern anxiety and aimlessness "hip"—Paula Fox's *Desperate Characters*, Lois Gould's *Such Good Friends*, and Sue Kaufman's *Diary of a Mad Housewife* were all popular examples of this trend. *Play It as It Lays* was thought to be one of the finest examples of this sensibility, and it earned Didion some of the strongest reviews of the year.

Not surprisingly, given the difference in their literary temperaments, Pauline pounced with her review of the film version of *Play It as It Lays*, released in the fall of 1972. The story of Maria's plight struck her as "the ultimate princess fantasy"—that is, a study of a woman "too sensitive for this world— you see the truth, and so you suffer more than ordinary people, and can't function." It wasn't only the sensibility of the novel that annoyed her, it was Didion's celebrated style, which Pauline found "ridiculously swank." She found *Play It as It Lays* absurdly self-conscious, "a writer's performance, with every word screwed tight, and a designer's feat, the sparse words placed in the spiritual emptiness of white pages." Her review included a rather personal swipe at Didion, who, she reported, "wanted Frank Perry to direct—possibly because he had already glorified the suffering little-girl-woman in *Diary of a Mad Housewife* . . . The adaptation is a novelist's wish fulfillment: narration that retains the most 'eloquent' passages in the book, dialogue virtually intact, and a transfer to the screen of the shattered-sensibility style by means of quick scenes that form a mosaic."

It was a review that brought a civil retort from Didion's husband John Gregory Dunne, who took Pauline to task for getting her facts wrong. Sometime earlier, at an evening they had spent together at an Academy Awards party at the home of the literary agent Lynn Nesbit, Dunne and Didion had mentioned to Pauline that Frank Perry would be directing *Play It as It Lays*. Pauline regarded Perry as one of the most humorless and flatfooted of directors and asked—incredulously, Dunne remembered—why they wanted him. "I replied that actually we wanted Sam Peckinpah to do the picture, and that Sam wanted to do it," Dunne wrote. "The studios reacted to Sam's doing a picture about a woman as if it were suggested that Hitler do a film about the Jewish question. With Sam out, it became academic who directed." Mike Nichols was interested, but negotiations with him broke down, and Perry had put up his own money to finance the script, making his assignment "a simple matter of economics."

A few weeks later Dunne wrote to her again, to tell her that he was reviewing her forthcoming collection, called *Deeper into Movies*, for *the Los Angeles Times*. "I confess a certain ambivalence about the book," he wrote. "I think you're the best movie critic in America, but I'm not altogether sure that's a compliment."

At year's end, she was completely let down by Sam Peckinpah's latest, *The Getaway*, a violent picture about a bank robbery, which she described as "the most completely commercial film Peckinpah has made, and his self-parasitism gives one forebodings of emptiness. When a director repeats his successful effects, it can mean that he is getting locked in and has stopped responding to new experience. (Hitchcock is the most glaring example.) *The Getaway* is long and dull and has no reverberations except of other movies, mostly by Peckinpah."

Peckinpah wrote to Pauline from Durango, Mexico, where he had been living ever since the filming of *Pat Garrett and Billy the Kid*. Illness had plagued the shoot, and he told her that he had at one point been forced to work with a fever of 104 degrees. But his tone in the letter was again apologetic, as it had been when she reviewed *Straw Dogs*: "Sorry you didn't get my crude attempt at satire with *Getaway*," he wrote. "It was a put on but few people realised [*sic*] it. . . . You said a great thing in your *Getaway* review about a director repeating himself. I am afraid I will be doing that for quite a while, until I get enough money to do the kind of scripts I believe in. But I suppose I will always be concerned with violence as that seems to be the only thing I am paid for. . . . I gather from brief excerpts that you are still as tough, talented and opinionated as ever, which is as it should be." Still smarting from not getting to film *Deliverance*, a project he had coveted, he added that he didn't see how such a fine novel could "be made into such a shitty film and be nominated for three awards. I don't like your town but Hollywood is really a dunghill." As a postscript, he added that "Rex and Judith loved" *The Getaway*: "That says something doesn't it?"

The pace of moviegoing that Pauline maintained at this time was extraordinary: As always, she saw many films that she didn't care to cover, and in her December 23, 1972, column for *The New Yorker*, she contributed substantial essays on five films, including Robert Altman's latest, *Images*. The study of the world of a schizophrenic woman who can no longer sort out reality from fantasy, it was a good representative of the kind of modestly budgeted film with a highly personal point of view that was being made regularly in the early 1970s. Altman had written the script several years before in Los Angeles and claimed not to have altered one word of it. Like all of his films of this period, *Images* didn't cost much. Altman admitted that the story was probably influenced mostly by Bergman's *Persona*, but he always stressed that he hadn't meant it to be a precise study in schizophrenia; "I trust instinct more than any study of logical conclusions," he later said.

Pauline thought *Images* didn't work, but she went easy on it in her review because of her respect for Altman's gifts, which she found "almost frighteningly non-repetitive." Altman showed every sign of continuing to expand as an artist—even in this "empty, trashy chic film," a "psychological thriller with no psychological content, so there's no suspense and the climax has no power." Her review ended in something of a defensive mode: "It's possible that this formidably complicated man has as many facets as this gadgety movie's tiresome prisms, and that in reaching out instinctively and restlessly he's learning techniques that he hasn't yet found a use for. My bet is that he will; when he's bad he's very bad, but when he's good he's extraordinary."

The message in that final paragraph seemed to be that the end result might be all-important in the work of other directors, but it was less so in Altman: In his films, the intention was given greater weight. For the most revered and influential film critic in America to take this position with a director did not necessarily do the director great favors in Hollywood. Pauline's reviews may have made it a bit easier for Altman to get funding, but it also made him the object of many other directors' resentment. Altman himself liked to tell people that he admired Pauline for never being in anyone's pocket, but there is plenty of evidence that he spent considerable time wooing her. He loved having lengthy meals with her, at which the liquor flowed freely. Even more than most directors, Altman took an intense interest in the fate of his films; his wife, Kathryn, recalled him obsessively telephoning the management of the New York theaters where his pictures had opened and asking them how many receipts had been tallied for each showing. He felt that the critics could make or break him, and he wasn't at all above courting the most important ones.

Rene Auberjonois, who acted in *Images*, lived in Manhattan, on West Ninety-third Street, just around the corner from Pauline and Gina. He frequently ran into Pauline while waiting for a bus, and they would chat about whichever film he was doing. In Ireland, on the set of *Images*, Altman asked Auberjonois to do him a favor, which made the actor deeply ill at ease. "He made me sit down and write a postcard to Pauline Kael about being in Ireland and making the film. I felt incredibly awkward about it, because I didn't really know her at all, but he assumed that because I lived around the corner from her, it would be all right for me to write a personal note to a film critic. I remember sitting there and not knowing what to say, and it was sent off, and I never heard from her."

By now Pauline was hearing frequently from stars and directors whose work she had reviewed. She regarded Carol Burnett as "probably the most gifted comedienne this country has ever produced," but she thought her new film, Martin Ritt's *Pete 'n' Tillie*, about a mismatched husband and wife, was a waste of her talents. Pauline thought Burnett's work in *Pete 'n' Tillie* was "grimly controlled" and "an unnecessarily confined and schoolmarmish performance." Her review brought her a letter of gratitude from Burnett, in which the actress admitted that she had known something was wrong during the filming but had been unable to figure out what it was.

Pauline also received a letter from Sydney Pollack, director of Robert Redford's new film *Jeremiah Johnson*, but it wasn't one of thanks. Pauline disliked the movie partly because she had thought that Redford would evolve into "a new kind of hip and casually smart screen actor, and he's already jumped into mythic-man roles in which tired, aging stars can vegetate profitably." For much of the film, mountain man Jeremiah Johnson wages a war against the Crow Indians who have killed his wife and child; at the end comes a scene in which the Crows' chief, signaling an end to hostilities, gives Johnson a sign of peace. Pauline wrote, "Jeremiah signals him back, giving him the finger." Pollack wrote her a lengthy response, saying that she had misinterpreted the gesture, and that he could

> only assume that by that point you were so bored with the film that you were half asleep, since there is no other way to understand how you could see Johnson giving the finger to the Crow Chief. He quite clearly raises his hand in a salute. . . . The whole attempt, poorly done or not, was to present both the Indian and white man as they were, *without* judgment, according to my best efforts at research. . . . Now, I have been called a bum by some very prestigious critics the world over, including yourself, and while it tends to kill my appetite for a few days . . . those are the rules. But I have never been so completely misunderstood or misinterpreted as in those last few lines of your review.

Pauline was disappointed when at the end of the year the New York Film Critics Circle awarded Ingmar Bergman's *Cries and Whispers* the year's Best Picture prize over *The Godfather.* She was equally displeased when Laurence Olivier (for *Sleuth*) triumphed over Marlon Brando—the result of an unusual and precedent-setting circumstance. She was also disappointed that Liv Ull-mann (*Cries and Whispers, The Emigrants*) won Best Actress over her favorites, Cicely Tyson and Liza Minnelli.

Pauline had recently begun exchanging letters with a young screenwriter named Robert Getchell, who had asked his agent to send along his new script "to save me the buck twenty." Getchell's screenplay concerned a Southwestern housewife named Alice who suddenly finds herself widowed and takes to the road with her young boy, in pursuit of the singing career she long ago abandoned. Getchell had written it with Shirley MacLaine in mind, and MacLaine had been eager to do it and had planned to try to get Peter Bogdanovich to direct; then she had gone to work on the presidential campaign of George McGovern, "never to be heard from again," Getchell wrote.

Pauline read the script with fascination, and while she found it sharp and witty and tough and beautifully observed, she suggested a few improvements. "The idea should be for them to keep going with lots of engagement," she wrote to Getchell, "to get something out of life along the way—not to look for a happy end." She added that she thought it should be directed by Altman, choosing not to think about the dilemma that might lie ahead if Getchell's script were to be filmed and she were to review it for *The New Yorker*.

The run of good films that appeared in late 1972 did not carry over to the new year: Most of the movies Pauline reviewed from January to March were disappointments. The major event of the winter months was the publication of her latest volume of criticism, *Deeper into Movies*, once again by Little, Brown. In her author's note Pauline stated that this collection was "a record of the interaction of movies and our national life during a frantic time when three decades seem to have been compressed into three years and I wrote happily—like a maniac—to keep up with what I thought was going on in movies—which is to say, our national theater." She added, "Right now, movie critics have an advantage over critics in most other fields: responsive readers. And it can help you to concentrate your energies if you know that the subject is fresh and that your review may make a difference to some people."

It was a sentiment that was picked up in the opening paragraph of the front-page notice in *The New York Times Book Review* on February 18, 1973. The reviewer was the eminent literary critic Irving Howe, who opened with the observation, "Right now, movie criticism in America seems livelier, more pungent than literary criticism. . . . Movies have recently carried a sharper air of excitement than have books; and some people have begun to develop, or fumble toward, a film esthetic." Howe admired Pauline's "crisp sentences," "aggressive wit," and the fact that "she brings to her movies a grounding in literary culture such as some movie reviewers take to be merely 'linear' and others don't even know they need." He admired the fact that "her approach to a new film is empiric and careful, not too different from that which a good critic of drama or fiction would employ." There was a caveat, however. "Sometimes she drops into a sort of brawling, Marie Dressler–like posture to assault the position of high-brow seriousness from which, in the main, she works." He questioned her "excessive praise for movies like *M\*A\*S\*H* and *McCabe & Mrs. Miller*" and picked apart her taste in advocating for films such as *Fiddler on the Roof*, *The Conformist*, and *The Last Picture Show*: "I suspect either that, as a result of seeing too many movies, her standards are slipping or she is kidding. And it doesn't look as if she's kidding." Howe took an academic's viewpoint of what he considered her principal weakness—that she did not "work out of a secure critical tradition. Its absence allows her a pleasing freedom of improvisation, but makes very hard the achievement of reflective depth and delicate judgment." The other reviews were excellent, and, for the fourth consecutive time, a Kael collection enjoyed brisk sales.

In the summer of 1973 Pauline took time out from her lecture appearances to accept an offer from *The New York Times Book Review* to write about the latest project by Norman Mailer: a coffee-table-sized illustrated biography of Marilyn Monroe, titled simply *Marilyn*. Pauline had never been a fan of Mailer; in 1968 she had panned his film *Wild '90*, calling it "the worst movie that I've stayed to see all the way through." While she certainly recognized Mailer's literary gifts (just as she recognized Joan Didion's), she didn't particularly respond to them; these representatives of New Journalism were mostly showing off too self-consciously for her taste, and she recoiled from Mailer's brand of literary machismo.

The very idea of Mailer on Monroe was bound to make her a little dubious from the outset. To Pauline, Monroe was at best an overripe, teasing blond comedienne who became adept at a kind of "self-satire," and Pauline thought that Monroe's "slow reaction time made her seem daffy, and she tricked it up into a comedy style." Pauline had found Monroe amusing in her one all-out carnal temptress role, as Rose Loomis in the 1953 Henry Hathaway thriller *Niagara*. But by 1973, the Monroe cult, campaigning to have the star considered a potentially great actress consistently deprived of the right material, had built to fever pitch. The woods were full of actors who claimed to have been present at the famous Actors Studio class in which Monroe played a scene from Eugene O'Neill's *Anna Christie* with Maureen Stapleton, reportedly to revelatory effect. (Her performance as Roslyn in *The Misfits*, written by her husband Arthur Miller, makes a persuasive argument that she was not everything that was being said of her. Miller may have had the best intentions of giving her something meaty to dig into as an actress, but she simply could not pull it off: her interminable pauses between lines are a heavy-handed cue to us that she's being "emotional" and derail any chance she has of getting a real performance tempo going.)

Part of the problem Pauline had with Mailer's take on Monroe was that he was trying to mine the legend for more than it was worth. "Who knows what to think about Marilyn Monroe or about those who turn her sickness to metaphor?" Pauline wondered. "I wish they'd let her die." She found that Mailer inflated Monroe's career "to cosmic proportions. She becomes 'a proud, inviolate artist,' and he suggests that 'one might literally have to invent the idea of a soul in order to approach her.' He pumps so much wind into his subject that he's trying to make Marilyn Monroe worthy of him, a subject to compare with the Pentagon and the moon."

Yet she found some of his insights impressively acute. He was especially good on Monroe's early years in an orphanage and how they may have been the foundation of her constant lying and a need to compartmentalize her life.

"His strength—when he gets rolling—isn't in Freudian guesses but in his fusing his knowledge of how people behave with his worst suspicions of where they really live," wrote Pauline. She also admired his description of the Hollywood machine and "the psychological and sexual rewards the studio system offered executives."

The book was a case of split personality, as Pauline saw it: "a rip-off all right but a rip-off with genius." She admitted that Mailer came up with "a runaway string of perceptions and you have to recognize that, though it's a bumpy ride, the book still goes like a streak." Ultimately, however, *Marilyn* suffered from the author's need to inflate its subject and wallow in his own theorizing; in the end, it became "Mailer's way to perform character assassination with the freedom of a novelist who has created fictional characters." The book finally was undone for her by "malevolence that needs to be recognized . . . Neither the world nor Marilyn Monroe's life should be seen in Norman Mailer's image."

Pauline's review of *Marilyn* became one of the most widely discussed pieces of criticism of the year, and, as she had predicted, it did nothing to prevent the book from being one of the year's most popular releases. Her appearance in the *New York Times Book Review* did, however, lead to a baffling encounter with William Shawn. When she dropped by *The New Yorker* offices over the summer, she ran into him, and he asked her why she hadn't let him have the review for the magazine. "What for?" Pauline replied. "You wouldn't have printed it."

"That's right," Shawn sighed.

# CHAPTER SIXTEEN

In the summer of 1973 Pauline was, like so many other Americans, riveted by the television coverage of the Watergate hearings. She knew that "The Current Cinema" was not the place for political grandstanding, but she made her feelings about the Nixon administration known while appearing on a symposium in Manhattan in early 1973. As *Newsweek* quoted her: "I live in a rather special world. I only know one person who voted for Nixon. Where they are, I don't know. They're outside my ken. But sometimes when I'm in a theater I can feel them."

When she returned to her *New Yorker* post in the fall of 1973, she offered her observations on the dominant mood in the country: "The Watergate hearings have overshadowed the movies this summer, yet the corruption that Watergate has come to stand for can be seen as the culmination of what American movies have been saying for almost a decade." The country was sinking deeper into a state of hopelessness. "The Vietnam War has barely been mentioned on the screen," Pauline wrote, but she rightly felt that you could sense its presence in many of the era's most intriguing films, from *They Shoot Horses, Don't They?* to *Midnight Cowboy* to action films such as *The French Connection*, in which "there was no virtuous side to identify with and nobody you really felt very good about cheering for." It worried her that films now embraced such "a depressive uncertainty," a trend she didn't see as representing artistic growth, but rather as an easy response to world events. "When Vietnam finished off the American hero as righter of wrongs, the movie industry embraced corruption greedily," she wrote; "formula movies could be energized by infusions of brutality, cynicism, and Naked Apism, which could all be explained by Vietnam and called realism. Moviemakers could celebrate violence and pretend, even to themselves, that they were doing the public a service."

The first movie she reviewed that fall picked up on this theme: *The Last American Hero*, directed by Lamont Johnson, and based on an *Esquire* article by Tom Wolfe from nearly a decade earlier, told the story of Junior Johnson (rechristened Junior Jackson for the film), a backwoods boy who starts out trafficking his father's moonshine and winds up a star on the stock-car racing circuit. The script concerned the idea that "corruption seems to be inescapable: if you want to win, you learn to take orders even from people whose idea of winning you don't understand. . . . The film says that to win you give up everything you care about except winning."

Pauline loved the film, which turned out to be another underdog for her to champion. She reported that Twentieth Century–Fox had cut the picture badly, losing some of its most important scenes, and then given it a pitifully limited opening in the South, pushing it as an action film when it was really a thoughtful character study. When it didn't do well, the studio decided it had a loser on its hands, one that couldn't possibly go over in urban areas, and gave it a limp one-week engagement in New York. Despite the fact that the studio didn't bother about setting up any press screenings, Pauline sought out the film—it was *Pretty Poison* all over again. In her review, she suggested that if the movie could manage to find some kind of audience—several of the other reviews were also good—"perhaps someone in the head office at Fox could do the sane, decent thing and restore the cuts?"

Johnson thought that he had gotten "a screwing" by the studio when the film was released, so when he read Pauline's favorable review, he dropped her a note thanking her. "I invited her to lunch, and we got drunk and had a marvelous time," he remembered. "She was a marvelous character. Marvelous gestures. She reminded me of Zasu Pitts. She would tear at her bosom and roll her eyes in disgust or dismay or delight about something. Extremities were her big suit. The fact that she was as enthusiastic about me as she was spread happily through the industry."

Pauline's first column that season highlighted a characteristic of hers that would come increasingly under fire as the decade wore on. Her opening comments on the state of films during Watergate America, combined with her review of *The Last American Hero*—a film that did not warrant the in-depth analysis of one by Bertolucci or Coppola or Altman—made for a long article. Several of her colleagues had begun to snipe about the length of her pieces. "I am sorry to say that I think *The New Yorker* did her in by giving her unlimited space," said Judith Crist. "And I think the older readers didn't have the patience, whereas the younger readers were the devotees."

At the New York Film Festival in the fall of 1973, Pauline saw another movie that seduced her completely: Martin Scorsese's *Mean Streets*. It was the thirty-year-old director's fourth feature, and its subject returned him to his early days, growing up in Little Italy on Manhattan's Lower East Side.

*Mean Streets*, shot for around $500,000, is the story of Charlie Capp, Jr. (Harvey Keitel), who has grown up in Little Italy and now is trying to make his way to a more respectable life uptown, running a restaurant and nightclub. Charlie possesses a fatal flaw: he doesn't have the demonic single-mindedness to make it in the brutal environment in which he's grown up. As far as his uncle Giovanni (Cesare Danova) is concerned, Charlie has two liabilities in particular—his epileptic girlfriend, Teresa (Amy Robinson), whom Giovanni considers a waste because she's physically damaged goods; and her brother, Charlie's good friend Johnny Boy (Robert De Niro), a volatile, gleefully stupid punk who plays dangerous games with loan sharks. Johnny Boy, for all his shortcomings, has an honesty that eludes Charlie. While Johnny Boy is a law unto himself, Charlie has a fatuous side. He wants to be upwardly mobile, but he isn't tough enough to do just anything to get there: he can't bring himself to turn his back on either Teresa or Johnny Boy. He is exactly what Johnny Boy calls him—"a fuckin' politician."

As a slice of Italian-American New York life, *Mean Streets* was less concerned with a well-structured story line than with making the brutal circumstances of the characters' lives practically come through the skin of the actors. In the opening sentence of her *New Yorker* review, Pauline dubbed *Mean Streets* "a true original of our period, a triumph of personal filmmaking." She loved the way the picture portrayed the mercurial nature of violence, which "breaks out so unexpectedly that you can't believe it, and is over before you've been able to take it in. The whole movie has this effect; it psyches you up to accept everything it shows you." Pauline felt that the true novelty of *Mean Streets* was the way in which it delved into "the psychological connections between Italian Catholicism and crime, between sin and crime." She thought that *The Godfather*, and now *Mean Streets*, had tapped into some previously unexplored connection between the characters' lawless, hedonistic lives and the powerful sense of guilt they had absorbed from their Catholic education and family life.

The most surprising review Pauline wrote during this period was of *The Way We Were*, a nostalgic romantic drama directed by Sydney Pollack and written by Arthur Laurents. *The Way We Were* was one of the hit films of the time that connected with the nostalgia craze that had arisen in the early 1970s. But the adoration for the past also implied a decided ambivalence about the present—a topic Pauline had been writing about in "The Current Cinema" for years. The student protest movement had begun to run out of steam by 1972, and by 1973, with the cessation of American military action in Vietnam, young rebels seemed tired, confused, unsure of how to channel their energies. "We were easily discouraged," wrote essayist Joyce Maynard, "quick to abandon hope for change and to lose interest." Pauline may have been a tremendous advocate of the movies that grew out of the atmosphere of unrest in the late '60s and early '70s, but she had always been curiously unpredictable on the question of open rebellion. Organized activism and protest were not anything she cared to involve herself with, given their group mentality, and she tended to counsel her young friends, caught up in campus rebellion, to channel their energies into what they dreamed of doing for a living—particularly if they wanted to write. As attuned to the times as she may have been, she had hung on to her old-school, Greatest Generation approach to work, and any trace of sentimentality about the ennobling virtue of organized activism had long since vanished.

The nostalgia movement had been slower to come into mainstream movies than it had to fashion and the theater, but *The Way We Were* was a sure sign of its arrival, and of the general shift in public tastes that would evolve over the next several years. A sentimental love story about a smart, committed girl who falls in love with a man who can't take a stand on anything, it wasn't at all Pauline's kind of movie. But her unexpected approval of the picture probably could be boiled down to a single factor—Barbra Streisand.

*The Way We Were* traced the unlikely and uneasy love that develops between Katie Morosky, an outspoken Jewish political activist, and Hubbell Gardiner (Robert Redford), an apolitical WASP with a talent for writing. The two meet in the 1930s at Columbia University, where Katie is deeply involved in the student Communist Party and takes everything she does seriously—too seriously. Despite her humorlessness, her dedication and intellectual spark attract Hubbell, who, in classic WASP tradition, lives his life trying not to offend anyone. The two commence a love affair a few years after leaving Columbia, and they eventually marry. When Hubbell is offered a screenwriting contract with a major Hollywood studio, they head west, and it is there that their marriage slowly comes apart in the climate of the Communist witch hunts. The film ended with a touching coda in the early '50s, back in New York: Katie, her political fervor undiminished, is handing out leaflets on a street corner, and Hubbell, also unchanged except for a new girlfriend, bumps into her for one last conversation. Both now see that their marriage was doomed, but their affection for each other is intact.

*The Way We Were* was launched on choppy waters. Redford had been reluctant to take the part of Hubbell, because he thought—correctly—that the story was really Katie's story and he would wind up playing second fiddle to Barbra Streisand. Once Redford was on board, Laurents got the word that he was fired. The director, Sydney Pollack, blamed it on the producer, Ray Stark, and Stark blamed it on Pollack. According to Laurents's memoir, eleven writers were brought in, including Alvin Sargent and Dalton Trumbo, the latter an original member of the Hollywood Ten. None of them reworked the script to Stark's satisfaction, and soon enough, he had rehired Laurents. But there were further travails ahead: The political content made the studio nervous, because they feared it might dwarf the love story.

With Streisand on Laurents's side, some of the crucial lines about the blacklist stayed in the film. But Laurents lost one important scene, one in which Hubbell tells Katie that someone has informed on her. The studio that employs him has told him that unless Katie clears herself by naming names before HUAC, he will lose his studio contract. Katie responds, painfully, "It's amazing how decisions are forced upon us willy-nilly." The scene was excised, and Pollack later said, rather defensively, that all of the cuts made were justified—that "it's hardly the definitive film about McCarthyism. It was never intended to be." To Laurents, the loss was heartbreaking. To those in the audience who pondered the scene's meaning at all, it now appeared that Hubbell and Katie were breaking up because he had slept with his old flame (Lois Chiles).

*The Way We Were* was hardly a first-class film, but Pauline responded to it, albeit with qualification—likening it to "a torpedoed ship full of gaping holes which comes snugly into port." She found that the sentimental sequences, story holes, Marvin Hamlisch's heavy-handed score, and the "bewildering" time chronology were all outweighed by "the chemistry of Barbra Streisand and Robert Redford." She thought that Streisand had "miraculous audience empathy" and that she "caught the spirit of the hysterical Stalinist workhorses of the thirties and forties—both the ghastly desperation of their self-righteousness and the warmth of their enthusiasm." She considered that playing Katie was a risk for Streisand, because it required her to be "defensive and aggressive in the same breath"—exactly the qualities that many moviegoers (men, in particular) had always objected to in her persona. But Pauline believed Streisand to have made a "gradual conquest of the movie public" and thought she and Redford made *The Way We Were* "hit entertainment and maybe even memorable entertainment"—a line that was quoted in large type at the top of the movie's print ads.

In the end, however, Pauline seriously overestimated Streisand's acting ability. In Katie's big telephone scene, in which she sobs her heart out to Redford because she isn't attractive enough for him, Streisand was poorly directed, and in the scene in which she lashes out at Hubbell's friends for their lack of political commitment, she made Kate seem strident and humorless.

All in all, her Katie seemed slightly self-conscious—the work of an actress gunning to be taken seriously.

Robert Altman's next film was a riff on the film noir genre, based very loosely on a novel by one of the masters of the detective story, Raymond Chandler. *The Long Goodbye* took Chandler's private-eye hero, Philip Marlowe, and transported him to early '70s Los Angeles. According to Altman, his idea was to make the story "Rip Van Marlowe"—the detective essentially wakes up thirty years later with his own code of ethics intact, but finds that everything around him has changed. The plot—Marlowe is implicated in a crime when he does an old friend a favor by driving him to Tijuana, and the friend's wife turns up murdered—was negligible in terms of how it unfolded. What mattered most, as was always the case with Altman's films, was the atmosphere and the people. Altman, along with his scenarist, Leigh Brackett (who had coscripted Howard Hawks's Marlowe classic *The Big Sleep*), created a stunningly atmospheric portrait of modern L.A., with its lacquered blondes, blocked alcoholic writers, and assorted drifters, loonies, and movie industry wannabes and hangers-on. Most detective films turn on details that are so precisely controlled that the audience may not feel it has time to breathe, but *The Long Goodbye* was exhilarating in its looseness. Altman was aided immeasurably by the superb camerawork of Vilmos Zsigmond, who used his film-flashing technique to make the movie look like old postcards of L.A.; he also kept the camera moving continually, giving the audience a quiet, sustained sensation of being on a voyage of discovery.

*The Long Goodbye* was another project to appeal to Pauline's white-knight impulse: Its L.A. opening in March 1973 was met with stinging reviews and grossed only $10,300 in the opening week. A misleading advertising campaign that made it look like a sleek detective thriller didn't help. It was pulled from distribution and given a new campaign much closer to the ironic spirit of the film. Only then did it open in New York, and while it was too late for it to become the blockbuster it might have been, at least it turned out to be a hit in Manhattan, where it got mostly favorable reviews and enjoyed a good run.

For Pauline, *The Long Goodbye* was another Altman masterpiece, and she was beginning to despair of his ever finding a mass audience again. "Maybe the reason some people have difficulty getting into Altman's wavelength is that he's just about incapable of overdramatizing," she wrote. "He's not a pusher." In a judgment that sounded suspiciously auteurist, she praised Altman's contribution at the expense of Leigh Brackett's, saying that although

Brackett's name was on the picture as scenarist, "when you hear the improvised dialogue you can't take this credit literally." Elliott Gould, for whom *The Long Goodbye* represented a return to stature after two years in the box-office wilderness, felt that the comment about Brackett was not quite fair. "But I understand Pauline," Gould said. "When we showed the picture at the empty Grauman's Chinese Theater before it opened, I was there and Leigh was there. I felt it was like an American jazz performance that Bob allowed me to do. I'm talking to myself all the time, because there's no one to talk to except my cat. I said to Leigh Brackett, 'Does this validate the work that you did?'" Brackett, fortunately, liked the end result.

While Pauline was hardly alone in enjoying friendships with filmmakers—Richard Schickel and Judith Crist, among others, fraternized with directors and stars, though they maintained their reputations as tough, honest critics—her relationships were more problematic. Because her praise could be more passionate than that of any other critic, it was all the more traumatic for the artists when she turned on them with that same degree of passion.

A particularly complicated case arose with Woody Allen. She had enjoyed two of his recent comedies, *Bananas* and *Everything You Always Wanted to Know About Sex*, feeling that he had come a long way from the facile unevenness of his first solo directorial feature, *Take the Money and Run*. To Pauline, Allen's recent work suggested he was "an erratic comic genius," and she admired the fact that Allen had "found a nonaggressive way of dealing with urban pressures. He stays nice; he's not insulting, like most New York comedians, and he delivers his zingers without turning into a cynic." For Pauline, Allen's "essential sanity" was "the base from which he takes flight."

Pauline thought that Allen's new picture, *Sleeper*, a comedy set in 2173, was the most stable and most sustained of his films, "without the lapses that had found their way into his earlier work." In it, Allen starred as the thirty-five-year-old owner of the Happy Carrot health food restaurant in Greenwich Village, who is admitted to the hospital for a peptic ulcer and wakes up two hundred years later. Allen had written to Pauline late in 1972 that *Sleeper* was a Buster Keaton–type comedy, though not in the pure Keaton spirit because of the intrusion of sound. Allen and Pauline had a friendly, long-running argument about the impact of sound on comedy, with Allen taking the position that sound prevented the great comics from achieving total reality. While Pauline found *Sleeper* consistently funny, something was missing: She felt that "Allen's new sense of control over the medium and over his own material seems to level out the abrasive energy. You can be with it all the way, and yet it doesn't impose itself on your imagination—it dissolves when it's finished."

Pauline saw deeply into the appeal Allen had for the 1970s movie audience: He was the brainy, nerdy kid who had always been beaten up on the school grounds but had managed to triumph because of his brains and wit, which, despite layers of insecurity and paranoia, he always believed in. Allen was the smart, irreverent observer of the social revolution that had been shaking up America since the '60s, but although this brand of comedy was popular with young people—his script for *Sleeper* took gentle jabs at the NRA and the Nixon administration—he was anything but subversive. Quite the opposite: He was too much of a misfit to be a genuine hero of the youth movement, and he was a nostalgist with a deep love for traditional pop culture. Pauline was probably right when she judged that Allen had a misguided attraction to healthy conformity: "The battered adolescent," she wrote, "still thinks that that's the secret of happiness."

Over a period of several years, Allen saw Pauline socially and frequently wrote to her when he happened to be out in California filming. He enjoyed having discourse with someone he considered to be such a superb critic, and the subjects of his letters varied widely. He wrote to her praising her advocacy of films such as *McCabe & Mrs. Miller*. He sent her the script for his comedy *Everything You Always Wanted to Know About Sex*, asking her to read it and make any suggestions for changes. He wasn't afraid to disagree with her: He didn't like *Sounder* at all, and he thought that *Straw Dogs* was nothing remotely approaching a work of art, fascist or otherwise. Certainly, however, Allen cultivated her strenuously, going so far as to take her side after Peter Bogdanovich's rebuttal to "Raising Kane" appeared in *Esquire*, assuring her that it would fail to get any serious attention at all. He also knew that he always had a sympathetic ear whenever he complained to her about the indignities suffered by talented directors in Hollywood, writing to her in the summer of 1973 about the creative bankruptcy that he found so stifling.

During Christmas week, a film opened that exploded box-office records around the country: William Friedkin's *The Exorcist*—a thriller based on William Peter Blatty's bestselling novel about the demonic possession of a twelve-year-old girl. Pauline was offended by the movie's grotesqueries, but she was even more outraged by its attempts at an overlay of seriousness on a basic horror story. Pauline, whose distrust of organized religion had only intensified with the years, thought Blatty's musings about the afterlife and the other side to be a lot of medieval nonsense, and she opened her review with a full-barrel attack: "When you see him on TV talking about communicating with his dead mother, your heart doesn't bleed for him, your stomach turns for him." She chose to interpret *The Exorcist* as a public relations effort on behalf of the Catholic Church, and she wanted desperately to see it exposed as such. (Friedkin, for his part, was a non-Catholic who recalled "learning about the Catholic Church while I was doing that film.") To her *The Exorcist* was the grossest sort of study in manipulation; she saw "no indication that Blatty or Friedkin has any feeling for the little girl's helplessness and suffering, or her mother's, any feeling for God or terror of Satan."

*The Exorcist* had been a difficult film to get off the ground, despite the book's success. According to Friedkin, three top directors—Arthur Penn, Stanley Kubrick, and Mike Nichols—turned it down, largely because they didn't think it would be possible to cast as the possessed Regan a young girl who could do everything that the script demanded of her. "The whole movie was balanced on that," Friedkin remembered. "There was an open call for a thousand girls. Linda Blair never came to the open call. Her mother brought her in. [Until then] I thought I was going to have to do it with a sixteen-year-old. No one else came close." The Warners publicity stated that Friedkin had actually looked at some five hundred girls, and Pauline seized on this fact for one of the most lacerating observations she ever put down on paper. "I wonder about those four-hundred and ninety-nine mothers of the rejected little girls. . . . They must have read the novel; they must have known what they were having their beautiful little daughters tested for. When they see *The Exorcist* and watch Linda Blair urinating on the fancy carpet and screaming and jabbing at herself with the crucifix, are they envious? Do they feel, 'That might have been my little Susie—famous forever'?"

Blatty was incensed by her review and lit into her on television and in print interviews, though he apologized by letter a few months later. Friedkin was also upset about her attack, though he admitted that she had perhaps scored a point when she called *The Exorcist* "the biggest recruiting poster the Catholic Church has had since the sunnier days of *Going My Way* and *The Bells of St. Mary's*." "I found it wrong-headed," said Friedkin. "On the other hand, I know many people who went into the priesthood because of that. I remember meeting James Cagney toward the end of his life, and he had seen it, and he said, 'Young man, I've got a bone to pick with you. I had a barber for twenty years, and he saw the movie and he left being the barber to enter the priesthood.' I said, 'I'm sorry, sir.' Kael was probably right—but it wasn't *intended* that way."

*The Exorcist* would eventually gross in the neighborhood of $165 million. Its success was also an early harbinger of sweeping change in the industry that not even Pauline could have predicted.

Fortunately, there was Robert Altman, who was proving to be not only in artistic command but highly prolific. *Thieves Like Us*, his newest picture, was released in February 1974. Filmed in and around Jackson, Mississippi, on a budget of $1.25 million, *Thieves Like Us* was an unusual film for Altman in that it followed its source material, a novel by Edward Anderson about a trio of bank robbers during the Depression, rather closely.

By now Pauline anticipated Altman's new films with such fervor that she decided to make a visit to the set of *Thieves Like Us*. She knew that the material was very close to that of *Bonnie and Clyde*, but she read Anderson's novel and liked it, and she was curious to see how Altman would transform it. Pauline's presence was a major event for the cast and crew, who felt her support for their work as keenly as Altman did. "I remember her walking in and seeing her for the first time," the screenwriter Joan Tewkesbury said, "and you just wanted to rush up and say, 'My God, I think you're wonderful—and thank you!' And she just went straight for Bob, and we thought . . . okay. She walked around and looked and they talked." Tewkesbury recalled that it was obvious that Pauline preferred the company of big men in the movie industry to hanging out with other women. To her, Pauline resembled a major cultural figure such as the photojournalist Margaret Bourke-White. "What you got was this sense of women who really had to come through the journalistic ranks, which meant they were competing with the boys and not with each other," said Tewkesbury. "So you got very short shrift from these girls."

*Thieves Like Us* was a beautifully sustained piece of work, and because it was more plot-driven than Altman's earlier films, it had the potential to capture a wider audience. For Pauline, it was yet another Altman triumph; it had "the pensive, delicate romanticism of *McCabe*, but it isn't hesitant or precarious . . . It's the closest to flawless of Altman's films—a masterpiece." She had long loved to describe the dry, cautious writing of some of her fellow critics as "saphead objectivity"; there was none of that in her review of *Thieves Like Us*:

> Robert Altman spoils other directors' films for me; Hollywood's paste-up, slammed-together jobs come off a faulty conveyor belt and are half chewed up in the process. I think I know where just about all the elements come from in most American movies (and in most foreign movies, too) and how the mechanisms work, but I don't understand how Robert Altman gets his effects, any more than I understand how Renoir

did (or, for that matter, how Godard did from *Breathless* through *Weekend*, or how Bertolucci does). When an artist works right on the edge of his unconscious, like Altman, not asking himself why he's doing what he's doing but trusting to instinct (which in Altman's case is the same as taste), a movie is a special kind of gamble.

In both New York and Los Angeles, her colleagues began to grumble: Pauline was not keeping a healthy distance from her pet director. At the San Francisco Film Festival in the fall of 1973, Altman spoke at a retrospective of his own work, telling audiences that "Pauline Kael saved *McCabe & Mrs. Miller* when the studio and the distributors were going to junk it, and she did the same for *The Long Goodbye*. Naturally I agree with everything she said." Pauline's detractors predicted that, sooner or later, it all had to end badly. One thing that delighted them: Her rapturous support failed to keep *Thieves Like Us* from being a box-office disappointment.

Pauline's 1973–74 season at *The New Yorker* ended with a pair of "road" pictures about criminals on the lam: Steven Spielberg's *The Sugarland Express* and Terrence Malick's *Badlands*. In *The Sugarland Express* a daffy blonde named Lou Jean goads her husband to escape from a Texas prerelease prison so they can kidnap their child, whom the welfare department has taken from them and placed in foster care. Pauline rightly thought that she sensed the influence of Robert Altman in the film's clear-eyed and perceptive, but never condescending, view of America. She recognized immediately Spielberg's gift for camera technique and jazzy visual storytelling: "In terms of the pleasure that technical assurance gives an audience, this film is one of the most phenomenal debut films in the history of movies." She loved that Spielberg had managed to get a naturalistic performance out of Goldie Hawn as the blissfully oblivious Lou Jean, who revels in her newfound celebrity and never stops believing that everything is going to work out just fine. Most important, Spielberg loved the art form and knew how to use it: "If there is such a thing as a movie sense—and I think there is (I know fruit vendors and cabdrivers who have it and some movie critics who don't)—Spielberg really has it."

She was bored, however, by *Badlands*, which she judged to be yet another oppressively sour film about the dead end of American life, with no ray of light and not much humor. She found this study of two killers named Kit (Martin Sheen) and Holly (Sissy Spacek) in flight through the Plains states "an intellectualized movie—shrewd and artful, carefully styled to sustain its low-key view of dissociation. Kit and Holly are kept at a distance, doing things for no explained purpose; it's as if the director had taped gauze over their characters, so that we wouldn't be able to take a reading on them." *Badlands* wasn't playful enough for Pauline; the violence had no comic edge to it, and she was bound to tire of Holly's "poetic" voice-over narration.

Her review, however, caused her unexpected difficulties with William Shawn. When he read her March 8, 1974, column while it was in production, he cornered her in *The New Yorker* offices. Terrence Malick was a Harvard friend of Shawn's son, Wallace. Shawn said, "I guess you didn't know that Terry is like a son to me."

"Tough shit, Bill," Pauline answered, as she prepared for her six-month layoff.

In June 1974 Pauline delivered the address at the 142nd commencement exercises of Wesleyan University. Over the past few years she had begun to amass a string of honorary doctoral degrees from various universities around the country. On June 18, 1972, Columbia College awarded her a Doctor of Arts and Letters, and on May 27, 1973, she gave the commencement address at Smith College, which also conferred an Honorary Doctorate of Letters upon her. On June 19, 1973, she gave a speech, "The Effects of Movies," at the commencement exercises at Kalamazoo College, where she received a Doctorate of Humane Letters. While her opinions on the general state of academia hadn't changed, she enjoyed speaking before graduating classes and getting a chance to mingle with the students.

A few months earlier, on April 18, 1974, Pauline received her most distinctive honor to date when *Deeper into Movies* received the National Book Award in the category of Arts and Letters. In addition to the citation, the award carried a cash prize of $1,000. Janet Flanner presented her with the award, praising her not only as a writer but as a *New Yorker* colleague, causing Pauline to hang her head humbly. In her acceptance speech, she said, "Movie criticism is a happy, frustrating, slightly mad job. You can't help knowing how ridiculous you appear when you interpose your words between the public and the vast machinery of advertising and publicity. Often you know you're going to be made to look a fool. And so I'm particularly grateful for this award, as a recognition for those of us who try to sort out what's going on in the mass media, without getting swept up in the circus. Thank you."

Pauline's life had never been as exhilarating as it was now. Her existence revolved around going to movies, talking about movies, lecturing on movies, being interviewed about movies. Not only had the National Book Award put an official seal on her status, but that year she also received the Front Page Award from the Newswomen's Club of New York, for the Best Magazine Column of 1974. Once she had been described as *one* of America's most important and influential film critics, but now, there were few other qualifiers. She had achieved what she had always craved—major stardom— and with stardom came power.

The National Society of Film Critics was her pet group, far more than the New York Film Critics Circle. While the NYFCC was populated with critics who had been established long before Pauline's arrival in New York, the NSFC boasted a number of new members whose careers she had nurtured. "With her review of *Last Tango*, I think," observed Howard Kissel, then the film reviewer for *Women's Wear Daily*, "she began to sense that she did have a power. And I think she had this notion that if the critics had a cabal, they could be more powerful." Several of her colleagues felt she was overestimating the force that a group such as the NSFC could wield. "I would say film critics have power when it comes to some little movie that could be overlooked otherwise," said Kissel. "But in terms of what Hollywood wants to sell—no."

Already the legend of Pauline's inner circle of critic protégés was building. Inclusion in the group was pursued, often desperately, by outsiders. But there were no guarantees of safety at any point. David Denby was a writer in his late twenties who had a burning ambition to become a critic. Pauline met him in 1967, while he was a student at the Columbia University School of Journalism. She got along well with Denby, who assumed an enviable position in the Kael circle, spending many late nights into morning at the Turin, listening in rapt fascination as she debated with her other guests and, as Denby recalled, mowed down "the reputations of virtually every writer in town."

At this point Denby felt that he had been inducted into the literary boot camp of his dreams. Pauline might endlessly hector him and her other protégés about their thoughts and opinions, constantly pressing them to go further and deeper in their writing, to sort out and sharpen their ideas on the page. She could openly badger them about what she considered their middle-brow taste, but she was so witty and engaging that "those who didn't turn away in anger were convinced that she was rough on them for their own good. At least, that was the promise." She enjoyed playing the role of the tough fourth-grade teacher that so many writers crave: She held the young critics she took up to a dizzyingly high standard, going over their articles line by line—endlessly devoted, it seemed, to showing them how to improve their work. About one article of Denby's that was in progress, Pauline said, "It's shit, honey . . . and if you don't make it better I'll stick pins in you." Toward the end of Denby's time at Columbia, she suggested him for a film critic's post at *The Atlantic Monthly*, and he got the job.

The problem was that, by Denby's own admission, he was so drawn to, so dominated by, Pauline's voice on the printed page that it crept into his own writing. She recognized her influence, too, and few things rankled her more than the awareness that her acolytes were blindly devoted to her. She loved being surrounded by like-minded people, but slavish imitators eventually invited her contempt. As far as Denby was concerned, Pauline's followers had to go along with the general outline of her thinking, but they couldn't be too obeisant; they had to demonstrate that they could think for themselves. When Pauline noticed the imitative streak in Denby's writing, she wasn't pleased. At some point during her *New Yorker* stint in 1972–73, Denby recalled, she telephoned him to tell him that she didn't think he had the right stuff. "You're too restless to be a writer," she proclaimed. A few hours later, knowing that she had wounded him, she phoned again, telling him, "I've thought about this seriously, honey. You should do something else with your energy."

In Denby's case the student had for some time begun to be suspicious of the teacher and revolt against the rules of Pauline's private academy. He had come to doubt some of her opinions (her rave for *Fiddler on the Roof* particularly baffled him) and claimed to have been present at a lunch at a Chinese restaurant in New York at which she had laid the director Nicholas Ray out flat, pitilessly analyzing his films one by one and altogether dismissing a good many of them, to the point that "Ray, his face cast down into his shrimp and rice, said hardly a word."

So, when greeted with Pauline's announcement that he was not fit for a career as a writer, Denby nervously disagreed with her and did the only thing he felt he could do: He withdrew from her life. They continued to see each other at professional gatherings in the years that followed—Denby would be film critic for *New York* and later *The New Yorker*—but Pauline never recanted her opinion. Denby would later recall the acute discomfort of being cast out not only by Pauline but by many of her acolytes, whom he had mistakenly considered friends. He would go on to an enviable career as a critic and commentator, but the hurt and humiliation that Pauline's rejection brought remained with him for years.

She had a similarly conflicted relationship with another of her rebels, Paul Schrader. Since turning down the movie-reviewing post in Seattle that she had urged him to take, Schrader had been living in Los Angeles, trying to be a screenwriter. By 1973 he had finished a number of original scripts and, swallowing his pride, sent Pauline four of them—*Taxi Driver*, *The Yakuza*, *Déjà Vu*, and *Rolling Thunder*. Schrader wrote to her about them in May of that year, clearly wanting her to approve of the path he had taken. He told her that he considered *Taxi Driver* the best of the lot.

Pauline took the screenplay of *Taxi Driver* to bed with her late one night, expecting to leaf through only a few pages before dropping off to sleep. She was so riveted by it, however, that she read the entire script before dawn broke. She was unnerved by the characterization of Travis Bickle, the dissociative cabdriver so obsessed with purging the scum of New York, that she was unable to sleep with the script in the bedroom. Eventually she took it into another room, stacked a pile of other things on top of it, and went back to bed.

In mid-1974 *Taxi Driver* was green-lighted by Columbia Pictures. Schrader was in New York and had dinner with Pauline and the Chicago film reviewer Roger Ebert at the Algonquin. Perhaps because she didn't want to admit she had been wrong about which vocation he should choose, she never said much to Schrader about his script. All she offered about *Taxi Driver* that night was that she felt Robert De Niro would never be able to do justice to the part of Travis Bickle.

In December 1974, when *The Godfather, Part II* was released, Pauline changed her mind about De Niro. The second *Godfather* film, once again directed masterfully by Francis Ford Coppola, was both a prequel and a sequel, picking up the story of Vito Corleone from his Sicilian childhood, and jumping ahead in time to the 1950s, when the new don, the cold-blooded Michael Corleone (Al Pacino), is establishing the family's base of operations in Nevada. *The Godfather, Part II* was that rarest of all sequels: Unfolding at three hours and twenty minutes, it had much greater depth and breadth than the first film. Pauline found that she came close to not having "the emotional resources to deal with the experience of this film. Twice, I almost cried out at acts of violence that De Niro's Vito committed. I didn't look away from the images, as I sometimes do at routine action pictures. I wanted to see the worst; there is a powerful need to see it. You need these moments as you need the terrible climaxes in a Tolstoy novel. A great novelist does not spare our feelings (as the historical romancer does); he intensifies them, and so does Coppola." She admitted that she found *The Godfather, Part II* so overwhelming that "about midway, I began to feel that the film was expanding in my head like a soft bullet." Her review was a fine example of something she always sought to do—let the reader in on her thought processes. She thought that Michael's closed-off self—his inability to have a single moment of happiness—came through brilliantly in Al Pacino's performance. "Is it our imagination, or is Michael's face starting to rot?" Pauline wondered of the film's early scenes. She thought that De Niro, as young Vito, had "the physical audacity, the grace, and the instinct to become a great actor—perhaps as great as Brando." Most of all, she expressed great admiration for Coppola, whose approach she found "openhanded: he doesn't force the situations. He puts the material up there, and we read the screen for ourselves." She found that "the sensibility at work in this film is that of a major artist. We're not used to it: how many screen artists get the chance to work in the epic form, and who has been able to seize the power to compose a modern American epic? And who else, when he got the chance and the power, would have proceeded with the absolute conviction that he'd make the film the way it should be made? In movies, that's the inner voice of the authentic hero." It was one of her most deeply felt pieces of the period, and it elicited a note of praise from Penelope Gilliatt, who called it "a magnificent piece."

It was Francis Ford Coppola's year: He had released another, almost equally remarkable film a few months earlier—*The Conversation*, a harrowingly intimate story of a professional electronics surveillance expert whose life's work has created a sick obsession with his own privacy. With its minimal dialogue and music, *The Conversation* had much in common with *Blow-Up*, but it was a far more vital and less pretentious film. Because it was released in the summer of 1974, Pauline missed reviewing it for *The New Yorker*, but she did manage to get comments on it into a special essay she wrote for the magazine in August, "On the Future of Movies."

That *The Conversation* had not done well in general release, she wrote, was classic proof of the corruption of the studio heads, who couldn't accept that Coppola was "in a position (after directing *The Godfather*) to do what he wanted to do; they're hurt that he flouts their authority, working out of San Francisco instead of Los Angeles. And they don't really have any respect for *The Conversation*, because it's an idea film." Paramount, she claimed "didn't *plan* on *The Conversation* being a success, and nothing now is going to make them help it become one." Pauline identified what she saw as a steadily encroaching trend: Young audiences were no longer quite so willing to take a chance on an unusual, quiet, complicated picture as they might have been a few years ago. She was right that the atmosphere was changing—possibly because the spirit of organized protest had seriously faded and the disillusionment in the wake of Watergate was having a numbing effect on so much of American social and cultural life. It was becoming apparent that "audiences like movies that do all the work for them. . . . They don't mind being banged over the head—the louder the better." While she didn't state it explicitly, "On the Future of Movies" clearly conveyed her concern that the Altmans and Scorseses and Coppolas were going to face difficulties in the years to come. Cutesy comedies like *The Sting* and slam-bang thrillers like *The Exorcist* were what audiences seemed to crave, and they were benefiting from all of the studios' backing, while smaller films like *Thieves Like Us* and *The Conversation* vanished. She overstated her case, however, when she claimed, "The movie companies used to give all their pictures a chance, but now they'll put two or three million, or even five, into selling something they consider surefire, and a token—a pittance—into the others." Although blockbuster marketing was steadily on the rise, and the audience numbers were giving it validation, she neglected to mention that old Hollywood had frequently trashed some of its finest work by not releasing it properly—Fred Zinnemann's *The Member of the Wedding*, Charles Laughton's *Night of the Hunter*, and Orson Welles's *Touch of Evil* being but three examples from the 1950s.

Near the end of "On the Future of Movies," she made another pitch for the artist in Hollywood:

> Perhaps no work of art is possible without belief in the audience—the kind of belief that has nothing to do with facts and figures about what people actually buy or enjoy but comes out of the individual artist's absolute conviction that only the best he can do is fit to be offered to others. . . . An artist's sense of honor is founded on the honor due others. Honor in the arts—and in show business, too—is giving of one's utmost, even if the audience does not appear to know the difference, even if the audience shows every sign of preferring something easy, cheap, and synthetic. The audience one must believe in is the great audience: the audience one was part of as a child, when one first began to respond to great work—the audience one is still part of.

It was a compelling argument, but Fred Goldberg, vice president of United Artists, wrote Pauline a sharp letter objecting to her claim that Paramount hadn't properly supported *The Conversation*. Goldberg claimed that the studio had spent $95,000 on advertising for the film's pre-opening and first week, including two full-page ads in *The New York Times*, one of them quoting the film's many laudatory reviews. Goldberg pointed out that $95,000 was an impressive budget for a theater containing 589 seats. The effort had paid off for one week, because the New York gross was excellent—$30,000—but despite big ads throughout the New York run, the gross began to dip quickly. Goldberg added that if Pauline thought that after that kind of backing, Paramount still did not want *The Conversation* to be a success, it was a sign that she was playing to her prejudices and didn't "really care about the business end of motion pictures." He accused her of underestimating the real power of selling a film—word of mouth in the audience—which no one could ever predict. In closing, he added that he still considered her "a hell of a writer."

In October 1974, Pauline wrote a review of Karel Reisz's *The Gambler*, the story of a New York City English professor (James Caan) with a gambling addiction. She judged it as "strikingly well-edited and . . . dramatically supercharged and compelling." But it was one of Pauline's least favorite kinds of picture, one that was too worked out and schematic. Speaking, as she loved to do, directly to the audience, she wrote that it was "complete without us, and there's nothing for us to do except receive it, feel wiped out, and genuflect."

The screenplay for *The Gambler* was written by the young James Toback, who was not at all pleased when he read Pauline's review. She felt that the movie tried to tell the audience that "the secret of gambling is that gamblers are self-destructive people who want to lose." She thought compulsive gambling had a much simpler source: "The poor bastard who buys a two-dollar ticket he can't afford is hoping to change his life with the two dollars. How else can he change it?"

Not long afterward Toback met Pauline, who was attending a screening in New York with Gina, and quickly confronted her. "I always enjoy reading you," Toback said, "so I was really disturbed to find that the one critic I enjoy reading totally missed the boat on my movie. I'm not talking about whether you liked it or didn't—you just got it wrong. You were so blind with your own personal fury that you didn't actually get what's right on the screen for someone who's listening to hear." Pauline, curious, wanted him to explain. Toback continued, "The whole point in the review was that the movie says gamblers gamble to lose. And that is an idiotic statement. The opposite is in the movie."

As they were getting into the elevator, Pauline suggested that they go out to dinner, so that Toback could explicate further on what he felt she had missed. Over a lengthy meal at O'Neal's he and Pauline talked into the night, while Gina remained silent. "For a while I just felt awkward and tried to direct some of my comments toward her," he recalled, "but I saw after a while that this was probably not unusual."

There was another point in Pauline's review of *The Gambler* that stung Toback. She had commented that the picture featured "a lot of characters, but there is really only one, and he is the author's surrogate, the brilliant young Jewish prince, professor of literature to ghetto blacks, potential great novelist, and gambler." After their dinner, he and Pauline became fast friends, and over time, he thought he understood the source of her comment about his being a Jewish prince. Toback had in fact come from a well-to-do New York family, while Pauline had come from working-class stock. "She never liked to talk about being Jewish," Toback observed. "It was never anything she really identified with. At the same time, she had a real social and cultural antagonism for Jews she felt were sort of pretenders to society. She felt the character in *The Gambler* was that, and therefore I must be." To Toback, Pauline's conflicts about being Jewish were securely rooted in her relationship with her father, a working-class man who was looked down on by certain strata of society—in particular, by other, wealthier Jews. Toback believed that Pauline had grown up eager to establish herself as a personal force, but that it was important to her that she do this without betraying her father and what he was. She would not look down on him. "She thought, 'I'm just what he was. I just happen to be writing interestingly about a popular art. And you don't have to know what John Simon knows to be the best at it.'"

At year's end she saw another movie that enabled her to dig into a film the way she liked to do—*Alice Doesn't Live Here Anymore*. Pauline's suggestion to Robert Getchell that it would be perfect for Robert Altman hadn't come to fruition, although the finished film, with its evocative portrayal of the world of dive bars baking in the Arizona sunshine, had an Altman feel. Ellen Burstyn, who had been cast in the lead, had seen *Mean Streets* and eventually decided that Martin Scorsese would be able to bring to the story the grit she felt it needed.

*Alice* was a movie that the critics were bound to embrace; dozens of reviews mentioned that the movie had come along at just the right point, given the paucity of good women's roles onscreen. Pauline, too, liked *Alice* very much, and what she came up with for *The New Yorker* was one of her most complex—and baffling—reviews of the '70s.

She wrote that it was "one of the rare films that genuinely deserve to be called controversial . . . *Alice* is thoroughly enjoyable: funny, absorbing, intelligent even when you don't believe in what's going on—when the issues it raises get all fouled up."

She referred to *Alice* as "the first angry-young-woman movie"—as portrayed by Ellen Burstyn, Alice had a sharp edge, and her temper was quick to rise to the surface. But she liked the way Scorsese handled the scenes with Alice and her fresh-mouthed son (Alfred Sutter), as well as his avoidance of phony Hollywood warmth. Pauline's difficulty in getting her mind around *Alice* was most likely due to her uneasiness with what she took to be the movie's feminist agenda. And in taking this position, she jumped to conclusions about Burstyn's performance for which she could not possibly have had the least foundation:

> Burstyn appears to be so determined not to play a teasing, fake-tender woman that she flings women's-movement into her work before she's absorbed it as an actress and discovered what she can use and what she can't. And so instead of seeing Alice we're seeing the collision of Alice with Ellen Burstyn's consciousness as of this moment in history. I think we'd connect more fully with Alice if Burstyn weren't trying to turn the role into a statement. On the other hand, there's a stimulation and excitement in what Burstyn is attempting. I don't really like most of her acting here—her rhythm seems a beat off—yet I'm held by what she's trying to do, and by her need to play against stereotypes. Without her ferocious attack, *Alice* might seem no more than a slight, charming comedy.

By writing "The trouble with Ellen Burstyn's performance is that she's playing against something instead of playing a character," Pauline was speculating on the private thought processes of the actress—something she could have had no idea about. She accused Burstyn of striking "so many of those discordant notes that she must think it's a sign of liberation for Alice to be defiantly short-tempered." It was crystal-ball gazing, pure and simple—and quite out of critical bounds.

Despite the fact that her review of *Alice* was essentially a positive one, her comments about Ellen Burstyn wounded the actress. Only four years earlier Burstyn had written Pauline a warm thank-you letter for a positive review of her performance in Paul Mazursky's *Alex in Wonderland*. After the *Alice* review appeared, however, Pauline was not a topic Burstyn was fond of discussing.

Later in February Pauline wrote a review that would, indirectly, come to have enormous impact on her career. Hal Ashby's *Shampoo* was one of the most lavishly praised films of the '70s—a thoughtfully observed and well-acted film about George (Warren Beatty, who also produced and coscripted it), a sexually rapacious Beverly Hills hairdresser who jumps from bed to bed on the eve of the presidential election of 1968. It was designed as a contemporary comedy of manners, and the screenplay, coauthored by Robert Towne, had a subtle, knowing humor and a great sense of structure: It was a little like a Congreve play for the pre-Nixon era.

Pauline, in synch with her colleagues, felt that *Shampoo* "might have been no more than a saucy romp . . . But the way it has been done, the joke expands the more you think about it. *Shampoo* is light and impudent, yet like the comedies that live on, it's a bigger picture in retrospect." What she loved most about it, perhaps, was its honest, dead-on portrayal of how people in a privileged society such as Beverly Hills viewed sex, and its perception of the L.A. experience that no other movie had ever quite captured: It expressed "the emotional climate of the time and place. Los Angeles has become what it is because of the bright heat, which turns people into narcissists and sensuous provocateurs. The atmosphere seems to infantilize sex: sexual desire is despiritualized; it becomes a demand for immediate gratification."

For Warren Beatty, *Shampoo* represented a personal triumph. Since *McCabe & Mrs. Miller*, he had worked fairly steadily in a string of disappointing pictures, but nothing he had done since *Bonnie and Clyde* had had much impact. Pauline found his performance as George in *Shampoo* genuinely impressive; she knew that George wasn't "an easy role; I don't know anyone else who could have played it." In the review she included a line that sounded a bit close to the kind of review that seemed designed to be easily excerpted in movie advertising: She called *Shampoo* "the most virtuoso example of sophisticated kaleidoscopic farce that American moviemakers have ever come up with." It was an early sign of the "absolutist" streak in her reviewing, a tendency that had been fairly latent up until recent years. From this point on, however, she would often describe films and performances in terms of extremes—the best or the worst examples in history.

Directly on the heels of *Shampoo* she undertook what was the boldest move of her career to date. Robert Altman's new picture, *Nashville*, had begun filming in the summer of 1974, and it was the director's most ambitious project yet—an attempt to catch the spirit and pulse of mid-'70s America by way of a story set in the country music capital. Although the tone of *Nashville* was intimate, the film unfolded on a broad canvas: There were twenty-four principal characters in all, several of them played by major stars. Among them were the stud country singer Tom Frank (Keith Carradine), Opal (Geraldine

Chaplin), a sycophantic groupie posing as a BBC reporter, the strung-out country star Barbara Jean (Ronee Blakley), the adulterous gospel singer Linnea (Lily Tomlin), and third-party presidential candidate Hal Phillip Walker (Thomas Hal Phillips).

Pauline made a brief visit to the set of *Nashville* to tape an interview with Altman to be broadcast on European television. As she had when she showed up for the filming of *Thieves Like Us*, she saw enough to give her a good idea of what the director was after—and of course, his choice of a pop-culture subject like Nashville was already to her liking. "She was very entertaining and interesting and funny about herself—self-deprecating," Michael Murphy, who was in the cast, remembered. "Bob was one of the guys who, if you crossed him, he'd let you know about it. He yelled at her a couple of times, and she'd say, 'Oh, Bob . . .' And then she would come back with a good review or a not-so-good review, and they'd be friends again. He didn't court her in the same way a lot of people would. He courted her, but he was himself, and he wasn't paying homage, really. He was very happy that she understood him and what he was trying to do."

Murphy also sensed something else beneath Pauline's convivial surface: "I always had a feeling about Pauline—that there was a certain kind of disdain, from the beginning—that I was not really worthy of being in these movies, that there were a lot of people who were better than I was. She would give me a shot in some review, but I would see her someplace, and I liked her, and she liked me. And eventually, I got a good review from her!"

Sue Barton, director of publicity for Altman's production company, Lion's Gate Pictures, remembered Pauline's visit to the *Nashville* set and her fascination as she sat with the director, watching the dailies. "Bob was very flattered by how wonderful she thought he was," recalled Barton. "I would say she was slightly star-struck. She was so important to the filmmakers, and she had so much power. Being able to quote Pauline Kael was probably the best thing you could ever wish for. She was this little person with her little glasses and her little bowl haircut. She was far from beautiful, and this aspect of her personality allowed her to be with beautiful and interesting people and have a lot of clout. And everybody wanted her to be their friend. Bob was a genuine talent and a genuine eccentric, and that was her love for him."

*Nashville*'s shooting schedule stretched to a little over seven weeks, and then the extensive editing process began. By early 1975 the picture was still not quite completed, but Altman wanted to show it in New York, and Lion's Gate issued invitations to a select few, including Pauline. She was stunned by how brilliant *Nashville* had turned out to be, and throughout the screening, she gasped, clapped her hands together, laughed loudly, and took notes furiously. The next day she telephoned Lion's Gate to ask if it would be acceptable for her to review the film in advance; she knew what the box-office fate of most of Altman's pictures had been, and she had dug around enough to get the sense that *Nashville*'s distributor, Paramount Pictures, wasn't fully behind the movie. The person who took her call told her, "That's what the screening was for." This was the answer Pauline wanted to hear: *Nashville* was scheduled for a summer release, and unless she leaped into action now, the chance to review it would go to Penelope Gilliatt. And Pauline knew that no matter what Gilliatt wrote, her review couldn't possibly help the film find its audience.

She talked Shawn into letting her run the review in advance, and it appeared in the March 3, 1975, issue of *The New Yorker*. It opened with one of her favorite devices, the rhetorical question:

Is there such a thing as an orgy for movie-lovers—but an orgy without excess? At Robert Altman's new, almost-three-hour film, *Nashville*, you don't get drunk on images, you're not overpowered—you get elated. I've never before seen a movie I loved in quite this way: I sat there smiling at the screen, in complete happiness. It's a pure emotional high, and you don't come down when the picture is over; you take it with you. In most cases, the studio heads can conjecture what a director's next picture will be like, and they feel safe that way—it's like an insurance policy. They can't with Altman, and after United Artists withdrew its backing from *Nashville*, the picture had to be produced independently, because none of the other major companies would take it on. U.A.'s decision will probably rack up as a classic boner, because this picture is going to take off into the stratosphere—though it has first got to open. (Paramount has picked up the distribution rights but hasn't yet announced an opening date.) *Nashville* is a radical, evolutionary leap.

In that one paragraph, she accomplished several things: She cued the reader that she had given herself over, without reservation, to the film; she heckled the studios for not supporting Altman; and she proclaimed, before its release, that it was going to be a box-office smash. She admitted that "*Nashville* isn't in final shape yet, and all I can hope to do is to suggest something of its achievement." But she found the movie a profound comment on "the great American popularity contest. Godard was trying to achieve a synthesis of documentary and fiction and personal essay in the early sixties, but Godard's Calvinist temperament was too cerebral. Altman, from a Catholic background, has what Joyce had: a love of the supreme juices of everyday life. He can put unhappy characters on the screen . . . and you don't wish you didn't have to watch them; you accept their unhappiness as a piece of the day, as you do in *Ulysses*." Despite her antagonistic feelings toward the Catholic Church, this was a further expression of her belief that the Catholic upbringings of Coppola, Scorsese, and Altman was key to their success: Simply put, she believed that the Catholic fixation on guilt and sin and mystery had triumphed, in artistic terms, over the traditional Protestant obsessions with repression, self-denial, and an iron work ethic. Kathryn Altman, the director's wife, would dismiss this idea years later, but Joan Tewkesbury somewhat agreed with Pauline, feeling that Altman, like many Catholics who have rejected their faith, was fascinated by "all of those things that are forbidden when you're a kid. But it wasn't conscious, and if you had said that to Bob, he would have told you you were full of shit."

For Pauline, *Nashville* was the greatest example yet of Altman's ability to characterize Americans in a way that had the flavor of satire, yet was so affectionate and complex and true that it went far beyond satire. The movie's comment on America in one of its pivotal moments in history—post-Watergate—was rich and flavorful but never ungenerous, never a cheat, never an easy exposé, in the way that so many films such as *Midnight Cowboy* had been for years. *Nashville* was a brilliant success, in large part, because Altman included the audience in the experience of telling his story as much as he had included his actors. "Altman wants you to be part of the life he shows you," Pauline wrote, "and to feel the exhilaration of being alive. . . . For the viewer, *Nashville* is a constant discovery of overlapping connections. The picture says, This is what America is, and I'm part of it. *Nashville* arrives at a time when America is congratulating itself for having got rid of the bad guys who were pulling the wool over people's eyes. The movie says that it isn't only the politicians who live the big lie—the big lie is something we're all capable of trying for." She ended with a great, crashing, symphonic chord: She called *Nashville* "the funniest epic vision of America ever to reach the screen."

Pauline remained on a high about *Nashville* for weeks afterward, and it helped to sustain her through her disappointment in Barbra Streisand's latest vehicle, a sequel to her Oscar-winning Fanny Brice story, *Funny Lady*. Streisand had been reluctant to do the film, but she had acquiesced to the producer, Ray Stark, to whom she was under contract. *Funny Lady* was leaden and stale and charmless, but what shattered Pauline was that her favorite female star had taken on those same qualities. She found that what Streisand did in the film was "no longer singing, it's something else—that strident overdramatiza-tion that turns a song into a big number. The audience's attention is directed away from the music and onto the star's feat in charging it with false energy. Streisand is out to knock you cold, and you get cold, all right." At the end of her review, she admitted to her readers, "The main problem I had with *Funny Lady* is that I fell out of like with Barbra Streisand." She observed that Strei-sand's "volatility is gone; something rigid and overbearing and heavy seems to be settling into her manner. She may have gone past the time when she could play a character; maybe that's why she turns Fanny Brice into a sacred monster. Has Streisand lost sight of the actress she could be?"

The review provided a kind of vindication for Streisand, who was not so stung by Pauline's barbs that she couldn't see she had been right not to want to do the film in the first place. Pauline was delighted when Streisand phoned her to tell her she thought her comments were just, but Ray Stark, who objected violently to the review, wrote Pauline a strong letter of complaint. She answered him in crusader mode, still trying to use her power for the good of those she considered to be the most gifted in the business:

> Dear Ray,
>
> We'll have to talk about it. If I was unjust to Barbra, that could be because I wasn't pinning enough responsibility on you. Mainly I think we see the film so differently because of our opposing views of Streisand: I think she has it in her to be a great artist and I gather that you don't. If she doesn't, then what she does in *Funny Lady* hardly matters. But if she does, then it's a terrible, self-destructive waste.
>
> But we also disagree about movies: you really believe in the forties—you still want directors to be employees. Ray, you're too smart not to know that the directors you call the good ones are second-rate. And you're too rich not to take a gamble sometimes on the first-rate.

From this point on, Pauline often saw herself as more than a critic. Her reviews became more urgent, more emotional, more haranguing. She seemed to feel that mere criticism wasn't sufficient, that she might be the only thing standing between some of Hollywood's biggest talents and some form of creative bankruptcy.

# CHAPTER EIGHTEEN

*Nashville* went into general release in the summer of 1975, and Pauline's description of it as "the funniest epic vision of America ever to reach the screen" was trumpeted in the print ads. As usual, when the film opened in New York, Altman, accompanied by Joan Tewkesbury, beat a path to the theater where it was playing, checking the movie lines at each showing. *Nashville* wound up costing only a little over $2 million, and with Pauline's news-making advance rave, and the other, mostly positive reviews that came in over the summer, it was expected that the movie would have little trouble becoming a hit, as she had predicted.

Many of her fellow critics, however, were incensed that she had published the early review. They chose to view her action less as a case of passionate advocacy for a deserving picture than as an example of galloping arrogance and opportunism. They had all waited until the distributor had set up official press screenings—why couldn't she? Those who had never trusted her trusted her even less now.

Some were quite vocal in their disapproval. A week after her review appeared in *The New Yorker*, Vincent Canby wrote a lengthy piece in *The New York Times* that opened with an assertion that Pauline hadn't seen the "real" *Nashville*—that there had been no finished soundtrack, that it had been edited since she had viewed it, and might well have further cuts prior to general release. His tone was snide: "If one can review a film on the basis of an approximately three-hour rough cut, why not review it on the basis of a five-hour rough cut? A ten-hour one? On the basis of a screenplay? The original material if first printed as a book? On the basis of a press release? Gossip items?" He then launched into a merciless parody of her prose style, using an imaginary review of Elia Kazan's forthcoming *The Last Tycoon*: "*The Last Tycoon* bombs like a paper bag full of water. It goes splat all over you and you wait there, like an idiot, hoping that someone will wipe you off." (Perhaps not coincidentally, Canby had dedicated his new novel, *Living Quarters*, to Penelope Gilliatt.) In June, just after the film's release, Rex Reed ridiculed Pauline on *The Merv Griffin Show*. He called Altman "really not very talented" and used Pauline's *Nashville* review as evidence that she was "always foaming at the mouth about something."

While it was much discussed among serious film-lovers, the huge potential country-and-western audience didn't take to *Nashville*, and the movie
suffered in those circles from poor word of mouth. The film proved to be too
long, full of too many characters, its point of view a little too sophisticated
for much of rural America. *Nashville* didn't speak to the country as a whole
in the way that Altman had hoped and Pauline had imagined it would. It
would make back its cost and then some, but it was hardly the blockbuster
she had anticipated. Joan Tewkesbury recalled, "Nobody got rich. But it created a kind of firestorm that allowed everybody to keep working, so that was
the payoff."

In the spring of 1975, Pauline picked up two more honorary degrees. On
May 13, Haverford College awarded her a Doctor of Humane Letters; the
citation read, in part, "In the twilight land of flickering forms she is an outpost
of literacy, keeping Mythos safely chained to Logos. Her service is to the best
in our imagined selves." Five days later she received a Doctor of Humane
Letters from Paul E. Bragdon, the president of Reed College in Portland,
Oregon. On June 1 she was an honored guest at the hundredth annual commencement of the Massachusetts College of Art. She made a few appearances
on the lecture circuit, then returned to New York, where she and Gina packed
up their belongings at 333 Central Park West and moved full-time up to Great
Barrington. The Turin had simply become too expensive, and her salary at
*The New Yorker* remained too low for it to be feasible for her to maintain a
residence in Manhattan. Over the years, she had continued to complain about
living in the city, often telling people that life in New York meant being forced
to clear off your work area to set the table for dinner. She reveled in the fresh
air and quiet of Great Barrington, but the move did present one practical
obstacle: She still didn't drive and relied on Gina as her chauffeur. An arrangement was made with *The New Yorker* that she would come to town every two
weeks, see a group of movies back-to-back, stay at the Royalton Hotel in
midtown, and then return to Great Barrington to finish writing her reviews,
with express mail services taking the place of bicycle messengers.

As usual she spent much of the summer making preparations for her fall
season at *The New Yorker*. This partly involved reading a stack of books and
plays whose film versions were due to be released. As always, she clipped
newspaper articles she thought might be pertinent to some of her reviews.
She also watched news programs religiously and made careful notes on matters that she thought might be addressed in her own writing.

In July, she made her usual midsummer solo appearance in *The New Yorker* with a lengthy tribute to Cary Grant that she had been working on for some time. "Cary Grant—The Man from Dream City" was by far the most perceptive analysis of the actor's appeal that had been written to date. The essay was far more than an appreciation of Grant; it was also a penetrating examination of the screwball comedy genre. There were a few echoes of her view of Herman Mankiewicz in "Raising Kane" when she wrote, "Cary Grant is your dream date—not sexless but sex with civilized grace, sex with mystery. He's the man of the big city, triumphantly suntanned. Sitting out there in Los Angeles, the expatriate New York writers projected onto him their fantasies of Eastern connoisseurship and suavity."

Pauline's comments on the Grant legend were extraordinarily acute. She felt that one of the keys to his appeal was his odd, sexy reticence: "He draws women to him by making them feel he needs them, yet the last thing he would do would be to come right out and say it." She felt he was "not the modern kind of actor who taps his unconscious in his acting. Part of his charm is that his angers are all externally provoked; there are no internal pressures in him that need worry us, no rage or rebelliousness to churn us up." Instead, "We could admire him for his timing and nonchalance; we didn't expect emotional revelations from Cary Grant . . . He appeared before us in his radiantly shallow perfection, and that was all we wanted of him."

The most influential film that summer was Steven Spielberg's second feature, *Jaws*, which Pauline thought showed all the confidence, wit, and command of technique that she admired in his debut theatrical film, *The Sugarland Express*. *Jaws* was the kind of jazzy, comedy-inflected thriller she loved, a film that didn't take itself too seriously and represented, as far as she was concerned, the best that American pop culture had to offer—a junk-food film made with craft and wit and style. She wrote that it might well be "the most cheerfully perverse scare movie ever made."

The film opened on June 20, just nine days after *Nashville*, in a wide-release pattern—no starting in a few theaters and waiting for word of mouth to build. With a major television ad campaign paving the way, *Jaws* became one of the biggest moneymakers in history in a remarkably short time, eventually grossing a staggering $458 million—dwarfing *The Exorcist*'s earnings of two years earlier. It established an overnight marketing revolution in Hollywood; the summer blockbuster had been born. Because Pauline admired the film and its director, she failed to perceive where its astonishing success might lead, and how it might ultimately make life more difficult for many of the artists she had spent years championing.

Pauline had a better time than usual at that year's New York Film Festival;

she believed that the great artistic explosion that had ignited films in the late '60s might really endure for a time. There were several American movies she liked, one of which was Michael Ritchie's *Smile*, a comedy set in small-town America about the fictional Young American Miss teenage beauty pageant. It was, in a way, a cousin of *Nashville*, making its comments through the filter of an established American pop institution. Also like *Nashville, Smile* had a definite post-Watergate feel about it: the characters of Big Bob (Bruce Dern) and Brenda (Barbara Feldon), the principal organizers of the pageant, were determined to hold on to their sunny, superficial views of the world despite the fact that America had changed for good.

Ritchie had gotten the idea for *Smile* when he had been a judge at Santa Rosa's Junior Miss pageant; several of the acts for the film's talent competitions, including the packing of a suitcase and Annette O'Toole's "Sincerity Strip," were lifted from real-life beauty contests. Even the long sequence of the Jaycees Exhausted Rooster ceremony, which involved inductees kissing a raw chicken's behind, was taken from life. "Michael Ritchie really had the pulse of America in the most loving way," recalled Barbara Feldon. "He had both the sharpest satirical eye and the most loving touch. At the time we were shooting in Santa Rosa, and when I saw it put together, I was stunned that it wasn't mean. It was very sweet, actually."

Pauline thought Ritchie's direction was a bit uneven, but still she couldn't help admiring *Smile*. "There hasn't been a small-town comedy in so long," she wrote, "that this fresh, mussy [*sic*] film seems to be rediscovering America."

She was especially delighted by the festival's final showing: François Truffaut's *The Story of Adèle H.* The director had been on a self-imposed sabbatical for a few years, writing and studying and searching for inspiration for a new film. Pauline felt his exile had been worthwhile, for his new film affected her as none of his movies had in years. *The Story of Adèle H.* was an unusual choice of subject matter for Truffaut: Adèle (Isabelle Adjani), the younger daughter of Victor Hugo, who has grown up on the isle of Guernsey, where her famous father lives in exile, falls in love with a British lieutenant. They have an affair in England, but the lieutenant wearies of her, and is happy to leave her behind when he is transferred with his regiment to Nova Scotia. But she is determined to repossess him and, defying convention, follows him, hounding him, humiliating him—doing anything to make sure he becomes hers. She manages to sabotage his engagement to another woman of wealth and position, all the while growing more and more desperate and finally going insane.

Pauline was temperamentally drawn to stories such as *Adèle H.*—stories in which women were portrayed acting out their darkest passions, throwing off societal expectations of them, displaying a willingness to go as far as their romantic obsessions could take them. It was for the same reason that she loved the novels of Edna O'Brien, with their fearless confrontation of "the shocking messiness of love"; she prized O'Brien for her "perceptions of what I thought no one else knew—and I wasn't telling."

Pauline considered *Adèle H.* the first genuinely great movie to emerge from Europe since *Last Tango in Paris*. What she admired most was the way that Truffaut managed to tell his story in a way that was both "romantic *and* ironic: he understands that maybe the only way we can take great romantic love now is as craziness, and that the craziness doesn't cancel out the romanticism—it completes it. Adèle's love isn't corrupted by sanity; she's a great crazy. She carries her love to the point where it consumes everything else in her life, and when she goes mad, it doesn't represent the disintegration of her personality; it is, rather, the final integration."

The big American movie of 1975—the movie that captured the hearts of the public in the way that Pauline had hoped *Nashville* would—was *One Flew Over the Cuckoo's Nest*, Milos Forman's adaptation of the 1962 novel by Ken Kesey. Its story of Randle McMurphy, who leads a rebellion among the inmates of an Oregon state mental hospital, was closely tied to the political turmoil of the '60s, with the inmates standing in for America's free-spirited, searching youth, and the maddeningly calm and manipulative Nurse Ratched being viewed as a reflection of Nixon's silent majority. These associations were inevitable, and because Kesey's novel had been so popular, particularly with college students, an even reasonably faithful film version of it was probably destined to be a hit.

But *One Flew Over the Cuckoo's Nest* received mixed reviews when it opened in November, with several critics complaining that the novel had been over-simplified. Howard Kissel felt that a few years earlier, the good guys vs. bad guys scheme would have "led to a victory for the good guys. Now it is the bad guys who triumph—for no apparent reason other than to intensify the emotional blow to the audience."

In her *New Yorker* review, Pauline took issue with the "long literary tradition behind this man's-man view of women as the castrater-lobotomizers," but she thought the film deserved credit for making Kesey's comic-strip fantasy about freedom and repression human and more realistic. She found it "a powerful, smashingly effective movie" and praised Milos Forman for grasping "how crude the poet-paranoid system of the book would look on the screen now that the sixties' paranoia has lost its nightmarish buoyancy. . . . Forman could have exploited the Watergate hangover and retained the paranoid simplicities that helped make hits of *Easy Rider* and *Joe,* but instead he . . . has taken a less romantic, more suggestive approach." She thought that McMurphy was a great role for Jack Nicholson, with his "half smile—the calculated insult that alerts audiences to how close to the surface his hostility is." She thought McMurphy was "so much of a Nicholson role that the actor may not seem to be getting a chance to do much new in it. But Nicholson doesn't use the glinting, funny-malign eyes this time; he has a different look—McMurphy's eyes are farther away, muggy, veiled even from himself. You're not sure what's going on behind them."

The opening of a new Stanley Kubrick film had become an occasion for Pauline to dread. In the wake of *2001* and *A Clockwork Orange,* Kubrick had been all but deified by the media; the combination of his reputation as one of filmland's true intellectuals and his attention-getting ways of making movies had many critics and reporters poised to salute his every effort as a Great Cultural Landmark. The new project was *Barry Lyndon,* based on Thackeray's novel about a penniless Irish rogue who rises to dizzying wealth and social position in the mid–eighteenth century. Kubrick's film moved at a perfect adagio tempo that was nevertheless surprisingly novel and hardly ever dull.

Pauline acknowledged the film's visually arresting quality and found its first segments mesmerizing. She thought the novel had probably intrigued Kubrick because of its "externalized approach," which he had devised a way of matching in stately pictorial terms. But she felt he had missed Thackeray's lighthearted, satirical tone. For her, the movie wore out its welcome fairly soon. "As it becomes apparent that we are to sit and admire the lingering tableaux," she wrote, "we feel trapped. It's not merely that Kubrick isn't releasing the actors' energies or the story's exuberance but that he's deliberately holding the energy level down." She couldn't help jabbing Kubrick in a rather personal way when she wrote of her disappointment in seeing the picture's "slack-faced and phlegmatic" star, Ryan O'Neal, "his face straining with the effort to be what the Master wants—and all that Kubrick wants is to use him as a puppet." Every frame of it was a reflection of the director's self-importance. "Kubrick isn't taking pictures in order to make movies, he's making movies in order to take pictures," she wrote. She also expressed her desire that Kubrick "would come home to this country to make movies again, working fast on modern subjects" such as his early, expert noir thriller *The Killing.*

*Barry Lyndon* divided the New York critics, ten of whom, led by *Time*'s

Richard Schickel and *The New York Times*'s Vincent Canby, wrote favorably of it, with eight writing unfavorably. There was further divisiveness at that year's voting for the New York Film Critics Circle Awards, which Rex Reed reported in his column in the *Daily News*. "I think it is important to remind everyone that *Barry Lyndon* was the head-on favorite of many of the voters," he complained, "losing out in the third ballot only because the absentee critics lost their rights to proxies. I was voting for *Barry Lyndon* all the way." Reed, like many others, was incensed that *Nashville* took the Best Picture prize both from the NYFCC and the National Society of Film Critics.

When Sam Peckinpah's *The Killer Elite* was released that winter, Pauline wrote an odd essay for "The Current Cinema" titled "Notes on the Nihilist Poetry of Sam Peckinpah." Less a review than a lengthy mash note, it offered an enormous amount of ammunition to her critics; Andrew Sarris could hardly be blamed if he felt that Pauline was becoming more of an auteurist than he had ever been. She liked *The Killer Elite*, which she found "intensely, claustrophobically exciting." But the essay was most concerned with her admiration for her maverick friend, who continued to spit in the faces of the movie executives who thought they knew how to handle artists:

> As the losing battles with the moneymen have gone on, year after year, Peckinpah has—only partly sardonically, I think, begun to see the world in terms of the bad guys (the studio executives who have betrayed him or chickened out on him) and the people he likes (generally actors), who are the ones smart enough to see what the process is all about, the ones who haven't betrayed him yet. Hatred of the bad guys—the total mercenaries—has become practically the only sustaining emotion in his work, and his movies have become fables about striking back.

And later:

> Peckinpah has become so nihilistic that filmmaking itself seems to be the only thing he believes in. He's crowing in *The Killer Elite*, saying, "No matter what you do to me, look at the way I can make a movie." The bedeviled bastard's got a right to crow.

All of this was unquestionably sincere. But it was too much—Pauline was all but turning Peckinpah into a Christlike figure in the pages of *The New Yorker*. If Pauline admired the "craziness" in artists, Peckinpah gave it to her in spades. She failed to see that her idolatry of him was a kind of romanticism, that perhaps the executives who tried to keep him on track during the course of making a film might possibly have a legitimate point of view as well.

Pauline and Peckinpah continued to keep up a close correspondence. In 1976, he wrote to her from England, where he was filming *Cross of Iron* and coping with a trying sabbatical from alcohol:

> If God had not meant man to drink he would not have invented the grape or the process known as distillation. . . . I enjoy living a life of sobriety and piety and do not look forward to the 17th of this month when my liver will give me the okay to begin again my needed ways of self-destruction. But I have found that being sober constantly is somewhat of a letdown, as I have been waking up without a hangover (the one I have been nursing so carefully for some 20 odd years). I feel like I have lost an old friend, but he is just one of many that I have lost on this film.

Some people gossiped that Pauline was sleeping with Peckinpah, and still others thought there was a romantic connection between her and her good friend Richard Albarino, a handsome, energetic New York writer whose company Pauline enjoyed because his intellectual tempo was similar to hers. But those closer to her knew better. The fact was that Pauline had been finished with men for some time. "She was done completely," said James Toback. "One hundred percent. And if you wanted to misinterpret her life about the ones who were sort of escorting her, the one that you could have misinterpreted was Dick Albarino. It had the appearance of that, but that was not true."

Having missed the opportunity to write about Paul Mazursky's *Blume in Love*, Pauline was delighted to celebrate his next movie, *Next Stop Greenwich Village*, an autobiographical account of his days as a young actor in New York. She parted company with her fellow critics, however, when she reviewed Lina Wertmuller's *Seven Beauties* in the winter of 1976, a film that was acclaimed in *The New York Times* as "Miss Wertmuller's *King Kong*, her *Nashville*, her *8½*, her *Navigator*, her *City Lights*." "If *Seven Beauties* is all these things, what is it?" Pauline wondered. This film about the misadventures of a Neapolitan man during World War II who runs afoul of the Nazis and is sent to a concentration camp where he pathetically tries to win favor with a female commandant was, Pauline thought, "beyond annoyance . . . it's extremely ambitious, and I think it's a gloppy mess." She disliked Wertmuller's films—she hadn't responded to the much-acclaimed *Swept Away*, either, complaining that "the characters never shut up"—and noted that it was futile to discuss "the stated ideas in a Wertmuller film because they can't be sorted out . . . The way Lina Wertmuller makes movies, she has to believe that disorder is creative. She plunks in whatever comes to mind, and rips through the scenes. It's all bravura highs and bravura lows, without any tonal variation," all the while believing that she was "raising the consciousness of the masses."

She also strayed from the herd with her review of Martin Scorsese's *Taxi Driver.* Pauline, of course, had a long history with the project, and the end result was just as unnerving as she had imagined it would be that night two years earlier, when she had read the script in bed and then been afraid to have it in the room with her. Perhaps no mainstream film—not even *Midnight Cowboy*—had so fully explored the seamy side of New York, which in 1976 was still a grim, crime-ridden city in which old-time residents bemoaned the ugly decline of neighborhoods such as Times Square, where much of the movie's action took place. The character of Iris, the twelve-year-old hooker played by Jodie Foster—the focal point of Travis's reformer's zeal—was a movie first, and genuinely disturbing. There is an unnerving sequence in which Travis attempts to date Betsy, the campaign worker portrayed by Cybill Shepherd, by taking her to a porn film in Times Square. And there is the depiction of Travis's insane assassination plot aimed at the political candidate Palantine. Like *Nashville*, *Taxi Driver* considered the violence that marginalized outsiders could inflict on those who occupied center stage.

In time, *Taxi Driver* would be held up as one of the richest examples of the bold new directorial sensibility that had sprung up in American films of the 1970s. So it is surprising to read the reviews it received on its initial release. Many, like Vincent Canby's, were positive. But there was plenty of negative press, too. Andrew Sarris disliked "its life-denying spirit, its complete lack of curiosity about the possibilities of people. Between Scorsese's celebrated Catholic guilt and Schrader's celebrated Protestant guilt even a Checker cab would groan under such a burden of self-hatred."

It must have been difficult for Pauline to write about the film, given her history with Schrader, and in the review she pointedly did not go into any detail about Schrader's contribution; she simply mentioned that he wrote the script. All the credit was given to Martin Scorsese, whom she thought "may just naturally be an Expressionist . . . Scorsese's Expressionism isn't anything like the exaggerated sets of the German directors; he uses documentary locations, but he pushes discordant elements to their limits, and the cinematographer, Michael Chapman, gives the street life a seamy, rich pulpiness." Although she initially told Schrader that De Niro wouldn't be up to playing Travis, she thought that he had given a wondrous performance: He had "used his own emptiness—he's reached down into his own anomie. Only Brando has done this kind of plunging, and De Niro's performance had something of the undistanced intensity that Brando's had in *Last Tango*." She wrote, "No other film has ever dramatized urban indifference so powerfully; at first, here, it's horrifyingly funny, and then just horrifying."

Ultimately, Pauline saw *Taxi Driver* as a brilliant expression of her own fears about New York. In the screening room where she first viewed the film—Bernard Herrmann's score had not yet been added—she sat in stunned silence at the ending, in which Travis winds up being acclaimed as a hero and resumes his restless night-driving search, which will surely explode in violence once again. Her friend Joseph Hurley recalled that when the movie was over, she leaned back in her seat and cried, *"He's still out there!"*

In the spring of 1976 Pauline's fifth collection appeared, covering the period of her *New Yorker* reviews from September 1972 to March 1975. The working title had been the jokey *All the Way with Movies*, but when she had tested it on her friends and none of them liked it, she switched it to *Reeling*. This time she paid a price for the wildly passionate enthusiasm she expressed in her reviews.

Once again coverage of her book occupied the prestigious front page of *The New York Times Book Review*. Once again, it was no longer enough to hail it as an important volume of criticism; by now, Pauline occupied such a significant place in the literary as well as popular culture that some deeper perspective was needed. The illustration the *Times* chose was a constellation of star shapes filled with the head shots of various artists, including Robert Altman, Barbra Streisand, Marlon Brando, and Martin Scorsese. Pauline's face dominated—the biggest star of all.

The assigned reviewer was Robert Brustein, the erudite theater critic. His essay opened on a positive note with a generous mention of Pauline's "animation and charm as a movie reviewer." Brustein felt that "at a time when many critics are expressing feelings of dejection, even a sense of apocalypse about their subjects, Miss Kael continues to write about movies with the breathless delirium of one smitten with young love."

Brustein expressed his concern, however, that she had become too much of a clucking mother hen concerning the fates of the movies and directors she loved, and that her writing was "becoming larded with hyperbole."

> I don't mean to quarrel with Miss Kael's opinions. I enjoyed most of these movies myself. . . . No, what disturbs me about these quotes is the promotional quality of the language and the way her enthusiasm is just

beginning to fade over into press agentry. Like most influential critics, Miss Kael must be aware that she is writing not only for the reader but for the advertising agency—movie ads now reprint her reviews some-times in their entirety—but in her wholly laudable efforts to bring good movies to the attention of as many people as possible, she has, willy-nilly, become a cog in the marketing mechanism of the very system she deplores.

Brustein went on to say that her energetic style was best digested by read-ing only a few reviews at a time. "It is always an entertaining book," he wrote, "and piece by piece a brilliant one, but taking it in large doses, you may get frazzled by all the feverish energy, flashing like St. Elmo's fire, around so many ephemeral works."

She was likewise criticized for her hyperbole in *The Village Voice*'s review, written by Richard Gilman—and illustrated with a doctored photo of Pauline wearing star-shaped sunglasses. While acknowledging her formidable gifts as a writer, Gilman wrote, "What she so often practices now, setting the lead for her fellows, is an amalgam of idiosyncratic opinion, star gazing, myth-mongering, politics, sociological punditry, and intervention as a kind of co-worker in the medium. It may be in tune with the times, may be much more satisfying to many readers than the tradition (her popularity of course suggests that it is), but it's surely different from criticism as we've known it."

Gilman's most damning words came in characterizing her involvement with directors, writers, and other people in the industry, which he interpreted as a "desire to relieve the lonely detachment of the commentator by an active role, a direct hand in it all. I mean by this her notorious abandonment of critical neutrality, the scandalous apotheosis of *Nashville* before it was finished; the trafficking with certain directors and screenwriters as evangelist and would-be colleague."

Pauline was incensed by many of the carping reviews that *Reeling* received, but at least one of them led to an enduring friendship. Greil Marcus, the rock critic and books columnist for *Rolling Stone*, published a review of *Reeling* that also accused her of lapsing into hyperbole. "Everything had to be the greatest, the best, the newest," he recalled. "And it seemed to be out of control, and I didn't know what this was about." When Marcus's review appeared, Pauline telephoned him at his home in Berkeley. "Did you really mean all that stuff that you wrote about me?" she asked. Marcus said that he did. "Well," said Pauline, "my daughter agrees with you, but I don't. I'm coming to Berkeley and would like to meet you."

The Marcuses invited her to dinner, and when she arrived at their house, she looked around and asked where the other guests were. "She just sort of expected that there would be a big party for her," Marcus said. "Which it had never occurred to us to do. We had a marvelous time, and she lived up to all our fantasies, which is to say, she was extreme in her opinions—extreme in her likes and dislikes, whether it had to do with movies or books or food or anything."

The spring of 1976 was occupied with a heavy promotional tour for *Reeling*, which started with lectures at the College of Marin, Berkeley, the Los Angeles Film Festivals (Filmex), Immaculate Heart College, and the University of Colorado at Boulder. There were numerous radio and television interviews, including an hour-long appearance on Los Angeles's KNBC-TV. She also was eager to appear on several of the national talk shows whose invitations she had previously declined, including those of Mike Douglas, Dinah Shore, and Phil Donahue. She wrote to her editor Billy Abrahams that she would be "happy to do any radio or TV that comes up, but wish to avoid newspaper and magazine interviews, as I am too tempting a target for bitchy reporters."

By the summer of 1976 Pauline had a new agent, Perry Knowlton of Curtis, Brown Ltd. Peter Davison of the Atlantic Monthly Press was delighted and wrote Knowlton a congratulatory note, advising him, "She is not lacking in exigence as an author, nor, I'm sure you will find, as a client." But the publisher was relieved that at last she was handling her business affairs over to a proper agent, having been without one since dispensing with Robert Mills's services several years earlier.

She had a number of new projects in the offing, one of which was a collection of her capsule reviews. Knowlton offered it to Billy Abrahams for an advance of $75,000. Abrahams balked at the asking price and offered $25,000, which Pauline turned down out of hand. There was also *Lays of Ancient Hollywood*, a collection of essays on actors, with "Cary Grant—The Man from Dream City" as its centerpiece. But Abrahams again found Knowlton's request for $75,000 "too high by far," and passed; the long-planned book never materialized.

In the fall of 1976 Pauline saw a movie at the New York Film Festival that she admired very much—the Swiss director Alain Tanner's *Jonah Who Will Be 25 in the Year 2000*, the story of a group of left-leaning men and women who are attempting to adjust to the fact that the social revolution they anticipated in the '60s has not come to pass. It was a witty and quietly provocative talkfest, austerely but beautifully photographed, and while some critics objected to its odd structure—John Simon found the people in it "as uncomfortable to watch as a backless chair is to sit in"—Pauline thought it "a marvelous toy, weightless, yet precise and controlled." She was indulgent of what would become the year's smash hit, *Rocky*, saying that the picture was "shameless, and that's why—on a certain level—it works. What holds it together is innocence." She was won over by Sylvester Stallone's performance in the title role, as a down-and-out debt collector who gets a chance at the world heavyweight boxing title. "Stallone has the gift of direct communication with the audience," Pauline wrote. "Rocky's naïve observations come from so deep inside him that they have Lewis Carroll enchantment."

The young writer Carrie Rickey, a former student of Pauline's old friend Manny Farber, accompanied Pauline the night she saw *Rocky* (which happened to be Election Night, 1976) and would remember the evening for reasons apart from the movie. After the screening, Pauline and Rickey went to her room at the Royalton and watched the election returns. Pauline, who supported Jimmy Carter, was incensed when Rickey admitted that she had cast an absentee ballot in her native California for Eugene McCarthy. "She screamed at me for doing that," recalled Rickey. "She lectured me on why I needed to be for Carter. We also had a very interesting conversation about whether *Nashville* predicted Carter—this weird populist governor from a Southern state augured for a Carter win."

Rickey also remembered Pauline's lack of interest in the feminist movement. Rickey was quite intrigued by the contrast between the female and male aesthetics in film. "I had proposed back then that the women who directed movies—and there weren't a lot of them—used longer takes and not a lot of cuts. I thought their rhythm was inimical to mainstream cinema, which was more quick cuts and actions. Pauline said, 'Stay away from that feministic stuff'—her word—'it's going to kill your career.'"

The picture that excited Pauline most in late 1976 was an unexpected one: Brian De Palma's *Carrie*. Based on a novel by Stephen King, *Carrie* was a horror tale about the drab, unpopular high school girl (Sissy Spacek) dominated by her crazed, fundamentalist mother but gifted with powers of telekinesis. The film climaxed at the senior prom, where, after her sadistic high school classmates humiliate her by rigging the election so that she is voted prom queen and then dumping a bucket of pig's blood on her, she exacts a horrifying revenge on all of them. In *Carrie*, De Palma went far beyond the parameters of the typical horror film, infusing it with a great deal of warmth and humor, and a rather astute point of view about growing up in 1970s America. It had a nasty, funny, subversive feel, and was perhaps the ideal horror film for the post-Watergate era. Pauline had admired aspects of De Palma's low-budget efforts in the 1960s, but with *Carrie*, she felt he had arrived onscreen as a major talent. And the acclaim she heaped on him caused a great deal of eye-rolling among her colleagues, who felt that the director had turned out nothing more than a well-crafted commercial product.

Pauline thought *Carrie* had "a beautiful plot," and she laid another of her superlatives on De Palma, who, in her judgment, had "the wickedest baroque sensibility at large in American movies." She loved the teasing sense of humor and pulp sensibility that he brought to the horror movie. To Pauline, *Carrie* seemed to be taking off from a number of other movies, including *Psycho*, *The Way We Were*, and one of her favorite classic bad films, 1935's *She*, with Helen Gahagan. In his 1960s films, she pointed out, De Palma had used mostly stationary camera setups, but here his camera swirled dizzingly in scene after scene, particularly the romantic moment with Carrie and her dream date (William Katt) at the senior prom, in which the audience has the sensation of dancing along with the couple and getting completely drawn into the most gloriously romantic night of poor Carrie's wretched life. She celebrated De Palma's emergence as a stylish, tongue-in-cheek director. "He's uncommitted to anything except successful manipulation," she wrote, "when his camera conveys the motion of dreams, it's a lovely trick. He can't treat a subject straight, but that's all right; neither could Hitchcock. . . . Everything in his films is distanced by his persistent adolescent kinkiness; he's gleefully impersonal."

If her elevation of De Palma's "persistent adolescent kinkiness" into some kind of major achievement baffled many of Pauline's friends as well as her enemies, it was her review, in the end, that carried the day for De Palma and his cast. Nancy Allen, who played the movie's chief villainess, remembered vividly the day that Pauline's review appeared. "I think that Brian was just thrilled," she said. "And disgusted at the same time, because the studio wasn't treating it like it was anything better than a slasher picture." De Palma quickly became one of the directors Pauline felt compelled to promote. Allen remembered that she had the reputation for being a bit chilly toward her pet directors' wives and girlfriends, but she found Pauline warm and friendly. "She liked Brian a lot and there I was, the girlfriend. I didn't know if I would be accepted or not. She was very pleasant and said hello and smiled sweetly. I remember thinking, *Okay, that was all right*. She was possessive. They were her guys."

But if Pauline led the critical chorus in praise of *Carrie*, she was in the front row of the booing section for one of the most extravagantly praised and talked-about movies of the year, Sidney Lumet's satire on the television industry,

*Network.* Lumet was not the real creative force behind the picture—that distinction belonged to the screenwriter, Paddy Chayevsky, who had long since established himself as the satirist for the masses. *Network* appealed to a wide audience, partly because everyone could grasp its shrill, loud message, and also because it presented itself as a movie that was really about something *important*. Perhaps it was the film's combination of intellectual posturing and outrageous satire that seduced the critics, many of whom gave it excellent reviews. The television newsmen themselves took a much dimmer view of the picture. CBS's Walter Cronkite called it "a fantasy burlesque that might be considered an interesting, amusing divertissement, but nothing more," and NBC's Edwin Newman denounced it as "incompetent."

Pauline loathed the movie, observing that Chayefsky had become "like a Village crazy, bellowing at you: blacks are taking over, revolutionaries are taking over, women are taking over. He's got the New York City hatreds, and ranting makes him feel alive." She felt that Chayefsky's thesis that television "is turning us into morons and humanoids" was insupportable. "TV may have altered family life and social intercourse; it may have turned children at school into entertainment seekers. But it hasn't taken our souls, any more than movies did, or the theatre and novels before them." The movie was unremitting in its assault on the audience. She complained that Chayefsky had failed to provide audiences with a good, satiric farce because he wrote "directly to the audience—he soapboxes. He hardly bothers with the characters; the movie is a ventriloquial harangue," aided by Lumet, who kept "the soliloquies going at a machine-gun pace." But while an enthusiastic review from Pauline could often help a film's box-office fortunes, a damning review from her had little impact if a movie was destined to connect with the public consciousness— which *Network* certainly did: *Network*'s *"I'm as mad as hell and I'm not going to take this anymore!"* became more widely quoted than any movie line since "I'm going to make him an offer he can't refuse."

In her spare time Pauline continued to be a TV news junkie, and nothing that transpired on the American political and cultural scenes seemed to escape her notice. She was an avid TV watcher in other ways, too, some of her favorites being *The Carol Burnett Show*, *The Mary Tyler Moore Show*, and the comedy phenomenon that had premiered on NBC in the fall of 1975, *Saturday Night Live*. She was less enthusiastic about many of the well-intentioned made-for-television films of the time, though she did like her friend Lamont Johnson's *The Execution of Private Slovik*, starring Martin Sheen. (It made up for her distaste for Johnson's *Lipstick*, a graphic rape drama starring Margaux and

Mariel Hemingway that had been hampered by studio interference. When Johnson ran into Pauline at a screening of the film in New York, she got up from her seat as the final credits were rolling and whispered, "I'm not going to write about this one, darling.")

As 1976 drew to a close, Pauline expressed her growing disappointment in Barbra Streisand, whose latest film, *A Star Is Born*, represented what she felt was another step in the wrong direction. Most stars, at some point, become obsessed with delivering the image that they want their public to believe in—and often, the one that the public itself wants to believe. For Pauline, Streisand had now reached this juncture in her career. Her portrayal of Esther Hoffman in *A Star Is Born* was in effect a rejection of her earlier brash New York Jewish girl persona. The bigger the star she was becoming, the more she seemed to want to be loved. Pauline found "she acts a virtuous person by not using much energy. She seems at half-mast, out of it, and you don't get engrossed in reading her face, because she's reading it for you. She wants to make sure we get what's going on all the time. That kills any illusion—that and the camera, which is always on her a second too soon, and seconds too long, emphasizing how admirable she is, how strong yet loving. How gracious, too." *A Star Is Born* was done in because all the sting was taken out of the plot—now it was "a drippy love story about two people who love each other selflessly." She felt that Streisand had taken a one-dimensional, colorless role, with no indication in the script that Esther might have a hint of ruthless ambition that would make her rise to stardom more interesting.

The musical orchestrations, which Pauline characterized as "fake gospel, fake soul, fake disco, or fake something else" didn't help, either. But the saddest waste, as far as she was concerned, was of her beloved star. "Streisand has more talent than she knows what to do with, and the heart of a lion," she wrote. "But she's made a movie about the unassuming, unaffected person she wants us to think she is, and the image is so truthless she can't play it."

John Gregory Dunne and Joan Didion had written the script, but later they all but disowned the picture after it was turned over to Streisand and her coproducer husband, Jon Peters. After Pauline's damning review appeared, Dunne wrote to her, "Yours was the only notice I saw that proceeded from the proper assumptions about the story and the kind of star it attracted. . . . To give Barbra her due, she always knew that, given the nature of the material, the man had to have the better part. She asked us to switch the parts around, but we said the man would come out like Chance Wayne [the gigolo in Tennessee Williams's *Sweet Bird of Youth*]. . . . We are now quite amused . . . by the movie, in large part because of the amount of money it is making."

Dunne concluded by saying he hoped to see Pauline when she was in L.A. that spring: "Perhaps we can get together. I'm only a parttime shit."

Considering her fame, and the stable if not completely secure financial position she was in, it was odd that Pauline traveled to Europe so infrequently. That May, however, she did agree to serve on the jury at the 1977 Cannes Film Festival. It was welcome recognition of her stature from the international film community, but the experience itself was not a positive one. The jury included the chair, Roberto Rossellini, plus Jacques Demy, Carlos Fuentes, Benoîte Groult, and Marthe Keller. Shortly after her arrival Keller was pulled aside by Robert Favre Le Bret, the festival's president, who informed her that a solid commercial choice was needed for the top prize, the coveted Palme d'Or, and that he was instructing her to vote for Ettore Scola's *A Special Day*, starring Marcello Mastroianni and Sophia Loren—a film with the potential to be a great commercial success. Keller, incensed, went to the jury members the next day and told them what had transpired. Over the next few days the jurors were approached one by one—with Pauline, the one that Le Bret had reason to fear the most—being the last. The end result was they all tacitly agreed not to vote for *A Special Day*—a film most of them admired—on principle. Instead the Palme d'Or went to Paolo and Vittorio Taviani's *Padre Padrone*. "I will remember all my life," Keller said, "the morning the Palme d'Or was announced—Le Bret said on the radio that the women who wanted to make some salade niçoise, they would not find any tomatoes, because people were throwing them at the jury today. Pauline got completely wild."

Keller spent a great deal of time with Pauline at Cannes. "We had, in private, a great relationship. We went all the time to see the movies together. She had very good manners—but not in the theater when she saw the movie." At a screening of Marguerite Duras's *Le Camion,* with Gérard Depardieu, Pauline started to scream when she saw the actor's name in the credits. "Before it started, she was saying very bad things about him," Keller recalled.

James Toback remembered that she viewed her summer at Cannes as "a horrible experience." He felt that Pauline had, despite her elevated position, retained a heavy streak of provincialism that was rooted in her defensiveness about her upbringing. To yield to the intoxication of a major European cultural event such as Cannes simply would be a betrayal of her entire background. "She was not comfortable in Europe because she was not the pope," Marthe Keller observed. "There are highly intelligent people, lots of them, in our business in Europe. In America, some of them were a little bit more superficial. I think she was too smart to be only a critic. I think there was somewhere a frustration in her. I thought she was so smart, but there was something mean killing her smartness."

The summer at Cannes also brought about a small eruption in her harmonious relationship with Robert Altman. There had been trouble earlier, when Pauline had seen his first picture since *Nashville*, *Buffalo Bill and the Indians*. After the screening, which was attended by many in Altman's inner circle, Pauline sat in silence. It was the first Altman picture since *Brewster McCloud* that she thought was a fizzle, and she was wondering how to let the director know. Finally, she leaned over to him at dinner and whispered that she thought the editing should be speeded up a bit to give the picture more momentum. Altman was drunk, and he exploded at her, telling her to be a big girl and get up and share her opinion with everyone else in the room.

It was a tense moment, followed by another at Cannes, where Altman's new film, *Three Women*, starring Sissy Spacek and Shelley Duvall, was being shown. "I was at Cannes, because Shelley won a prize there for it," recalled Altman. "And I remember seeing Pauline at the airport, and she said, 'I loved the first part of the movie, Bob, but I hated the second part.' I said, 'That's like I'm showing you my new kid, and you say, 'I love his head but I can't stand his body.' So you didn't like it. Forget it."

But the director didn't forget that Pauline had failed to advocate for *Three Women* when she was in a powerful position on the Cannes jury. Marthe Keller bumped into him at Elaine's restaurant in Manhattan not long after, and he refused to speak to her. For Keller, that was the price paid for being a juror: "You have one person who loves you forever, and you have twenty-five people who hate you."

The 1936 graduating class of San Francisco's Girls' High School
(Pauline is in the front row, tenth from the right).

Detail: Pauline, front row, center.

James Broughton, the father of Pauline's only child, Gina James.

Pauline cutting her friend Linda Allen's hair, at Pauline's house on Oregon Street, Berkeley, 1964.

Gina James, Berkeley, 1964.

The members of the New York Film Critics Circle, 1970.
BACK ROW (standing): Bernard Drew, Pauline, A. H. Weiler, William Wolf,
Frances Herridge, Frances Taylor, Archer Winsten, Robert Salmaggi, Judith
Crist. FRONT ROW (seated): Ann Guarino, Wanda Hale, Kathleen Carroll.

Pauline on the New Journalism panel at the 1972 More Conference.
Photographed by Jill Krementz; all rights reserved.

Pauline receiving the National Book Award from Janet Flanner.
Photographed by Jill Krementz; all rights reserved.

A 1975 appearance on PBS, with Robert MacNeil and Woody Allen.

Pauline's one and
only stint as a juror at
the Cannes Film
Festival, 1977, with
producer-actor
Jacques Perrin.

Always a reluctant New Yorker, Pauline found the perfect retreat in Great Barrington, Massachusetts.

Pauline at home in Great Barrington.

Pauline's writing desk: order was always extremely important to her.

Pauline with one of her *New Yorker* editors, William Whitworth.
Photographed by Jill Krementz; all rights reserved.

Pauline in her office at *The New Yorker*.
Photographed by Jill Krementz; all rights reserved.

September 15, 1980          Jill Krementz

Pauline with her close friend Polly Frost.

Pauline's eightieth birthday party, June 1999.

# CHAPTER NINETEEN

Unlike many of her colleagues, who thought it was appropriate to be entertained by press agents and publicists, Pauline maintained a strict code when it came to accepting gifts or even meals out. If she liked and respected the people, she treated them fairly—if not, she could be withering. Marion Billings, who worked on many of Martin Scorsese's best pictures, was a publicist Pauline particularly admired. They met at a screening for *Mean Streets*, became friends, and for years had a regular lunch date at Armando's, an Italian restaurant on West Seventy-sixth Street. Billings would make it clear that she was on an expense account, but Pauline never permitted her to pick up the check. "She respected me because I didn't lie," Billings recalled. At one point early in their friendship, Pauline gave her a copy of *Kiss Kiss Bang Bang*, inscribed "For Marion—and there are all those others that out of charity I haven't mentioned, but which are engraved on our behinds instead of our hearts. Love, Pauline." Some of the others could try their best to ingratiate themselves with her, but it didn't work. Sally Ann Mock of *The New Yorker* remembered one Christmas in the mid-'70s when a steady stream of bottles of liquor and boxes of chocolates was sent to Pauline from various publicists. Mock's job that holiday season was to pack them all up and send them back.

Michael Sragow, film critic for *The Baltimore Sun*, among other publications, once observed that 1977 was a pivotal year in the American movie industry—the year when film artistry quite suddenly reached a plateau as a number of changes began to make themselves felt throughout Hollywood. Pauline had guessed wrong about the long-term impact of a couple of the young-lion directors who had burst forth early in the decade, namely Peter Bogdanovich and William Friedkin. After three spectacular box-office successes in a row—*The Last Picture Show*, *What's Up, Doc?*, and *Paper Moon*—Bogdanovich suffered three consecutive flops: *Daisy Miller*, *At Long Last Love*, and *Nickelodeon*. Friedkin, after the enormous success of both *The French Connection* and *The Exorcist*, came up with the disappointing *Sorcerer*.

Another factor whose influence Pauline didn't quite fully appreciate was the enormous box-office (and critical) success of *Jaws*. The danger it presented was that the blockbuster was now becoming the backbone of the industry—something upon which every studio was beginning to depend. The studios increasingly wanted the safe guarantees of audience polls, demographic studies, and bank-approved stars. Low-budget films that were deemed lacking in mass appeal were routinely denied a big marketing and publicity push and might return only a few hundred thousand dollars at the box office. The studio executives were losing confidence in their ability to build a hit on good, basic story material, making it unlikely that a *M\*A\*S\*H* or *McCabe & Mrs. Miller* could get financing. One sign that the producers didn't really know which direction to go in was the decline of the sort of serious contemporary subjects that had flourished only a few years ago. The great dialogue between screen and audience that Pauline had dreamed of now showed every sign of being in jeopardy. The more she talked to her friends about the corrupt, moneygrubbing ways of Hollywood, the more she felt compelled to do something about the situation.

She addressed this state of affairs in an essay she wrote before her six-month layoff in March 1977. In "Where We Are Now" she cited the rise of high-quality television films such as *Roots* and *Sibyl*, and that she had come to feel she was missing nothing in the cinema by staying home to watch them. "The movie studios aren't putting up a fight," she wrote. "The lassitude of the studio heads—in for a year or two, or just a half year, and then moving around in the conglomerate chess game—is a sign of their powerlessness. Suddenly, there are no strong men at the top. Heads of production come and go without having had a chance to build a reputation."

In mid-1977 another blockbuster was released and became so successful, with such a sharp eye on the youth audience, that it made *Jaws* seem like a faint ripple. George Lucas's *Star Wars* was the mammoth hit of the era, and it penetrated the public consciousness in a way that was almost alarming. Children and teenagers went back to see it again and again. The *Star Wars* merchandising machine—action figures, lunch boxes, posters—swept through the world. It was not a movie Pauline was temperamentally disposed to admire: She found Lucas's preoccupation with childhood thrills faintly depressing. "There's no breather in the picture, no lyricism," she wrote. She objected to it because it was a big toy with "no emotional grip . . . It's an epic without a dream." And yet audiences were deliriously eager to follow Lucas on his journey back to childhood. Pauline's two-paragraph commentary on *Star Wars* in the fall of 1977 was more than a dismissal: It was an indication that her audience, the great audience she believed in, had begun to lose its way.

"I told her from the beginning that Spielberg was going to be responsible for a huge shift in money toward kids and movies," recalled James Toback. "I told her, this is something you're missing the boat on. Forget whether you think he's a lousy director or a good director—the significance of Steven Spielberg has very little to do with what is on the screen. He, along with George Lucas, is completely shifting where money will be spent on movies from now on. The audience that is going to be appealed to is going to go way down in age. Movies are going to be made for twelve-year-old boys, and there's going to be a sliver of money spent, relatively speaking, on the rest of us. And that's what she was missing. I said, *Jaws* and *Star Wars* are going to change the whole structure of Hollywood. You could see it and feel it. And that is not a phenomenon that she ever really labeled."

In the fall of 1977 Pauline reviewed Fred Zinnemann's *Julia*, based on a celebrated segment of Lillian Hellman's bestselling memoir, *Pentimento*. In it, Hellman recalled, in a tone of tastefully restrained heroism, how in the 1930s she had gone deep into Nazi Germany on a dangerous mission to smuggle $50,000 to her old childhood friend Julia, who was involved in the underground resistance. Pauline had highly conflicted feelings about Hellman as a playwright. Despite her fond memories of Tallulah Bankhead in *The Little Foxes*, she believed that Hellman's precisely embroidered dramas laid out in neat arrangements of black and white represented the brand of immaculate craftsmanship that had seriously arrested the development of the American theater. But there was also already considerable evidence that the "Julia" episode had at the very least been partially invented. "She was quite obsessed with the fact that Hellman was a liar," said Richard Albarino, "and that the story was fabricated. It wasn't because of her politics. Pauline seemed to be like an old-time Adlai Stevenson liberal. Very moderate—not leftish. She didn't like excess in any of these things. She had a great deal of admiration for the establishment and liked order—which I think is reflected in her review."

Pauline's greatest difficulty with *Julia*, however, involved Jane Fonda. There had been signs that the actress might not fulfill the promise she had shown in *They Shoot Horses, Don't They?* and *Klute*. Since winning the Academy Award for the latter, Fonda had filmed only sporadically and not very substantially, choosing instead to involve herself in a stream of high-profile political causes— a direction Pauline felt was a betrayal of her natural gifts. Years later, Fonda's biographer, Patricia Bosworth, recalled that in an interview Pauline held Fonda up as an example of a grandstanding actor who had buried herself in politics. "She thought it was ridiculous that actors dissipated their talents by becoming political," Bosworth remembered. "She thought it was silly, and she had no respect for it at all."

*Julia* paid a highly romanticized tribute to female friendship—Pauline called it "classical humanist" filmmaking—and as such it was hailed as an important picture, particularly coming after so many years that had witnessed such a paucity of good opportunities for leading actresses. The very small company of bankable female stars included Fonda, Barbra Streisand, and Goldie Hawn. The press, therefore, was eager to suggest that *Julia* was at the fountainhead of 1977 pictures ushering in a new Era of the Woman. In a *New York Times* interview, Fonda felt the need to point out that the relationship between Lillian and Julia in the film was "not neurotic or sexually aberrant." She also held forth on the importance of pictures such as *Julia*. "Women in movies have always been defined in terms of men, or they are victims. . . . It is very important to make movies about women who grow and become ideological human beings and totally committed people. We have to begin to put that image into the mass culture."

The media jumped on *Julia* in just the way Fonda and the film's producers had hoped. The picture was the focal point of a big *Newsweek* article called "Hollywood's New Heroines," about the upcoming spate of pictures for women—including Herbert Ross's *The Turning Point,* Paul Mazursky's *An Unmarried Woman*, and Richard Brooks's *Looking for Mr. Goodbar,* based on Judith Rossner's bestselling novel, a fictionalized account of a sexually promiscuous New York City schoolteacher who was murdered by a man she picked up in a singles bar. Pauline had admired the book's "pulpy morbidity" and "erotic, modern-Gothic compulsiveness" but felt that Brooks had undermined a good opportunity by turning the film into a "windy jeremiad" about the dangers of a sexually liberated society, a pompous, moralizing drama that was essentially "an illustrated lecture on how nice girls go wrong." Pauline could not understand this point of view: She didn't see what was wrong with single women cruising bars, writing, "It's what nice people do when they're not feeling so nice, or when they can't stand the complications of relationships." And while she had previously admired Diane Keaton's casual, affectless acting style in Woody Allen's comedies, she felt that in *Goodbar* the star had lacked "a powerful enough personality to bull her way through the huffing and puffing of Richard Brooks." Pauline found it difficult to rejoice in the success of *Julia* and *Looking for Mr. Goodbar* simply because they provided substantial roles for actresses. She didn't see how "women's films" could possibly help women unless they were *good* films.

She was delighted, however, by Steven Spielberg's new film, *Close*

*Encounters of the Third Kind*, about a random group of people whose lives are changed forever by a vision from outer space. *Close Encounters* was the latest step in Spielberg's appeal to the mass comic-book imagination, and Pauline thought he had delivered a wonderful picture suffused with "a child's playfulness and love of surprises . . . You can feel the pleasure the young director took in making it." She thought the sequence in which the extraterrestrials' spaceship hovers over a Wyoming mountaintop as the awestruck earthlings look on was "one of the peerless moments in movie history—spiritually reassuring, magical, and funny at the same time." Spielberg may not have had "the feelings for words which he has for images," but he was worth another of her superlatives: He was "probably the most gifted American director who's dedicated to sheer entertainment." The pleasure she took in the wonders of a *Close Encounters* or the Gothic teenage-pop sensibility of a *Carrie* was beginning to make her critics question whether she was becoming too enamored of the shiny-new-toy aspect of movies at the expense of depth and profundity.

But it was another piece of Hollywood pop that really animated her that Christmas season—John Badham's *Saturday Night Fever*, with John Travolta as Tony, a working-class Italian-American kid from Brooklyn who lives out his fantasies on the dance floor of a disco hall called the Odyssey. For Pauline it was a fascinating social document, a look at "how the financially pinched seventies generation that grew up on TV attempts to find its own forms of beauty and release." Pauline loved the picture's mise-en-scène: The scenes in the disco suggested "a TV-commercial version of Art Deco; the scenes there are vividly romantic, with the dancers in their brightest, showiest clothes, and the lights blinking in burning neon-rainbow colors, and the percolating music of the Bee Gees . . . These are among the most hypnotically beautiful pop dance scenes ever filmed."

She was especially intrigued by *Saturday Night Fever*'s star:

> There is a thick, raw sensuality that some adolescents have which seems almost preconscious. In *Saturday Night Fever*, John Travolta has this rawness to such a degree that he seems naturally exaggerated: an Expressionist painter's view of a young prole. . . . His large, wide mouth stretches across his narrow face, and his eyes—small slits, close together—are, unexpectedly, glintingly blue and panicky. Walking down the street in his blood-red shirt, skintight pants, and platform soles, Tony moves to the rhythm of the disco music in his head. It's his pent-up physicality— his needing to dance, his becoming himself only when he dances—that draws us into the pop rapture of this film.

.    .    .

One of the greatest mysteries of Hollywood in the 1970s is why it took the film industry so long to deal with the Vietnam War. Since the signing of the Paris Peace Accords and swift withdrawal of American troops in early 1973, the defining conflict of an entire generation had seldom surfaced onscreen. It was fitting that Jane Fonda, the Hollywood star most publicly associated with the antiwar movement, was the driving force behind the first major studio film in some time to take on the Vietnam experience at home.

Fonda often referred to Hal Ashby's *Coming Home* in interviews as her "baby"—the movie she cared about more than any of the others she had made. She had been very frank in interviews about her difficulty getting cast in films ever since winning the Academy Award for *Klute*. In the mid-1970s, with the steady erosion of the American counterculture, the major studios were reluctant to take a chance on an actress whose views on the Vietnam War had been so unpopular with such a large sector of the public. The remnants of Nixon's silent majority held Fonda in contempt, and the younger audience that had rallied behind her was no longer ablaze with the spirit of protest; many of those former activitists seemed battle-fatigued, eager to get on with their lives. With the lack of belief in institutions, which had cast a pall over the country since Watergate, Americans seemed to be pulling into themselves more than they had in years: The pursuit of private pleasure and prosperity was steadily dwarfing concern over the public good.

Because of this prevailing climate, there was some doubt that a drama about Vietnam's effect on the home front would be able to capture an audience of any size. *Coming Home*, set in Los Angeles, involved Sally Hyde (Fonda's character), the wife of a gung-ho marine officer (Bruce Dern) assigned to Vietnam. While her husband is away, she begins working as a volunteer in a veterans' hospital. There she meets Luke (Jon Voight), a former high school classmate; once a star athlete, he's now a paraplegic. The two of them begin an affair, and gradually, Sally's consciousness is raised—the times begin to change her, in ways that will ultimately destroy her marriage.

Ashby had had a difficult time getting a workable screenplay in hand, and the end result showed it. Pauline found the movie to be "a mixture of undeveloped themes, and is so thinly textured that Ashby has filled in the dead spaces by throwing a blanket of rock songs over everything. (It's disconcerting to hear words like 'strawberry fields forever' when you're trying to listen to what people are saying to each other.)" And while she thought that the film was "evocative of that messy time; it's permeated with free-floating anxiety," she didn't like the performances of either Fonda or Dern. Fonda, she felt, was "trying to act without her usual snap, and the result is so unsure she comes flutteringly close to a Norma Shearer performance."

She considered Dern miscast because he seemed equally deranged before and after going to Vietnam. And one of the things that disturbed her most was the simpleminded comparison of the husband's workmanlike lovemaking with the crippled Luke's ability to bring Sally to a thrilling orgasm. "There's a strong enough element of self-admiration in the film's anti-Vietnam attitudes," she wrote. "It's not enough that Hyde is wrong about the war; he's got to be a lousy lover, too." Despite Ashby's handiwork in the editing room, there was no arguing with his own assessment: "We started before we were ready."

In February Paul Schrader's debut film as a director opened. It was *Blue Collar*, about a trio of Detroit auto workers who attempt to blackmail their union and wind up getting crushed underfoot for their trouble. Pauline found it too heavy-handed: "*Blue Collar* says the system grinds all workers down, that it destroys their humanity and their hopes," she wrote. She thought Schrader might have made a decent film had he focused on the friendship of the three men and how it is destroyed in the process of trying to get rich. But she believed he lacked the necessary wit and invention; she felt that the humorless streak revealed in *Taxi Driver* defeated Schrader here.

While the industry was busily congratulating itself for having realized that there was a profitable market in films about real women's issues (*Julia*, *The Turning Point*, and *Looking for Mr. Goodbar*), the crest of this particular wave came in February, with the release of a movie that struck a much deeper nerve. Paul Mazursky's *An Unmarried Woman* dealt with a subject that was becoming much discussed in the late '70s: women who found a way of coping, often quite happily and successfully, without a man. The women's movement had only pressed itself deeper into the general culture as the decade went by, and as far as many were concerned, the progress hadn't unrolled at a fast-enough rate. As yet, there were very few female CEOs. Hollywood was still very much an old boys' club, although in the mid-'70s, Pauline's friend Marcia Nasatir made history by becoming the first woman vice president and head of production at United Artists; Sherry Lansing would not ascend to the presidency of Twentieth Century–Fox until 1980. Still, the spirit of the women's movement was very much alive in the literary and entertainment worlds. It was there in the success of nonfiction works such as Nancy Friday's bestselling study of identity, *My Mother/My Self*, and novels such as Marilyn French's *The Women's Room*, which sold more than 20 million copies worldwide. In entertainment, the changing times were more present on the small screen than they were in the movies. *The Mary Tyler Moore Show* had achieved a landmark success by presenting a woman spinning through her thirties without being married, and the woman alone cropped up in sitcoms such as *Rhoda*, *Phyllis*, and *Alice*. Even Edith Bunker, the sheltered Queens housewife on CBS's iconic hit *All in the Family*, was shown to be working toward some kind of stronger sense of herself as the decade moved on. An increasing number of made-for-television films explored subjects of great concern to women, ranging from *A Case of Rape*, with Elizabeth Montgomery, to *Strangers: The Story of a Mother and Daughter*, with Gena Rowlands and Bette Davis.

*An Unmarried Woman* was the story of an upper-middle-class woman (Jill Clayburgh) who discovers that her stockbroker husband, Martin (Michael Murphy), has fallen in love with another woman and is leaving her. In one scene that particularly resonated with audiences at the time, Erica walks away from Martin dry-eyed and shell-shocked, as the camera swirls around her in one continuous take—until she vomits in a trash can. It was a movie that put the zeitgeist center stage: Erica's friend Sue (Pat Quinn) observes, "It was so much easier in the '60s. Vietnam. Assassination. The Black Panthers. There was a helluva lot to do. You can't even find a decent cause these days." And there is a revealing exchange between Erica and her precocious teenage daughter, Patti (Lisa Lucas):

> PATTI: I mean, everybody I know is either miserable or divorced. I don't
>     want that.
> ERICA: There's a lot of happily married couples.
> PATTI: Name three.
> ERICA: I'll have to think about it.

Michael Murphy didn't grasp the impact of certain aspects of the script when he first read and rehearsed it. "We thought that Martin pissing Erica off was just sort of a mechanism to get her off on her own and dishing with the girls. But the weight of that marriage became more prominent than any of us thought it would. It took on some weight of its own. Sometimes with movies that happens." After *An Unmarried Woman* was released, Murphy got up one Sunday and walked down Third Avenue to the theater where the film was playing. "There's this line, and they're mostly women. I thought, *Holy Toledo, what's going on here?* And that's when I realized something culturally was happening. For many years, both genders hated me. I was the first of the whiny yuppies, you know? I had women wrinkling their noses at me. There were guys who looked down at me. My own agent called me and said, 'Don't expect you're going to get a lot of work from this.'"

Pauline found the film "funny and buoyant besides. It's an enormously friendly, soft-edged picture," and she loved the performance of Jill Clayburgh, whose "floating, not-quite-sure not-quite-here quality is just right"; perhaps it was even appropriate that "that camera isn't in love with her—she doesn't seem lighted from within." She did agree with her fellow critics, however, that some of the movie's points were hit a little too glancingly. She thought that Mazursky was "a superb shaggy screenwriter and rarely less than deft, but he touches so many women's-liberation bases that you begin to feel virtuous, as if you'd been passing out leaflets for McGovern."

The picture became problematic once it introduced a too-perfect man for Erica, in the person of Saul Kaplan (Alan Bates), a smart, sexy, understanding, and successful painter who wants to spirit her away to Vermont for the summer. But the movie ends with Erica not sure that Saul is the answer; she prefers to continue exploring her own single status. Surprisingly, Pauline objected less to Saul's perfection than to the fact that Erica hesitates to be with him; she felt that at that point in the story, the audience lost interest in what happened to Erica, because it was difficult to tell "whether she's struggling toward independence or embracing the generalized anxiety and dissatisfaction in the culture and sinking into it." She suspected that the director's "ambiguous ending, which is a way of postponing *his* decision, suggests that he can't get through to his own creation. He doesn't know what's going on in Erica's head." Perhaps James Broughton had been right all those years ago—Pauline was in many ways an Ibsenist at heart.

There was a reason that Pauline's enthusiasm had grown shriller, more insistent, in the recent years: Outstanding movies with a lively, original sensibility had been coming along much more infrequently than they had just a few years earlier. The life was seeping out of the film movement of the 1970s, and she knew it. All the more reason, then, to intensify her advocacy for the movies she loved, even for those that she thought simply showed promise: In the new, blockbuster-oriented Hollywood, artists were having a harder time than ever before.

Around this time, her judgment began to seem as if it had gotten knocked slightly askew, leading her to praise films that struck many readers as being something less than she claimed. She appeared at times to be reviewing the sensibility behind the film rather than the end result. "She at that point in her movie criticism was becoming a kineticist," observed Richard Albarino. "She loved the kinetics of movies. She was a sensualist. That kinetic style of filmmaking bowled her over—movies that were exciting in that way, with real feeling behind them." She seemed to feel that if she concentrated hard enough, she could transform her reader's opinions.

Toward the end of her 1977–78 *New Yorker* stint, she reviewed two films that appealed to that sense. One was James Toback's latest, *Fingers*, a drama about the bizarre duality that marks the life of Jimmy Fingers, a debt collector who dreams of becoming a concert pianist. While other reviewers gave the unruly film mostly negative notices, Pauline raved about it. She loved the idea that "Jimmy needs to be an exciting, violent, emotional man, a man who's at war with himself, who has so much going on that he's shooting sparks, hitting highs and lows." Even if much of the film seemed "still locked up in the writer-director's head," she loved it because he showed every sign of having "true moviemaking fever." In describing one of her favorite scenes—one in which the prizefighter Dreems (played by Toback's close friend Jim Brown) knocks two girls' heads together—she abandoned all restraint: "The shock is in the speed of Dreems's action: the film views him not as thinking fast but as not needing to think—as not being sicklied o'er with the white man's pale cast of thought." George Malko remembered vividly the impact it had on her in the theater: "The only time I ever felt Pauline levitate in the seat next to me was when Jim Brown takes the two young girls and cracks their heads together. Pauline gasped, *'Oooh!'* and literally left her seat."

In her review of *Fingers*, Pauline had written, "Normality doesn't interest Toback. He's playing the literary adolescent's game of wanting to go crazy so he can watch his own reaction." No doubt she felt she was paying a compliment to a kindred spirit, but her remark angered the director even more than the "Jewish prince" comment in her review of *The Gambler*, and once more, he called her on it. "You refer to the literary adolescent's way of playing crazy," Toback snapped at her. "I went clinically insane for eight days under LSD, at nineteen, as you well know. It was the seminal event of my life. And you, who have *never* experienced insanity, don't know what the fuck you're talking about. And for you to deliberately throw in a line like that is embarrassing and lightweight and not worthy of you." Pauline was quite taken aback: By now Toback was a close friend and a regular companion at screenings.

Another film that brought her kineticist's reaction was Brian De Palma's latest, *The Fury*. Like *Carrie*, it dealt with a form of telekinesis, this time belonging to two young people who share a psychic gift and as a result are being used as pawns by the U.S. government, which plots to employ them as secret intelligence weapons. Pauline shrugged off *The Fury*'s ramshackle plot and gushed that it went "so far beyond anything in his last film, *Carrie*, that that now seems like child's play . . . De Palma is one of the few directors in the sound era to make a horror film that is so visually compelling that a viewer seems to have entered a mythic night world. . . . We can hear the faint, distant sound of De Palma cackling with pleasure." Again, she found few critics who agreed with her, let alone shared her unrestrained enthusiasm. When she wrote, "No Hitchcock thriller was ever so intense, went so far, or had so many 'classic' sequences," even many of her die-hard fans wondered if she might temporarily have gone off the rails.

At a lecture Pauline had delivered at Lincoln Center in the 1960s, she had been introduced as "the author of *I Lost It at the Movies*." John Simon, sitting in the audience, had loudly intoned, "What she lost was her taste." Now, many were wondering if he might not have had a point. What her readers had no way of knowing—perhaps even she did not know—was that she was attempting to shed a layer of skin. Her passion for the movies had reached another level, one that would take her in another direction entirely.

S everal of the big studio films released in the summer of 1978 crystallized for Pauline a trend she had seen building in recent years: People she talked with suddenly seemed wary of the visceral side of films. The edginess, the eruptions of violence and volatile emotions that had made the *Godfather* films, *Straw Dogs*, *Taxi Driver*, and *Carrie* among the most-talked-about movies of the decade now seemed anathema to many in the audience. The counterculture spirit that had once fed some of the best moviemaking was all but drying up. Ever since the fall of Saigon in the spring of 1975, Vietnam had been rapidly fading in the public memory as a meaningless mistake that was best forgotten; to many, those who had served in the war were now viewed less as tragic victims than as unfortunate losers. College campuses were no longer a center of any kind of organized dissent; instead, membership in fraternities and sororities—the essence of comfort-seeking conformity—had spiked; the soft-edged Bee Gees songs from *Saturday Night Fever* could be heard blasting from the upstairs windows of every Sigma Chi house in the country. A wave of complacency had swept over American life, making its presence felt on the screen, both large and small: On television, the new "adult" era ushered in by *Room 222*, *All in the Family*, and *The Mary Tyler Moore Show* had been dwarfed by feel-good nostalgia comedies such as *Happy Days* and *Laverne & Shirley*, and bubble-headed farces such as *Three's Company*.

In terms of her own writing life, Pauline felt that the recent social changes in America had helped to create an unhealthy moviegoing climate in which audiences flocked to tame, tidy films and avoided messy, provocative ones. She expressed her concerns in her opening essay of the fall of 1978, "Fear of Movies," in which she posited her theory that "Discriminating moviegoers want the placidity of *nice* art—of movies tamed so that they are no more arousing than what used to be called polite theatre." Among the biggest offenders were Warren Beatty's *Heaven Can Wait*, which earned some of the year's best reviews but which she described as having "no desire but to please, and that it's only compulsiveness; it's so timed and pleated and smoothed that it's sliding right off the screen." She was stunned that the summer-movie audience turned up in relatively small numbers for three of her favorites, Sam Peckinpah's *Convoy*, Martin Scorsese's *The Last Waltz*, and Irvin Kershner's *Eyes of Laura Mars*. Pauline's defense of *Convoy*, however, made her an easy target for her critics:

> The trucks give the performances in this movie, and they go through changes: when the dust rises around them on rough backcountry roads, they're like sea beasts splashing spume; when two of them squeeze a little police car between their tanklike armored bodies, they're insect titans. The whole movie is a prankish road dance, and the convoy itself is a protest without a cause: the drivers are just griped in general and blowing off steam. They want the recreation of a protest.

But Pauline was unrepentant. She thought that both *Convoy* and *Eyes of Laura Mars*, a thriller about a murderer who stabs the eyes of his victims, displayed what to her was the most important quality a filmmaker could have: moviemaking fever. Unlike some of her colleagues, Pauline refused to see *Laura Mars* as any kind of feminist commentary; in fact, it was her refusal to take a "topical" view of movies of the time—such as hailing *Looking for Mr. Goodbar* and *An Unmarried Woman* as major advances for women's films simply because they dealt with issues of contemporary concern—that was partly the reason that so many of those connected with *The Village Voice* despised her writing. Her enthusiasm for *Convoy* and *Laura Mars* fueled the mounting criticism that she was an advocate of sensationalism in the movies: that being turned on as an audience member was more important to her than any real cogency in the writing or direction—the very thing she had been railing about back in the sixties in essays such as "Are Movies Going to Pieces?" However unfair that disparagement may have been, it was probably inevitable for a critic who, in the words of the film historian Jeanine Basinger, "took risks—she was not careful. She was bold—and her boldness made people take shots at her." But it was an accusation that would cling to her in the years to come.

"Fear of Movies" also included Pauline's sharp observations of Woody Allen's latest, *Interiors*, a study of a well-educated, upper-middle-class WASP family of New Yorkers that has been unraveling for years. The film's dialogue, which managed to be both arid and archly literary, and the austere, earth-toned production design and conspicuously somber, sedate direction and photography, along with its concerns with the problems of a group of intellectually striving Manhattanites, all added up to a movie that seemed to Pauline as if its director was desperately begging to be taken seriously. She wondered, "How can Woody Allen present in a measured, lugubriously straight manner the same sorts of tinny anxiety discourse that he generally parodies?" To her, the film's presentation of a WASP dilemma was a mask for classic Jewish concerns. "Surely at root the family problem is Jewish: it's not the culture in general that imposes these humanly impossible standards of achievement—they're a result of the Jewish fear of poverty and persecution and the Jewish reverence for learning." *Interiors* was "a handbook of art-film mannerisms," and she feared that in the end, Allen's obsession with repressive good taste "is just what may keep him from making great movies." (In this, she turned out to be amazingly prescient.) Pauline was delighted to have the chance to overturn the "official" verdict of Penelope Gilliatt, who had reviewed *Interiors* in *The New Yorker* only weeks earlier, saying of Allen, "This droll piece of work is his most majestic so far."

Pauline was also displeased with Robert Altman's latest, *A Wedding*. The movie had probably come about for all the wrong reasons: While Altman was shooting *Three Women*, a reporter from *Mother Jones* had asked him what he was going to film next; exasperated with her vapid questions, he recalled, he answered, "A wedding. . . . I'm taking this crew, and we'll be doing weddings. Somebody gets married, and we'll go and film it. I was really shitty. About that time we broke for lunch, and I went into this motel room with two or three other staff, and I said, 'You know, that's not a bad idea.'"

In *A Wedding*, it appears that Altman wanted to accomplish something similar to what he had achieved in *Nashville*—a revealing inside look at a bedrock American institution. Like *Nashville* it featured a big, attractive cast (including Carol Burnett, Vittorio Gassman, and Mia Farrow), but it had too many characters—forty-eight compared with *Nashville*'s twenty-four—and the film's tone this time was sour, not generous, without *Nashville*'s constant surprises and twists. To Pauline, it was "like a busted bag of marbles—people are running every way at once." She objected to its condescending tone: Altman, she felt, "doesn't like the characters on the screen; he's taking potshots at them, but he doesn't show us what he's got against them." The movie's cynical tone saddened her, and her disappointment in Altman was crystallized by her choice of a title for the review—"Forty-eight Characters in Search of a Director."

Pauline's growing disappointment in the movies she had been seeing had an odd, dispiriting effect on those who loyally read her each week. While there was truth to the accusation that her writing at times became hyperbolic, those reviews from the early to mid-'70s continued to convey an enthusiasm that was addictive. By the fall of 1978, however, many of her readers may have felt that they were experiencing withdrawal from a powerful drug. The great champion of the creative flowering of earlier in the decade took it personally that that period seemed all but over, and at times, her writing showed it.

She was, however, in excellent form with her review of Ingmar Bergman's *Autumn Sonata*. It was a prestige project, a work by an acknowledged master that also featured a topical theme—the bitter conflict of a mother and daughter. *Autumn Sonata* told the story of Charlotte (Ingrid Bergman, in her first film with the director), a famed Swedish concert pianist who goes to visit her daughter, Eva (Liv Ullmann), married to a country parson. The daughter is a study in pent-up rage, which she blames on her mother's years of neglect.

The critics, many of them impressed by the mere idea of a collaboration between the two Bergmans, were generally respectful of the film, although most of the praise was qualified; Andrew Sarris, for one, admitted that at some point he "began tuning out on Eva's tirade." *Autumn Sonata* was the kind of story Pauline was temperamentally disposed to dislike. She resented that Bergman presented Eva's point of view "as the truth. Not just the truth as she nearsightedly sees it but the truth." The audience was given no real opportunity to see Charlotte's point of view, and as a result, the movie seemed like a long, shrill whine. "It's like the grievances of someone who has just gone into therapy—Mother did this to me, she did that to me, and that and that and that," Pauline wrote. "Eva is vengeful and overexplicit and humorless; she takes no responsibility for anything. Without any recognition of the one-sidedness, Ingmar Bergman lays it on so thick—makes it all so grueling—that we have to reject it."

It was unquestionably a genuine reaction to the movie's point of view—but it could hardly have escaped the attention of those close to her that the relationship between Charlotte and Eva bore certain resemblances to that between Pauline and Gina. Pauline's daughter had developed into a lovely woman who looked far younger than thirty and had retained her gentle, soft-spoken manner. (Pauline's friend the writer Martha Sherman Bacon observed in a letter that Gina resembled a Gainsborough portrait, *A Child of Quality in Peasant Dress*.) Mother and daughter's relationship had had its fractious moments at various points in the past few years. By now Gina had given up dance and become seriously interested in painting. Outwardly, Pauline seemed very supportive of her work. But the silver cord remained as tightly attached as ever, and Pauline could commit herself to Gina's creative interests only to the point that they didn't threaten her own needs for her daughter's time and attention. Simultaneously, she encouraged Gina and worried that she might abandon her. Many friends felt that if Gina had expressed a desire to pursue a career as an artist elsewhere, Pauline would have done her best to dissuade her from it. She had simply grown too accustomed to having her daughter close by. Carrie Rickey remembered a phone conversation between her own mother and Pauline in the mid-'70s in which Pauline stressed how important it was for mothers to meddle in their daughters' lives and set them on the right path.

Some who were close to the two women felt that Gina had assumed the mother role at times: Whenever Pauline drove herself with deadlines, drank too much, and didn't get enough sleep, Gina would urge her to maintain a better health regimen and take care of herself. Pauline had become friendly with a young movie-lover named Al Avant, who later angered her by gently encouraging Gina to go her own way. "He was always pushing her to get out and start her own life and pointing out to her that Pauline was dominating her life, which was true," said Richard Albarino. Eventually, he recalled, Al Avant "was cast out in no uncertain terms. Pauline didn't mind people being friendly, but she objected to him counseling Gina into active rebellion against her, because she totally depended on Gina."

In addition to her growing dissatisfaction with the run of new movies, Pauline was not particularly happy with her situation at *The New Yorker*. She continued to do battle with William Shawn over tone and language in her copy, and after more than ten years of the same arguments, she was suffering from battle fatigue. Shawn, for his part, was just as exasperated as he once had been about Pauline's insistence on using sexual and scatological language that he deemed inappropriate for the magazine. Their arguments had lost none of their sting over the years; as always, Pauline seemed to enjoy pushing Shawn to the limits, trying to find a crack in his gentlemanly decorum. "I can remember a couple of times, at least, seeing him turn so red when they would start arguing," remembered William Whitworth, who served as Pauline's immediate editor for a time in the 1970s. "She would never let it go. Shawn had had a heart attack, and I thought a couple of times that he might fall over on the floor right there in the office. She was the only person in the process who didn't treat him the way the world of journalism did, and the way the rest of us did, as a very special little person—which he was. She treated him like one of the guys and talked to him that way, with a lot of wisecracks."

One memorable confrontation with Shawn came in late 1978, when Pauline submitted her review of *Goin' South*, a raucous Western comedy starring and directed by Jack Nicholson. "The problem Shawn had with her over and over had to do with her trying to sneak naughty words into the text and being really overtly, lip-smackingly appreciative of any sexual situations in the movie and wanting to make those as vivid as possible," said Whitworth. In the opening sentence of her review of *Goin' South*, Pauline rendered a vivid description of Nicholson, an actor she was still trying to come to terms with: "He bats his eyelids, wiggles his eyebrows, and gives us a rooster-that-fully-intends-to-jump-the-hen smile." Shawn's note in the galley margin read, "This piece pushes her earthiness at us, as if she wants to see how far she can push us, too. It's the tone of the whole review."

Later in the same review she wrote of the actor, "He's like a young kid pretending to be an old coot, chawing toothlessly and dancing with his bottom close to the earth." Shawn wrote in the margin, "Her earthiness, her focus on body functions." The description of Nicholson's bottom being close to the earth was deleted, as was a later reference to Nicholson's being "a commercial for cunnilingus." Shawn circled the phrase and wrote, "This has to come out. We can't or won't print it." Whitworth recalled that in all the years he worked at *The New Yorker*, he never saw Shawn make such an adamant decree; it was his customary style to try to get his way via gentle persuasion.

Late in 1978 a film was released that Pauline thought had a good deal of the guts and vision that the decade's greatest films had shown. Michael Cimino's second feature, *The Deer Hunter*, concerned a group of Pennsylvania steel-mill workers whose lives are shattered by their experience serving in Vietnam. Robert De Niro starred as the distant, mysterious Michael, who saves his buddy Nick (Christopher Walken) when they are captured by the Vietcong and, in the movie's most harrowing sequence, forced to play a deadly game of Russian roulette. As a director, Cimino was not afraid to be expansive: the Russian Orthodox wedding sequence, which became famous, went on for twenty-five minutes. (Rutanya Alda, who played the bride, Angela, recalled that the filming of it required sixteen- and eighteen-hour working days, with Cimino shooting all of the rehearsals to catch the most spontaneous moments.) Pauline thought the film's "long takes and sweeping, panning movements are like visual equivalents of Bruckner and Mahler: majestic, yet muffled," and that despite its structural flaws, it was "an astonishing piece of work, an uneasy mixture of violent pulp and grandiosity, with an enraptured view of common life—poetry of the commonplace."

Jane Fonda, while campaigning for her own Vietnam project, *Coming Home*, spoke out angrily against *The Deer Hunter* because of its depiction of the Vietcong, and despite her enthusiasm for the film Pauline was inclined to agree, finding it one of the few big Hollywood movies of the era to display a right-wing sensibility, in which Cimino betrayed "his xenophobic yellow-peril imagination. It's part of the narrowness of the film's vision that there is no suggestion that there ever was a sense of community among the Vietnamese which was disrupted. . . . The impression a viewer gets is that if we did some bad things over there we did them ruthlessly but impersonally; the Vietcong were cruel and sadistic. The film seems to be saying that the Americans had no choice, but the V.C. enjoyed it." She guessed that many would dismiss the movie because of its "traditional isolationist message: Asia should be left to the Asians, and we should stay where we belong, but if we have to go over there we'll show how tough we are." Yet despite her reservations, Pauline could see that *The Deer Hunter* showed evidence of tremendous artistry. Once more she had plenty of praise for Robert De Niro, who had developed into an actor capable of illuminating an opaque character. "We have come to expect a lot from De Niro: miracles," she wrote. "And he delivers them—he brings a bronze statue almost to life." (In later years, Pauline's friend Daryl Chin would tease her about her early support of De Niro, saying, "Pardon me—he's someone you babysat!")

Her review of *The Deer Hunter* was one of the most vital pieces she had written in some time, demonstrating again her Agee-like talent for working out her feelings on the page. The future *Entertainment Weekly* film critic Owen Gleiberman was still a student at the University of Michigan at Ann Arbor when Pauline's review of *The Deer Hunter* appeared. "When I see something as huge, as rich, and as garbled as *The Deer Hunter*, regardless of how secure I am with my own feelings," Gleiberman wrote to her, "I feel slightly off balance until I get a look at what you had to say. And what you've said has, I believe, made a difference in my life."

At year's end Pauline saw the most purely enjoyable movie she'd seen in years—Philip Kaufman's remake of the 1956 low-budget science fiction classic *Invasion of the Body Snatchers*. The original version, about a community being systematically supplanted by pods from outer space that hatch perfect, desensitized human replicas, had been a surprise hit when it was released and was still a favorite in campus revivals, as it had come to be read as a biting commentary on the McCarthyist paranoia of the '50s. The remake swapped the original's small-town California setting for San Francisco but retained the paranoid atmosphere.

Pauline thought that for pure movie thrills, the new *Invasion of the Body Snatchers* was "the American movie of the year—a new classic." She approved of the change of scene, because Kaufman and the screenwriter, W. D. (Rick) Richter, had beautifully captured the strays and eccentric artists that populated San Francisco. What better setting for a movie about the dangers of creeping conformity? She felt that eccentricity was "the San Francisco brand of humanity. . . . There's something at stake in this movie: the right of freaks to be freaks—which is much more appealing than the right of 'normal' people to be normal." She also had special praise for Veronica Cartwright, who played the film's second female lead. Cartwright was an actress whose work Pauline had been following closely for some time. In her review of Cartwright's 1975 film, *Inserts*, Pauline had compared her to Jeanne Eagels—"a grown-up, quicksilver talent." Writing about *Invasion*, she observed that Cartwright possessed "such instinct for the camera that even when she isn't doing anything special, what she's feeling registers. She doesn't steal scenes—she gives them an extra comic intensity."

"Sweetie, you need a publicist—nobody knows you," Pauline told Kaufman when they met at a Chinese restaurant shortly after the release of *Invasion of the Body Snatchers*. Kaufman declined the idea of a publicity push, but he and Pauline maintained a pleasant friendship for years. "She recognized that *Body Snatchers* was in large part a comedy," said Kaufman. "Pauline put her finger on it. It's meant to be playful. We had such a great time making it, and everyone connected with it had a great sense of humor."

Not long after her review of *Body Snatchers* appeared, Pauline also had the opportunity to meet Cartwright in New York. They had a drink at the Plaza, and Pauline was full of questions and advice on what Cartwright might do next. James Toback joined them briefly, because Pauline wanted him to interview Cartwright for a possible role in an upcoming film. "She was obsessed with James Toback," Cartwright remembered. "I mean *obsessed*. It was almost motherly. She wanted to make sure a meeting was set up between us, and it was almost like she was trying to guide him through something."

When Toback left for another appointment, Pauline and Cartwright remained behind to finish their cocktails. Evening was coming on, and Pauline invited Cartwright to attend a screening with her that night. Cartwright, who was having difficulties with her then-boyfriend, thanked her but begged off, mentioning her need to deal with her problems at home. Pauline could not hide her disappointment. "I had the weirdest feeling she was offended," Cartwright observed. "I don't know quite what happened, but she never reviewed me after that. She mentioned me, but she never picked me out in anything else. She was determined not to say anything."

Pauline's growing sense of dissatisfaction with the films she was seeing took a particularly harsh turn in her treatment of Paul Schrader's new film, *Hardcore*, starring George C. Scott as a strict Midwestern Calvinist whose daughter disappears on a church youth-group trip to Los Angeles; when a private detective he has hired determines that the girl is appearing in hard-core porn movies, Scott's character goes out to L.A. to try to find her and bring her home.

Years later, Paul Schrader admitted, "I was never happy with how that ended up. I don't think the film works. I changed the whole ending—the ending never worked." Schrader was also upset that the producer, Daniel Melnick, had pulled a casting switch on him. Initially, the part of the hooker who befriends Jake and helps in his quest to find his daughter was to be played by Diana Scarwid. "Danny Melnick didn't want to fuck her," Schrader recalled. "He said, 'I'm not going to put a girl in there that I don't want to fuck.' So I put a lightweight actress [Season Hubley] in there against George, and that killed the whole section."

Pauline found *Hardcore* dreary. To her, Schrader did not exhibit anything close to the true moviemaking fervor of a Phil Kaufman or a Brian De Palma, despite his knack for coming up with "powerful raw ideas for movies." Schrader had shot *Hardcore* on location in real L.A. porn shops and peep shows, but for Pauline the movie was short on ambience. "Schrader doesn't enter the world of porno"; she wrote, "he stays on the outside, looking at it coldly, saying 'These people have nothing to do with me.'" The character of Jake was not developed enough to suit her—there was no indication that he might be tempted or titillated by the world of porn—and the film's approach to its subject was "cautious and maddeningly opaque." It was her final paragraph, though, that verged on cruelty:

> The possibility also comes to mind that the porno world is Schrader's metaphor for show business, and that, in some corner of his mind, he is the runaway who became a prostitute. He has sometimes said that he regards working in the movie business as prostitution, and *Hardcore* looks like a film made by somebody who finds no joy in moviemaking. (Paul Schrader may like the idea of prostituting himself more than he likes making movies.) Several veteran directors are fond of calling themselves whores, but, of course, what they mean is that they gave the bosses what they wanted. They're boasting of their cynical proficiency. For Schrader to call himself a whore would be vanity: he doesn't know how to turn a trick.

It was so devastating a critique that it was almost impossible for Schrader not to take it personally. At the time he was already making his next film,

*American Gigolo*, and he simply tried to shake off Pauline's judgment. To others, however, who knew of her history with Schrader, as both friend and mentor, it was astonishing that she could write about him in such a manner.

Her final review of the 1978–79 season was of Walter Hill's *The Warriors*, which involved a meeting of all New York City's street gangs to put aside rivalries and organize so they can outnumber the police force three to one and take over the city. Pauline ignored the fact that many of the actors playing the gang members looked like TV commercial actors; she found the film "like visual rock" and "mesmerizing in its intensity. It runs from night until dawn, and most of the action is in crisp, bright Day-Glo colors against the terrifying New York blackness; the figures stand out like a jukebox in a dark bar. There's a night-blooming psychedelic shine to the whole baroque movie." Again, it was a review that suggested that the greatest gift a movie could deliver was a gut-level thrill; matters of construction and detail were of secondary importance.

Pauline's review of *The Warriors* was significant in that it seemed likely to be the last piece that she would write for *The New Yorker*. She had honestly believed that she would eventually be able to unseat Penelope Gilliatt and take over "The Current Cinema" on a full-time basis, but since Shawn remained stubbornly loyal to Gilliatt, that possibility seemed ever more remote. An even bigger concern was that she had reached the point where she questioned the degree of her own influence with readers. When she began writing regularly for the magazine eleven years earlier, she had wanted to shake up the way *New Yorker* readers thought, to reshape their ideas about which movies were worth seeing. She now believed that she had succeeded only in a partial and limited way. She was particularly piqued that she had not been able to have an effect on the tastes of most of the senior writers and editors at *The New Yorker*, who dutifully continued to attend art films by Fassbinder and Bresson that they thought were good for them, and looked askance at her praise for *Carrie*, *The Fury*, and *The Warriors*. She complained that the only ones at the magazine who listened to her about which movies to see were the young fact-checkers and messengers. There was also a significant sector of New York's intelligentsia that had never forgiven her for not covering innovative and experimental works and some of the more obscure foreign films. She was beginning to fear that she was, in the words of Alan Jay Lerner, serenading the deaf and searching the eyes of the blind.

At this rather confusing juncture, she was approached by Warren Beatty with an offer of work in Hollywood. Over the years Beatty had occasionally mentioned that he thought her ideas and level of taste could have even greater impact if she were to work in the film industry in some capacity. She had thanked him for his kindness and demurred, but the idea had stayed in the back of her mind. And, as the great eruption of '70s moviemaking had dwindled, she began to wonder if Beatty wasn't right. Perhaps she might be able to make a difference where it mattered most—by improving the level of what was put into production.

Pauline believed that she understood a lot of the reasons for the decline in film quality. The movie companies, as she told an interviewer, had succeeded in taking "the risk factor out of financing movies, by selling them in advance to TV, international TV, cable, Home Box Office, as well as selling them in advance to theaters." It was simply easier for the studios to back projects that could be sold ready-made to television—and because of the need to appeal to the general tastes and safe standards of the TV audience, it was harder than ever to get financing for a project with real edge that would have to be substantially edited and partially redubbed for network showings. To Pauline's way of thinking, Hollywood at its best had succeeded by combining the two qualities that had distinguished *The Godfather*—commerce and art. But now, the businessmen seemed to have inherited the earth.

Beatty presented her with a persuasive argument for heading west: Wouldn't it be much better, instead of pointing out where movies had gone wrong after they had been made, if she could perform the same function by analyzing the scripts and advising on casting before production began? Pauline pondered the decision for a long time, and when she learned that the first project she would work on was a James Toback picture called *Love and Money* that Beatty's company was set to make, she became much more interested. *Love and Money* was a noirish drama about a Los Angeles bank employee who becomes involved in financial and political intrigue in Central America. Pauline, believing Toback to be an artist who hadn't yet been allowed the opportunity to hit his full creative stride, now saw an opportunity to help him. Negotiations between her lawyer, Kenneth Ziffren, and Beatty's legal team began.

It was not a decision she entered into lightly. Many critics dreamed of going to Hollywood, and most of them, it seemed, had a script tucked away in a drawer, ready to show at the right moment to the stars and directors with whom they came in contact. Some had actually developed serious screenwriting careers, such as Frank S. Nugent, *The New York Times* movie critic from 1936 to 1940, who had gone west and written John Wayne pictures such as

*Fort Apache* and *The Quiet Man*. James Agee had worked on an even higher level with the scripts for *The African Queen* and *Night of the Hunter*.

With Penelope Gilliatt still occupying her post for half the year, Pauline did not feel that she owed unwavering loyalty to *The New Yorker*. She had been explicit about her feelings on the matter, and William Shawn had refused to listen—getting rid of Gilliatt seemed something he simply could not and did not want to do. She met with Shawn and told him of her decision. After offering some basic words of caution about the dangers of venturing into the viper's nest of Hollywood production, he agreed to a leave of absence.

It is surprising that, knowing as much as she did about Hollywood politics, Pauline felt confident in her choice. But she was nearly sixty, aching for a change of pace, and she felt it was then or never. Many of her friends at *The New Yorker* were saddened by her decision—it felt as if an era was ending, and indeed it was, in more ways than one. Around the time she filed her last column, Nora Ephron wrote to tell her how much she would miss reading her. Her old nemesis Ray Stark also contacted her: "Now we can be friends again—I hope."

A number of people close to her attempted to talk her out of her plan. Whatever problems she had encountered at *The New Yorker*, after all, she had essentially been in the company of gentlemen and gentlewomen—too much so, at times, for her taste and temperament. She believed she had been too tough for *The New Yorker*, and she believed that she was tough enough to withstand anything that Hollywood could hand her. Warren Beatty was famous for being a master manipulator, and several friends warned her that he probably wanted to bring her out to Hollywood to neutralize her. "He wanted to hunt her down, and get her," observed Paul Schrader. "If she was a twenty-two-year-old starlet, he would get her in one way. If she was a sixty-year-old film critic, he would get her another way." But Pauline was an enthusiast, and with enthusiasm went a certain naïveté that does not exist in the heart of a true cynic.

On the occasion of her departure, the fact-checking department composed an extended limerick, with numerous jabs at Penelope Gilliatt:

> There was a fine writer named Pauline
> Who chose judging films as a calling
> But she shared half her chores
> With the Empress of Bores
> A limey whose work was appalling

So Pauline became a producer
A calling where deadlines are looser
And if she ever needs
Some new stars to play leads
We hope our debuts won't traduce her.

From now on those of us who CK
Current Cin will be seen much more than TK
With Penelope here
Fucking up her career
Oy vey, will we miss La PK!

Her X-rated prose was too jarrin'
To the boss of the mag she was star in
Though the alternative critic
Leaves us near paralytic
Still we wish her the best with old Warren!

# CHAPTER TWENTY-ONE

T here is a famous story about Fred Zinnemann, the veteran director of *From Here to Eternity*, *A Man for All Seasons*, and *The Nun's Story*, being interviewed in the 1980s by a young, arrogant studio executive with no knowledge of movie history, for a job directing a major new studio film.

"So," said the executive, having done no homework whatsoever on the director's distinguished career. "Tell me—what have you done?"

"You first," said Zinnemann.

While Pauline's desire to go to work in Hollywood was unquestionably driven by her desire to have an effect on how movies got made, she had a much simpler motivation as well—money. Her half-year's salary at *The New Yorker* was still insufficient for her and Gina to live at any consistent level of comfort, and as she approached sixty, she became increasingly concerned about building up a nest egg. She worried that her meager earnings at the magazine would never be enough to provide Gina with any kind of decent inheritance. And now she faced the prospect of more money than she had ever seen in her life.

Kenneth Ziffren's negotiations with Warren Beatty's lawyer, David Saunders of Mitchell, Silberberg & Knupp, were complicated and protracted. "Now I know what Warren meant when he said that his attorneys must get paid by the word," Ziffren wrote to Pauline, adding that it would "probably take the whole weekend" to examine the contract that Saunders had sent over. In the end Ziffren worked out a very attractive deal for her: She would receive a salary of $150,000 a year, payable in monthly installments. The agreement stipulated that if one of the films she worked on wound up being produced, her annual salary would rise to $175,000 for the second picture and to $200,000 for the third and any succeeding ones. Ziffren also secured a payment of $750 weekly for Richard Albarino to act as Pauline's associate producer on *Love and Money*. She was granted the right to remove her credit on any picture, provided that Beatty decided to remove his. And there were various other perks thrown in, including reimbursement for transportation, since she still didn't drive.

One thing was clear to everyone close to her: Despite the fact that she had left the door open by only requesting a leave of absence from *The New Yorker*, she was not at all sure she would ever return. Pauline viewed her job with Beatty as the first step in a complete career change but was careful in her comments to the press, saying that if the job didn't pan out, she would return to criticism. Ziffren recalled, "She was keen to break loose from what she had been doing all her professional life and to try to do it from another chair, or another typewriter, so to speak."

Pauline's work on *Love and Money* began in Great Barrington, before she moved west. To Albarino, James Toback was someone who viewed himself as a kind of laboratory for his own fantasies. "He never wrote or made anything that he hadn't experienced first," observed Albarino. "He can't write fiction; he can only write diaries, and dramatize them." The immediate problem was that Pauline thought the script for *Love and Money* was a mess. She and Albarino would have late-night meetings at her room at the Royalton to discuss the script's problems. Eventually the deadline for submitting the script loomed, and Pauline panicked. Horrified by the thought that the first picture her name would be linked with might be a dud, she telephoned Albarino and told him that she needed him to rewrite the script in ten days. Over a meeting at the Harvard Club, Toback agreed to let them rework it, despite the fact that it was likely to change dramatically once casting was completed and filming began. Albarino quit his job, drove up to Great Barrington, and went to work. At that time of year it was bitterly cold in Massachusetts, and he and Pauline stayed up for several nights, fortifying themselves with brandy as they worked away. She seemed oddly protective of Toback at times: When Albarino devised a lengthy, Bertolucci-like tracking sequence around a bungalow, of which he was rather proud, Pauline rejected it, protesting that Toback would never know how to direct it.

As the week wore on Albarino realized that the current ending didn't work. At around ten o'clock one night, he drove to a local supermarket, where he suddenly came up with a way to fix it. He rushed back to Pauline's and told her his idea. She approved of it, and he sat down to write. "I typed about four words," said Albarino, "and she burst in and said, 'Is it done?' I broke down crying. That's how fraught this circumstance was."

With the script completed, Pauline and Albarino flew out to Hollywood together. A few evenings later she reported to him that the script had met with general enthusiasm. Behind the scenes, however, all was not well. For one thing, both Beatty and Toback were growing weary of Albarino's lengthy digressions during meetings. They weren't sure he was the right person for the project, but Pauline appeared to be quite dependent on him.

Pauline found a second-floor apartment in Beverly Hills. It was a lovely old-style L.A. setting, and she quickly made herself at home there. She took taxis to and from her office at Paramount, where Beatty was headquartered, and enjoyed getting caught up with old friends such as Joe Morgenstern and Piper Laurie, Marcia Nasatir, Paul Mazursky, and Irvin Kershner.

In a short time, Pauline demonstrated her lack of finesse at the game of studio politics. It led her to deliver a number of blunt judgments to various executives, who weren't used to being spoken to quite so sharply. She and Toback also had major disagreements about various aspects of *Love and Money*. Disagreements, of course, are a standard part of the production process in Hollywood, but Pauline had had no experience in this atmosphere. Her battles with William Shawn over copy may have been ongoing, but the process of putting together a movie involved far more people and ideas, and she was not accustomed to such a complex mix of opinions and points of view from creative, marketing, and merchandising personnel.

One principal conflict between Pauline and Toback involved the sanctity of the script. Toback looked at it in much the same way that Altman did—as a constantly evolving work in progress. He knew that on the set any number of changes would be made, because he regarded a script as nothing more than "a blueprint which may or may not work." Pauline, however, thought that her greatest asset as a producer was attentiveness to the screenplay; she believed that many potentially good films of recent years had gone off the rails because the producers hadn't cared enough to weigh in on the writing. "I found it impossible to work with her," Toback remembered, "because she was fetishistic about the script. There are certain things that work theoretically that don't work practically. She was insistent on mapping things out, with the most precise and neat sense of certainty, in a way that made me feel she had never actually been on a set."

Both Pauline and Toback were also becoming increasingly anxious about another project that was occupying more and more of Beatty's attention: a large-scale drama based on the lives of the socialist revolutionary John Reed and his wife, Louise Bryant. It had became clear, once Pauline arrived in Hollywood, that Beatty was far more interested in making that film than he was *Love and Money*. She was dead set against the Reed film and repeatedly tried to talk Beatty out of doing it, warning him that it was a pompous, grandiose idea, and accusing him of trying to reinvent himself as the new David Lean.

After several weeks of arguing with Pauline over the script of *Love and Money*, Toback went to Beatty and told him that he was not going to be able to function with her as the film's producer. Beatty assured him that it would be foolish, if not suicidal, of him to drop the most powerful movie critic in America from his movie, but Toback was adamant. Beatty finally agreed to accede to his demand, on the condition that he be allowed to tell Pauline that the whole idea of dropping her was Toback's and that he, Beatty, did not support it.

A meeting was called at the Beverly Wilshire Hotel, with Beatty, Toback, Pauline, and Albarino. "I feel very badly," she said when informed of the decision. "This is not the way I wanted it to work out. I don't feel it's necessary to stop working, but if Jim does, I guess I have to accept it." Beatty was true to his word, telling her repeatedly that her dismissal was not his idea and that he thought it was a mistake.

The firing of Pauline from *Love and Money* also presented Beatty with a very real practical problem: He had sold Paramount's CEO, Barry Diller, on the idea of Toback and Pauline as a team. By 1980, Diller, in his late thirties, was riding high. As CEO and chairman of Paramount Pictures, he was a wizard at promotion, and he saw to it that Paramount's marketing budgets were beefed up to unheard-of levels. He also rejected the notion of opening big movies slowly and gradually, allowing word of mouth to build. Diller felt this process backfired more often than it succeeded, and drove home the new method of mass release, getting audiences into theaters before a wide received opinion had been formed.

At Paramount, Diller had scored enormous successes with *Saturday Night Fever* and *Grease*. He was a great admirer of Pauline's, and both his and Beatty's reputations had risen even higher when word got out that they had managed to sign up the country's most important critic. It was seen as a joke on the New York establishment: Hollywood money was still all-powerful— even Pauline Kael could be bought. Now, however, Beatty would have to inform Diller that he was delivering only half of the package, and predicted that Diller would withdraw financing for *Love and Money*, which is ultimately what came to pass. The project bounced over to Lorimar, where it eventually got made. But Pauline's name—along with Albarino's—was removed from it.

Only one trace of her influence on the movie remained: She had insisted that Toback cast her old comedy idol Harry Ritz in a key role. Even that fizzled, however: Toback went to Las Vegas, interviewed Ritz, and agreed that he would be fine in the part. Once filming began at Lorimar, though, Ritz lasted only a single day. "He was confused," recalled Toback. "He had a lot of trouble with his lines. He didn't know whether he was any good." At the end of the day's shooting, Ritz called Toback into his trailer and begged to be released from the film. "You have to let me go back to Las Vegas," he said. "I can't do this. I'm going to embarrass you. I'm going to embarrass the movie. I'm not up to it." He was replaced by the director King Vidor.

In order to allow them all—Diller included—to save face, Beatty arranged a new deal for Pauline with Paramount. She was to stay on as a "creative production executive," helping to develop a number of potential screen projects. The new contract stipulated that she would suggest ideas for films, read novels and scripts, comment on works in progress, and suggest directors, actors, producers, and other talent for specific projects. She started the new post on May 1, 1979. Her contract ran for five months, at a salary of $50,000—a considerable drop from her producer's salary, but still far more than *The New Yorker* had paid her. Pauline later recalled that this position consisted of sitting in an office and talking to various producers who happened to drop by, offering her opinions on a wide range of story ideas. She remembered that most people were extremely courteous—partly, she thought, because they respected her, but also because they feared her and the possibility that she might write poisonous things about her experience in Hollywood.

News of Pauline's difficulties was inevitably leaked to the press, and *Newsweek* quoted one studio insider as saying that she "did a masterful job of alienating everybody within six weeks." Pauline claimed that she was pleased to be relieved of her producing duties because "producers just stand around and wring their hands," and asserted that her new post was much more to her liking. But her new job soon became even more problematic than the old one had been. There was a distinct hierarchy at Paramount: Diller was the studio chief; Michael Eisner, an old ABC-TV colleague who had helped launch the monster hits *Happy Days* and *Laverne & Shirley,* and whom Diller had induced to join Paramount, was CEO; and Donald Simpson was senior vice president of worldwide production. Unfortunately for Pauline, Simpson was the one who effectively ran studio operations—and the executive to whom she was directly answerable. Simpson would soon become a Hollywood legend, one of the individuals who changed the industry permanently with his "marketing first, production second" paradigm. He helped refine the idea that a movie blockbuster did not require careful planning before being presented to the studios; a mammoth hit could spring from a pitch that lasted no more than thirty seconds. Sometimes it could even spring from a single line, a single idea—as long as it was something the marketing executives could sell. This became known as "high concept," memorably described by Simpson's biographer, Charles Fleming, as "a supercharged, simpleminded creature, an Aesop's fable on crystal meth." Pauline's own notions about developing properties ran completely opposite to Simpson's, and she soon found herself caught in the crossfire of studio politics.

One of the difficulties was that Simpson had not been involved in the hiring of Pauline; Beatty had cut the deal directly with Diller, who ultimately handed her over to Simpson. According to Toback, Simpson had been enraged, feeling that he had been treated like a studio errand boy. It was he who made the decision to kill *Love and Money*, and he decided, on principle, to block whatever Pauline proposed. Years later he told Toback that when Pauline was put under his supervision, "It was a cake put in my lap, and all I had to do was take out my knife. Rarely in life can you pay back an insult so easily and so quickly."

Surviving studio correspondence bears out that this was the state of affairs in which Pauline found herself mired. She attempted to launch a number of projects after being taken off *Love and Money*. One was *Quinces*, an original script by her good friend and Great Barrington neighbor, the humorist Roy Blount, Jr. It went nowhere, and everything for which she subsequently expressed enthusiasm was routinely shot down by Simpson. "Dear Pauline," he wrote to her in late July, "as we discussed last Friday night at the Brian De Palma movie, this is a piece of material that we are not interested in. We just don't believe in it as a movie." On another occasion, referring to a script called *Dixianne*, Simpson wrote, "Eisner and I have reviewed one more time and, unfortunately, it is still pass. Clearly this is a case of oversight versus foresight. At least, as Roy Blount Jr. would say, 'You're batting 500.' Warmest regards, Don Simpson."

Soon enough she realized that it was not possible for her to survive in this environment. She was appalled by the coarse behavior of some of the executives, particularly at one casting session, in which she witnessed a selection of actresses' eight-by-ten head shots divided into two piles: "Would fuck her" and "Wouldn't fuck her." She had assumed that people would want to listen to what she had to say, and she quickly understood that while they might be polite on the surface, they regarded her as completely disposable. She was hurt, angry, and humiliated, and in the end, only one project she was keen on—*The Elephant Man*, the story of Joseph Merrick, a deformed man who lived in London during the Victorian era—managed to find its way into production, under the brilliant direction of David Lynch.

Many people who knew her well speculated that her hiring by Paramount had all been part of an elaborate plan by Beatty after her damning review of *Heaven Can Wait*. "Warren's power to charm cannot be overestimated," observed the actor-writer Buck Henry. "Everyone he has ever worked with has had knock-down drag-out fights with him, and yet they—or at least many of them—come back for more. And the fact is that he is great fun to spend time with when there isn't some horrible problem." Pauline, however, seems never to have accused Beatty of tricking her. In interviews after leaving Hollywood, she always stressed how fairly and decently she had been treated by Beatty. She gently dismissed the whole matter by saying that she had underestimated the demands of movie producing—that she had realized, early on, that she was not the kind of person to corral a group of creative people and ride herd on them until they did what she wanted. "An awful lot of the time in Hollywood was spent mulling over the same things," she said, "because you talk to people and two days later they come back and talk over the same problems, and I got very impatient. It's hard not to show it."

There was truth in all of this—but the biggest truth of all was that she simply missed writing, and the power base that had gone with it. Now that she gotten a close view of what went on in Hollywood, she felt that she had gained an advantage that no other film critic really had. Now she really knew something about how movies were—or weren't—made, and she could impart that knowledge to her readers. She did discuss other career possibilities— Kenneth Ziffren recalled that there was some talk about how she might use her talents effectively in the theater—but in the end, she decided that what she wanted most was to return to *The New Yorker*.

While she was still in Hollywood, she had lunch with Paul Schrader at Nickodell's, an old-time Melrose Place restaurant that was the unofficial commissary of Paramount Pictures. Once they had gotten settled in, Schrader explained his reason for wanting to see her. Pauline had commented to someone at an industry party that he was a good writer who would never make a good director. From Schrader's viewpoint, this was extremely damaging: She was, after all, speaking not to her readers in the pages of *The New Yorker* but to people in the movie business who would make decisions about whether or not to hire him. "You are trying to destroy my career from the inside," Schrader told her, "and I've got to call you on it." Schrader recalls that Pauline gave him a "typical kind of mealy-mouthed response—'I didn't really mean it that way'—like any politician."

In the meantime, *The New Yorker* was having some rather public problems of its own. In March, shortly after Pauline had written her farewell review of *The Warriors*, the magazine had published a profile of the celebrated British author Graham Greene, written by Penelope Gilliatt. In April, William Shawn received a letter from the writer Michael Mewshaw, who offered compelling evidence that Gilliatt was guilty of plagiarism: Entire sentences and phrases, as well as a number of paraphrased ideas and sentences, had been lifted directly from an article Mewshaw had written for *The Nation* in mid-1977, one that was later reprinted in both *The London Magazine* and the Italian publication *Grazia*. Gilliatt's final paragraph had consisted of fourteen sentences, eight of which were stolen from Mewshaw. Mewshaw's attorney had urged him to pursue high-cost damages, but because the magazine had a high reputation, and because it had run positive reviews of two of his novels, Mewshaw asked Shawn for only $1,000, in addition to a printed acknowledgment that Gilliatt had plagiarized his piece.

A few days later Shawn received a letter from Graham Greene himself, who stated that after he counted fifty errors and misquotations in Gilliatt's published profile, he gave up reading it. It was a shocking embarrassment for *The New Yorker*, which, under Shawn's guidance, had successfully maintained a reputation for irreproachable professional standards. A key part of that reputation had been the magazine's fact-checking department, which still kept up a watch so fastidious that it drove some authors to distraction. But it was not the first time Gilliatt had come under fire for "borrowing" from other writers. In 1974 Sandra Berwind, a professor of English at Bryn Mawr, had written to Shawn complaining that Gilliatt, in her review of Paul Mazursky's *Harry and Tonto*, had borrowed heavily from W. B. Yeats's *Essays and Introductions*.

Berwind's complaints prompted a telephone call from Shawn, who obsequiously thanked her for her letter, then said, "I suppose, Professor Berwind, that in your line of work you come upon students who plagiarize. And I suppose you are understanding at times and forgive them?" Shawn vacillated throughout his conversation with Berwind, who remembered him as being "kind of patronizing. No indication of doing one thing or the other."

In 1978 Andy Holtzman, film program coordinator for the New York Shakespeare Festival, accused Gilliatt of showing up twenty-five minutes late for a screening of the documentary film *Deal*, ignoring the festival's attempts to schedule another screening, and then publishing a negative review in *The New Yorker*. Holtzman suggested reassigning the film to Pauline, but again, the complaint about Gilliatt fell on deaf ears.

For years Gilliatt's drinking had been a well-known problem among film producers, publicists, critics, and *The New Yorker* staff. Howard Kissel recalled a screening that he attended in the late 1970s. Gilliatt had failed to show up for it, and after delaying the start time as long as possible, a nervous team of publicists had screened the film without her. After the movie was finished, Kissel and his fellow critics attempted to exit the screening, but they couldn't leave the room: Gilliatt, blind drunk, had arrived late and passed out against the door.

Not even Shawn, however, could completely ignore the Michael Mewshaw matter, and *The New Yorker* agreed to the writer's demands for a $1,000 payment. But Shawn, in enabler mode, told Mewshaw that Gilliatt had been plagued by personal problems, and persuaded him to drop his request for a printed acknowledgment of her plagiarism. Instead, he placed her on a leave of absence from the magazine.

Pauline was able to keep a close eye on these events, thanks to many members of *The New Yorker*'s editorial staff who were loyal to her and were reliable sources on the Gilliatt affair. One of them, Patti Hagan, wrote to her in Los Angeles that the fact-checking department had uncovered all of the similarities in the Gilliatt and Mewshaw articles and reported them to Shawn. According to Hagan, Gilliatt had gone to Shawn's office and talked her way out of it, and Shawn had ordered all of her copy restored; now that the matter had become a public embarrassment, he was putting the blame on the fact-checkers.

By the end of 1979 Pauline had not renewed her five-month contract with Paramount, and her Hollywood episode came to an end (though she always claimed that she had received other offers that would have enabled her to remain in Hollywood). To the press she remarked that she hadn't had enough energy to accomplish her goals at Paramount. "Frankly, many producers aren't doing the job that they should; the director is asked to carry too large a burden," she told *The Hollywood Reporter*. She put the blame for the high quotient of misguided movies on the producers: Often, actors were miscast, rewrites were abandoned, the thread of the movie was lost, simply because the producer had failed to do his job.

She contacted Shawn and told him that she would like to return to her old post—a proposition that was much more attractive to her now that Penelope Gilliatt's future with the magazine was in question. It wasn't a matter, however, of simply saying she wanted to come back. Shawn had to decide what to do about Roger Angell, Susan Lardner, and Renata Adler, all of whom had taken a turn writing "The Current Cinema." Pauline headed back to New York and waited to hear how Shawn would prepare for her reentry. She busied herself with lecture appearances, including a visiting writers' symposium at Vanderbilt University on March 26, at which she spoke of the decline in quality movies. "You work for a long time to become a writer," she complained to the audience, "and then your subject is cut out from under you."

She was stunned when she discovered that Shawn did not want her to rejoin the staff. She had assumed that, given her reputation, it would be relatively easy to work out the details. Her fame was at its height. Her new publisher, Holt, Rinehart and Winston, where Billy Abrahams had recently moved, was preparing to bring out her new collection. And now, after all she had done to raise the magazine's visibility and attract younger readers, Shawn was saying he didn't want her.

Pauline delivered the shocking news to the staff editor William Whitworth, who immediately went to Shawn's office to discuss the matter. It was an unwritten rule that one was not supposed to question Shawn's staff decisions, but Whitworth managed to bring up the matter of Pauline tactfully. "He went into a long explanation that she had corrupted herself by adopting the ways and standards of Hollywood," Whitworth remembered. "He talked for some time. When something was immoral, that was one of the magic words for him—'corrupted.' He would explain it to you like a teacher or a theologian—at length. I went away just stunned. It was so unexpected and impractical. This was when movies were really something in the culture. I just thought she was tremendously important to us."

Whitworth appealed to Shawn a few days later, pointing out that the leave of absence that Pauline had taken implied that she would be able to return when her Hollywood period was finished. It was the kind of point of honor on which Shawn was always quite vulnerable, and after listening to Whitworth's entreaties, he reluctantly agreed that Pauline could resume her position. Eventually it was worked out that she would begin writing full-time for the magazine in the fall of 1980.

In the years to come Pauline would always be extremely reticent about the details of her time in Hollywood. If pressed by an interviewer, she would give her own carefully orchestrated version of what had transpired, but the experience had clearly left its mark on her. As Jeanine Basinger said, "I had the feeling that what had happened to her there shocked her. She was not a woman who failed at things. She had a sense of shame and failure, and I think she buried it."

# CHAPTER TWENTY-TWO

In April 1980 Holt, Rinehart and Winston brought out Pauline's new collection of reviews, titled *When the Lights Go Down* (a title suggested by a stranger she met a dinner party in Los Angeles). The new volume covered her reviews and essays from July 1975 to March 1979. Now that her reputation as America's foremost movie critic seemed all but unassailable, it was ironic that she could no longer expect unqualified raves when she published a new book. Her impact and influence had to be examined closely for subtext and possible negative influences.

Taking note of her increasing tendency to rhapsodize on the page, Michael Wood in *The New York Times Book Review* wrote, "What has happened, I think, is not that she has lost her touch or her taste, but that she has tried to ride her enthusiasms too hard and her astringent language won't take it. I can't think of a single bad film she's praised, but her recent work is littered with extravagant claims for merely amiable or seriously skewed movies." Wood pointed out, in his largely favorable review, that she was extremely persuasive about audiences' potentially damaging leeriness about violence in "Fear of Movies," and he stressed, "Whatever mellowness has crept into her writing, there are no signs at all of fatigue."

Andrew Sarris gave her a good lashing in an odd, risky review published in *The Village Voice*. "When Pauline scolds the industry," Sarris wrote, "she seems to be flailing at phantoms from the past. She has no more control over the raging unconscious of today's unbridled movies than anyone else, but she never gives up trying to shape the future." Much more damning was his strong suggestion that she was deeply corrupt. Citing her positive review of *Fingers*, a movie he disliked, he wrote, "a more candid critic than Pauline might have felt impelled to inform her *New Yorker* readers that this alleged denizen of Dostoevskian depths was her constant escort at screenings. It is not that I care whether Pauline chooses to be seen in public with James Toback. It is simply that her *politique* often seems to consist of setting one standard for people she knows and another for people she doesn't. She thus acts as an unflagging apologist for Sam Peckinpah and Irvin Kershner, whatever their failings, while heaping a steady torrent of abuse on Don Siegel and Alan Pakula, whatever their virtues."

The promotional tour that had been arranged for *When the Lights Go Down* was daunting—and a clear indication that public interest in Pauline was high. On April 1 she appeared on *The Dick Cavett Show*, joking about the avalanche of hate mail she had received for her positive reviews of *Mean Streets* and *Invasion of the Body Snatchers*, contrasted with only two letters for her favorable review of *Last Tango in Paris*. She expressed her regret that Robert Altman's latest films didn't display the same affection for their characters that his earlier ones had, and she skillfully downplayed her Hollywood episode by claiming that her six-month leave from *The New Yorker* had been coming up anyway—that she had simply prolonged it slightly.

Six days later she was a guest on the late-night talk show hit *Tomorrow*, with Tom Snyder. One day later, she did interviews for *Women's Wear Daily* and National Public Radio's *All Things Considered*. On April 9, she had interviews with the *New York Post* and with Arlene Francis on New York's WOR radio. Then she was off to Boston for interviews with *The Boston Globe*, *The Christian Science Monitor*, *The Real Paper*, WGBH-TV, and WB2 Radio, plus a lecture at the Rabb Lecture Hall. After that, she was off on a grueling lecture tour, including appearances in Detroit, Chicago, Dallas, Houston, Los Angeles, San Francisco, and Toronto.

During one of her L.A. appearances, she was startled during the question-and-answer session when a man raised his hand and asked, "Why are you shaking?" Recently she had noticed a very slight tremor in her hands, but she had put it down to nerves, and she was astonished that it would be visible to someone sitting halfway across a large auditorium.

At *The New Yorker* Pauline at last had what she had always wanted—the entire reviewing post, with a commensurate raise in salary. Her schedule was adjusted slightly: Now she came down to New York every other week, checked into the Royalton for four days, and saw two movies each night, returning to Great Barrington to write her column. Often Gina or one of Pauline's friends in the Berkshires drove her both ways.

After a pleasant trip to Colombia with Gina and their friend the author Jaime Manrique, she returned in the magazine's June 9, 1980, issue, with a negative review of Stanley Kubrick's latest, *The Shining*, a supernatural tale that boasted great technological advances but fell flat as a thriller. While Pauline enjoyed Jack Nicholson's performance early in the film—"He has a way of making us feel that we're in on a joke—that we're reading the dirty, resentful thoughts behind his affable shark grins"—more of him was less as the movie went on. She thought that he was too ideally cast: "His performance begins to seem cramped, slightly robotized. There's no surprise in anything he does, no feeling of invention."

Her big "comeback" piece, however, came in the June 23, 1980, issue, with a lengthy essay titled "Why Are Movies So Bad? Or, The Numbers." Some have viewed it as her revenge on Hollywood for her mistreatment there; in fact, she offered no explanation about her time in Hollywood, assuming that informed readers would understand her position. What she was really doing was giving her readers a glimpse of what she had learned "out there," and the essay was Pauline at her stinging best. Taking precise (if unspoken) aim at Don Simpson, she opened fire on the new breed of studio executives—ignorant, uneducated, and unfeeling where movies were concerned, who thought only about box-office grosses, and never about giving an audience something that might prove deeply satisfying. The conglomerates in charge of the studios were painted with the blackest part of her brush: She described them as filled with men who were attracted to the film world because it gave them the opportunity to elevate their status by rubbing shoulders with famous stars and directors. Part of the trouble was that they began to see themselves as genuinely creative people:

> Very soon they're likely to be summoning directors and suggesting material to them, talking to actors, and telling the company executives what projects should be developed. How bad are the taste and judgment of the conglomerate heads? Very bad. They haven't grown up in a show-business milieu—they don't have the background, the instincts, the information of those who have lived and sweated movies for many years.

She believed the central problem was that the studio heads had "discovered how to take the risk out of moviemaking . . . If an executive finances what looks like a perfectly safe, stale piece of material and packs it with stars, and the production costs skyrocket way beyond the guarantees and the picture loses many millions, *he* won't be blamed for it—he was playing the game by the same rules as everybody else. If, however, he takes a gamble on a small project that can't be sold in advance—something that a gifted director really wants to do, with a subtle, not easily summarized theme and no big names in the cast—and it loses just a little money, his neck is on the block."

It was a loss to American letters that Pauline, away in Hollywood, missed the opportunity to review the most ambitious undertaking of the decade—the movie that was, whether it was intended to be or not, the cumulative event of the 1970s: Francis Ford Coppola's Vietnam epic *Apocalypse Now*. Despite the movie's horrendous production problems—shooting in the Philippines was shut down for some months—Pauline correctly perceived that the film signified the audience's "readiness for a visionary, climactic, summing-up movie. We felt that the terrible rehash of pop culture couldn't go on, mustn't go on—that something new was needed. Coppola must have felt that, too, but he couldn't supply it." She was distressed, however, to see that a film with such brilliant isolated sequences was, in her words, "an incoherent mess"; she felt that the director had simply gotten lost. (Robert Getchell recalled that when he and Pauline went to see the movie in Westwood, she held her nose as they walked out of the theater.)

Pauline didn't get behind James Bridges's evocative *Urban Cowboy*, about aimless Texas oil-rig workers who compete to ride a mechanical bull, but she was entranced by Debra Winger, whom she described as having "a quality of flushed transparency. When she necks on the dance floor—and she's a great smoocher, with puffy lips like a fever blister—her clothes seem to be under her damp skin. (She's naked all through the movie, though she never takes her clothes off.)" Winger had the kind of sensual, electric presence that Pauline had once loved in the young Jane Fonda.

She again came out powerfully on behalf of Brian De Palma for his latest, *Dressed to Kill*, a compendium of Hitchcockian themes and takeoffs. There were a few genuinely frightening scenes in *Dressed to Kill*, but her response to the movie seemed excessive: She found it De Palma's most sustained piece of work, in which he had "perfected a near-surreal poetic voyeurism—the stylized expression of a blissfully dirty mind." But despite her exuberant description of some of the movie's lengthier set pieces, many readers found her review unpersuasive if not simply wrong-headed.

Why did Pauline prefer De Palma's work to Hitchcock's, when the younger director was essentially reworking over many themes developed by the master? Perhaps it was the understanding of female psychology that De Palma showed. (Hitchcock's movies are full of scenes with women that make one's skin crawl—a prime example being the sequence in his 1955 version of *The Man Who Knew Too Much*, in which James Stewart sedates Doris Day before telling her that their son has been kidnapped.) Her friend David Edelstein thought that she also favored the lushness of DePalma's visual palette—his emphasis on pure sensuality.

*When the Lights Go Down* was still selling nicely by midsummer. One prominent publication, however—*The New York Review of Books*—had not weighed in on the book until mid-August, when it ran a lengthy review by Renata

Adler. The sniping notices that Pauline had received over the years—particularly for *Reeling*—were of a type that nearly every writer had to deal with in the course of a career. But the piece in *The New York Review of Books* was another matter altogether: It was the most devastating critical attack on Pauline's career ever published. The cover line, "The Sad Tale of Pauline Kael," was an indication of what was to come; the review itself was titled "The Perils of Pauline," a formula that had already been exhausted in any number of newspaper and magazine pieces about her. More than just a review of *When the Lights Go Down*, Adler's essay was a broadside against Pauline's lofty reputation, an aggressive attempt to discredit her—with the nation's literary community occupying a ringside seat.

Certainly an attack on America's most celebrated movie critic was a "box-office" concept, and Renata Adler was an inspired choice to write it. She was a well-known contributor to the publication, a sometime film critic with impressive credentials (*The New York Times* and, most recently, *The New Yorker*). and an acclaimed fiction writer. The passionate, emotional, argumentative Pauline confronted with the dispassionate, chiseled-prose Adler—two more temperamentally opposed writers would have been difficult to imagine.

Pauline had been annoyed by many of Adler's recent reviews for *The New Yorker*; in particular, she was incensed by Adler's dismissal of Carroll Ballard's *The Black Stallion*, which Pauline considered one of the best films of a bad year. And with her tony educational background (Bryn Mawr, Harvard, the Sorbonne, a law degree from Yale) and frequently reported-on social connections, Adler was the sort of darling of the East Coast intellectual establishment that Pauline had for so long viewed with contempt.

An advance copy of *The New York Review of Books* issue that featured "The Perils of Pauline" was sent to Pauline with a note from the publication's editor, Robert Silvers, in the event that Pauline wanted to reply.

Adler's essay began with a lengthy two columns in which she outlined her thoughts on what made a good critic in the arts, and why the best ones inevitably found themselves played out after a certain period and moved on to write about other topics. For another two and a half columns she expressed her qualified admiration for Pauline's work from the 1950s up through her first few years at *The New Yorker*, stating that she had "continued to believe that movie criticism was probably in quite good hands with Pauline Kael."

The bomb was dropped midway through the fifth column, when Adler stated that *When the Lights Go Down* was "jarringly, piece by piece, line by line, and without interruption, worthless." She went on to detail her complaints—that Pauline's work had taken on "an entirely new style of *ad hominem* brutality and intimidation; the substance of her work has become little more than an attempt, with an odd variant of flak advertising copy, to coerce, actually to force numb acquiescence, in the laying down of a remarkably trivial and authoritarian party line."

In 1976, when *Reeling* was published, John Simon had, while expressing his admiration for Pauline as a stylist, objected to her coarseness of spirit and taste, in terms of both language and her championing of certain movies he considered lowbrow: "She is a lively writer with a lot of common sense, but also one who, in a very disturbing sense, is common." Adler echoed this theme in her review, complaining that Pauline had "lost any notion of the legitimate borders of polemic. Mistaking lack of civility for vitality, she now substitutes for argument a protracted, obsessional invective—what amounts to a staff cinema critics' branch of *est*." Adler—not coincidentally, perhaps, an ardent admirer of William Shawn's editing style—lamented Pauline's use of images of "sexual conduct, deviance, impotence, masturbation; also of indigestion, elimination, excrement. I do not mean to imply that these images are frequent, or that one has to look for them. They are relentless, inexorable." Among the words and phrases that bothered her: "just a belch from the Nixon era"; "you can't cut through the crap in her"; "plastic turds"; and "tumescent filmmaking."

Adler also attacked Pauline for her repeated use of "the mock rhetorical question," such as "Were these 435 prints processed in a sewer?" "Where was the director?" and "How can you have any feelings for a man who doesn't enjoy being in bed with Sophia Loren?" These questions, she felt, were "rarely saying anything; they are simply doing something. Bullying, presuming, insulting, frightening, enlisting, intruding, dunning, rallying."

There was more: Adler took issue with Pauline's use of "you" to indicate what the audience was feeling, when she would have more civilly, in Adler's view, said "I." Like Robert Brustein, Andrew Sarris, and even Pauline's friend Greil Marcus, she found fault with the surfeit of hyperbole, and she objected, seemingly on moral grounds, to comments such as the one Pauline wrote about Paul Schrader, in *Hardcore*—not knowing how to turn a trick—which Adler felt represented "a new breakthrough in vulgarity and unfairness." She also theorized that Pauline had taken advantage of *The New Yorker*'s famously genteel editing process, in which writers are "free to write what, and at what length, they choose." While disagreements with writers of feature articles could be dealt with simply by postponing the running of the piece, movie reviews demanded constant currency; Pauline's work had to be run, week in and week out, essentially forcing *The New Yorker* either to fire her or "to accommodate her work. The conditions of unique courtesy, literacy, and civility, of course, were what Ms. Kael was most inclined by temperament to test. Her excesses got worse." Reading Pauline in book form was a very different experience from reading her from week to week, Adler wrote, because "It is difficult, with these reviews, to account for, or even look at, what is right there on the page."

"The Perils of Pauline" quickly became an incendiary topic of conversation in New York literary circles. It was hard to remember when any established writer had launched such a damning dismissal of one of her own kind. *Time* and *New York* ran full-scale feature articles on the scandal. In *The Village Voice*, Andrew Sarris gave his seal of approval to Adler's broadside, but the publication also ran a scathing article by Pauline's friend James Wolcott, who mercilessly limned Adler as "Princess Renata," a writer who "when not dusting off her diplomas . . . writes about journalistic chores—book reviewing, movie reviewing, investigative reporting—with the pained, annoyed tone of a royal bride stranded in one of the empire's scruffier provinces." Letters to the editor poured into *The New York Review of Books*. "Renata Adler should see a psychiatrist," her young critic friend at the *Los Angeles Herald Examiner*, Michael Sragow, wrote to Pauline. "Hope you're bearing this latest injustice with your usual fortitude and good humor, which is what you've been displaying in your reviews." Several other friends came to Pauline's rescue in print, including Gary Arnold, who denounced Adler to *New York* as "one of the dunces of the profession."

One person who didn't rise to her defense was William Shawn, who characteristically tried to calm the waters. "That's just how Renata reacts to Pauline," he told a reporter. "One has to permit all writers a certain amount of idiosyncrasy." Many at the magazine speculated that Shawn agreed with Adler's assessment of Pauline's work, but in interviews, the editor worked hard to maintain a neutral stance, saying, "There are boundaries beyond which the magazine can't go. But you have to give Pauline the benefit of the doubt as to her intentions and needs. If at times she finds it necessary to use unconventional language, that has to be allowed."

Many of Pauline's friends, James Wolcott among them, felt that the Adler piece was something of an inside job, given the close relationship of both Adler and Penelope Gilliatt to one of Pauline's chief antagonists, Vincent Canby. (Gilliatt did send Pauline a sympathetic note when Adler's essay was published. Gilliatt wrote that such an outrage "shouldn't happen to anyone, let alone to anyone who writes." She added, "And you certainly know how much I have *always* admired your humanity and zeal.")

Pauline attempted to stay above the fray, telling *Time*'s reporter simply,

"I'm sorry that Ms. Adler doesn't respond to my writing. What else can I say?"
Privately, however, she was deeply wounded by Adler's harsh words. Despite
her sharpness with others in print, she had always maintained a conscience
about what she wrote, and she often told friends that she would have had to
have been a complete boor not to feel a twinge of sadness and discomfort
when she ran into someone whose films she had savaged. She had always
known how painful it was for an artist to be the object of a full-scale critical
attack: Now she had experienced it personally.

She went back to work, and it is impossible to know exactly what effect, if
any, on her day-to-day writing Adler's criticism had had. Certainly there
seemed to be no difference in tone or substance or style, at least not immediately. The run of movies that fall wasn't bad: She loved *The Stunt Man*, starring
Peter O'Toole, and considered its director, Richard Rush, "a kinetic-action
director to the bone; visually, he has the boldness of a comic-strip artist"; she
found "a furious aliveness in this picture." And she was completely won over
by Jonathan Demme's *Melvin and Howard*, which opened the 1980 New York
Film Festival. Pauline compared Demme's intuitive gifts at creating characters onscreen with Jean Renoir's; she thought *Melvin and Howard* "a comedy
without a speck of sitcom aggression: the characters are slightly loony the way
we all are sometimes (and it seldom involves coming up with cappers or with
straight lines that somebody else can cap). When the people on the screen do
unexpected things, they're not weirdos; their eccentricity is just an offshoot
of the normal, and Demme suggests that maybe these people who grew up
in motor homes and trailers in Nevada and California and Utah seem eccentric because they didn't learn the 'normal,' accepted ways of doing things."
    The fall of 1980 saw the release of the one movie she had managed to help
get onto the assembly line in Hollywood—*The Elephant Man*. (Some critics
would have recused themselves, but Pauline saw no conflict of interest.) Pauline had liked David Lynch's *Eraserhead*, and she thought that he had brought
his powerful imagination to full flower in his new picture. The story of the
unfortunate, deformed Englishman John Merrick was handled with remarkable grace, and without hysteria or sentiment. "*The Elephant Man* has the
power and some of the dream logic of a silent film," Pauline wrote, "yet there
are also wrenching, pulsating sounds—the hissing steam and the pounding
of the start of the industrial age."
    In late October she published a long review of Woody Allen's latest, *Star-
dust Memories*, the most annihilating piece of criticism she had done for some
time. Pauline thought the director had been in decline for a while. She had

admired the sweetness of feeling that came through in his 1977 hit *Annie Hall*, but she was bothered by the picture's New York chauvinism and sneering attitude toward Los Angeles, and Allen's self-deprecating treatment of his Jewishness worked on her nerves. In her notes for the movie (she didn't review it), she wrote of Allen's character, the uptight Jewish comedian Alvy Singer, "He only shows you what you see anyway." She thought *Annie Hall* was a promising idea that wasn't delved into deeply enough and never quite found its real subject because it veered off into a tale of two cities—New York versus L.A. She had also had major reservations about Allen's 1979 picture *Manhattan*, which Andrew Sarris hailed as the first great film of the seventies; Pauline was disturbed that Allen chose to focus on the narcissism and career issues of three mixed-up people as being representative of what was wrong with all of New York, and she hooted at the idea that all of this neurosis was shown in contrast to the purity of the teenage girl played by Mariel Hemingway. "What man in his forties," she wrote, with chilling prescience, "could pass off a predilection for teen-agers as a quest for true values?"

In *Stardust Memories*, Allen played Sandy Bates, a famous comedy director who wants to be taken seriously and find himself as an artist, but no one will let him. Pauline was annoyed by the movie's sour narcissism; she thought that Allen was trying to become the Jewish Fellini. "Throughout *Stardust Memories*," she wrote, "Sandy is superior to all those who talk about his work; if they like his comedies, it's for freakish reasons, and he shows them up as poseurs and phonies, and if they don't like his serious work, it's because they're too stupid to understand it. He anticipates almost anything that you might say about *Stardust Memories* and ridicules you for it." There was no question in Pauline's mind that Sandy was a mouthpiece for Allen's true feelings about himself; she cited a comment he had made to *Newsweek*: "When you do comedy, you're not sitting at the grown-ups' table, you're sitting at the children's table." In her reviews of *Stardust Memories*, she painted him as another kind of traitor, too: For years Allen's unmade-bed looks and wired, smart Jewish humor had made him "a new national hero." Now he seemed to be rejecting all that as well. Pauline considered it "a horrible betrayal when he demonstrates that despite his fame he still hates the way he looks and that he wanted to be one of *them*—the stuffy macho Wasps—all along." She closed with a stinging slap: "If Woody Allen finds success very upsetting and wishes the public would go away, this picture should help him stop worrying."

There was a time when Pauline had been invited to Allen's New Year's Eve parties, events filled with many bright lights among New York's intelligentsia. On one invitation, Allen wrote that even if she didn't like most of the people there, she'd have him to talk to for laughs. He was apologizing in advance for the guests at his party. Pauline had seen right through him, and she used it in her review of *Stardust Memories*. After that, her friendship with Allen froze solid.

She was also disappointed in Martin Scorsese's new picture, *Raging Bull*, in which Robert De Niro played the middleweight boxing champion Jake LaMotta. Like Allen, Scorsese seemed to have gotten carried away with his own seriousness. She thought *Raging Bull* wasn't content to be a human drama about the glory days and inevitable decline of a famous prizefighter; it aimed to be "a biography of the genre of prizefight films." And it wasn't even content to be that: "It's also about movies and about violence, it's about gritty visual rhythm, it's about Brando, it's about the two *Godfather* pictures—it's about Scorsese and De Niro's trying to top what they've done and what everybody else has done." It was meant to be the apotheosis of all the great, tough pictures of the seventies about Italian-American urban life, but it had a muffled impact, in Pauline's view, because "You can feel the director sweating for greatness, but there's nothing *under* the scenes." She also found De Niro's much-acclaimed performance didn't have the impact that was intended. "What De Niro does in this picture isn't acting, exactly," she wrote. "Though it may at some level be awesome, it definitely isn't pleasurable. De Niro seems to have emptied himself out to become the part he's playing and then not got enough material to refill himself with."

Pauline was annoyed the following year when the eight Academy Award nominations for *The Elephant Man* did not include one for Freddie Francis's cinematography. She was also upset that the Academy ignored her new favorite, Debra Winger, for *Urban Cowboy*. At the New York Film Critics Circle voting that year, she had gotten behind *Melvin and Howard*, her friend Irvin Kershner's sequel to *Star Wars*, *The Empire Strikes Back*, and—inexplicably—*Dressed to Kill* for Best Picture; O'Toole, Alan King (for Sidney Lumet's comedy *Just Tell Me What You Want*), and Kurt Russell (for *Used Cars*) for Best Actor; Debra Winger, Mary Steenburgen, Dyan Cannon (for *Honeysuckle Rose*), and Shelley Duvall (as Olive Oyl in Robert Altman's film of the famous comic strip *Popeye*), for Best Actress. She was chagrined when *Ordinary People* took the prize for Best Picture, but happy that *Melvin and Howard* earned citations for Best Director (Jonathan Demme) and Best Screenplay (Bo Goldman).

At *The New Yorker* Pauline had been edited for some time by Gardner Botsford, someone she was fond of, but eventually there was a reshuffling, and Daniel Menaker was assigned to her. It seemed a good fit: Menaker, who had started at the magazine in 1969 as a fact-checker, was a longtime movie fan, and he was bright and eager to succeed. "I would say that of all of the nonfiction writers I worked with, there certainly was no one else with whom I did less," recalled Menaker. He noticed early on that she wasn't seeking from her editor a response to the content of what she wrote. "She wanted someone to help make sure her inflections and feelings were what she meant them to be," Menaker recalled. "She would be more likely to say, rather than 'Do you think a comma should go there?,' 'Do you think people will get the fact that I sort of admired, but also had real questions about, this particular actor?' It was more like tonalities. It wasn't like editing. Well, I guess it was, in a way—she knew what I meant. I was more like a reader or a sounding board or an audience."

Pauline was well liked by the magazine's support staff—the copy editors, fact-checkers, and messengers who were more or less at her service. Her rapport with them was not unlike Joan Crawford's camaraderie with the crew members on her movies. "I don't think she had a snobby bone in her body toward such people," said Menaker. "But these people were no threat to her. She had a good common touch, a good, decent comportment with them. There were occasions when I saw her get kind of cross in one way or another, but she very seldom got angry. What she would do is look or act sort of bewildered or flummoxed, and that was a sign of her displeasure." Most often, Pauline would become aggravated when a fact-checker had unintentionally given away something in a review to a source, but she seldom made an issue out of it.

To close friends Pauline complained that Shawn had, in a subtle way, been treating her differently since her return from Hollywood. Perhaps, having been persuaded despite his original instincts to take her back, he felt compelled to convey his disapproval in other ways. Once it seemed that he might have gotten some degree of perverse enjoyment out of their wrangles over copy—he was well known for being susceptible to the emotional demands of many of the women on the staff. Now he seemed much of the time to avoid her. "She loved to provoke Shawn," remembered Menaker. "Pauline would put stuff in to madden him—I think she'd even say, 'This will get his goat.'" But Shawn's attitude toward Pauline was also complex: As much as he respected her and was grateful for the attention she had brought to "The Current Cinema," he also seemed resentful of her. She had grown beyond his power to control. Shawn's genial, paternal attitude had never worked particularly well with Pauline, yet they seemed strangely fond of each other on some level—like Beatrice and Benedict. "I think they really got off on this partnership of mutual dislike," said Menaker. "He was weary and resigned, but I just can't believe that he didn't enjoy the game a little bit."

.    .    .

In 1980 Pauline had asked a casual acquaintance of hers, a painter named Warner Friedman, to come by the house in Great Barrington. Gina, who was living in her own house near Pauline's, had become immersed in her painting—she would choose volcanoes as one of her chief subjects—and Pauline asked Warner to give her daughter some advice on how to frame some of her pictures. Before long Warner and Gina were dating. Warner was not intimidated by Pauline but he remembered that she maintained something of a coolness toward him once he and Gina began seeing each other. He and Gina developed a large circle of painter friends, and whenever Pauline was around them, she would mutter, "Painting, painting, *painting*!" Warner felt that she was somewhat bothered by the fact that so many of their circle were struggling and showed no sign of being close to any kind of commercial success. More to the point, he recalled, she was dying for someone to ask her about the movies.

Now that she was back from her aborted Hollywood foray, it seemed more important than ever that she gather a close circle of moviegoing friends around her. Many of them could be described, with some accuracy, as acolytes. However much Pauline loved passing judgment, it is clear that her inner circle craved her approval. It had become the talk of the industry that she preferred to surround herself with younger people—the word was that she loved to play the mentor, the lecturer, and wanted to be surrounded by those who didn't challenge her views, who dutifully nodded at every word that came out of her mouth. Once, when Warren Beatty saw her at a screening with several of her young critic friends in tow, he remarked, "Here comes Ma Barker and her gang." These adoring young protégés would come to be known as the Paulettes, a term clearly intended to imply slavish imitation and sycophancy, and its accuracy would be debated by both friends and enemies of Pauline's for decades to come. No one is absolutely certain who coined the label "Paulettes"—some credit the critic Richard Corliss—but it stuck. (After her death David Denby would even title a *New Yorker* remembrance of her "My Life as a Paulette.") Whatever the source of the term, it is equally true that it was accurate in the case of some of her followers—and deeply unfair in the case of others.

The Paulettes had been in formation for some time before they found themselves so neatly labeled. In 1976, following a screening of *Carrie*, Joseph Hurley, a mutual friend of Pauline and Joseph Morgenstern, had spent an evening with Pauline and several of her younger followers—among them Carrie Rickey and Al Avant—and was distressed by what he witnessed there. He hadn't liked *Carrie* at all and felt that the others had ganged up on him for not agreeing with Pauline's favorable opinion of the movie, trying to make him look like a fool. He found it even more distasteful for people as young and inexperienced as Rickey and Avant to be gleefully mowing down the reputations of many fine film artists. To Hurley, their behavior reeked of the worst kind of New York snobbery. The following morning he dashed off a scorching letter to Pauline, accusing her of encouraging such behavior.

One of Pauline's favorite young friends was Ray Sawhill. He had written to her about her review of *Nashville* while he was still a student at Princeton, and, as was often the case, it marked the beginning of a friendship. Sawhill had a keen, probing intelligence, a quick wit, and he was friendly and unpretentious—Pauline's kind of person. Their tastes certainly weren't completely congruent—Sawhill was far more interested in avant-garde cinema than Pauline was—but once he had moved to New York and she got to know him, he became a steady companion at screenings and dinners. Sawhill eventually became an arts reporter at *Newsweek*, an experience he grew to dislike because he felt that the magazine didn't care much about how to convey information to its readers, only about how to package it. Pauline took a great interest in his career and was constantly prodding him to be a movie critic. The problem was that Sawhill didn't particularly *want* to be a movie critic; he was drawn to other kinds of writing, as well, and by his own admission, he was not much of a careerist. As a result he became Pauline's favorite "bad boy"—the one in her circle who often wouldn't do what she told him to. Pauline was perpetually exhorting Sawhill to write huge critical pieces on spec and send them to the top magazines, as a way of securing a regular writing post, but he often ignored her advice—to the degree that, once, she shook her fist at him and railed, "You make me so mad!" But clearly, Sawhill's independence from her was also a quality she respected.

Another of Pauline's favorites was Michael Sragow, whom she had gotten to know in the 1970s when he was a student at Harvard. When Sragow began writing criticism for the *Los Angeles Herald Examiner* and then *Rolling Stone*, Pauline would call to tell him what she thought about a particular review. "Most of her criticism was not that hard if you understood the tenor of what she said," Sragow observed. "One of the joys of coming up in that era was that there was real argument, and it was zesty and not always fighting. I think you had to be in the same sort of ballpark of perceiving what was on the screen to have the kind of friendship where you would discuss movies with her. But I think she was kind of bored if you only thought what she thought, if you didn't bring your own eyes to it."

Another young writer whose career Pauline took great interest in was David Edelstein. Unlike some of the acolytes who felt that the way to get along with Pauline was to agree with her, Edelstein did not find that she dictated opinions to him. Rather, he found her extremely sensitive about letting him find his own way in his thinking about movies, as if she understood that he was still a work in progress and she didn't want to influence him unduly. He felt that her interest in being surrounded by a group had less to do with wanting to be Ma Barker, or the Queen Bee, than with her love of being the member of an audience. "Pauline had enormous insight into people," said Edelstein. "For someone who was a critic, she was extraordinarily other-directed. She would get people spouting their opinions and sometimes she would use them. She would use it in a way that was orchestrated in a way that was beyond anything anybody could have done. But she loved to be surprised."

For Pauline, being a spectator continued to be the best thing life could offer. Carrie Rickey remembered an Italian restaurant in Times Square of which Pauline was particularly fond. For dessert she always ordered zaba-glione, the custard dessert that was made at the table—something Rickey suspected she relished because she was both attending a performance and granting an audience. Her old friend Linda Allen recalled a visit that Pauline made to Berkeley when she attended a family reunion. Pauline asked Allen to come over for a visit, and when Allen arrived, she found Pauline's grand-nieces and grand-nephews playing rambunctiously in the backyard. "She was watching them, like a movie," Allen said. "She said at one point, 'I want to see how this comes out.'"

If Pauline thought, however, that her protégés were going in the wrong direction, or if she suddenly felt that she had misjudged their potential, she could drop them with amazing swiftness. This was the fate of Carrie Rickey. Around the time Pauline left for Hollywood, Rickey was given a job as an art critic for *The Village Voice.* Pauline seemed delighted; she frequently called Rickey to ask her questions about various painters or exhibits. In the midsummer of 1980 the *Voice* gave Rickey the job she had had her eye on all along—film critic, as an alternate to Andrew Sarris. The Renata Adler piece had come out by then, as well as Sarris's piece in the *Voice* in which he backed up Adler's point of view. When Rickey called Pauline to commiserate, she noticed immediately that Pauline seemed uninterested in discussing the Adler essay. She talked briefly about the Sarris article, denouncing him to Rickey as sexless and telling her that his marriage to Molly Haskell was a sham. Then Rickey told her that she had just gotten the film critic's post. There was a long silence on the other end of the line.

"Well," Pauline finally said. "They didn't ask me. If they had, I would have told them to hire Jim Wolcott."

"The conversation was over," said Rickey years later, "and so was our friendship."

In 1982 Rickey interviewed for a job at *Rolling Stone*. She had been led to believe that it was as good as hers, when she was suddenly informed that she was out of the running: One of the editors had called Pauline, who pronounced against Rickey. Although Rickey went on to work successfully at *The Philadelphia Inquirer*, at the time she felt professionally blackballed. "I thought," she remembered, "I was fine when I was an acolyte. But she didn't want me as a peer."

At the end of 1980, *Heaven's Gate*, Michael Cimino's epic Western about the conflict between settlers and cattlemen in Johnson County, Wyoming, was released by United Artists—to disastrous reviews. Pauline didn't find it quite the abomination that many other critics did, but she believed Cimino had gotten so wrapped up in creating a certain atmosphere that he had completely lost sight of his story, which rambled along incoherently. "It's a movie you want to deface; you want to draw mustaches on it, because there's no observation in it, no hint of anything resembling direct knowledge—or even intuition—of what people are about," Pauline wrote. Running nearly three hours and forty minutes, *Heaven's Gate* had cost in excess of $36 million— possibly up to $50 million—and the press was quick to paint it as a symbol of the worst excesses of directorial freedom in Hollywood. United Artists withdrew it quickly and cut it by more than an hour, but it flopped again on rerelease. In time, *Heaven's Gate* was seen as the final, cataclysmic gasp of the great auteurist period of the past decade, but the process of getting a movie made in Hollywood had been getting more and more complicated for some time. *Heaven's Gate*, if anything, became a convenient excuse for the studio heads, who would increasingly refuse to green-light a project unless an entire publicity campaign could be built around one good line—the Don Simpson legacy. The marketing executives were steadily taking over, and now that her bruises were beginning to heal, Pauline was relieved not to have remained in Hollywood.

In March of 1981 she saw Louis Malle's *Atlantic City*, starring Burt Lancaster and Susan Sarandon. Her chief pleasure was in seeing the screen work of the brilliant playwright John Guare. Like Pauline, Guare had an aversion to the carefully orchestrated "problem" dramas of playwrights such as William Inge, which told the audience, "Little Sheba might not Come Back but don't worry, we'll learn from this experience and everything will be all right. I was beginning to see that Great White Way naturalism is to reality what sentimentality is to feeling."

Pauline loved the ecstatic flow of Guare's work, and the way in which great ideas, genre spoofs, and free-floating, imagistic dialogue all bumped into one another. "You're not struck with the usual dramatic apparatus—the expository dialogue and the wire-pulling to get the characters into the planned situations. Instead, you get gags, which prove to be the explanation." She admitted, "Though I have a better time in the theater at John Guare's plays than I do at the plays of any other contemporary American, I would not have guessed that his charmed, warped world and his dialogue, which is full of imagery, could be so successfully brought to the screen."

On May 7, 1981, Pauline appeared in a public debate with a onetime idol, Jean-Luc Godard, held at the Marin Civic Center in Mill Valley, California. The event had attracted a crowd of some two thousand people, and on the way there, Godard was quite charming to Pauline. Once they got onstage, however, his tone changed. Their debate turned out to be a long, rambling conversation in which Godard seemed perennially on the offensive against Pauline, who had taken a dim view of some of his more recent pictures. She persistently attempted to keep the conversation on a fairly linear track, while Godard just as persistently attempted to venture off on other paths. He launched the session by criticizing her for "Why Are Movies So Bad? Or, The Numbers." He didn't accept the degree of blame she placed on the conglomerates behind the studios, and felt that critics, Pauline included, needed to take more responsibility for the level of movies being released. Critics, he said, were "using their power in the same direction that the businessmen of the movies are"—meaning that advertising influenced how reviews were written. Pauline tried to defend *The New Yorker*'s strict separation of advertising and editorial matters, but Godard dismissed the argument.

Using Michael Cimino as an example, he attacked the press for overpraising *The Deer Hunter* while blatantly condemning *Heaven's Gate*, a picture which, to his eye, had a number of admirable elements. "It has a lot of magnificent things that the director cannot follow through on—for very obvious reasons which we can analyze," he protested. "But the reviewers never say that, and never try to help someone who is very arrogant, as Cimino is, to make a better picture next time." He attacked one of Pauline's favorites, Brian De Palma, for not adequately preparing his scripts, and compared him unfavorably with Hitchcock. He also stated that he felt criticism should be a kind of science, a comment that Pauline told him was downright perverse. The conversation ambled on, and as the evening's presenter, Sydney Goldstein of City Arts and Lectures, recalled, "It was a chilling ride back to the city."

The summer of 1981 saw the release of the year's greatest commercial success, *Raiders of the Lost Ark*, the George Lucas–Steven Spielberg tribute to old movie serials, starring Harrison Ford. The picture had a tongue-in-cheek tone that appealed to the snobs in the audience who wanted to feel they weren't "just" looking at an adventure movie. It appealed to an incredibly wide base, but Pauline regarded it as a perfect symbol of the rise of the marketing executives; in her review of the picture, she pointed out that marketing budgets often surpassed total production budgets, a practice that "could become commonplace." She found *Raiders* didn't allow you "time to breathe—or to enjoy yourself much, either. It's an encyclopedia of high spots from the old serials, run through at top speed and edited like a great trailer—for flash." At last, she could see the direction in which *Jaws* had led. Its excesses were especially a pity, she thought, because both Lucas and Spielberg were loaded with moviemaking talent. She observed that if Lucas "weren't hooked on the crap of his childhood—if he brought his resources to bear on some projects with human beings in them—there's no imagining the result." But it's doubtful that Lucas paid attention to her admonishment—not in the face of the $230 million gross racked up by *Raiders*.

Pauline had stumbled through the year, mostly indifferent to the films she was seeing, until the summer brought Brian De Palma's *Blow Out*, the story of a sounds-effects specialist (John Travolta) who one night witnesses a man driving off a bridge and into a river. The man in the car turns out to be the governor of Pennsylvania, who was preparing a campaign for the presidency; he dies, but the hero manages to rescue a girl who was also in the car, and soon the two of them find themselves embroiled in a case of high-level conspiracy. It was, as Pauline noted, a movie that had overtones of political events of recent years— ranging from Chappaquiddick to Watergate. Several critics dismissed it as a routine takeoff on *Blow-Up*, but Pauline found it to be "the first movie in which De Palma has stripped away the cackle and the glee." It was "hallucinatory, and it has a dreamlike clarity and inevitability, but you'll never make the mistake of thinking that it's only a dream. Compared with *Blow Out*, even the good pictures that have opened this year look dowdy." And then she took one of her giant steps, as if defying the critics who attacked her for being hyperbolic: "I think De Palma has sprung to the place that Altman achieved with films such as *McCabe & Mrs. Miller* and *Nashville* and that Coppola reached with the two *Godfather* movies—that is, to the place where genre is transcended and what we're moved by is an artist's vision." Despite its virtues, *Blow Out* didn't receive particularly strong reviews, and it muddled along at the box office.

The most heralded actress's performance of the summer left her cold—Meryl Streep in Karel Reisz's *The French Lieutenant's Woman*. She had admired Streep on the New York stage, particularly as a comedienne, and written warmly of her performance as Linda in *The Deer Hunter*. But Pauline generally preferred actors who conveyed some kind of ripe sensuality, inflected with a certain craziness or messiness. This was particularly true of her favorite female stars, from Bette Davis to Debra Winger. She had already pegged Streep as a highly cerebral actress, and wrote: "We never really get into the movie because, as Sarah, Meryl Streep gives an immaculate, technically accomplished performance, but she isn't mysterious. She's pallid and rather glacial. . . . Meryl Streep's technique doesn't add up to anything. We're not fascinated by Sarah; she's so distanced from us that all we can do is observe how meticulous Streep—and everything else about the movie—is."

Pauline was just beginning to feel that she had recovered from the wounds inflicted by Renata Adler's essay when she was hit by another attack—one that was, in its way, even more unsettling.

# CHAPTER TWENTY-THREE

It was the unlikeliest of films that caused Pauline so much difficulty in late 1981. George Cukor's *Rich and Famous* was an anachronism for the early '80s—a new version of John Van Druten's musty Broadway comedy *Old Acquaintance*, about the tumultuous friendship of two women writers, one with a serious literary reputation, the other the author of trashy bestsellers. The play had been previously filmed in 1943, with Bette Davis and Miriam Hopkins as the battling friends. Now it had been updated, spanning the period from 1959 to 1981, with Jacqueline Bisset as the serious one and Candice Bergen, fresh from her surprising comedic success in Alan J. Pakula's *Starting Over*, as the trashmonger. *Rich and Famous* earned a certain niche in film history because, at eighty-one, George Cukor was the oldest director on record to have helmed a major studio picture.

What perplexed Pauline most about the film was her strong feeling that the entire movie was suffused with a gay sensibility. This was fine in the campier scenes, in which an outrageously over-the-top Bergen was used "almost as if she were a big, goosey female impersonator," in Pauline's words. The problem came in the scenes in which the picture strained to take a serious look at why Bisset's character was so bottled up creatively and emotionally. One sequence in particular bothered Pauline. In it, Bisset is picked up by a hot young boy, takes him back to her room at the Algonquin, and watches with anxious lust as he slowly removes his clothes. "She begins to kiss his abdomen passionately, gratefully," wrote Pauline. "It's gruesomely silly. . . . This picture might have been *made* by young hustlers." At the end of her review, she offered, "*Rich and Famous* isn't camp, exactly; it's more like a homosexual fantasy. Bisset's affairs, with their masochistic overtones, are creepy, because they don't seem like what a woman would get into."

Pauline didn't foresee that her remarks would upset her readers, and perhaps if they had been written by a gay man, they might not have. But coming from a heterosexual woman, they were perceived by many as hostile; by 1981, the lines in the war for sexual equality had been drawn much more boldly than they had been before. In identifying Bisset's character with what she thought of as the masochistic side of gay cruising, she misstepped by failing to explain herself adequately: She was speaking specifically of the gay men she knew for whom sex and genuine intimacy were two different things. For Pauline, casual sex onscreen didn't need to be accompanied by an explanation or apology, or loads of sober, melancholy rationale—this was exactly what had disturbed her about *Looking for Mr. Goodbar*. But her comment about Bisset's affairs was perilously close to the one she had made about the Rod Steiger character in *The Sergeant*, and it appeared to some of her offended readers that her thinking on gay issues hadn't advanced since 1968. Many of her gay readers might once have unquestioningly been seduced by her language and the force of her personality; now many of them demanded accountability.

The gay press was quick to register its outrage, with a full-scale attack launched by Stuart Byron in *The Village Voice*. "However much male gay life has followed promiscuous patterns not available to straights until the advent of the postpill paradise, the gay fantasy has always been exactly the same as the straight fantasy: love and happiness with one person forever." The *Voice*, of course, had long had it in for her: it was the home base of Andrew Sarris, and the paper's critics deplored the fact that Pauline didn't toe the line on feminism and gay rights—and certain staff members even felt that she had never fully embraced her own Jewishness. "The reason the *Voice* hated her was that she wasn't politically correct," said David Edelstein. "It's as simple as that. They didn't consider her tastes particularly feminist. De Palma they found unbearable. They were cultural commissars there."

Many of her friends leaped to her defense. James Wolcott was stunned by the backlash from her *Rich and Famous* review. "Pauline was so advanced on gay things in her sensibility, in the people she had around her," he said. "The Stuart Byron thing bothered her because she knew it wasn't true, and when something like that was said other people would pick up on it. She would say, 'Haven't they seen what a lousy movie it is?' 'You're going to make this movie the basis of your stand about gay portrayals and sensibility—*this* thing?' It was a sore point."

Pauline believed in giving readers a precise description of the emotions a film generated in her, even if the words she used to describe them were tough, even coarse. Years earlier, when she had used the phrase "fag phantom of the opera" to describe Rod Steiger's role in *No Way to Treat a Lady*, she had chosen the term both for rhythm and to convey the cheap, low-camp nature of the character. Likewise, shortly after her *Rich and Famous* review appeared, she wrote about *Pixote*, Hector Babenco's superb film about the horrible lives of child criminals in Brazil. Describing a character played by Jorge Juliao, she wrote that he was "a soft creature, flamingly nelly—an imitation of a young girl without parody." Her use of the word "nelly" may have rankled William Shawn—but again, it was the word she thought best conveyed her feeling for the character. "Effeminate" would have been too tame, too predictable. A key to her profound connection with readers had always been her rich use of the vernacular; she wrote in the current jargon, and she thought her readers should be able to take it. "If I make these jokes," she told her friend Daryl Chin, "it's because I have so many gay friends and I assume they all understand."

While some movie fans were offended by her review of *Rich and Famous* on behalf of George Cukor—he was widely known to be gay, and it was considered that she had disrespected him by painting *Rich and Famous* as a gay fantasy—it was mostly her army of avid gay readers who felt that she had betrayed them, and they vented their anger in letters that poured into the offices of *The New Yorker*. Pauline was disturbed by the violence of some of them, and to those angered readers whose letters and phone calls she answered, she explained that she had simply been trying to point out the difference in nuance between gay and heterosexual encounters.

During the creative and social upheaval of the 1960s and '70s, Pauline's tough-mindedness and intellectual daring had been a perfect match for what was taking place in the movies. But times had changed. Ronald Reagan had been elected on a platform that effectively included a war on liberalism, and the economic downturn and perceived lack of leadership in the Jimmy Carter administration had helped create an enormous swing to the right in U.S. politics. The protection of corporate interests was paramount on Reagan's list of concerns, and Pauline constantly fretted that the new, money-driven culture ushered in by his election was having a devastating effect on the movies.

Yet, while what wound up on the screen was becoming blander and safer, society was, paradoxically, becoming more polarized, and many people were becoming much more militant about the issues that concerned them. The days when a mainstream publication such as *Time* could characterize homosexuality as an affliction were long gone. With the impending AIDS crisis, which would devastate the world in the 1980s and '90s, many publications would find it a delicate matter to criticize gay subject matter or sensibility on any level. The zeitgeist was changing—and the reaction to Pauline's review of *Rich and Famous* was an indication that it was changing in ways that were alien to her values.

For her part, Pauline made no effort to moderate her use of astringent language just because some of her readers objected to it. In a November review of Milos Forman's *Ragtime*, she stunned some readers with her description of the director's concept of the Gibson girl Evelyn Nesbit, played by Elizabeth McGovern: "Forman appears to see Evelyn as some sort of open-mouthed retard." Again she was drawing from ordinary American speech—"retard" was a common expression for anyone who engaged in dull, stupid behavior— and therefore considered the term acceptable.

At the end of 1981 she surprised everyone with an ecstatic review for Herbert Ross's *Pennies from Heaven*, calling it "the most emotional movie musical I've ever seen." Based on the BBC TV series, *Pennies from Heaven* was an emotionally jarring look at the quietly desperate life of an Illinois sheet-music salesman, played by the comedian Steve Martin. The novelty of the movie, which captured in amazing detail the sadly evocative paintings of Edward Hopper, was that the characters lip-synched to popular recordings from the '30s to express themselves. "Despite its use of Brechtian devices," Pauline wrote, "*Pennies from Heaven* doesn't allow you to distance yourself. You're thrust into the characters' emotional extremes; you're right in front of the light that's shining from their eyes. And you see the hell they go through for sex and money." Herbert Ross was not a director for whom she ever had much regard, but this time she thought he had surpassed himself: "There's something new going on—something thrilling—when the characters in a musical are archetypes yet are intensely alive. . . . This picture shows that the talent to make great movie musicals is out there, waiting." She pushed hard for the movie in her review, because she had a strong sense that the studio, MGM, wouldn't know what to do with it, and she was right: *Pennies from Heaven* suffered from a halfhearted marketing campaign and failed completely at the box office.

The movie on which her fans were most eager to read her verdict was Warren Beatty's *Reds*, which had a splashy opening in December. She did not recant her opinion that it was a mistake for Beatty to have taken on such an ambitious project—the story of the American journalist John Reed and his eventual undoing as a pawn in the Bolshevik Revolution—but she admitted that it was a film made with "an enormous amount of dedication and intel- ligence. It's absorbing, and you feel good will toward it." Nevertheless, she felt that *Reds* didn't work, largely because Beatty hadn't decided which aspects of his sprawling story interested him most. She loved the interviews with survivors from John Reed's era—including Henry Miller, Hamilton Fish, Rebecca West, Dora Russell, and Adela Rogers St. John—but felt the prob- lem was that they were "all much peppier and more vital than the actors."

One of the biggest difficulties Pauline had with *Reds* was the casting of Diane Keaton, Beatty's girlfriend at the time, as Reed's fellow journalist and revolutionary, and his wife, Louise Bryant. She felt the movie did Bryant a disservice by presenting her as "a tiresome, pettishly hostile woman," and that it never really grappled with the question of how talented or how opportunistic Bryant was. "It takes Keaton a long time to get any kind of bearings; at the start her nervous speech patterns are anachronistic—she seems to be playing a premature post-hippie neurotic," Pauline wrote.

She admired much about Beatty's performance in the film, finding him "remarkably subtle in the way he tunes in to whoever is in a scene with him," though she felt that he was still trying to sell his nice-boy image to the audience; he was too "bewildered, shaggy, eager" and didn't tap enough into the darker side of John Reed. In the end, *Reds* was "extremely traditional, and in movies traditional means derivative . . . [it is] the least radical, the least innovative epic you can imagine."

Her review of *Reds* led to yet another showdown with Shawn. In order to describe the relationship between John Reed and Louise Bryant as Beatty had conceived it, Pauline had written that the movie showed Reed to be "pussywhipped." Shawn tried to get her to change it to "henpecked," which she laughed at and rejected. The argument went back and forth between them, until Shawn finally told her in no uncertain terms that "pussywhipped" would not be printed in *The New Yorker*. (It's a shame, in a way, since many who saw *Reds* must agree that it's the only word to describe the onscreen relationship.)

There is no surviving correspondence from *The New Yorker* that addresses the question of whether Pauline should have been allowed to review *Reds*, given her history with Beatty and Paramount. Certainly Shawn must have considered the potential conflict carefully before allowing her to go ahead. "There was no way that she was going to be able to see *Reds* with an open mind," said James Toback. "And she actually hit Warren, in a semiconscious or unconscious desire to stick to him, by attacking Diane Keaton's performance. It was her way of saying, 'You, who of all men should know how to bring out the best in a woman, have taken your girlfriend, the female star, and come up with a performance that's not good.' If she was going to say something to nail him, that was it." Roy Blount, Jr., remembered going with Pauline to the screening of *Reds* and seeing the Paramount publicists hovering fearfully around her. "Oh, God, they were so damned nervous. It was in this little bitty screening room in New York, and they were just sort of hanging on her for a reaction." *Reds* had substantial earnings as one of the Christmas season's big prestige pictures, but its eventual take of around $32 million was not quite enough to earn back its staggering production cost—the result that Pauline had predicted when Beatty was developing the project at Paramount.

At the voting for the 1981 New York Film Critics Circle, Pauline did her usual campaigning for her favorites. For the Best Picture prize, she favored *Blow Out, Pennies from Heaven,* and *Atlantic City;* for Best Director, Brian De Palma for *Blow Out,* Walter Hill for *Southern Comfort,* and Louis Malle for *Atlantic City.* Her picks for Best Actor included Burt Lancaster for *Atlantic City* and John Travolta for *Blow Out,* plus Andre Gregory for *My Dinner with Andre* (cowritten by and costarring William Shawn's son, Wallace). For Best Actress her finalists included Faye Dunaway (*Mommie Dearest*), Bernadette Peters (*Pennies from Heaven*), and Marília Pera (*Pixote*). Lancaster was the only one of her choices who won in the end—and she was especially chagrined to see the Best Picture award go to *Reds.*

Throughout 1982 there was still the occasional marvelous personal film that she loved writing about and did her best to champion. One was Alan Parker's marital drama *Shoot the Moon,* about which she observed, "I'm a little afraid to say how good I think *Shoot the Moon* is—I don't want to set up the kind of bad magic that might cause people to say they were led to expect so much that they were disappointed." Bo Goldman, whose script for *Melvin and Howard* she had admired so much, had come through again, with a story that wasn't "just about marriage; it's about the family that is created, and how that whole family reacts to the knotted, disintegrating relationship of the parents." She felt that Diane Keaton had redeemed herself for her weak performance in *Reds,* and Albert Finney, playing her tormented husband, was her match—they gave "the kind of performances that in the theater become legendary." Pauline's advocacy did not help *Shoot the Moon,* which grossed only a little more than $7 million on a budget of $12 million.

As the year went on, she also admired Jean-Jacques Beineix's French thriller *Diva,* thinking the director someone "who understands the pleasures to be had from a picture that doesn't take itself very seriously." And she was delighted by Steven Spielberg's captivating fantasy *E.T. The Extra-Terrestrial,* which she described as "a dream of a movie—a bliss-out." She was encouraged to see Spielberg applying his prodigious imagination to a touching, human story; to her, it made up for the mechanical excesses of *Raiders of the Lost Ark:* "He's like a boy soprano lilting with joy all through *E.T.,* and we're borne along by his voice."

It was reassuring when she celebrated the return to form of Robert Altman with *Come Back to the Five & Dime, Jimmy Dean, Jimmy Dean.* She was fond of telling people that she couldn't quite account for Altman's talent—that when he was on his game, he was remarkable, but when he was off it, one would never guess that he had any talent at all. *Come Back to the Five & Dime, Jimmy Dean, Jimmy Dean* began life as a play by Ed Graczyk, which Altman directed on Broadway in early 1982. It got downbeat reviews and ran for only fifty-two performances. Graczyk had written the kind of well-made play that had become a staple of Broadway in the '40s and '50s—the kind in which the characters' self-delusions and hypocrisies are systematically revealed—the sort of thing that seemed antithetical to Altman's intuitive style. It concerned the reunion of a James Dean fan club on the twentieth anniversary of the star's death, and Pauline thought that in its "fake-poetic, fake magical way, it reeks of the worst of William Inge, of Tennessee Williams misunderstood." After its failure onstage Altman had filmed it for under $1 million with most of the same cast. Cher, Sandy Dennis, Karen Black, and Kathy Bates all reprised their roles, and Pauline thought that what the director had gotten out of them was remarkable:

> If the roles made better sense, the actresses might not be able to plunge so far down into themselves or pull up so much emotion. It's *because* this glib, religioso play is so derivative that the actors have found so much depth in it. When actors peel away layers of inhibition, they feel they're uncovering "truth" and it's traditional for directors and acting teachers to call it that. But this truth may be derived from their stored-up pop mythology—atrocity stories from sources as diverse as comic books, TV, and Joan Didion, and tales of sacrificial heroes and heroines that go back beyond the birth of movies to the first storytellers. "Truthful" acting may be affecting to us because it represents the sum total of everything the actors have been affected by.

Pauline found the movie "a genuine oddity—like *Night of the Iguana* performed by a company of seraphim." But Altman's old magic relit the screen, and Pauline's joy in welcoming him back was almost palpable:

> Altman keeps looking at the world, and it's never the same; what we're responding to is his consciousness at work (and play). The sunlight coming through the shop's glass front and the dusty pastel colors are part of the film's texture, along with the women's hair and heads and hands, which are always touching, moving. Present and past interpenetrate, and Altman keeps everything in motion. (The close-ups are pauses, not full stops.) His feeling for the place is almost as tactile as his feeling for the performers. When the characters' passions well up the camera is right there, recording the changes in their neck muscles, their arms, their cheeks. But it never crowds them.

. . .

One of the fascinating aspects of the careers of so many movie stars is that their peak years are usually over so quickly. What seemed fresh and spontaneous and original about them—the very qualities that made the public take to them in the first place—can seem like mannerisms and limitations. Only a few years earlier, Jane Fonda had seemed primed for a long run as the screen's premier actress, but after her stiff performances in *9 to 5* and *On Golden Pond*, it was clear her peak years were finished. Meryl Streep was rapidly rising as the most important actress on the screen, complete with the validation of uniformly excellent reviews and a *Time* cover story, but Pauline continued to resist her charms. Streep's much-celebrated technique was just that to Pauline—lacking the warm glow of a genuine personality behind it. In *Still of the Night*, Streep's 1982 psychological thriller, Pauline thought the actress didn't "resemble a living person; her face is gaunt, her skin has become alabaster. She seems to have chosen to do a Meryl Streep parody; she's like some creature from the moon trying to be a movie star."

Streep's big film of the year, and the one that would win her her second Academy Award, was *Sophie's Choice*, based on William Styron's bestselling novel about a Polish holocaust survivor living with her abusive boyfriend in Brooklyn. The film was, for Pauline, "encrusted with the weighty culture of big themes: evil, tortured souls, guilt." In her review, she did a masterful job at identifying again what troubled her most about the actress:

> Streep is very beautiful at times, and she does amusing, nervous bits of business, like fidgeting with a furry boa—her fingers twiddling with our heartstrings. She has, as usual, put thought and effort into her work. But something about her puzzles me: after I've seen her in a movie, I can't visualize her from the neck down. Is it possible that as an actress she makes herself into a blank and then focuses all her attention on only one thing—the toss of her head, for example, in *Manhattan*, her accent here? Maybe, by bringing an unwarranted intensity to one facet of a performance, she in effect decorporealizes herself. This could explain why her movie heroines don't seem to be full characters, and why there are no incidental joys to be had from watching her. It could be that in her zeal to be an honest actress she allows nothing to escape her concep- tion of a performance. Instead of trying to achieve freedom in front of the camera, she's predetermining what it records.

Years later, in an interview, Streep admitted that Pauline's review of *Sophie's Choice* affected her deeply. "I'm incapable of not thinking about what Pauline wrote, and you know what I think?" the actress said. "That Pauline was a poor Jewish girl who was at Berkeley with all these rich Pasadena WASPs with long blond hair, and the heartlessness of them got her." Certainly many of the actresses Pauline admired most onscreen were Jewish—from Sylvia Sidney and Paulette Goddard to Barbra Streisand, Goldie Hawn, and Debra Winger. But Streep's theory ignores the fact that Pauline was overwhelmed by many beautiful blond women on the screen—from Catherine Deneuve to Michelle Pfeiffer.

Pauline was also baffled by the latest appearance of Robert De Niro, one of the screen actors in whom she had placed the most hope. De Niro was reunited with Martin Scorsese for *The King of Comedy*, in which the actor played a sociopath named Rupert Pupkin, who wants nothing more than to become a star TV comic. He obsessively worships Jerry Langford (Jerry Lewis), star of a Johnny Carson–style late-night program, and when he has exhausted every possible attempt to get Langford to pay attention to him, Rupert kidnaps the star, telling the police he will release him only in exchange for a ten-minute spot on the show.

*The King of Comedy* turned out to be far more prescient about the future of television than *Network* ever dreamed of being: Rupert does indeed make a hit with the audience, gets a big book deal, and lands on the cover of several national magazines after serving only a light sentence. At the end of the film, Jerry Langford walks past a store window and sees Rupert on TV. The movie presaged Morton Downey, Jr., and Monica Lewinsky—figures who took the low road as a way of spinning celebrity.

But Pauline dismissed *The King of Comedy* as "quiet and empty," and she thought that Scorsese "designs his own form of alienation in this movie—it seems to teeter between jokiness and hate." Most surprising was her view of De Niro, whom she felt gave a hollow, chilly performance as Pupkin, never endowing him the sort of humanity that might trigger a strong emotional response in the audience. What De Niro achieved in *The King of Comedy*, she believed, was close to what he had done in *Raging Bull*. It was "anti-acting":

Performers such as John Barrymore and Orson Welles and Laurence Olivier have delighted in putting on beards and false noses, yet, no matter how heavy the disguise, they didn't disappear; they still had spirit, and we could feel the pleasure that they took in playing foul, crookback monsters and misers—drawing us inside and revealing the terrors of the misshapen, the deluded. A great actor merges his soul with that of his characters—or, at least, gives us the illusion that he does. De Niro in disguise denies his characters a soul. It's not merely that he hollows himself out and becomes Jake La Motta, or Des the priest in *True Confessions*, or Rupert Pupkin—he makes them hollow, too, and merges with the character's emptiness.

Since they met in 1980, Gina's relationship with Warner Friedman had blossomed, and on March 17, 1982, she gave birth to their son, William James. Like Pauline, Gina had a deep desire to have a child, but she was not entirely certain about marriage. Then, on Will's first birthday, Friedman and Gina invited a group of friends, including Pauline, over to celebrate at Friedman's house in Sheffield, Massachusetts. He had secretly called a justice of the peace to show up and marry him and Gina before the gathering, and when he announced his plan, Pauline's voice emerged loud and clear from the group: "Oh, shit." She was no less skeptical about marriage than she had ever been—and the thought that Friedman would now have an even greater claim on Gina's attention was jarring to her.

Friedman and Pauline often disagreed. She became very angry one evening when he said that all actors were stupid, and on another occasion when, after several drinks, he pronounced, "Movies are not art." He characterized Pauline's relationship with Gina as "a distant closeness" and recognized that, as independent as Pauline was, she needed Gina to be close by. Gina, for her part, clearly harbored certain resentments against Pauline. She was angry with herself that she had not rebelled against her mother and insisted on having a proper education—a point on which many of Pauline's friends sympathized with her. Mother and daughter had one important trait in common: they were both self-contained about their emotions, very conscious of not allowing tensions between them to be played out before others. Friedman recalled a time when Gina was hospitalized for some minor surgery. "Pauline sort of showed a little affection," he recalled, "and Gina was annoyed by it. As close as they seemed, they were not demonstrative."

# CHAPTER TWENTY-FOUR

For some years Billy Abrahams had been urging Pauline to publish a collection of her capsule reviews, which by now were an institution in *The New Yorker*'s front-of-book section. She had amassed more than eleven thousand of these pieces, some of them dating back to her days writing program notes for the Berkeley Cinema Guild. Noting the success that Leonard Maltin had had with his own collection of brief reviews, Abrahams urged her to gather her own, and when it became clear that *Lays of Ancient Hollywood* would not materialize, the project became a priority. Videocassettes of movies were soon to hit the market, and Abrahams knew that if movies on tape led to the anticipated revolution in home viewing, Pauline's book was likely to be very popular indeed. She chose the title herself—*5001 Nights at the Movies*. Assembling and editing the collection was a massive task, but when Holt, Rinehart and Winston brought it out in 1982, *The Boston Globe*'s Mark Sweeney called it "an incomparable dip-in book," and the *Chicago Tribune*'s Richard Christiansen dubbed it "a browser's delight." It sold very well and eventually had even greater success as a paperback—the only thing that baffled readers was the inclusion of movies such as *Car Wash* and *Straight, Place and Show*, with the Ritz Brothers—at the expense of staples such as *Gone With the Wind* and *The Wizard of Oz*. Sharp-eyed readers may have noticed that she altered her view of at least one film, Robert Bresson's *Diary of a Country Priest*. In *Kiss Kiss Bang Bang* she had called it "one of the most profound emotional experiences in the history of film"; now she still found it great, but qualified her opinion, judging that the slow rhythm might make viewers feel that they were "dying with the priest. The film may raise the question in your mind: Does Bresson know what a pain this young man is?"

Whatever her feelings about the quality of the films she was reviewing, Pauline's enthusiasm for writing was undiminished. William Whitworth once observed that of all the staff writers at *The New Yorker*, no one exhibited the zeal for sitting down to work that she did. By now she was no longer pleased with Daniel Menaker as her direct editor, and requested that he be replaced. William Shawn called Menaker in and said, "I don't want you to take this personally. You lasted a long time with her. But Miss Kael feels that you may not have the time and attention to give her the sort of editorial help she needs."

Pauline's idea of the attention she wished for from an editor primarily involved sitting in her office and reading her column aloud to him, with a small electric fan blowing behind her. "Whenever she came across something that she felt didn't sound like her, she would change it. I had been learning all along from other writers that when you have a genuine voice, you have to listen to it and listen to it carefully. The dark side of that was incredible tedium, after a while. It was more like being a silent witness than it was being an editor. I suppose my impatience showed through."

In 1983 Pauline received the Award for Distinguished Journalism from the Newswomen's Club of New York. She was pleased by the honor, but she had continued to resist any feminist interpretation of her career. She was not comfortable with the increasing labeling of "male" and "female" art and culture and was also ill at ease with the streak of militant anger present in the thinking of so many hard-core feminists. She thought, to paraphrase the writer Suzanne Gordon, that there was a great difference between male objectification and male appreciation, and she did not see that much good could come from the sexes being increasingly isolated from each other.

In June 1983 she turned sixty-four, and was conscious of a certain physical decline. That summer she suffered a long period of back pain that made it difficult for her to sit in screenings for long periods of time. More worrisome was the frequent tightness in her chest, which struck her when she picked up the mail each day in Great Barrington and began walking back up the hill to her house. She had developed hypertension and tried treating it with the beta blocker Diltiazem, which only made her depressed; her doctors put her on Dyazide, which proved a more effective way of treating her blood pressure. She suffered several more bouts of severe flu, and still had a slight tremor in her hands, which she attributed to the advancing years.

The summer of 1983 was an unrewarding time to be writing movie criticism. Her review of *Flashdance* could easily have been interpreted by some Hollywood insiders as an open attack on the man who produced it, Don Simpson—but it is doubtful that Pauline would have liked the film no matter who happened to be at the helm. She trounced it as a "lulling, narcotizing musical; the whole damn thing throbs. It's a motorized anatomy lesson, designed to turn the kids on and drive older men crazy. It's soft-core porn with an inspirational message, and it's maybe the most calculating, platinum-hearted movie I've ever seen." She welcomed Woody Allen back, guardedly, with her review of *Zelig*, his documentary satire about a chameleon-like personality who inserts himself into the lives of many of the great figures of the century. She felt it was a small success that had been wildly overrated: "The film has a real shine, but it's like a teeny carnival that you may have missed—it was in the yard behind the Methodist Church last week."

That fall, she enjoyed herself tremendously at Philip Kaufman's *The Right Stuff*, based on Tom Wolfe's book about the marketing of Project Mercury's groundbreaking team of astronauts. She wrote that the entire film gave off "a pleasurable hum" and that "like Tom Wolfe, Phil Kaufman wants you to find everything he puts in beguilingly wonderful and ironic. That's the Tom Wolfe tone, and to a surprising degree Kaufman catches it and blends it with his own." What intrigued her most was the way in which Kaufman, "far more of an anti-establishmentarian than Tom Wolfe," had taken the book's "reactionary cornerstone: the notion that a man's value is determined by his physical courage . . . Yet the film's comedy scenes are conceived in counterculture terms."

Years later, Kaufman still wasn't certain about Pauline's term "reactionary cornerstone." "Someone told me she saw it with a group of her followers," he said, "and I don't know if that was a Pauline reaction, purely. The movie was all about the wives and female courage, and all of these things—women holding up. Every scene in the movie was an aspect of the right stuff. It wasn't all about macho stuff. In fact, a lot of it was downplaying that. Pauline saw a movie once and sometimes she might see it in a mood or with certain people and the mood of the room—and you just have to live with that. I would never think of calling Pauline to try to explain my work to her."

She was delighted by Barbra Streisand's directorial debut with *Yentl*, released in November. She thought the movie "rhapsodic," and a welcome musical return to the screen for the star. "Her singing voice takes you farther into the character; the songs express Yentl's feelings—what she wants to say but has to hold back," Pauline wrote. "Her singing is more than an interior monologue. When she starts a song, her hushed intensity makes you want to hear her every breath, and there's high drama in her transitions from verse to chorus." Pauline had always resented that Streisand had in the past come under fire for her perfectionism, and toward the end of the review, her partisanship came glaring through: "And now that she has made her formal debut as a director, her work explains why she, notoriously, asks so many questions of writers and directors and everyone else—that's her method of learning. And it also explains why she has sometimes been unhappy with her directors: she really did know better."

The year's most universally acclaimed big studio picture was James L. Brooks's *Terms of Endearment*. It had a good premise: the uneasy relationship between an unusual, strong-minded, exceptional-in-some-ways mother

(Shirley MacLaine) and her much less exceptional daughter (Debra Winger), whose life swings out of control when she enters into a bad marriage and later develops terminal cancer. Pauline loathed it, feeling that Brooks had directed "the actors with both eyes on the audience." Winger confirmed Pauline's faith in her; she found her performance "incredibly vivid," but in the end, the film's manipulative style irritated her: "If *Terms* had stayed a comedy," she wrote, "it might have been innocuous, but it had to be ratified by importance, and it uses cancer like a seal of approval. Cancer gives the movie its message: 'Don't take people for granted; you never know when you're going to lose them.' At the end, the picture says, 'You can go home now—you've laughed, you've cried.' What's infuriating about it is its calculated humanity." *Terms of Endearment* was about as close as the major Hollywood studios seemed to be willing to get to complex, problematic subject matter, and the savvy moviegoer was beginning to perceive the decision-by-committee mentality that had gone into such movies.

Music continued to play an enormous role in Pauline's life at home. She listened to a wide range of recordings—everything from opera to Aretha Franklin. She considered opera a great, all-consuming art form, like movies, and she could be thrilled by it without possessing an encyclopedic knowledge of it. (She once telephoned opera aficionado John Simon because she didn't recognize Verdi excerpts being played in Bertolucci's *1900*.) Her musical tastes made for a fascinating parallel with her taste in movies. In general, she preferred the subtlety of jazz to the all-out, hearty razzmatazz of Broadway show tunes; one of her favorite recordings was Billie Holiday's "Getting Some Fun out of Life." In the realm of classical music, she was extremely resistant to the composers who wore their profundity on their sleeve. For this reason she never fully warmed to Mahler and Bruckner ("There wasn't a lot of room for bombast," observed David Edelstein) while she had a deep love for the music of Handel and Gluck and other early-music composers, because she admired their economical structure—they created exciting, passionate music that was also formally disciplined. One of the singers whose records she played most often was the great American countertenor Russell Oberlin—an unusual preference, since at the time countertenors had nothing like the wider acceptance they later achieved.

Reviewing *Amadeus*, Milos Forman's screen version of Peter Shaffer's long-running play, Pauline was amused by the playwright's vision of the relationship between the respected middlebrow court composer Antonio Salieri and the wildly gifted young Mozart: "Shaffer has Salieri declaring war on Heaven for gypping him, and determined to ruin Mozart because God's voice is speaking through him. . . . He's the least humble of Christians—he seems to expect God to give him exact value for every prayer he has ever delivered." Where she took issue with the movie, however, was in its suggestion that Salieri was right: She thought that Shaffer erred "by showing you Mozart as a rubber-faced grinning buffoon with a randy turn of mind, as if that were all there was to him, [and it] begins to lend credence to Salieri's mad notion that Mozart doesn't have to do a thing—that his music is a no-strings-attached, pure gift from God." Still, she was surprised how much she liked the film, in large part because of F. Murray Abraham's performance—she considered him "a wizard at eager, manic, full-of-life roles, and he gives Salieri a cartoon animal's obsession with Mozart—he's Wile E. Coyote."

The year 1984 was significant in several ways. In April, Pauline's seventh collection of reviews, *Taking It All In*, was published by Holt, Rinehart and Winston, covering her *New Yorker* pieces from June 1980 to June 1983. She presented it at a sales conference in Washington, D.C. Judy Karasik, an employee at Holt at the time, remembered the excitement that surrounded Pauline's appearances. "I was sitting next to her," remembered Karasik, "and I'd never seen anyone so nervous before speaking in my life. Her hands were sweating so profusely that I believed that drops were pouring off of them. She sort of held them at her side and sort of shook them. She was trembling, and breathing oddly. Then she got up there and was so brilliant."

Reviewing the book in *The New York Times Book Review*, Gerald Mast called Pauline's work "fiercely impressionistic and aggressively untheoretical," and praised her "powerful perceptions and terrific writing." He went on to say that he found her self-confidence in her own impressions somewhat exhausting at times—he felt that, occasionally, he longed for her to ponder the meaning of a film rather than state it so boldly. And he objected to her review of *Rich and Famous*—not for the reasons Stuart Byron had, but because he felt that she had not adequately considered, or even mentioned, George Cukor's long career in dialogue comedy. "No auteurist critic, of the sort Miss Kael so vehemently despises, would ever have done so poor a job at *thinking* about this director," Mast wrote.

By the mid-1980s the nature of movie criticism itself had begun to change dramatically. In keeping with the tone in recent Hollywood films, reviewing had become lighter and more "entertainment" driven. Increasingly, national newsmagazines put movies on their covers that they thought were likely to connect with a wide sector of the public and become iconic. While Pauline did not object to movies getting cover stories in *Time* and *Newsweek*, she was quite aware that this meant that magazine publishers brought pressure to bear on their reviewers to write about the films in question positively—a practice she abhorred.

TV critics had a new visibility, thanks mostly to the success of the Chicago-based reviewers Gene Siskel and Roger Ebert, who became popular in the mid-1970s with a local TV program of film reviews that eventually became known as *Sneak Previews*. Siskel and Ebert had a regular-guy appeal, a shoot-from-the-hip, commonsense style of addressing their viewers. Their reviews were short and punchy and argumentative, always capped by a "Thumbs Up" or "Thumbs Down" summation. The format caught on, and in 1978, they moved to PBS. In 1982 their audience grew substantially when they changed their show's title to *At the Movies* and went into national syndication. Siskel and Ebert became enormous pop-culture figures, and signaled a major change in what people wanted from film reviewing. They weren't critics, exactly—at least not on their television show—but consumer guides, for whom the ultimate point was to let the audience know whether or not they should spend their hard-earned money at the box office. Siskel and Ebert were at the forefront of the "sound bite" movement—their message was fast, punchy, memorable, and made few demands of their viewers. It was also effective: The director Albert Brooks remembered that his 1985 film *Lost in America* had a limited release; the week after Siskel and Ebert gave the movie two "Thumbs Up," it tripled its business.

The New York Film Critics Circle, meanwhile, remained as divided as ever. It was widely perceived that there were two basic camps, one led by Sarris and the other by Kael. It had become a game with those members who didn't avidly belong to one camp or the other to see which came out on top in each year's voting process. Rumors continued to the effect that Pauline commandeered her followers and "suggested" to them how they might vote, a charge that was difficult to prove. Certainly she didn't get her way in the final voting with any degree of consistency. The same held true for the National Society of Film Critics. David Ansen remembered his excitement at being inducted into the society, but at the first meeting, the level of venom in the room was shocking. "Pauline's archenemy, Richard Schickel, was there," recalled Ansen. "I couldn't believe the behavior that was going on. He was acting like a sort of naughty, nasty frat boy and he was literally making insulting comments about Pauline's legs. He didn't say it to her face. There were a lot of great feuds—not overtly between Pauline and Andrew Sarris. The only times I would see them in the same room were at these voting meetings, and they tended to ignore each other." Ansen rejected the idea that Pauline insisted on people's slavishly agreeing with her views on movies. On several occasions she would tell him that she had admired a review he had written for *Newsweek*, and at times his opinion had differed significantly from her own.

In early 1985 Pauline surprised her longtime readers by sharply deviating from her reviewing past: She gave her approval to a David Lean picture, *A Passage to India*, based on the famous E. M. Forster novel. While the book was not the sort that she responded to as enthusiastically as she had *The Bostonians* or the great Russian novels, she did feel that *A Passage to India* was "suggestive and dazzlingly empathic."

She believed Lean's film version to be "an admirable piece of work, because the director's control"—the very quality for which she had attacked him earlier—had "a kind of benign precision . . . because of the performers (and the bright-colored, fairy-tale vividness of the surroundings.)" Lean's reading of the book was "intelligent and enjoyable, and if his technique is to simplify and to spell everything out in block letters, this kind of clarity has its own formal strength. It may not be the highest praise to say that a movie is orderly and dignified or that it's like a well-cared-for, beautifully oiled machine, but of its kind this *Passage to India* is awfully good."

What intrigued her most about the film was that it seemed "informed by a spirit of magisterial self-hatred. That's its oddity: Lean's grand 'objective' manner—he never touches anything without defining it and putting it in its place—seems to have developed out of the values he attacks. It's an imperial bookkeeper's style—no loose ends. It's also the style that impressed the Indians, and shamed them because they couldn't live up to it. It's the style of the conqueror—who is here the guilt-ridden conqueror but the conqueror nevertheless." Forster did not neatly tie up the novel's situations; Lean was a careful, precise filmmaker who arranged everything neatly in place. "What's remarkable about the film is how two such different temperaments as Forster's and Lean's could come together," Pauline wrote.

For Pauline, the most exhilarating movie of the summer of 1985 was John Huston's mob family comedy *Prizzi's Honor*. Huston was in the midst of his late-career resurgence, which had begun with *The Man Who Would Be King*; *Prizzi's Honor* was a beautifully sustained satire—the characters are delightfully corrupt, discussing murder in the same calm, matter-of-fact terms that most families use to discuss house payments and insurance matters. Pauline wrote, "If John Huston's name were not on *Prizzi's Honor*, I'd have thought a fresh new talent had burst on the scene, and he'd certainly be the hottest new director in Hollywood. . . . It's like *The Godfather* acted out by The

Munsters, with passionate, lyrical arias from Italian operas pointing up their low-grade sentimentality." At seventy-eight, Huston's touch was as sure as it been in his glory days; Pauline approved of Jack Nicholson, who she thought would "do anything for the role he's playing, and he has a just about infallible instinct for how far he can take the audience with him." She also heralded the breakthrough of the director's daughter, Anjelica Huston, who played the family granddaughter Maerose like "a Borgia princess, a high-fashion Vampira who moves like a swooping bird and talks in a honking Brooklynese that comes out of the corner of her twisted mouth. . . . she has the imperiousness of a Maria Callas or a Silvana Mangano."

For all her excitement there was a certain lack of cohesiveness in her review of *Prizzi's Honor* that she had seldom shown. It seemed overlong, and not quite all of a piece, as if she were so astonished to find a film this good that she was no longer quite sure how to convey her enthusiasm.

ew actors ever drew forth Pauline's venom in quite the same way that
Clint Eastwood did. As the years rolled on, her dislike for his particular brand of monotone machismo had ripened into near-contempt.
She considered it a sign of the way movies had gone off track that Martin
Scorsese was now (she believed) in decline, and Robert Altman was all but a
back number—yet Eastwood's star remained as potent as ever. His one-
dimensional screen personality had weathered the years, and unlike old-time
action and Western stars such as Randolph Scott and Joel McCrea, he wasn't
appearing in increasingly marginalized vehicles. Rather, there was a new
weight, even a self-conscious "importance" about his films. When he began
to be hailed as an artist for involving himself with more serious subject matter, Pauline was dumbfounded.

*Pale Rider*, released in the summer of 1985, was a good example: a Western about a Mysterious Stranger who appears to help a scraggly band of gold
miners stand up to an evil land baron. Eastwood played this ethereal avenger
role with a straight face, and Pauline hooted at the pretensions of the high-
toned Western: "This tall, gaunt-faced Stranger sometimes wears clerical garb
and is addressed as Preacher," she wrote. "When he takes off his shirt, his
back has shapely bullet holes, like stigmata, and when he opens his mouth
sententious words of wisdom fall out of it—gems like 'There's plain few problems can't be solved with a little sweat and some hard work.' If this is how
people beyond the grave talk, I'd just as soon they didn't come back to visit."
The movie, however, was a hit, and Eastwood continued to maintain, in
Pauline's words, "a career out of his terror of expressiveness." Several of Pauline's friends thought her vilification of Eastwood revealed a certain attraction
to him. "A lot of people thought she was really turned on by Clint Eastwood,"
said Ray Sawhill. "He was the big, macho, alpha male, and Pauline just loved
beating up on him. And I think there were reasons *why* she loved beating up
on him."

Her disappointment in the path taken by Scorsese surfaced once more in
her review of *After Hours*, the director's comic nightmare about a man who
loses his money and spends an insane night stumbling through flakiest SoHo.

*After Hours* had the chaotic, nothing-can-go-right structure of a bad dream, and it had amusing performances and bits of business, but Pauline thought Scorsese's tone couldn't sustain itself. "His work here is livelier and more companionable than it has been in recent years; the camera scoots around, making jokes—or, at least, near-jokes," she wrote. "But the movie keeps telling you to laugh, even though these near-jokes are about all you get. Soon it becomes clear that the episodes aren't going anywhere—that what you're seeing is a random series of events in a picture that just aspires to be an entertaining trifle and doesn't make it." It disturbed her that Scorsese seemed to be "using his skills . . . like a hired hand, making a vacuous, polished piece of consumer goods—all surface."

In some ways, the essential Pauline hadn't changed over the years: In the mid-'80s she was still much more inclined to embrace an oddball trifle such as *Pee-wee's Big Adventure* ("I liked the movie's unimportance. It isn't *saying* anything") than she was a big-budget, prestige picture like Sydney Pollack's *Out of Africa* ("Meryl Streep has used too many foreign accents on us, and this new one gives her utterances an archness, a formality—it puts quotation marks around everything she says") or Steven Spielberg's *The Color Purple*. The film, based on the enormously popular novel by Alice Walker about the lifetime of indignities suffered by Celie, a poor, battered, sexually abused Georgia black woman, before she eventually finds her own path to self-respect, marked Spielberg's first venture into human drama, and Pauline didn't think he showed much talent for it. "Spielberg's *The Color Purple* is probably the least authentic in feeling of any of his full-length films," she wrote; "the people on the screen are like characters operated by Frank Oz. . . . The movie is amorphous; it's a pastoral about the triumph of the human spirit, and it blurs on you."

For Pauline it was never enough to take on starkly dramatic subject matter—one had to do something with it. On this particular point, she got into further trouble with another picture she covered at the same time, Claude Lanzmann's nine-hour-plus documentary on the Nazi death factories, *Shoah*, which was released to an almost universally rapturous critical reception at the end of 1985.

Pauline's unsentimental attitude toward her Jewish background hadn't changed over the years. The idea that she might be one of the "chosen" struck her as absurd, and she resented the sense of entitlement she perceived in many members of the New York Jewish literary community. She had no more tolerance for the religious feelings of Jews than she had for those of Christians. Charles Simmons remembered a night when he invited Jack Greenberg, an attorney and later dean of Columbia College, Greenberg's wife, and Pauline all to dinner at his apartment. Simmons made a baked ham, and when they all sat down to dinner, Mrs. Greenberg exclaimed, "I can't eat that!" "Oh, for Chrissake, are you kidding?" snapped Pauline. "That medieval bullshit?" Simmons quickly prepared Mrs. Greenberg a plate of scrambled eggs, but he recalled thinking that Pauline's attitude was so contemptuous because she considered such thinking irrational.

Pauline sat through the entire length of *Shoah* (in two parts) at regular showings in a theater, not at a private screening, since she wanted to gauge the audience's response. She later wrote that the large crowd for the first section had largely dwindled away by the time the second was shown (though this was denied by her old friend Dan Talbot, who had acquired the film's distribution rights in New York). *Shoah* was the most comprehensive film ever made about the death-camp experience, but Pauline felt it contained few moments of genuine beauty. Lanzmann's approach to his subject struck her as highly self-conscious and arty, played out at a punishing length. She hated the insistent way that the camera kept returning ominously to the railroad tracks that led to the camps. She believed that everyone who saw *Shoah* was being asked to surrender unconditionally to the view of Nazi horrors that it presented, and she was unable to find that level of surrender within herself.

Her colleague Jane Kramer at *The New Yorker* agreed with her about *Shoah*. "I hated it," Kramer recalled. "I just thought, the poeticized landscape, the heavy symbolism. When you think that it followed a movie as brilliant and intimate as *The Sorrow and the Pity*? Lanzmann was such a sanctimonious presence—kind of like the Elie Wiesel of filmmakers. He sure as hell wasn't the Primo Levi. You look at those two writers about Auschwitz, and the depth and humanity of Levi and the capital gains of Wiesel. He was arrogant and self-serving."

Pauline turned in her review of *Shoah*, and Shawn called her into his office as soon as he had read it. He did not want to publish it at all, and they had a series of heated discussions over it. Shawn held the piece for two weeks, which enraged her—she felt like a schoolgirl being reprimanded for having written an honest essay. Finally she was able to get it into print, on two conditions: that it was strategically placed at the end of the column that led with her reviews of *Out of Africa* and *The Color Purple*, and that she added an opening that prepared the reader for what was to follow. It wasn't Pauline's style to offer an apologia for her views or to prepare her readers for a soft landing, but Shawn was immovable on this point. Grudgingly she provided the introduction:

> Probably everyone will agree that the subject of a movie should not place it beyond criticism. . . . I ask the forbearance of readers for a dissenting view of a film that is widely regarded as a masterpiece. I found *Shoah* logy and exhausting right from the start, and when it had been going on for an hour or longer, I was squirming restlessly, my attention slackening.

She followed this equivocal opening with an objection to Lanzmann's interviewing techniques: "We watch him putting pressure on people—pouncing on a detail here or there—and we register the silences, the hesitancies, the breakdowns . . . sitting in a theatre seat for a film as full of dead spaces as this one seems to me a form of self-punishment." She went on to compare *Shoah* unfavorably with the level of moral complexity presented in *The Sorrow and the Pity*, with "so many widely differing instances of collaboration and resistance, and such a steady accumulation of perspectives." In *Shoah* Lanzmann seemed to be stacking the deck to show an entire world of blind cruelty, and as a result, she felt there was no way into the movie. It wasn't quite so much what the film was saying as its way of saying it that disturbed her. "It's not just the exact procedures used in the extermination process that Lanzmann is hunting down," she wrote. "He's after the Gentiles' attitudes toward the process. *Shoah* presents a world in which a Gentile rarely shows any human feeling toward a Jew. The Polish peasants who saw Jewish children being thrown into vans by their feet don't seem to have been upset, or even touched." She believed that Lanzmann's principal motive in making the film "appears to be to show you that the Gentiles will do it to the Jews again if they get a chance." It was a tough and provocative line of thinking, but toward the end of her review, she nearly tumbled off the path of her argument when she said, "The film is diffuse, but Lanzmann is blunt-minded: he's out to indict the callous. If you were to set him loose, he could probably find anti-Semitism anywhere." It was a stunning lapse of judgment, considering that Lanzmann was looking for anti-Semitism in the most obvious of places—the death camps. While Pauline's intellectual honesty was admirable, it was difficult to shake off the feeling that her thinking was influenced by other factors, of which she was only partly conscious.

Lillian Ross recalled,

> The *Shoah* reaction was especially peculiar. I went with Shawn to the two screenings of the documentary, and we agreed with most critics that it was a significant contribution to the record of the horrific Nazi period in history. The documentary was not being offered for judgment

of its cinematic technical virtues. Shawn tried to clarify its role, in talking to Pauline Kael about it. With his inimitable patience, he always tried earnestly to reason with anyone clinging stubbornly to unreasonable prejudice or purposes. It might be that Kael's megalomaniacal possession of anything called film led to her resentment of the director Claude Lanzmann as an interloper in her territory, and therefore she insisted that *Shoah* had to be reviewed only as a movie. It might be that Kael's own Jewish heritage accounted for her need to harbor complicated and perverse ways of demonstrating that she was free of the painful abhorrence of the holocaust felt by other people. I don't know. Shawn ran her 'review' as she insisted.

Shawn's fears about Pauline's response to the movie proved justified: Her comments proved antagonistic to the Jewish community, in New York and elsewhere. There was an immediate outcry from the respected critic Alfred Kazin, from *The New Republic*'s Leon Wieseltier, and from her by now regular adversary, *The Village Voice*, represented this time by J. Hoberman. Wieseltier went so far as to suggest that she didn't see *Shoah*'s worth because the movie refrained from depicting the violence to which she was obviously addicted; he said she might have liked it better if it had been directed by Brian De Palma.

One of the most incensed readers was Dan Talbot, who wrote a long letter of protest to Pauline, and copied Shawn on it:

> I'm upset about how unmoved you represent yourself in the face of such emotionally disturbing testimony in the movie. . . . I simply cannot understand how you were unable to respond in some way and even fail to write about survivor Simon Srebnik's visit, for the first time in over thirty years, to Chelmno, where 400,000 Jews were murdered. His account of what happened at Chelmno in the 1940's is surely one of the most moving episodes ever put on film. This scene occurs at the beginning of the film. Minutes later, Mordechai Podchelebink, the second survivor of Chelmno . . . recounts in very poetic Yiddish how he placed his wife and children in the grave at Chelmno and then asked to be killed. The Germans kept him alive; they said he was strong enough to work. He is crying as he tells this tragic epic. How is it possible not to respond deeply—Jew or Gentile—to all this?
>
> . . . Did you learn something? Did you know before seeing the film that children under four rode the death trains free of charge

while those under ten went half-fare? And that these trains were booked by German travel agents? And paid for by the proceeds of confiscated Jewish property? That the Jewish workers in the gas chambers were not allowed to use the words "corpse" or "dead bodies" but instead "puppets" and "rags"? Can you imagine a great fiction writer improving upon all this? Don't you at least think that Lanzmann's selection of material out of 350 hours of footage he shot is done with the mind and heart of a great artisan, if not an artist?

He closed his lengthy letter with a telling observation: "You're often on target but some forces outside of film criticism prevented you from experiencing this work in a whole way."

Shawn called Talbot and confided that, although he had never censored one of the magazine's critics, he had seriously considered not running the review. Pauline did not respond to Talbot's letter, and they did not speak for an entire year.

A number of Pauline's other friends parted company with her in their views on *Shoah*. Owen Gleiberman—then a young critic at *The Boston Phoenix*, and one who liked the film very much—thought that her review was one of her greatest efforts, and that it actually showed deep respect for the profundity of the Holocaust. David Edelstein had also admired *Shoah*, and couldn't help wondering if part of her resistance to the film had to do with her deep-rooted suspicion of any religious group. "She had so little use for doctrine, or for Torah scholarship, or any of that crap," said Edelstein. "She was as dismissive of it as anyone I've ever known. Uncomprehending. But I do believe that she couldn't have written what she wrote if she didn't on some level believe in an oversoul, some sort of interconnectedness that I think the great artists tap into and that she tapped into when she wrote about their work. I am sure she would snort like crazy if she heard me talk about it in those terms. I believe that she was an extremely spiritual person without being in any way, shape, or form a believer. I've met many skeptics, and in some ways they're extremely obnoxious in their bottom-line dismissal of the idea of transcendence. They are so wedded to this idea that any discussion of the spirit is a delusion, that they can't even give themselves to great art in a way that Pauline would recognize. Pauline could be transported—she could go to another place without identifying it as religious."

On the subject of *Shoah*, Pauline herself remained unrepentant. Nine years after her review appeared, she told *The New Yorker*'s Hal Espen that "a

Holocaust movie should not be sacrosanct simply because of the subject. I think most of the reviewers were willing to call the director of *Shoah* a great filmmaker because he'd taken on a great subject. They used to treat Stanley Kramer as a great filmmaker, too, especially when he made the nuclear-disaster movie *On the Beach*." Perhaps she tired of the way her thoughts on *Shoah* shadowed her, though: Nearly a decade later, when *For Keeps*, a compendium of her selected criticism, was published, the review was not included.

As the time came to vote on the New York Film Critics Circle Awards, Pauline lined up behind *Prizzi's Honor* for Best Picture, and pushed for Jack Nicholson to win Best Actor and John Huston Best Director for *Prizzi*, and Jessica Lange (*Sweet Dreams*) and Coral Browne (*Dreamchild*) for Best Actress. That year her tastes prevailed, for the most part: *Prizzi's Honor* did win prizes for Best Picture and for Nicholson, John Huston, and Angelica Huston, while Norma Aleandros took Best Actress for *The Official Story*. Woody Allen took the Screenplay prize for *The Purple Rose of Cairo*. Pauline was disappointed only in the Best Documentary prize, which went to *Shoah*.

The first half of 1986 continued to bring few films that fully engaged Pauline. She was quite taken with Paul Mazursky's *Down and Out in Beverly Hills*, a reworking of Jean Renoir's classic comedy *Boudu Saved from Drowning*, and she thought the movie's view of the new money of Beverly Hills was wonderfully soft-edged and beautifully realized—the kind of generous-spirited social satire she always loved. For some years she had been an unabashed fan of Bette Midler, but she also perceived that hers was the kind of outsized talent that was going to have difficulty finding the right movie roles. In *Down and Out in Beverly Hills*, Pauline thought that Midler had "never before been this seductive on the screen. This is only the fourth picture she has starred in, and you see a softer, less funky Midler; she's playing the role of a bored, dissatisfied housewife who has something extra—a warped charm rather like that of Teri Garr, but riper, juicier." She found Geraldine Page giving one of the year's most acclaimed performances in *The Trip to Bountiful*, nearly as actressy as she had back in 1961 in the screen version of *Summer and Smoke*. And she resisted joining in the chorus of praise hurled at Woody Allen's new picture, *Hannah and Her Sisters*, about the romantic entanglements of three New York women. Pauline's notes are especially revealing here: "Allen's idea of movie acting is the reading of lines," she scribbled to herself. "It doesn't just repeat his work, it repeats itself." In her printed review she wrote, "The movie is a little stale, and it suggests the perils of inbreeding. It might be time for Woody

Allen to make a film with a whole new set of friends, or, at least, to take a long break from his sentimentalization of New York City." Pauline often told friends that she wanted to carry a Harpo Marx seltzer bottle around with her and use it to squirt certain characters on the screen who irritated her. Writer Allen Barra remembered that she considered Sam Waterston as the smug architect in *Hannah and Her Sisters* a good candidate for squirting. "I don't want to hurt him," she said. "I just want to squirt him."

Early 1986 was a frantic period: Pauline spent whatever little time was left between *New Yorker* deadlines promoting her latest collection of reviews, *State of the Art*, published by Dutton, where Billy Abrahams had moved and where she had followed him. In the introduction she cued readers to her thoughts on the changes in the movie industry during the 1980s, which she chose to signify by departing from her usual sexually tinged book title. (The original choice had been *Spitting Images*.) "It seemed time for a change; this has not been a period for anything like Grand Passions. I hope that *State of the Art* will sound ominous and sweeping and just slightly clinical." While promoting the book, she told interviewers that although she admired the technological advances in cinematography and sound, she was constantly disappointed that the movies had lost the riskiness they'd developed in the previous decade—now they were simply too square for her. Ultimately, *State of the Art* didn't sell nearly as well as many of her previous books had done: The net sales of the clothbound and paperback versions combined added up to 14,944.

For much of the 1980s Pauline had suffered from fairly steady bouts of heart trouble—the lining of her heart was perilously thin, and she had attacks of angina. She tried not to yield to it and to continue with her punishing schedule, but she did suffer a couple of collapses in screening rooms, and she carried nitroglycerine pills in her purse. Trent Duffy, who had worked as a production editor and indexer on several of her books, remembered the subject coming up while she was doing the promotional tour for *State of the Art*. Duffy was escorting her from one Fifth Avenue bookstore to another. It was a bitterly cold December, and Pauline insisted on taking a taxi everywhere. Duffy was surprised, since they were going only from Fifty-seventh Street to Fifty-third Street, but Pauline, who was holding a scarf over her face, told him that her doctor had asked her not to spend any time in the cold when the temperature was below thirty degrees. "This bum ticker of mine," she muttered.

In the winter of 1986 Pauline was delighted to celebrate the release of

Stephen Frears's *My Beautiful Launderette*. With the major studios steadily turning out such dross, it was small, independent pictures such as *My Beautiful Launderette*, made for less than $1 million, that were drawing an enthusiastic audience—the viewers who used to be defined as the "art house" crowd. Pauline loved this spiky love story set in punk-infested South London, about two young men, Omar and Johnny (Gordon Warnecke and Daniel Day-Lewis), who inject some life into their seedy neighborhood by opening a spiffed-up, trendy laundromat. Pauline wrote, "Frears is responsive to grubby desperation and to the uncouthness and energy in English life—he's responsive to what went into the punk-music scene and to what goes into teen-age gang life." She found that "Frears's editing rhythms that seem so right are actually very odd. *My Beautiful Launderette* doesn't feel like any other movie; it's almost as if he's cutting to the rhythm of Pakistani-accented English—to what you can hear even in the quirky lilt of the title." She loved Day-Lewis's performance as the constantly daring Johnny, and she loved the movie's light, unself-conscious portrayal of two men in love: "This Johnny wants to make something of himself, and he'll go through more than his share of humiliation to do it," she wrote. "He also enjoys wooing the cuddly Omar. He can't resist touching Omar with his tongue when they're out on the street, right in front of the launderette, with white-racist rowdies all around them. He can't resist being frisky, because it's dangerous, and that makes it more erotic."

The fact that *My Beautiful Launderette* and other "small pictures" (such as James Ivory's *A Room with a View*) were able to break through and find their audience was heartening to Pauline. The fates of most films now seemed pegged solely on the question of how big a noise could be made about them. This and this alone was seen by the industry—and by a growing part of the audience—as the sole measure of their worth. The strong, cautionary words, the advocacy for smart, risky, creative filmmaking that Pauline had poured forth in her column for years may have been more important than ever, but they seemed increasingly futile. The movie executives who had once read her with great fascination, even when she destroyed their films, now were far less interested in what she had to say. The marketing lords had figured out a way to make certain films—many films—critic-proof. Don Simpson's power had reached its apex, while Pauline's was on the decline.

All of this was very much on her mind when she reviewed *Top Gun*, a Tom Cruise action picture about fighter pilots that became one of the top box-office hits of the summer of 1986. It was produced by Don Simpson and Jerry Bruckheimer, and Pauline wrote, "Selling is what they think moviemaking is about.

The result is a new 'art' form: the self-referential commercial. *Top Gun* is a recruiting poster that isn't concerned with recruiting but with being a poster."

Still, she advocated steadfastly for the few signs of life she saw on the movie scene. One came with David Lynch's latest, *Blue Velvet*. The film belonged to a rather overworked genre: the study of a small town whose calm exterior masks sexual perversities and violent tensions. But this was nothing for the mainstream bestseller mentality, such as *Kings Row* or *Peyton Place*: In exploring the unexpected horrors that lurk in the little town of Lumberton, *Blue Velvet* took many audience members to a place they weren't entirely sure they wanted to be. As the odd, clean-cut, yet slightly bent Jeffrey, whose coming of age is the final destination point of the bizarre plot, Kyle MacLachlan gave what Pauline termed "a phenomenal performance." The film, she thought, was "the work of a genius naïf. If you feel that there's very little art between you and the filmmaker's psyche, it may be because there's less than the usual amount of inhibition. Lynch doesn't censor his sexual fantasies, and the film's hypercharged erotic atmosphere makes it something of a trance-out, but his humor keeps breaking through, too."

She also loved the spirit of twenty-nine-year-old Spike Lee's *She's Gotta Have It*, which was shot in black and white in twelve days for around $175,000 and grossed more than $7 million—around the same amount as the studio-backed *Blue Velvet*. Pauline thought Lee had the rarest gift of all—"what for want of a better term is called 'a film sense.' It's an instinct for how to make a movie move—for how much motion there should be in a shot, for how fast to cut the shots, for how to make them flow into each other rhythmically." And she was delighted by Jonathan Demme's *Something Wild*, largely because Demme possessed "a true gift for informality . . . I can't think of any other director who is so instinctively and democratically interested in everybody he shows you. Each time a new face appears, it's looked at with such absorption and delight that you almost think the movie will flit off and tell this person's story."

At the 1986 New York Film Critics Circle Awards, she supported *Blue Velvet*, although she would have been happy to see *Something Wild* win. Unfortunately, she was thwarted across the board: *Hannah and Her Sisters* swept the prizes, winning Best Picture, Best Director for Woody Allen, and Best Supporting Actress for Dianne Wiest. The NYFCC, however, ignored the film that won that year's Academy Award for Best Picture, Oliver Stone's *Platoon*. Pauline spent the first paragraph of her review laying out Stone's (to her) suspect background: Yale dropout, failed, nomadic writer, decorated soldier in Vietnam, postwar druggie, then NYU film student under Martin Scorsese.

"We can surmise," Pauline wrote (perhaps somewhat unfairly), "that Stone became a grunt in Vietnam to 'become a man' and to become a writer. As *Platoon*, a coming-of-age film, demonstrates, he went through his rite of passage, but, as *Platoon* also demonstrates, he became a very bad writer—a hype artist." She recognized that Stone was trying to show the madness brought on by Vietnam in a more visceral way than it had ever been shown before, but, despite such touches as the use of her old sparring partner Samuel Barber's *Adagio for Strings* as counterpoint for the bloody battle scenes, *Platoon* lacked the poetry, however misshapen, of *The Deer Hunter*. "The results are overwrought," Pauline wrote, "with too much filtered light, too much poetic license, and too damn much romanticized insanity."

By this time Gina and Warner Friedman had separated. Pauline had feared that marriage would destroy their relationship, and she had wanted to save them both the heartbreak. Gina and Will moved in with Pauline briefly before finding another house nearby. Warner continued to visit Pauline after he and Gina were divorced. One thing they had in common was a love of watching boxing matches on television, and they were often joined by Allen Barra.

One person for whom Pauline showed unconditional affection was Will. Her friends were amazed by how completely she doted on him—and he in turn adored her. Will always called her "Pauline"—never "Grandma." Once, when Will was a small child, Warner and Gina had gone away for an overnight trip and left Will in Pauline's care. Gina asked her mother to be sure to keep a close eye on him, and Pauline replied, 'I'll watch him with my own life.'

She continued to love life in Great Barrington and the big house with its spacious rooms and overflowing bookshelves. She enjoyed going to several of the local restaurants, including the Inn on the Green and the Castle Street Grill. But if she dined at a place that was under par, she would sigh, "I can do better than this myself." She did enjoy cooking at home and typically preferred simple meals with fresh ingredients—lots of vegetables and pasta. By now she had stopped drinking as a general health precaution. She missed her strong shots of Myers's Rum and Wild Turkey, but learned to get the utmost out of endless pots of tea and bottles of water.

Her relations with most of the local business owners were fairly harmonious, with the occasional ripple. Once, Warner had taken her to a hardware store to buy some supplies. It happened to be Mother's Day, and the proprietor gave her a gift, adding in a condescending tone, "Because you look like you're a mother or a grandmother." "Fuck you, Charlie," Pauline replied. "Do you know I've written ten books?"

Pauline continued to work hard to promote younger writer friends that she considered had something exceptional to offer. Ray Sawhill by now had a serious girlfriend, a bright and attractive young writer named Polly Frost. Many of the male Paulettes felt that Pauline was unduly harsh on their wives and girlfriends, but in this case, Pauline had introduced the couple. She had immediately taken to Frost, who had studied the harpsichord but now had a serious interest in being a writer. Pauline sensed in Frost what she had sensed in Sawhill: Neither of them was interested in her as a cult leader or career champion, but as an entertaining, warm, lively person who was fun to talk with over a meal. Her conversations with Frost revolved around clothes, food, and animals more than it did movies. Frost's gift was for humor, and Pauline helped her get several pieces published in *The New Yorker* and *The Atlantic Monthly*. But she almost always believed that criticism was the path her protégés should take, and she began prodding Frost to write movie reviews.

One of the flaws in her mentoring style was that her pride in her own past often led her to give bad career advice to young writer friends. "She was about to go back to San Francisco when Shawn gave her a buzz and hired her at *The New Yorker*," said Sawhill. "But somehow, in her mind, this turned into: She got what she worked for—it wasn't just a great stroke of luck that turned her life around. It was—finally, the universe has been proven a just one." And Pauline was certain that if the writers she was encouraging would only sit down and write a big piece on spec, magazine editors would see how brilliant they were and have to hire them. "She would be let down if I would say, 'I'm killing myself writing these pieces and nobody's publishing them,'" said Sawhill. "Somehow, she really thought it would work, and in many cases, it didn't."

Pauline also continued to advocate strongly for both David Edelstein and James Wolcott. She had been trying for some time to interest Shawn in Wolcott, but the editor always demurred, saying that he didn't think Wolcott was quite right for *The New Yorker*. She also tried to persuade Billy Abrahams to bring out a book of Wolcott's collected pieces. As early as 1982, she had written to Abrahams that Wolcott's movie columns for *Texas Monthly* were "absolutely first rate. The amazing thing about his writing—whether it's the freelance pieces in *The New Republic* or in *The New York Review of Books* or one of his regular columns—is that it overlaps and forms a body of witty criticism. There hasn't been anything like him since the young Tynan. . . . Why don't you nab him?"

One person who resisted being drawn into Pauline's circle was the gifted young critic Owen Gleiberman. Like many others, Gleiberman's friendship with her began when he wrote her a fan letter while still a college student. He was writing reviews for the University of Michigan's student newspaper, and Pauline encouraged him to send her some samples, writing back and offering praise and constructive criticism in some detail. They eventually met in 1980 in New York, shortly after her return from Hollywood, and at first Gleiberman seemed poised to become a Paulette.

Although Gleiberman was as flattered by Pauline's attention as most of her protégés were, he also was very aware of the complexities involved in her mentorship. He believed that she was most comfortable when her younger "discoveries" did work she could respect and honestly praise, work that showed originality and spark, yet she was also quite conscious of keeping them in the position of being an acolyte. It was the same complex that David Denby had observed years earlier, and in many cases the fate of the Paulettes seemed to rest on the question of their individual temperament: How willing were they were to remain in Pauline's shadow?

In the 1980s *The Boston Phoenix* served as a kind of farm team for the Paulettes who had their eye on success in bigger, New York jobs: Janet Maslin, Steven Schiff, and David Edelstein had all put in their time at the *Phoenix* before moving on to higher-profile reviewing posts. Gleiberman took this route as well, and had spent two and a half years on the newspaper, happily working as a second-string movie critic, when he received a call from Clay Felker. The genius behind *New York* was now in decline, and was trying to revive some of his lost glory by starting a small newspaper, a sort of precursor to the successful *Seven Days*, known as *The East Side Express*. He had read some of Gleiberman's reviews in the *Phoenix* and asked him to be his first-string movie critic. Gleiberman agreed, staying on at the *Phoenix* while free-lancing for Felker's publication.

Once Gleiberman began working for the short-lived *East Side Express*, he found himself reviewing many of the same films Pauline wrote about for *The New Yorker*. Often he disagreed with her—Bob Fosse's *Star 80*, which he liked and Pauline detested, being a case in point. His career advanced to the point that he was put up for membership in the National Society of Film Critics, which initially he was denied. When discussing his disappointment about that decision with Pauline one day, she told him that she felt that a number of the members had not believed his work for *The East Side Express* to be at the same level of what he was doing for the *Phoenix*.

"Nobody was reading my reviews in *The East Side Express*," Gleiberman recalled. "They read what you sent in. I knew she was lying to me. And what

I said to myself was, *I cannot trust what she's saying.* And I decided right there to end my friendship with Pauline, because I realized that she would lie to her critic acolytes in order to keep them in line. She was a great, fascinating woman who had her dark side." There was no dramatic falling-out between Pauline and Gleiberman; they remained on cordial but relatively distant terms for the rest of her life. But Gleiberman's experience with her was as shocking, perhaps even traumatic, as, in a different way, Denby's had been. Gleiberman always considered himself the truest of all the Paulettes because he had realized that he had to be himself. "To be true to what Pauline taught us," he said, "you had to break with her."

# CHAPTER TWENTY-SIX

For years one of the chief topics of conversation among staff members at *The New Yorker* had been the eventual retirement of William Shawn. There was much concern about the magazine's lack of a succession plan. Given *The New Yorker*'s love of promoting from within, various staff members had been put forth as possible heirs to Shawn's mantle, and all were deemed unsuitable for one reason or another. By the mid-1980s the magazine industry had changed as dramatically as the movie industry had: Few if any other publications now had the same degree of sensitivity about the separation of editorial and advertising departments. Making money and capturing the endlessly sought-after young demographic were more important than ever, and at many publications, the state of advertising was the overwhelming consideration when the owners were considering which grade to put on the editor's report card.

Shawn had weathered a number of tense situations in the past several years; one had come in 1976, when several staff members brought the threat of unionization to a head. *The New Yorker* had never been a union house, and in a memo written to the staff in the fall of 1976, Shawn articulated his opposition:

Dozens of people had advanced . . . from typist or secretarial jobs into jobs as checkers or proofreaders; or gone from jobs as checkers or proofreaders to Talk reporters or messengers into jobs as editors or into writing for the magazine. Everything has been open to everybody. The organization has not been stratified or rigid. This openness and this freedom of movement have been basic for the way *The New Yorker* works. This is a place in which scores of people, over the years, have learned and have found themselves. We have not thought in job "categories." People here have been thought of as individuals and treated as individuals, with a good deal of latitude for individual temperaments and work habits, and even idiosyncrasy. This is, in fact, a magazine of individualists. I think that a union might introduce a rigidity in the way the office functions, hinder the free flow of people from one kind of work to another, reduce the opportunity for experiment, and reduce the emphasis on the individual. I also think that it would tend to polarize the office.

Shawn won the battle over unionization, but as time went on, it was increasingly clear that he could not really face the idea of a succession plan. Even many of those who loved and respected him had long recognized his enormous capacity for manipulation; by now, it seemed that he was unwilling to entertain the notion of a *New Yorker* without himself at the helm. Even the old-time company man Brendan Gill had written in his memoir, published on the occasion of the magazine's fiftieth anniversary in 1975, "If Shawn were to give up some of his duties as editor, it might have the welcome effect of freeing him to write more. For it is as a writer that he could still achieve, if he so wishes, a second and equally distinguished career."

Those who kept a close eye on such matters were aware that *The New Yorker* was not keeping pace in the competitive 1980s marketplace. Circulation and advertising were on the decline, and the magazine's longtime owner, Peter Fleischmann, was in failing health and wearying of the responsibility of presiding over the publication; eventually, as the majority stockholder, he sold all of his shares to Samuel I. Newhouse, Jr., head of the immense publishing and media corporation Advance Publications. In May 1985, for a final payment in the neighborhood of $170 million, Newhouse became *The New Yorker*'s new owner. For a time it seemed that Newhouse might honor the magazine's family-oriented process of advancement by naming the veteran editor Chip McGrath to succeed Shawn. That plan fell through, however, and in January 1987, Newhouse sent a memo to staff members informing them that a new editor would be brought in from the book industry: Robert A. Gottlieb, the highly regarded editor in chief of Alfred A. Knopf—a firm that happened to be owned by Newhouse.

Many longtime members of the magazine staff were devastated that Shawn would be dismissed in such a manner. A letter was composed to Gottlieb, informing him of the staff's "powerful and apparently unanimous expression of sadness and outrage over the manner in which a new editor has been imposed upon us." It went on to explain to Gottlieb that "*The New Yorker* has not achieved its preeminence by following orthodox paths of magazine publishing and editing, and it is our strange and powerfully held conviction that only an editor who has been a long-standing member of the staff will have a reasonable chance of assuring our continuity, cohesion, and independence." The document was signed by all but a handful of staff members—and Pauline was one of the latter. Although Pauline had remained offended by what she considered his casual treatment of her since her return from Hollywood, her refusal to sign the letter was not a personal matter: She simply felt that the time had come. On Friday, February 13, 1987, William Shawn exited the publication where he had begun work in 1933.

"He was a great editor, but he *was* eighty," Pauline said to a crowd of advertisers at one of *The New Yorker*'s promotional luncheons at the Beverly Hills Hotel in May 1987. She went on to assure them that "with Bob Gottlieb replacing Bill Shawn at *The New Yorker*, the magazine still will hold on to the values you like, and, if anything, it'll be more readable." Late in 1987, however, she was happy to write a letter of support for Shawn, who was eager to take on some challenging retirement projects and had applied to the John D. and Catherine T. MacArthur Foundation for a fellowship. Pauline's letter hailed him as "an amazing man—dedicated to what he believes to be the best writing," and urged the MacArthur Foundation to give him the fellowship because it would "constitute a vote of confidence in an eighty-year-old man of letters. It would be a beautiful gesture."

Readers who were anticipating a difficult adjustment to a new editor were surprised by how little the scope of the magazine changed once Gottlieb assumed control. Like Shawn, he was very much a hands-on editor, and there was still frequent coverage of subjects that might not be done in depth elsewhere. Pauline was scarcely affected; she was still allowed a generous amount of space, although she wasn't always writing as long as she had in the past—partly because of a certain diminishing of her energy, but also because it was getting harder for her to justify spending so much time on inferior films.

At year's end she was once again able to praise John Huston, who, at eighty and struggling with emphysema, had directed a screen version of James Joyce's "The Dead"—a detailed account of an annual party and supper given by a pair of spinster music teachers on the Feast of the Epiphany in 1904 Dublin, thought by many to be the finest short story in the English language. Huston had, in Pauline's words, "never before blended his actors so intuitively, so musically," as he had in these "funny, warm family scenes that might be thought completely out of his range." (Huston had actually spent twenty years living in Galway.) He had done what Pauline thought every great artist needed to do: He had enlarged his vision as he aged. Huston died shortly after completing the filming in the summer of 1987.

*Broadcast News*, another year-end release in 1987, was a much more penetrating look at the world of television news than the grandiose and pretentious *Network*, and it became a big hit with audiences, grossing more than

$50 million on its release. Directed, produced, and scripted by James L. Brooks, *Broadcast News* was the story of a changing TV news industry. The traditional, hard-research-and-reporting route is represented by the driven, brainy producer Jane (Holly Hunter) and solid, reliable newsman Aaron (Albert Brooks), who dreams of having a shot at anchoring the news. The increasingly popular news-as-entertainment route is represented by the vapid, poorly informed, but charismatic and audience-savvy reporter Tom (William Hurt). The following exchange typified the movie's essential conflict:

> TOM: I don't write. But that didn't stop me from sending my audition tapes to the bigger stations and the networks.
> JANE: It's hard for me to advise you, since you personify something that I truly think is dangerous.

As a news junkie, Pauline had watched the content of network news being debased for years, and her years of watching brilliantly informed her review of the picture:

> Basically, what the movie is saying is that beautiful, assured people have an edge over the rest of us, no matter how high our I.Q.s are. But, by applying this specifically to the age of television, Jim Brooks used it as the basis for a satirical critique of what TV is doing to us. On the surface, at least, he's saying that Aaron represents substance and integrity, while handsome, slick Tom—a faker who's essentially an actor-salesman—represents TV's corruption of the news into entertainment. The picture suggests that this view is the lowdown on TV: it satirizes anchorman punditry by showing the rising star as a boob with a smooth, practiced manner. And its thesis may give moviegoers a tingle, because it connects with some of what we see anchormen doing: reading sentences so rhythmically that the meaning is lost, asking questions of the reporters and then not following through even when their answers raise much bigger questions, smiling so falsely that it seems to rot their facial muscles.

While *Broadcast News* was an intelligent, tartly observed look at a major shift in America's culture, Pauline found it ultimately too neat and facile. "There's not even a try for any style or tension in *Broadcast News*," she wrote. "It's all episodic, like a TV series. . . . Jim Brooks has made a movie about three people who lose themselves in their profession, and it's all cozy and clean and clever. He plays everything right down the middle. He can't seem to imagine having a conflicted, despairing relationship with your profession."

Still, she felt essential goodwill toward the picture, and she admired the performances of all three stars. But she didn't feel that *Broadcast News* was good enough to sweep the New York Film Critics Circle's 1987 awards— which it did.

As always, Pauline could be counted on not to fall in line with her fellow critics, many of whom found Louis Malle's latest effort, *Au revoir les enfants,* among the year's finest pictures. It was an embroidered account of an episode from Malle's childhood, when the Catholic boarding school he attended hid a number of Jewish boys among the students—boys who were later uncovered by the Gestapo and sent to Auschwitz. It was a dignified, stately, nobly restrained piece of moviemaking, and the critics, while admiring Malle's craftsmanship, were also quite moved by the subject matter itself. Malle made no bones about saying to the press that he considered it his finest achievement.

As always, this sort of serious self-awareness was a red flag to Pauline, who thought that *Au revoir les enfants* suffered from an overdose of subdued good taste that kept the audience at a steady remove from the story. "The camera is so discreet it always seems about ten feet too far away," she wrote. She found that Gaspard Manesse, as Julien Quentin, the character Malle based on himself, was a bit of a blank, "directed so that he never engages us; we can't look into him, or into anyone else." The end of her review was vintage Pauline, exhorting her readers not to allow themselves to be easily manipulated by Malle's story:

> Yes, it gets to you by the end. How could it not? But you may feel pretty worn down—by how accomplished it is, and by all the aching, tender shots of Jean [the Jewish boy in hiding]. He's photographed as if he were a piece of religious art: Christ in his early adolescence. There's something unseemly about the movie's obsession with his exotic beauty—as if the French-German Jews had come from the far side of the moon. And does he have to be so brilliant, and a gifted pianist, and courageous? Would the audience not mourn him if he were just an average schmucky kid with pimples?

The old guard at *The New Yorker* mostly gave a cold shoulder to the film version of Jay McInerney's bestselling 1984 paperback original, *Bright Lights, Big City,* which became a kind of *Catcher in the Rye* for the coked-up club crowd of 1980s Manhattan. The main character, Jamie, was based on

McInerney himself, in the days when he briefly served as a fact-checker at *The New Yorker* while submerging himself in the downtown disco scene. There were a number of characters lifted directly from the offices of *The New Yorker*, among them Jamie's fellow fact-checker Yasu Wade, a character that was a direct hit at Pauline's good friend Craig Seligman, who had long since left the magazine and was pursing a writing career on the West Coast. (McInerney described Wade/Seligman as "too fastidious to do anything dangerous or dirty. You suspect that his sexual orientation is largely theoretical. He'd take a hot piece of gossip over a warm piece of ass any day of the week.") Pauline thought the movie was flat and rather humorless, but she couldn't resist singling out what for her was its high point: John Houseman's performance as the magazine's weary editor in chief, based all too clearly on William Shawn. She told friends that Houseman's pained look was the very essence of William Shawn's soul.

Perhaps none of the gifted directors of the 1970s displayed the degree of stagnation, a decade-plus later, that Woody Allen did. With *Another Woman*, released in the fall of 1988, he demonstrated that his fascination with the remoteness and emotional aridity of Manhattan intellectuals and artists hadn't receded—or developed. Gena Rowlands played a cold philosophy professor who rents an apartment for the purpose of writing a book; she is distracted by the next-door conversations, through the vent, of a therapist and her patients—one patient in particular, a coming-unglued pregnant woman (Mia Farrow). The professor becomes obsessed with the woman, who gradually leads her to confront the things in life she has missed. The professor was a distant cousin to Geraldine Page's perfection-obsessed mother in *Interiors*. But by now, Allen had worn down his concern for these characters to the point where the grooves were off them; his insights now seemed the kind that '70s college students would come up with after a few hits on the bong. Pauline put it succinctly: "Woody Allen's picture is meant to be about emotion, but it has no emotion. It's smooth and high-toned; it's polished in its nothingness."

As always, she preferred off-center comedy to message drama that took itself too seriously. She was intoxicated by Pedro Almodóvar's *Women on the Verge of a Nervous Breakdown*, a comedy about sexual chaos in modern Madrid, painted in bold strokes and Day-Glo colors. It was a daring comedy, "a hallucinogenic Feydeau play," as Pauline described it, and she thought that Almodóvar seemed like "Godard with a human face—a happy face." But she disliked Barry Levinson's *Rain Man*, a story of the relationship between a two-bit bum named Charlie (Tom Cruise) and his brilliant, autistic brother Raymond (Dustin Hoffman). Pauline acknowledged the wit in Hoffman's performance, but she thought it had "nowhere to go. It becomes a repetitive, boring feat, though the boringness can be construed as fidelity to the role (and masochists can regard it as great acting)." She thought that in Hoffman's "mind's eye he's always watching the audience watch him." She regarded Tom Cruise as "an actor in the same sense that Robert Taylor was an actor. He's patented: his knowing that a camera is on him produces nothing but fraudulence." For dismissing *Rain Man* as "wet kitsch," she was flooded with letters accusing her of bigotry toward autistic people.

In the spring of 1989 Dutton published Pauline's latest collection of reviews, *Hooked*, covering the period of July 1985 to June 1988, for which she had received an advance of $17,500, with Billy Abrahams once again her editor. *Publishers Weekly* complained, "A disquieting note . . . is the insensitive review of the Holocaust documentary *Shoah*," but admitted that "on the whole, Kael's genuine excitement about film sustains the book." *Hooked* sold in the neighborhood of 13,250 net copies in hardcover and 1,650 in paperback.

Blockbuster movies had risen to a position of unprecedented dominance in the film market, and the big one of the summer of 1989 was Tim Burton's *Batman*. Pauline loved the thirty-year-old director's "macabre sensibility, with a cheerfulness that's infectious," and she thought that "this powerfully glamorous new *Batman*, with sets angled and lighted like film noir, goes beyond pulp; it gallops into the cocky unknown." When a big special-effects-driven picture was executed this well, Pauline did not object to its possibly dwarfing worthy smaller pictures.

For some time a definite weariness seemed to be coloring Pauline's weekly reviewing. She hadn't written a truly surprising, expansive, out-on-the-ledge review since the *Shoah* controversy three years earlier. In her review of Brian De Palma's *Casualties of War*, however, she regained some of her old vitality. It was a movie that allowed her to make the most profound emotional connection she had made in years; despite the marked difference in subject matter, *Casualties of War* might be considered her *Shoeshine* of the late '80s. (She even referenced the De Sica film in the first paragraph of her review of the De Palma.) Based on a horrific crime that had taken place in Vietnam in 1966, *Casualties of War* depicted a group of American G.I.s who get brutally ambushed by Vietcong. When one of them is killed, their sergeant (Sean Penn) snaps, and hatches a plan to retaliate by abducting a Vietnamese girl and raping her. *Casualties of War* provided Pauline with an opportunity to go into her long-abandoned confessional mode:

> We in the audience are put in the man's position: we're made to feel the awfulness of being ineffectual. This lifelike defeat is central to the movie. (One hot day on my first trip to New York City, I walked past a group of men on a tenement stoop. One of them, in a sweaty sleeveless T-shirt, stood shouting at a screaming, weeping little boy perhaps eighteen months old. The man must have caught a glimpse of my stricken face, because he called out, "You don't like it lady? Then how do you like this?" And he picked up a bottle of pink soda pop from the sidewalk and poured it on the baby's head. Wailing sounds, much louder than before, followed me down the street.)

Pauline thought that *Casualties of War* showed De Palma plumbing emotional depths that might not have been previously expected of him. She found the picture demonstrated "such seductive, virtuosic control of film craft that he can express convulsions in the unconscious." But the most dazzling dimension of her lengthy review was the connection she made with some of his earlier thrillers. "In essence, it's feminist," she wrote—a judgment that seemed aimed directly at the sensibilities of *The Village Voice* critics:

> I think that in his earlier movies De Palma was always involved in examining (and sometimes satirizing) victimization, but he was often accused of being a victimizer. Some moviegoers (women, especially) were offended by his thrillers; they thought there was something reprehensibly sadistic in his cleverness. He *was* clever. When people talk about their sex fantasies, their descriptions almost always sound like movies, and De Palma headed right for that linkage: he teased the audience about how susceptible it was to romantic manipulation. *Carrie* and *Dressed to Kill* are like lulling erotic reveries that keep getting broken into by scary jokes. He let you know that he was jerking you around and that it was for your amused, childish delight, but a lot of highly vocal people expressed shock. This time, De Palma touches on raw places in people's reactions to his earlier movies; he gets at the reality that may have made some moviegoers too fearful to enjoy themselves. He goes to the heart of sexual victimization, and he does it with a new authority. The way he makes movies now, it's as if he were saying, "What is getting older if it isn't learning more ways that you're vulnerable?"

Pauline's was the most impassioned review that *Casualties of War* would receive—and she was stunned when she found herself the object of yet another backlash. *The Village Voice* ran a cover story titled "De Palma's Latest Outrage." (The headline was, in fact, a blatant misrepresentation of the article, which happened to be written by Allen Barra, who wrote the newspaper a letter informing readers that the title was not his choice.) None of this controversy, however, helped *Casualties of War* achieve box-office success—a failure that Pauline took extremely hard.

Daniel Day-Lewis had broken through in the mid-'80s as a screen actor to be reckoned with, but Pauline found that his performances varied considerably. (She had found him notably lacking in James Ivory's *A Room with a View*.) In *My Left Foot*, the Irish writer-director Jim Sheridan's life story of Christy Brown, an Irishman born with cerebral palsy who learned to paint with his foot and became an enormously successful artist, writer, and rounder—Day-Lewis won her over. She opened her review with a detailed account of the scene in the picture in which Brown is devastated by the announcement of his beloved teacher (Fiona Shaw) that she is going to marry someone else, which she described as perhaps "the most emotionally wrenching scene I've ever experienced at the movies. The greatness of Day-Lewis's performance is that he pulls you inside Christy Brown's frustration and rage (and his bottomless thirst). There's nothing soft or maudlin about this movie's view of Christy." She found Day-Lewis possessed of the sensual, imaginative daring that she loved in Laurence Olivier, and she compared his performance with Olivier's as Richard III. Day-Lewis won the New York Film Critics Circle Best Actor prize for *My Left Foot*, and Pauline was seated next to him at the awards presentation, held at the Algonquin Hotel. He was terribly shy, but Pauline worked hard to bring him out, patting him on the hand and asking him questions until he was smiling and quite animated.

In August, Pauline attended a family reunion at her sister Anne's house in Berkeley. She continued to have great affection for Anne, who had recently retired from Lowell High School after a long and distinguished teaching career there. The years had improved the relationship between her and Rose somewhat, but they were still anything but close.

While in Berkeley, Pauline connected with her old friend from the Cinema Guild days, Linda Allen. Pauline struck Allen as being a little heavier than she had remembered, with slightly hunched shoulders and noticeably less energy. But, as she wrote in an unpublished essay about Pauline, "The wide eyes still miss nothing." It was Gina who had changed more, Allen thought:

she looked "surprisingly unlike herself as a girl, especially with her spacious, curved, pure-looking forehead covered with bangs. . . . Very different from the fragile, quiet dancer and child artist; still an artist, though, and definitely shy."

There was a reason that Pauline seemed less robust to Allen. For some time she had been feeling increasingly fatigued and had had a great deal of trouble keeping her balance, especially when she was walking against a strong wind. In New York she had fallen on the street a number of times, breaking her nose more than once. The tremor in her hands had intensified over the years, but whenever she consulted her doctors they had assured her it was nothing more than a benign tremor—no cause for alarm. Friends were slow to notice her symptoms, partly because she had always had a certain fluttery, birdlike quality, especially when she was having an intense reaction to something. By late 1989 she realized she could no longer maintain the illusion that there was nothing seriously wrong with her: Every instinct told her otherwise.

She consulted another doctor. This time, she mentioned that her tremor would sometimes surface in one hand, sometimes in the other. The doctor, concerned, sent her to a neurologist, whose tests confirmed what she had feared for some time: She had Parkinson's disease. Her neurologist explained to her that unlike other degenerative conditions that attack the central nervous system, such as Lou Gehrig's, Parkinson's was often quite responsive to treatment—particularly in the case of elder onset—and that she might be able to manage a more or less normal life for a number of years. Still, the news was a terrible blow to her. Until she had reached her sixties, she had had few health concerns. To find herself suddenly forced to focus on her own fragile condition was an exceedingly difficult thing for a woman who had often shot through life feeling invincible.

In October 1989 Pauline invited Allen Barra and his wife, Jonelle, to attend a screening, but the film was so poor that she decided against reviewing it. She invited the Barras out to dinner at a Chinese restaurant on Eighth Avenue, and as they were sitting at a window table, Pauline looked up to see a man knifed in the middle of the street. The man fell to the ground, and Barra went out to stay with him until the police and ambulance arrived. Barra remembered that Pauline "was cool the entire time. Didn't say a word. Gina told me afterward that it shook her so badly that she couldn't function for a couple of days. That cemented her loathing of New York. I don't know how many times she said, 'Oh, dearie, it would be so nice to see you later on in the day, because I just can't stand it in this awful city.'"

By now there was another new actress to add to her pantheon. She thought that Diane Keaton, forgiven at last for *Reds*, had hit her stride in movies ranging from *Crimes of the Heart* to *Baby Boom*. Debra Winger's career already seemed to be fading, something that disappointed Pauline terribly. She liked Christine Lahti, Rae Dawn Chong, Ellen Barkin, Lesley Anne Warren, Pamela Reed, and the beautiful and gifted Michelle Pfeiffer, whose talent had first impressed Pauline in *Natica Jackson* on PBS-TV. When Stephen Frears was preparing to film *Dangerous Liaisons*, he had settled on Kelly McGillis for the pivotal role of the cruelly manipulated Mme. de Tourvel. Pauline was already displeased with him for having cast Glenn Close as the scheming Marquise de Merteuil (an opinion she would change when the film was released), and when she went out to dinner with him suggested several other actresses for the part of Mme. de Tourvel—among them, Pfeiffer. She sent him a VHS tape of *Natica Jackson*, and Frears, won over, gave the actress the role. She gave a beautiful performance, as she did in her new film, Steve Kloves's *The Fabulous Baker Boys*. Pauline hailed Pfeiffer's arrival with her usual flair: "With Pfeiffer in deep-red velvet crawling on the piano like a long-legged Kitty-cat and sliding down to be closer to the pianist, something new has been achieved in torrid comedy."

In December a film opened that would usher in one of the most profitable and influential movie trends of the 1990s: Disney's animated feature version of Hans Christian Andersen's fairy tale *The Little Mermaid*. Pauline, who had little patience for most of the enormously popular Disney features of the 1930s, '40s, and '50s, was delighted that her grandson, Will, was more drawn to exotic, exciting adventure stories. She made short work of *The Little Mermaid*, which she found no less treacly than vintage Disney had been:

Are we trying to put kids into some sort of moral-aesthetic safe house? Parents seem desperate for harmless family entertainment. Probably they don't mind this movie's being vapid, because the whole family can share it, and no one is offended. We're caught in a culture warp. Our children are flushed with pleasure when we read them *Where the Wild Things Are* or Roald Dahl's sinister stories. Kids are ecstatic watching videos of *The Secret of NIMH* and *The Dark Crystal*. Yet here comes the press telling us that *The Little Mermaid* is "due for immortality." People are made to feel that this stale pastry is what they should be taking their kids to, that it's art for children. And when they see the movie they may believe it, because this *Mermaid* is just a slightly updated version of what their parents took them to. They've been imprinted with Disney-style kitsch.

*The Little Mermaid* took in more than $100 million at the box office and achieved a merchandising success that Walt Disney himself might only have dreamed of, opening the door for the studio's astonishing resurgence in the 1990s.

The following year brought many pictures she liked very much, including two released at the end of 1989, Paul Mazursky's *Enemies: A Love Story* and Bruce Beresford's *Driving Miss Daisy*, the latter inadvertently causing her yet more trouble in the by-now advanced era of political correctness. *Driving Miss Daisy* had enjoyed great success as an Off-Broadway play by Alfred Uhry, about the growing friendship between a cantankerous Southern Jewish woman and her cagey, independent-minded black chauffeur. She praised Beresford for underplaying the "coziness and slightness" of the original material, and at the voting of the New York Film Critics Circle in December 1989, *Driving Miss Daisy* was one of four films—the others being *Enemies: A Love Story, The Fabulous Baker Boys,* and *My Left Foot*—that Pauline supported for the major awards.

The strategic voting of the NYFCC had long been a challenge. Choices that received a handful of votes in the first ballot could wind up being triumphant in the third and fourth ballots because, as the field of possible winners narrowed and shifted, critics were often more concerned with blocking their least favorite choices than with backing their number-one preferences. It was a frustrating process, and one person who most objected to it was Georgia Brown, a critic at *The Village Voice*, Andrew Sarris having decamped for *The New York Observer*. Brown found *Driving Miss Daisy*'s view of black servitude offensively regressive and sentimental. And when she saw its star Jessica Tandy building a groundswell of support, with none at all going to her costar, Morgan Freeman, she got angry. Her anger intensified as she saw her own favorite, Spike Lee's *Do the Right Thing*, losing ground in the balloting process.

Brown's article on the NYFCC process, "Bite the Ballot," published in the *Voice* in early 1989, featured a single illustration: a publicity photo of Pauline. After outlining her frustrations with the voting process, she shifted blame in Pauline's direction for the move against *Do the Right Thing*. "Does Kael orchestrate campaigns inside the film societies?" Brown asked. "She may. Last year while being inducted into the NYFCC, the then chairman warned

that I might receive some 'lobbying' phone calls before the December voting."
That was the most cogent piece of evidence Brown could summon against
Pauline, and in her rambling, unfocused article, she strongly suggested that
Pauline was guilty of (a) organizing her acolytes in a voting bloc—a point she
might have been able to prove had she done her homework—and (b) out-and-
out racism because she didn't back *Do the Right Thing*—an argument that
wasn't really argued at all. Brown's article received more attention than it
merited and proved to be more damaging than it had any right to be, serving
as a sad reminder that the idea and intent behind a movie had become more
significant than the results onscreen.

# CHAPTER TWENTY-SEVEN

Pauline's physical condition worsened at a faster rate than she and her doctors had anticipated. Although it was not yet preventing her from keeping up her regular reviewing duties, the task of writing was becoming more and more arduous; she found that the words didn't pour out of her at the rate they once had. There was no ignoring the fact that the Parkinson's was affecting her memory; she would start to call a longtime friend or acquaintance, but the name wouldn't surface. She had always had an excellent memory—for details, for facts, for entire scenes and stretches of dialogue in movies that she hadn't seen for decades—and more and more she would have to rely on the fact-checkers at *The New Yorker* to back her up on certain details in a movie review. (Fortunately, it was part of the checkers' job to go to the movies and take notes, a policy that had been instituted years earlier as a method of dealing with Penelope Gilliatt's lapses.)

One night in 1990 Pauline sat through a screening of Penny Marshall's *Awakenings,* based on Oliver Sacks's book about treating comatose patients with the drug L-dopa. While it was difficult for her to watch the film, given her struggles to become accustomed to life with Parkinson's, still, she didn't go soft on the movie, which she considered a betrayal of the most compelling aspects of its source.

To make matters worse, she was saddened by most of the movies that were being released. She was not taken in by Michael Moore's *Roger & Me,* a documentary about the economic devastation in the wake of the closing of eleven General Motors plants in Flint, Michigan. Audiences responded enthusiastically to Moore's muckraking spirit and were eager to hail him as a new truth-teller and counterculture hero, but Pauline found the film shockingly mean-spirited; she hated the way Moore scored cheap laughs off the poor people of Flint who were simply trying to get by any way they could. "The picture is like the work of a slick ad exec," she wrote. "It does something that is humanly very offensive: *Roger & Me* uses its leftism as a superior attitude."

There were, unfortunately, signs of her fatigue showing up on the pages of *The New Yorker.* She liked Stephen Frears's *The Grifters,* based on Jim Thompson's book about a trio of con artists, but she wasn't quite able to convey the movie's pulse and originality in her review. She also liked Martin Scorsese's latest, *Goodfellas*, and while she thought the film missed greatness because Scorsese and his scriptwriter, Nicholas Pileggi (who adapted his own book), hadn't shaped the material, she acknowledged that "the moviemaking has such bravura that you respond as if you were at a live performance."

She took aim at one of the year's biggest, *Dances with Wolves*, the drama about a Civil War soldier who befriends the Sioux and eventually becomes a tribal member. "There's nothing affected about Costner's acting or directing," she wrote. "You hear his laid-back, surfer accent; you see his deliberate goofy faints and falls, and all the close-ups of his handsomeness. This epic was made by a bland megalomaniac. (The Indians should have named him Plays with Camera.) You look at that untroubled face and know he can make everything lightweight."

In December she made the very last of her lost-cause pitches, this time for Karel Reisz's *Everybody Wins*, with Debra Winger as a flaked-out hooker involved in a mystery in a small New England town. The movie was sneaked into release early in 1990 and bombed, but now, nearly a year later, Pauline exhorted her readers to catch it on VHS. She had a touching observation about the fate of *Everybody Wins* that indicated the depths of her discouragement: "For a brief period in the late sixties and early seventies, moviegoers seemed willing to be guided through a movie by their intuition and imagination; if this slyly funny picture about the spread of corruption had been released then, it might have been considered a minor classic."

It was that period that she hoped, against all evidence to the contrary, might somehow be resuscitated in some form or another. But what had happened to the movies went far beyond the blockbuster mentality and the studio's obsession with repeated formulas and marketing strategies. The past decade had seen a steady erosion of the pride of place in the culture that movies had once held. A great deal of that development was a function of the video revolution: The ideas of movies as an event, an actual performance unfolding before you, was no longer relevant; now films could be experienced over several nights at home, robbing them of the impact they once had on audiences. In New York the booming video industry had proved to be the death knell of the great abundance of revival theaters. Critics, as a result, were fated to become less and less important. It was a good time for Pauline to stop regular reviewing.

One evening that January she had shown up at the Broadway Screening Room to see Paul Mazursky's new comedy, *Scenes from a Mall*, costarring Woody Allen and Bette Midler. One of the few people in attendance was

Owen Gleiberman, who got into a conversation with her about Jonathan Demme's latest, *Silence of the Lambs*. Pauline hadn't liked it at all—she felt Demme was selling out by making a highly commercial story in which he wasn't particularly interested and that didn't play to any of his strengths as a director. She seemed to sense that *Silence of the Lambs* was going to be a big hit for him, which it was—it would even earn him the Academy Award for Best Director. "The movies are so shitty now," she sighed to Gleiberman.

The lights went down, and *Scenes from a Mall* began. It was abysmal—a shocking comedown from a director she had always believed in, a director who had continued to deepen his craft and vision over more than twenty years.

She was seventy-one, and she was tired and in failing health—and the movies weren't worth the time and effort anymore. She notified *The New Yorker* of her decision: Her review of the Steve Martin comedy *L.A. Story*, in the magazine's February 11, 1991, issue, would be her last. A reviewing career that had begun at the magazine with *Bonnie and Clyde* would end with *L.A. Story*.

By March the news of her retirement had been made public. It received major coverage in many leading newspapers and magazines, where it was viewed as the end of a spectacular era. "For a brief, golden time in the '70s . . . it must have seemed as if the movies themselves had caught up with her vision of what they ought to be: subversive and supple, erotic and multilayered and alive," wrote David Ansen in *Newsweek*. "But the passionate cinematic 'energy' she sought became increasingly supplanted by a crass, bludgeoning energy that was like a cruel parody of the kinds of movies she fought for. Kael may have changed the face of criticism, but she's always been playing a bigger, more impossible game—to change the movies themselves, and us with them." "At worst, she wasn't far from a film-world version of Walter Winchell, conducting vendettas and boosting intimates," wrote Tom Carson in *L.A. Weekly*. "These habits are unseemly; they detract from Kael's greatness. They don't change the fact that greatness is the right word." Pauline herself put a much lighter spin on it, telling the press that she would still write occasionally for *The New Yorker*. As far as giving up regular reviewing was concerned, she insisted that no should be sorry on her behalf—after all, now she wouldn't ever have to sit through another Oliver Stone movie.

In fact, she had occupied the spotlight for so long, in a more vital and ongoing way than any other movie critic ever had, that stepping out of it was not easy. On May 2, 1991, she was awarded the Mel Novikoff Award at the San Francisco Film Society, for a body of work that "enhanced and expanded the filmgoing public's knowledge and appreciation of world cinema."

(She wasn't feeling well enough to fly to California, and her friend Michael Sragow accepted on her behalf.) Journalists still telephoned her for quotes, young filmmakers still showed up on her doorstep in Great Barrington seeking her advice, film companies still inundated her with video copies of their latest releases. She continued to keep up with everything, weighing in with her younger critic friends about new movies, still trying to have an influence on what was being written about them—and in many cases, succeeding.

In the fall of 1991 *Movie Love*, a collection of her last three years of *New Yorker* reviews, was brought out by Dutton. *The Los Angeles Times Book Review* said that it provided "welcome reading at a time when film criticism seems to have been reduced to 'a 10!' and 'Two Thumbs up.'" A few months after the book's release, her hometown honored her by proclaiming a Pauline Kael Day during Petaluma History Week. By now Petaluma had become a gentrified community with more than a little of Ye Olde Country Village atmosphere— far too precious for Pauline's taste. She again offered the genuine excuse of ill health and declined to show up to celebrate her honor.

Life for the Paulettes had become quite different, in many cases, now that Pauline was in retirement. For one thing, they lacked the advantage of attending screenings with her and going out afterward to a restaurant to talk over the movie they had just seen, sparking thoughts and ideas in many directions. For another, the world at large didn't seem as welcoming to them without Pauline as their mentor. People who had branded them—unfairly, in some cases—as imitators now felt the freedom to dismiss them. Without her, there seemed to be much less point in being a Paulette. A number of them felt betrayed when they failed to become the powerful force that she had once been.

At *The New Yorker*, meanwhile, Terrence Rafferty had been moved into the first-ranking film critic's position. Initially, Pauline had supported him, but she grew to believe that his approach was too dry and that he wasn't focusing on the right movies or responding to them in the proper way. To back up Rafferty, Robert Gottlieb hired Pauline's friend Michael Sragow. She was delighted that James Wolcott had landed a staff position at the award-winning *Texas Monthly*—one of the smartest magazines around. She prodded Polly Frost in the direction of movie criticism, and Frost eventually began reviewing for *Harper's Bazaar* and *Elle*. Pauline regularly read Steve Vineberg's work for *The Threepenny Review*, and encouraged his work as a stage director. She came to see a production of John Guare's *Marco Polo Sings a Solo* that Vineberg staged, and urged him to move to New York to try his work as a director full-time; she was baffled when he told her that he loved his job at the College of

the Holy Cross and wanted to keep it. The passing of time had done nothing
to diminish her disdain for academic life.

There remained a serious degree of competition among the Paulettes, one
that heated up if it was felt that she was favoring one—as when she recommended David Edelstein over the others for a series of positions. (She began
telling friends that she thought Edelstein should succeed Terrence Rafferty
at *The New Yorker*.) Often, there were extreme tensions in the Great Barrington
house if a group of Paulettes had been invited for a weekend; the sense of
competitiveness over who was closest to Pauline was almost palpable. One
person who remained wary of many of the rowdier and more outspoken Paulettes was Gina, who regarded some of them as users and manipulators, and
was skeptical about her mother's intense engagement with them.

Many of the Paulettes were hesitant about introducing their wives and
girlfriends to their mentor. When James Wolcott became seriously involved
with the talented writer and editor Laura Jacobs, who eventually became his
wife, he told her that he wasn't going to introduce her to Pauline because
Pauline wouldn't like her. Besides Polly Frost, however, she was fond of Stephanie Zacharek, another critic for *The Boston Phoenix*, who eventually married
the film critic and essayist Charles Taylor, whose career Pauline had followed
with interest for some time. Zacharek had idolized Pauline when she was
growing up, and the day that Taylor took her to meet Pauline in Great Barrington, Zacharek was extremely nervous. She was an attractive redhead, and
Pauline put her at ease immediately by opening the door and saying, "Oh—you
have Annette O'Toole's hair!"

Oddly enough, she had rather kind feelings toward Molly Haskell, who
was married to her chief agitator, Andrew Sarris. Pauline was quick to point
out that she thought Sarris had a lively intelligence, and that she had refrained
from commenting on his work after "Circles and Squares"—the so-called feud
between them was mostly maintained by Sarris over the years. "Pauline felt
that Molly, once she married Sarris, really hampered herself," observed Wolcott, "because there was no way that she was not going to bow to his greater
authority. She felt that Molly never became the critic she might have been,
because she took up so many of Andy's tastes and sensibilities. Even when she
differed, she had to explain *why* she differed."

Similarly, Pauline often regretted that the wives of important artists took
such a backseat to their husbands. When she had dinner with Satyajit Ray, a
director whose work she had admired for decades, she found his wife, Bijoya,
to be extremely bright and poised. But she noticed that when Ray began to
speak, Bijoya became silently adoring. At one point in their conversation,

Pauline mildly challenged one of Ray's opinions about a movie. The director froze, and his wife gave Pauline a look to indicate that she had deeply offended the great man.

Her younger friends admired her for hanging on to her democratic spirit; spending time with Pauline was a teaching experience that went beyond the bounds of talking about writing. Charles Taylor remembered, "I once said, in a fit of frustration, 'Stupid people drive me crazy.' And she said, 'You know, some people just aren't bright. They can't help that.'" Another time, Polly Frost was with Pauline at a party where one of the other guests was complaining about her recent experience on jury duty. "These people were all housewives, and what do they know?" she snapped. Pauline turned to her and said, "And what did *your* mother do?"

In late 1994, with several of Pauline's earlier volumes having gone out of print, Dutton published *For Keeps*, a huge compendium of her reviews, spanning her entire career. By February 1995 it appeared in the number-six position on *The Village Voice Literary Supplement*'s list of hardcover bestsellers. (By January 1996, it had sold more than 18,000 copies in hardcover—an excellent run.) Pauline had gone carefully through all of her published reviews and essays, in conjunction with Billy Abrahams, and carefully excerpted the pieces of writing she considered her best. (Perhaps because she had battle fatigue, she omitted several of her more controversial reviews, including the ones of *The Children's Hour*, *The Sergeant*, *Rich and Famous*, and *Shoah*.) In her author's note she discussed the pleasures of a lifetime of reviewing films. "I'm frequently asked why I don't write my memoirs," she wrote. "I think I have." Many friends and colleagues continued to prod her to do a memoir, however, including Peggy Brooks, who spent a weekend with Pauline and Charles Simmons in Great Barrington in September of 1994. "I kept bringing up the idea of her work on an autobiography," Brooks wrote to Abrahams. "She was resistant at first, but it seemed both to Charles and me, that towards the end, she was starting to think about it seriously. I know it's difficult for her physically to write now, but her head is in such sharp shape, I think she could do a fascinating book, different from any other of hers." The memoir never came to pass.

One of her greatest pleasures continued to be her grandson. Will, now ten, was an energetic, quixotic boy who didn't seem particularly interested in either his studies or athletics—several friends observed that he seemed to live almost in a world of his own. His interests were few but intense. He loved action figures and action movies—Bruce Lee was a favorite. He was fascinated by space—any television documentary on black holes was certain to capture his attention—and he loved his enormous collection of big, unbreakable Carnegie animals. Pauline indulged him in all of these, never attempting to steer him toward a more "serious" path. She thought that children should be left alone, allowed to find their own way, and she happily joined him in watching Bruce Lee movies. She seemed intent on giving her seal of approval to Will's uncomplicated pursuit of pop culture in the same sense that she had once tried to tell her readers that there was no need to feel guilty about enjoying kitsch and trash.

Warner Friedman often worried that his son's interests weren't broad enough and would try to encourage him to paint and to attend museums with him. He also asked Allen Barra to try to get Will interested in sports. Barra spent a fair amount of time practicing baseball with him; while Will was a very good batter, he lacked the patience to master fielding. When Barra came for visits, he often brought his young daughter, Maggie, to play with Will. Barra had taken an active role in helping to shape Maggie's reading tastes and had instructed her to read both *Tom Sawyer* and Arthur Conan Doyle's Sherlock Holmes stories. Pauline's reaction bordered on hostility. "Oh, just let her grow up," she would say. "I never understood her attitude on things like that," Barra recalled. "Here was a perfect opportunity for Will to learn about art. And Pauline could have given so much to him, and she didn't."

Pauline kept abreast of the changes that continued to sweep through *The New Yorker* offices. After five years Si Newhouse had judged Robert Gottlieb's editorial tenure unsatisfactory—advertising had declined sharply, and the magazine was losing $5 million a year—and replaced him with Tina Brown, the thirty-eight-year-old British editor who had successfully relaunched *Vanity Fair* and transformed it into a top celebrity magazine. Many of the old-guard writers and reporters suddenly found themselves bounced from their long-standing (and frequently unproductive) jobs. The content changed considerably, with much greater emphasis on current events and far less focus on the magazine's literary and cultural subjects. Carefully crafted features on cultural figures such as the Irish author Molly Keane, the producer Irene Mayer Selznick, and the famously dyspeptic novelist Marcia Davenport appeared far less frequently; topicality was now critical.

A number of insiders, as well as many longtime readers, resented the new direction, feeling that Brown had subverted the unique mission and tone of the magazine, but Pauline believed that Brown's arrival made for a welcome and exciting change. (She often asked friends if they really thought anyone would miss Ved Mehta's interminable, old-fashioned articles.) Pauline was also pleased when Brown, at long last, engaged James Wolcott as a staff writer—a sign that the magazine was cultivating some livelier voices. She was unhappy, however, when Brown terminated Michael Sragow as movie critic.

By the mid-1990s Pauline's Parkinson's symptoms had grown debilitating. While in the house, she relied on her four-pronged cane—she joked that it wasn't very dashing, but it did the job. Outside, however, she was constantly fearful of falling, and felt quite uneasy if she didn't have someone's arm to support her. Visits to New York were impossible—she made her last trip there in 1992. Public appearances were also no longer feasible, and she hated to go to plays or concerts or movies: When her shaking was at its worst, she noticed that she made the seats around her vibrate, and she didn't want to distract her fellow audience members.

Twice a week she took massage therapy from a doctor in Otis, Massachusetts—Pauline thought he was a little like a hippie version of Jeff Bridges. She looked forward to her sessions for two reasons: Her doctor was unimpressed with her celebrity and frequently told her why he thought she'd been wrong about certain movies; most important, the therapy brought forth good results, making her muscles much more supple.

Although she tried not to lose her sense of humor, she wasn't very good at witnessing her own diminuendo. Her fading memory was a particular source of irritation: She told Ray Sawhill that during the day, she would often wonder if the words she couldn't come up with would ever come back to her. They did—at night, when she was in bed. She also experienced in a highly personal way the cold and condescending way in which people discriminate against the elderly: In stores in Great Barrington, she was frequently ignored by clerks who didn't want to contend with an elderly woman with a cane and the shakes. For someone who had always possessed a strong sense of pride and independence, such episodes were humiliating.

She continued to take pride in the developing careers of the Paulettes. Hal Hinson had secured a reviewing spot at *The Washington Post*, David Edelstein was doing fine work at *Slate*, Michael Sragow was the lead film critic at the *San Francisco Examiner*. More than ever, she was a devoted champion of James Wolcott—who in 1997 left *The New Yorker* and returned to *Vanity Fair*, where he had once been a contributing editor. He was hired to write columns on media and pop culture, which he would presumably be able to do in more of a no-holds-barred way than *The New Yorker* had permitted. Pauline wasn't mad about *Vanity Fair*, which she found too brassy and insubstantial and celebrity-driven, but she looked forward to seeing what Wolcott came up with.

In the magazine's April 1997 issue, she found out. In a column titled

"Waiting for Godard," Wolcott wrote a devastating piece about the Paulettes, branding them as a band of hopeless imitators who had squandered their own talents by falling under Pauline's spell. "They write as advocates, both feet on the accelerator," he wrote. "They still write as if 'trash' (the good kind—blatant, vital, sexy) were in danger of being euthanized by the team of Merchant Ivory. Gentility is the enemy—we're drowning in crinoline! they cry. Bring back hot rods and cheap lipstick." Wolcott was reasonably careful not to place Pauline herself in his crosshairs, but he didn't really need to: Without saying so directly, his article heavily implied that she had encouraged sycophancy and slavish devotion. Pauline was stunned that someone whose career she had worked so assiduously to advance could have written such a piece. Of course, Wolcott had learned a great deal from her: "Waiting for Godard" was, in its own way, as much of an attention-getter for him as "Circles and Squares" had once been for her. Articles were written about it, radio broadcasts were devoted to it, and the term "Paulette" became familiar to a wide reading public. Pauline refrained from commenting on "Waiting for Godard" publicly, but, unsurprisingly, Wolcott instantly became persona non grata among his fellow Paulettes. "He's a careerist creep," observed Charles Taylor. "I think that Wolcott simply decides what is going to advance him and takes the pose. I read that piece, and that piece hurt Pauline. That piece *really* hurt her. The loss of him as a friend hurt her."

Wolcott acknowledged that "Waiting for Godard" severed their friendship, although it is difficult to tell if he considered that a strong possibility at the time he was writing the piece. "I knew she wasn't happy about it," he said. "James Toback told me later on that she was really pissed. I think that piece was overkill. I feel bad about it. I had just re-upped with *Vanity Fair*, so I was trying to build up a head of steam—not so much about Pauline but about the other people. . . . I didn't think people would carry on the grudges for fifteen years."

Despite the fact that "Waiting for Godard" created a permanent split between Wolcott and Pauline, she continued to read his work with interest. During one of her treatments at Massachusetts General Hospital in the late 1990s, she asked Steve Vineberg to bring her a copy of *Vanity Fair* so she could read Wolcott's latest column.

As the 1990s wore on, Gina had to deal with her own health problems in addition to caring for her mother. She suffered a bout with cancer, which was treated successfully, in addition to a prolonged and draining case of Lyme disease that left a few lingering effects in its wake. Pauline's Parkinson's had by now made it impossible for her to manage a knife and fork properly, which meant that she stopped going to restaurants for a time. Eventually she was put on a more intensive round of medication that stabilized her shaking condition and enabled her to lead a much more normal life. The problem was, the stronger medicine gave her hallucinations. She saw live bears—"no cartoons, no lyricism—just realism," she told Ray Sawhill—at the edge of her vision. Once she watched as a third arm came out of her chest to grapple with her other two arms. When she reached out to crush the third arm, she watched in terror and amazement as it shattered into bits; she told friends it reminded her of the end of *Zabriskie Point*. Eventually, the hallucinations receded, and she joked that she had occasionally reached out to pat the animals that appeared before her.

When she didn't feel up to climbing the stairs to her second-floor bedroom, she would stay downstairs in the living room, reading and keeping up with the news. She had an exercise bicycle installed there, which she was supposed to use to keep herself as limber as possible. She slept deeply, but not for long periods of time—often, five hours was the limit. She told Ray Sawhill that her declining health made her all the more "desperate to read and to take in everything . . . I think I've never been so eager to learn and to do things as I am now." She loved keeping up with television news and watching *The Sopranos*, *Saturday Night Live*, and *Sex and the City*. She also made her way through the steady stream of cassettes of new movies that producers and directors were constantly sending her. Sometimes a screening of a new picture was arranged for her at a local movie theater.

In January 1999 an article by the film director Wes Anderson appeared in *The New York Times* that many of her friends and followers found deeply insulting. "My Private Screening with Pauline Kael" described Anderson's efforts to arrange a screening of his new film, *Rushmore*, for her at the Triplex in Great Barrington. Anderson seemed to have intended the piece to be wry, but it came across as mean-spirited and condescending, portraying Pauline as a frail, out-of-touch woman operating in a state of confusion. Anderson wrote a letter to the *Times* saying that he hadn't intended to mock her. "I thought, when I read that, this is what's wrong with Wes Anderson's movies," said Steve Vineberg. "The guy is tone deaf."

As she grew older Pauline became increasingly hunched and began to shrink dramatically: By 2000 she had lost a total of four inches in height. She depended on friends to take her out to dinner and movies and support her to keep her from falling. The worst part about this, she said, laughing, was that she had to make deals to see movies she would otherwise have no interest in viewing: When she persuaded a friend to accompany her to *American Psycho*, she had to promise to go with that friend to see *Keeping the Faith*, starring Ben Stiller.

Stephanie Zacharek remembered that even as Pauline's condition worsened, she seemed amazingly responsive to the world around her; her powers of observation had scarcely dimmed at all. "Sometimes, Charlie and I would go to little shops on the way out to visit her, and I would show her what I had bought—a scarf or something—and I would say, 'Oh, my God, I shouldn't be spending money right now.' And she would say, 'You have to buy these things when you're young when you have the figure to wear them, because when you're older, and you have the money, your figure will be gone.'" Even when she was feeling her worst, there were certain pleasurable constants in her life. Fresh flowers were always welcome—"They're more delicious than food now," she once told George and Elizabeth Malko.

As Pauline grew more fragile, her views softened: Pauline in the stormy weather of bad health was far more conciliatory than the Pauline of her younger, feistier days. Ray Sawhill and Polly Frost, David Edelstein, Silvana Nova, and Craig Seligman were on hand as much as possible to help out. Roy Blount, Jr., who lived nearby, was a loyal neighbor, always checking in to see if she needed anything done around the house. Steve Vineberg frequently drove her to doctor's appointments at Massachusetts General. Once, Vineberg took his visiting mother and Pauline out to lunch at a restaurant in Great Barrington. As he drove along, his mother in the front seat and Pauline in the back, Pauline commented, "You look so restive sitting up there next to your mother. I wish I could sit with my mother." It was the first time Vineberg could ever recall her mentioning Judith.

Several of Pauline's other friends, however, noticeably dropped out. "A number of people around any diva start to think that that person's like them, and start to project," remarked Polly Frost. "And a good diva, like Pauline, allows people to project. It's power. But Pauline couldn't play Pauline anymore, and a lot of people disappeared." They had seen the power player they desperately wanted her to be, but they hadn't seen past the persona.

One night in Great Barrington, sometime in the late 1990s, she was having dinner with Taylor and Zacharek. Also dining in the restaurant was George Roy Hill, who also had been diagnosed with Parkinson's. Their previous battles—even the letter that opened with "Listen, you miserable bitch"—were immediately forgotten. Pauline clutched his hand warmly and gave him the name of her massage therapist, promising him that the therapy would do him a world of good.

Despite the general softening of her temperament, she could still snap.

After surgery for a congested carotid artery, Pauline came out of the anesthesia to hear the surgeons and nurses talking about the actor Matthew Modine. "He's never any good," Pauline whispered. Another time, she was sharing a hospital room with a gregarious woman who kept telling Pauline about her love for Jesus. Finally an exasperated Pauline said, "Well, honey, from the look of things, he hasn't done much for you lately!"

As Will grew older, he retained his sweet, friendly nature. Some friends noticed, however, that his interests didn't seem to be broadening and deepening in the way that might have been expected. He would become quite obsessive about certain movies—such as *Braveheart* and *Last of the Mohicans*—films with action and heroism. He loved the outdoors—particularly hiking in the Berkshires—but he still showed little interest in reading, and Pauline seemed no more inclined than ever to encourage him. He entered Bard College at Simon's Rock, an experimental institution in Great Barrington. He dropped out, then went back. Gina worried about her son a great deal, and wondered if he might have some sort of serious medical condition—but Pauline mostly turned a blind eye to Will's resistance to a traditional path.

In 1999 the National Book Critics Circle awarded Pauline the Ivan Sandrof Award for Contribution to American Arts and Letters. That June, she celebrated her eightieth birthday with an enormous party at the Great Barrington house. It was a beautiful late spring day, and in attendance were her closest friends: Polly Frost and Ray Sawhill, Charles Taylor and Stephanie Zacharek, Steve Vineberg, Michael Sragow, Arlene Croce, David Edelstein, Allen and Jonelle Barra. Wallace Shawn was there, unofficially representing her *New Yorker* years. Her sister Anne flew out from Berkeley, and the two of them sat together at the party, looking diminutive and birdlike. She invited some people to whom she had not been close for years, such as David Denby—but no invitation was issued to James Wolcott. With Pauline's ignorance about technology and which appliances were better than others, she had never owned a first-class television set. Several of her critic friends chipped in and bought her a big, state-of-the-art television, which delighted her. (When Gina bought a new computer, however, Pauline didn't go near it, but only eyed it suspiciously.)

Also present was Roy Blount, Jr., who composed a poem for the occasion:

> "Presenting Creation, more or less,"
> Said Jehovah.
> "Oh. What a mess," Pauline observed.

So he gave it form.
Roundish. Molten cooling to warm.

"Has it occurred to you to let there be light?"

"By golly," Jehovah said, "you're right."

But light revealed a certain void.

"You might try creating celluloid,
And then a projector," said Pauline,
"For showing images on a screen."

"Look, it's one thing you're not afraid of me,
But don't get so far ahead of me!
What are those images gonna be of?"
Exclaimed Jehovah—"Vengeance? Love?"

"A couple of characters wouldn't hurt."

So Jehovah grabbed two handfuls of dirt.

"Mm," said Pauline, "you've got something there.
You're casting Cary Grant and Cher?"

"No. For Eve I want someone *deep*,"
He said, "I'm making Meryl Streep.
And who really cares whom I make first male?
A first-mate type. Think Alan Hale."

"Oh God," said Pauline, "a feminist flick,
With the Holy Ghost as the only dick."

"No," he huffed, his face getting red,
"A serious film, with a message," he said.

"Oh why does my sinking heart suspect
You're letting Stanley Kramer direct?"

"So be it," Jehovah thundered, and that
Is why "The Fall of Man" fell flat.

And also why, when Edison came
To visit Pauline one day and claim,

"I've made a *moving* picture," she
Patted his hand and said, "We'll see."

And seen we have, with feelings and eyes
Her vision's done much to aesthetize.
Here's to Orson and Bogie and Katie,
And towering over them, Pauline at 80.

In telephone conversations with a number of old friends and colleagues, she expressed regret that she might have treated them unfairly when she was in her heyday. In September 2000, Carrie Rickey received a call from a mutual friend, Francis Davis, who told her that Pauline wanted to speak with her. Rickey called the house in Great Barrington, and in the course of a ninety-minute conversation, Pauline at one point said, "I don't know what you know, but I know I've done some things to you that were not okay." Rickey told her that it was all in the past and not to burden herself with it. After she hung up the phone, she wept uncontrollably—she had had the conciliatory conversation with Pauline that she had never been able to have with her own mother.

An endless stream of writers still sought her out for interviews, demanding to know what she thought of the current stream of films and directors. There was still an army of readers who felt cut adrift without her to lean on as their guide to the world of moviemaking. Two of the more prominent were Francis Davis, who recorded a lengthy conversation with her that he eventually published in book form as *Afterglow*, and Susie Linfield, a respected New York journalist and professor who requested Pauline's permission to write a full-scale biography. Linfield conceived of her book as more of an interior look at Pauline's life than a conventional biography, and sent Pauline a lengthy and well-presented proposal, but Pauline declined to participate.

In the spring of 2001 Pauline received word that she had been chosen for a prestigious fellowship administered by Columbia University's National Arts Journalism Program. The Distinguished Lectureship in Criticism, which had previously gone to writers such as Patricia Bosworth and Pauline's friend Arlene Croce, offered an honorarium of $20,000, to be paid that September, and required one visit to Columbia in the fall or spring semesters, during which time she would present a lecture to the elite of Columbia's community. Given the state of her health, it was arranged that the balance of her participation would take place via teleconferencing and videoconferencing from Great Barrington. Pauline was as happy about the cash prize as she was about the honor, and she looked forward to the presentation of the fellowship, scheduled for October 4 at Columbia's Kathryn Miller Bache Theater.

In late August 2001, Polly Frost was sitting with Pauline at her bedside.

Frost had never seen Will's favorite film, *Braveheart*, and when he began agitating for her to watch it with him, Frost said to Pauline that she thought it was the right thing to do. At one point, the leading lady, Sophie Marceau, lashed out at Mel Gibson. "You tell him, girlie!" whispered Pauline, like the 1930s heroine she had always imagined herself being.

Her friend Dennis Delrogh had been to see Coppola's *Apocalypse Now: Redux*, with much original footage restored. Delrogh pointed out that Andrew Sarris still hadn't liked the movie.

"Of course," said Pauline. "He's smart."

Around the same time, Pauline's old friend Erhard Dortmund telephoned her from Oregon to ask how she was feeling. The nurse brought the telephone to her. After a few whispered exchanges, Pauline asked Dortmund what he was reading. As it happened, he was in the middle of Philip Roth's *The Dying Animal*.

On Monday, September 3, 2001, Michael Sragow telephoned Pauline at home. Her voice was weaker than ever, but she told him that Gina had been taking very good care of her. They spoke a bit about mutual friends, including Lamont Johnson. "Isn't he amazing?" Pauline whispered. Sragow could tell it was impossible for her to speak for much longer, and told her goodbye.

A little less than two hours later, Craig Seligman telephoned Sragow to tell him Pauline had died.

# CHAPTER TWENTY-EIGHT

On November 30, 2001, a memorial tribute to Pauline was presented at the Walter Reade Theater by the Film Society of Lincoln Center and *The New Yorker*. George Malko hosted the event. Gina was the first speaker, and her comments were remarkably brave and unsentimental:

> As a mother, Pauline was exactly what you would expect from reading her or knowing her. Taste, judgment, being right were crucial. Her inflexibility pleased her. She was right—and that was it. My mother had tremendous empathy and compassion, though how to comfort, soothe, or console was a mystery that eluded her. Pauline tried to make me aware of people's needs and she taught me to be considerate of other people's feelings. But when Pauline spoke to someone about their work as if it had been produced by a third party, it had repercussions. There was fallout. In my youth, I watched what she left, unaware, in her wake: flickering glimpses of crushed illusions, mounting insecurities, desolation. Those she was not dismissive of, those who valued her perception, judgment, integrity, and extreme forthrightness, did feel her sting, but also felt she was totally real and that she affirmed and valued them as human beings. She could see the possibilities. Pauline's greatest weakness, her failure as a person, became her great strength, her liberation as a writer and critic. She truly believed that what she did was for everyone else's good, and that because she meant well, she had no negative effects. She refused any consideration of that possibility and she denied any motivations or personal needs. . . . This lack of introspection, self-awareness, restraint, or hesitation gave Pauline supreme freedom to speak up, to speak her mind, to find her honest voice. She turned her lack of self-awareness into a triumph.

Gina was followed by Craig Seligman, who spoke of the good fortune he'd had, not only in becoming friends with his literary idol, but in finding her such fun to be around. "She was funny and lethal right up to the end," said Seligman. "One day when she was near death and I was trying to divert her with chatter about working as an editor, I said, 'It never ceases to amaze me how many people who call themselves writers actually can't write.' And she said, very weakly, 'Yes—they say things like 'It never ceases to amaze me.'"

Robert Altman gave a rambling speech about Pauline's championing of his work—it was easy to imagine her mentally editing his remarks—while Arlene Croce shared affectionate reminiscences of being with Pauline and Gina the day that they found the Great Barrington house, and of crossing Fifth Avenue with Pauline to avoid running into Otto Preminger. John Bennet, one of her later editors at *The New Yorker*, recalled her constant fussing over revisions. ("It's a piece of crap, but maybe I can do something with it.") Jonathan Demme, Marcia Nasatir, and an obviously shaken David Edelstein all took their turns at the podium. Malko read a brief note from Anne Wallach, who was unable to attend the service. And Roy Blount, Jr., read the poem he'd composed for Pauline's birthday, concocting different voices for Pauline and the Almighty.

It had been decided that the last voice should be Pauline's. The lights went down. A series of recordings with Pauline reading from her reviews and talking about the movies were played. The audience sat transfixed, listening to that soft, sensual voice with its rising and falling cadences, its easy western rhythm and accent.

Malko took the stage again. "Pauline really believed all her life that she was lucky to be able to do what she wanted to do," he said. "But we were the lucky ones. Thank you, Pauline."

Then the audience quietly filed out of the theater, as quiet as if they were critics leaving a screening, accompanied by the Baroque music that Pauline loved.

It is always tempting—too tempting—to try to draw great lessons from the lives of those writers whom we have spent a lifetime admiring. As Polly Frost observed, their pull is too powerful: We insist on trying to determine what kind of legacy the person has left, now that she is no longer there to explain the world to us. "Upon sober reflection," said Arlene Croce at Pauline's memorial tribute, "I have to say that I haven't understood anything in this country since—well, since Pauline stopped writing about the movies."

One of the most powerful truths to be gleaned from examining Pauline's life is that it was, throughout its span, a triumph of instinct over an astonishing intellect. Her highly emotional responses to art were what enabled her to make so indelible a mark as a critic. On the surface, it might seem that any critic does the same thing, but it's doubtful that any critic ever had so little barrier between herself and her subject. She connected with film the way a great actor is supposed to connect with his text, and she took her readers to places they never could have imagined a mere movie review could transport them.

To call what she did reviewing, of course, is to trivialize it. She was not writing snappy, easily quoted opinions that would fit neatly into twelve column inches. She brought us into the experience of sitting next to her in a darkened movie theater. She generously shared her passion and knowledge and insights, made us feel that we were a part of the magic and chaos and wreckage unfolding up there on the screen. She made us feel the way we feel during a great performance in the theater—that we're part of what's happening onstage.

Pauline's biggest professional disappointment was that she lived to see the infantilization of the great moviegoing audience she had always dreamed of and believed in. "Now people watch movies so they can stay kids," said her friend Armond White in a 2009 interview. Pauline would have agreed with him. She also would have been shattered to witness the way in which the role of the film critic has been eclipsed—not only by studio marketing practices but even more by the Internet, with its system of validating the critical opinion of anyone who owns a computer.

But Pauline's great victory was that, like a visionary novelist, she widened the scope of her art—she redefined the possibilities of how a critic could think, and how a critic's work might benefit the art form itself. At a certain point she abandoned the idea of writing about anything but the movies. She may have been able to bring her critical gifts to bear on other subjects, and affected us similarly. What mattered most was that she gave completely and exhaustively of herself, until the day came when physically she had nothing left to give. To Ray Sawhill, her reviews weren't pieces of criticism so much as exhilarating pieces of performance art, played out in the pages of *The New Yorker*.

We should be grateful that once she found her subject, she never deserted it, never grew bored with it—the trap that awaits nearly every critic. Her almost childlike optimism about the screen's possibilities, even her unsuccessful time in Hollywood, was an attempt to draw herself closer to her subject. She lived her entire life the way so many of us do only for a brief time as college students, staying up all night in coffee shops with our ragged copies of Henry James and Vladimir Nabokov and Flannery O'Connor, reading and debating, unable, yet, to imagine that we could ever grow weary of the world of books and music and movies and ideas.

Perhaps Pauline's life's work, and the unflagging, joyful energy she brought to it, are best illuminated by a story that Marcia Nasatir loved to tell. It was

September 1971, and the past week had seen the death of Nikita Khrushchev and Richard Nixon's being named *Time*'s Man of the Year; Nasatir's son Seth had just been sent over to Vietnam. Nasatir called Pauline to tell her how overwhelmed she felt by it all.

Pauline listened. There was a momentary silence.

"And to think," Pauline finally said, "there's not even a decent movie to see."

# ACKNOWLEDGMENTS

This book began for me many years ago in Oregon, when I was a seventh-grade student and first came across Pauline Kael's *Kiss Kiss Bang Bang* at the Tillamook County Library. Much of what she said about *Blow-Up* and *Morgan!* and other films of the sixties was lost on me—this kind of movie never made it to the Tillamook Coliseum—but I devoured "Notes on 280 Movies" at the back of the book. Movie criticism to me meant the reviews in *The Oregonian*, written by the local critic, who, I could tell even at that early age, couldn't write. But here was a woman who could—her sentences had such drive and pulse and snap that they took complete hold of me. I found I committed great chunks of them to memory, the way, as a good little schoolboy, you're supposed to memorize "The Rime of the Ancient Mariner" or the prologue to *The Canterbury Tales*. I knew, of course, that at Beaver Elementary School, you couldn't really stand up in the classroom and recite, "Author-director Joseph Mankiewicz's bad taste, exhibited with verve, is more fun than careful, mousy, dehydrated good taste," and not expect your classmates to wonder if you'd lost it. So I kept reading Pauline Kael quietly. This wasn't diligent reading, like my progression through the novels of John Steinbeck. This was impassioned reading.

When I was eighteen, my parents gave me a subscription to *The New Yorker*, and all through college—the late 1970s and early 1980s, I went to the movies with a kind of breathless excitement; there were very few films that opened in my little college town that I didn't see. And Pauline Kael was my guide. She explained things to me, introduced me to things I hadn't seen, angered me when I thought she'd been unfair or prejudiced. Best of all, by her example, she toughened me up intellectually. I don't know at which point it occurred to me that I really didn't know much about her life, beyond the bare externals that she revealed in interviews—her pride in her West Coast roots, her preference for country living over New York City—but I wondered why, with the unceasing flow of biographies, no one had attempted to write the story of Kael's life. Partly, I found out, it was because she had consistently discouraged any such attempts. She had memorably stated her position in the introduction to her final published collection, *For Keeps*, in 1994: "I'm frequently asked why I don't write my memoirs. I think I have." I took her point. Pauline's life was not a highly dramatic or even a particularly eventful one in terms of marriages and love affairs. I discovered to my surprise that she had not traveled widely, and that her curiosity had been unflagging but in some ways oddly limited. Her life had been consumed by reading and going to the movies and writing about them. Still, she had known many important and gifted people in both the moviemaking and literary worlds, and she had lived through, responded to, and influenced some very exciting times. Maybe her life wouldn't make a book that was chock-full of thrilling events. But I was sure there was a way to show how her life was really a spectacular playing out of her own artistic enthusiasms, to show how she interacted with the changing world of movies.

There were a few disappointments along the way. I sought the cooperation of Pauline's daughter, Gina James. She promised she would give the matter serious thought, but eventually decided against participating in any way. She was a kind and friendly presence on the other end of the phone, however, and to my knowledge she has not done anything to stand in the way of the book. For that I am grateful to her.

The majority of Pauline's friends wanted to talk about her, wanted to talk about what she had brought into their lives, and what they missed about her now that she was gone.

Much of my central research was conducted at Pauline's archive at the Lilly Library at Indiana University, Bloomington. This is a wonderful institution I have made use of while working on earlier books, and I am grateful to the Lilly's courteous, efficient, supportive staff. For someone who claimed she didn't want a biography written, Pauline preserved much of her past meticulously. My thanks to Indiana University for giving it such a good home, and for maintaining it so well.

As I delved into the film history of the 1960s and '70s, I spent countless hours at the Lincoln Center Library for the Performing Arts. Once again, I am grateful to the library's helpful staff.

I also undertook crucial research at Berkeley University; the California State Historical Society; the Film and Television Archives of the University of California at Los Angeles; Boston University's Howard Gotlieb Archival Research Center (special thanks to Vita Paladino and Sean Noel); the Jewish Museum of New York City; Hampshire College; Kent State University (which houses the James Broughton collection); the Margaret Herrick Library of the Motion Picture Academy of Arts and Sciences, Pacifica Radio Archive; the New York Public Library (which houses the archives of *The New Yorker*); the Paley Center for Media; the Petaluma Historical Library and Museum; Petaluma Regional Library; the Harry Ransom Humanities Research Collection at the University of Texas, Austin (particularly for use of the Robert Mills Collection); the San Francisco Public Library; the Sonoma County Library; Special Collections at Stanford University (the

William Abrahams papers); the University of Oregon Libraries; Yale University's Sterling Memorial Library (the Dwight Macdonald collection) and Beinecke Rare Book and Manuscripts Library.

For assistance with my research, I am grateful to Mara Caden, Jean M. Cannon, Rebecca Feldhaus, Sonia Finley, Tristan Kraft, Beth Higgins, Craig Simpson, Shannon Sullivan, and Tracy Turner.

For me, the best part of preparing to write a biography is the chance to interview the people who knew the subject. Deepest gratitude to those who took the time to speak with me: Richard Albarino, Rutanya Alda, David Young Allen, Linda Allen, Nancy Allen, Kathryn Altman, Robert Altman, David Ansen, Rene Auberjonois, Bruce Baillie, Bob Balaban, Carroll Ballard, Allen Barra, Sue Barton, Jeanine Basinger, Thomas Baum, Jane Beirn, Sandra Berwind, Marion Billings, Alan Blackman, Roy Blount, Jr., Peter Bogdanovich, Patricia Bosworth, Chris Bram, Harry Breitrose, Meredith Brody, Albert Brooks, Marjorie Broughton, Hilda Burton, Ernest Callenbach, Dyan Cannon, Joel Canarroe, Carol Carey, Kathleen Carroll, Veronica Cartwright, Charles Champlin, Carol Channing, Daryl Chin, Richard Christiansen, George Christy, Paul Coates, Judith Crist, Patrick Crow, Richard Daniels, Francis Davis, David Del Tredici, Dennis Delrogh, Erhard Dortmund, Trent Duffy, Karen Durbin, David Edelstein, Barbara Feldon, Suzanne Finstad, Jack Foley, William Friedkin, Warner Friedman, Polly Frost, Robert Getchell, Owen Gleiberman, Bruce Goldstein, Sydney Goldstein, Ricky Ian Gordon, Elliott Gould, Bob Greensfelder, John Guare, Donald Gutierrez, James Harvey, Buck Henry, Hal Hinson, Rebecca Hughes, Tresa Hughes, Joseph Hurley, James Ivory, Lamont Johnson, Simon Johnson, Howard Kaminsky, Kenneth Kann, Judy Karasik, Philip Kaufman, Marthe Keller, Howard Kissel, Shirley Knight, Jane Kramer, Richard Kramer, Stephen Kresge, Edward Landberg, David Littlejohn, George Litto, Becket Logan, Phillip Lopate, Tom Luddy, Sidney Lumet, Nick Macdonald, Elizabeth Macklin, George and Elizabeth Malko, Tom Mankiewicz, Jaime Manrique, Greil Marcus, Paul Mazursky, Patrick McGilligan, Sheila McGrath, Daniel Menaker, Sally Ann Mock, Joseph Morgenstern, Michael Murphy, Linda Olle, Ariel Parkinson, Pat Patterson, James Pegolotti, James Pritchard, Joe Regan, Alan Rich, Carrie Rickey, Janna Ritz, Dan Rosenblatt, Lillian Ross, Dana Salisbury, Alvin Sargent, Andrew Sarris, Ray Sawhill, Paul Schrader, Lorenzo Semple, Jr., Charles Simmons, John Simon, Joel Singer, Hoyt Spelman, Michael Sragow, Sam Staggs, Nancy Steinbeck, Howard Suber, Dan Talbot, James Tamulis, Charles Taylor, Joan Tewkesbury, David Thomson, James Toback, Lee Tsiantis, Carol Van Strum, Steve Van Strum, Steve Vineberg, Bret Wallach, Jessica Walter, Armond White, William Whitworth, Frederick Wiseman, James Wolcott, Colin Young, Stephanie Zacharek, and Kenneth Ziffren.

Thanks to Ann Bassart, who allowed me to look over Pauline's former home on Oregon Street in Berkeley, my former professors at Oregon State University, Kerry Ahearn and Michael Oriard, to Ron and Howard Mandelbaum at Photofest, Marilyn Horne, and to Linda Allen for her generosity in providing some previously unpublished photos of Pauline. Deepest thanks to Jill Krementz for her amazing generosity.

Many of the movies mentioned here I saw in the 1970s, at the Whiteside and State theaters in Corvallis, Oregon, in the company of my friend Cynthia Peterson. Writing this book has brought back many happy movie-going memories.

For constant support, advice, and encouragement, I thank a wonderful group of friends: Ronald Bowers, Clifford Capone, Bob Demyan, Lauren Flanigan, Craig Haladay, Omus and Jessica Hirshbein, Anne Lawrence, John Manis, Arlo McKinnon, Cheryl McLean, Francesca Mercurio, Steven and Lisa Mercurio, the late Geoff Miller, Eric Myers, David Niedenthal, Patricia O'Connell, Fred Plotkin, Judy Rice, Kathryn Leigh Scott, Helen Sheehy, Michael Slade—and Erik Dahl, whose phone calls are always one of the best parts of the day. And thanks most of all to my partner, Scott Barnes, for his extreme patience and loving presence.

At *Opera News*, my employer for more than twenty years, I have the pleasure of working with a movie-loving editor in chief, F. Paul Driscoll, who was never too busy with his own deadlines and life to offer insightful comments about my work on the book. Thanks also to editorial production coordinator Elizabeth Diggans for her wise judgment and for being the best colleague I've ever had, associate editor Louise T. Guinther for her eagle-eyed copyediting, and art director Greg Downer for his help with photos. Thanks also to Oussama Zahr, Adam Wasserman, Tristan Kraft, Kathy Beekman, Fred Cohn, Susan Albert, and Beth Higgins, for making coming in to work a pleasure, every day.

I am grateful to Viking's Francesca Belanger, Sharon Gonzalez, and Kyle Davis and to the astute copy editor, John McGhee, for the keen attention they have shown to this project.

The best for last. There are two people who have enhanced my professional life in ways I never imagined possible: my inimitable and irreplaceable agent, Edward Hibbert, and one of New York's finest—my editor Rick Kot.

Brian Kellow
New York City
April 2011

# NOTES

INTRODUCTION:

page ix **"too many erotic sequences"**: "The World Looks at Films": *Atlas* (September 1971).

ix **"I certainly did not set out to do a film about incest. . . . But I began exploring"**: *The New York Times*, March 19, 1989.

ix **"not only the prudent, punctilious surface"**: Pauline Kael, "The Current Cinema," *The New Yorker* (October 23, 1971).

ix **"but the volatile and slovenly life underneath"**: Ibid.

ix **"the only shock is the joke"**: Ibid.

x **"the Muhammad Ali of film critics"**: Author interview with Richard Daniels, January 18, 2010.

x **"How many times . . . thirty years"**: Pauline Kael, speech at Oregon State University, April 1976.

xi **"Definitely her engagement was libidinal"**: Author interview with Hal Hinson, July 20, 2009.

xi **"I am the most grateful human being in the world"**: David Frost interview with Joan Crawford, *The David Frost Show*, 1970.


CHAPTER ONE

1 **"Judith Kael resented her lot"**: Author interview with Bret Wallach, September 16, 2009.

1 **"who runs her fingers over books as if they were magic objects"**: Pauline Kael, "The Current Cinema," *The New Yorker* (November 28, 1983).

3 **"affection radiated at about two degrees above absolute zero"**: Author interview with Bret Wallach, September 16, 2009.

4 **"a community of idealists"**: Kenneth L. Kann, *Joe Rappaport: Life of a Jewish Radical* (Philadelphia: Temple University Press, 1981), 178.

4 **"retained a Jewish identity"**: Ibid.

4 **"bore an unmistakable resemblance to the *shtetl*"**: Ibid.

5 **"the one white Jew in Petaluma"**: Ibid.

5 **"she loved to eat and cook"**: Author interview with Stephanie Zacharek, September 4, 2009.

5 **"Such wonderful evenings"**: Kenneth L. Kann, *Comrades and Chicken Ranchers: The Story of a California Jewish Community* (Ithaca, N.Y.: Cornell University Press, 1993), 61.

5 **"Yiddish books—the classical writers, history, politics"**: Ibid.

5 **"We were so eager for the movie to go on"**: Pauline Kael, *The Citizen Kane Book* (New York: Bantam, 1971).

5 the **"Three Amazons"**: Author interview with Dana Salisbury, September 20, 2009.

6 **"only in a vague sort of way,"**: Author interview with Stephanie Zacharek, September 4, 2009.

6 **"Chicken ranching?"**:, Kann, *Comrades and Chicken Ranchers*, 65.
6 **"a celebration and glorification of materialism"**: Kael, *I Lost It at the Movies*, 79.
6 **"not the legendary west"**: Ibid., 82.
7 **"The summer nights arc very long"**: Ibid., 88.
7 **"My father, who was adulterous"**: Ibid., 89.
7 **"He put up everything he had as security"**: Ibid., 65.

## CHAPTER TWO

9 **"Pauline had no patience or even any kind of feeling for her mother"**: Author interview with Dana Salisbury, September 20, 2009.
9 **"these ideas had saved her life"**: Ibid.
9 **"All of us have probably had the feeling"**: Pauline Kael, "The Current Cinema," *The New Yorker* (March 13, 1978).
10 **"The youngest in a large family has a lot of of advantages"**: *Mandate* (May 1983).
10 **"I was quick to understand things"**: Ibid.
11 **"Pauline looked down with such contempt on my aunt Rose"**: Ibid.
12 **"one of the best of the social-protest films"**: Pauline Kael, *5001 Nights at the Movies* (New York: Holt, Rinehart and Winston, 1982), 348.
12 **"How do you live?"**: Howard J. Green and Brown Holmes, screenplay of *I Am a Fugitive from a Chain Gang*, 1932.
12 **"The girls we in the audience loved were delivering wisecracks"**: Leo Lerman, "Pauline Kael Talks About Violence, Sex, Eroticism and Women & Men in the Movies": *Mademoiselle* (July 1972), 15.
12 **"suggested an element of lunacy and confusion in the world"**: Ibid., 16.
13 **"She was crazy, ga-ga, over my dad,"**: Author interview with Janna Ritz, February 5, 2009.
13 **"Though she came from the theatre"**: Kael, *5001 Nights at the Movies*, 403.
13 **"remarkable modernism"**: Ibid.
13 **"an amazing vernacular actress"**: Ibid., 30.
13 **"halfway human"**: Ibid., 599.
14 **"extraordinary sensual presence"**: Ibid., 116.
14 **"shiny and attractive"**: Ibid., 859.
14 **"I don't know of any other scene"**: Kael, *The New Yorker* (November 27, 1971).
15 **"the embodiment of the sensational side of '30s movies"**: Kael, *5001 Nights at the Movies*, 466.
15 **"hypes it with an intensity"**: Kael, *5001 Nights at the Movies*, 170.
15 **"a gooey collection of clichés"**: Ibid., 173.
15 **"slams her way through them in her nerviest style"**: Ibid.
15 **"that made the picture seem almost folk art"**: Pauline Kael, *Kiss Kiss Bang Bang* (Boston: Atlantic–Little, Brown, 1968), 41.
15 **"I think I understand what my father meant"**: Ibid., 43.
16 **"term-paper pomposity"**: *Mandate* (May 1983).
17 **"the English are the inheritors of civilization and style"**: Untitled college paper by Pauline Kael, housed at the Lilly Library, Indiana University.
17 **"immersed in a sensibility"**: *Interview* (April 1989).
18 **"the liveliest of his novels"**: Kael, *The New Yorker* (August 6, 1984).
18 **"a more earthly kind of greatness"**: Ibid.

18 **"the best novel in English about what at the time was called 'the woman question'"**: Ibid.

18 **"She would come in and inspect the cream on my arms"**: *Mandate* (May 1983).

18 **"Oh, that's how to do it"**: *Interview* (April 1989).

19 **"Renoir isn't a sociologist"**: Pauline Kael, *I Lost It at the Movies* (Boston: Atlantic–Little, Brown,1965), 109.

19 **"a triumph of clarity and lucidity"**: Ibid., 110.

19 **"perhaps the most influential of all French films"**: Ibid., 111.

19 **"There was always a circle of people around Pauline"**: *People* (April 18, 1983).

20 **"Sissie Symmes"**: Ekbert Faas, *Young Robert Duncan: Portrait of the Poet as Homosexual in Society* (Santa Barbara: Black Swallow Press, 1983).

20 **"He was attracted to strong-mother-archetype women"**: Author interview with Jack Foley, October 9, 2008.

21 **"Don't be foolish—you don't love me—you will never love me"**: Undated note from Pauline Kael to Robert Duncan, housed at the Lilly Library, Indiana University.

21 **"For Christ's sake be analyzed!"**: Ibid.

21 **"[T]here appears to be nothing between Communist involvement and smug indifference"**: Kael, *The New Yorker* (October 15, 1973).

## CHAPTER THREE

24 **"When I was first told, in 1921"**: R. P. Blackmur, general introduction to *The Wings of the Dove (The Laurel Henry James)* (Dell: New York, 1958).

25 **"a wonderful movie . . . really the most exciting photography"**: Letter from Pauline Kael to Violet Rosenberg, February 10, 1941.

25 **"the most sustained in quality"**: Ibid.

25 **"I'm fairly sure that in the long run it would turn out disastrously"**: Letter from Kael to Rosenberg, March 21, 1941.

26 **"fairly dull"**: Ibid.

26 **"awfully vulgar-funny—really quite something"**: Ibid.

26 **"not too poor"**: Ibid.

26 **"the most beautiful shot of Frances Dee"**: Ibid.

26 **"Communication (orally)"**: Ibid.

26 **"a rather complex essay"**: Ibid.

26 **"We've been working together just about every waking moment"**: Letter from Kael to Rosenberg, May 9, 1941.

26 **"It was tremendous fun"**: *Interview* (April 1989).

27 **"trouble with Bob is he feels guilty"**: Pauline Kael notes, undated.

28 **"I haven't invested a sou in pleasure clothes"**: Letter from Kael to Rosenberg, February 28, 1942.

28 **"look at them all over and feel delighted"**: Ibid.

28 **"a schlock classic"**: Pauline Kael, *5001 Nights at the Movies* (New York: Holt, Rinehart and Winston, 1982), 536.

28 **"special, appealingly schlocky romanticism"**: Ibid., 122.

29 **"patriotic and shiny-faced"**: Studs Terkel, *The Good War* (New York: Pantheon, 1989), 123.

29 **"a heavy confusion of young men"**: Ibid.

30 **"Pleasing news for a change"**: Letter from Kael to Rosenberg, April 15, 1943.

30 **"a modern but not moderne chalet":** John Gruen, *Menotti: A Biography* (New York: Macmillan, 1978), 50.

30 **"One would have to be an imbecile":** Letter from Kael to Rosenberg, February 18, 1944.

30 **"Bob is terribly sweet to me":** Letter from Kael to Rosenberg, October 19, 1943.

31 **"hurried and a little too chic.":** Letter from Kael to Rosenberg, November 5, 1944.

31 **"I am looking forward to a magazine which will stand for the principles":** Letter from Kael to Dwight Macdonald, December 13, 1943.

31 **"who have suffered in modern society persecution, excommunication":** *Politics* (August 1944).

32 **"At least I don't have a fad for *your* music":** Letter from Kael to Rosenberg, undated.

32 **"He has pride and vanity at a maximum":** Ibid.

32 **"I almost feel as if it had become a layer":** Letter from Kael to Rosenberg, 1945.

32 **"masterpiece art":** *Film Comment* (May–June 1977).

32 **"termite art":** Ibid.

32 **"feels its way through walls of particularization":** Ibid.

32 **"I can't see any difference between writing about a porno movie":** Ibid.

33 **"an excited audience is never depressed":** David Parkinson, ed., *The Graham Greene Film Reader: Reviews, Essays, Interviews and Film Stories* (New York: Applause, 1993), xxii.

33 **"amuses but he doesn't excite":** Ibid., xxix.

33 **"Movies are such common and lowly stuff":** *The New Republic* (December 28, 1938).

33 **"the only unaffected trouper in the bunch":** *The New Republic* (September 20, 1939).

34 **"It would have a little more stature as a 'religious' film":** *The Nation* (May 13, 1944).

34 **"It seems to me that she is quite limited":** *The Nation* (April 14, 1945).

35 **"funnier, more adventurous, more intelligent":** *The Nation* (February 5, 1944).

35 **"Yet the more I think about the film":** Ibid.

35 **"Any critic writing for a large publication":** *News Workshop* (June 1954).

36 **"pictures are a great intellectual exercise":** Ibid.

36 **"eastern college people":** Letter from Kael to Rosenberg, November 26, 1945.

36 **"they'll work for almost anything":** Ibid.

CHAPTER FOUR

37 **"I don't think properly on the typewriter":** Letter from Pauline Kael to Violet Rosenberg, undated.

38 **"He offered me three gifts":** James Broughton, *Coming Unbuttoned* (San Francisco: City Lights, 1993), 3–4.

38 **"He looked like he was the concept that Marlowe was working on in *Doctor Faustus*":** Author interview with Ariel Parkinson, November 29, 2009.

39 **"adored babies but disliked children":** James Broughton, *Coming Unbuttoned* (San Francisco: City Lights, 1993), 1.

39 **"She deplored little magazines"**: Broughton, 68.

39 **"She was not sympathetic to avant-garde enterprise"**: Author interview with Ernest Callenbach, September 9, 2008.

39 **"She liked the word 'precious'"**: Author interview with Bruce Baillie, November 5, 2010.

40 **"He 'threw her out'"**: Author interview with Joel Singer May 29, 2008.

40 **"Pauline is Pauline"**: Author interview with Dana Salisbury, September 2009.

40 **"what sounded like such a solid thing"**: Letter from Robert Horan to Pauline Kael, undated.

40 **"excepting the fact"**: Letter from Horan to Kael, July 25, 1949.

40 **"When it happens to you"**: Author interview with Meredith Brody, February 28, 20 11.

41 **"The pictures of Gina are a delight"**: Letter from Horan to Kael, July 25, 1949.

41 **"I'm Gina!" "I'm a baby!"**: Gina James's baby book, May–June 1950, housed at the Lilly Library, Indiana University.

41 **"a farce for people who read and write"**: *Orpheus in Sausalito*, play by Pauline Kael, housed at Lilly Library.

41 **"The world doesn't find you"**: Ibid.

42 **"There is not an unintelligent line in** *The* [sic] *Shadow of a Man***"**: *The Santa Barbara Star*, November 2, 1950.

42 **"brash, confident, pugnacious"**: Original screen story by Pauline Kael, *The Brash Young Man*, housed at the Lilly Library.

42 **"He became modest and shy"**: Ibid.

42 **"Mr. Benjamin Burl's infatuation"**: Ibid.

43 **"no"**: Ibid.

43 **"about the substance and quality of a slick-paper magazine story"**: Columbia Pictures reader report on *The Brash Young Man*, housed at the Lilly Library.

43 **"its first best chance would be with the magazines"**: Ibid.

44 **"I was never hungry in my life"**: Author interview with Warner Friedman, May 12, 2009.

44 **"You never were?"**: Ibid.

45 **"When** *Shoeshine* **opened in 1947"**: Pauline Kael, *I Lost It at the Movies* (Boston: Atlantic–Little, Brown,1965), 114.

46 **"somewhat segmented art-film audience"**: *City Lights*, winter 1953.

46 **"When the mass audience becomes convinced"**: Ibid.

46 **"The Chaplin of** *Limelight* **is no irreverent little clown"**: Ibid.

46 **"surely the richest hunk of self-gratification"**: Ibid.

46 **"My dear, you are a true artist"**: Ibid.

46 **"The camera emphasis on Chaplin's eyes"**: Ibid.

## CHAPTER FIVE

48 **"The new wide screen surrounds us"**: Pauline Kael, *I Lost It at the Movies* (Boston: Atlantic–Little, Brown, 1965), 323–24.

48 **"When Senator McCarthy identifies himself"**: Ibid., 328.

49 **"the type of thing I have been trying to get hold of for a long time"**: Letter from Penelope Houston to Pauline Kael, July 23, 1954.

50 **"What keeps** *you* **going?"**: Pauline Kael, "The Current Cinema," *The New Yorker* (July 4, 2005).

51 **"She was the closest thing to somebody who had my kind of vision about movies":** Author interview with Edward Landberg, May 24, 2008.

51 **"I hadn't written notes":** Ibid.

52 **"There was a little resistance to the notion":** Author interview with Stephen Kresge, June 15, 2008.

52 **"one of the first imaginative approaches to the musical as a film form":** Pauline Kael, Berkeley Cinema Guild notes for *Sous les toits de Paris.*

52 **"not really so 'great' as its devotees claim":** Kael, Berkeley Cinema Guild notes for *Red River.*

52 **"My parents hardly ever went to the movies":** Author interview with Carol van Strum, February 11, 2010.

53 **"They were doing it":** Ibid.

53 **"Landberg was very remote":** Author interview with Ariel Parkinson, November 29, 2009.

54 **"We were married for something like a year":** Author interview with Edward Landberg, May 24, 2008.

54 **"Pauline and Ed Landberg came for dinner one night":** Author interview with Ariel Parkinson, November 29, 2009.

54 **"I soon found out that I couldn't stand this woman":** Author interview with Edward Landberg, May 24, 2008.

55 **"Like a public building designed to satisfy the widest public's concept of grandeur":** "Movies, the Desperate Art," Daniel Talbot, ed., *Film: An Anthology* (Berkeley: University of California Press, 1959), 52.

55 **"about as magical as a Fitzpatrick travelogue":** Ibid.

55 **"protagonists in any meaningful sense":** Ibid., 65.

56 **"been quick to object to a film with a difficult theme":** Ibid., 57.

56 **"She was one of the most ethical people I ever knew":** Author interview with David Young Allen, September 9, 2009.

57 **"Cinema Studio and Guild!":** Remarks by Gina James, memorial tribute to Pauline Kael, November 30, 2001.

57 **"Her mind was always moving five times faster":** Author interview with Donald Gutierrez, July 21, 2009.

57 **"She had a motherly side":** Author interview with Ernest Callenbach, September 9, 2008.

58 **"She started damning his poems":** Author interview with Donald Gutierrez, July 21, 2009.

59 **"Her attention to Gina would go on and off like a searchlight":** Author interview with Stephen Kresge, June 15, 2008.

60 **"Does a poet edit his own poetry?":** Ibid.

60 **"She was overwhelmed in his presence":** Ibid.

60 **"She got Gina and me out of the house":** Author interview with David Young Allen, September 9, 2009.

## CHAPTER SIX

61 **"She was kind of a champion of mine":** Author interview with Alan Rich, February 21, 2009.

61 **"I remember running into Pauline on Telegraph Avenue":** Ibid.

63 **"I would like to suggest that the educated audience":** Pauline Kael, *I Lost It at the Movies* (Atlantic–Little, Brown, 1965), 31.

63 **"large generalizations in order to be suggestive":** Ibid., 31.

63 "incense burning": Ibid., 32.

63 "audiences of social workers": Ibid., 34.

63 "It is a depressing fact": Ibid., 41.

64 "The codes of civilized living ": Ibid., 129–130.

64 "a study of the human condition at the higher social and economic levels": Ibid., 148.

65 "cinematic masterpiece": Ibid., 142.

65 "The irony of this hyped-up, slam-bang production": Ibid., 143, 146.

65 "overwrought, tasteless, and offensive": Ibid., 150.

65 "irresistible evocation of the mood of Mark Twain": Ibid., 150.

66 "The injustice of it is almost perfect": John Osborne and Nigel Kneale, screenplay of *Look Back in Anger*, 1959.

66 "a conventional weakling": Kael, *I Lost It at the Movies*, 68.

66 "about the failures of men and women": Ibid., 69.

67 "Aren't we supposed to feel sorry for these girls": Ibid., 176.

67 "very expansive guy": Author interview with Bob Greensfelder, October 3, 2008.

67 "sleepy and bored": Pauline Kael, KPFA broadcast, November 22, 1961.

68 "the most simple and traditional and graceful of all modern Westerns": Pauline Kael, *5001 Nights at the Movies* (New York: Holt, Rinehart and Winston, 1982), 629.

69 "interviews with Quakers and Unitarians": Pauline Kael, KPFA broadcast, December 8, 1962.

69 "Do you really want to be endlessly confirmed": Ibid.

69 "And you I suppose": Ibid.

69 "a million words delivered without remuneration is a rather major folly": Kael, KPFA broadcast, March 27, 1963.

69 "if KPFA is not a station": Ibid.

70 "although some of her charges made that an attractive possibility": Letter from Trevor Thomas to KPFA subscribers, April 17, 1963.

70 "Despite your implacable harassment of me in print": Letter from Dwight Macdonald to Pauline Kael, November 27, 1963.

70 "one of the best I've read": Ibid.

70 "the most urgent task for American film criticism . . . a rationale for . . . Critical practice": Letter from Dwight Macdonald to John Simon Guggenheim Foundation, November 27, 1963.

70 "cinema has become": Ibid.

70 "Miss Kael has little income independent from what she earns by her pen": Ibid.

71 "She had a style that appealed to a lot of people:": Author interview with John Simon, March 6, 2008.

71 "Her main trouble was, of course": Ibid.

71 "She felt that it would make me more important than I am": Ibid.

71 "marvelous ambiguity and split in the content": Pauline Kael, panel discussion at Donnell Library, September 1963.

71 "enjoying Hud's anarchism": Ibid.

71 "That's sociology": Ibid.

71 "I am worried about Pauline Kael's position": Ibid.

72 "to assuage their own boredom": Ibid.

72 "I've never been bored, John": Ibid.

72 "wants to be a great film—it cries out its intentions": Pauline Kael, *I Lost It at the Movies*, 192.

72 "surprisingly like the confectionary dreams": Ibid., 263.
72 "And isn't it rather adolescent to treat the failure of love with such solemnity?": Ibid., 184.
72 "For whom does love last?": Ibid.
73 "Pauline had her blind spots": Author interview with Colin Young, June 12, 2009.

## CHAPTER SEVEN

75 "The strong director imposes his own personality": Andrew Sarris, *The American Cinema: Directors and Directions, 1929–1968* (New York: E. P. Dutton), 31.
75 "Ultimately, the auteur theory": Ibid., 30.
76 "If I had not been aware of Walsh": Gerald Mast and Marshall Cohen, eds., *Film Theory and Criticism* (New York: Oxford University Press, 1979), 665.
76 "Would Sarris not notice the repetition": Pauline Kael, *I Lost It at the Movies* (Boston: Atlantic–Little, Brown, 1965), 294.
76 "The greatness of critics like Bazin in France": Ibid., 295.
76 "technical competence": Ibid.
76 "The greatness of a director like Cocteau": Ibid., 296.
76 "the distinguishable personality of the director as a criterion of value": Ibid.
76 "The smell of a skunk": Ibid., 297.
77 "because Hitchcock repeats": Ibid.
77 "not so much a personal style as a personal theory of audience psychology": Ibid., 298.
77 "interior meaning": Ibid., 302.
77 "extrapolated from the tension": Ibid., 302.
77 "the opposite of what we have always taken for granted in the arts": Ibid.
77 "Their ideal auteur is the man who signs a long-term contract": Ibid.
77 "I suspect that the 'stylistic consistency'": Ibid., 306.
78 "What's the matter?": Author interview with Andrew Sarris, February 17, 2009.
78 "She was always on the boil": Ibid.
78 "I wasn't as worldly and aggressive": Ibid.
78 "Pauline acted as if I were a great menace of American criticism": Ibid.
78 "attack on the theory received more publicity": Sarris, *The American Cinema*, 26.

## CHAPTER EIGHT

80 "Growing numbers of middle-class consumers": Todd Gitlin, *The Sixties: Years of Hope, Days of Rage* (New York: Bantam, 1987), 16.
80 "The rock 'n' roll generation": Ibid., 6.
81 "The Associated Press picked up the editorial": Author interview with Judith Crist, July 17, 2008.
82 "*The Group* is the book that Mary McCarthy's admirers have been waiting for": Pauline Kael, unpublished review of *The Group*, September 1963.
83 "rather fruitless to care so much about how fairly": Letter from Elizabeth Hardwick to Pauline Kael, September 14, 1963.

83 **"the general recommendations which are truly not too radical":** Letter from Peter Davison to Pauline Kael, July 16, 1964.
83 **"some of the very best pieces were marred by being too long":** Ibid.
84 **"It's *all right*, I want to say":** Eudora Welty, "Is Phoenix Jackson's Grandson Really Dead?," *Critical Inquiry* (September 1974), 220.
84 **"were restless and talkative":** Pauline Kael, *I Lost It at the Movies* (Boston: Atlantic–Little, Brown, 1965), 15.
84 **"accepts lack of clarity":** Ibid.
85 **"boob who attacks ambiguity and complexity":** Ibid.
85 **"more and more people":** Ibid.
85 **"There are very few American film critics":** *Library Journal*, undated review.
85 **"the artistry, literacy, fine style and clearheaded reasoning":** *Publishers Weekly*, undated review.
85 **"Never dull, blazingly personal, provokingly penetrating":** *Kirkus Reviews*, undated review.
85 **"I am not certain just what Miss Kael thinks she lost at the movies":** *The New York Times Book Review*, March 14, 1965.
86 **"the surest instinct":** Ibid.
86 **"That she is able to analyze":** Ibid.
86 **"always gratifying when a friend":** Letter from James Broughton to Pauline Kael, April 2, 1965.
86 **"My good wishes to you and Gina":** Ibid.
86 **"Billy dear":** Various correspondence from Pauline Kael to William Abrahams.
86 **"I don't really want to do it":** Letter from Pauline Kael to Robert Mills, February 9, 1965.
87 **"I think there was a moment":** Author interview with David Young Allen, September 2, 2009.
87 **"I know you love California":** Author interview with Dan Talbot, October 7, 2008.
87 **"the cover seems to illustrate the title":** Letter from Robert Mills to Marcia Nasatir, November 8, 1965.
87 **"In the evenings, especially, Bob and Pauline drank and talked":** Author interview with Tresa Hughes, September 20, 2009.
88 **"People shouldn't marry you":** Play by Pauline Kael, *Wearing the Quick Away*, housed at the Lilly Library, Indiana University.
88 **"how my thumbnails got worn down":** "It's Only a Movie": speech by Pauline Kael given at Dartmouth College, October 1965.
89 **"goes against the grain":** Ibid.
89 **"a world more exciting":** Ibid.
89 **"something we wanted":** Ibid.
89 **"Surely only social deviates":** Ibid.
89 **"large-scale campaigns designed to cut him down":** Pauline Kael, *Kiss Kiss Bang Bang* (Boston: Atlantic–Little, Brown, 1968), 191.
89 **"His greatness is in a range that is too disturbing":** Ibid., 195.
89 **"still the most exciting American actor on the screen":** Ibid.
90 **"The only thing she was really lacking":** Author interview with Sidney Lumet, February 13, 2009.
90 **"rather brusque and strict":** Author interview with Shirley Knight, February 21, 2009.

90  **"I remember doing so many takes"**: Author interview with Jessica Walter, March 30. 2009.

90  **"He'll do a bunch of takes"**: Author interview with Shirley Knight, February 21, 2009.

91  **"We had a good dinner and a lot to drink"**: Author interview with Sidney Lumet, February 13, 2009.

91  **"My job"**: Ibid.

91  **"I thought, this is a very dangerous person"**: Ibid.

91  **"changed the way their readers viewed the world"**: Marc Weingarten, *The Gang That Wouldn't Write Straight* (New York: Crown, 2005), 7.

92  **"What really offended me"**: Author interview with Sidney Lumet, February 13, 2009.

92  **"he would not try to reshape the scenario"**: Kael, *Kiss Kiss Bang Bang*, 71.

92  **"I had heard it was going to be butchery"**: Author interview with Sidney Lumet, February 13, 2009.

CHAPTER NINE

93  **"Appreciation courses have paralyzed reactions"**: Pauline Kael, *McCall's* (February 1966).

93  **"rather like watching an old movie"**: Pauline Kael, *McCall's* (March 1966), 24.

94  **"stately, respectable and dead"**: Pauline Kael, *McCall's* (April 1966), 36.

94  **"watching a giant task of stone masonry"**: Ibid.

94  **"that will probably have to bankrupt several studios before a halt is called"**: Ibid.

95  **"the single most repressive"**: Pauline Kael, *McCall's* (May 1966).

95  **"You begin to feel"**: Ibid.

95  **"The reviews became less and less appropriate"**: *Newsweek* (May 30, 1966).

95  **"What would you like us to do with all this money?"**: Letter from Robert Mills to Pauline Kael, June 7, 1966.

96  **"ploddingly intelligent and controlled"**: Pauline Kael, *Kiss Kiss Bang Bang* (Boston: Atlantic–Little, Brown, 1968), 132.

96  **"I could hardly get a word in edgewise"**: Author interview with Joseph Morgenstern, May 8, 2009.

97  **"a modernized version of an earlier, romantic primitivist notion"**: Kael, *Kiss Kiss Bang Bang*, 20.

97  **"so appealing to college students"**: Ibid., 22.

97  **"And if it be said that this is sociology"**: Ibid.

97  **"could find good use for another one or two hundred dollars a check"**: Letter from Robert Mills to Robert Evett, December 12, 1966.

97  **"Judy Crist!"**: Author interview with Judith Crist, June 10, 2008.

98  **"Your agent was right"**: Ibid.

98  **"She wanted to explain to me"**: Ibid.

98  **"the fervor and astonishing speed"**: Kael, *Kiss Kiss Bang Bang*, 32.

99  **"the casting superb and the performance beautiful"**: Ibid., 200.

99  **"the best of Griffith, John Ford"**: Ibid.

99  **"And Welles—the one great creative force in American films in our time"**: Ibid.

99  **"movies made by a generation bred on movies"**: Kael, *Kiss Kiss Bang Bang*, 115.

101 **"a cheap piece of bald-faced slapstick"**: *The New York Times*, August 7, 1967.
101 **"How do you make a good movie in this country without being jumped on?"**: Pauline Kael, "The Current Cinema," *The New Yorker* (October 21, 1967).
102 **"they were able to use the knowledge"**: Ibid.
102 **"*Bonnie and Clyde* keeps the audience in a kind of eager, nervous imbalance"**: Ibid.
102 **"Audiences at *Bonnie and Clyde* are not given a simple, secure basis for identification"**: Ibid.
102 **"The trouble with the violence in most films"**: *The New York Times*, September 17, 1967.
102 **"the whole point of *Bonnie and Clyde* is to rub our noses in it"**: Kael, *The New Yorker* (October 21, 1967).
103 **"*Bonnie and Clyde* as a danger to public morality"**: Ibid.
103 **"it has put the sting back into death"**: Ibid.

## CHAPTER TEN

105 **"You cannot keep *The New Yorker* out of the hands"**: Ben Yagoda, *About Town: The New Yorker and the World it Made* (New York: Scribner, 2000), 59.
106 **"William Shawn respected, admired, and enjoyed the movie reviews of John McCarten and Brendan Gill"**: Author interview with Lillian Ross, August 1, 2009.
107 **"It was totally fictitious"**: Author interview with John Simon, March 6, 2008.
107 **"The only thing she wanted me to do"**: Ibid.
107 **"I think a certain Anglophilia crept into it very early on"**: Marc Smirnoff, *The Oxford American* (Spring 1992), reprinted in *Conversations with Pauline Kael*, Will Brantley, ed. (Jackson: University Press of Mississippi, 1996), 157.
108 **"Mr. Shawn was always polite and courteous"**: Author interview with Jane Beirn, February 20, 2009.
109 **"seemed to seek combat"**: Author interview with Lillian Ross, August 1, 2009.
109 **"*The New Yorker* has a long-standing tradition of squalor"**: Ved Mehta, *Remembering Mr. Shawn's New Yorker: The Invisible Art of Editing* (Woodstock, N.Y.: Overlook, 1998), 111.
109 **"The emotional shorthand of television"**: Pauline Kael, "The Current Cinema," *The New Yorker* (March 16, 1968).
110 **"presence is so strong "**: Kael, *The New Yorker* (March 30, 1968).
110 **"this fag phantom of the opera"**: Ibid.
111 **"Does playing a homosexual paralyze him as an actor?"**: Kael, *The New Yorker* (January 18, 1969).
111 **"There is something ludicrous and at the same time poignant"**: Ibid.
112 **"a volatile mixture of fictional narrative"**: Kael, *The New Yorker* (April 6, 1968).
112 **"less a document of Maoist thought"**: Richard Brody, *Everything Is Cinema: The Working Life of Jean-Luc Godard*, (New York: Henry Holt, 2008), 306.
112 **"We all know that an artist can't discover anything for himself"**: Kael, *The New Yorker* (April 6, 1968).
112 **"funny, and they're funny in a new way"**: Ibid.
112 **"probably never have a popular, international success"**: Kael, *The New Yorker* (October 5, 1968).
113 **"a great original work"**: Ibid.

113 **"perhaps the briefest statement "**: Pauline Kael, *Kiss Kiss Bang Bang* (Boston: Atlantic–Little Brown, 1968), introduction.

113 **"Katharine Hepburn is probably the greatest actress of the sound era"**: Ibid., 353.

114 **"she-Shaw of the movies"**: *Newsweek* (May 20, 1968).

114 **"blessedly brilliant"**: Ibid.

114 **"If Miss Kael has a particular bent as a film critic"**: *The New York Times Book Review*, May 5, 1968.

114 **"going great guns at the moment"**: Letter from William Abrahams to Robert Mills, June 6, 1968.

115 **"the best film critic since Agee"**: Letter from Louise Brooks to Pauline Kael, May 26, 1962.

115 **"You could have knocked me over with Audrey Hepburn"**: Letter to Pauline Kael from Louise Brooks, September 13, 1968.

115 **"Going through the index "**: Ibid.

115 **"Your picture on the dust cover "**: Ibid.

115 **"In life . . . fantastically gifted people"**: Kael, *The New Yorker* (September 28, 1968).

115 **"It has been commonly said . . . that the musical *Funny Girl*"**: Ibid.

115 **"Most Broadway musicals are dead"**: Ibid.

116 **"She is not quite up to the task"**: *The New York Morning Telegraph*, September 20, 1968.

116 **"The one thing you cannot fault her with is that she is unique"**: Ibid.

116 **"She simply drips as unself-consciously"**: Kael, *The New Yorker* (September 28, 1968).

117 **"Glamour is what Julie Andrews doesn't have"**: Kael, *The New Yorker* (October 26, 1968).

117 **"merely coarsen[ed] her shining nice-girl image"**: Ibid.

117 **"When an actress has been a star for a long time"**: Kael, *The New Yorker* (November 9, 1968).

118 **"She hated that kind of thing"**: Author interview with Jane Kramer, February 24, 2009.

118 **"there was a always a fair amount of drama in getting the copy out of Penelope Gilliatt"**: Author interview with Jane Beirn, February 20, 2009.

119 **"Gina was a lovely girl"**: Author interview with Tresa Hughes, September 20, 2009.

119 **"I think she had more of a sense of fellowship and community on the West Coast"**: Ibid.

119 **"Brian would say, 'I've got only three three minutes of film'"**: Author interview with Rutanya Alda, April 26, 2009.

120 **"I did my own share of soul-wrestling"**: *Interview* (April 1989).

120 **"a direct and lucid movie"**: Kael, *The New Yorker* (December 28, 1968).

120 **"almost magical lack of surprise"**: Ibid.

120 **"In film, concentrating on a few elements gives those elements such importance"**: Ibid.

121 **"She was sore because she was only paid half a salary"**: Author interview with Jane Kramer, February 24, 2009.

122 **"There is so much talk now about the art of the film"**: *Harper's* (February 1969).

122 **"because it's smart in a lot of ways that better-made pictures aren't"**: Ibid.

122 **"But they are almost the maximum of what we're now getting from American movies"**: Ibid.

122 **"At the movies we want a different kind of truth"**: Ibid.

122 **"connects with their lives in an immediate"**: Ibid.

123 **"I don't trust anyone who doesn't admit"**: Ibid.

123 **"obscenely self-important"**: Ibid.

123 **"a celebration of cop-out"**: Ibid.

123 **"to think of himself as a myth-maker"**: Ibid.

123 **"Trash has given us an appetite for art"**: Ibid.

123 **"She's such a sweet girl"**: Tagline for *Pretty Poison*.

124 **"When I discovered that *Pretty Poison* had opened without advance publicity or screenings"**: Kael, *The New Yorker* (November 2, 1968).

124 **"When she was on somebody's side"**: Author interview with Lorenzo Semple, Jr., October 5, 2008.

124 **"I'm going to bring a friend along"**: Ibid.

124 **"a habit of hers when she went out to dinner"**: Ibid.

125 **"the spray of venom"**: Pauline Kael, "The Current Cinema," *The New Yorker* (September 27, 1969).

125 **"grotesque shock effects"**: Ibid.

125 **"the simple, *Of Mice and Men* kind of relationship at the heart of it"**: Ibid.

126 **"What is new about *Easy Rider*"**: Ibid.

127 **"a basic decency and intelligence in his work"**: Ibid.

127 **"really seem to have the style for anything"**: Ibid.

127 **"facetious Western"**: Ibid.

127 **"destroys one's sense of mood and time and place"**: *Life* (October 24, 1969).

127 **"The dialogue is all banter"**: Kael, *The New Yorker* (September 27, 1969).

127 **"Listen, you miserable bitch"**: Letter from George Roy Hill to Pauline Kael, September 26, 1969.

128 **"Americans talk a lot about marital infidelity"**: Columbia Pictures publicity handout, *Bob & Carol & Ted & Alice*.

128 **"I felt obliged to note that I did not believe"**: New York *Daily News*, October 6, 1969.

128 **"When it was offered to me"**: Author interview with Elliott Gould, June 13, 2009.

128 **"unpleasant"**: *The New York Times*, September 17, 1969.

128 **"I read Canby's review"**: Author interview with Paul Mazursky, September 2, 2009.

129 **"*Bob & Carol & Ted & Alice* is a slick, whorey movie"**: Kael, *The New Yorker* (October 4, 1969).

129 **"taken the series of revue sketches"**: Ibid.

129 **"looks a bit like Lauren Bacall and a bit like Jeanne Moreau"**: Ibid.

129 **"Someone tapped me on the shoulder from behind"**: Author interview with Dyan Cannon, June 13, 2009.

129 **"probably the most sophisticated intelligence"**: Kael, *The New Yorker* (October 18, 1969).

129 **"the most insidious kind of enemy"**: Ibid.

129 **"*High School* is so familiar"**: Ibid.

130 **"Many of us grow to hate documentaries"**: Ibid.

130 **"Joe is a very soft-spoken, kind guy":** Author interview with Frederick Wiseman, October 8, 2008.

130 **"The impression I had was that she felt I didn't need her":** Ibid.

130 **"Dear Sir: I think I've figured it out":** Letter from Cornelius Freeman to *The New Yorker*, November 28, 1969.

130 **"There was a time":** Letter from Leslie E. Jones to *The New Yorker*, November 1969.

130 **"They're looking for 'truth'":** Kael, *The New Yorker* (September 27, 1969).

131 **"Grim":** Author interview with Carrie Rickey, May 9, 2009.

131 **"How're you going to feed it?":** James Poe and Robert E. Thompson, screenplay of *They Shoot Horses, Don't They?*, 1969.

131 **"I'm tired of losing!":** Ibid.

131 **"She doesn't try to save some ladylike part of herself":** Kael, *The New Yorker* (December 20, 1969).

132 **"a good chance of personifying American tensions":** Ibid.

132 **"Somewhere along the line":** Kael, *The New Yorker* (January 3, 1970).

132 **"is alive to":** Ibid.

132 **"to be liberated from period clothes":** Ibid.

132 **"not using decadence as a metaphor for Naziism":** Ibid.

132 **"Visconti, though drawn to excess":** Ibid.

132 **"I have rarely seen a picture I enjoyed less":** Ibid.

133 **"a B-25 pilot":** Twentieth Century–Fox publicity handout, *M*A*S*H*.

133 **"Bob had gotten fired from Warners":** Author interview with George Litto, June 4, 2010.

133 **"Did you hear that?":** Author interview with Rene Auberjonois, September 2, 2009.

133 **"He was referring to a conversation":** Ibid.

134 **"I remember the sound engineer":** Ibid.

134 **"Donald Sutherland and I became very close during the process":** Author interview with Elliott Gould, June 13, 2009.

135 **"We were completely under the radar":** Author interview with Rene Auberjonois, September 2, 2009.

135 **"This picture wasn't released—it escaped":** Robert Altman, interview for Twentieth Century–Fox DVD release, *M*A*S*H*.

135 **"a marvelously unstable comedy":** Kael, *The New Yorker* (January 24, 1970).

135 **"competence is one of the values the movie respects":** Ibid.

135 **"I've rarely heard four-letter words used so exquisitely well":** Ibid.

135 **"When the dialogue overlaps":** Ibid.

135 **"Many of the best recent American movies leave you feeling":** Ibid.

136 **"His pictures showed life taking its course":** Author interview with Elliott Gould, June 13, 2009.

136 **"After so many movies that come on strong":** Kael, *The New Yorker* (March 4, 1970).

136 **"Pauline Kael is my favorite movie critic":** *The New York Times*, undated.

137 **"While I miss the polemics":** Ibid.

137 **"One doesn't want to talk about how Tolstoi got his effects":** Pauline Kael, "Trash, Art and the Movies": *Harper's* (February 1969).

137 **"By neglecting to analyze technique":** *The New York Times Book Review*, February 22, 1970.

137 **"About film art":** Ibid.

137 **"In her youth, as the author avows":** Ibid.

139 **"I never adapted to New York":** *People* (April 18, 1983).
139 **"for her film criticism":** Citation from the American Academy of Arts and Letters and the National Institute of Arts and Letters, May 26, 1970.
140 **"Gimme a P, Gimme a G":** Letter from Michael B. Pulman, Department of History, Florida State University, to *The New Yorker*, May 23, 1971.
140 **"could focus under the most intense sedation—alcohol":** Author interview with Jane Kramer, February 24, 2009.
141 **"My sense was that they stayed out of each other's way almost intentionally":** Ibid.
141 **"My personal feeling—more than personally—is that Pauline did not have any respect, particularly, for Penelope":** Author interview with Sally Ann Mock, February 27, 2009.

## CHAPTER TWELVE

143 **"there was an obvious hunger for film":** Toby Talbot, *The New Yorker Theater and Other Scenes from a Life at the Movies* (New York: Columbia University Press, 2009), 53.
144 **"at one end of the table were the intellectuals":** Author interview with Judith Crist, July 17, 2008.
144 **"I always felt that there was an assumption":** Author interview with Kathleen Carroll, February 25, 2009.
144 **"Headliners and by-liners help us do the job":** *The New York Times*, September 15, 1968.
145 **"I have slept through more productions of this dated play":** New York *Daily News*, June 1, 1973.
145 **"Well, when he shows up at screenings":** Author interview with Judith Crist, July 17, 2008.
146 **"Pauline! Of course, *you* come to all the finest pictures":** Author interview with John Simon, March 6, 2008.
146 **"There were a lot of directors":** Author interview with Paul Schrader, August 31, 2009.
146 **"It used to be that understood that no matter how low your estimate of the public intelligence was":** Pauline Kael, "The Current Cinema," *The New Yorker* (October 3, 1970).
147 **"no contemporary American subject provided a better test of the new movie freedom than student unrest":** Ibid.
147 **"the recently developed political consciousness":** Ibid.
147 **"slanted to feed the paranoia of youth":** Ibid.
147 **"members of the audience responded on cue":** Ibid.
147 **"manipulation of the audience is so shrewdly, single-mindedly commercial":** Ibid.
148 **"not caring, and not believing anything":** Ibid.
148 **"She *owned* Gina":** Author interview with Charles Simmons, June 29, 2009.
149 **"tone deaf about the effects of things on people":** Author interview with Dana Salisbury, September 20, 2009.
149 **"I think George lifted Barbra, in a way":** Author interview with Buck Henry, April 27, 2009.
149 **"Were Hepburn and Tracy this good together":** Kael, *The New Yorker* (November 14, 1970).
149 **"to see Streisand":** Ibid.

149  **"like thousands of girls"**: Ibid.
150  **"a good idea in theory, a bad one in practice"**: Kevin Brownlow, *David Lean: A Biography* (New York: St. Martin's Press, 1996), 585.
150  **"no driving emotional energy"**: Kael, *The New Yorker* (November 21, 1970).
150  **"gush made respectable"**: Ibid.
150  **"a lousy lay"**: Brownlow, 586.
151  **"We'll give you color"**: Ibid.
151  **"The book has been promoted from the start"**: Kael, *The New Yorker* (December 26, 1970).
151  **"should bring joy to millions"**: New York *Daily News*, January 12, 1971.
151  **"It deals in private passion at a time when we are exhausted from public defeats"**: Ibid.
152  **"You don't want to be a minister"**: Paul Schrader, *Schrader on Schrader & Other Writings* (London: Faber & Faber, 1990), 291.
152  **"some cold chitchat"**: Ibid., 292.
153  **"I don't trust critics who say they care only for the highest and the best"**: Kael, *The New Yorker* (January 23, 1971).
153  **"free-spirited"**: Ibid.
153  **"have been so sold on Pop and so saturated with it that they appear to have lost their bearings in the arts"**: Ibid.
153  **"In most cases, the conglomerates"**: Ibid.
153  **"they understand that their job is dependent on keeping everybody happy"**: Ibid.
154  **"I don't have any doubts about movies being a great art form"**: Ibid.
154  **"summery richness"**: Kael, *The New Yorker* (March 20, 1971).
154  **"no emotional head of steam"**: Ibid.
154  **"Our desire for grace and seductive opulence is innocent"**: Kael, *The New Yorker* (March 27, 1971).


CHAPTER THIRTEEN

156  **"You have no say at all"**: Patrick McGilligan, *Backstory 2: Interviews with Screenwriters of the 1940s and 1950s* (Berkeley: University of California Press, 1991).
157  **"I hear you're pretty good in seminars but boring as a lecturer"**: Author interview with Howard Suber, July 28, 2010.
158  **"Why would the biggest film critic in America"**: Ibid.
158  **"all the time, but not as a distinguished visitor"**: Author interview with Tom Mankiewicz, December 16, 2008.
159  **"bitter experiences"**: Howard Suber interview with Sara Mankiewicz, housed at the Lilly Library, Indiana University.
159  **"A brand-new bicycle"**: Ibid.
160  **"to write and produce a work of fiction"**: Deposition of Orson Welles, April 1949.
160  **"When an actor becomes the role offstage"**: Note written by Pauline Kael, housed at the Lilly Library.
161  **"Well . . . it's a trivial point"**: Author interview with Howard Suber, July 28, 2010.
161  **"*Citizen Kane* is perhaps the one American talking picture"**: Pauline Kael, "Onward and Upward with the Arts," *The New Yorker* (February 20/27, 1971).
161  **"*Citizen Kane* . . . isn't a work of special depth"**: Ibid.

161 **"conceived and acted as entertainment in a popular style"**: Ibid.

162 **"conventional schoolbook explanations for greatness"**: Ibid.

162 **"to miss what makes it such an American triumph"**: Ibid.

162 **"never been rivaled in wit and exuberance"**: Ibid.

162 **"may for a brief period"**: Ibid.

162 **"When I got into it"**: Ibid.

162 **"idiotic indiscretion"**: Ibid.

163 **"Men cheated of their due"**: Ibid.

163 **"such worship generally doesn't help"**: Ibid.

163 **"Welles isn't in it"**: Ibid.

163 **"Gothic atmosphere"**: Ibid.

163 **"I already know what happened"**: Author interview with Howard Suber, July 28, 2010.

163 **"had been advertised as a one-man show"**: Kael, "Onward and Upward," *The New Yorker* (February 20/27, 1971).

164 **"has lived all his life in a cloud of failure"**: Ibid.

164 **"98% hustling and 2% moviemaking"**: DVD, *Citizen Kane*, Turner Home Entertainment, 2001.

164 **"a first-rate account and I am a better man for having read it"**: Letter from Nunnally Johnson to Pauline Kael, March 5, 1971.

164 **"the references to Mank's drinking"**: Ibid.

164 **"There have always been the Welles idolators"**: Author interview with Tom Mankiewicz, December 16, 2008.

164 **"a highly intelligent and entertaining study"**: *The New York Times*, October 31, 1971.

164 **"superficial and without one quotable line"**: Ibid.

164 **"he was the one who did in fact put it all together"**: Ibid.

165 **"loaded with error and faulty supposition presented as fact"**: *Esquire* (June 1972).

165 **"were to collaborate in writing the prefatory material to the published screenplay"**: Ibid.

165 **"full credit for whatever use she made of it"**: Ibid.

165 **"That is 100 percent, whole-cloth lying"**: *Esquire* (June 1972).

165 **"vivified the material"**: Ibid.

165 **"twaddle"**: Ibid.

166 **"The revisions made by Welles"**: Ibid.

167 **"How am I going to answer this?"**: Author interview with Peter Bogdanovich, September 26, 2009.

167 **"Don't answer"**: Ibid.

## CHAPTER FOURTEEN

168 **"I don't really care much about the story in a film"**: Commentary by Robert Altman, DVD, *McCabe & Mrs. Miller*, Warner Bros., 2002.

169 **"saddened and disgusted"**: Rona Barrett broadcast, Channel 5, June 2, 1971.

169 **"rated R, presumably for rotten"**: Ibid.

169 **"got up and walked out"**: Ibid.

169 ***"McCabe & Mrs. Miller* is a beautiful pipe dream of a movie"**: Pauline Kael, "The Current Cinema," *The New Yorker* (July 3, 1971).

169 **"so indirect in method"**: Ibid.

169 **"the theatrical convention that movies have generally clung to"**: Ibid.

169 **"Will a large enough American public accept"**: Ibid.

170  "Seeing *Sunday Bloody Sunday*": Kael, *The New Yorker* (October 2, 1971).
170  "MRS. GRENVILLE: Darling, you keep throwing in your hand": Penelope Gilliatt, *Sunday Bloody Sunday: The Original Screenplay of the John Schlesinger Film* (New York: Dodd, Mead, 1971), 89.
171  "Peter Finch's Dr. Daniel Hirsh": Kael, *The New Yorker* (October 2, 1971).
171  "the characters here all are coping": Ibid.
171  "instantly recognizable as a classic": Ibid.
171  "lost his stridency": Ibid.
171  "what few people who write for the screen think to do": Ibid.
171  "mistake the film for the filmmaker": Author interview with William Friedkin, May 10, 2008.
172  "bland, barren, gray look": *The Village Voice*, February 24, 1972.
172  "It's a dismal town": Ibid.
172  "I have visions of Pauline Kael in the year 2001": Ibid., October 14, 1971.
172  "turn into a bludgeon to beat other filmmakers with": Kael, *The New Yorker* (October 9, 1971).
172  "worked-up, raunchy melodrama": Ibid.
172  "exploitative of human passions and miseries": Ibid.
172  "a lovingly exact history of American small-town life": Ibid.
172  "perhaps what TV soap opera would be if it were more honest": Ibid.
173  "For several decades": Ibid.
173  "still feeling that they represented something preferable ": Ibid.
173  "part of the truth of American experience": Ibid.
173  "Pauline misses the point": Author interview with Peter Bogdanovich, September 26, 2009.
173  "It would have taken *Winchester '73*": Larry McMurtry, *The Last Picture Show* (New York: Dial Press, 1966), 204.
173  "If Bogdanovich replaces Hopper": Kael, *The New Yorker* (October 9, 1971).
174  "I told him that Pauline had said it was a picture that even Richard Nixon would like": Author interview with Peter Bogdanovich, September 26, 2009.
174  "I don't know if that's a compliment or not": Ibid.
174  "I thought Pauline was deaf to feminism": Author interview with Karen Durbin, January 12, 2010.
175  "the best high of all": Joan Didion and John Gregory Dunne, screenplay of *Panic in Needle Park,* 1971.
175  "everyone seems to be dressed for a mad ball": Kael, *The New Yorker* (October 30, 1971).
175  "It is literally true": Ibid.
175  "often irrational and horrifying brutal": Ibid.
175  "extraordinarily well made": Ibid.
175  "what we once feared mass entertainment might become": Ibid.
176  "primarily an American Jewish contribution": Kael, *The New Yorker* (November 13, 1971).
176  "probably the only successful attempt ": Ibid.
176  "the Jews as an oppressed people": Ibid.
176  "self-hatred and self-infatuation": Ibid.
176  "Younger members of the audience—particularly if they are Jewish": Ibid.
176  "Thank you for your in *depth* critique": Letter from Norman Jewison to Pauline Kael, March 15, 1972.
177  "man in his natural state": *The New York Times*, January 4, 1972.

177 **"directed toward cuteness at every opportunity"**: *Life* (February 4, 1972).

177 **"a viciously rigged game"**: Ibid.

177 **"If such a catastrophe has indeed occurred"**: *The Village Voice*, December 20, 1971.

177 **"a victory in which we share"**: Kael, *The New Yorker* (January 1, 1971).

177 **"symptomatic of a new attitude in movies"**: Ibid.

177 **"corrupt"**: Ibid.

178 **"At the movies"**: Ibid.

178 **"right-wing fantasy"**: Kael, *The New Yorker* (January 15, 1972).

179 **"falling to the water in an instant extended to eternity"**: Kael, *The New Yorker* (January 29, 1972).

179 **"take the façade of movie violence"**: *The New York Times*, February 26, 1995.

179 **"got so wound up in the aesthetics of violence"**: Kael, *The New Yorker* (March 21, 1970).

179 **"profoundly depressing"**: Letter from Sam Peckinpah to Pauline Kael, May 22, 1970.

180 **"You can't make violence real to audiences today"**: Kevin J. Hayes, *Sam Peckinpah Interviews* (Jackson: University of Mississippi Press, 2008), 102.

180 **"The vision of *Straw Dogs* is narrow and puny"**: Kael, *The New Yorker* (January 28, 1972).

180 **"intuitions as a director are infinitely superior to his thinking"**: Ibid.

180 **"stale anti-intellectualism"**: Ibid.

180 **"one of the few truly erotic sequences in film"**: Ibid.

180 **"the punches that subdue the wife"**: Ibid.

180 **"The rape has heat to it"**: Ibid.

180 **"The thesis that man is irretrievably bad and corrupt is the essence of fascism"**: *The New York Times*, January 2, 1972.

180 **"What I am saying, I fear"**: Kael, *The New Yorker* (January 29, 1972).

180 **"Fascist, God how I hate that word"**: Letter from Sam Peckinpah to Pauline Kael, February 21, 1973.

181 **"Doesn't Kael know *anything* about sex?"**: Hayes, 100.

181 **"*Cabaret* is a great movie musical"**: Kael, *The New Yorker* (February 19, 1972).

181 **"distinctive, acrid flavor—a taste of death on the tongue"**: Ibid.

182 **"The grotesque amorality in *Cabaret* is frightening"**: Ibid.

182 **"you can create a new organic whole"**: Ibid.

182 **"the best popular movies come out of a merger of commerce and art"**: Kael, *The New Yorker* (March 18, 1972).

182 **"tenaciously intelligent"**: Ibid.

182 **"mellowed in recent years"**: Ibid.

183 **"those old men who carry never-ending grudges"**: Ibid.

183 **"Organized crime is not a rejection of Americanism"**: Ibid.

183 **"one of the most intricately balanced moral dilemmas imaginable"**: Kael, *The New Yorker* (March 25, 1972).

183 **"Inexplicably"**: Ibid.

## CHAPTER FIFTEEN

186 **"improbable one"**: Author interview with Erhard Dortmund, February 9, 2009.

186 **"She would throw a little dart in"**: Author interview with James Wolcott, August 3, 2010.

187 **"Sometimes I would just sit there silent as a stone":** Author interview with James Morgenstern, May 8, 2009.

187 **"She thought that the editorial department should be doing more":** Author interview with Hoyt Spelman, January 15, 2009.

187 **"fossil":** Author interview with Joseph Morgenstern, May 8, 2009.

188 **"Pauline was one of the women":** Author interview with Karen Durbin, January 12, 2010.

188 **"that a Negro family can be as dreary as a white family":** "Trash, Art and the Movies": *Harper's* (February 1969).

188 **"never pushes a moment too hard":** Pauline Kael, "The Current Cinema," *The New Yorker* (September 30, 1972).

188 **"the singular good fortune":** Ibid.

188 **"to strive for classical plainness":** *The New York Times*, September 25, 1972.

188 **"no resemblance whatsoever to reality as I observed it":** *The New York Times*, November 12, 1972.

188 **"Are they available only for fantasies":** *Life* (October 20, 1972).

189 **"heavy and glazed":** Kael, *The New Yorker* (November 4, 1972).

189 **"Factually it's a fraud, but emotionally it delivers":** Ibid.

189 **"Pop music provides immediate emotional gratifications":** Ibid.

189 **"want Billie Holiday's hard, melancholic sound":** Ibid.

190 **"Everything outside this place is bullshit":** Bernardo Bertolucci and Franco Arcalli, screenplay of *Last Tango in Paris*, 1972.

191 **"our marriage was nothing more than a foxhole for you":** Ibid.

191 **"Listen, you dumb dodo":** Ibid.

191 **"drenched":** Author interview with George Malko, April 15, 2009.

191 **"Bernardo Bertolucci's *Last Tango in Paris*":** Kael, *The New Yorker* (October 28, 1972).

192 **"having a seizure onstage":** Ibid.

192 **"a study of the aggression in masculine sexuality":** Ibid.

192 **"Americans seem to have lost the capacity for being scandalized":** Ibid.

192 **"might have been easier on some":** Ibid.

192 **"this is a movie people will be arguing about":** Ibid.

192 **"I've tried to describe":** Ibid.

193 **"Bertolucci and Brando have altered the face of an art form":** Kael, *The New Yorker* (October 28, 1972).

193 **"I remember we came out of the movie":** Author interview with Charles Simmons, June 29, 2009.

193 **"I saw *Last Tango*, not with her":** Ibid.

193 **"stylistically wasteful and excessive":** *The Village Voice*, February 1, 1973.

193 **"its best scenes are isolated from each other":** Ibid.

194 **"Under ordinary circumstances":** Ibid.

194 **"That . . . was her last tango with Sarris":** Author interview with Hoyt Spelman, January 15, 2009.

194 **"the ultimate princess fantasy":** Kael, *The New Yorker* (November 11, 1972).

194 **"too sensitive for this world":** Ibid.

194 **"ridiculously swank":** Ibid.

194 **"a writer's performance":** Ibid.

195 **"wanted Frank Perry to direct":** Kael, *The New Yorker* (November 11, 1972).

195 **"I replied that actually we wanted Sam Peckinpah to do the picture":** Letter from John Gregory Dunne to Pauline Kael, November 20, 1972.

195 **"a simple matter of economics":** Ibid.

195 **"I confess a certain ambivalence about the book":** Letter from John Gregory Dunne to Pauline Kael, December 5, 1972.

196 **"Sorry you didn't get my crude attempt":** Letter from Sam Peckinpah to Pauline Kael, February 21, 1973.

196 **"be made into such a shitty film":** Ibid.

196 **"Rex and Judith loved":** Ibid.

196 **"I trust instinct more than any study of logical conclusions":** David Thompson, *Altman on Altman* (London: Faber & Faber, 2006), 74.

196 **"almost frighteningly non-repetitive":** Kael, *The New Yorker* (December 23, 1972).

197 **"He made me sit down and write a postcard to Pauline Kael":** Author interview with Rene Auberjonois, September 2, 2009.

197 **"grimly controlled":** Kael, *The New Yorker* (December 30, 1972).

197 **"an unnecessarily confined and schoolmarmish performance":** Ibid.

197 **"a new kind of hip and casually smart screen actor":** Ibid.

198 **"Jeremiah signals him back, giving him the finger":** Ibid.

198 **"only assume that by that point you were so bored with the film":** Letter from Sydney Pollack to Pauline Kael, January 5, 1973.

198 **"to save me the buck twenty":** Letter from Robert Getchell to Pauline Kael, December 31, 1972.

198 **"The idea should be for them to keep going with lots of engagement":** Note by Pauline Kael on screenplay of *Alice Doesn't Live Here Anymore*, 1974.

199 **"a record of the interaction of movies and our national life":** Pauline Kael, *Deeper into Movies* (Boston: Atlantic–Little, Brown, 1973), xv.

199 **"Right now, movie critics have an advantage":** Ibid.

199 **"Right now, movie criticism in America seems livelier":** *The New York Times Book Review*, February 18, 1973.

199 **"crisp sentences":** Ibid.

199 **"aggressive wit":** Ibid.

199 **"she brings to her movies a grounding in literary culture":** Ibid.

199 **"Sometimes she drops into a sort of brawling":** Ibid.

199 **"excessive praise":** Ibid.

199 **"I suspect either that, as a result of seeing too many movies":** Ibid.

200 **"the worst movie that I've stayed to see":** Kael, *The New Yorker* (January 20, 1968).

200 **"self-satire":** *The New York Times Book Review*, July 23, 1973.

200 **"slow reaction time made her seem daffy":** Ibid.

200 **"Who knows what to think about Marilyn Monroe ":** Ibid.

200 **"to cosmic proportions":** Ibid.

201 **"His strength—when he gets rolling":** Ibid.

201 **"a rip-off all right":** Ibid.

201 **"a runaway string of perceptions ":** Ibid.

201 **"Mailer's way to perform character assassination":** Ibid.

201 **"malevolence that needs to be recognized":** Ibid.

201 **"What for?":** Pauline Kael, Introduction, *For Keeps*, (New York: Dutton, 1994), iii.

201 **"That's right":** Ibid.

CHAPTER SIXTEEN

202 **"I live in a rather special world":** *Newsweek* (February, 1973).

202 **"The Watergate hearings"**: Pauline Kael, "The Current Cinema," *The New Yorker* (October 1, 1973).

202 **"The Vietnam War has barely been mentioned on the screen"**: Ibid.

202 **"there was no virtuous side to identify with"**: Ibid.

202 **"a depressive uncertainty"**: Ibid.

202 **"When Vietnam finished off the American hero as a righter of wrongs"**: Ibid.

203 **"corruption seems to be inescapable"**: Ibid.

203 **"perhaps someone in the head office at Fox"**: Ibid.

203 **"I invited her to lunch"**: Author interview with Lamont Johnson, April 6, 2009.

203 **"I am sorry to say"**: Author interview with Judith Crist, July 17 2008.

204 **"a fuckin' politician"**: Martin Scorsese and Mardik Martin, screenplay of *Mean Streets*, 1973.

204 **"a true original of our period"**: Kael, *The New Yorker* (October 8, 1973).

204 **"breaks out so unexpectedly"**: Ibid.

204 **"the psychological connections"**: Ibid.

204 **"We were easily discouraged"**: Joyce Maynard, "I Remember," *New York* (August 18, 1975).

206 **"It's amazing how decisions are forced upon us willy-nilly"**: Arthur Laurents's screenplay of *The Way We Were*, 1973.

206 **"it's hardly the definitive film about McCarthyism"**: *American Film* (April 1978).

206 **"a torpedoed ship full of gaping holes which comes snugly into port"**: Kael, *The New Yorker* (October 15, 1973).

206 **"bewildering"**: Ibid.

206 **"miraculous audience empathy"**: Ibid.

206 **"caught the spirit of the hysterical Stalinist workhorses"**: Ibid.

206 **"defensive and aggressive in the same breath"**: Ibid.

206 **"a gradual conquest of the movie public"**: Ibid.

206 **"hit entertainment and maybe even memorable entertainment"**: Ibid.

207 **"Maybe the reason some people have difficulty getting into Altman's wavelength"**: Kael, *The New Yorker* (October 22, 1973).

207 **"He's not a pusher"**: Ibid.

208 **"when you hear the improvised dialogue"**: Ibid.

208 **"But I understand Pauline"**: Author interview with Elliott Gould, September 9, 2009.

208 **"an erratic comic genius"**: Kael, *The New Yorker* (December 31, 1973).

208 **"found a nonaggressive way"**: Ibid.

208 **"essential sanity"**: Ibid.

208 **"the base from which he takes flight"**: Ibid.

208 **"without the lapses that had found"**: Ibid.

208 **"Allen's new sense of control over the medium"**: Ibid.

209 **"The battered adolescent . . . still thinks that's the secret of happiness"**: Ibid.

210 **"When you see him on TV"**: Kael, *The New Yorker* (January 7, 1974).

210 **"learning about the Catholic Church while I was doing that film"**: Author interview with William Friedkin, May 10, 2008.

210 **"no indication that Blatty"**: Ibid.

210 **"The whole movie was balanced on that"**: Author interview with William Friedkin, May 10, 2008.

210 **"I wonder about those four-hundred and ninety-nine mothers"**: Kael, *The New Yorker* (January 7, 1974).

210 **"the biggest recruiting poster":** Ibid.
210 **"I found it wrong-headed":** Author interview with William Friedkin, May 10, 2008.
211 **"I remember her walking in":** Author interview with Joan Tewkesbury, February 4, 2009.
211 **"What you got was this sense of women":** Ibid.
211 **"the pensive, delicate romanticism of *McCabe*, but it isn't hesitant or precarious":** Kael, *The New Yorker* (February 4, 1974).
211 **"saphead objectivity":** Pauline Kael, *Time* (March 14, 1968).
211 **"Robert Altman spoils other directors' films for me":** Kael, *The New Yorker* (February 4, 1974).
212 **"Pauline Kael saved *McCabe & Mrs. Miller*":** Letter from Grover Sales to Pauline Kael, October 22, 1973.
212 **"In terms of the pleasure that technical assurance gives an audience":** Kael, *The New Yorker* (March 18, 1974).
212 **"If there is such a thing as a movie sense":** Ibid.
212 **"an intellectualized movie—shrewd and artful":** Kael, *The New Yorker* (March 18, 1974).
213 **"I guess you didn't know that Terry is like a son to me":** *Modern Maturity* (March–April, 1998).
213 **"Tough shit, Bill":** Ibid.
213 **"Movie criticism is a happy, frustrating, slightly mad job":** Pauline Kael, acceptance speech, National Book Awards, April 18, 1974.

## CHAPTER SEVENTEEN

214 **"With her review of *Last Tango*, I think":** Author interview with Howard Kissel, July 2, 2008.
214 **"I would say film critics have power":** Ibid.
214 **"the reputations of virtually every writer in town":** David Denby, "My Life as a Paulette," *The New Yorker* (October 20, 2003).
215 **"those who didn't turn away in anger":** Ibid.
215 **"It's shit, honey":** Ibid.
215 **"You're too restless to be a writer":** Ibid.
215 **"I've thought about this seriously, honey":** Ibid.
215 **"Ray, his face cast down into his shrimp and rice":** Ibid.
216 **"the emotional resources":** Pauline Kael, "The Current Cinema," *The New Yorker* (December 23, 1974).
217 **"about midway":** Ibid.
217 **"Is it our imagination":** Ibid.
217 **"the physical audacity":** Ibid.
217 **"openhanded":** Ibid.
217 **"the sensibility at work":** Ibid.
217 **"a magnificent piece":** Letter from Penelope Gilliatt to Pauline Kael, December 17, 1974.
217 **"in a position":** Kael, *The New Yorker* (August 5, 1975).
217 **"didn't *plan* on *The Conversation* being a success":** Ibid.
218 **"audiences like movies that do all the work for them":** Ibid.
218 **"The movie companies used to give all their pictures a chance":** Ibid.
218 **"Perhaps no work of art is possible without belief in the audience":** Ibid.

219 **"really care about the business end":** Letter from Fred Goldberg to Pauline Kael, August 22, 1974.
219 **"a hell of a writer":** Ibid.
219 **"strikingly well-edited":** Kael, *The New Yorker* (October 14, 1974).
219 **"complete without us":** Ibid.
219 **"the secret of gambling ":** Ibid.
219 **"The poor bastard who buys a two-dollar ticket":** Ibid.
219 **"I always enjoy reading you":** Author interview with James Toback, May 21, 2009.
220 **"For a while I just felt awkward:** Ibid.
220 **"a lot of characters":** Kael, *The New Yorker* (October 14, 1974).
220 **"She never liked to talk about being Jewish":** Author interview with James Toback, May 21, 2009.
220 **"She thought, 'I'm just what he was":** Ibid.
220 **"one of the rare films that genuinely deserve to be called controversial":** Kael, *The New Yorker* (January 13, 1975).
221 **"the first angry-young-woman movie":** Ibid.
221 **"Burstyn appears to be":** Ibid.
221 **"The trouble with Ellen Burstyn's performance is that she's playing against something instead of playing a character":** Ibid.
221 **"so many of those discordant notes":** Ibid.
222 **"might have been no more than a saucy romp ":** Kael, *The New Yorker* (February 17, 1975).
222 **"the emotional climate of the time and place":** Ibid.
222 **"an easy role":** Ibid.
222 **"the most virtuoso example of sophisticated kaleidoscopic farce":** Ibid.
223 **"She was very entertaining and interesting and funny about herself ":** Author interview with Michael Murphy, October 15, 2009.
223 **"I always had a feeling about Pauline":** Ibid.
223 **"Bob was very flattered by how wonderful she thought he was":** Author interview with Sue Barton, October 23, 2008.
224 **"That's what the screening was for":** Jan Stuart, *The* Nashville *Chronicles: The Making of Robert Altman's Masterpiece* (New York: Simon & Schuster, 2000), 281.
224 **"Is there such a thing as an orgy for movie-lovers":** Kael, *The New Yorker* (March 3, 1975).
224 **"*Nashville* isn't in final shape yet":** Ibid.
224 **"The great American popularity contest":** Ibid.
225 **"all of those things":** Ibid.
225 **"Altman wants you to be part of the life he shows you":** Ibid.
226 **"no longer singing":** Kael, *The New Yorker* (March 17, 1975).
226 **"The main problem I had with *Funny Lady*":** Ibid.
226 **"volatility is gone":** Ibid.
226 **"Dear Ray":** Letter from Pauline Kael to Ray Stark, April 15, 1975.

## CHAPTER EIGHTEEN

227 **"the funniest epic vision of America ever to reach the screen":** Pauline Kael, "The Current Cinema," *The New Yorker,* March 3, 1975.
227 **"If one can review a film":** *The New York Times,* March 9, 1975.

227  *The Last Tycoon* **bombs like a paper bag full of water**: Ibid.
227  **"really not very talented"**: Jan Stuart, The Nashville *Chronicles: The Making of Robert Altman's Masterpiece* (New York: Simon & Schuster, 2000), 285.
227  **"always foaming at the mouth about something"**: Ibid.
228  **"Nobody got rich"**: Author interview with Joan Tewkesbury, February 4, 2009.
228  **"In the twilight land of flickering "**: Doctor of Humane Letters citation to Pauline Kael, Haverford College, May 13, 1975.
229  **"Cary Grant is your dream date"**: Kael, *The New Yorker* (July 14, 1975).
229  **"He draws women to him"**: Ibid.
229  **"not the modern kind"**: Ibid.
229  **"We could admire him"**: Ibid.
229  **"the most cheerfully perverse scare movie ever made"**: Kael, *The New Yorker* (November 8, 1976).
230  **"Michael Ritchie really had the pulse of America"**: Author interview with Barbara Feldon, November 4, 2010.
230  **"There hasn't been a small-town comedy in so long"**: Kael, *The New Yorker* (October 6, 1975).
231  **"the shocking messiness of love"**: Kael, *The New Yorker* (February 12, 1972).
231  **"perceptions of what I thought no one else knew—and I wasn't telling"**: Kael, *The New Yorker* (February 12, 1972).
231  **"romantic** *and* **ironic"**: Kael, *The New Yorker* (October 27, 1975).
231  **"Now it is the bad guys"**: *Women's Wear Daily*, November 17, 1975.
231  **"long literary tradition"**: Kael, *The New Yorker* (October 27, 1975).
231  **"a powerful, smashingly effective movie"**: Ibid.
231  **"how crude the poet-paranoid system"**: Ibid.
232  **"half smile"**: Ibid.
232  **"so much of a Nicholson role"**: Ibid.
232  **"externalized approach"**: Kael, *The New Yorker* (December 29, 1975).
232  **"As it becomes apparent"**: Ibid.
232  **"slack-faced and phlegmatic"**: Ibid.
232  **"his face straining with the effort to be what the Master wants"**: Ibid.
232  **"Kubrick isn't taking pictures in order to make movies"**: Ibid.
233  **"I think it is important to remind everyone"**: New York *Daily News*, January 2, 1976.
233  **"intensely, claustrophobically exciting"**: Kael, *The New Yorker* (January 12, 1976).
233  **"As the losing battles"**: Ibid.
233  **"Peckinpah has become so nihilistic"**: Ibid.
234  **"If God had not meant man to drink"**: Letter from Sam Peckinpah to Pauline Kael, December 14, 1976.
234  **"She was done completely"**: Author interview with James Toback, May 21, 2009.
234  **"Miss Wertmuller's** *King Kong*": Kael, *The New Yorker* (February 16, 1976).
234  **"If** *Seven Beauties* **is all these things, what is it?"**: Ibid.
234  **"beyond annoyance"**: Ibid.
234  **"the characters never shut up"**: Ibid.
235  **"the stated ideas"**: Ibid.
235  **"raising the consciousness of the masses"**: Ibid.
235  **"its life-denying spirit"**: *The Village Voice*, February 16, 1976.
235  **"may just naturally be an Expressionist"**: Kael, *The New Yorker* (February 9, 1976).

235 **"used his own emptiness":** Ibid.
236 **"No other film":** Ibid.
236 *"He's still out there!":* Author interview with Joseph Hurley, February 6, 2009.
236 **"animation and charm as a movie reviewer":** *The New York Times Book Review,* April 4, 1976.
236 **"I don't mean to quarrel with Miss Kael's opinions":** Ibid.
237 **"It is always an entertaining book":** Ibid.
237 **"What she so often practices now":** *The Village Voice,* June 11, 1976.
237 **"desire to relieve the lonely detachment":** Ibid.
237 **"Everything had to be the greatest":** Author interview with Greil Marcus, November 12, 2010.
237 **"Did you really mean all that stuff that you wrote about me?":** Ibid.
238 **"She just sort of expected":** Ibid.
238 **"happy to do any radio or TV that comes up":** Letter from Pauline Kael to William Abrahams, March 16, 1976.
238 **"She is not lacking in exigence as an author":** Letter from Peter Davison to Perry Knowlton, June 14, 1976.
238 **"too high by far":** Letter from William Abrahams to Perry Knowlton, undated.
239 **"as uncomfortable to watch as a backless chair is to sit in":** John Simon, *New York* (November 15, 1976).
239 **"a marvelous toy":** Kael, *The New Yorker* (October 18, 1976).
239 **"shameless, and that's why—on a certain level—it works":** Kael, *The New Yorker* (November 29, 1976).
239 **"Stallone has the gift of direct communication with the audience":** Ibid.
239 **"She screamed at me for doing that":** Author interview with Carrie Rickey, May 9, 2009.
239 **"I had proposed back then that the women who directed movies":** Ibid.
239 **"Stay away from that feministic stuff":** Ibid.
240 **"a beautiful plot":** Kael, *The New Yorker* (November 22, 1976).
240 **"the wickedest baroque sensibility at large in American movies":** Ibid.
240 **"He's uncommitted to anything except successful manipulation . . . when his camera conveys the motion of dreams":** Ibid.
240 **"I think that Brian was just thrilled":** Author interview with Nancy Allen, May 30, 2010.
240 **"She liked Brian a lot and there I was, the girlfriend":** Ibid.
241 **"a fantasy burlesque":** *Women's Wear Daily,* November 12, 1976.
241 **"incompetent":** Ibid.
241 **"like a Village crazy":** Kael, *The New Yorker* (December 6, 1976).
241 **"is turning us into morons and humanoids":** Ibid.
241 **"TV may have altered family life and social intercourse":** Ibid.
241 **"directly to the audience—he soapboxes":** Ibid.
241 **"the soliloquies going at a machine-gun pace":** Ibid.
241 *"I'm as mad as hell":* Paddy Chayevsky, screenplay of *Network,* 1976.
241 **"I'm going to make him an offer he can't refuse":** Francis Ford Coppola, screenplay of *The Godfather,* 1972.
242 **"I'm not going to write about this one, darling":** Author interview with Lamont Johnson, April 26, 2009.
242 **"she acts a virtuous person":** Kael, *The New Yorker* (January 10, 1977).
242 **"a drippy love story about two people who love each other selflessly":** Ibid.
242 **"fake gospel":** Ibid.
242 **"Streisand has more talent than she knows what to do with":** Ibid.

242 **"Yours was the only notice I saw":** Letter from John Gregory Dunne to Pauline Kael, January 24, 1977.

243 **"I will remember all my life":** Author interview with Marthe Keller, November 8, 2010.

243 **"We had, in private":** Ibid.

243 **"Before it started":** Ibid.

243 **"a horrible experience":** Author interview with James Toback, May 21, 2009.

243 **"She was not comfortable in Europe":** Author interview with Marthe Keller, November 8, 2010.

244 **"I was at Cannes":** Author interview with Robert Altman, June 19, 2004.

244 **"You have one person who loves you forever":** Author interview with Marthe Keller, November 8, 2010.


CHAPTER NINETEEN

245 **"She respected me because I didn't lie":** Author interview with Marion Billings, October 23, 2008.

245 **"For Marion":** Inscription to Marion Billings from Pauline Kael, *Kiss Kiss Bang Bang.*

246 **"The movie studios aren't putting up a fight":** Pauline Kael, "The Current Cinema," *The New Yorker* (February 28, 1977).

246 **"There's no breather in the picture, no lyricism":** Kael, *The New Yorker* (September 26, 1977).

246 **"no emotional grip":** Ibid.

247 **"I told her from the beginning":** Author interview with James Toback, May 21, 2009.

247 **"She was quite obsessed with the fact that Hellman was a liar":** Author interview with Richard Albarino, November 9, 2010.

247 **"She thought it was ridiculous":** Author interview with Patricia Bosworth, June 28, 2010.

248 **"classical humorist":** Kael, *The New Yorker* (October 10, 1977).

248 **"not neurotic or sexually aberrant":** *The New York Times*, October 31, 1976.

248 **"Women in movies have always been defined in terms of men":** *The New York Times*, October 31, 1976.

248 **"pulpy morbidity":** Kael, *The New Yorker* (October 24, 1977).

248 **"erotic, modern-Gothic compulsiveness":** Ibid.

248 **"windy jeremiad":** Ibid.

248 **"an illustrated lecture on how nice girls go wrong":** Ibid.

248 **"It's what nice people do":** Ibid.

248 **"a powerful enough personality":** Ibid.

249 **"a child's playfulness and love of surprises":** Kael, *The New Yorker* (November 28, 1977).

249 **"one of the peerless moments in movie history":** Ibid.

249 **"probably the most gifted American director who's dedicated to sheer entertainment":** Ibid.

249 **"how the financially pinched seventies generation ":** Kael, *The New Yorker* (December 26, 1977).

249 **"a TV-commercial version of Art Deco":** Ibid.

249 **"There is a thick, raw sensuality that some adolescents have which seems almost preconscious":** Ibid.

250 **"a mixture of undeveloped themes":** Kael, *The New Yorker* (February 20, 1978).

250 **"evocative of that messy time":** Ibid.
251 **"trying to act without her usual snap":** Ibid.
251 **"There's a strong enough element of self-admiration":** Ibid.
251 **"We started before we were ready":** *The New York Times*, February 19, 1978.
251 ***Blue Collar* says the system grinds all workers down":** Kael, *The New Yorker* (February 27, 1978).
252 **"It was so much easier in the '60s":** Paul Mazurky's screenplay of *An Unmarried Woman*, 1978.
252 **"PATTI: I mean, everybody I know is either miserable or divorced":** Ibid.
252 **"We thought that Martin pissing Erica off":** Author interview with Michael Murphy, October 15, 2009.
252 **"There's this line, and they're mostly women":** Ibid.
253 **"funny and buoyant besides":** Kael, *The New Yorker* (March 6, 1978).
253 **"floating, not-quite-sure not-quite-here quality is just right":** Ibid.
253 **"a superb shaggy screenwriter and rarely less than deft":** Ibid.
253 **"whether she's struggling toward independence":** Ibid.
253 **"She at that point in her movie criticism was becoming a kineticist":** Author interview with Richard Albarino, November 23, 2009.
254 **"Jimmy needs to be an exciting, violent, emotional man":** Kael, *The New Yorker* (March 13, 1978).
254 **"still locked up in the writer-director's head":** Ibid.
254 **"The shock is in the speed of Dreems's action":** Ibid.
254 **"The only time I ever felt Pauline levitate":** Author interview with George Malko, April 15, 2009.
254 **"Normality doesn't interest Toback":** Kael, *The New Yorker* (March 20, 1978).
254 **"You refer to the literary adolescent's way":** Author interview with James Toback, May 21, 2009.
254 **"so far beyond anything in his last film, *Carrie*":** Ibid.
255 **"No Hitchcock thriller was ever so intense":** Ibid.
255 **"What she lost was her taste":** Author interview with Joe Regan, November 10, 2010.

## CHAPTER TWENTY

256 **"Discriminating moviegoers want the placidity of *nice* art":** Pauline Kael, "The Current Cinema," *The New Yorker*, September 25, 1978.
256 **"no desire but to please":** Ibid.
257 **"The trucks give the performances in this movie":** Ibid.
257 **"took risks":** Author interview with Jeanine Basinger, November 19, 2010.
258 **"How can Woody Allen present":** Ibid.
258 **"Surely at root the family problem is Jewish":** Ibid.
258 **"This droll piece of work is his most majestic so far":** Penelope Gilliatt, "The Current Cinema," *The New Yorker* (August 7, 1978).
258 **"A wedding. . . . I'm taking this crew, and we'll be doing weddings":** Author interview with Robert Altman, June 19, 2004.
258 **"like a busted bag of marbles":** Kael, *The New Yorker* (September 25, 1978).
258 **"doesn't like the characters on the screen":** Ibid.
259 **"began tuning out on Eva's tirade":** *The Village Voice*, November 6, 1978.
259 **"as the truth":** Kael, *The New Yorker* (November 6, 1978).

259 **"It's like the grievances of someone who has just gone into therapy"**: Ibid.

260 **"He was always pushing her to get out "**: Author interview with Richard Albarino, November 23, 2009.

260 **"was cast out in no uncertain terms"**: Ibid.

260 **"I can remember a couple of times, at least, seeing him turn so red when they would start arguing"**: Author interview with William Whitworth, November 30, 2009.

260 **"The problem Shawn had with her over and over"**: Ibid.

261 **". . . he bats his eyelids"**: Kael, *The New Yorker* (November 27, 1978), galley proof courtesy of William Whitworth.

261 **"This piece pushes her earthiness at us"**: Ibid.

261 **"He's like a young kid pretending to be an old coot"**: Ibid.

261 **"Her earthiness, her focus on body functions"**: Ibid.

261 **"a commercial for cunnilingus"**: Ibid.

261 **"This has to come out"**: Ibid.

261 **"long takes and sweeping, panning movements"**: Kael, *The New Yorker* (December 18, 1978).

261 **"an astonishing piece of work"**: Ibid.

261 **"his xenophobic yellow-peril imagination"**: Ibid.

262 **"traditional isolationist message: Asia should be left to the Asians"**: Ibid.

262 **"We have come to expect a lot from De Niro: miracles"**: Ibid.

262 **"Pardon me—he's someone you babysat!"**: Author interview with Daryl Chin, November 16, 2010.

262 **"When I see something as huge, as rich"**: Letter from Owen Gleiberman to Pauline Kael, March 13, 1979.

262 **"the American movie of the year—a new classic"**: Kael, *The New Yorker* (March 15, 1976).

262 **"the San Francisco brand of humanity"**: Ibid.

263 **"a grown-up, quicksilver talent"**: Ibid.

263 **"such instinct for the camera that even when she isn't doing anything special"**: Kael, *The New Yorker* (March 13, 1979).

263 **"Sweetie, you need a publicist—nobody knows you"**: Author interview with Philip Kaufman, May 7, 2009.

263 **"She recognized that *Body Snatchers* was in large part a comedy"**: Ibid.

263 **"She was obsessed with James Toback"**: Author interview with Veronica Cartwright, April 26, 2009.

263 **"I had the weirdest feeling she was offended"**: Ibid.

264 **"Danny Melnick didn't want to fuck her"**: Author interview with Paul Schrader, August 31, 2009.

264 **"powerful raw ideas for movies"**: Kael, *The New Yorker* (February 19, 1979).

264 **"Schrader doesn't enter the world of porno"**: Ibid.

264 **"cautious and maddeningly opaque"**: Ibid.

264 **"The possibility also comes to mind"**: Ibid.

265 **"like visual rock"**: Kael, *The New Yorker* (March 5, 1979).

265 **"mesmerizing in its intensity"**: Ibid.

266 **"the risk factor out of financing movies"**: *In These Times* (May 1980).

267 **"Now we can be friends again"**: Letter from Ray Stark to Pauline Kael, March 29, 1979.

267 **"He wanted to hunt her down, and get her"**: Author interview with Paul Schrader, August 31, 2009.

267 **"There was a fine writer named Pauline"**: Undated poem from various staff members of *The New Yorker*.

## CHAPTER TWENTY-ONE

269 **"So. . . . Tell me"**: Author interview with James Toback, May 21, 2009.

269 **"Now I know what Warren meant"**: Letter from Kenneth Ziffren to Pauline Kael, 1979.

269 **"probably take the whole weekend"**: Ibid.

270 **"She was keen to break loose from what she had been doing"**: Author interview with Kenneth Ziffren, June 19, 2009.

270 **"He never wrote or made anything that he hadn't experienced first"**: Author interview with Richard Albarino, November 23, 2009.

270 **"I typed about four words"**: Ibid.

271 **"a blueprint which may or may not work"**: Author interview with James Toback, May 21, 2009.

271 **"I found it impossible to work with her"**: Ibid.

272 **"I feel very badly"**: Ibid.

272 **"He was confused"**: Ibid.

273 **"You have to let me go back to Las Vegas"**: Ibid.

273 **"did a masterful job of alienating"**: *The New York Times*, May 15, 1979.

273 **"a supercharged, simpleminded creature"**: Charles Fleming, *High Concept: Donald Simpson and the Hollywood Culture of Excess* (New York: Doubleday, 1998), 14.

274 **"It was a cake put in my lap"**: Author interview with James Toback, May 21, 2009.

274 **"Dear Pauline . . . as we discussed last Friday night"**: Memo from Don Simpson to Pauline Kael, July 25, 1979.

274 **"Eisner and I have reviewed one more time"**: Memo from Don Simpson to Pauline Kael, undated.

274 **"Warren's power to charm cannot be overestimated"**: Author interview with Buck Henry, April 29, 2009.

275 **"You are trying to destroy my career from the inside"**: Author interview with Paul Schrader, August 31, 2009.

276 **"I suppose, Professor Berwind"**: Author interview with Sandra Berwind, February 21, 2009.

277 **"Frankly, many producers aren't doing the job that they should"**: *The Hollywood Reporter*, May 16, 1980.

277 **"You work for a long time to become a writer"**: Remarks by Pauline Kael at Visiting Writers Symposium at Vanderbilt University, March 26, 1980.

278 **"He went into a long explanation"**: Author interview with William Whitworth, November 30, 2009.

278 **"I had the feeling that what had happened to her there shocked her"**: Author interview with Jeanine Basinger, November 19, 2010.

## CHAPTER TWENTY-TWO

279 **"What has happened, I think"**: *The New York Times Book Review*, April 6, 1980.

279 **"Whatever mellowness has crept into her writing"**: Ibid.

279 **"When Pauline scolds the industry"**: *The Village Voice*, July 2–8, 1980.

279 **"a more candid critic than Pauline"**: Ibid.

280 **"Why are you shaking?"**: Audio interview between Pauline Kael and Ray Sawhill, 2000.

280 **"He has a way of making us feel that we're in on a joke"**: Pauline Kael, "The Current Cinema," *The New Yorker* (June 9, 1980).

280 **"His performance begins to seem cramped, slightly robotized"**: Ibid.

281 **"Very soon they're likely to be summoning "**: Kael, *The New Yorker* (June 23, 1980).

281 **"discovered how to take the risk out of moviemaking"**: Ibid.

282 **"readiness for a visionary, climactic, summing-up movie"**: Ibid.

282 **"an incoherent mess"**: Television interview with Pauline Kael, *Live at Five*, fall 1982.

282 **"a quality of flushed transparency"**: Kael, *The New Yorker* (July 21, 1980).

282 **"perfected a near-surreal poetic voyeurism—the stylized expression of a blissfully dirty mind"**: Kael, *The New Yorker* (August 4, 1980).

283 **"continued to believe that movie criticism"**: *The New York Review of Books*, August 14, 1980.

283 **"jarringly, piece by piece, line by line, and without interruption, worthless"**: Ibid.

283 **"an entirely new style of** *ad hominem* **brutality and intimidation"**: Ibid.

284 **"She is a lively writer with a lot of common sense"**: *The New Leader* (March 30, 1973).

284 **"lost any notion of the legitimate borders of polemic"**: *The New York Review of Books*, August 14, 1980.

284 **"sexual conduct, deviance"**: Ibid.

284 **"just a belch from the Nixon era"**: Ibid.

284 **"you can't cut through the crap in her"**: Ibid.

284 **"plastic turds"**: Ibid.

284 **"tumescent filmmaking"**: Ibid.

284 **"the mock rhetorical question"**: Ibid.

284 **"Were these 435 prints processed in a sewer?"**: Ibid.

284 **"Where was the director?"**: Ibid.

284 **"How can you have any feelings"**: Ibid.

284 **"rarely saying anything"**: Ibid.

284 **"a new breakthrough in vulgarity"**: Ibid.

284 **"free to write what"**: Ibid.

284 **"to accommodate her work"**: Ibid.

285 **"It is difficult, with these reviews"**: Ibid.

285 **"Princess Renata"**: *The Village Voice*, August 6–12, 1980.

285 **"when not dusting off her diplomas"**: Ibid.

285 **"Renata Adler should see a psychiatrist"**: Letter from Michael Sragow to Pauline Kael, July 28, 1980.

285 **"one of the dunces of the profession"**: *New York*, August 11, 1980.

285 **"That's just how Renata reacts to Pauline"**: Ibid.

285 **"shouldn't happen to anyone"**: Letter from Penelope Gilliatt to Pauline Kael, July 30, 1980.

286 **"I'm sorry that Ms. Adler doesn't respond to my writing"**: *Time* (July 27, 1980).

286 **"a kinetic-action director to the bone"**: Kael, *The New Yorker* (September 29, 1980).

286 **"a furious aliveness in this picture"**: Ibid.

286  **"a comedy without a speck of sitcom aggression"**: Kael, *The New Yorker* (October 13, 1980).

286  **"*The Elephant Man* has the power and some of the dream logic of a silent film"**: Kael, *The New Yorker* (October 27, 1980).

287  **"He only shows you what you see anyway"**: Pauline Kael, undated notes taken after a screening of *Annie Hall*, 1977.

287  **"What man in his forties"**: Kael, *The New Yorker* (October 27, 1980).

287  **"Throughout *Stardust Memories* . . . Sandy is superior to all those who talk about his work"**: Ibid.

287  **"When you do comedy"**: Ibid.

287  **"a new national hero"**: Ibid.

287  **"a horrible betrayal"**: Ibid.

287  **"If Woody Allen finds success very upsetting"**: Ibid.

288  **"a biography of the genre of prizefight films"**: Kael, *The New Yorker* (December 8, 1980).

288  **"it's also about movies and about violence"**: Ibid.

288  **"You can feel the director sweating for greatness"**: Ibid.

288  **"What De Niro does in this picture isn't acting"**: Ibid.

289  **"I would say that of all the nonfiction writers"**: Author interview with Daniel Menaker, April 1, 2009.

289  **"She wanted someone to help make sure"**: Ibid.

289  **"I don't think she had a snobby bone in her body"**: Ibid.

289  **"She loved to provoke Shawn"**: Ibid.

289  **"I think they really got off"**: Ibid.

290  **"Painting, painting, *painting*!"** Author interview with Warner Friedman, August 12, 2009.

290  **"Here comes Ma Barker and her gang"**: *Vanity Fair*, April 1997.

291  **"You make me so mad!"**: Author interview with Polly Frost, March 20, 2009.

291  **"Most of her criticism was not that hard"**: Author interview with Michael Sragow, September 12, 2008.

292  **"Pauline had enormous insight into people"**: Author interview with David Edelstein, July 31, 2009.

292  **"She was watching them, like a movie"**: Author interview with Linda Allen, November 14, 2009.

292  **"Well"**: Author interview with Carrie Rickey, May 9, 2009.

293  **"The conversation was over"**: Ibid.

293  **"I thought . . . I was fine when I was an acolyte"**: Ibid.

293  **"It's a movie you want to deface"**: Kael, *The New Yorker* (December 22, 1980).

293  **"Little Sheba might not Come Back but don't worry"**: John Guare, *The War Against the Kitchen Sink* (Smith & Kraus: Lyme, New Hampshire, 1996), x, xi.

294  **"You're not stuck with the usual dramatic apparatus"**: Kael, *The New Yorker* (March 23, 1980).

294  **"Though I have a better time"**: Ibid.

294  **"using their power in the same direction that the businessmen of the movies are"**: Debate between Jean-Luc Godard and Pauline Kael, reprinted in *Camera Obscura*, 1982.

294  **"It has a lot of magnificent things"**: Ibid.

294  **"It was a chilling ride back to the city"**: Author interview with Sydney Goldstein, February 20, 2009.

295  **"could become commonplace"**: Kael, *The New Yorker* (June 25, 1981).

295  **"time to breathe"**: Ibid.

295  **"weren't hooked on the crap of his childhood":** Ibid.
295  **"the first movie in which De Palma":** Kael, *The New Yorker* (July 27, 1981).
295  **"hallucinatory":** Ibid.
295  **"I think De Palma has sprung to the place ":** Ibid.
296  **"We never really get into the movie because, as Sarah":** Ibid.


CHAPTER TWENTY-THREE

297  **"almost as if she were a big, goosey female impersonator":** Pauline Kael, "The Current Cinema," *The New Yorker* (October 26, 1981).
297  **"She begins to kiss his abdomen passionately, gratefully":** Ibid.
297  **"It's gruesomely silly."** Ibid.
298  **"The reason the *Voice* hated her":** Author interview with David Edelstein, July 31, 2009.
298  **"Pauline was so advanced on gay things in her sensibility":** Author interview with James Wolcott, August 3, 2010.
298  **"fag phantom of the opera":** Kael, *The New Yorker* (March 30, 1968).
298  **"a soft creature, flamingly nelly":** Kael, *The New Yorker* (November 9, 1981).
299  **"If I make these jokes":** Author interview with Daryl Chin, November 16, 2010.
299  **"Forman appears to see Evelyn as some sort of open-mouthed retard":** Kael, *The New Yorker* (November 23, 1981).
300  **"the most emotional movie musical":** Kael, *The New Yorker* (December 21, 1981).
300  **"Despite its use of Brechtian devices":** Ibid.
300  **"There's something new going on—something thrilling":** Ibid.
300  **"an enormous amount of dedication and intelligence":** Ibid.
300  **"all much peppier and more vital than the actors":** Ibid.
300  **"a tiresome, pettishly hostile woman":** Ibid.
301  **"It takes Keaton a long time to get any kind of bearings":** Ibid.
301  **"pussywhipped":** Author interview with Ray Sawhill, March 20, 2009.
301  **"henpecked":** Ibid.
301  **"There was no way that she was going to be able to see *Reds* with an open mind":** Author interview with James Toback, May 2009.
301  **"Oh, God, they were so damned nervous":** Author interview with Roy Blount, Jr., September 15, 2008.
302  **"I'm a little afraid to say how good":** Kael, *The New Yorker* (January 18, 1982).
302  **"just about marriage":** Ibid.
302  **"the kind of performances that in the theater become legendary":** Ibid.
302  **"who understands the pleasures to be had":** Kael, *The New Yorker* (April 19, 1982).
302  **"a dream of a movie—a bliss-out":** Kael, *The New Yorker* (June 14, 1982).
302  **"He's like a boy soprano lilting with joy all through *E.T.*":** Ibid.
303  **"fake-poetic, fake magical way":** Kael, *The New Yorker* (November 15, 1982).
303  **"If the roles made better sense":** Ibid.
303  **"a genuine oddity":** Ibid.
303  **"Altman keeps looking at the world":** Ibid.
304  **"resemble a living person":** Kael, *The New Yorker* (December 13, 1982).
304  **"encrusted with the weighty culture of big themes: evil, tortured souls, guilt":** Kael, *The New Yorker* (December 27, 1982).
304  **"Streep is very beautiful at times":** Ibid.

304 **"I'm incapable of not thinking about what Pauline wrote"**: *The Guardian*, Apirl 18, 1997.

305 **"anti-acting"**: Kael, *The New Yorker* (March 7, 1983).

305 **"Performers such as John Barrymore and Orson Welles and Laurence Olivier"**: Ibid.

306 **"Oh, shit"**: Author interview with Warner Friedman, August 12, 2009.

306 **"Movies are not art"**: Ibid.

306 **"a distant closeness"**: Ibid.

306 **"Pauline sort of showed a little affection"**: Ibid.


CHAPTER TWENTY-FOUR

307 **"an incomparable dip-in book"**: *The Boston Globe*, October 29, 1982.

307 **"a browser's delight"**: *The Chicago Tribune*, December 5, 1982.

307 **"one of the most profound emotional experience in the history of film"**: Pauline Kael, *Kiss Kiss Bang Bang* (Boston: Little Brown, 1968), 259.

307 **"dying with the priest"**: Pauline Kael, *5001 Nights at the Movies* (New York: Holt, Rinehart and Winston, 1982), 189.

307 **"I don't want you to take this personally"**: Author interview with Daniel Menaker, April 1, 2009.

308 **"Whenever she came across something that she felt didn't sound like her"**: Ibid.

308 **"lulling, narcotizing musical"**: Pauline Kael, "The Current Cinema," *The New Yorker* (June 27, 1983).

308 **"The film has a real shine"**: Kael, *The New Yorker* (August 8, 1983).

309 **"a pleasurable hum"**: Kael, *The New Yorker* (October 17, 1983).

309 **"like Tom Wolfe"**: Ibid.

309 **"far more of an anti-establishmentarian than Tom Wolfe"**: Ibid.

309 **"reactionary cornerstone"**: Ibid.

309 **"Someone told me she saw it with a group of her followers"**: Author interview with Philip Kaufman, May 7, 2009.

309 **"rhapsodic"**: Kael, *The New Yorker* (November 28, 1983).

309 **"Her singing voice takes you farther"**: Ibid.

309 **"And now that she has made her formal debut as a director"**: Ibid.

310 **"the actors with both eyes on the audience"**: Kael, *The New Yorker* (December 12, 1983).

310 **"incredibly vivid"**: Ibid.

310 **"If *Terms* had stayed a comedy . . . it might have been innocuous"**: Ibid.

310 **"There wasn't a lot of room for bombast"**: Author interview with David Edelstein, July 31, 2009.

310 **"Shaffer has Salieri declaring war on heaven for gypping him"**: Kael, *The New Yorker* (October 29, 1984).

311 **"by showing you Mozart as a rubber-faced grinning buffoon"**: Ibid.

311 **"a wizard at eager, manic, full-of-life roles"**: Ibid.

311 **"I was sitting next to her"**: Author interview with Judy Karasik, April 8, 2009.

311 **"fiercely impressionistic and aggressively untheoretical"**: *The New York Times Book Review*, April 15, 1984.

311 **"powerful perceptions and terrific writing"**: Ibid.

311 **"No auteurist critic"**: Ibid.

312 **"[Pauline's] archenemy, Richard Schickel, was there"**: Author interview with David Ansen, December 23, 2008.

313 **"suggestive and dazzlingly empathic"**: Kael, *The New Yorker* (January 14, 1985).

313 **"a kind of benign precision"**: Ibid.

313 **"intelligent and enjoyable"**: Ibid.

313 **"informed by a spirit of magisterial self-hatred"**: Ibid.

313 **"What's remarkable about the film is how two such different temperaments"**: Ibid.

313 **"If John Huston's name were not on *Prizzi's Honor*"**: Kael, *The New Yorker*, (July 1, 1985).

314 **"do anything for the role he's playing"**: Ibid.

314 **"a Borgia princess"**: Ibid.

CHAPTER TWENTY-FIVE

315 **"This tall, gaunt-faced Strange"**: Pauline Kael, "The Current Cinema," *The New Yorker* (August 12, 1985).

315 **"a career out of his terror of expressiveness"**: Ibid.

315 **"A lot of people thought she was really turned on by Clint Eastwood"**: Author interview with Ray Sawhill, April 11, 2009.

316 **"His work here is livelier and more companionable than it has been in recent years"**: Kael, *The New Yorker* (September 23, 1985).

316 **"using his skills"**: Ibid.

316 **"I liked the movie's unimportance"**: Kael, *The New Yorker* (November 4, 1985).

316 **"Meryl Streep has used too many foreign accents on us"**: Kael, *The New Yorker* (December 30, 1985).

316 **"Spielberg's *The Color Purple* is probably the least authentic in feeling"**: Ibid.

317 **"I can't eat that!"**: Author interview with Charles Simmons, June 29, 2009.

317 **"Oh, for Chrissake"**: Ibid.

317 **"I hated it"**: Author interview with Jane Kramer, February 24, 2009.

318 **"Probably everyone will agree that the subject of a movie should not place it beyond criticism"**: Kael, *The New Yorker* (December 30, 1985).

318 **"We watch him putting pressure on people"**: Ibid.

318 **"so many widely differing instances of collaboration and resistance"**: Ibid.

318 **"It's not just the exact procedures"**: Ibid.

318 **"appears to be to show you"**: Ibid.

318 **"The film is diffuse"**: Ibid.

318 **"The *Shoah* reaction was especially peculiar"**: Author interview with Lillian Ross, August 1, 2009.

319 **"I'm upset about how unmoved you represent yourself"**: Letter from Dan Talbot to Pauline Kael, January 3, 1986.

320 **"You're often on target"**: Ibid.

320 **"She had so little use for doctrine"**: Author interview with David Edelstein, July 31, 2009.

320 **"a Holocaust movie should not be sacrosanct"**: Kael, *The New Yorker* (December 30, 1985).

321 **"never before been this seductive on the screen"**: Kael, *The New Yorker* (February 10, 1986).

321 **"Allen's idea of movie acting is the reading of lines"**: Notes from Pauline Kael's screening of *Hannah and Her Sisters*.

321 **"It doesn't just repeat his work, it repeats itself"**: Ibid.

321 **"The movie is a little stale"**: Kael, *The New Yorker* (February 24, 1986).

322 **"I don't want to hurt him. . . . I just want to squirt him"**: Author interview with Allen Barra, July 16, 2009.

322 **"It seemed time for a change"**: Pauline Kael, introduction, *State of the Art* (New York: Dutton, 1985).

322 **"This bum ticker of mine"**: Author interview with Trent Duffy, February 17, 2009.

323 **"Frears is responsive to grubby desperation"**: Kael, *The New Yorker* (March 10, 1986).

323 **"Frears's editing rhythms that seem so right are actually very odd"**: Ibid.

323 **"This Johnny wants to make something of himself"**: Ibid.

323 **"Selling is what they think moviemaking is about"**: Kael, *The New Yorker* (June 16, 1986).

324 **"a phenomenal performance"**: Kael, *The New Yorker* (September 22, 1986).

324 **"the work of a genius naïf"**: Ibid.

324 **"what for want of a better word is called a 'film sense,'"**: Kael, *The New Yorker* (October 6, 1986).

324 **"a true gift for informality"**: Kael, *The New Yorker* (November 17, 1986).

325 **"We can surmise"**: Kael, *The New Yorker* (January 12, 1987).

325 **"The results are overwrought"**: Ibid.

325 **"I'll watch him with my own life"**: Author interview with Warner Friedman, August 12, 2009.

325 **"I can do better than this myself"**: Author interview with Polly Frost, April 10, 2009.

325 **"Because you look like you're a mother or a grandmother"**: Author interview with Warner Friedman, August 12, 2009.

325 **"Fuck you, Charlie"**: Ibid.

326 **"She was about to go back to San Francisco"**: Author interview with Ray Sawhill, March 20, 2009.

326 **"She would be let down if I would say"**: Ibid.

326 **"absolutely first rate"**: Letter from Pauline Kael to William Abrahams, February 4, 1982.

327 **"Nobody was reading my reviews in *The East Side Express*"**: Author interview with Owen Gleiberman, February 18, 2009.

328 **"To be true to what Pauline taught us"**: Ibid.

## CHAPTER TWENTY-SIX

329 **"Dozens of people had advanced"**: William Shawn to the staff of *The New Yorker*, fall 1976.

330 **"If Shawn were to give up some of his duties as editor"**: Brendan Gill, *Here at The New Yorker* (New York: Random House, 1975; quoted from DaCapo paperback edition), 381.

330 **"powerful and apparently unanimous expression of sadness"**: Letter to Robert A. Gottlieb from the staff of *The New Yorker*, January 13, 1987.

330 **"*The New Yorker* has not achieved its preeminence by following orthodox paths of magazine publishing and editing"**: Ibid.

331 **"He was a great editor"**: Pauline Kael, remarks to audience at *New Yorker* luncheon, Beverly Hills Hotel, May 7, 1987.

331 **"with Bob Gottlieb"**: Ibid.

331 "an amazing man—dedicated to what he believes to be the best writing": Letter from Pauline Kael to Samuel M. Grupper, MacArthur Fellows Program, December 22, 1987.

331 "constitute a vote of confidence in an eighty-year-old man of letters": Ibid.

331 "never before blended his actors so intuitively, so musically," Pauline Kael, "The Current Cinema," *The New Yorker* (December 14, 1987).

331 "funny, warm family scenes that might be thought completely outside his range": Ibid.

332 "TOM: I don't write": James L. Brooks's screenplay of *Broadcast News*, 1987.

332 "Basically, what the movie is saying": Kael, *The New Yorker* (January 11, 1988).

332 "There's not even a try for any style or tension in *Broadcast News*": Ibid.

333 "The camera is so discreet it always seems about ten feet too far away": Kael, *The New Yorker* (February 22, 1988).

333 "directed so that he never engages us": Ibid.

333 "Yes, it gets to you by the end": Ibid.

334 "too fastidious to do anything dangerous or dirty": Jay McInerney, *Brights Lights, Big City* (New York: Vintage Books, 1984), 19.

334 "Woody Allen's picture is meant to be about emotion": Kael, *The New Yorker* (October 31, 1988).

334 "a hallucinogenic Feydeau play": Kael, *The New Yorker* (November 14, 1988).

334 "Godard with a human face—a happy face": Ibid.

335 "nowhere to go": Kael, *The New Yorker* (February 16, 1989).

335 "mind's eye he's always watching the audience watching him": Ibid.

335 "an actor in the same sense that Robert Taylor was an actor": Ibid.

335 "wet kitsch": Ibid.

335 "A disquieting note": *Publishers Weekly* (September 9, 1988).

335 "on the whole, Kael's genuine excitement about film sustains the book": Ibid.

335 "macabre sensibility": Kael, *The New Yorker* (July 10, 1989).

335 "this powerfully glamorous new *Batman*": Ibid.

336 "We in the audience are put in the man's position": Kael, *The New Yorker* (August 21, 1989).

336 "such seductive, virtuosic control of film": Ibid.

336 "In essence, it's feminist": Ibid.

336 "I think that in his earlier movies": Ibid.

337 "the most emotionally wrenching scene I've ever experienced at the movies": Kael, *The New Yorker* (October 2, 1989).

337 "The wide eyes still miss nothing": Unpublished memoir by Linda Allen.

338 "surprisingly unlike herself": Ibid.

338 "was cool the entire time": Author interview with Allen Barra, July 16, 2009.

339 "With Pfeiffer in deep-red velvet crawling on the piano like a long-legged Kitty-cat": Kael, *The New Yorker* (October 16, 1989).

339 "Are we trying to put kids into some moral-aesthetic safe house?": Kael, *The New Yorker* (December 11, 1989).

340 "coziness and slightness": Kael, *The New Yorker* (December 25, 1989).

340 "Does Kael orchestrate campaigns inside the film societies?": *The Village Voice*, February 4, 1988.

## CHAPTER TWENTY-SEVEN

342 **"The picture is like the work of a slick ad exec"**: Pauline Kael, "The Current Cinema," *The New Yorker* (January 8, 1990).

343 **"the moviemaking has such bravura that you respond as if you were at a live performance"**: Kael, *The New Yorker* (November 19, 1990).

343 **"There's nothing affected about Costner's acting or directing"**: Kael, *The New Yorker* (December 17, 1990).

343 **"For a brief period in the late sixties and early seventies"**: Ibid.

344 **"The movies are so shitty now"**: Author interview with Owen Gleibman, February 18, 2009.

344 **"For a brief, golden time in the '70s"**: *Newsweek* (March 18, 1991).

344 **"At worst, she wasn't far from a film-world version of Walter Winchell"**: *L. A. Weekly*, March 22, 1991.

344 **"enhanced and expanded the filmgoing public's knowledge and appreciation of world cinema"**: Citation, Mel Novikoff Award, San Francisco Film Society, May 2, 1991.

345 **"welcome reading at a time when film criticism"**: *The Los Angeles Times Book Review*, September 22, 1991.

346 **"Oh—you have Annette O'Toole's hair!"**: Author interview with Charles Taylor, June 15, 2009.

346 **"Pauline felt that Molly, once she married Sarris"**: Author interview with James Wolcott, August 3, 2010.

347 **"I once said, in a fit of frustration"**: Author interview with Charles Taylor, June 15, 2009.

347 **"These people were all housewives"**: Ibid.

347 **"And what did *your* mother do?"**: Author interview with Polly Frost, April 11, 2009.

347 **"I'm frequently asked"**: Pauline Kael, introduction, *For Keeps* (New York: Dutton, 1994).

347 **"I kept bringing up the idea of her work on an autobiography"**: Letter from Peggy Brooks to William Abrahams, September 29, 1994.

348 **"Oh, just let her grow up"**: Author interview with Allen Barra, July 16, 2009.

350 **"They write as advocates, both feet on the accelerator"**: James Wolcott, "Waiting for Godard," *Vanity Fair* (April 1997).

350 **"He's a careerist creep"**: Author interview with Charles Taylor, June 15, 2009.

350 **"I knew she wasn't happy about it"**: Author interview with James Wolcott, August 3, 2010.

351 **"no cartoons, no lyricism—just realism"**: Audio interview between Pauline Kael and Ray Sawhill, 2000.

351 **"desperate to read and to take in everything"**: Ibid.

351 **"I thought, when I read that, this is what's wrong with Wes Anderson's movies"**: Author interview with Steve Vineberg, August 26, 2008.

352 **"Sometimes, Charlie and I would go to little shops on the way out to visit her"**: Author interview with Stephanie Zacharek, September 4, 2009.

352 **"They're more delicious than food now"**: Author interview with George and Elizabeth Malko, April 15, 2009.

352 **"You look so restive sitting up there next to your mother"**: Author interview with Steve Vineberg, August 26, 2008.

352 **"A number of people around any diva":** Author interview with Polly Frost, March 20, 2009.

353 **"He's never any good":** Author interview with Ray Sawhill, March 20, 2009.

353 **"Well, honey, from the look of things":** Author interview with Steve Vineberg, August 26, 2008.

353 **"Presenting Creation, more or less":** Poem by Roy Blount, Jr., composed for Pauline Kael's eightieth birthday, June 19, 1999.

355 **"I don't know what you know":** Author interview with Carrie Rickey, May 9, 2009.

356 **"You tell him, girlie!":** Author interview with Polly Frost, April 11, 2009.

356 **"Of course. He's smart":** Author interview with Dennis Delrogh, April 5, 2011.

356 **"Isn't he amazing?":** Author interview with Michael Sragow, October 21, 2008.


CHAPTER TWENTY-EIGHT

357 **"As a mother, Pauline was exactly what you would expect from reading her or knowing her":** Remarks by Gina James, memorial tribute to Pauline Kael, November 30, 2001.

357 **"She was funny and lethal right up to the end":** Remarks by Craig Seligman.

358 **"It's a piece of crap":** Remarks by John Bennet.

358 **"Pauline really believed all her life that she was lucky to be able to do what she wanted to do":** Remarks by George Malko.

358 **"Upon sober reflection":** Remarks by Arlene Croce.

359 **"Now people watch movies so they can stay kids":** *New York* (February 23, 2009).

360 **"And to think . . . there's not even a decent movie to see":** Remarks by Marcia Nasatir.

# BIBLIOGRAPHY

Adler, Renata. *Gone: The Last Days of* The New Yorker. New York: Simon & Schuster, 1999.

Agee, James. *Agee on Film*. New York: McDowell, Oblensky, 1958.

Anderson, Paul Thomas (ed.). *Altman on Altman*. London: Faber and Faber, 2006.

Bertin, Celia. *Jean Renoir: A Life in Pictures*. Baltimore: The John Hopkins Press, 1991.

Biskind, Peter. *Easy Riders, Raging Bulls: How the Sex 'n' Drugs 'n' Rock and Roll Generation Saved Hollywood*. New York: Simon & Schuster, 1998.

———. *Star: How Warren Beatty Seduced America*. New York: Simon & Schuster, 2010.

Brantley, Will (ed.). *Conversations with Pauline Kael*. Jackson: University Press of Mississippi, 1996.

Björkman, Stig (ed.). *Woody Allen on Woody Allen*. London: Faber and Faber, 1995.

Brody, Richard. *Everything Is Cinema: The Working Life of Jean-Luc Godard*. New York: Henry Holt, 2008.

Broughton, James. *Coming Unbuttoned*. San Francisco: City Lights, 1993.

Brownlow, Kevin. *David Lean: A Biography*. New York: St. Martin's Press, 1996.

Carroll, Peter. *It Seemed Like Nothing Happened: The Tragedy and Promise of America in the 1970s*. New York: Holt, Rinehart and Winston, 1982.

Crist, Judith, *The Private Eye, the Cowboy and the Very Naked Girl: Movies from Cleo to Clyde*. New York: Holt, Rinehart and Winston, 1968.

———. *Take 22: Moviemakers on Moviemaking*. New York: Viking, 1984.

Crowther, Bosley. *The Lion's Share*. New York: E. P. Dutton, 1957.

Davidson, Michael. *The San Francisco Renaissance: Poetics and Community at Midcentury*. New York: Cambridge University Press, 1991.

Davis, Francis. *Afterglow: A Last Conversation with Pauline Kael*. New York: Da Capo, 2002.

Dunne, John Gregory. *The Studio*. New York: Farrar, Straus and Giroux, 1969.

Faas, Ekbert. *Young Robert Duncan: Portrait of the Poet as Homosexual in Society*. Santa Barbara: Black Sparrow Press, 1983.

Finstad, Suzanne. *Warren Beatty: A Private Man*. New York: Harmony Books, 2005.

Fleming, Charles. *High Concept: Don Simpson and the Hollywood Culture of Excess*. New York: Doubleday, 1998.

Foley, Jack (ed.). *All: A James Broughton Reader*. Brooklyn, N.Y.: White Crane Press, 2006.

Fonda, Jane. *My Life So Far*. New York: Random House, 2005.

Gill, Brendan. *Here at* The New Yorker. New York: Random House, 1975.

Gilliatt, Penelope. *Jean Renoir: Essays, Conversations, Reviews*. New York: McGraw-Hill, 1975.

———. *Sunday Bloody Sunday*. New York: Dodd, Mead, 1971.

Gitlin, Todd. *The Sixties: Years of Hope, Days of Rage*. New York: Bantam, 1987.

Gruen, John. *Menotti: A Biography*. New York: Macmillan, 1978.

Guare, John. *The War Against the Kitchen Sink*. Lyme, N.H.: Smith & Kraus, 1996.

Harris, Mark. *Pictures at a Revolution: Five Movies and the Birth of the New Hollywood*. New York: The Penguin Press, 2008.

Harvey, James. *Movie Love in the Fifties*. New York: Alfred A. Knopf, 2001.

Hayes, Kevin (ed.). *Sam Peckinpah Interviews*. Jackson: University Press of Mississippi, 2008.

Hellman, Lillian. *An Unfinished Woman*. Boston: Little, Brown, 1969.

———. *Pentimento*. Boston: Little, Brown, 1973.

Howe, Irving. *World of Our Fathers*. New York: Harcourt Brace Jovanovich, 1976.

Jackson, Kevin. *Schrader on Schrader*. London: Faber and Faber, 1990.

Kael, Pauline. *The Citizen Kane Book* ("Raising Kane"). New York: Bantam, 1971.

———. *Deeper into Movies*. Boston: Atlantic–Little, Brown, 1973.

———. *5001 Nights at the Movies*. New York: Holt Rinehart and Winston, 1982.

———. *For Keeps*. New York: Dutton, 1994.

———. *Going Steady*. Boston: Atlantic–Little, Brown, 1970.

———. *Hooked*. New York: Dutton, 1989.

———. *I Lost It at the Movies*. Boston: Little, Brown, 1965.

———. *Kiss Kiss Bang Bang*. Boston: Little, Brown, 1968.

———. *Movie Love*. New York: Dutton, 1991.

———. *Reeling*. Boston: Little, Brown, 1976.

———. *State of the Art*. New York: Dutton, 1985.

———. *Taking It All In*. New York: Holt, Rinehart and Winston, 1984.

———. *Where the Lights Go Down*. New York: Holt, Rinehart and Winston, 1980.

Kann, Kenneth L. *Comrades and Chicken Ranchers: The Story of a California Jewish Community*. Ithaca, N.Y.: Cornell University Press, 1993.

———. *Joe Rappaport: Life of a Jewish Radical*. Philadelphia: Temple University Press, 1981.

Kaufmann, Stanley. *A World on Film*. New York: Harper & Row, 1966.

Kirshenblatt-Gimblett, Barbara, and Jonathan Karp (eds.). *The Art of Being Jewish in Modern Times*. Philadelphia: University of Pennsylvania Press, 2008.

Lasar, Matthew. *Pacifica Radio: The Rise of an Alternative Network*. Philadelphia: Temple University Press, 1999.

Laurents, Arthur. *Original Story: A Memoir of Broadway and Hollywood*. New York: Alfred A. Knopf, 2000.

Lax, Eric. *Woody Allen: A Biography*. New York: Alfred A. Knopf, 1991.

Libo, Kenneth, and Irving Howe. *We Lived There Too*. New York: St. Martin's Press, 1984.

Long, Robert Emmet. *James Ivory in Conversation*. Berkeley and Los Angeles: University of California Press, 2005.

Lopate, Phillip. *American Movie Critics*. New York: Library of America, 2006.

———. *Totally Tenderly Tragically: Essays and Criticism from a Lifelong Love Affair with the Movies*. New York: Anchor Books, 1998.

McCarthy, Mary. *The Group*. New York: Harcourt Brace Jovanovich, 1963.

McGilligan, Patrick. *George Cukor: A Double Life*. New York: St. Martin's Press, 1991.

———. *Backstory 2: Interviews with Screenwriters of the 1940s and 1950s*. Berkeley: University of California Press, 1991.

Mair, George. *The Barry Diller Story: An Inside Look at Hollywood's Power Player*. New York: John Wiley & Sons, 1997.

Mann, William. *Kate: The Woman Who Was Hepburn*. New York: Henry Holt, 2006.

Mast, Gerald, and Marshall Cohen. *Film Theory and Criticism*. New York: Oxford University Press, 1979.

Mazursky, Paul. *Show Me the Magic*. New York: Simon & Schuster, 1999.

Meade, Marion. *Dorothy Parker: What Fresh Hell Is This?* New York: Villard, 1987.

Mehta, Ved. *Remembering Mr. Shawn's New Yorker: The Invisible Art of Editing*. Woodstock, N.Y.: Overlook, 1998.

Metzker, Isaac. *A Bintel Brief, Volume II: Letters to the* Jewish Daily Forward. New York: Viking, 1981.

Parkinson, David (ed.). *The Graham Greene Film Reader: Reviews, Essays, Interviews and Film Stories*. London: Carcanet Press, 1993.

Parish, Robert Graham. *The RKO Gals*. New York: Arlington, 1974.

Phillips, Julia. *You'll Never Eat Lunch in This Town Again*. New York: Random House, 1991.

Rinehart, Katherine J. *Petaluma: A History in Architecture*. Charleston, S.C.: Arcadia, 2005.

Ross, Lillian. *Here But Not Here*. New York: Random House, 1998.

———. *Picture*. New York: Rinehart & Company, 1952.

Sarris, Andrew. *The American Cinema: Directors and Directions 1929–1968*. New York: E. P. Dutton, 1968.

———. *Confessions of a Cultist: On the Cinema, 1955/1969*. New York: Touchstone, 1971.

Schickel, Richard. *Clint Eastwood*. New York: Alfred A. Knopf, 1996.

———. *Matinee Idylls: Reflections on the Movies*. Chicago: Ivan R. Dee, 1999.

Schrader, Paul. *Schrader on Schrader & Other Writings*. London: Faber & Faber, 1990.

Seligman, Craig. *Sontag & Kael: Opposites Attract Me*. New York: Counterpoint, 2004.

Simon, John. *Reverse Angle: A Decade of American Films*. New York: Crown, 1982.

Snyder, Gary. *The Real Work: Interviews and Talks, 1964–1979*. New York: New Directions, 1980.

Stuart, Jan. *The Nashville Chronicles: The Making of Robert Altman's Masterpiece*. New York: Simon & Schuster, 2000.

Talbot, Toby. *The New Yorker Theater and Other Scenes from a Life at the Movies*. New York: Columbia University Press, 2009.

Terkel, Studs. *The Good War: An Oral History of World War II*. New York: Pantheon, 1984.

Thompson, David. *Altman on Altman*. London: Faber & Faber, 2006.

Weingarten, Marc. *The Gang That Wouldn't Write Straight*. New York: Crown, 2005.

Wreszin, Michael. *A Moral Temper: The Letters of Dwight Macdonald*. Chicago: Ivan R. Dee, 2001.

Wright, William. *Lillian Hellman: The Image, the Woman*. New York: Simon & Schuster, 1986.

Yagoda, Ben. *About Town:* The New Yorker *and the World it Made*. New York: Scribner, 2000.

Zuckoff, Mitchell. *Robert Altman: The Oral Biography*. New York: Alfred A. Knopf, 2009.

# INDEX

Grateful acknowledgment is made for permission to reprint or quote from the following writings:

Poem by Roy Blount, Jr., by permission of Roy Blount, Jr.
Letter from Peggy Brooks, by permission of Peggy Brooks
Letters from John Gregory Dunne, by permission of Joan Didion
Letter from Robert Getchell, by permission of Robert Getchell
Letter from Owen Gleiberman, by permission of Owen Gleiberman
Letter from George Roy Hill, by permission of the Estate of George Roy Hill
Letters and other writings by Pauline Kael, by permission of Gina James, in the Pauline Kael
Collection, Lilly Library, Indiana University, Bloomington, Indiana
Letters from Dwight Macdonald, Dwight Macdonald Papers, Manuscripts and Archives,
Yale University Library
Letter from Robert Mills, by permission of Fred Mills, in the collection of the Harry Ransom
Humanities Research Center, The University of Texas at Austin
Poem by *New Yorker* staff members, *New Yorker* records, Manuscripts and Archives Division,
The New York Public Library, Astor, Lenox and Tilden Foundations
Letters from Sam Peckinpah, by permission of Kristen Dennis
Letter from Sydney Pollack, by permission of the Sydney Pollack family
Letter from Grover Sales, by permission of Georgia Sales
Letter from Michael Sragow, by permission of Michael Sragow
Letter from Daniel Talbot, by permission of Daniel Talbot
Letter from Ken Ziffren, by permission of Ken Ziffren


Photograph credits

Insert page 1 (top and bottom): Photograph by Walter A. Scott, used by permission of Gina
James, in the Pauline Kael Collection, Lilly Library, Indiana University, Bloomington, Indiana
2 (top): Courtesy Joel Singer
2 (bottom), 3 (top): Photograph by James Cano, 1964, courtesy Linda Allen
3 (bottom): Courtesy Kathleen Carroll
4 (top and bottom), 7 (top and bottom): Photographed by Jill Krementz, all rights reserved
5 (top and bottom): Photofest
6 (top and bottom), 8 (top): Courtesy Polly Frost
6 (center): Courtesy Allen Barra
8 (bottom): By permission of the photographer, James Hamilton